Heinrich August Wilhelm Meyer

Critical and exegetical handbook to the Epistle to the Romans

Vol. 1

Heinrich August Wilhelm Meyer

Critical and exegetical handbook to the Epistle to the Romans
Vol. 1

ISBN/EAN: 9783337730109

Printed in Europe, USA, Canada, Australia, Japan

Cover: Foto ©ninafisch / pixelio.de

More available books at **www.hansebooks.com**

Just published, in demy 8vo, price 10s. 6d.,

The Bible Doctrine of Man.

(Seventh Series of Cunningham Lectures.)

By JOHN LAIDLAW, D.D.

'"An important and valuable contribution to the discussion of the anthropology of the sacred writings, perhaps the most considerable that has appeared in our own language.'—*Literary Churchman.*

'The work is a thoughtful contribution to a subject which must always have deep interest for the devout student of the Bible.'—*British Quarterly Review.*

'Dr. Laidlaw's work is scholarly, able, interesting, and valuable. . . . Thoughtful and devout minds will find much to stimulate, and not a little to assist, their meditations in this learned and, let us add, charmingly printed volume.'—*Record.*

'On the whole, we take this to be the most sensible and reasonable statement of the Biblical psychology of man we have met.'—*Expositor.*

'The book will give ample material for thought to the reflective reader; and it holds a position, as far as we know, which is unique.'—*Church Bells.*

'The Notes to the Lectures, which occupy not less than 180 pages, are exceedingly valuable. The style of the lecturer is clear and animated; the critical and analytical judgment predominates.'—*English Independent.*

Just published, Second Edition, demy 8vo, 10s. 6d.,

The Training of the Twelve;

OR,

EXPOSITION OF PASSAGES IN THE GOSPELS EXHIBITING THE TWELVE DISCIPLES OF JESUS UNDER DISCIPLINE FOR THE APOSTLESHIP.

BY

A. B. BRUCE, D.D.,

PROFESSOR OF DIVINITY, FREE CHURCH COLLEGE, GLASGOW.

'Here we have a really great book on an important, large, and attractive subject—a book full of loving, wholesome, profound thoughts about the fundamentals of Christian faith and practice.'—*British and Foreign Evangelical Review.*

'It is some five or six years since this work first made its appearance, and now that a second edition has been called for, the Author has taken the opportunity to make some alterations which are likely to render it still more acceptable. Substantially, however, the book remains the same, and the hearty commendation with which we noted its first issue applies to it at least as much now.'—*Rock.*

'The value, the beauty of this volume is that it is a unique contribution to, because a loving and cultured study of, the life of Christ, in the relation of the Master of the Twelve.'—*Edinburgh Daily Review.*

T. and T. Clark's Publications.

'This series is one of great importance to the biblical scholar; and, as regards its general execution, it leaves little or nothing to be desired.'—*Edinburgh Review.*

KEIL AND DELITZSCH'S
INTRODUCTION TO AND COMMENTARIES ON THE OLD TESTAMENT.

In 27 Volumes, demy 8vo.

MESSRS. CLARK have resolved to offer complete sets of this work at the Original Subscription Price of £7, 2s. 0d. Single volumes may be had, price 10s. 6d.

In crown 8vo, Eighth Edition, price 7s. 6d.,

THE SUFFERING SAVIOUR;
OR, MEDITATIONS ON THE LAST DAYS OF THE SUFFERINGS OF CHRIST.

By F. W. KRUMMACHER, D.D.

'The work bears throughout the stamp of an enlightened intellect, under the teaching of the Holy Spirit, and of a profound study of the Word of God.'—*Record.*

'The reflections are of a pointed and practical character, and are eminently calculated to inform the mind and improve the heart. To the devout and earnest Christian the volume will be a treasure indeed.'—*Wesleyan Times.*

BY THE SAME AUTHOR.

Just published, Second Edition, in crown 8vo, price 7s. 6d.,

DAVID, THE KING OF ISRAEL:
A PORTRAIT DRAWN FROM BIBLE HISTORY AND THE BOOK OF PSALMS.

At the close of two articles reviewing this work, the *Christian Observer* says: 'Our space will not permit us to consider more at large this very interesting work, but we cannot do less than cordially commend it to the attention of our readers. It affords such an insight into King David's character as is nowhere else to be met with; it is therefore most instructive.'

In demy 8vo, price 7s. 6d.,

SERMONS TO THE NATURAL MAN.

By WILLIAM G. T. SHEDD, D.D.,
Author of 'A History of Christian Doctrine,' etc.

'Characterised by profound knowledge of divine truth, and presenting the truth in a chaste and attractive style, the sermons carry in their tone the accents of the solemn feeling of responsibility to which they owe their origin.'—*Weekly Review.*

In One Volume, crown 8vo, price 5s., Third Edition,

LIGHT FROM THE CROSS:
SERMONS ON THE PASSION OF OUR LORD.

Translated from the German of A. THOLUCK, D.D.,
Professor of Theology in the University of Halle.

'With no ordinary confidence and pleasure, we commend these most noble, solemnizing, and touching discourses.'—*British and Foreign Evangelical Review.*

In Three Volumes, 8vo, price 31s. 6d.,

A COMMENTARY ON

THE GOSPEL OF ST. JOHN.

By F. GODET, D.D.,
PROFESSOR OF THEOLOGY, NEUCHATEL.

'This work forms one of the battle-fields of modern inquiry, and is itself so rich in spiritual truth that it is impossible to examine it too closely; and we welcome this treatise from the pen of Dr. Godet. We have no more competent exegete, and this new volume shows all the learning and vivacity for which the Author is distinguished.'—*Freeman.*

BY THE SAME AUTHOR.

Just published, in Two Volumes, 8vo, price 21s.,

A COMMENTARY ON

THE GOSPEL OF ST. LUKE.

Translated from the Second French Edition.

'We are indebted to the Publishers for an English translation of the admirable work which stands at the head of this review. . . . It is a work of great ability, learning, and research.'—*Christian Observer.*

'Marked by clearness and good sense, it will be found to possess value and interest as one of the most recent and copious works specially designed to illustrate this Gospel.'—*Guardian.*

BY THE SAME AUTHOR.

In Two Volumes, 8vo, Vol. I. now ready, price 10s. 6d.,

A COMMENTARY ON

ST. PAUL'S EPISTLE TO THE ROMANS.

'We have looked through it with great care, and have been charmed not less by the clearness and fervour of its evangelical principles than by the carefulness of its exegesis, its fine touches of spiritual intuition, and its appositeness of historical illustration.'—*Baptist Magazine.*

Just published, in demy 8vo, Fourth Edition, price 10s. 6d.,

MODERN DOUBT AND CHRISTIAN BELIEF.

A Series of Apologetic Lectures addressed to Earnest Seekers after Truth.

By THEODORE CHRISTLIEB, D.D.,
UNIVERSITY PREACHER AND PROFESSOR OF THEOLOGY AT BONN.

Translated, with the Author's sanction, chiefly by the Rev. H. U. WEITBRECHT, Ph.D., and Edited by the Rev. T. L. KINGSBURY, M.A.

'We recommend the volume as one of the most valuable and important among recent contributions to our apologetic literature. . . . We are heartily thankful both to the learned Author and to his translators.'—*Guardian.*

'We express our unfeigned admiration of the ability displayed in this work, and of the spirit of deep piety which pervades it; and whilst we commend it to the careful perusal of our readers, we heartily rejoice that in those days of reproach and blasphemy so able a champion has come forward to contend earnestly for the faith which was once delivered to the saints.'—*Christian Observer.*

DR. LUTHARDT'S WORKS.

In Three handsome crown 8vo Volumes, price 6s. each.

'We do not know any volumes so suitable in these times for young men entering on life, or, let us say, even for the library of a pastor called to deal with such, than the three volumes of this series. We commend the whole of them with the utmost cordial satisfaction. They are altogether quite a specialty in our literature.'—*Weekly Review.*

APOLOGETIC LECTURES
ON THE
FUNDAMENTAL TRUTHS OF CHRISTIANITY.
Fifth Edition.
BY C. E. LUTHARDT, D.D., LEIPZIG.

'From Dr. Luthardt's exposition even the most learned theologians may derive invaluable criticism, and the most acute disputants supply themselves with more trenchant and polished weapons than they have as yet been possessed of.'—*Bell's Weekly Messenger.*

APOLOGETIC LECTURES
ON THE
SAVING TRUTHS OF CHRISTIANITY.
Fourth Edition.

'Dr. Luthardt is a profound scholar, but a very simple teacher, and expresses himself on the gravest matters with the utmost simplicity, clearness, and force.'—*Literary World.*

APOLOGETIC LECTURES
ON THE
MORAL TRUTHS OF CHRISTIANITY.
Third Edition.

'The ground covered by this work is, of course, of considerable extent, and there is scarcely any topic of specifically moral interest now under debate in which the reader will not find some suggestive saying. The volume contains, like its predecessors, a truly wealthy apparatus of notes and illustrations.'—*English Churchman.*

Just published, in demy 8vo, price 9s.,

ST. JOHN THE AUTHOR OF THE FOURTH GOSPEL.
BY PROFESSOR C. E. LUTHARDT,
Author of 'Fundamental Truths of Christianity,' etc.
Translated and the Literature enlarged by C. R. GREGORY, Leipzig.

'A work of thoroughness and value. The translator has added a lengthy Appendix, containing a very complete account of the literature bearing on the controversy respecting this Gospel. The indices which close the volume are well ordered, and add greatly to its value.'—*Guardian.*

'There are few works in the later theological literature which contain such a wealth of sober theological knowledge and such an invulnerable phalanx of objective apologetical criticism.'—*Professor Guericke.*

Crown 8vo, 5s.,

LUTHARDT, KAHNIS, AND BRÜCKNER.
The Church: Its Origin, its History, and its Present Position.

'A comprehensive review of this sort, done by able hands, is both instructive and suggestive.'—*Record.*

CRITICAL AND EXEGETICAL

COMMENTARY

ON

THE NEW TESTAMENT.

BY

HEINRICH AUGUST WILHELM MEYER, Th.D.,
OBERCONSISTORIALRATH, HANNOVER.

From the German.

THE TRANSLATION REVISED AND EDITED, WITH THE SANCTION OF
THE AUTHOR, BY

WILLIAM P. DICKSON, D.D.,
PROFESSOR OF DIVINITY IN THE UNIVERSITY OF GLASGOW.

PART IV.
THE EPISTLE TO THE ROMANS.
VOL. I.

EDINBURGH:
T. & T. CLARK, 38 GEORGE STREET.
MDCCCLXXXI.

PRINTED BY MORRISON AND GIBB,

FOR

T. & T. CLARK, EDINBURGH.

LONDON, ...	HAMILTON, ADAMS, AND CO.
DUBLIN, . . .	ROBERTSON AND CO.
NEW YORK, ...	SCRIBNER AND WELFORD.

CRITICAL AND EXEGETICAL

HANDBOOK

TO

THE EPISTLE TO THE ROMANS.

BY

HEINRICH AUGUST WILHELM MEYER, Th.D.,

OBERCONSISTORIALRATH, HANNOVER.

TRANSLATED FROM THE FIFTH EDITION OF THE GERMAN BY

Rev. JOHN C. MOORE, B.A.,

HAMBURG.

VOL. I.

EDINBURGH:
T. & T. CLARK, 38 GEORGE STREET.
MDCCCLXXXI.

GENERAL PREFACE

BY THE EDITOR.

AMONG the many valuable contributions with which the scholars and theologians of Germany have enriched the literature of New Testament exegesis, the *Kritisch-exegetischer Kommentar über das Neue Testament* of Dr. Meyer has been pronounced by the almost unanimous verdict of competent judges the best, as it is unquestionably the most careful and elaborate, work of its kind. The title indicates with sufficient clearness its distinctive character as at once critical and exegetical, although the former element stands in subordination to the latter. The critical remarks prefixed to each chapter present a lucid statement of the evidence with reference to all questions of any moment affecting the constitution of the text, and are especially valuable for the concise explanations which they give of the probable origin of the various readings, and of the grounds which, in a conflict of evidence and of critical opinion, have determined Dr. Meyer's own judgment. But, terse and discriminating as is its textual criticism, a still higher value belongs to the exegesis which forms the pith and marrow of the book. While there are many commentaries of more or less excellence which occupy themselves with the theological import of Scripture, with popular exposition or with homiletic illustration, and others which are largely devoted to historical criticism—as it is called, although it is in reality too often mere arbitrary speculation—Dr. Meyer has chosen and has steadily cultivated the special field of exegesis pure and simple. His sole aim is to ascertain the grammatical and historical meaning of Scripture in accordance with the legitimate principles, and in the use of the proper resources, of interpretation, leaving the result thus obtained to be turned to due account by the theologian, the preacher, or the critical inquirer for their respective purposes. That the primary sense of Scripture can be rightly arrived at only by the method of grammatico-historical interpretation, is now admitted on all hands; and it is acknowledged that all Christian theology must rest on the foundation of sure and solid exegesis. The theologian must presume the processes, and must accept the assured results, of interpretation; nor can the preacher be regarded as duly equipped for his work, unless he is able to draw directly from the fountain-head— *integros accedere fontes atque haurire* — and to quicken and deepen his Christian insight by fresh and daily renewed study of the living word.

In this, as in other departments of science, the best results have been attained by dividing labour and specialising research, and Dr. Meyer has, by the concentration of his energies for upwards of forty years on the exegetical study of the New Testament, made the field essentially his own. The Commentaries on the Gospels, on Acts, and on the Epistles to the Romans, Corinthians, Galatians, Ephesians, Philippians, Colossians, and Philemon proceed from his own hand, and have all of them been revised and enlarged in successive editions—several even a fifth time. For the completion of the work on the same general plan he called in the services of able colleagues—Dr. Lünemann for the Epistles to the Thessalonians and Hebrews, Dr. Huther for the Pastoral and the Catholic Epistles, and Dr. Düsterdieck for the Apocalypse. The labours of Meyer in New Testament exegesis may be regarded as correlative and complementary to those of Winer in New Testament Grammar. While Winer rescued

the grammar of the New Testament idiom from the dogmatism
and caprice which had prevailed before his time, and rendered it,
in the confident but just language of his title-page, "the sure[1]
foundation of New Testament exegesis," he dealt, from the nature
of the case, merely with the isolated phenomena as illustrations.
Meyer undertook the task of applying the same principles and
methods to the interpretation of the New Testament as a whole.
This work he has accomplished with rare exegetical tact and
unrivalled philological precision. We say, unrivalled; for—
without derogating from the merits of other labourers in the
same field, and without denying the excellence more especially
of various recent monographs formed after his model—it may
safely be affirmed that his work remains, in its own line and
in its most characteristic features, unequalled. The only book
which, as covering the same ground, may be fairly brought into
comparison with it is the "Kurzgefasstes exegetisches Handbuch
zum Neuen Testament" of de Wette—a masterpiece of exegetical
skill, unquestionably well entitled to a place by its side. Each
work has its own special excellences; and no one has acknowledged the merits of Meyer more frankly than de Wette himself,
who repeatedly refers, as does also Meyer on his part, to the help
which each derived from the labours of the other—to the can-
dour with which they accepted, or the fairness with which they
controverted, as the case might be, each other's views—and who
pronounced Meyer, even at the outset of his exegetical career,
an expositor distinguished by thoroughness (Gründlichkeit),
correct perception, and sure judgment. The Handbook of de
Wette is marked by a singular power of condensation and
felicity of clear and terse expression; but the Commentary of
Meyer is superior in philological accuracy, and in the fulness
with which it sets forth not only the grounds on which his own

---

[1] Mr. Moulton, in his most accurate and admirable translation of Winer, omits
the word "sure," probably deeming it unnecessary any longer to affirm what
nobody now denies.

interpretation rests, but also the reasons which may be urged in support of, or in opposition to, the interpretations of others— a feature which gives special value to it as a practical discipline for the student of exegesis. And—independently of other considerations—the work of Dr. Meyer possesses the marked advantage of having undergone to a much greater extent successive revisions *at the hands of its author*, and has thus been enriched, not only by the working in of results gathered in the interval from the labours of others, but also by the ample fruits of the author's own more extended experience and more mature judgment. The first part of de Wette's Handbook appeared in 1836, and it was completed in 1848, while his death took place in 1849. The first part of Dr. Meyer's Commentary appeared in 1832, and it has ever since been receiving alterations and additions down to the spring of the present year. No doubt the work of de Wette has been reissued, since his death, in various editions by able and careful scholars, such as Brückner, Messner, and Moeller. But in this case we have no assurance, that the manipulation which the work has undergone is such as would have been approved by the mature judgment of the author, or even that it may be consistent with his known principles and views. Indeed, a lately reissued part of the work—the Commentary on Acts, as edited by Overbeck—presents a flagrant instance to the contrary. For Dr. Overbeck has not only made additions of his own, which amount to nearly two-thirds of the whole book, but—with a liberty, which in this country we should deem wholly unwarrantable, and strangely disrespectful to the memory of a man so distinguished as de Wette—he has overlaid the original work with a running commentary of tedious minuteness, written in support of critical views, to which de Wette had, in the preface to his own last edition, declared himself wholly opposed.[1] In Dr. Meyer's case, on the other hand, we have the

---

[1] De Wette's words—sufficiently remarkable—are to this effect : "That I have not entered more at length into a refutation of the destructive criticism of Baur,

latest judgments of the great exegete himself, as he passes under review the fresh contributions to the literature of the subject, and in their light re-examines his earlier positions, and recalls, modifies, or vindicates anew his conclusions. Nothing indeed is more remarkable in connection with Dr. Meyer's work than the results furnished by a comparison of its successive editions, as evincing the diligence with which he read and digested every new academic dissertation that might throw light on his subject, the impartiality and truth-loving spirit with which his mind remained open to fresh light and was ready to change or modify its interpretation wherever there seemed due ground, and the assiduous care with which he revised every sentence. The interleaved sheets—at present in my possession—shewing the corrections and additions made by Dr. Meyer on the fourth edition in preparation for the fifth, furnish, in their MS. erasures and copious marginal annotations, even a more striking illustration of the extent and variety of this alteration than the subjoined specimen, taken *ad aperturam,* in which I have underlined the portions changed.[1] This constant process of alteration

may possibly occasion disappointment in some quarters; but, besides that it would have required more space than I have at my disposal, I deem such a refutation superfluous. Extravagant criticism of this sort nullifies itself; and the only benefit arising from it is, that by exceeding all bounds it awakens the feeling of a necessity for imposing self-restraint." In the face of this condemnation Dr. Overbeck has superinduced on the work of de Wette an elaborate treatise carrying out in detail that very criticism, and thereby—whatever might under other circumstances be its value—fundamentally altering the standpoint and perverting the character of the book. The pleas by which he attempts to vindicate his course are wholly inadequate to justify so unprecedented a violation of the respect due to a great name and a great book, as is the publication, under cover of a new edition, of views diametrically opposed to the last judgment of the author.

[1] Rom. v. i. The underlining shows the extent of the alterations.

Fourth Edition.

V. 1.[1] Οὖν folgert aus dem ganzen vorigen Abschnitt 3, 21—4, 25, und zwar formell so weiterführend, dass δικαιωθέντες

Fifth Edition.

V. 1.[1] Οὖν folgert aus dem ganzen vorigen Abschnitt 3, 21—4, 25, und zwar formell so weiterführend, dass δικαιωθέντες

[1] Ueber V. 1-8. s. *Winzer* Commentat. Lips. 1832.

[1] Ueber V. 1-8. s. *Winzer* Commentat. Lips. 1832. Ueber das ganze Kap.: *Stölting* Beitäge z. Exegese d. Paul. Briefe, Gött. 1869. p 3 ff.

and addition serves to account, in a great measure, for the somewhat awkward form of many of the sentences, broken up as they are by subsequent parenthetical insertions, or prolonged by the appending of fresh clauses not contemplated at the outset.

Fourth Edition.	*Fifth Edition.*
gleich nach διὰ τὴν δικαίωσιν ἡμ. mit sieghaftem Nachdrucke wieder an die Spitze tritt. In welcher *beglückenden Heilsgewissheit* die Gläubigen vermöge ihrer durch den Glauben eingetretenen Rechtfertigung (δικαιωθέντες) sich befinden (nicht ihre *Heiligung*, wie *Rothe* will), soll nun geschildert werden. — εἰρήνην ἔχ. π. τ. Θεόν] Der Gerechtfertigte ist nicht mehr in dem Verhältnisse eines Menschen, dem Gott feind sein muss und ist (ἐχθρὸς Θεοῦ, V. 9 f.) sondern *Frieden* (nicht allgemein: *Befriedigung*, Genüge, wie *Th. Schott* meint) hat er in seinem Verhältnisse zu Gott. Es ist *der* Friede, der im bewussten objectiven Zustande der Versöhnung besteht, das Gegentheil des Zustandes, in welchem man dem göttlichen Zorne verfallen ist. Mit der Rechtfertigung tritt dieser Friede als sofortige und dauernde Folge derselben ein. Daher δικαιωθέντες — ἔχομεν (vrgl. Act. 9, 31. Joh. 16, 33.). Und *durch Christum* (διὰ τοῦ κυρίου etc.) ist dieser Besitz vermittelt, was sich zwar von selbst versteht, aber nach der Stärke und Fülle der eigenen Glaubenserfahrung des Ap. sehr natürlich noch besonders hervortritt, um an diese objective Ursache des Friedensstandes wie triumphirend auzuknüpfen, was wir ihr hinsichtlich des fraglichen Punktes zu verdanken haben V. 2. — πρός (von der ethischen Beziehung, *Bernhardy* p. 265.) wie Act. 2, 47. 24, 16. Vrgl. Herodian. 8, 7. 8.: ἀντὶ πολέμου μὲν εἰρήνην ἔχοντες πρὸς θεούς. Plat. Pol. 5. p. 465. B.: εἰρήνην πρὸς	gleich nach διὰ τὴν δικαίωσιν ἡμ. mit sieghaftem Nachdrucke wieder an die Spitze tritt. In welcher *beglückenden Heilsgewissheit* die Gläubigen vermöge ihrer durch den Glauben eingetretenen Rechtfertigung sich befinden, soll nun näher dargelegt, nicht aber soll *ermahnt* werden (*Hofm.* nach der Lesart ἔχωμεν), "unser Verhältniss zu Gott ein Friedensverhältniss sein zu lassen" (durch Glaubens*leben*), wobei der Nachdruck, welcher doch offenbar zunächst auf δικαιωθ. und dann auf εἰρήνην ruht, auf διὰ τοῦ κυρίου ἡμ. Ἰ. Χ. liegen soll. — εἰρήνην ἔχ. π. τ. Θεόν] Der Gerechtfertigte befindet sich nicht mehr in dem Verhältnisse eines Menschen, dem Gott feind sein muss und ist (ἐχθρὸς Θεοῦ, V 9 f.), sondern *Frieden* (nicht allgemein: *Befriedigung*, Genüge, wie *Th. Schott* meint) besitzt er in seinem Verhältnisse zu Gott. Das ist *der* Friede, der im bewussten objectiven Zustande der Versöhnung besteht, das Gegentheil des Zustandes, in welchem man dem göttlichen *Zorne* und dem *sensus irae* verfallen ist. Mit der Rechtfertigung tritt dieser Friede als sofortige und dauernde Folge derselben ein.[1] Daher δικαιωθέντες — ἔχομεν (vrgl. Act. 9, 31. Joh. 16, 33.). Und *durch Christum* (διὰ τοῦ κυρίου etc.) als den εἰρηνοποιός, ist ihm dieses *pacem obtinere* (*Bremi* ad Isocr. Archid. p. 111.) vermittelt, was sich zwar von selbst versteht, aber nach der Stärke und Fülle der eigenen Glaubenserfahrung des Ap. sehr natürlich noch besonders wieder hervortritt, um

[1] Vrgl. *Dorner* d. Rechtfert. durch d. Glauben p. 12. f.

In estimating the character and value of Dr. Meyer's work, it is essential that we should always bear in mind the precise standpoint from which it is written. That is simply and solely, as we have already indicated, the standpoint of the exegete, who endeavours in the exercise of his own independent judgment to arrive, by the use of the proper means, at the historical sense of Scripture. His object is not to seek support for the doctrines, nor does he bind himself or regulate his operations by the definitions or decisions of any particular Church. On the contrary, he reaches his results by a purely exegetical process, and places them, when so found, at the disposal of the Church. Under these circumstances, it is not perhaps surprising that these results do not in all respects accord with the traditional interpretation, or with the received doctrines, of the Church to which he belonged (the Lutheran). But as little is it surprising, on the

Fourth Edition.

ἀλλήλους οἱ ἄνδρες ἄξουσιν. Legg. 12. p. 955. B. Alc. I. p. 107. D. Nicht zu verwechseln mit dem göttlich gewirkten *innern* Frieden (von welchem Phil. 4, 7. εἰρήνη τοῦ Θεοῦ zu fassen ist, vrgl. Kol. 3, 15.); sondern dieser ist das subjective Correlat des objectiven εἰρήνη πρὸς τ. Θεόν.

Fifth Edition.

an diese objective Ursache des Friedenstandes wie triumphirend anzuknüpfen, was wir ihr hinsichtlich des fraglicher Punktes zu verdanken haben V. 2. Um so weniger ist Grund vorhanden, διὰ τοῦ κυρίου etc. an εἰρήνην anzuschliessen (*Stölting*); es gehört wie πρὸς τ. Θεόν nach der Stellung von ἔχομεν zu diesem Worte. — πρός (von der ethischen Beziehung, *Bernhardy* p. 265.) wie Act. 2, 47. 24, 16. Vrgl. Herodian. 8, 7. 8: ἀντὶ πολέμου μὲν εἰρήνην ἔχοντες πρὸς θεούς. Plat. Pol. 5. p. 465. B.: εἰρήνην πρὸς ἀλλήλους οἱ ἄνδρες ἄξουσιν. Legg. 12. p. 955. B. Alc. I. p. 107. D., Xenoph. u. A. Nicht zu verwechseln mit dem göttlich gewirkten Gemüthszustand des *Seelen*friedens, von welchem Phil. 4, 7. εἰρήνη τοῦ Θεοῦ zu fassen ist, vrgl. Kol. 3. 15.; sondern dieser ist das subjective Correlat des objectiven Verhältnisses der εἰρήνη, welche wir πρὸς τ. Θεόν haben, obwohl mit letzterer untrennbar verbunden.

other hand, that the longer Dr. Meyer prosecuted the study of Scripture from his own standpoint, the closer was the approximation of his general results to the conclusions embodied in the great Confessions of the Protestant Church. Some petulant critics, indeed, who seem slow to give to any that differ from them credit for that love of the truth to which they themselves lay claim, have sneered at the comparatively conservative and orthodox issues of his later exegesis; but no one has ventured openly to affirm that these issues were reached otherwise than by the consistent and conscientious application of his exegetical principles. The general result in Dr. Meyer's case—which is only what may be reasonably expected, unless we are to suppose that the great body of earlier interpreters have studied Scripture wholly in vain—coincides with the well-known statement of Winer, that "the controversies among interpreters have usually led back to the admission that the old Protestant views of the meaning of Scripture are the correct ones."[1] If the study of this book is fitted to supersede a mere blind attachment to foregone conclusions, it is no less adapted to counteract the too prevalent tendency in our own day to empty Scripture of all definite and

[1] In the Preface to the *fourth* edition of his Commentary on Romans, issued in 1865, Meyer has some interesting remarks as to the phases of opinion which had come and gone (or nearly so) within his own experience. "We older men," he says, "have seen the day when Dr. Paulus and his devices were in vogue; he died without leaving a disciple behind him. We passed through the tempest raised by Strauss some thirty years ago; and with what a sense of solitariness might its author now celebrate his jubilee! We saw the constellation of Tübingen arise, and, even before Baur departed hence, its lustre had waned. A fresh and firmer basis for the truth which had been assailed, and a more complete apprehension of that truth—these were the blessings which the waves left behind; and so will it be when the present surge has passed away. What Strauss says by way of censure on Schleiermacher—that he had himself lashed with cords to the mast of faith in Christ, in order that he might pass by the dangerous island of criticism unharmed—will always (in the sense in which it held true of *that* Ulysses) redound to his praise. The Church and its science will continue bound to the strong mast of faith in Christ, and bound to it with the cords—that cannot be torn asunder—which the New Testament has woven in its living word. Only in the event of these bands giving way would the voices of criticism prove siren-songs leading it to destruction."

objective significance, or to find in it just what suits the sentiments or wishes of the seeker.

Much impressed by frequent use with the value of the work, I have long cherished a wish that its contents might be made available in an English dress to the professional student of Scripture, who might not be able to consult it with facility in the original; and when sometime ago Messrs. Clark obtained the consent of the German publishers to the issue of an English translation, I undertook at their request, and with the readily given sanction of Dr. Meyer, to edit the work. I was induced to do so, not only because it seemed important that the translation of such a work should be executed on uniform principles, and on a common plan—which it was not likely to be, if its several parts were rendered by different translators acting independently—but also because it appeared desirable that a work of so technical a character, the value of which largely depends on the minute accuracy of the rendering, should be revised and passed through the press by some one more or less familiar with its professional use. It has frequently happened that translations otherwise good have been disfigured by blunders springing from the want of this special knowledge on the part of the translators.[1] I trust

---

[1] I subjoin a few illustrations, out of a great many culled from various sources, which have come at different times under my own observation, and which may suffice to indicate the character of the mistakes into which translators not specially conversant with the subject under discussion are apt to fall:—Zusammensetzung des Worts, "connection of the words;" den gewichtigen Gleichbau, "the forcible comparison;" was betrifft der Structur, "as regards the style;" prinzipiell, "principal;" in einer ... Rection, "in a direction;" zu interpungiren, "to interpolate;" sächliche Objecte, "sensible objects;" sinnliche Vorstellung, "ingenious representation;" sinnfällig, "spirit-crushing;" in dem ergänzten Vordersatze, "in the enlarged premise;" technischer Terminus, "technical terminus;" unverträglich, "unbearable;" Vorwurf, "theme;" Ausweg, "elucidation;" Vorhaltung des thatsächlichen Bestandes, "reproach against the actual resistance offered;" ein Anklang unserer Stelle, "a corroboration of our passage;" Hellenen, "Hellenists;" verzweifelnde Verachtung, "doubtful repute;" Cult, "culture;" absonderlich, "ingenious;" Attraction, "contraction;" den von Hofm. angezogenen Belegen gemäss, "not in conformity to the accompaniments added to it by H.;" thatsächliche Belege zu, "actual consequences of;" eigentlicher Sinn, "actual sense;" mit Accus. der Person und der Sache, "with the accusative of the person

that the present translation—on which no small pains have been bestowed both by the translators and by the reviser—may be found tolerably free from these grosser errors; although, on looking into it afresh, I find not a few instances in which the effort to reproduce the form as well as the matter of the original may occasion some perplexity to the English reader, and there are others where I am by no means certain that we have seized or have clearly enough expressed the meaning. This specially applies to some of the passages in which Dr. Meyer deals with the new interpretations so copiously thrown out by the subtlety of Dr. von Hofmann of Erlangen, whose ingenious refinements and obscurities—to which I suppose Dr. Meyer's strong language towards the close of his Preface to the German edition to allude —are by no means easy to render. The changes which, in the fulfilment of my somewhat delicate task, I have ventured to make may not—I can well suppose—always appear to the translators as improvements; and it is but fair to them that I should accept the responsibility of the form in which their translation appears.

In reproducing so great a masterpiece of exegesis, I have not thought it proper to omit any part of its discussions or of its references—however little some of these may appear likely to be of interest or use to English scholars—because an author such as Dr. Meyer is entitled to expect that his work shall not be tampered with, and I have not felt myself at liberty to assume

and on the case generally;" als der Welt verfallen, "as adapted to the world;" das Richturtheil, "the right sentence;" dem sittlichen Dünkel, "individuals in moral darkness;" eine schleppende Wiederholung, "a repetition too long delayed;" der so gewandt die griechische Schriftsprache handhabende, "who so cleverly applied to his use utterances of the Greek Scriptures;" Medium (used of the "middle" voice) "the medium;" ist erst Folge, "is the first consequence;" ein schiefer Gedanke, "a deeper thought;" frei nach der LXX, "entirely from the LXX;" anschauliche Bezeichnung, "a subjective relation;" der nachsätzliche δέ, "the emphatic δέ;" "Reihe und Glied, "row and member;" thetischer, "theistic;" unter dogmatischen Händeln sein Leben verlor, "lost his life by ecclesiastical visitation;" Beides halbirend, "preserving both;" Philo *l.c.* "Philo *passim*;" Isidorus Hispalensis, "Isidore of Spain;" Theophil. ad Autol., "Theophylact ad Autol.;" Beyschlag (proper name), "a bye-blow."

that the judgment of others as to the expediency of any omission would coincide with my own. Nor have I deemed it necessary to append any notes of dissent from, or of warning against, the views of Dr. Meyer, even where these are decidedly at variance with opinions which I hold. Strong representations were made to me that it was desirable to annex to certain passages notes designed to counteract their effect, but it is obvious that, if I had adopted this course in some instances, I should have been held to accept or approve of the author's views in other cases where I had not inserted any such *caveat*. The book is intended for, and can in fact only be used with advantage by, the professional scholar. Its general exegetical excellence far outweighs its occasional doctrinal defects; and, in issuing it without note or comment, I take for granted that the reader will use it, as he ought, with discrimination. He will find a valuable exhibition of complementary views in the American translation of Dr. Lange's Commentary, accompanied with elaborate notes by Dr. Schaff, and issued in this country by Messrs. Clark, while the logical sequence and doctrinal significance of the Epistle will be found specially developed in the Commentary of Dr. Charles Hodge.

The translation of the present volume has been made with care by the Rev. John C. Moore. I have revised it throughout, and carried it through the press. I subjoin to this Preface a note of the Exegetical Literature of the Epistle to the Romans, and of the Pauline or Apostolic Epistles generally; because information respecting it is often desired, and is only to be gathered from such works as Walch's *Bibliotheca Theologica*, Winer's *Handbuch der theologischen Literatur*, Darling's *Cyclopaedia Bibliographica*, and other sources, which are not always accessible to the student. I have also indicated, in general, the official position of the writers, and the date of their death. A notice is also prefixed to this volume—once for all—of some abbreviations, etc. used throughout the work.

The General Preface, specially written by Dr. Meyer for the English translation, will now be read with a deeper interest, as it was the last production of his pen. As these sheets were passing through the press—and while recent accounts had testified to the almost unimpaired vigour with which he was still pursuing in a green old age the revision of his Commentary—the news arrived of his death, after a very brief illness, on the 21st of June. The life of a scholar presents in general little of outward incident; but the following brief outline of the leading facts in his career, which has been kindly furnished to me by his son Dr. Gustav Meyer, will not be without interest.

Heinrich August Wilhelm Meyer was born on 10th January 1800 at Gotha, where his father was shoemaker to the Court. He attended the Gymnasium of his native town, where he was imbued by Schulze, Doering, and Rost with the most earnest zeal for the study of the classical languages, and, while at school there, he laid the foundation of those sure and solid attainments, and of that grammatical acuteness and precision, by the application of which to exegesis he has acquired so well founded a reputation in the theological world. At the age of eighteen he finished his school course with the greatest distinction as *primus omnium*, and entered the University of Jena, with a view to study theology under the guidance of Gabler, Danz, and Schott, while he also attended the prelections of Luden on History and of Fries on Philosophy. After two years and a half of study there he left Jena, passed his examination, and went to Grone near Göttingen, to act as resident tutor in the Academy of Pastor Oppermann, whose daughter he afterwards married. In January 1823, after having been examined afresh, he was appointed to the pastoral cure of the hamlet of Osthausen. On the dying out of the Gotha line, Osthausen was annexed to the Duchy of Meiningen. While settled there, he issued his edition of the *Libri symbolici ecclesiae Lutheranae*, which was published in 1830 by Vandenhoeck and Ruprecht at Göttingen. He had already acquired, in the year 1827, by *Colloquium* from the Consistory of Hannover the necessary recognition *ad eundem* in that kingdom, and in January 1831 he became pastor at Harste near Göttingen. Here he commenced the work, to which with untiring zeal he devoted himself (mostly during the earliest hours of the morning) down to the end of his life—his Commentary on the New Testament. In the autumn of 1837 he was called to Hoya as Superintendent, and after four years was transferred to Hannover as Consistorialrath, Superintendent and Pastor Primarius in the Neustädter Kirche. In 1845 the degree of Doctor of Theology was conferred on him by the Theological Faculty of Göttingen. A very painful abdominal affection in the year 1846, which compelled him to refrain entirely from work for a considerable period, tended to mature his resolution to give up a position which involved too great an amount of labour, and to devote himself to the Consistory alone. He did so accordingly in the summer of 1848. In May 1861 he received the title of Oberconsistorialrath. On the 1st October 1865 he retired, retaining at first the superintendence of certain examinations, which however he soon also gave up. During the night of the 15th June in the present year he was seized with intussusception, which proved beyond the reach of medical skill, and which, after a painful illness, put an end to his busy life on the 21st of June.

If the great work, on which rests his fame, shall meet in this country with but a tithe of the acceptance which it has found in Germany, those who have taken part with me in reproducing it will not account their labour lost.

W. P. D.

GLASGOW COLLEGE, *September* 1873.

EXEGETICAL LITERATURE OF THE EPISTLE.

[For Commentaries, and collections of Notes, embracing the whole New Testament, see Preface to the Commentary on the Gospel of St. Matthew. The following list includes works which deal with the Apostolic or the Pauline Epistles generally, or which treat specially of the Epistle to the Romans. Works mainly of a popular or practical character have, with a few exceptions, been excluded, since, however valuable they may be on their own account, they have but little affinity with the strictly exegetical character of the present work. Several of the older works named are of little value; others are chiefly doctrinal or controversial. Monographs on chapters or sections are generally noticed by Meyer *in loc.* The editions quoted are usually the earliest; *al.* appended denotes that the work has been more or less frequently reprinted. † marks the date of the author's death, c. = circa, an approximation to it.]

ABAILARD (Peter), † 1142, Scholastic : Commentariorum super S. Pauli Epistolam ad Romanos libri v. [Opera.]

ALESIUS [or HALES] (Alexander), † 1565, Prof. Theol. at Leipzig : Disputationes in Epistolam ad Romanos, cum P. Melancthonis praefatione.
8°, Vitemb. 1553.

ALEXANDER Natalis. See NOEL (Alexandre).

ALTING (Jacobus), † 1679, Prof. Theol. at Gröningen : Commentarius theoretico-practicus in Epistolam ad Romanos. [Opera.]
2°, Amstel. 1686.

AMBIANENSIS (Georgius), † 1657, Capuchin monk at Paris : Trina Pauli theologia . . . seu omnigena in universas Pauli epistolas commentaria exegetica, tropologica et anagogica.   2°, Paris. 1649-50.

AMBROSIASTER [or PSEUDO-AMBROSIUS], c. 380, generally identified with Hilarius the Deacon : Commentarius in Epistolas xiii. B. Pauli. [Ambrosii Opera.]

ANSELMUS [or HERVEUS], c. 1100 : Enarrationes in omnes S. Pauli Epistolas.   2°, Paris. 1533.

AQUINAS (Thomas), † 1274, Scholastic : Expositio in omnes Epistolas S. Pauli.   2°, Basil. 1475 *al.*

ARBOREUS (Joannes), c. 1550, Prof. Theol. at Paris : Commentarius in omnes Pauli Epistolas.   2°, Paris. 1553.

ARETIUS (Benedictus), † 1574, Prof. Theol. at Berne : Commentarii in omnes Epistolas D. Pauli, et canonicas.   2°, Morgiis, 1683.

BALDUIN (Friedrich), † 1627, Prof. Theol. at Wittenberg : Commentarius in omnes Epistolas apostoli Pauli . . . (Separately, 1608-1630).
4°, Francof. 1644 *al.*

BAUMGARTEN (Sigmund Jakob), † 1757, Prof. Theol. at Halle: Auslegung
des Briefes Pauli an die Römer.   4°, Halae, 1749.
BAUMGARTEN-CRUSIUS (Ludwig Friedrich Otto), † 1843, Prof. Theol. at Jena:
Commentar zum Römerbrief.   8°, Jena, 1844.
BEDA Venerabilis, † 735, Monk at Jarrow: Expositio in Epistolas Pauli
[a Catena from the works of Augustine, probably by Florus Lug-
dunensis, c. 852], *et* In Epistolas septem catholicas liber. [Opera.]
BEELEN (Jean-Théodore), R. C. Prof. of Or. Lang. at Louvain: Commen-
tarius in Epistolam S. Pauli ad Romanos.   8°, Lovani, 1854.
BELSHAM (Thomas) † 1829, Unitarian minister in London: The Epistles of
Paul the Apostle translated, with an exposition and notes.
                                       4°, Lond. 1822.
BENECKE (Wilhelm), † 1837, retired Hamburg merchant: Der Brief Pauli
an die Römer erläutert;   8°, Heidelb. 1831.
Translated . . . .   8°, Lond. 1854.
BISPING (August), R. C. Prof. Theol. at Münster: Exegetisches Handbuch
zu den Briefen der Apostels Paulus.   8°, Münster, 1854-8 *al*.
BOEHME (Christian Friedrich), † 1844, Pastor at Lucka near Altenburg:
Epistola Pauli ad Romanos Graece cum commentario perpetuo.
                                       8°, Lips. 1806.
BRAIS (Etienne de), c. 1680, Prof. Theol. at Saumur: Epistolae Pauli ad
Romanos analysis paraphrastica cum notis.   4°, Salmurii, 1670.
BRENT (Johann), † 1570, Provost at Stuttgard: Commentarius in Epistolam
ad Romanos.   2°, Francof. 1564 *al*.
BROWN (David), D.D., Prof. Theol. Free Church College, Aberdeen: Com-
mentary on the Epistle to the Romans, embracing the last results of
criticism.   12°, Glasg. 1860.
BROWN (John), D.D., † 1858, Prof. Exeg. Theol. to the United Presbyterian
Church, Edinburgh: Analytical Exposition of the Epistle of Paul
. . . to the Romans.   8°, Edin. 1857.
BRUNO, † 1101, Founder of the Carthusian Order: Commentarius in omnes
Epistolas Pauli.   2°, Paris. 1509.
BUCER (Martin), † 1551, Prof. Theol. at Cambridge: Metaphrasis et enar-
ratio in Epistolam Pauli ad Romanos.   2°, Basil. 1562.
BUGENHAGEN (Johann), † 1558, Prof. Theol. at Wittenberg: Interpretatio
Epistolae Pauli ad Romanos.   8°, Hagenoae, 1523.
BULLINGER (Heinrich), † 1575, Pastor at Zürich: Commentarii in omnes
Epistolas apostolorum.   2°, Tiguri, 1537 *al*.

CAJETANUS [Tommaso da Vio], † 1534, Cardinal: Epistolae S. Pauli et
aliorum apostolorum ad Graecam veritatem castigatae et juxta
sensum literalem enarratae.   2°, Venet. 1531 *al*.
CALIXTUS (Georg), † 1656, Prof. Theol. at Helmstadt: Expositiones litterales
in Epistolas ad Romanos, ad Corinthios priorem et posteriorem, ad
Galatas, ad Ephesios, ad Philippenses, ad Colossenses, ad Thessa-
lonienses . . . et ad Titum.   4°, Helmstadii, 1664-66.

CALVIN [CHAUVIN] (Jean), †1564: Commentarii in omnes Epistolas Pauli apostoli atque etiam Epistolam ad Ebraeos; necnon in Epistolas canonicas. 2°, Genevae, 1551 *al.*
CAPELLUS [CAPPEL] (Louis), † 1658. See ACTS.
CARPZOV (Johann Benedict), †1803, Prof. Theol. and Greek at Helmstadt: Stricturae theologicae et criticae in Epistolam Pauli ad Romanos... 8°, Helmstad. 1758.
CASSIODORUS (Magnus Aurelius), † 563, Chancellor of the Ostrogoth empire: Complexiones in Epistolas apostolorum, in Acta et in Apocalypsim quasi brevissima explanatione decursas. . . . 8°, Florent. 1721 *al.*
CATARINO (Ambrogio). See POLITI (Lanzelotto).
CHALMERS (Thomas), D.D., † 1847, Principal of F. C. College, Edinburgh: Lectures on the Epistle of Paul the Apostle to the Romans. 12°, Glasg. 1842 *al.*
CHRYSOSTOMUS (Joannes), † 407, Archbishop of Constantinople: Homiliae in Epistolas Pauli. [Opera.]
CHYTRAEUS [or KOCHHAFE] (David), † 1600, Prof. Theol. at Rostock: Epistola Pauli ad Romanos, brevi ac dialectica dispositione partium et grammatica declaratione textus . . . explicata. 8°, n. p. 1599.
CLAUDE (Jean), † 1687, Minister at the Hague: Commentaire sur l'Epître aux Romains. [Oeuvres.]
CONTARINI (Gasparo), † 1542, Cardinal: Scholia in Epistolas Pauli. [Opera.] 2°, Paris. 1571 *al.*
CONTZEN (Adam), † 1618, Jesuit at Mentz: Commentaria in Epistolam S. Pauli ad Romanos. 2°, Colon. 1629.
CONYBEARE (William John, M.A.), HOWSON (John Saul), D.D.: Life and Epistles of St. Paul. 4°, Lond. 1852 *al.*
COX (Robert) M.A., P. C. of Stonehouse, Devon: Horae Romanae, or an attempt to elucidate St. Paul's Epistle to the Romans, by an original translation, explanatory notes, and new divisions. 8°, Lond. 1824.
CRAMER (Johann Andreas), † 1788, Prof. Theol. at Kiel: Der Brief Pauli an die Römer aufs neue übersetzt und ausgelegt. 4°, Leip. 1784.
CRELL (Johann), † 1633, Socinian teacher at Racow: Commentarius in Epistolam Pauli ad Romanos, ex praelectionibus ejus conscriptus a Jona Schlichtingio . . . . 8° Racov. 1636.
CRUCIGER [CREUZINGER] (Kaspar), †1548, Pastor at Leipzig: Commentarius in Epistolam Pauli ad Romanos. 8°, Vitemb. 1567.

DALE (John): Analysis of all the Epistles of the New Testament. 12° Oxf. 1652.
DAMASCENUS (Joannes), † 754, Monk at S. Saba: Ex universa interpretatione J. Chrysostomi excerpta compendiaria in Epistolas S. Pauli. [Opera.]
DELITZSCH (Franz), Prof. Theol. at Leipzig: Brief an die Römer aus dem griechischen Urtext in das hebräische uebersetzt und aus Talmud und Midrasch erläutert. 8° Leip. 1870.

DICKSON (David), † 1662, Prof. Theol. at Glasgow and Edinburgh : Expositio analytica omnium apostolicarum Epistolarum. . . . 4°, Glasg. 1645. *and* Analytical Exposition of all the Epistles.   2°, Lond. 1659.
DIEU (Louis de), † 1642, Prof. in the Walloon College at Leyden : Animadversiones in Epistolam ad Romanos. Accessit spicilegium in reliquas ejusdem apostoli, ut et catholicas epistolas.
4°, Lugd. Bat. 1646.
DIONYSIUS CARTHUSIANUS [DENYS DE RYCKEL], † 1471, Carthusian monk : Elucidissima in divi Pauli Epistolas commentaria.   8°, Paris. 1531.

EDWARDS (Timothy), M.A., Vicar of Okehampton, Devon : Paraphrase, with critical annotations on the Epistles to the Romans and Galatians, with an analytical scheme of the whole.   4°, Lond. 1752.
EST [ESTIUS] (Willem Hessels van), † 1613, R. C. Chancellor of Douay : In omnes beati Pauli et aliorum apostolorum Epistolas commentarius.
2°, Duaci, 1614-16, *al.*
EWALD (Georg Heinrich August), Prof. Or. Lang. at Göttingen : Die Sendschreiben des Apostels Paulus übersetzt und erklärt.
8°, Götting. 1857.
EWBANK (William Withers), M.A., Incumbent at Everton : Commentary on the Epistle of Paul to the Romans . . .   8°, Lond. 1850-51.

FABER Stapulensis (Jacobus) [Jacques Lefevre d'Etaples], † 1536, resident at Nerac : Commentarius in Epistolas Pauli . . .   2°, Paris. 1512 *al.*
FAYE (Antoine de la), † 1616, Prof. at Geneva : Commentarius in Epistolam ad Romanos.   8°, Genevae, 1608.
FELL (JOHN), †1686, Bishop of Oxford: A Paraphrase and annotations upon all the Epistles of St. Paul, by Abraham Woodhead, Richard Allestry and Obadiah Walker. Corrected and improved by Dr. John Fell. [First issued anonymously in 1675.]   8°. Lond. 1708.
FERME (Charles), † 1617, Principal of Fraserburgh College : Analysis logica in Epistolam ad Romanos.   12°, Edin. 1651 *al.*
FERUS [WILD] (Johannes), † 1554, Cathedral Preacher at Mentz : Exegesis in Epistolam Paulli ad Romanos.   8°, Paris. 1559.
FEUARDENT (François), † 1612, Franciscan preacher at Paris : Commentarius in Epistolam ad Romanos.   8°, Paris, 1599.
FLATT (Johann Friedrich von), † 1821, Prof. Theol. at Tübingen : Vorlesungen über den Brief Pauli an die Römer, herausgegeben von Ch. D. F. Hoffmann.   8°, Tübing. 1825.
FLORUS Lugdunensis, c. 852.   See BEDA.
FORBES (John), LL.D., Prof. of Oriental Languages at Aberdeen : Analytical commentary on the Epistle to the Romans, tracing the train of thought by the aid of parallelism.   8°, Edinb. 1868.
FRITZSCHE (Karl Friedrich August), † 1846, Prof. Theol. at Rostock : Pauli ad Romanos Epistola. Recensuit et cum commentariis perpetuis edidit.   8°, Halis, 1836-43.

FROMOND (Libert), † 1653, Prof. Sac. Scrip. at Louvain : Commentarius in omnes Epistolas Pauli apostoli et in septem canonicas aliorum apostolorum epistolas.   2°, Lovan. 1663 *al.*

GAGNÉE (Jean de), † 1549, Rector of the University of Paris : Brevissima et facillima in omnes divi Pauli et canonicas epistolas scholia.
8°, Paris, 1543 *al.*
GERHARD (Johann), † 1637, Prof. Theol. at Jena : Adnotationes posthumae in Epistolam at Romanos, cum Analectis Jo. Ernesti Gerhardi.
4°, Jenae. 1666 *al.*
GLÖCKLER (Conrad), : Der Brief des Apostel Paulus an die Römer erklärt.
8°, Frankf.-a.-M. 1834.
GOMAR (François), † 1641, Prof. Theol. at Gröningen : Analysis et explicatio Epistolarum Pauli ad Romanos, Gal. Philipp. Coloss. Philem. Hebraeos. [Opera.]   2°, Amstel. 1644.
GRÖNEWEGEN (Henricus), † 1692, Minister at Enkhuizen : Vytleginge van den Zendbrief Paulli aan de Romeynen.   4°, Gorinchem, 1681.
GUALTHER [WALTHER] (Rudolph), † 1586, Pastor at Zurich : Homiliae in omnes Epistolas apostolorum.   2°, Tiguri, 1599.
GUILLIAUD (Claude), † 1550, Theological Lecturer at Autun : Collationes in omnes Epistolas Pauli.   4°, Lugd. 1542 *al.*

HALDANE (Robert), of Airthrey, † 1842 : Exposition of the Epistle to the Romans, with remarks on the Commentaries of Dr. Macknight, Prof. Tholuck, and Prof. Moses Stuart.   12°, Lond. 1842 *al.*
HAYMO, † 853, Bishop of Halberstadt [or REMIGIUS] : Commentarius in Epistolas S. Pauli.   2°, Paris. 1556 *al.*
HEMMING [or HEMMINGSEN] (Niels), † 1600, Prof. Theol. at Copenhagen : Commentarius in omnes Epistolas apostolorum.
2°, Lips. 1572 *al.*
HEMSEN (Johann Tychsen), † 1830, Prof. Theol. at Göttingen : Der Apostel Paulus, sein Leben, Wirken, und siene Schriften herausgegeben von F. Luecke.   8°, Götting. 1830.
HENGEL (Wessel Albert van), Prof. Theol. in Leyden : Interpretatio Epistolae Pauli ad Romanos.   8°, Lugd. Bat. 1854-9.
HERVEUS DOLENSIS, c. 1130, Benedictine.   See ANSELMUS.
HESHUSIUS (Tilemann), † 1588, Prof. Theol. at Helmstadt : Commentarius in omnes Epistolas Pauli.   2°, Lips. 1605.
HIPSTED (Johann), † 1681, Prof. in Gymnasium at Bremen : Collationes philologicae in Epistolam ad Romanos.   4°, Bremae, 1675.
HODGE (Charles), D.D., Prof. Theol. at Princeton : Commentary on the Epistle to the Romans.   8°, Philadelphia, 1835 *al.*
HOFMANN (Johann Christian Konrad von), Prof. Theol. at Erlangen : Die Heilige Schrift Neuen Testaments zusammenhängend untersucht. III. Theil. Brief an die Römer.   8°, Nördlingen, 1868.

HUGO DE S. VICTORE, † 1141, Monk at Paris: Quaestiones circa Epistolas Pauli. [Opera.]

HYPERIUS [GERHARD] (Andreas), † 1564, Prof. Theol. at Marburg: Commentarii in Pauli Epistolas. 2°, Tiguri, 1583.

JATHO (Georg Friedrich), Director of Gymnasium at Hildesheim: Pauli Brief an die Römer nach seinem inneren Gedankengange erläutert.
8°, Hildesheim, 1858-9.

JOWETT (Benjamin), M.A., Master of Balliol College, Oxford: The Epistles of St. Paul to the Thessalonians, Galatians, Romans, with critical notes and dissertations. 8°, Lond. 1855.

JUSTINIANI [GIUSTINIANI] (Benedetto), † 1622, S. J. Prof. Theol. at Rome: Explanationes in omnes Pauli Epistolas [et in omnes catholicas].
2°, Lugd. 1612-21.

KISTEMAKER (Johann Hyazinth), † 1834, R. C. Prof. Theol. at Münster: Die Sendschreiben der Apostel (und die Apocalypse), übersetzt und erklärt. 8°, Münster, 1822-3.

KLEE (Heinrich), † 1840, R. C. Prof. Theol. at Münich: Commentar über des Apostel Pauli Sendschreiben an die Römer. 8°, Mainz, 1830.

KNIGHT (Robert): A Critical Commentary on the Epistle of St. Paul the Apostle to the Romans. 8°, Lond. 1854.

KÖLLNER (Wilhelm Heinrich Dorotheus Eduard), c. 1850, Prof. Theol. at Göttingen: Commentar zu dem Briefe des Paulus an die Römer.
8°, Darmst. 1834.

KREHL (August Ludwig Gottlob), † 1855, Prof. Pract. Theol. at Leipzig: Der Brief an die Römer ausgelegt. 8°, Leip. 1849.

LANFRANC, † 1089, Archbishop of Canterbury: Commentarii in omnes D. Pauli Epistolas. [Opera.]

LAPIDE (Cornelius à) [VAN DEN STEEN], † 1637, S. J. Prof. of Sacred Scripture at Louvain: Commentaria in omnes D. Pauli Epistolas.
2°, Antwerp. 1614 et al.

LAUNAY (Pierre de), Sieur de La Motte: Paraphrase et exposition sur les Epistres de S. Paul. 4°, Saumur et Charenton, 1647-50.

LEEUWEN (Gerbrand van), † 1721, Prof. Theol. at Amsterdam: Verhandeling van den Sendbrief Paulli aan de Romeynen.
4°, Amst. 1688-99.

LEWIN (Thomas), M.A.: The life and Epistles of S. Paul.
8°, Lond. 1851.

LIMBORCH (Philipp van), † 1712, Arminian Prof. Theol. at Amsterdam: Commentarius in Acta Apostolorum et in Epistolas ad Romanos et ad Ebraeos. 2°, Roterod. 1711.

LIVERMORE (Abiel Abbot), Minister at Cincinnati: The Epistle of Paul to the Romans, with a commentary and revised translation, and introductory essays. 12°, Boston, U. S., 1855.

LOCKE (John), † 1704. See GALATIANS.
LOMBARDUS (Petrus), † 1160, Scholastic : Collectanea in omnes Epistolas
    D. Pauli ex. SS. Patribus.   2°, Paris. 1535 *al.*

MACKNIGHT (James), D.D., † 1800, Minister at Edinburgh : A new literal
    translation . . . of all the apostolical Epistles, with a commentary
    and notes, philological, critical, explanatory and practical . . .
                                                       4°, Edin. 1795 *al.*
MAIER (Adalbert), R. C. Prof. Theol. at Freiburg: Commentar über den
    Brief Pauli an die Römer.   8°, Freiburg, 1847.
MARTYR (Peter) [VERMIGLI], † 1562, Prof. Theol. at Strasburg : In Episto-
    lam ad Romanos commentarii . . .   2°, Basil. 1558, *al.*
MEHRING (H. J. F.) : Der Brief Pauli an die Römer uebersetzt und erklärt.
                                                       8°, Stettin, 1859.
MELANCHTHON (Philipp), † 1560, Reformer: Adnotationes in Epistolas
    Pauli ad Romanos et Corinthios . . . 4°, Basil. 1522.—Commentarii
    in Ep. Pauli ad Romanos. 8°, Argent. 1540.—Epistolae Pauli ad
    Romanos scriptae enarratio . . .   8°, Vitemb. 1556 *al.*
MELVILLE (Andrew), † 1622, Principal of St. Mary's College, St. Andrews :
    Commentarius in divinam Pauli Epistolam ad Romanos . . .
                                                       8°, Edin. 1849.
MOMMA (Willem), † 1677, Pastor at Middelburg : Meditationes posthumae
    in Epistolas ad Romanos et Galatas.   8°, Hag. Com. 1678.
MORISON (James), D.D. Prof. Theol. to the Evangelical Union, Glasgow :
    An exposition of the Ninth chapter of Paul's Epistle to the Romans.
    8°, Kilmarnock, 1849. *And* A critical exposition of the Third chap-
    ter . . .   8°, Lond. 1866.
MORUS (Samuel Friedrich Nathanael), † 1792, Prof. Theol. at Leipzig:
    Praelectiones in Epistolam Pauli ad Romanos. Cum ejusdem versi-
    one Latina, locorumque quorundam N. T. difficiliorum interpre-
    tatione. Ed. J. T. S. Holzapfel.   8°, Lips. 1794.
MUSCULUS [or MEUSSLIN] (Wolfgang), † 1563, Prof. Theol. in Berne : In
    Epistolam ad Romanos commentarius.   2°, Basil. 1555 *al.*

NIELSEN (Rasmus), Prof. Theol. at Copenhagen : Der Brief Pauli an die
    Römer entwickelt . . .   8°, Leip. 1843.
NOEL (Alexandre) [NATALIS], † 1724, Dominican teacher of Church History
    at Paris : Expositio litteralis et moralis in Epistolas D. Pauli.
                                                       2°, Paris. 1710.

OECUMENIUS, c. 980, Bishop of Tricca : Commentaria in Acta Apostolorum,
    in omnes Pauli Epistolas, in Epistolas catholicas omnes . . .
                                                       2°, Veronae, 1532 *al.*
OLTRAMARE (Hugues), Minister at Geneva : Commentaire sur l'Epître aux
    Romains. [I—V. 11.]   8°, Genève, 1843.

ORIGENES, † 254, Catechete at Alexandria : Fragmenta in Epistolas Pauli.
[Opera.]
OSORIO (Jeronymo), † 1580, Bishop of Sylvas: In Epistolam Pauli ad
Romanos libri quatuor. [Opera.] 2°, Romae, 1592.

PAREUS [or WAENGLER] (David), † 1622, Prof. Theol. at Heidelberg: Commentarius in Epistolam ad Romanos. 4°, Francof. 1608 *al.*
PAULUS (Heinrich Eberhard Georg), † 1851. See GALATIANS.
PEILE (Thomas Williamson), D.D., Vicar of Luton : Annotations on the apostolical Epistles, designed chiefly for the use of students of the Greek text. 8°, Lond. 1848-52.
PELAGIUS, c. 420, British monk: Commentarii in Epistolas S. Pauli. [Hieronymi Opera.]
PHILIPPI (Friedrich Adolph), Prof. Theol. at Rostock : Commentar über den Brief an die Römer. 8°, Erlangen and Frankf. 1848-52.
PICQUIGNY (Bernardin) [BERNARDINUS A PICONIO], Cistercian monk : Epistolarum Pauli triplex expositio, cum analysi, paraphrasi et commentariis. 2°, Paris, 1703.
POLITI (Lanzelotto) [AMBROGIO CATARINO], † 1553, Archbishop of Conza: Commentarius in omnes divi Pauli et alias septem canonicas Epistolas. 2°, Romae, 1546 *al.*
POSSELT (August), c. 1715, Pastor at Zittau: Richtige Erklärung der Epistel Pauli an die Römer . . . 4°, Zittau, 1696.
PRIMASIUS, c. 550, Bishop of Adrumetum : Commentaria in Epistolas Pauli. [Bibl. Max. Patrum. X.]
PRZIPZCOV or PRZYPKOWSKY (Samuel), † 1670, Socinian teacher : Cogitationes sacrae ad omnes Epistolas apostolicas.
2°, Eleutheropoli [Amstel.], 1692.
PURDUE (Edward), M.A. : A Commentary on the Epistle to the Romans, with a revised translation. 8°, Dubl. 1855.
PYLE (Thomas), D.D., †1756, Vicar of Lynn : A Paraphrase, with some notes on the Acts of the Apostles and on all the Epistles of the New Testament. 8°, Lond. 1725 *al.*

QUISTORP (Johann), † 1648, Superintendent at Rostock : Commentarius in omnes Epistolas Paulinas. 4°, Rostoch, 1652.

RABANUS MAURUS, † 856, Archbishop of Mentz : Enarrationum in Epistolas B. Pauli libri triginta. [Opera.]
RAMBACH (Johann Jakob), † 1735, Superintendent in Giessen : Ausführliche und gründliche Erklärung der Epistel Pauli an die Römer.
4°, Bremae, 1738.
Introductio historico-theologica in Ep. P. ad Romanos, cum Martini Lutheri Praefatione variis observationibus exegeticis illustrata. 8°, Halae, 1727.

REICHE (Johann Georg), Prof. Theol. in Göttingen: Versuch einer ausführlichen Erklärung des Briefes Pauli an die Römer, mit historischen Einleitung und exegetisch-dogmatischen Excursen.
8°, Götting. 1833-4.
Commentarius criticus in Novum Testamentum, quo loca graviora et difficiliora lectionis dubiae accurate recensentur et explicantur. Tom I.—III. Epistolas Paulinas et catholicas continentes.
4° et 8°, Götting. 1853-62.
REITHMAYR (Franz Xaver), † 1871, R. C. Prof. Theol. at Munich : Commentar zum Briefe an die Römer. 8°, Regensburg, 1845.
REMIGIUS (of Auxerre), † 899. See HAYMO.
ROLLOCK (Robert), † 1598, Principal of the University of Edinburgh Analysis dialectica in Pauli apostoli Epistolam ad Romanos . . .
8°, Edin. 1594 al.
RÜCKERT (Leopold Immanuel), c. 1845, Prof. Theol. at Jena ; Commentar über den Brief an die Römer. 8°, Leip. 1831.

SADOLETO (Jacopo), † 1547, Cardinal: Commentarius in Epistolam ad Romanos. 8°, Venet. 1536 al.
SALMERON (Alphonso), † 1585, Jesuit: Commentarii in Epistolas S. Pauli. [Opera.]
SCHLICHTING (Jonas), † 1664. See CRELL (Johann).
SCHMID (Sebastian), † 1696, Prof. Theol. at Strassburg: Commentarii in Epistolas Pauli ad Romanos, Galatas et Colossenses, una cum paraphrasi epistolae prioris ad Corinthios, utriusque ad Thessalonicenses, prioris ad Timotheum, epistolae ad Philemonem et cantici Mariae. [Previously issued separately.] 4°, Hamb. 1704.
SCHMID (Christian Friedrich), † 1778, Prof. Theol. at Wittenberg : Annotationes in Epistolam Pauli ad Romanos, philologicae, theologicae et criticae. 8°, Lips. 1777.
SCHOTT (Theodor) : Der Römerbrief seinem Endzweck und seinem Gedankengang nach ausgelegt. 8°, Erlangen, 1858.
SEDULIUS Scotus Hiberniensis, c. 800 ? : In omnes S. Pauli epistolas collectaneum. 2°, Basil. 1528.
SEMLER (Johann Salomon), † 1791, Prof. Theol. at Halle: Paraphrasis Epistolae Pauli ad Romanos cum notis et translatione vetusta.
8°, Halis, 1769.
SELNECCER (Nicolaus), † 1592, Prof. Theol. in Leipzig : In omnes Epistolas Pauli apostoli commentarius plenissimus. 2°, Lips. 1595.
SHUTTLEWORTH (Philip Nicholas), D.D., Bishop of Chichester: A Pamphrastic translation of the apostolical Epistles, with notes.
8°, Oxf. 1829 al.
SLADE (James), †1860, Rector of West Kirby : Annotations on the Epistles; being a continuation of Mr. Elsley's Annotations.
8°, Lond. 1824 al.

Soto (Domingo de), † 1560, Prof. Theol. at Salamanca: Commentarius in Epistolam Pauli ad Romanos. 2°, Antverp. 1550.
Spener (Philipp Jakob), † 1705, Provost at Berlin: Auslegung des Briefes an die Römer aufs neue herausg. von H. Schott. 8°, Leip. 1859 al.
Steinhofer (Friedrich Christoph), † 1761: Erklärung des Epistel Pauli an die Römer; mit einem Vorwort von J. T. Beck.
8°, Tübing. 1851.
Stengel (Liborius), † 1835, R. C. Prof. Theol. at Freiburg: Commentar über den Brief des Paulus an die Römer . . .
8°, Freiburg, 1836.
Stenersen (Stener Johannes), † 1835, Prof. of Church History at Christiania: Epistolae Paulinae perpetuo commentario illustratae. Vol. I. Ep. ad Rom. Voll. II. III. Epp. ad Corinth. IV. Ep. ad Galat.
8°, Christiania, 1829-34.
Stuart (Moses), † 1852, Prof. of Sacred Literature at Andover: A Commentary on the Epistle to the Romans, with a translation and various excursus . . . 8°, Andover, 1832 al.

Taylor (John), D.D., † 1761, Minister at Norwich: A Paraphrase with notes on the Epistle to the Romans: to which is prefixed a Key to the apostolic writings. 4°, Lond. 1745 al.
Terrot (Charles Hughes), D.D., Bishop, Edinburgh: The Epistle to the Romans, with an introduction, paraphrase and notes.
8°, Lond. 1828.
Theodoretus, † c. 458, Bishop of Cyrus: Commentarius in omnes Pauli Epistolas. [Opera, et] 2°, Lond. 1636.
Theodorus, † 429, Bishop of Mopsuestia: Commentarii in Epistolas Pauli. [Fragments in the Catenae, collected by Fritzsche: Theodori Mops. Commentaria in N. T. 1847. From Galatians to Philemon, in a Latin translation, incorporated in Rabanus Maurus.]
Theophylactus, c. 1070, archbishop of Acris in Bulgaria: In D. Pauli Epistolas commentarius Graece et Latine cura A. Lindselli . . .
2°, Lond. 1636 al.
Tholuck (Friedrich August Gottreu), Prof. Theol. at Halle: Auslegung des Briefes Pauli an die Römer, nebst fortlaufenden Auszügen aus den exegetischen Schriften der Kirchenväter und Reformatoren. 8°, Berl. 1824 al.—Translated by the Rev. Robert Menzies, D.D.
8°, Edin. 1842.
Til (Salomon van), † 1713, Prof. Theol. at Leyden: De Sendbrieven van Paullus aan de Romeinen en Filippensen, ontleedt, verklaardt en betoogt. 4°, Haarlem, 1721.
Commentarius in quatuor Pauli Epistolas, nempe priorem ad Corinthios, Ephesios, Philippenses, ac Colossenses.
4°, Amstel. 1726.
Titelmann (Franz), 1553, Provincial of Capuchins at Rome: Elucidatio in omnes Epistolas apostolicas. 8°, Antwerp, 1532 al

TOLETUS [FRANCISCO DE TOLEDO], † 1596, S. J. Cardinal : Commentarius et annotationes in Epistolam Pauli ad Romanos.
4°, Romae, 1602 al.
TURNER (Samuel Hulbeart), D.D., † 1861, Prof. of Biblical Interpretation at New York : The Epistle to the Romans, in Greek and English. With an analysis and exegetical commentary. 8°, New York, 1853.
TURRETINI (Jean-Alphonse), † 1737, Prof. Theol. at Geneva : In Pauli ad Romanos Epistolae capita priora xi, praelectiones criticae, theologicae et concinuatoriae. 4°, Lausannae, 1741.

UMBREIT (Friedrich Wilhelm Karl), † 1860, Prof. Theol. at Heidelberg : Der Brief an die Römer, auf dem Grunde des Alten Testaments ausgelegt. 8°, Gotha, 1856.

VAREN (August), † 1684, Prof. Theol. at Rostock : Paulus evangelista Romanorum succincta divinissimae . . . Epistolae ad Romanos analysi et exegesi repraesentatus. 8°, Hamb. 1696.
VAUGHAN (Charles John), D.D., Master of the Temple : St. Paul's Epistle to the Romans, with notes. 8°, Camb. 1857.—Third edition, enlarged.
8°, Lond. and Camb. 1870.
VITRINGA (Kempe), †1722, Prof. Theol. at Franeker : Verklaringe over de agt eerste capittelen van de Brief Paulli aan de Romeinen.
4°, Franek. 1729.
VORST (Koonrad), † 1629, Prof. Theol. at Leyden : Commentarius in omnes . Epistolas apostolicas, exceptis secunda ad Timotheum, ad Titum, ad Philemonem et ad Ebraeos. 4°, Amstel. et Harder. 1631.

WALFORD (William), † 1850, Pastor at Uxbridge : Curae Romanae : notes on the Epistle to the Romans. 12°, Lond. 1846.
WEINGART (Johann Friedrich), Pastor at Grossfahnern, Gotha : Commentarius perpetuus in Pauli Epistolam ad Romanos. [Et In decem Apostoli Pauli epistolas, quas vulgo dicunt epistolas minores.]
8°, Gothae, 1816.
WEINRICH (Georg), † 1629, Prof. Theol. at Leipzig : Commentarii in Epistolas Pauli. 4°, Lips. 1620.
WELLER (Jakob), † 1664, Chief Chaplain at Dresden : Adnotationes in Epistolam Pauli ad Romanos . . . collectae opera Jo. Schindleri.
4°, Brunsvigae, 1654.
WILLET (Andrew), † 1621, Prebendary of Ely : Hexapla, that is, a sixfold commentarie upon the most divine Epistle . . . to the Romanes.
2°, Lond. 1620.
WILSON (Thomas), c. 1620, Minister at Canterbury : A Commentary on the most divine Epistle of St. Paul to the Romans.
4°, Lond. 1614 al.

WINZER (Julius Friedrich), † 1845, Prof. Theol. at Leipzig: Adnotationes ad loca quaedam Epistolae Pauli ad Romanos. 4°, Lips. 1835.
WITTICH (Christoph), † 1687, Prof. Theol. at Leyden: Investigatio Epistolae ad Romanos . . . una cum paraphrasi. 4°, Lugd. Bat. 1685.
WOODHEAD (Abraham). See FELL (John).

ZACHARIAE (Gotthilf Traugott), † 1777, Prof. Theol. at Kiel: Paraphrastische Erklärung des Briefes Pauli an die Römer. 8°. Götting. 1786.

ABBREVIATIONS.

al., et al. = and others; and other passages; and other editions.

ad or *in loc.*, refers to the note of the commentator or editor named on the particular passage.

comp. = compare. " Comp. on Matt. iii. 5" refers to Dr. Meyer's own commentary on the passage. So also " See on Matth. iii. 5."

codd. = codices or manuscripts. The uncial manuscripts are denoted by the usual letters, the Sinaitic by א.

min. = codices *minusculi*, manuscripts in cursive writing. Where these are individually quoted, they are marked by the usual Arabic numerals, as 33, 89.

Rec. or Recepta = Textus receptus, or lectio recepta (Elzevir).

l. c. = *loco citato* or *laudato*.

ver. = verse, vv. = verses.

f. ff. = and following. Ver. 16 f. means verses 16 and 17. vv. 16 ff. means verses 16 and two or more following.

vss. = versions. These, when individually referred to, are marked by the usual abridged forms. *E.g.* Syr. = Peschito Syriac ; Syr. p. = Philoxenian Syriac.

p. pp. = page, pages.

e. g. exempli gratia.

sc. = *scilicet.*

N. T. = New Testament. O. T. = Old Testament.

κ.τ.λ. = καὶ τὰ λοιπά.

The colon (:) is largely employed, as in the German, to mark the point at which a translation or paraphrase of a passage is introduced, or the transition to the statement of another's opinions.

. . . . indicates that words are omitted.

The books of Scripture and of the Apocrypha are generally quoted by their usual English names and abbreviations. Ecclus. = Ecclesiasticus. 3 Esd., 4 Esd. [or Esr.] = the books usually termed 1st and 2d Esdras.

The classical authors are quoted in the usual abridged forms by book, chapter, etc. (as Xen. *Anab.* vi. 6, 12) or by the paging of the edition generally used for that purpose (as Plat. *Pol.* p. 291 B. of the edition of H. Stephanus). The names of the works quoted are printed in *Italics*. Roman numerals in small capitals are used to denote books or other internal divisions (as Thuc. iv.) ; Roman numerals in large capitals denote volumes (as Kühner, II.).

The references to Winer's Grammar, given in brackets thus [E. T. 152], apply to the corresponding pages of Dr. Moulton's English translation.

PREFACE

SPECIALLY WRITTEN BY THE AUTHOR FOR THE ENGLISH EDITION.

———◆———

IT cannot but be of great importance in the interests of a thorough, sure, and comprehensive knowledge, that the results of progressive effort and research in the wide domain of the sciences should be mutually exchanged and spread from people to people, and from tongue to tongue. In this way of a living fellowship of mind, penetrating to the farthest limits of civilisation, the various scientific peculiarities of national development and culture are necessarily more and more elevated into common property as regards their excellences, while their several defects and shortcomings are reciprocally compensated and supplied; and thus the honest efforts and labours of individuals, pressing forward in common towards a deeper and clearer knowledge, are at once encouraged by their mutual respect and stimulated by a generous rivalry. Especially, and in an eminent degree, does this hold true within the sphere devoted to the highest object of human effort—the sphere of scientific theology. To the cultivation of this science, in accordance with its healthy life springing from the Divine Word and with its destination embracing time and eternity, belongs in an eminent sense the noble vocation of applying every gift received from God freely and faithfully to the service of the great whole—the building up of His kingdom. In its view the nations with their various characteristic powers, capacities, and tongues, are members of the one body, to which they are to hail each other as belonging in the fellowship of the one Head, which is Christ, and of the one Spirit, whose motions and influences are not restrained by any limits of nation or of language.

From this point of view it cannot but be in every sense a matter for congratulation that in our day more than formerly those literary works of German theology, which have on their native soil obtained a fair position in the literature of the science to which they relate, should by translation into the English tongue have that more extended field opened up to them, whose only limit is the ever-increasing diffusion and prevalence of that language in both hemispheres. Thus German theological labour goes forth into the wide world; becomes at home in distant lands and in a foreign dress; communicates what has been given to it, in order, by the mutual working of the Spirit, to receive in its turn from abroad; stimulates so far as in it lies, in order that it may itself find stimulus and furtherance, instruction and correction; and in all this lends its aid, that the divided theological strivings of the age and the various tendencies of religious national character may be daily brought closer together, and united in the eternal focus of all genuine science, which is truth and nothing but truth—and in the realm of theology the highest truth of all, that of divine revelation.

In the transplanting of the literary products of German theology to the soil of the English language the well-known publishing house of the Messrs. T. & T. Clark of Edinburgh have earned special distinction; and their efforts, supported by select and able professional scholars, have already found, and continue increasingly to find, an appreciation corresponding to their merits both in British and American circles. I have therefore readily and willingly given my consent to the proposal of the above-mentioned honourable publishers to set on foot and to issue an English translation of my Commentary on the New Testament; and with no less readiness have my esteemed German publishers, Vandenhoeck and Ruprecht in Göttingen, declared their agreement to it. I earnestly wish that the version thus undertaken, the first portion of which is given to the public in the present volume, may not fail to receive, in the field of the English language and of the science which it represents, an indulgent and kindly reception, such as, during a long series of years, has been accorded to the German work by the German theological public. And if I venture to couple with this wish some measure of a hope corresponding to it, I am induced to do so simply by the fact that even in the German idiom these works have already found their way, in no inconsiderable numbers, both to England and America.

Respecting the object and intention of my Commentaries no special explanation is needed, since, in point of fact, these are obvious on the face of them. They aim at exactly ascertaining and establishing on due grounds the *purely historical sense of Scripture.* This aim is so clear and so lofty, that all the produce of one's own thoughts and subjective speculation must fall entirely into the background, and must not be allowed to mix up anything of its own with what objectively stands forth in the revelation of the New Testament and simply seeks to be understood just *as* it so stands. For exegesis is a historical science, because the sense of Scripture, the investigation of which is its task, can only be regarded and treated as a historical fact; as positively given, it can only be known, proved, established, and set forth so as to be clearly and surely understood, by the positive method of studying the grammar, the *usus loquendi,* and the connection in detail as well as in its wider and widest sense. Exegetical research therefore cannot regard any definitions of the doctrinal system of a Church as binding or regulative for its operations, as if forsooth, in cases where the Confession has spoken, its duty were to seek only what it was *à priori* directed to seek, and thereupon to find only what it so seeks. No! it is just when perfectly unprejudiced, impartial, and free—and thus all the more consciously and consistently guided simply and solely by those historically given factors of its science—that it is able with genuine humility to render to the church, so far as the latter maintains its palladium in the pure Word of God, real and wholesome service for the present and the future. Unhappily the Church of Rome, by its unchangeable tradition beyond the pale of Scripture, and now completely by its Vaticanum, has refused to receive such service in all points affecting its peculiar doctrine. But with the Evangelical Church it is otherwise. However deep may be the heavings of conflicting elements within it, and however long may be the duration of the painful throes which shall at last issue—according to the counsel of God and when His hour has come—in a happier time for the church when men's minds shall have attained a higher union, the pure word of Scripture, in its historical truth and clearness and in its world-subduing divine might, disengaged from every addition of human scholasticism and its dividing formulae, must and shall at length become once more a wonderful power of peace unto unity of faith and love. The Evangelical Church bears inalienably in its bosom the Word as the living and imperishable leaven of that final development.

Such is the ideal goal, which the scientific exposition of Scripture, while it desires nothing else than to elucidate and further the true historical understanding of Scripture, may never lose sight of in regard to the church, which is built on the Word But how limited is the measure of the attainments and of the gifts conferred upon the individual! and how irresistibly must it impel him, in the consciousness of his fragmentary contributions, to the humbling confession, "Not as though I had already attained!" Nevertheless let each strive faithfully and honestly according to what has been given to him, for that noble goal in the field of Scripture-science, in firm assurance that

God can bless even what is little and be mighty in what is weak. And so may the gracious God and Father of our Lord Jesus Christ accompany my humble labours on His Word, as they are now going forth in the dress of another language to far distant brethren, with the blessing on which all success depends, that they may conduce to the knowledge of His Truth, to the service of His Church, and to the glory of His Holy Name.

Dr. HEIN. AUG. WILH. MEYER,
Oberconsistorialrath.

Hannover, *March* 1873.

PREFACE

TO THE GERMAN EDITION.

ORTY years have now elapsed since my Commentaries on the New Testament were first given to the public. The first edition of the first volume—the weak commencement—appeared in January 1832. A scientific work, which has passed through a long course of development and still continues that course, has always a history—a biography—of its own, which of course is intimately interwoven with that of its author. Yet in this retrospect I can only be filled with praise and thanksgiving to the divine grace; of myself I have nothing to say. The indulgence of friendly readers, which I have experienced so long, will not, I hope, fail to be still extended to me, when my day's work is drawing to its end.

This fifth edition of the Commentary on the Epistle to the Romans is based—as was of course to be expected, and may be inferred from the increase in the number of the sheets—on a new and careful revision of the fourth edition, which was issued in 1865. This enlargement—although in particular instances much has been abridged or even deleted—could not be avoided, if on the one hand the more recent publications relating to the Epistle were to meet with due attention,[1] and if on the other hand

---

[1] I could not take into consideration the treatise of Dr. Eklund: "σαρξ vocabulum, quid ap. Paulum significet," Lund, May, 1872, which, cautiously proceeding by a purely exegetical method, in the definition of the ethical side of that

the general plan of the book—according to which it has to provide along with the exposition itself a critical view of the interpretations contrasting with it, and so of the detailed history of the exegesis—was to be preserved.

But on what portion of the New Testament could the labour and trouble—which are being continually renewed, wherever exegetical science conscientiously strives to reach its pure and clear historic aim—be less spared than on this, the grandest and richest in contents of all the Apostle's letters ? Especially at the present time. The Epistle to the Romans still stands forth as a never silent accuser confronting the Roman ecclesiasticism, which has strained to the uttermost spiritual arrogance in the dethroned head, and Loyolist submissiveness in the members, of its hierarchy (*perinde ac si essent cadavera*); it is still the steadfast divine charter of the Reformation, as formerly our Luther found mainly in it the unyielding fulcrum by the aid of which he upheaved the firmly-knit Roman structure from its old foundations. Amidst the vehement and pretentious conflicts, which continually surround us in the field of evangelic belief, we still have in this Epistle—just because it sets clearly before us the pure apostolic Gospel in its deepest and most comprehensive scope—the clearest and most prominent criterion for the recognition of what belongs to the pith and marrow of the Confession, in order that we may distinguish with steadfast eye and conscience that which is essential from all the fleeting, temporary,

notion arrives substantially at the explanation of Augustine and Luther—a result, nevertheless, in which I am still precluded from concurring, as regards the Epistle to the Romans, by the contrast of σάρξ and νοῦς, as well as that of σάρξ and the moral ἐγώ in ch. vii.—I must here also make supplementary mention of Hilgenfeld's dissertation "*Petrus in Rom und Johannes in Kl. Asien*" (*Zeitschrift*, 1872. 3) ; in it he declares himself in favour of the nearly contemporary martyrdom of Peter and Paul in Rome as a historically accredited fact, and, as I must still even after the doubts of Lipsius assume, with just reason, even as respects its independence of the Simon legend.—During the very printing of this Preface there have come into my hands the two dissertations by Harmsen, who defends the reference of the doxology in ix. 5 to God, and Hilgenfeld, who maintains the genuineness of chapters xv. and xvi. (in the latter's *Zeitschrift*, 1872. 4).

controversial or scholastic forms, with which it has become connected and interwoven through the historical relations of ecclesiastical symbols; a distinction, to which even the Introduction to the Formula Concordiae, although this most of all bears the theological impress of the time, significantly enough points, and which better meets the exigencies of the restless present than the overbearing cry—recklessly transcending limit or measure—after unity of doctrine, which yet does not remove or even so much as conceal the dissensions among the criers themselves. The unity which they desire—were it uniformly established, as it were in the lump, for *all* doctrinal definitions of the Confession—would be Roman, and the very negation of truth and truthfulness in the church, because it would be contrary to the *freedom of conscience in the understanding of Scripture,* which has its ground and support, its standard and limit, and the holy warrant of its upright confidence, not *beyond the pale of* Scripture, but *in* it, and in it *alone.*

Let us only advance with clearness along the straight path of pure historical exegesis, in virtue of which we have always to *receive* what Scripture gives to us, and never to *give* to it aught of our own. Otherwise we run a risk of falling into the boundless maze of an interpretation of Scripture at our own pleasure, in which artificial and violent expedients are quickly enough resorted to, with a view to establish results which are constructed from foregone premises, and to procure doctrines which are the creations—obtruded on Scripture—of a self-made world of thought and its combinations. Exegetes of this sort—whose labours, we may add, are usually facilitated by a lack of sure and thorough philological culture,[1] and of needful respect for linguistic authorities—

---

[1] We theologians are far too much given to neglect a comprehensive and precise knowledge of the Greek grammar. If the exegete of the present day supposes himself adequately furnished with such a Grammar as that of Rost (whose memory, as my former Gymnasial teacher, I gratefully revere) he is mistaken; it is no longer sufficient. We ought not to overlook the *progress* of philology in the field of the classics, but should be diligent in turning to account, for the New Testament, whatever the contributions of the *present day* furnish. Otherwise we neglect

have the dubious merit of provoking *refutation* more than others do, and thereby indirectly promoting the elucidation of the true sense of Scripture. Yet they may, as experience shows, attain for a time an influence, especially over younger theologians who have not yet reached the steadiness and soberness of mature exegetic judgment, by the charm of novelty and of a certain originality, as well as of a dialectic art, which veils its mistakes so that they are not at once recognised—an influence under which good abilities are misled and learn to be content with extracting from the words of Scripture a meaning, which, originating from their own presuppositions, belongs really to themselves. Indeed, if such a mode of handling Scripture, with its self-deceptions and with its often very singular caprices, could become dominant (which, looking to the present state and progress of science, I do not reckon possible), there would be reason to fear that gradually the principle of Scripture authority, which preserved in its full objectivity is the aegis of the evangelical churches, would become *illusory*. All the worse and more confusing is it, when such an exegesis employs as the organ of presenting and communicating its views a mode of expression, the quaint drapery of which hinders us from clearly discerning the substance of the meaning lying beneath it, and in fact frequently permits the effort of translating it into current forms of speech which cannot mislead to be attended with but dubious success.[1]

an eminently important part of our duty. I cannot but here recommend very urgently to the theologian, in the interest of pure exegesis, the second edition of Kühner's Large Grammar (in two parts, 1869-1872)—to which my citations will always henceforth refer—as the most complete and most solid work on the structure of the Greek language regarded from the present standpoint of science. This entirely remodelled edition is a glorious monument of thorough and comprehensive erudition, and of clear and ripe familiarity with the genius of the language of classic Hellenism.

[1] In presence of such wretched evils of style we may be allowed to recall the simple rule, which the epigrammatist bids the rhetoricians (*Anthol. Pal.* xi. 144, 5 f.) lay to heart:

Νοῦν ὑποκεῖσθαι δεῖ τοῖς γράμμασι καὶ φράσιν αὐτῶν
εἶναι κοινοτέραν, ὥστε νοεῖν ἃ λέγεις.

For the critical remarks the part of the *editio octava* of Tischendorf's New Testament, which includes the present Epistle, was in good time to be turned to account. As it deviates in many cases from the *editio septima*, and this diversity is partly due to a modification of the critical principles adopted, I have deemed it advisable to specify not merely the readings of the *octava*, but also those of the *septima*. The one I have indicated by *Tisch.* (8), the other by *Tisch.* (7); but where the two editions agree, I put merely *Tisch.*

With confidence then in God, who sits as Ruler and knows how to guide all things well, this work is left to make its way once more into the much agitated theological world. May He ward off harm, so far as it contains what is erroneous, and grant His blessing, so far as it may minister to the correct, unstinted, and undisguised understanding of His revealed Word.

Dr. MEYER.

Hannover, 24*th July* 1872.

THE
EPISTLE OF PAUL TO THE ROMANS.

INTRODUCTION.

§ 1. SKETCH OF THE APOSTLE'S LIFE.

PAUL, who received this Roman name, according to Jerome, *Catal.* 5—and from Acts xiii. 9, this view seems the most probable [1]—on occasion of the conversion of Sergius Paulus the Roman Proconsul of Cyprus, but was at his circumcision named שָׁאוּל,[2] was the son of Jewish parents belonging to the tribe of Benjamin (Rom. xi. 1; Phil. iii. 5), and was born at Tarsus[3] (Acts ix. 11, xxi. 39, xxii. 3), a πόλις μεγάλη καὶ εὐδαίμων (Xen. *Anab.* i. 2, 23) of ancient renown, founded according to the legend by Perseus, in Cilicia. The year of his birth is quite uncertain (A.D. 10-15 ?); but it is certain that he was of Pharisaic descent (see on Acts xxiii. 6), and that his father was a Roman citizen (see on Acts xvi. 37). He therefore possessed by birth this right of citizenship, which subsequently had so important a bearing on his labours and his fate

---

[1] See the particulars on Acts xiii. 9.

[2] Since both names were generally current, every attempt to explain their meaning in reference to *our* Paul is utterly arbitrary—from that of Augustine, according to whom he was called *Saul* as *persecutor* (as Saul persecuted David), and *Paulus* as *praedicator* (namely, as the *minimus apostolorum*, 1 Cor. xv. 9), down to Umbreit's play on the word פָּעַל (the *made* one, created anew) in the *Stud. u. Krit.* 1852, p. 377 f., and Lange's fancy that the Apostle was called the *little*, because he overcame Elymas as the little David overcame Goliath.

[3] Not at *Gischala* in Galilee, according to the statement of Jerome, *de Vir. ill.* 5 (comp. also what he says on Philem. 23), which cannot be taken into consideration after the Apostle's own testimony (see especially Acts xxii. 3), unless with Krenkel (*Paulus d. Ap. d. Heiden*, 1869, p. 215) we distrust the accounts of the Book of Acts even in such a point lying beyond the scope of its dogmatic tendency.

(Acts xxii. 27 f.). Of his first youthful training in his native city, where arts and sciences flourished (Strabo, xiv. 5, 13, p. 673), we know nothing; but it was probably conducted by his Pharisaic father in entire accordance with Pharisaic principles (Phil. iii. 5; Gal. i. 14), so that the boy was prepared for a Pharisaic rabbinical school at Jerusalem. While yet in early youth (Acts xxii. 3, xxvi. 4, comp. vii. 58; Gal. i. 14; Tholuck, in the *Stud. u. Krit.* 1835, p. 364 ff.; also in his *Vermischte Schr.* II. p. 274 ff.) he was transferred to Jerusalem, where he had perhaps even then relatives (Acts xxiii. 16), though there is no evidence that the entire family migrated thither (Ewald). He entered a training-school of Pharisaic theology, and became a rabbinic pupil of the universally honoured (Acts v. 34) Gamaliel (Acts xxii. 3), who, notwithstanding his strict orthodoxy (Lightfoot, *ad Matth.* p. 33), shows himself (Acts v. 34 ff.) a man of wise moderation of judgment.[1] In accordance with a custom, which was rendered necessary by the absence of any regular payment of the Rabbins and was very salutary for their independence (see on Mark vi. 3, and Delitzsch, *Handwerkerleben zur Zeit Jesu*, 1868, V.), the youthful Saul combined with his rabbinical culture the learning of a trade—tentmaking (Acts xviii. 3)—to which he subsequently, even when an apostle, applied himself in a way highly honourable and remarkably conducive to the blessing of his official labours, and for that reason he felt a just satisfaction in it (Acts xviii. 3, xx. 34; 1 Thess. ii. 9; 2 Thess. iii. 7 ff.; 1 Cor. iv. 12, ix. 6, xii. 15; 2 Cor. xi. 8, xii. 13). At the feet of Gamaliel he of course received an instruction which, as to form and matter, was purely rabbinic; and hence his epistles exhibit, in the mode in which they unfold their teaching, a more or less distinct rabbinico-didactic impress. But it was natural also that his susceptible and active mind should not remain unaffected by Hellenic culture, when he came into contact with it; and how could he escape such contact in Jerusalem, whither Hellenists flocked from all quarters under heaven? This serves to explain

---

[1] See traits of the mild liberality of sentiment, which marked this grandson of the celebrated Hillel, quoted from the Rabbins in Tholuck, *l.c.* p. 378. The fact that nevertheless the youthful Saul developed into a zealot cannot warrant any doubt, in opposition to Acts viii. 34 ff., as to his having been Gamaliel's pupil (such as Hausrath expresses, *neut. Zeitgesch.* II. p. 419 ff.).

a dilettante[1] acquaintance on his part with Greek literary works, which may certainly be recognized in Acts xvii. 28, if not also in 1 Cor. xv. 33 (Tit. i. 12); and which, perhaps already begun in Tarsus, may have been furthered without its being sought by his subsequent relations of intercourse with Greeks of all countries and of all ranks. It is impossible to determine how much or how little of the virtues of his character, and of the acuteness, subtlety, and depth of lofty intellect which he displayed as apostle, he owed to the influence of Gamaliel; for his conversion had as its result so entire a change in his nature, that we cannot distinguish—and we should not attempt to distinguish—what elements of it may have grown out of the training of his youth, or to what extent they have done so. We can only recognize this much in general, that Saul, with excellent natural gifts, with the power of an acute intellect, lively feelings, and strong will, was, under the guidance of his teacher, not merely equipped with Jewish theological knowledge and dialectic art, but had his mind also directed with lofty national enthusiasm towards divine things; and that, however deeply he felt sin to be the sting of death (Rom. vii. 7 ff.), he was kept free (Phil. iii. 6) from the hypocritical depravity which was at that time prevalent among Pharisees of the ordinary type (Schrader, II. p. 23 ff.; comp. also Keim, *Gesch. Jesu*, I. p. 265). Nevertheless it is also certain that the moderation and mildness of the teacher did not communicate themselves to the character of the disciple, who, on the contrary, imbibed in a high degree that prevailing rigour of Pharisaism, the spirit of which no Gamaliel could by his individual practical wisdom exorcise. He became a distinguished zealot for the honour of Jehovah and the law (Acts xxii. 3), as well as for Pharisaic principles (Gal. i. 14), and displayed all the recklessness and violence which are wont to appear, when fiery

[1] The exaggerations of the older writers (see *e.g.* Schramm, *de* STUPENDA *eruditione Pauli*, Herborn. 1710) are pure inventions of fancy. So too is Schrader's opinion, that Paul had by Greek culture prepared himself to be a Jewish missionary, a proselytiser. It cannot even be proved that he formed his diction on the model of particular authors, such as Demosthenes (Köster in the *Stud. u. Krit.* 1854, p. 305 ff.). The comparisons instituted with a view to establish this point are too weak and general. How many similar parallels might be collected, *e.g.* from Plato, and even from the tragedians! On the whole the general remark of Jerome, at Gal. iv. 24, is very appropriate: "*P. scisse, licet non ad perfectum, literas saeculares.*"

youthful spirits concentrate all their energies on the pursuit of an idea embraced with thorough enthusiasm. His zeal was fed with abundant fuel and more and more violently inflamed, when the young Christian party growing up in Jerusalem became an object of hostility as dangerously antagonistic to the theocracy and legal orthodoxy (comp. Acts vi. 13, 14), and at length formal persecution broke out with the stoning of Stephen. Even on that occasion Saul, although still in a very subordinate capacity, as merely a youth in attendance,[1] took a willing and active part (Acts viii. 1, xxii. 20); but soon afterwards he came forward on his own account as a persecutor of the Christians, and, becoming far and wide a terror to the churches of Judaea (Gal. i. 22 f.), he raged against the Christians with a violence so resolute and persistent (Acts xxii. 3 f., xxvi. 10 ff.), that his conduct at this time caused him ever afterwards the deepest humiliation and remorse (1 Cor. xv. 8, 9; Gal. i. 13; Eph. iii. 8; Phil. iii. 6; comp. 1 Tim. i. 13). Yet precisely such a character as Saul—who, full of a keen but for the time misdirected love of truth and piety, devoted without selfish calculation his whole energies to the *idea* which he had once embraced as his highest and holiest concernment—was, in the purpose of God, to become the chief instrument for the proclamation and extension of the divine work, of which he was still for the moment the destructive adversary. A transformation so extraordinary required extraordinary means. Accordingly when Saul, invested with full powers by the Sanhedrin (Acts ix. 1, xxvi. 9), was carrying his zealous labours beyond the bounds of Palestine, there took place near Damascus (35 A.D.) that wonderful appearance to him of the exalted Jesus in heavenly glory (see on Acts ix. 3; 1 Cor. ix. 1, xv. 8) which arrested him (Phil. iii. 12),and produced no less a result than that Saul—thereby divinely called, and subsequently favoured with an inward divine revelation of the Son of God[2] (see on Gal. i. 15 f.)—gradually became,

[1] Not as a married man or already a widower, of about thirty years of age, (Ewald, Hausrath); comp. on Acts vii. 58.

[2] The attempts of the Tübingen school (especially of Baur and Holsten) to represent the Gospel of Paul as having originated from the intrinsic action of his own mind, and the event at Damascus as a visionary picture drawn from his own spirit, are noticed and refuted at Acts ix., and by Beyschlag in the *Stud. u. Krit.* 1870, 1. Compare generally Dorner, *Gesch. d. prot. Theol.* p. 829 ff.

under the further guidance of the divine Spirit and in the school of his own experiences so full of trial, the Apostle, who by the most extensive and most successful proclamation of the Gospel, especially among the Gentiles, and by his triumphant liberation of that Gospel from the fetters of Mosaism on the one hand and from the disturbing influences of the current theosophic speculations on the other, did more than all the other apostles— he, the Thirteenth, more than the Twelve, who had been called in the first instance for the δωδεκαφύλον of Israel (Gal. ii. 9 ; 1 Cor. xv. 10). His conversion was completed through Ananias, who was directed to him by means of an appearance of Christ (Acts ix. 10 ff); and, having been baptized, he at once after a few days, in the resolute consciousness of his spiritual life transformed with a view to his apostolic vocation (Gal. i. 16), preached in the synagogues of Damascus Jesus[1] as being the Son of God (Acts x. 19 f.). For all half-heartedness was foreign to him; now too he was, whatever he was, *thoroughly*, and this energetic unity of his profound nature was now sanctified throughout by the living spirit of Christ. His apostolic labours at Damascus, the birthplace of his regenerate life, lasted three years, interrupted however by a journey to *Arabia* (Gal. i. 17), the object of which most probably was to make merely a preliminary and brief trial of his ministry in a foreign field.[2]

[1] The chief facts in the life of Jesus could not but have been already known to him in a general way, whilst he was actively opposing the Christians at Jerusalem ; but now, for the first time, there dawned upon him the *saving knowledge* of these facts and of their *truth*, and his constant intercourse with believers henceforth deepened more and more this saving knowledge. Thus, following the living historical tradition within the circle of Christianity under the influence of the Christ revealed in him, he became the most important witness for the history of Jesus apart from the Gospels. Comp. Keim, *Geschichte Jesu*, I. p. 36 ff.; also Hausrath, *neut. Zeitgesch.* II. p. 457. But that he had seen Christ Himself, cannot be inferred from 2 Cor. v. 16 ; see on that passage.

[2] Schrader, Köllner, Köhler (*Abfassungen d. epistol. Schr.* p. 43 f.), Rückert, and Schott on Gal. *l.c.*, Holsten, Döllinger, Krenkel, and others, think that Paul withdrew immediately after his conversion to a neighbouring desert of Arabia, in order to prepare himself in retirement for his calling. Compare also Hausrath, *neut. Zeitgesch.* II. p. 455. This view is decidedly at variance with Acts ix. 19, 20, where the *immediate* public teaching at Damascus, a few days after the conversion, receives very studious prominence. But we should only have to assume such an inconsistency with the passage in Acts, in the event of that assumed object of the Arabian journey being *exegetically* deducible from the Apostle's own words in Gal. i. 17, which, however, is by no means the case.

Persecution on the part of the Jews—which was subsequently so often, according to the Divine counsel, the salutary means of extending the sphere of the Apostle's labours—compels him to escape from Damascus (Acts ix. 19-26; 2 Cor. xi. 32 f.); and he betakes himself to the mother-church of the faith on account of which he has suffered persecution in a foreign land, proceeding to Jerusalem (A.D. 38), in order to make the personal acquaintance of Peter (Gal. i. 18). At first regarded by the believers there with distrust, he was, through the loving intervention of Barnabas (Acts ix. 27 f.), admitted into the relation of a colleague to the apostles, of whom, however, only Peter and James the brother of the Lord were present (Gal. i. 19). His first apostolic working at Jerusalem was not to last more than fifteen days (Gal. i. 18); already had the Lord by an appearance in the temple (Acts xxii. 17 ff.) directed him to depart to the Gentiles; already were the Hellenists resident in the city seeking his life; and he therefore withdrew through Syria to his native place (Acts ix. 30; Gal. i. 20). Here he seems to have lived and worked wholly in quiet retirement, till at length Barnabas, who had appreciated the greatness and importance of the extraordinary man, went from Antioch, where just at that time Gentile Christianity had established its first church, to seek him out at Tarsus, and brought him thence to the capital of Syria; where both devoted themselves for a whole year (A.D. 43) without interruption to the preaching of the Gospel (Acts xi. 25, 26). We know not whether it was during this period (see Anger, *temp. rat.* p. 104 ff.), or during his sojourn in Cilicia (see Ewald, *apost. Zeit.* p. 440, ed. 3), that the Apostle became the subject of that spiritual ecstasy and revelation which, even after the

Luke, it is true, makes no mention at all of the Arabian journey; but for that very reason it is highly improbable that it had as its object a silent preparation for his official work. For in that case the analogous instances of other famous teachers who had prepared themselves in the desert for their future calling (Ex. xxiv. 18, xxxiv. 28; Deut. ix. 9; 1 Kings xix. 8), and the example of John the Baptist, and even of Christ Himself, would have made the fact seem too important either to have remained wholly unknown to Luke, or to have been passed over without notice in his history; although Hilgenfeld and Zeller suppose him to have omitted it *intentionally*. On the other hand, we cannot suppose that the sojourn in Arabia extended over the whole, or nearly the whole, of the three years (Eichhorn, Hemsen, Anger, Ewald, Laurent, and older expositors). See generally on Gal. i. 17.

lapse of fourteen years, continued to be regarded by him as so extremely remarkable (2 Cor. xii. 2-4).

But the great famine was now approaching, which, foretold at Antioch by the prophet Agabus from Jerusalem, threatened destruction to the churches of Judaea. On this account the brethren at Antioch, quite in the spirit of their new brotherly love, resolved to forward pecuniary aid to Judaea; and entrusted its transmission to Barnabas and Saul (Acts xi. 27-30). After the execution of this commission (A.D. 44), in carrying out which however Saul at least cannot have gone all the way to Jerusalem (see on Gal. ii. 1), the two men were formally and solemnly consecrated by the church at Antioch as apostles to the Gentiles (Acts xiii. 1-3); and Saul now undertook—at first with, but afterwards without, Barnabas—his missionary journeys so fruitful in results. In the course of these journeys he was wont, where there were Jews, to attempt the fulfilment of his office in the first instance among them, in accordance with what he knew to be the divine order (Rom. i. 16, xv. 8 ff.), and with his own deep love towards his nation (Rom. ix. 1 ff.); but when, as was usually the case, he was rejected by the Jews, he displayed the light of Christ before the Gentiles. And in all variety of circumstances he exhibited a vigour and versatility of intellect, an acuteness and depth, clearness and consistency, of thought, a purity and steadfastness of purpose, an ardour of disposition, an enthusiasm of effort, a wisdom of conduct, a firmness and delicacy of practical tact, a strength and freedom of faith, a fervour and skill of eloquence, a heroic courage amidst dangers, a love, self-denial, patience, and humility, and along with all this a lofty power of gifted genius, which secure for the Saul whom Christ made His chosen instrument the reverence and admiration of all time.[1]

[1] Comp. Holsten, *l.c. Evang. d. Paul. u. Petr.* p. 88 ff.; Luthardt, *d. Ap. Paul. e. Lebensbild,* 1869; Krenkel, *Paul. d. Ap. d. Heiden,* 1869; Hausrath, *neut. Zeitgesch.* II. 1872; Grau, *Entwickelungsgesch. d. neutest. Schriftth.* 1871, II. p. 10 f.; also Sabatier, *l'apôtre Paul, esquisse d'une histoire de sa pensée,* Strasb. 1870. Still the history of the spiritual development of the Apostle cannot be so definitely and sharply divided into periods as Sabatier has tried to do. See, against this, the appropriate remarks of Gess, *Jahrb. f. D. Theol.* 1871, p. 159 ff. The motive power and unity of all his working lay in his inward fellowship with Christ, with His death and resurrection—in the subjective living and moving in Christ, and of Christ in him. Comp. Grau. *l.c.* p. 15 ff.

In accordance with the narrative of Acts, three[1] missionary journeys of the Apostle may be distinguished; and in the description of these we may insert the remaining known facts of his history.

(1.) On his consecration as Apostle to the Gentiles, Paul went along with Barnabas the Cyprian, and with Mark accompanying them as apostolic servant, first of all to the neighbouring Cyprus; where, after his advance from Salamis to Paphos, his work was crowned by a double success—the humiliation of the *goetes* Elymas, and the conversion of the proconsul Sergius Paulus (Acts xiii. 6-12). Then Pamphylia, where Mark parted from the apostles (xiii. 13), Pisidia and Lycaonia became in turn fields of his activity, in which, together with Barnabas, he founded churches and organized them by the appointment of presbyters (xiv. 23). At one time receiving divine honours on account of a miracle (xiv. 11 ff.), at another persecuted and stoned (xiii. 50, xiv. 5, 19), he, after coming down from Perga to Attalia, returned to the mother-church at Antioch.

While Paul and Barnabas were here enjoying a quiet sojourn of some duration among the brethren (Acts xiv. 28), there came down from Judaea Pharisaic Christians jealous for the law, who required the Gentile converts to submit to circumcision as a condition of Messianic salvation (Acts xv. 1; Gal. ii. 4). It was natural that this demand should encounter a decided opponent in the highly enlightened and liberal-minded Paul, whose lively assurance of the truth, resting on revelation and upheld by his own experience, could tolerate no other condition of salvation than faith in Christ; and in consequence both he and the likeminded Barnabas became entangled in no small controversy (Acts xv. 2). The dispute involved the fundamental essence and independent standing of Christianity and the whole freedom of a Christian man, and was therefore of such importance that the church at Antioch, with a view to its settlement,

---

[1] The supposition that there were other *chief journeys*, which, it is alleged, are left unnoticed in the Acts (Schrader), is quite incompatible with the course of the history as there given. He must, however, have made many subordinate journeys, for the Book of Acts is far from giving a complete account of his labours, as is clearly shown by various intimations in the Epistles. For example, how many journeys and events not noticed in the Acts must be assumed in connection with 2 Cor. xi. 14 ff. ?

deputed their most influential men, Paul, who also received a revelation for this purpose (Gal. ii. 2), and Barnabas along with some others (Paul also took Titus with him, Gal. ii. 1), to proceed to Jerusalem (fourteen years after the Apostle's first journey thither, A.D. 52), and there discuss with the apostles and elders the points in dispute. And how happy was the result of this so-called *Apostolic Council!* Paul laid the Gospel which he preached to the Gentiles before the church, and the apostles in particular, with the best effect (Gal. ii. 2, 6); and, as to the point of circumcision, not even his apostolic associate Titus, a Gentile, was subjected to the circumcision demanded by members of the church who were zealous for the law. With unyielding firmness Paul contended for the truth of the Gospel. The apostles who were present—James, the brother of the Lord, Peter and John—approved of his preaching among, and formally recognized him as Apostle to, the Gentiles (Gal. ii. 1-10); and he and Barnabas, accompanied by the delegates of the church at Jerusalem, Judas Barsabas and Silas, returned to Antioch bearers of a decree (Acts xv. 28-30) favourable to Christian freedom from the law, and important as a provisional measure for the further growth of the church (Acts xvi. 4 f.), though not coming up to that complete freedom of the Gospel which Paul felt himself bound to claim, and for this reason, as well as in virtue of his consciousness of independence as Apostle to the Gentiles, not urged by him in his Epistles. Here they prosecuted afresh their preaching of Christ, though not always without disturbance on the part of Jewish Christians, so that Paul was compelled in the interest of Christian freedom openly to oppose and to admonish even Peter, who had been carried away into dissimulation, especially seeing that the other Jewish Christians, and even Barnabas, had allowed themselves to be tainted by that dissimulation (Gal. ii. 11 ff.). Paul had nevertheless the welfare of his foreign converts too much at heart to permit his wishing to prolong his stay in Antioch (Acts xv. 36). He proposed to Barnabas a journey in which they should visit those converts, but fell into a dispute with him in consequence of the latter desiring to take Mark (Acts xv. 37-39)—a dispute which had the beneficial consequence for the church, that the two men, each of whom was qualified to fill a distinct field of labour, parted from one another and never again worked in conjunction.

(2.) Paul, accompanied by Silas, entered on a second missionary journey (A.D. 52). He went through *Syria* and *Cilicia*, strengthening the Christian life of the churches (Acts xv. 41); and then through *Lycaonia*, where at *Lystra* (see on Acts xvi. 1) he associated with himself Timothy, whom he circumcised—apart however from any connection with the controversy as to the necessity of circumcision (see on Acts xvi. 3)—with a view to prevent his ministry from causing offence among the Jews. He also traversed *Phrygia* and *Galatia* (Acts xvi. 6), in the latter of which he was compelled by bodily weakness to make a stay, and so took occasion to plant the churches there (Gal. iv. 13). When he arrived at *Troas*, he received in a vision by night a call from Christ to go to *Macedonia* (xvi. 8 ff.). In obedience to this call he stepped for the first time on the soil of Europe, and caused Christianity to take permanent root in every place to which he carried his ministry. For in Macedonia he laid the foundation of the churches at *Philippi, Thessalonica,* and *Beroea* (Acts xvi. 12 ff., xvii. 1 ff., 10 ff.); and then, driven away by repeated persecutions (comp. also 1 Thess. ii. 1 f., i. 6)—but leaving Silas and Timothy behind in Beroea (Acts xvii. 14)—he brought to Christ His first-fruits even in *Athens*, where he was treated by the philosophers partly with contempt and partly with ridicule (Acts xvii. 16 ff.). But in that city, whence he despatched Timothy, who had in the meanwhile again rejoined him, to Thessalonica (1 Thess. iii. 1 ff.), he was unable to found a church. The longer and more productive was his labour in *Corinth*, whither he betook himself on leaving Athens (Acts xviii. 1 ff.). There, where Silas and Timothy soon joined him, he founded the church which Apollos afterwards watered (1 Cor. iii. 6, 10, iv. 15, ix. 1); and for more than a year and a half (Acts xviii. 11, 18; A.D. 53 and 54)—during which period he received support from Macedonia (2 Cor. xi. 9), as he had previously on several occasions from the Philippians (Phil. iv. 15 f.)—overcame the wisdom of the world by the preaching of the Crucified One (1 Cor. ii. 1 ff.). The relation here formed with his fellow-craftsman Aquila (Acts xviii. 1 ff.), who as a Roman emigrant was sojourning with his wife Priscilla in Corinth, could not fail to exercise essential influence on the Christian church at Rome (Rom. xvi. 3). In Corinth he wrote also at this time the first of his doctrinal Epistles preserved to us—those *to the Thessalonians*. Corinth was the terminus of his second missionary journey. From Corinth he started on his return, not however taking a direct course, but first making by way of *Ephesus* (whither he brought Aquila and Priscilla with him) a journey to Jerusalem to attend a festival (Acts xviii. 18-22; A.D. 55), whence, without prolonging his stay, he returned to the bosom of the Syrian mother-church. But he did not remain there long (Acts xviii. 23); his apostolic zeal soon impelled him to set out once more.

(3.) He made his *third* missionary tour through *Galatia* and *Phrygia*, strengthening the churches which he had founded from town to town (Acts xviii. 23); and traversed Asia Minor as far as *Ephesus*, where for nearly three years (A.D. 56-58) he laboured with peculiar power and fervour and with eminent success (Acts xix. 1–xx. 1), although also assailed by severe trials (Acts xx. 19; 1 Cor. xv. 32, comp. 2 Cor. i. 8). This sojourn of the Apostle was also highly beneficial for other churches than that at Ephesus; for not only did he thence make a journey to *Corinth*, which city he now visited for the second time (see on 2 Cor. *introd.* § 2), but he also wrote towards the end of that sojourn what is known to us as the *First Epistle to the Corinthians*, receiving subsequently intelligence of the impression made by it from Timothy, whom he had sent to Corinth before he wrote, as well as from Titus, whom he had sent after writing it. The Epistle to the *Galatians* was also issued from Ephesus. He was impelled to leave this city by his steadfast resolution now to transfer his labours to the far West, and indeed to Rome itself, but before doing so to revisit and exhort to steadfastness in the faith his Macedonian and Achaean converts (Acts xix. 21, xx. 2), as well as once more to go to Jerusalem (Acts xix. 21). Accordingly, after Demetrius the silversmith had raised a tumult against him (Acts xix. 24 ff.), which however proved fruitless, and after having suffered in Asia other severe afflictions (2 Cor. i. 8), he travelled through *Macedonia*, whither he went by way of Troas (2 Cor. ii. 12), and where, after that in addition to Timothy Titus also from Corinth had joined him, he wrote the *Second Epistle to the Corinthians*. He then remained three months in *Achaia* (Acts xx. 3), where he issued from Corinth—which he now visited for the third time (2 Cor. xii. 14, xiii. 1)—his Epistle *to the Romans*. Paul now regards his calling in the sphere of labour which he has hitherto occupied as fulfilled, and is impelled to pass beyond it (2 Cor. x. 15 f.); he has preached the Gospel from Jerusalem as far as Illyria (Rom. xv. 19, 23); he desires to go by way of Rome to Spain, as soon as he shall have conveyed to Jerusalem a collection gathered in Macedonia and Greece (Rom. xv. 23 ff.). But it does not escape his foreboding spirit that suffering and tribulation await him in Judaea (Rom. xv. 30 ff.).

The Apostle's missionary labours may be regarded as closed with this last sojourn in Achaia; for he now entered on his return journey to Jerusalem, in consequence of which the capital of the world was to become the closing scene of his labours and sufferings. Hindered solely by Jewish plots from sailing directly from Achaia to Syria, he returned once more to Macedonia, and after Easter crossed from Philippi to Troas (Acts xx. 3-6), where his companions, who had set out previously, awaited him. Coming thence to Miletus, he bade a last farewell with touching fervour and solemnity to the presbyters of his beloved church of Ephesus (Acts xx. 17 ff.); for he was firmly convinced in his own mind, filled as it was by the Spirit, that he was going to meet bonds and afflictions (xx. 23). At Tyre he was warned by the Christians not to go up to Jerusalem (xxi. 4); at Caesarea Agabus announced to him with prophetic precision the approaching loss of his freedom (xxi. 10 ff.), and his friends sought with tears to move him even now to return; but nothing could in the least degree shake his determination to follow absolutely the impulse of the Spirit, which urged him towards Jerusalem (xx. 22). He went thither (A.D. 59) with heroic self-denial and yielding of himself to the divine purpose, in like manner as formerly the Lord Himself made His last pilgrimage to the Jewish capital. Arriving there shortly before Pentecost—for his object was not only to convey to the brethren the gifts of love collected for them, but also to celebrate the national festival, Acts xxiv. 17—he was induced by James and the presbyters immediately on the following day to undertake, for the sake of the Judaists, a Nazarite vow (xxi. 17 ff.). But, while it was yet only the fifth day of this consecration (see on Acts xxiv. 11), the Asiatic Jews fell upon him in the temple, accusing him of having, as an enemy of the law and the temple, brought Gentiles with him into the holy place; and they would have killed him, had not the tribune of the fort Antonia rescued him by military force from their hands (xxi. 28-34). In vain he defended himself before the people (Acts xxii.), and on the following day before the Sanhedrin (xxiii. 1-10); but equally in vain was a plot now formed by certain Jews who had bound themselves by an oath to put him to death (xxiii. 11-22); for the tribune, when informed of it, had the Apostle conducted immediately to the Procurator Felix at Caesarea (xxiii. 23-35). Felix was base enough, in spite of Paul's excellent defence, to detain him as a prisoner for two years, in the expectation even of receiving a bribe; and on his departure from the province, from a wish to gratify the Jews, left the Apostle to be dealt with by Porcius Festus his successor (summer, A.D. 61), Acts xxiv. Even from the more equitable Festus, before whom the Jews renewed their accusations and Paul the defence of his innocence, he did not receive the justice that was his due; wherefore he found himself compelled to make a formal appeal to the Emperor (xxv. 1-12). Before this date however, whilst living in the hope of a speedy release, he had written at Caesarea his Epistles *to the Ephesians, Colossians*, and *Philemon* (which are usually assigned to the *Roman* captivity); see on Eph. *introd.* § 2. His appeal, notwithstanding the unanimously favourable opinions pronounced regarding him (Acts xxvi.) after his solemn defence of himself before King Agrippa II. and his sister (xxv. 13 ff.), was necessarily followed by his transference from Caesarea to Rome. During the autumn voyage, on which he was accompanied by Luke and Aristarchus, danger succeeded danger, after the Apostle's wise warnings were despised (Acts xxvii. 10, 11, 21); and it was only in consequence of his advice being afterwards followed (Acts xxvii. 30-36) that all were saved and, after the stranding of their vessel at Malta, happily landed to pass the winter on that island. In the following spring he saw Rome, though not—as it had been so long his earnestly cherished wish to visit it (Rom. i. 10 ff.)—as the free herald of the Gospel. Still he there enjoyed the favour—after receiving a custodia militaris—of being permitted to dwell in his own hired house and to continue without interruption his work of instruction among all who came to him. This mild imprisonment lasted two full years (from the spring of 62): and as at this time his intrepid fidelity to his office failed not to make oral proclamation of the kingdom of God (Acts xxviii. 30, 31; Phil. i. 12 ff.), so in particular the *Epistle to the Philippians*, which emanated from this time of captivity, is a touching proof of that fidelity, as well as of the love which he still received and showed, of the sufferings which he endured, and of the resignation and hope which alternated within him. This letter of love may be called his *swan's song*. The two years' duration of his further imprisonment did not decide his cause; and it does not make his release by any means self-evident,[1] for Luke reports nothing from this period respecting the progress of the Apostle's trial. But now all at once we lose all trustworthy accounts bearing on the further course of his fate; and only thus much can be gathered from the testimonies of ecclesiastical writers as historically certain, that he died the death of a martyr at Rome under Nero, and nearly at the same time[2] as Peter suffered crucifixion at the same place. See the testimonies in Credner, *Einl.* I. p. 318 ff.; Kunze, *praecip. Patrum testim., quae ad mort. P. spect.*, Gott. 1848; and generally Baur, *Paulus*, I. p. 243 ff. ed. 2; Wieseler, p. 547 ff.; Otto, *Pastoralbr.* p. 149 ff.; from the Catholic point of view, Döllinger, *Christenth. und Kirche*, p. 79 ff. ed. 2.

The question however arises, Whether this martyrdom (beheading) was the issue of his trial *at that time* (Petavius, Lardner, Schmidt, Eichhorn, Heinrichs, Wolf, *de altera Pauli captivit.* Lips. 1819, 1821, Schrader, Hemsen, Köllner, Winer, Fritzsche,

---

[1] In opposition to Stölting, *Beitr. z. Exeg. d. Paul. Br.* p. 195.

[2] Whether Peter suffered martyrdom somewhat earlier than Paul (Ewald), or some time later, cannot be made out from Clement, *Cor.* I. 5, any more than from other sources. Moreover this question is bound up with that as to the place and time of the composition of the First Epistle of Peter. But that Peter *never* came to Rome—as, following Baur and others, Lipsius, *Chronol. d. Röm. Bischöfe*, 1869, and *Quellen d. Röm. Petrussage*, 1872, and Gundert in the *Jahrb. f. D. Th.* 1869, p. 306 ff., seek to prove (see the earlier literature on the question in Bleek's *Einleitung*, p. 562)—cannot, in view of the church tradition, be maintained. The discussion of this question in detail belongs to another place.

Baur, Schenkel, de Wette, Matthies, Wieseler, Schaff, Ebrard, Thiersch, Reuss, Holtzmann, *Judenth. u. Christenth.* p. 549 f., Hausrath, Hilgenfeld, Otto, Volckmar, Krenkel, and others, including Rudow, *Diss. de argumentis historic., quibus epistolar. pastoral. origo Paul. impugnata est*, Gott. 1852, p. 6 ff.), or of a *second* Roman captivity, as has been assumed since Eusebius (ii. 22) by the majority of ancient and modern writers, including Michaelis, Pearson, Häulein, Bertholdt, Hug, Heidenreich, *Pastoralbr.* II. p. 6 ff., Mynster, *kl. theol. Schr.* p. 291 f., Guericke, Böhl, *Abfassungsz. d. Br. an Timoth. u. Tit.*, Berl. 1829, p. 91 ff., Köhler,[1] Wurm, Schott, Neander, Olshausen, Kling, Credner, Neudecker, Wiesinger, Baumgarten, Lange, *apost. Zeitalt.* II. i. p. 386 ff., Bleek, Döllinger, Sepp, Gams, *d. Jahr d. Märtyrertodes d. Ap. Petr. u. Paul.* 1867, Ewald, Huther and others. Since the testimony of Eusebius, *l.c.*, which is quite of a general character, confessedly has reference merely to a tradition (λόγος ἔχει), which was acceptable to him on account of 2 Tim. iv. 16 f., the historical decision of this question turns on the statement of Clemens Romanus.[2] He says, according to Dressel's text,[3] 1 Cor. 5: Διὰ ζῆλον καὶ ὁ Παῦλος ὑπομονῆς βραβεῖον ὑπέσχεν, ἑπτάκις δεσμὰ φορέσας, φυγαδευθεὶς, λιθασθεῖς. Κῆρυξ γενόμενος ἔν τε τῇ ἀνατολῇ καὶ ἐν τῇ δύσει, τὸ γενναῖον τῆς πίστεως αὐτοῦ

---

[1] Who, curiously enough, further assumes a third and fourth captivity.

[2] Nothing at all bearing upon our question can be derived from the testimony of Dionysius of Corinth, quoted by Euseb. ii. 25, to which Wiesinger still attaches weight. It merely affirms that Peter and Paul having come to Italy, there taught, and died as martyrs. Comp. Caius *ap.* Eus. *l.c.*, Iren. *Haer.* iii. 1; Tertull. *Scorp.* 15, *praescr.* 36; and even the κήρυγμα Πέτρου (Clem. *Strom.* vi. 5). These testimonies do not in the least suggest the idea of a *second* presence in Rome.

[3] Dressel follows the recension of Jacobson (Oxon. 1838, and 2d ed. 1840), who collated Cod. A anew, and carefully rectified its text of the epistle first issued by Patricius Junius (Oxon. 1633), followed substantially in that form by Cotelerius (Paris 1672), and then amended by Wotton (Cantabr. 1718). The variations however of the different revisions of the text, which is only preserved, and that in a very faulty form, in Cod. A, do not essentially affect the present question. Even the form in which Laurent (*neutest. Stud.* p. 105 ff., and in the *Stud. u. Krit.* 1870, p. 135 ff.) gives the text of the passage in Clement on the basis of Tischendorf's reproduction of Cod. A, is without influence on our question. This holds true also with respect to the latest critical editions of the Clementine Epistles by Hilgenfeld (*N. T. extra canonem*, 1866, I.), by Lightfoot (*S. Clement of Rome. The two Epistles*, etc. 1869), and by Laurent (*Clem. Rom. ad Cor. epistula*, etc. 1870).

κλέος ἔλαβεν, δικαιοσύνην διδάξας ὅλον τὸν κόσμον, καὶ ἐπὶ τὸ τέρμα τῆς δύσεως ἐλθών, καὶ μαρτυρήσας ἐπὶ τῶν ἡγουμένων. Οὕτως ἀπηλλάγη τοῦ κόσμου, καὶ εἰς τὸν ἅγιον τόπον ἐπορεύθη, ὑπομονῆς γενόμενος μέγιστος ὑπογραμμός. This passage, it is thought, indicates clearly enough that Paul before his death, passing beyond Italy, had reached the farthest limit of the West, Spain,[1] and that therefore a second Roman imprisonment must be assumed. See especially Credner, *Gesch. d. Kanon*, p. 51 ff.; Huther, *Pastoralbr. Einl.* p. 32 ff. ed. 3; Lightfoot *l.c.*, who understands by τέρμα τ. δ. *Gades*. In opposition to this view we need not seek after any different interpretation of τὸ τέρμα τ. δύσεως; whether it may be taken to signify *the western limit appointed to Paul* (Baur, Schenkel, Otto)—which certainly would be very meaningless—or the *line of demarcation* between East and West (Schrader, Hilgenfeld, *apost. Väter*, p. 109); or even the *centre* of the West (Matthies). But it is to be observed :—1st. that the language generally bears a highly rhetorical and hyperbolical character, and, were it only for this reason, it is very hazardous to interpret the "limit of the West" (τὸ τέρμα τῆς δύσεως) with geographical accuracy. And is not even the immediately preceding δικαιοσ. διδάξας ὅλον τὸν κόσμον a flourish of exaggeration? 2d. Clement does not speak of East and West from his own Roman stand-point, but, as was most naturally accordant with the connection and design of his statement, from the standpoint of Paul, into whose local relations he in thought transports himself. While the Apostle laboured in Asia, he was in the *East*: then he passed over to Greece, and thus had become, from his Oriental point of view, a herald also in the *West*. But in the last crisis of his destiny he came even to the far West, as far as Rome: and for this idea how naturally, in the midst of the highly coloured language which he was using, did the expression ἐπὶ τὸ τέρμα τῆς δύσεως ἐλθών suggest itself! It could not have been misunderstood by the readers, because people at Corinth could not but *know* the place where Paul met his death. 3d.

---

[1] So also Ewald, *apost. Zeit.* p. 620 ff. ed. 3, who supposes that, when Paul heard in Spain of the horrors of the Neronian persecutions, he hurried back to Rome to bear witness for Christianity; that there he was arrested, placed once more on trial, and condemned to death. According to Ewald the Book of Acts itself, at i. 8, points by way of anticipation to the Spanish journey.

Ἐπὶ τῶν ἡγουμένων denotes (in allusion to Matth. x. 18) the rulers generally, before whom Paul gave testimony concerning Christ (μαρτυρήσας), after he had reached this τέρμα τῆς δύσεως. If the latter denotes *Rome*, then we may without hesitation, on historical grounds, conclude that the rulers are those Roman magistrates before whom Paul made his defence in Rome. But if *Spain* should be the "goal of the West," we should find ourselves carried by the μαρτυρήσας ἐπὶ τῶν ἡγουμ. to some scene of judicial procedure *in Spain;* and would it not in that case be necessary to assume a sojourn of the Apostle there, which that very trial would render specially memorable? But how opposed to such a view is the fact, that no historical trace, at all certain, is preserved of any church founded by Paul in Spain! For the testimonies to this effect adduced by Gams, *Kirchengesch. v. Spanien*, p. 26, Sepp, *Gesch. der Ap.* p. 314, ed. 2, and others, contain nothing but traditions, which have merely arisen from the hypothetical Spanish journey of Paul. And to say with Huther that the Apostle had *travelled* (ἐλθών) to Spain, but had not *laboured* there, is to have recourse to an explanation at variance with the intrinsic character of Paul himself and with the context of Clement. Besides, according to Rom. xv. 23 f., Paul desired to transfer his *ministry*, that was accomplished in the East, to Spain. 4th. If ἐπὶ τὸ τέρμα τ. δύσεως ἐλθών was intended to transport the reader to Spain, then it would be most natural, since οὕτως sums up the previous participial clauses, to transfer the ἀπηλλάγη τοῦ κόσμου also to *Spain;* for just as this ἀπηλλ. τ. κ. is manifestly correlative to the δικαιοσύνην διδάξ. ὅλον τ. κόσμον, so εἰς τ. ἅγιον τόπον ἐπορεύθη corresponds with the ἐπὶ τ. τέρμα τ. δύσεως κ.τ.λ.; so that Paul, starting from the τέρμα τ. δύσεως, which he has reached, and where he has borne his testimony before the rulers, enters on his journey to the holy place. It is only, therefore, when we understand *Italy* as the western limit, that the language of Clement is in harmony with the historical circumstances of the case.[1] See, moreover, Lipsius,

---

[1] If we render μαρτυρήσας *martyrium passus* (Credner, Lange, and older writers), this result comes out the more clearly, since at all events Paul died in Rome; along with which indeed Döllinger further finds in ἐπὶ τῶν ἡγουμ. an evidence for the year 67 that has been the traditional date since Eusebius, *Chron.* (comp. also Gams, *Jahr d. Märtyrertodes*, etc.; and Sepp, *l.c.* p. 379), when Nero was absent and the *Prefects* ruled in Rome. See his *Christenth. u. Kirche*, p. 101, ed.

de Clem. Rom. ep. ad Cor. I. p. 129, and *Chronol. d. röm. Bischöfe*, p. 163 ff. It cannot withal be overlooked that in the so-called *Epist. Clem. ad Jacobum*, c. 1, there is manifestly an echo of our passage, and yet Rome alone is designated as the final goal of the Apostle's labours: τὸν ἐσόμενον ἀγαθὸν ὅλῳ τῷ κόσμῳ μηνύσαι βασιλέα, μέχρις ἐνταῦθα τῇ Ῥώμῃ γενόμενος, θεοβουλήτῳ διδασκαλίᾳ σώζων ἀνθρώπους, αὐτὸς τοῦ νῦν βίου βιαίως τὸ ζῆν μετήλλαξεν. After this the conjecture of Wieseler (and Schaff, *Hist. of Apost. Church*, p. 342), who, instead of ἐπὶ τὸ τέρμα as given by Junius, would read ὑπο τὸ τέρμα, and explain it "before the *supreme power* of the West," is unnecessary. It is decisive against this view that Jacobson, as well as Wotton, found ἐπὶ in the Cod. A, and that Tischendorf likewise has attested the existence of καὶ ἐπὶ as beyond doubt. But, besides, Wieseler's expedient would not be admissible on grounds of linguistic usage, for τέρμα in the sense assumed is only used with ἔχειν; see Eur. *Suppl.* 617, *Or.* 1343, Jacobs. *ad Del. epigr.* p. 287. From the very corrupt text of the *Canon Muratorii*,[1]

2. Against that chronological determination, see generally Baxmann, *dass Petr. u. Paul nicht am 29. Junius 67. gemartert worden sind*, 1867.

[1] The passage in question runs, "Acta autem omnium apostolorum sub uno libro sunt. Lucas optime Theophile comprindit (comprehendit), quia sub praesentia ejus singula gerebantur, sicuti et semote passionem Petri evidenter declarat, sed profectionem Pauli ab urbe ad Spaniam proficiscentis." Wieseler conjectures that after *proficiscentis* the word *omittit* has been left out; that *semote* means: at a separate place, viz. *not* in the Acts of the Apostles, but in the Gospel, xxii. 31-33. A very forced conjecture, with which nevertheless Volkmar (in Credner's *Gesch. d. Kanon*, p. 348) agrees, supposing that a *non* has dropped out after *proficiscentis*. Credner, *l.c.* p. 155 f., conjectured *semota* (namely *oca*, which is supposed to refer to John xxi. 18 ff., and Rom. xv. 24), and then *et* instead of *sed*. Otto, p. 154, would read *sic et* instead of *sed;* making the meaning: "Consequently (*sic*) he declares openly, that just as (*uti et*) in his absence the martyrdom of Peter took place, so likewise (*sic et*) the journey of Paul," etc. But how much must we thus introduce into the *semote!* Laurent alters into: "*semota passione ... et profectione*," etc. Various suggestions are made by others; see Ewald, *Jahrb.* VIII. p. 126, whose own procedure is the boldest. Hilgenfeld, *Kanon u. Krit. d. N. T.*, thinks that the author has "*guessed*" the martyrdom of Peter and the Spanish journey of Paul from the abrupt close of the Acts of the Apostles. Such a theory should have been precluded by the "*evidenter declarat*," for which indeed Ewald would read "*evidenter decerpit*" or "*decollat*. If we must resort to conjecture (and it is necessary), it seems the simplest course, instead of *et semote*, to insert *id semotam*, and then instead of *sed, et*. This would yield the sense: *as this circumstance (id)*, viz. the writing down only what took place in his presence, *evidently explains the exclu-*

nothing can be gathered bearing on our question, except that the author was already *acquainted with* the tradition of the journey to Spain afterwards reported by Eusebius; not, that he wished to *refute* it (Wieseler, p. 536). On the other hand, Origen (in Euseb. iii. 1: τί δεῖ περὶ Παύλου λέγειν ἀπὸ Ἱερουσαλὴμ μέχρι τοῦ Ἰλλυρικοῦ πεπληρωκότος τὸ εὐαγγέλιον τοῦ Χριστοῦ καὶ ὕστερον ἐν τῇ Ῥώμῃ ἐπὶ Νέρωνος μεμαρτυρηκότος) tacitly excludes the Spanish journey. The tradition regarding it arose very naturally out of Rom. xv. 24; (Jerome: "ad Italiam quoque et, *ut ipse scribit*, ad Hispanias—portatus est"), and served as a needed historical basis for the explanation of 2 Tim., acquiring the more general currency both on this account and because it tended to the glorification of the Apostle. It is further worthy of attention that the pseudo-Abdias, in his *Historia Apostolica*, ii. 7, 8 (in Fabricius, *Cod. Apocr.* p. 452 ff.), represents the execution as the issue of the captivity reported in the Acts. Had this author been a believer in a liberation, as well as in a renewed missionary activity and second imprisonment, he would have been the last to refrain from bringing forward wonderful reports regarding them. Substantially the same may be said of the *Acta Petri et Pauli* in Tischendorf, *Act. ap. apocr.* p. 1 ff.

Note.—If we regard the *Epistles to Timothy and Titus*—which, moreover, stand or fall *together*—as genuine, we *must* take, as Eusebius in particular has done with reference to 2 Tim., the tradition of the Apostle's liberation from Rome and of a second captivity there as an historical postulate,[1] in order to gain the room which cannot otherwise be found for the historical references of those Epistles,

---

sion (*semotam*) *of the passion of Peter and of the journey of Paul from Rome to Spain.* On both of these occasions the author accordingly thinks that Luke was not present, and thereby the fact that he has omitted them in his book is explained.

[1] This is the ground assumed by the latest expositors of the Pastoral Epistles, who maintain their genuineness, Wiesinger and Huther; whilst Rudow, again, in the already mentioned *Dissert.* 1852, only rejects the First Ep. to Timothy (comp. Bleek), and, calling in question a second captivity, ascribes the Second Ep. to Timothy to the first imprisonment, and the Ep. to Titus to the sojourn at Ephesus. So also Otto, with respect to the two last-named Epistles; but he regards the First Ep. to Timothy as a letter of instruction for Timothy in view of his mission to Corinth, consequently as nearly contemporaneous with the Ep. to Titus. See, in opposition to Otto, Huther on the *Pastoral Epistles, Introd.* ed. 3

and the latest possible time for their other contents. But the more defective the proof of the second imprisonment is, the more warranted remain the doubts as to the genuineness of these Epistles, which arise out of their own contents; while in virtue of these doubts the Epistles, in their turn, cannot themselves be suitably adduced in proof of that captivity. Besides, it cannot be left out of view that in all the unquestionably genuine Epistles which Paul wrote during his imprisonment every trace of the previously (Rom. xv. 24) cherished plan of a journey to Spain has vanished; and that in the Epistle to the Philippians, which was certainly not written till he was in Rome (i. 25 f., ii. 24), he contemplates as his further goal in the event of his liberation, not the far West, but Macedonia, or in other words a return to the East. From Acts xxiii. 11, however, no evidence can be adduced against the Spanish journey (as Otto contends), because in this passage there is no express mention of a *last* goal, *excluding* all further advance.

§ 2. The Christian Church at Rome.[1]

That the Christian Church in Rome had been in existence for a considerable time when Paul wrote to it, is clear from i. 8-13 and xiii. 11, 15; and that it was already a church formally constituted, may be gathered from the general analogy of other churches that had already been long in existence, from xii. 5 ff., and less certainly from xvi. 5. Especially may the existence of a body of presbyters, which was essential to church organization (Acts xiv. 23), be regarded as a matter of course. In the Acts of the Apostles the existence of the Church is presupposed (xxviii. 15) as something well known; and the author, who follows the thread of his *Apostle's* biography, had no occasion to narrate its origin or development.

The *origin* of the Roman Church cannot therefore be determined with certainty. It is not incredible that even during the lifetime of Jesus faith in Him had taken root, in individual cases, among the Roman Jews (comp. Clem. *Recogn.* i. 6). For

---

[1] See Th. Schott, *d. Römerbrief s. Endzweck u. Gedankengang nach*, Erl. 1858; Mangold, *d. Römerbr. u. d. Anfänge d. röm. Gem.* Marb. 1866; Wieseler in *Herzogs Encykl.* XX. p. 583 ff. (1866); Beyschlag in the *Stud. u. Krit.* 1867, p. 627 ff.; comp. also Grau, z. *Einführ. in d. Schriftth. N. T.*, Stuttg. 1868, and his *Entwickelungsgesch. d. neut. Schriftth.* II. 1871, p. 102 ff.; Sabatier, *l'apôtre Paul*, 1870.

among the pilgrims who flocked to the festivals at Jerusalem from all countries Romans also were wont to be present (Acts ii. 10), and that too in considerable numbers, because the multitude of Jews in Rome had since the time of Pompey become extraordinarily great (see Philo, *leg. ad Caj.* II. p. 568; Dio Cass. xxxvi. 6; Joseph. *Antt.* xvii. 11, 1), including Jews directly from Palestine (prisoners of war, see Philo, *l.c.*), of whom a large portion had attained to freedom, the rights of citizenship, and even wealth. Is it unlikely that individual festal pilgrims from Rome, impressed by the words and works of Jesus in Jerusalem, carried back with them to their homes the first seeds of the faith? To this view it cannot be objected (as by Reiche), that Christianity did not spread beyond the bounds of Palestine until after the miracle of Pentecost; for there is mention, in fact, in Matt. x. of the official *missionary activity* of the Apostles, and in Acts viii. 1 ff. of that of emigrants from Jerusalem. If the former and the latter did not labour in foreign lands until a subsequent period, this by no means excludes the possibility of the conversion of individual foreigners, partly Jews, partly proselytes, *who became believers in Jerusalem.* It is further probable that there were some Romans among the three thousand who came over to the Christian faith at the first Pentecost (Acts ii. 10); at least it would be very arbitrary to exclude these, who are expressly mentioned among the *witnesses* of what occurred at Pentecost, from participation in its *results.* Lastly, it is probable that the persecution which broke out with the stoning of Stephen drove some Palestinian Christians to take refuge even in the distant capital of the world, distinguished by its religious toleration, and in fact inclined to Oriental modes of worship (Athenaeus, *Deipnos.* I. p. 20 B., calls it ἐπιτομὴν τῆς οἰκουμένης, and says: καὶ γὰρ ὅλα τὰ ἔθνη ἀθρόως αὐτόθι συνῴκισται). For that this dispersion of the Christians of Jerusalem was not confined to Samaria and Judaea (an objection here urged by Reiche and Köllner), is proved by Acts xi. 19, where emigrants are mentioned who had gone as far as Phoenicia and Cyprus. And how easily might some find their way even to Rome, seeing that the brisk maritime intercourse between these places and Italy afforded them opportunity, and seeing that they might expect to find admittance and repose among their countrymen in Rome, who were strangers to the fanatical zeal of

Palestine. But although, in consequence of the constant intercourse maintained by the Jews at Rome with Asia, Egypt and Greece, and especially with Palestine (Gieseler, *Kirchengesch.* I. § 17), various Christians may have visited Rome, and various Jews from Rome may have become Christians, all the influences hitherto mentioned could not establish a Christian *congregational life* in Rome. Individual Christians were there, and certainly also Christian fellowship, but still no organized church. To plant such a church, there was needed, as is plain from the analogy of all other cases of the founding of churches with which we are acquainted, official action on the part of teachers endowed directly or indirectly with apostolic authority.

Who the *founder* of the Roman *congregational life* was, however, is utterly unknown. The Catholic Church names the Apostle *Peter;* concerning whom, along with the gradual development of the hierarchy, there has been a gradual development of tradition, that he came to Rome in the second year, or at any rate about the beginning of the reign of the Emperor Claudius (according to Gams, A.D. 41), to overcome Simon Magus, and remained there twenty-five years (Gams: twenty-four years and an indefinite number of days), till his death, as its first bishop. See Eusebius, *Chron.* (in Mai's *Script. vet. nov. coll.* VIII. p. 376, 378); and Jerome, *de vir. ill.* 1.[1] But that Peter in the year 44, and at the date of the apostolic conference in the year 52, was still resident in Jerusalem, is evident from Acts xii. 4, xv. 7, and Gal. ii. 1 ff. From Acts xii. 7 a journey to Rome cannot be inferred.[2] Further, that still later, when Paul was living at

---

[1] See, generally, Lipsius, *d. Quellen d. Röm. Petrussage,* Kiel, 1872. As to the way in which that tradition, the germs of which are found in Dionysius of Corinth (Euseb. *H. E.* ii. 25), gradually developed itself into the complete and definite form given above, see Wieseler, *chronol. Synops.* p. 571 ; regarding the motley legends connected with it, see Sepp, *Gesch. d. Ap.* p. 341, ed. 2 ; concerning the unhistorical matter to be eliminated from the report of Jerome, see Huther *on* 1 *Peter, Introd.;* comp. Credner, *Einl.* II. p. 382. The alleged presence of Simon in Rome is probably the mere product of a misconception, by which Justin, *Apol.* i. 26 (comp. Irenaeus, *Haer.* i. 23), explained an old inscription as referring to Simon Magus. Comp. also Uhlhorn, *d. Homil. u. Recogn. d. Clem.* p. 378 f.; Möller in *Herzogs Encykl.* XIV. p. 392 ff.; Bleek, p. 563 f.

[2] Even if Peter had actually, in the course of his foreign travels (1 Cor. ix. 5), visited Rome once in the time of Claudius (comp. on Acts xii. 17), which Ewald (*apost. Zeit.* p. 606 f. ed. 3.) concedes to ecclesiastical tradition, not calling in

Ephesus, Peter had not been labouring in Rome, is evident from Acts xix. 21, because Paul followed the principle of not interfering with another Apostle's field of labour (Rom. xv. 20 ; comp. 2 Cor. x. 16); and, had Peter been in Rome when Paul wrote to the Romans, he would have been saluted by the latter before all others; for the numerous salutations in ch. xvi. presuppose an accurate acquaintance with the teachers who were then in Rome. Peter cannot have been labouring in Rome at all before Paul himself was brought thither, because the former, as Apostle to the Jews, would have brought Christianity into closer contact with the Jewish population there than is apparent in Acts xxviii. 22. It is even in the highest degree improbable that Peter was in Rome prior to the writing of the Epistle to the Philippians—the only one which was certainly written by Paul in Rome—or at the time of its being written ; for it is inconceivable that Paul should not in this letter have mentioned *a fellow-Apostle,* and that one Peter, especially when he had to complain so deeply of being forsaken as at Phil. ii. 20. Consequently the arrival of Peter in Rome, which was followed very soon by his execution—and which is accredited by such ancient and strong testimony (Dionysius of Corinth, in Euseb. ii. 25 ; Caius, in Euseb. ii. 25 ; Origen, in Euseb. iii. 1; Irenaeus ; Tertullian, etc.) that it cannot be in itself rejected—is to be placed only towards the end of Paul's captivity, subsequent to the composition of the Epistle to the Philippians. If, therefore, the tradition of the Roman Church having been founded by Peter—a view disputed even by Catholic theologians like Hug, Herbst, Feilmoser, Klee, Ellendorf, Maier, and Stengel, who however are vehemently opposed by Windischmann, Stenglein, Reithmayr, and many others[1]

question even a meeting with Simon Magus there, yet we cannot regard this as involving the foundation of the Roman church and the episcopal position. Otherwise Paul would have intruded on another labourer's field. See the sequel.

[1] Döllinger, *Christenth. u. Kirche,* p. 95 ff. ed. 2, still seeks to support it on the usual grounds, and in doing so starts from the purely fanciful *à priori* premiss, that the Roman Church *must* have been founded by an Apostle, with the equally arbitrary conclusion : "and that Apostle *can only* have been Peter." He gives to the twenty-five years' duration of the Petrine *episcopatus* a curious roundabout interpretation, according to which the episcopate is made to mean merely *ecclesiastical dignity* in general ; see p. 317. The passage of Dionysius of Corinth in Euseb. ii. 25 is misinterpreted by him.—It ill accords with the Roman epis-

—must be entirely disregarded (although it is still defended among Protestants by Bertholdt, Mynster and Thiersch), it is on the other hand highly probable, that a Christian church was founded at Rome only subsequent to Paul's transference of his missionary labours to Europe; since there is no sort of indication, that on his first appearance in Macedonia and Achaia he anywhere found a congregation already existing. He himself in fact stood in need of a special direction from Christ to pass over to Europe (Acts xvi. 9 f.); and so another official herald of the faith can hardly before that time have penetrated as far as Italy. But, when Paul was labouring successfully in Greece, it was very natural that apostolic men of his school should find motive and occasion for carrying their evangelic ministry still further westward,—to the capital of the Gentile world. The expulsion of the Jews from Rome under Claudius (Sueton. *Claud.* 25; Acts xviii. 2) served, under Divine guidance, as a special means for this end. Refugees to the neighbouring Greece became Christians, Christians of the Pauline type, and then, on their return to Rome, came forward as preachers of Christianity and organisers of a church. We have historical confirmation of this in the instance of Aquila and Priscilla, who emigrated as Jews to Corinth, dwelt there with Paul for upwards of a year and a half, and at the date of our Epistle had again settled in Rome, where they appear, as previously in Ephesus (1 Cor. xvi. 19), according to Rom. xvi. 3 as teachers and the possessors of a house where the Roman church assembled.[1] It is probable that

copate of Peter that in Euseb. iii. 2, and Irenaeus, iii. 3, *Linus* is expressly named as the *first* Roman bishop; and in fact in the *Constit. ap.* vii. 46, 1, it is said that he was appointed by *Paul;* while Peter only nominated the *second* bishop (Clemens) after the death of Linus. According to this statement Peter had nothing to do with the founding of the Roman episcopate, and neither Paul nor Peter was bishop in Rome. On the whole it is to be maintained that *no* Apostle at all was bishop of a church. The apostolate and the presbyterate were two specifically distinct offices in the service of the Church. In *Rome* especially the succession of bishops can only be historically proved from Xystus onwards (*ob.* 125); see Lipsius, *l.c.*

[1] That this married pair came to Corinth, not as Christians, but as still Jews, and were there converted to Christianity through Paul, see on Acts xviii. 1, 2. Comp. Reiche, I. p. 44 f.; Wieseler, *l.c.* p. 586.—Moreover, that the *Christians* (Jewish-Christians) resident in Rome were driven into exile along with other Jews by the edict of Claudius, can neither be proved nor yet controverted from the well-known passage in Sueton. *Claud.* 25 (see on Acts xviii. 1); for at that time

others also, especially among the persons mentioned in ch. xvi., were in similar ways led by God; but it is certain that a chief place among the founders of the church belongs to Aquila and Priscilla; since among the many who are greeted by Paul in the 16th chap. he presents to them the *first* salutation, and that with a more laudatory designation than is accorded to any of the others.

Christianity, having taken root in the first instance among the *Jews,* found the more readily an entrance among the *Gentiles* in Rome, because the popular heathen religion had already fallen into a contempt inducing despair both among the cultivated and uncultivated classes (see Gieseler I. i. § 11-14; Schneckenburger, *neutest. Zeitgesch.* p. 59 f.; Holtzmann, *Judenthum u. Christenthum,* p. 305 ff.). Hence the inclination to Monotheism was very general; and the number of those who had gone over to Judaism was very great (Juvenal, *Sat.* xiv. 96 ff.; Tac. *Ann.* xv. 44, *Hist.* v. 5; Seneca, in Augustine, *de civ. Dei,* vii. 11; Joseph. *Antt.* xviii. 3, 5). How much attention and approval, therefore, must the liberal system of religion, elevated above all the fetters of a deterrent legal rigour, as preached by Aquila and other Pauline teachers, have met with among the Romans dissatisfied with heathenism! From the description of most of the persons named in ch. xvi., from the express approval given to the doctrine in which the Romans had been instructed, xvi. 17, vi. 17, and even from the fact of the composition of the letter itself, inasmuch as not one of the now extant letters of the Apostle is directed to a *non-Pauline* church, we may with certainty infer that *Pauline* Christianity was preponderant in Rome; and from this it is a further necessary inference that a very important part of the Roman church consisted of *Gentile-Christians.* This *Gentile-Christian* part must have been the *preponderating* one, and must have formed its *chief constituent* element (in opposition to Baur, Schwegler, Krehl, Baumgarten-Crusius, van Hengel, Volkmar, Reuss, Lutterbeck, Thiersch, Holtzmann, Mangold, Grau, and Sabatier), since Paul expressly and repeatedly designates and addresses the Romans in general as belonging to the ἔθνη (i. 6, 13, xi. 13); and asserts before them the importance

the Christian body, which at all events was very small and isolated, was not yet independent, but still united with the Jewish population.

of his calling as *Apostle to the Gentiles* (xv. 15 f., i. 5 ; comp. xvi. 4, 26). Comp. Neander, *Gesch. d. Pflanzung*, etc., ed. 4, p. 452 ff., Tholuck, Philippi, Wieseler, Hofmann. Indeed, we must presume in accordance with the apostolic agreement of Gal. ii. 7 ff., that Paul would not have written a doctrinal Epistle to the Romans, especially one containing his entire gospel, if the church had been, in the main, a church of the περιτομὴ and not of the ἀκροβυστία.[1] Even ch. vii. 1, where the readers are described as γινώσκοντες νόμον, as well as the numerous references to the Old Testament, and proofs adduced from it, are far from attesting the predominance of Jewish Christianity in Rome.[2] They are fully explained, when we recollect that in the apostolic age *all* Christian knowledge was conveyed through the channel of the Old Testament (xvi. 26); that an acquaintance with the law and the prophets, which was constantly on the increase by their being publicly read in the assemblies (comp. on Gal. iv. 21), was also to be found among the *Gentile-Christians;* and that the mingling of Jews and Gentiles in the churches, even without a Judaizing influence being exerted on the latter (as in the case of the Galatians), could not but tend to further the use of that Old Testament path which Christian preaching and knowledge had necessarily to pursue. The grounds upon which Baur (in the *Tübing. Zeitschr.* 1836, 3, p. 144 ff. 1857, p. 60 ff., and in his *Paulus*, I. p. 343 ff. ed. 2 ; also in his *Christenth. d. drei erst. Jahrb.* p. 62 ff. ed. 2; see also Volckmar, *d. Röm. Kirche,* p. 1 ff.; Holsten, *z. Ev. u. Paul. u. Petr.* p. 411) seeks to establish the preponderance of Jewish Christianity will be dealt with in connection with the passages concerned ; as will also the defence

---

[1] By this Epistle he would have gone beyond the line laid down by him for his own field of labour (comp. 2 Cor. x. 13 ff), and would have interfered in the sphere not assigned to him—the *Apostleship to the Jews.*

[2] Even in the Epistle of Clement, written in the name of the Roman Church, with its numerous O. T. references, the Gentile-Christian and Pauline element of thought predominates, although there is a manipulation of Pauline views and ideas in accordance with the "Christian legalism" (Ritschl, *altkath. K.* p. 274 ff.) of a later period. Comp. Lipsius, *de Clem. Rom. Ep. ad Cor. pr.* 1855 ; and Mangold, p. 167 ff. I cannot agree with Wieseler and others that this Epistle was written before the destruction of Jerusalem, but with Ritschl and others assign it to the time of Domitian ; comp. Cotelerius.

of that preponderance which Mangold has given, while correcting in many respects the positions of Baur. The middle course attempted by Beyschlag, *l.c.* p. 640—that the main element of the church consisted of native Roman *proselytes* to Judaism, so that we should regard the church as *Gentile-Christian* in its *lineage*, but as *Jewish-Christian* in its *habits of thought* — is unsupported by any relevant evidence in the Epistle itself, or by any indication in particular of a previous *state of proselytism.*

But even if there was merely a considerable portion of the Christian church at Rome consisting of those who had been previously Jews (as, in particular, xiv. 1 ff. refers to such), it must still appear strange, and might even cast a doubt upon the existence of a regularly organized church (Bleek, *Beitr.* p. 55, and *Einl.* p. 412; comp. Calovius and others), that when Paul arrives as a prisoner in Rome, and wishes to acquaint himself with the Jewish community there, the leaders of the latter make no mention of a Christian congregation at Rome, but evince merely a superficial cognisance of the Christian sect in general (Acts xxviii. 22). But the Jewish leaders are here speaking as *officials*, and, as such, are not inclined without special immediate occasion to express their views before the captive stranger as to the position of the Christian body which existed *in Rome itself.* A designation of the Christian sect *generally* in accordance with its notorious outward reputation—such as might bring it into suspicion—is enough for them; but as to the precise relation in which this sect stands to them in *Rome* itself they do not feel themselves called upon to say anything for the present, and, with discreet reserve, are therefore wholly silent respecting it. This narrative therefore of Acts is neither to be regarded as a fiction due to the tendency of the author (Baur, Zeller, Holtzmann), nor to be explained, arbitrarily and inadequately, by the expulsion of the Jews under Claudius (Olshausen), which had induced the Roman Jewish-Christians to separate themselves entirely from the Jews, so that on the return of the latter from exile the former remained unnoticed by them. Neither is it to be accounted for, with Neander—overlooking the peculiar character of Jewish religious interests—by the vast size of the metropolis; nor, with Baumgarten, by the predominance of the Gentile-

Christians there; nor yet, with older writers, by the hypothesis—unjust and incapable of proof—that the Roman Jews acted a dishonest and hypocritical part on the occasion. Not dishonesty, but prudence and caution are evinced in their conduct (comp. Schneckenburger, Philippi, Tholuck, Mangold), for the explanation of which we do not require, in addition to what they themselves express in ver. 22, to assume any special outward reason, such as that they had been rendered by the *Claudian measure* more shy and reserved (Philippi; comp. Ewald, *apost. Zeit.* p. 588, ed. 3); especially seeing that there is no just ground for referring the words of Suetonius, "Judaeos *impulsore Chresto* assidue tumultuantes Roma expulit" (*Claud.* 25), to disputes between Jews and Christians relative to the Messiahship of Jesus, contrary to the definite expression "tumultuare."[1]

We may add that our Epistle—since Peter cannot have laboured in Rome before it was written—is a *fact destructive of the historical basis of the Papacy*, in so far as the latter is made to rest on the founding of the Roman church and the exercise of its episcopate by that Apostle. For Paul the writing of such a didactic Epistle to a church of which he knew Peter to be the founder and bishop, would have been, according to the principle of his apostolic independence, an impossible inconsistency.

---

[1] The *Chrestus* of Suetonius was a Jewish agitator in Rome, who was actually so called. See on Acts xviii. 2, and Wieseler, p. 585. Every other interpretation is fanciful, including even the one given above, which is adopted by the majority of modern writers, among others by Baur, Holtzmann, Keim, Grau, and Mangold. Thiersch is peculiar in adding to it the groundless assertion that "the disturbances arose through the testimony of *Peter* to the Messiah in Rome, but that Peter had again left Rome even before the expulsion of the Jews by Claudius." Groundless is also the opinion of Philippi, that, if *Chrestus* is to be taken as an agitator, he must have been a pseudo-Messiah. The pseudo-Messiahs appeared much later. But after the analogies of Judas and Theudas, other insurgents are conceivable enough—enthusiasts for political freedom and zealots. Beyschlag, p. 652 ff., likewise taking *Chrestus* as equivalent to *Christus*, infers too rashly, from the passage in Suetonius, that the Roman Church was chiefly composed of proselytes, who, when the native-born Jews were expelled, *remained behind*. Märcker (*Lehre von der Erlös. nach d. Römerbr.* Meining. 1870, p. 3) rightly rejects the interchange of the names *Chrestus* and *Christus*.

§ 3. Occasion, Object and Contents of the Epistle.[1]

Long before writing this Epistle (ἀπὸ πολλῶν ἐτῶν, xv. 23) the Apostle had cherished the fixed and longing desire (Acts xix. 21) to preach the Gospel in person at Rome (i. 11 ff.)—in that metropolis of the world, where the flourishing of Christianity would necessarily exert an influence of the utmost importance on the entire West; and where, moreover, the special relation in which the church stood to the Apostle through its Pauline founders and teachers, and through the many friends and fellow-labourers whom he possessed in the city (ch. xvi.), claimed his ardent and loving interest. His official labours in other regions had hitherto prevented the carrying out of this design (i. 13, xv. 22). Now indeed he hoped that he should soon accomplish its realisation; but, partly because he wished first to undertake his collection-journey to Jerusalem (xv. 23-25), and partly because Spain, and not Rome (xv. 24-28), was to be the goal of his travels to the West, a lengthened sojourn in Rome cannot have formed part of his plan at that time. Accordingly, in pursuance of his apostolic purpose with reference to the Roman church, he could not but wish, on the one hand, no longer to withhold from it at least such a written communication of his doctrine, which he had so long vainly desired to proclaim orally, as should be suitable to the church's present need; and on the other hand, by this written communication to pave the way for his intended personal labours in such fitting manner as to render a prolonged stay there unnecessary. This twofold desire *occasioned* the composition of our Epistle, for the transmission of which the journey of the Corinthian deaconess Phoebe to Rome (xvi. 1) afforded an opportunity which he gladly embraced. He could not fail to possess a sufficient *acquaintance* with the circumstances of the church, when we consider his position towards the teachers saluted in ch. xvi., and the eminent importance of the church itself—of whose state, looking to the active intercourse between Corinth and Rome, he was certainly thoroughly informed—as well as the indications afforded by ch. xii. xiv. xv. That the Epistle was called forth

---

[1] See, besides the works quoted in § 2, Riggenbach in the *Luther. Zeitschr.* 1868, p. 33 ff.

by special communications made from Rome itself (possibly by Aquila and Priscilla) is nowhere apparent from its contents; on the contrary, such a view is, from the *general nature* of the contents, highly improbable. Of all the Apostle's letters, our present Epistle is that which has least arisen out of the necessity of dealing with special *casual* circumstances. According to Baur, the readers, as Jewish Christians (imbued also with erroneous Ebionite views), gave rise to the letter by their opposition to Paul, in so far, namely, as they saw in Paul's apostolic labours among the Gentiles a detriment to the Jews, contrary to the promises given to them by God, and therefore asserted the national privileges of their theocratic primacy in an exclusive spirit as opposed to the universalism of the Pauline teaching. Comp. also Schwegler, *nachapost. Zeit.* I. p. 285 ff.; Volckmar, *l.c.* p. 7 ff.; and also Reuss, *Gesch. d. N. T.* § 105 ff. ed. 4. In this view the Epistle is made to assume a specifically polemic character, which it manifestly has not (how very different in this respect the Ep. to the Galatians and those to the Corinthians!); it is assumed that the Church was a Jewish-Christian one; and an importance too great in relation to the whole, and indefensible from an exegetical point of view,[1] is attached to the section, chs. ix.-xi. (even in Baur's second edition, which contains on this point a partial retractation), while, on the other hand, the two last chapters have to be sacrificed to critical doubts that have no foundation. In no other Pauline Epistle is the directly polemical element so much in the background; and where it does find expression, it is only for the moment (as in xvi. 17-20),—a sure proof that it was least of all the concrete appearance and working of Antipaulinism which the Apostle had occasion in *this* Epistle to oppose. Against *that* enemy he would have waged a very different warfare, as is shown in particular in the case of the Epistle to the Galatians, so nearly allied in its contents. Nor is *that* enemy to be discovered in the weak in faith of xiv. 1 ff. Of course, however, Paul could not present *his* Gospel otherwise than in

---

[1] Baur previously, after his dissertation in the *Tüb. Zeitschr.* 1836, 3, found even the *princival theme* of the whole Epistle in chs. ix.-xi., for which chs. i.-viii. only serve as introduction. See against this view Huther's *Zweck u. Inhalt d.* 11 *ersten Kap. d. Römerbr.* 1846, p. 14 f. Baur, in his *Christenth. d. drei ersten Jahrh.* p. 62 ff. ed. 2, has modified his view on this point.

antagonism to the Jewish righteousness of works and arrogance, which it had already overcome and would continue to do so; for this antagonism belonged to the *essence* of his Gospel and had to assert itself, wherever there was Judaism—only in various forms and degrees according to the given circumstances—and therefore at Rome as well. The view of Thiersch (*Kirche im apostol. Zeitalt.* p. 166), that Paul desired to elevate the Jewish-Christian church, which had consisted of the simple followers of Peter, from their still somewhat backward standpoint to more enlarged views, rests on the erroneous opinion that Peter had laboured in Rome.

The *object* of our Epistle, accordingly, was by no means the drawing up of a systematic doctrinal system in general (see, against this view, Köstlin in the *Jahrb. f. Deutsche Theol.* 1856, p. 68 ff.; Grau, *Entwickelungsgesch.* II. p. 114); but it is not on the other hand to be restricted more specially than by saying: *Paul wished to lay before the Romans in writing, for their Christian edification* (i. 11, xvi. 25), *his evangelic doctrine*—the doctrine of the sole way of salvation given in Christ—*viewed in its full, specific character as the superseding of Judaism, in such a way as the necessities and circumstances of the Church demanded, and as he would have preached it among them, had he been present in person* (i. 11). The mode in which he had to accomplish this was determined by the circumstance, that he deemed it necessary for his object fully to set forth before the Roman church, in a manner proportioned to the high importance of its position, this Gospel as to which his disciples had already instructed them, *in the entire connection of its constituent fundamental principles.*[1] In no other letter has he done this so completely and thoroughly;[2] hence it is justly regarded as a grand scheme of his whole teaching,[3] in the precise

---

[1] Against which Hofmann unjustifiably urges ἀπὸ μέρους and ὡς ἐπαναμιμνῄσκων ὑμᾶς in xv. 15. See on that passage.

[2] So completely, that we can well enough understand how this Ep. could become the basis of Melancthon's *loci communes*.

[3] Comp. Hausrath, *neut. Zeitgesch.* II. p. 514 ff. Observe, at the same time, that though the Epistle deals very much with *legal notions*, this does not arise from its being destined for the *Romans* to whom Paul had become a *Roman* (Grau, *l.c.* p. 113), but from the very nature of the Pauline Gospel in general, and is therefore found *e.g.* also in the Epistle to the Galatians.

form which he held to be suitable for its presentation to the *Romans*. How much he must have had this at heart! How much he must have wished to erect such a complete and abiding memorial of *his* Gospel in the very capital of the Gentile world, which was to become the Antioch of the West! Not merely the present association of Jews and Gentiles in the church, but, generally, the essential relation in which, according to the very Pauline teaching, Christianity stood to Judaism, required him to subject this relation in particular, viewed in its strong antagonism to all legal righteousness, to an earnest and thorough discussion. This was a necessary part of his design; and consequently its execution, though on the whole based on a thoroughly didactic plan, nevertheless assumed, in the presence of the given points of antagonism, partly an apologetic, partly a polemic form, as the subject required; without however any precise necessity to contend against particular *doctrinal misconceptions among the Romans*, against divisions and erroneous views, such as had appeared, for example, among the Galatians and Corinthians; or against a Judaistic leaven brought with them by the Jews and Jewish-Christians who had returned to Rome (comp. Grau). The actual dangers for the moment in the Church were more of a moral than a dogmatic character—a remark which applies also to the opposition between the Gentile Christians, strong in faith, and the scrupulous Jewish Christians —and have merely given occasion to some more special notices (xiii. 1 ff.; xiv. 1 ff.), and hints (xvi. 1 ff.) in the hortatory portion of the Epistle. The Judaistic opponents of Pauline Christianity had not yet penetrated as far as Rome, and were not to arrive there till later (Ep. to the Philippians). It was therefore an untenable position when, even before the time of Baur, who assumed the object of the Epistle to be the *systematic and radical refutation of Jewish exclusiveness*, its aim was very frequently viewed as that of a *polemic against Jewish arrogance*, which had been specially aroused on account of the calling of the Gentiles (Augustine, Theodoret, Melancthon, Michaelis, Eichhorn, Schmidt, Flatt, Schott, and others [1]). The same may be said of the hypothesis

[1] Comp. van Hengel, who assumes that Paul desired to instruct the Romans *how to refute the subtleties of the Jews* with reference to the calling of the Gentiles, and to free them from errors and doubts thence arising.

that Paul wished, *in a conciliatory sense,* to obviate misunderstandings between Jewish and Gentile Christians (Hug). There is no evidence in the Epistle of actual circumstances to justify any such special definitions of its object; and even from xvi. 20 it cannot be assumed that Judaistic temptation had already begun (as Grau thinks). The *comprehensiveness* of the object of our Epistle—from which, however, neither the combating of Judaism, which arose naturally and necessarily out of the nature of the Pauline Gospel, nor (seeing that the *future* coming forward of his opponents could not be concealed from the Apostle) the *prophylactic* design of it, may be excluded—has been justly defended by Tholuck, Rückert, de Wette, Reiche, Köllner, Fritzsche, Philippi, Wieseler, Hausrath and others. Comp. Ewald, p. 317 f. Along with it, however, Th. Schott (comp. also Mangold, Riggenbach, Sabatier) has assumed a special *personally apologetic* purpose on the part of the Apostle;[1] namely that, being now on the point of proceeding with his Gentile mission-work in the far West, Paul wished to gain for his new labours a fixed point of support in the Roman church,[2] and on this account wished to instruct the Romans as to the significance and justification of the step, and to inspire them with full confidence regarding it, for which reason he exhibits to them in detail the nature and principles of his work. Against this view it may be urged, in general, that Paul nowhere gives expression to this special purpose, though the announcement of it would have been of decided importance, both

---

[1] Hofmann also makes the object of the Apostle *personal*. Paul assumes it to be a matter of surprise in Rome that he, the Apostle of the Gentiles, should have hitherto always kept aloof from the world's capital, and even now had not come to it. It might seem as if the church, that had arisen without his aid, had no interest for him; or as if he were afraid to proclaim the message of salvation in the great centre of Gentile culture. This twofold erroneous notion he was especially desirous to refute. As a proof how far he was from being thus afraid, he sets forth what in his view the message of salvation was, etc. etc. Thus he might hope that the church in the metropolis of the world would be just as steady a point of support for his ministry in the farthest West, as if it had been founded by himself. In this way, however, assumptions and objects are assigned to the Epistle which are not expressed in it, but are imputed to it on the ground of subordinate expressions, as will be shown in the exposition.

[2] Compare also Sabatier, *l'apôtre Paul*, p. 160 f., who at the same time affirms of the "grand missionaire:" *dont l'ambition était aussi vaste que le monde*. According to Sabatier, Paul gives down to chap. viii. the defence of his *doctrine*, and in chaps. ix.-xi. that of his *apostleship*.

for his own official interests and for the information of the Roman church (they could not read it between the lines either in the preface, vv. 1-15, or in the conclusion, xv. 14-44); and, in particular, that the Apostle's intention of visiting the Romans only in *passing through, without making a lengthened sojourn*, is incompatible with the assumed purpose which he is alleged to have formed regarding the church. Moreover, a justification on so great a scale of the *Gentile* mission would presuppose not a *Gentile*-Christian, but a *Jewish*-Christian, church and its requirements. Hence Mangold, holding the same view that the Epistle contains a *justification of the Gentile apostleship*, has the advantage of consistency in his favour; his theory is nevertheless based on the unsatisfactory ground adopted by Baur, namely, that the Church was Jewish-Christian. See, further, Beyschlag, *l.c.* p. 636 ff., and especially Dietzsch, *Adam u. Christus*, p. 14 ff.

As to *contents*, our Epistle, after the salutation and introduction (i. 1-15), falls into two main portions, a theoretical and a hortatory, after which follows the conclusion (xv. 14-xvi. 27). The *theoretic portion* (i. 16-xi. 36) bears its theme at the outset, i. 16, 17: "Righteousness before God, for Jews and Gentiles, comes from faith." Thereupon is established, in the first place, the necessity of this plan of salvation, as that which the whole human race required, Gentiles and Jews alike, because the latter also, even according to their own law, are guilty before God, and cannot attain to righteousness (i. 17-iii. 20). The nature of this plan of salvation is then made clear, namely, that righteousness really and only comes from faith; which is especially obvious from the justification of Abraham (iii. 21-iv. 25). The blessed results of this plan of salvation are, partly the blissful inward condition of the justified before God (v. 1-11); partly that justification through Christ is just as universally effective, as Adam's fall was once universally destructive (v. 12-21); and partly that true morality is not only not endangered by the manifestation of grace in Christ, but is promoted and quickened by it (chap. vi.), and made free from the fetters of the law (vii. 1-6). This last assertion demanded a defence of the law, as that which is in itself good and holy, but was abused by the sinful principle in man, against his own better will, to his destruction (vii. 17-25)—a sad variance of man with himself, which could not be removed through the law, but only through Christ, whose Spirit produces in us the freedom of the new divine life, the consciousness of adoption, and assurance of future glory (ch. viii.). From the lofty description of this blessed connection with Christ, Paul now suddenly passes to the saddening thought that a great part of that very Jewish people, so signally favoured of God, has rejected the plan of redemption ; and therefore he develops at length a Theodicée with regard to the exclusion, apparently irreconcileable with the divine promises, of so many members of the theocracy from the attainment of salvation in Christ (chs. ix.-xi.). The *hortatory portion* (chs. xii.-xv. 13) gives the essentials of the Pauline ethical system, partly in the form of general exhortations (xii. 1-21; xiii. 8-14), and partly in some special discussions which were deemed necessary in the circumstances of the Romans (xiii. 1-7, xiv. 1-xv. 13). The *conclusion* comprises in the first place—corresponding to the introduction (i. 8-15)—personal explanations with regard to the Apostle's intended journey by way of Rome to Spain (xv. 14-33); then the recommendation of Phoebe (xvi. 1 ff.) and salutations (xvi. 3-16); a warning with a closing wish (xvi. 17-20); some supplementary salutations with a second closing wish (xvi. 21-24); and, finally, a concluding doxology (xvi. 25-27).

"*This Epistle is the true masterpiece of the N. T., and the very purest Gospel, which is well worthy and deserving that a Christian man should not only learn it by heart, word for word, but also that he should daily deal with it as with the daily bread of men's souls. For it can never be too much or too well read or studied ; and the more it is handled, the more precious it becomes and the better it tastes.*"—Luther, *Preface.*

§ 4. Place and Time of Composition.—Genuineness of the Epistle.

Since the Apostle, when he composed his letter, was on the point of conveying to Jerusalem the proceeds of a collection made in Macedonia and Achaia (xv. 25-27), and intended to journey thence by way of Rome to Spain (xv. 28, comp. Acts xix. 21), we are thus directed to his last sojourn—of three months —in Achaia, Acts xx. 3. His purpose was to cross over directly from Achaia to Syria in order to reach Jerusalem, but he was led, owing to Jewish plots, to take quite a different route, namely, back through Macedonia (Acts xx. 3). This change in the plan of his journey had not been made when he wrote his Epistle; otherwise he would not have failed to mention in ch. xv.—where he had at vv. 25 and 31 very immediate inducement to do so—a circumstance so remarkable on account of its novelty and importance. We justly infer therefore—even apart from the fact that the composition of *such* an epistle presupposes a somewhat lengthened and quiet abode—that it was written before Paul again departed from Achaia. Although Luke mentions no particular city as the scene of the Apostle's three months' residence at that time, still it is, *à priori*, probable that he spent at least the greater part of the time in *Corinth*. For Corinth was the principal church of the country, and was in the eyes of the Apostle pre-eminently important and precious on account of his earlier labours there. But our attention is also directed to Corinth by the passages 1 Cor. xvi. 1-7, 2 Cor. ix. 4, xii. 20–xiii. 3, from which it is plain that, on his journey down from Macedonia to Achaia, Paul had chosen that city as the place of his sojourn, where he wished to complete the business of the collection, and from which he would convey the money to Jerusalem. Now, since the recommendation of the deaconess Phoebe from the Corinthian seaport Cenchreae (xvi. 1, 2), as well as the salutation from his host Gaius (xvi. 23, comp. with 1 Cor. i. 14), point to no other city than *Corinth*, we may, beyond all doubt, abide by it as the *place* of writing, and not with Dr. Paulus (*de orig. cp. P. ad Rom. paralip.* Jen. 1801, and *Römerbrief*, p. 231), on account of xv. 19 (see on that passage), put forward a claim on behalf of a town in Illyria. Theodoret has admirably proved in detail its composition at Corinth.

The *time* of composition accordingly falls in A.D. 59, when Paul regarded his ministry in the East as closed, and (see xv. 19, 23) saw a new and vast scene of action opened up to him in the West, of which Rome should be the centre and Spain the goal.

The *genuineness* is decisively attested by the testimonies of the orthodox church (the first express and special quotations from it are found in Irenaeus, *Haer.* iii. 16, 3, 9, while previously there are more or less certain echoes of its language or traces of its use),[1] as well as of the Gnostics Basilides, Valentinus, Heracleon, Epiphanes, and Theodotus; and there is not a single trace that even the Judaizing heretics, who rejected the authority of the Apostle, at all rejected the Pauline authorship of our Epistle. In order to warrant any doubt or denial of its authenticity, therefore, the most cogent internal grounds would need to be adduced; and in the utter absence of any such grounds, the worthless scruples of Evanson (*Dissonance of the four generally received Evangelists*, 1792, p. 259 ff.) and the frivolities of Bruno Bauer could find no supporters. The Epistle bears throughout the lively original impress of the Apostle's mind, and his characteristic qualities, in its matter and its form; is the chief record of *his* Gospel in its entire connection and antagonism; and is therefore also the richest original-apostolic charter and model of all true evangelical Protestantism. The opinion of Weisse (*philosoph. Dogm.* I. p. 146), which ultimately amounts to the suggestion of a number of interpolations as interwoven throughout the Epistle (see his *Beitr. z. Krit. d. Paul. Br.*, edited by Sulze, p. 28 ff.), rests simply on a subjective criticism of style, which has discarded all weight of external evidence.

The originality of the Epistle extends also to its *language*, the *Greek*, in which Paul dictated it to Tertius.[2] The note of the Syrian Scholiast on the Peschito, that Paul wrote his letter in *Latin*—a theory maintained also, but for a polemical purpose, by Hardouin, Salmeron, Bellarmine, Corn. à Lapide, and others—is based merely upon a hasty inference from the native language of the readers. Its composition in Greek however corresponds fully, not only with the Hellenic culture of the Apostle himself, but also with the linguistic circumstances of Rome (see Credner's *Einl.* II. p. 383 f.; Bernhardy, *Griech. Literat.* ed. 2, p. 483 ff.), and with the analogy of the rest of the ancient Christian writings addressed to Rome (Ignatius, Justin, Irenaeus, *et al.*).

That *the two last chapters* are genuine and inseparable parts of the Epistle, see in the critical remarks on ch. xv.

[1] Clem. *Cor.* i. 35; Polycarp, *ad Phil.* 6; Theoph. *ad Autol.* i. 20, iii. 14; letter of the Churches of Vienne and Lyons in Euseb. v. 1.

[2] The reason why Paul did not usually write his Epistles himself is to be sought, not in a want of practice in the writing of Greek—which is a supposition hardly reconcileable with his Hellenic culture—but in his apostolic position, in which—when, instead of the oral preaching for which he was called, he had to enter on written communication—friendly and subordinate hands were at his service. Comp. on Gal. vi. 11.

Παύλου ἐπιστολὴ πρὸς Ῥωμαίους.

The simplest and most ancient superscription is: πρὸς Ῥωμαίους in A B C ℵ.

CHAPTER I.

Ver. 1. Ἰησοῦ X.] Tisch., following B, reads Χριστοῦ Ἰησοῦ against decisive testimony. — In ver. 7 ἐν Ῥώμῃ, and in ver. 15 τοῖς ἐν Ῥώμῃ, are wanting in G. Börn.; and on ver. 7 the scholiast of cod. 47 remarks: τὸ ἐν Ῥώμῃ οὔτε ἐν τῇ ἐξηγήσει, οὔτε ἐν τῷ ῥητῷ μνημονεύει (who? probably the codex, which lay before the copyist). This quite isolated omission is of no critical weight; and is in no case to be explained by the very unnatural conjecture (of Reiche) that Paul in several Epistles (especially in that to the Ephesians) addressed the readers simply as Christians, and that then the place of residence was inserted by the copyists in accordance with the context or with tradition. In ver. 7 the omission might be explained by the reading ἐν ἀγάπῃ, which G and a few other authorities give instead of ἀγαπητοῖς; but, since τοῖς ἐν Ῥ. is wanting in ver. 15 also, another unknown reason must have existed for this. Perhaps some church, which received a copy of the Epistle from the Romans for public reading, may have, *for their own particular church-use,* deleted the extraneous designation of place, and thus individual codices may have passed into circulation without it. Rückert's conjecture, that Paul himself may have caused copies without the local address to be sent to other churches, assumes a mechanical arrangement in apostolic authorship, of which there is elsewhere no trace, and which seems even opposed by Col. iv. 16. — Ver. 8. ὑπέρ] A B C D* K, ℵ, min., Dam. read περί, which Griesb. has recommended, and Lachm. and Tisch. have adopted: justly, on account of the preponderant attestation, since both prepositions, though ὑπέρ less frequently (Eph. i. 16; Phil. i. 4), were used for the expression of the thought (in opposition to Fritzsche). — Ver. 13. The less usual position τινὰ καρπόν (Elz. κ. τ.) is established by decisive testimony; as also ὁ Θεὸς γάρ (Elz. ὁ. γ. Θ.) in ver. 19; and δὲ καί (Elz. τὲ καί) in ver. 27, although not on equally strong authority. — Instead of οὐ θέλω in ver. 13, D* E G, It. and Ambrosiaster read οὐκ οἴομαι. Defended by Rinck. But the very assurance already expressed in vv. 10, 11 might easily cause the οὐ θέλω to seem unsuitable here, if due account was not taken of the new element in the progress of the discourse contained in προεθέμην. — After εὐαγγ. in ver. 16 τοῦ Χριστοῦ (Elz.) is omitted on decisive authority; πρῶτον, however, which Lachmann has bracketed, ought not to be rejected on the inadequate adverse testimony of B G, Tert. as it might seem objectionable along with πιστεύοντι (not so in ii. 9 f.). — Ver. 24. The καί is indeed wanting after διό in A B C ℵ, min., Vulg. Or. al.; it was very easily passed over as superfluous; comp. ver. 26; ii. 1. Nevertheless Lachm. and Tisch. (8) have deleted it. — ἐν ἑαυτοῖς] Lachm. and Tisch. read ἐν αὐτοῖς, following A B C D* ℵ, min. But how frequently was the reflexive form neglected by the copyists. It occurred also in ver. 27 (B K). — Ver. 27. ἄρρενες] B D* G, 73, Or. Eus. Oec. read ἄρσενες. Adopted by Lachm. Fritzsche and Tisch. (7). Since two different forms cannot be supposed to have been used in the same verse, and in that which follows ἄρσενες ἐν ἄρσεσι is undoubtedly the true reading (only A* ℵ, min., and some Fathers reading uniformly ἄρρ. ἐν ἄρρ.), we must here adopt the form ἄρσενες almost invariably used in the N. T. (only the Apocal. has ἄρρ.). — Ver. 29. πορνείᾳ] wanting after ἀδικ. in A B C K ℵ, min., and several vss. and Fathers. Deleted by Lachm. Fritzsche, and Tisch., and rightly so; it is an interpolation introduced by those who did not perceive that the naming of this vice was not again appropriate here. It was written in the margin, and introduced at different places (for we find it *after* πονηρίᾳ also, and even after κακίᾳ), so that it in some instances even supplanted πονηρίᾳ. — The placing of κακίᾳ immediately after ἀδικίᾳ (Lachm. on weak authority), or according to A ℵ, Syr., after πονηρίᾳ (Tisch. 8), is explained by the aggregation of terms of a similar kind. — Ver. 31. After ἀστόργους Elz. and Scholz read ἀσπόνδους, which Mill condemned, and Lachm. and Tisch. have omitted. It is wanting in A B D* E G and ℵ*, Copt. Clar. Germ. Boern. and several Fathers. It is found before ἀστόργ. in 17, 76, Theophyl. Taken from 2 Tim. iii. 3. — Ver. 32. After ἐπιγνόντες, D E Bas. read οὐκ ἐνόησαν, and G, οὐκ ἔγνωσαν. That death is the wages of sin—this *Christian* doctrinal proposition seemed not at all to correspond with the *natural* knowledge of the *Gentiles*. — Instead of αὐτὰ ποιοῦσιν, ἀλλὰ καὶ συνευδοκοῦσι B reads αὐτὰ ποιοῦντες, ἀλλὰ καὶ συνευδοκοῦντες; so Lachm. in margin. This arose from the fact, that εἰσίν was erroneously taken for the chief verb in the sentence; or else it was a consequence of the introduction of οὐκ ἔγνωσαν, which in other witnesses led to the insertion of γάρ or δὲ after οὐ μόνον.

Vv. 1-7.—*The Apostolic salutation.*

Ver. 1. Παῦλος] See on Acts xiii. 9. — δοῦλος ... εὐαγγ. Θεοῦ is the exhaustive statement of his official dignity, proceeding from the general to the particular, by which Paul earnestly—as dealing with the Church of the metropolis of the world, which had as yet no personal knowledge of him—opens his Epistle as an official apostolic letter; without, however, having in view therein (as Flatt thinks) opponents and calumniators of his apostleship, for of the doings of such persons in Rome the Epistle itself contains no trace, and, had such existed, he would have set forth his dignity, not only positively, but also at the same time negatively (comp. Gal. i. 1). — In the first place Paul describes by δοῦλος 'I. X. *his relation of service to Christ*, as his Ruler, whose *servant* he is, and that *in general* (comp. on Phil. i. 1), just as the Old Testament עֶבֶד־יְהוָה expresses the relation of service to Jehovah, without marking off in itself exclusively any definite class, such as the prophetic or the priestly (see Josh. i. 1, xiv. 7, xxii. 4; Judg. ii. 8; Ps. cxxxi. 10; comp. Acts xvi. 17). This relation of entire dependence (Gal. i. 10; Col. iv. 12) is then *specifically and particularly* indicated by κλητὸς ἀπόστολος, and for this reason the former δοῦλος 'I. X. cannot be rendered merely in general *Christi cultor* (so Fritzsche), which is inadequate also at 1 Cor. vii. 22; Eph. vi. 6. Paul was *called* to his office, like all the earlier Apostles; he did not arrive at it by his own choice or through accidental circumstances. For the history of this divine calling, accomplished through the exalted Christ Himself, see Acts ix. (xxii. 26), and the remarks thereon. This κλητός presented itself so naturally to the Apostle as an essential element [1] in the full description of his official position which he meant to give (comp. 1 Cor. i. 1), that the supposition of a side-glance at uncalled teachers (Cameron, Glöckler) seems very arbitrary. — ἀφωρισμένος εἰς εὐαγγ. Θεοῦ] characterizes the κλητὸς ἀπόστολος more precisely: *set apart* (definitely separated from the rest of mankind) *for God's message of salvation*, to be its preacher and minister (see on Eph. iii.

---

[1] See Weiss in the *Jahrb. f. Deutsche Theol.* 1857, p. 97 ff.

7). The article before εὐαγγ. elsewhere invariably given in the N. T., is omitted here, because Paul views the message of God, of which he desires to speak, primarily under its *qualitative* aspect (comp. also van Hengel and Hofmann). Concrete definiteness is only added to it gradually by the further clauses delineating its character. This mode of expression implies a certain *festal* tone, in harmony with the whole solemn character of the pregnant opening of the Epistle: *for a gospel of God*, which He promised before, etc. Still we are not to understand, with Th. Schott, *a work* of proclamation, since εὐαγγ. is not the *work* of conveying a message, but the *message* itself. Θεοῦ is the genitive *subjecti* (*auctoris*), ver. 2, not *objecti* (Chrysostom). See on Mark i. 1. It is *God* who causes the message of salvation here referred to, which is *His* λόγος (Acts x. 36), to be proclaimed; comp. xv. 16; 2 Cor. xi. 7; 1 Thess. ii. 2, 8, 9; 1 Pet. iv. 17. The destination of Apostle to the *Gentiles* is involved in ἀφωρ. εἰς εὐ. Θ. though not expressed (against Beza and others). Further, since ἀφωρ. is parallel with the previous κλητός, it is neither to be explained, with Toletus and others, including Olshausen, by Acts xiii. 2, nor with Reiche, Ewald and van Hengel (following Chrysostom and others) by Gal. i. 15, comp. Jer. i. 5; but rather by Acts ix. 15 (σκεῦος ἐκλογῆς), comp. xxvi. 16 ff. The setting apart took place as a historical fact in and with his calling at Damascus. Entirely different is the mode of presenting the matter in Gal. i. 15, where ἀφορίσας με ἐκ κοιλ. μητρ. as the act of predestination in the counsel of God, is *placed before* the καλέσας, as the historically accomplished fact. The view of Drusius (*de sectis*, ii. 2, 6) and Schoettgen (comp. Erasmus and Beza), which Dr. Paulus has again adopted, viz. that Paul, in using the word ἀφωρ., alludes to his former *Pharisaism* ("the true Pharisee in the best sense of the word"), is based on the Peschito translation (see Grotius), but is to be rejected, because the context gives no hint of so peculiar a reference, for which also no parallel can be found in Paul's other writings.

Ver. 2. A more precise description of the character of this εὐαγγέλιον Θεοῦ, according to its concrete peculiarity, as far as ver. 5 inclusive, advancing and rising to a climax under the urgent sense of the sacredness of his office, which the Apostle has frankly to assert and to establish before the church of the metropolis of the world, personally as yet unknown to him.— ὃ προεπηγγείλατο κ.τ.λ.] How natural that the Apostle with his Old Testament training should, in the light of the New Testament revelation which he had received, first of all glance back at the connection divinely established in the history of salvation between the gospel which he served and ancient prophecy, and should see therein the *sacredness* of the precious gift entrusted to him! To introduce the idea of an *antithetic* design ("ut invidiam novitatis depelleret," Pareus, Estius, Grotius and others, following Chrysostom and Theophylact) is quite arbitrary, looking to the general tenor of vv. 1-7. The news of salvation God has *previously promised* (προεπηγγείλατο, 2 Cor. ix 5; Dio Cass. xlii. 32) *through His prophets*, not merely in so far as these, acting as the organs of God (αὐτοῦ), foretold the Messianic age, with the dawn of which the εὐαγγέλιον, as the "*publicum de Christo exhibito praeconium*" (Calovius), would necessarily begin, but they foretold also this *praeconium itself*, its future proclamation. See x. 18, xv. 21; Isa. xl. 1 ff., xlii. 4, lii. 1 ff.; Zeph. iii. 9; Ps. xix. 5, lxviii. 12; Deut. xviii. 15, 18. It is the less necessary therefore to refer ὅ, with Philippi and Mehring, to the *contents* of the gospel. — τῶν προφητῶν] is not to be limited, so as either to include merely the prophets *proper* in the narrower sense of the word, or to go back—according to Acts iii. 24, comp. xiii. 20—only *as far as Samuel.* The following ἐν γραφαῖς ἁγ. suggests, on the contrary, a reference to *all who in the O. T. have prophesied the gospel* (even Moses, David and others not excluded); comp. Heb. i. 1.— ἐν γραφαῖς ἁγίαις] Not: *in the holy Scriptures* (so most expositors, even Fritzsche), in which case the article must have been used; but qualitatively: *in holy writings.* The divine promises of the gospel, given through the prophets of God, are found in *such* books as, being God's records for His revelations, are *holy* writings. Such are the prophetic writings of the O. T.; thus designated so as to lay stress on their *qualitative* character. In a corresponding manner is the anarthrous γραφῶν προφητικῶν to be understood in xvi. 26.

Vv. 3, 4.[1] We must, with Lachmann and Tischendorf, set aside the view which treats τοῦ γενομένου . . . . νεκρῶν, and vv. 5, 6, as parentheses, because we have to deal with intervening

---

[1] Comp. Pfleiderer in Hilgenfeld's *Zeitschr.* 1871, p. 502 ff.

clauses which accord with the construction, not with insertions which interrupt it. See Winer, p. 526 [E. T. 707]. — περὶ τοῦ υἱοῦ αὐτοῦ] "Hoc refertur ad illud quod praecessit εὐαγγέλιον; explicatur nempe, de quo agat ille sermo bona nuntians," Grotius. So, also, Toletus, Cajetanus, Calvin, Justiniani, Bengel, Flatt, Reiche, Köllner, Winzer, Baumgarten-Crusius, Krehl, Umbreit, Th Schott, Hofmann, and others. But it may be objected to this view, on the one hand, that περί is *most naturally* connected with the *nearest* suitable word that precedes it; and on the other that εὐαγγ., frequently as it is used with the *genitive* of the object, nowhere occurs with περί in the N. T.;[1] and still further, that if this connection be adopted, the important thought in ver. 2 appears strangely isolated. Therefore, the connection of περί with ὃ προεπηγγ. is to be preferred, with Tholuck, Klee, Rückert, Fritzsche, Reithmayr, Philippi, van Hengel, Ewald, Mehring, and others, following Theodoret; so that *the great personal object* is introduced, *to which* the divine previous promise of the gospel *referred;* consequently, the *person concerning whom* was this promise of the future message of salvation. God *could not* (we may remark in opposition to Hofmann's objection) have previously promised the gospel *in any other way at all* than by speaking of Christ His Son, who was to come and to be revealed; otherwise his προεπαγγέλλεσθαι εὐαγγέλιον would have had no concrete tenor, and consequently no object. — τοῦ γενομένου *down to* νεκρῶν describes under a twofold aspect (κατὰ) the *exalted dignity* of Him who had just been designated by τοῦ υἱοῦ αὐτοῦ: (1) κατὰ σάρκα, He entered life as *David's* descendant; (2) κατὰ πνεῦμα ἁγιωσ., He was powerfully instated as Son of God by His resurrection. Nevertheless ὁ υἱὸς τοῦ Θεοῦ, in the words περὶ τοῦ υἱοῦ αὐτοῦ (not αὐτοῦ), is not by any means to be taken in the general, merely historical theocratic sense of *Messiah* (Winzer, *Progr.* 1835, p. 5 f.; comp. also Holsten, *z. Ev. d. Paul. u. Petr.* p. 424; and Pfleiderer, *l.c.*), because this is opposed to the constant usage of the Apostle, who *never* designates Christ as υἱὸς Θεοῦ otherwise[2] than from the

---

[1] Hofmann erroneously thinks that Paul *could* not have added the object of his divine message otherwise than by περί. He would have only needed to repeat the εἰς εὐαγγέλιον with rhetorical emphasis, in order then to add the object in the genitive (τοῦ υἱοῦ ἀ.). Comp. Dissen. *ad Dem. de cor.* p. 315.

[2] Comp. Gess, *v. d. Pers. Christi,* p. 89 ff.; Weiss, *bibl. Theol.* p. 309.

standpoint of the knowledge which God had given to him by revelation (Gal. i. 16) of the *metaphysical Sonship* (viii. 3, 32; Gal. iv. 4; Col. i. 13 ff.; Phil. ii. 6 ff. *al.*); and the hypothesis of a *modification* having taken place in Paul's view (Usteri, Köllner; see, on the other hand, Rückert) is purely fanciful. Here also the υἱὸς τοῦ Θεοῦ is conceived in the *metaphysical sense* as He who had proceeded out of the *essence* of the Father, like Him in substance (not, as Baur thinks, as organ of the Spirit, which is the purer form of human nature itself), and is sent by Him for the accomplishment of the Messianic counsel. But since it was necessary for this accomplishment that He should appear as *man*, it was necessary for Him,—and these essential modal definitions are now added to the υἱοῦ τοῦ αὐτοῦ,—*as* a human phenomenon, (1) to be *born* κατὰ σάρκα, and indeed of the seed of David,[1] and yet (2) to be actually *instated* κατὰ πνεῦμα, as that which, although from the time of His birth in appearance not different from other men (Phil. ii. 7; Gal. iv. 4), He *really was*, namely the Son of God. These two parallel clauses are placed in *asyndetic* juxtaposition, whereby the second, coming after the first, which is itself of lofty and honourable Messianic significance, is brought out as of *still greater importance*. See Bernhardy, p. 448; Dissen. *ad. Pind. Exc.* II., *de Asynd.* p. 275. Not perceiving this, Hofmann fails to recognise the contrast here presented between the two aspects of the Son of God, because Paul has not used κατὰ πνεῦμα δὲ ὁρισθέντος in the second clause. — κατὰ σάρκα] *in respect of flesh;* for the Son of God had a fleshly mode of being on earth, since His concrete manifestation was that of a *materially human* person. Comp. ix. 5; 1 Tim. iii. 16; 1 Pet. iii. 18; Phil. ii. 7; Rom. v. 15; 1 Cor. xv. 21; 1 Tim. ii. 5. To the σάρξ belonged in the case of Christ also, as in that of all men, the ψυχή as the principle of the animal life of man; but this sensuous side of His nature was not, as in all other men, the seat and organ of sin. He was not σαρκικός (vii. 14), and ψυχικός (1 Cor. ii. 14), in the ethical sense, like all ordinary men, although, in virtue of that sensuous nature, he was capable of

---

[1] But at the same time the idea of "an accommodation to the Jewish-Christian mode of conception" (Holsten, *z. Ev. Paul. u. Petr.* p. 427), is not to be entertained. Paul gives the two main epochs in the history of the Son of God, as they actually occurred and had been already prophetically announced.

being tempted (Heb. ii. 18; iv. 15). Although in this way His body was a σῶμα τῆς σαρκός (Col. i. 22), yet He did not appear ἐν σαρκὶ ἁμαρτίας, but ἐν ὁμοιώματι σαρκὸς ἁμαρτίας (Rom. viii. 2). *With reference to His fleshly nature*, therefore, *i.e.* in so far as He was a materially-human phenomenon, He was *born* (γενομένου, comp. Gal. iv. 4), *of the seed* (as descendant) *of David*, as was *necessarily* the case with the Son of God who appeared as the promised Messiah (Jer. xxiii. 5; Ps. cxxxii. 11; Matth. xxii. 42; John vii. 42; Acts xiii. 23; 2 Tim. ii. 8). In this expression the ἐκ σπέρματος Δαυΐδ is to be understood of the *male* line of descent going back to David (comp. Acts ii. 30, ἐκ καρποῦ τῆς ὀσφύος), as even the genealogical tables in Matthew and Luke give the descent of *Joseph* from David, not that of *Mary*;[1] and Jesus Himself, in John v. 27 (see on that passage), calls Himself, in contradistinction to His Sonship *of God*, son of a *man*, in which case the correlate idea on which it is founded can only be that of *father*hood. It is, therefore, the more erroneous to refer ἐκ σπ. Δαυ. to *Mary* ("ex semine David, i.e. ex virgine Maria," Melancthon; comp. also Philippi), especially since Paul nowhere (not even in viii. 3, Gal. iv. 4) indicates the view of a supernatural generation of the bodily nature of Jesus (Usteri, *Lehrbegr.* p. 328; Rich.

---

[1] In opposition to Hofmann, *Weissag. u. Erfüll.* II. p. 49 (comp. the Erlangen *Zeitschr.* 1868, 6, p. 359 f.), who generalizes the sense of the words in such a way as to convey the meaning that Christ appeared *as one belonging to the collective body which traces its descent back to David*. But in fact it is simply said that Christ was BORN *of the seed of David*. The reading γεννωμένου (in min., and MSS. used by Augustine) is a correct gloss; and Hofmann himself grants (*heil. Schrift N. T., in loc.*) that γίγνεσθαι ἐκ here signifies descent by *birth*. And even if γενομένου be taken as meaning : who *appeared*, who *came* (comp. on Mark i. 4; Phil. ii. 7; so Ewald), still the genetic relation to the σπέρμα of David remains the same. He *came* κατὰ σάρκα of the seed of David, and that in no other way than through His *birth*. This remark holds good also against other obscure evasions to which Hofmann resorts in his *Schriftbcw.* II. 1, p. 113; in his *heil. Schr. N. T.* he adheres substantially to his earlier view ("*come of the race which called itself after David, because tracing its descent to his ancestry*"). No, the σπέρμα of David is nothing else than his *semen virile*, out (ἐκ) of which, transmitted (comp. ἀπό, Acts xiii. 23) through the male line from γενεά to γενεά (Matth. i. 6 ff.), at length the Son of God κατὰ σάρκα—Christ, the David's son of promise—was born. See besides, against Hofmann, Rich. Schmidt, *l.c.* — Because Christ was ἐκ σπέρματος of David, He might also Himself be called σπέρμα of David, in the same way as He is called in Gal. iii. 16 σπέρμα Ἀβραάμ; and He is so called Matth. i. 1. Comp. further on ἐκ σπέρματος, in the sense of fatherhood, Soph. *O. C.* 214: τίνος εἶ σπέρματος . . . . πατρόθεν.

Schmidt, *Paulin. Christol.* p. 140 ff.; Pfleiderer, *l.c.*), even apart from the fact that the Davidic descent of the mother of Jesus can by no means be established from the N. T. It is the more unjustifiable, to pronounce the metaphysical divine Sonship without virgin birth as something *inconceivable*[1] (Philippi). — There now follows the *other*, second mode in which the Son of God who has appeared on earth is to be contemplated, viz. *with reference to the spirit of holiness*, which was in Him. The parallelism between κατὰ σάρκα and κατὰ πνεῦμα ἁγ., apparent even in the position of the two elements, forbids us to understand κατὰ πν. ἁγιωσ. as denoting the *presupposition and regulative cause* of the state of glorious power ascribed to the Son of God (Hofmann). In that case Paul must have used another preposition, conveying the idea *on account of*, perhaps διά with the accusative (comp. the διό, Phil. ii. 9), in order to express the thought which Hofmann has discovered, namely, that the holiness of His spirit, and therefore of His life, *was to make* His divine Sonship a state of glorious power. Regarding the view taken of ἐν δυνάμει in connection with this, see the sequel. Ἁγιωσύνη, in Paul's writings as well as in the Sept. (in Greek authors and in the other writings of the N. T. it does not occur), invariably means *holiness* (2 Cor. vii. 1; 1 Thess. iii. 13; Ps. xcvi. 6, xcvii. 12, cxliv. 5), not *sanctification* (as rendered by the Vulgate, Erasmus, Castalio, and many others, including Glöckler and Schrader). So also in 2 Macc. iii. 12. The *genitive* is the gen. *qualitatis* (Hermann, *ad Viger.* pp. 887, 891; Kühner, II. 1, p. 226), and contains the specific character of the πνεῦμα. This πνεῦμα ἁγιωσ. is, in contradistinction to the σάρξ, the other side of the being of the Son of God on earth; and, just as the σάρξ was the outward element perceptible by the senses, so is the πνεῦμα the inward mental element, the substratum of His νοῦς (1 Cor. ii. 16), *the principle and the power of His* INNER *life*, the intellectual and moral "Ego" which receives the communication of the divine—in short, the ἔσω ἄνθρωπος of Christ. His πνεῦμα also was *human* (Matth. xxvii. 50; John xi. 33, xix. 30)—altogether He was an *entire* man, and the Apollinarian conception is without support in the N. T. teaching—but it was the seat of the divine nature belong-

---

[1] This opinion rests on a premiss assumed *à priori*, on an abstract postulate, the propriety of which it is impossible to prove. Comp. on Matth. i. 18, *note*.

ing to His person; not excluding the specialty of the latter (in opposition to Beyschlag, *Christol.* pp. 212, 231), but being rather that which contained the metaphysical υἱότης Θεοῦ, or—according to the Johannine type of doctrine—the seat and the organ of the Λόγος, which became flesh in the human person of Jesus, as also of the fulness of the Holy Spirit which bore sway in Him (John iii. 34; Acts i. 2; 2 Cor. iii. 17). Consequently the πνεῦμα of Christ, although human (comp. Pfleiderer), was exalted above all other human spirits, because essentially filled with God, and thereby *holy*, sinless, and full of divine unpolluted life, as was no other human πνεῦμα; and for this reason His unique quality is *characterized* by the distinguishing designation πνεῦμα ἁγιωσύνης, *i.e. spirit full of holiness*. This purposely-chosen expression, which is not to be abated to the *studium* sanctitatis (van Hengel), must, seeing that the text sets forth the two sides of the *personal nature of Christ*, absolutely preclude our understanding it to refer to the πνεῦμα ἅγιον,[1] the *third* person of the divine Trinity, which is not meant either in 1 Tim. iii. 16, or in Heb. ix. 14. Nevertheless, the majority of commentators, since Chrysostom, have so explained it; some of them taking it to mean: " *secundum Sp. S. ei divinitus concessum* " (Fritzsche; comp. Beza, Calixtus, Wolf, Koppe, Tholuck, and others);[2] some referring it to the *miraculous working of the Holy Spirit* (Theodoret), or to the *bestowal* of the Spirit which took place through Christ (Chrysostom, Oecumenius, Theophylact, Luther, Estius, Böhme, and others). Since the contrast between σάρξ and πνεῦμα is not that between the human and the divine, but that between the bodily and the mental in human nature, we must also reject the interpretation which refers the words to the *divine nature* (Melancthon, Calovius, Bengel, and many others); in which case some take ἁγιωσύνη as equivalent to θεότης (Winzer); others adduce in ex-

[1] This is called in the *Test. XII. Patr.* p. 588, πνεῦμα ἁγιωσύνης, in so far as it *produces* holiness.
[2] Comp. also Zeller in the *theol. Jahrb.* 1842, p. 486. In his view (2 Cor. iii. 17), the πνεῦμα is the element of which the higher personality of Christ consists. According to Baur, *Paulus* II. p. 375, it is the *Messianic spirit*, the *intrinsic principle* constituting the Messiahship of Christ. According to Holsten, *z. Ev. d. Paul. u. Petr.* p. 425, it is in itself a *transcendent pneumatic force, which produces* the ἁγιωσύνη, a radiance of the divine πνεῦμα ἅγιον.

planation of πνεῦμα the here irrelevant πνεῦμα ὁ Θεός, John iv. 24 (Beza, Winzer, Olshausen, Maier, Philippi); others take the expression as substantially equivalent to the Johannine λόγος (Rückert; comp. Reiche, "the principle of His higher essence"), and thus have not avoided an Apollinarian conception. The correct interpretation is substantially given by Köllner, de Wette, Baumgarten-Crusius, Ewald (also in his *Jahrb.* 1849, p. 93), and Mehring. Comp. Hofmann ("spirit which supposes, wherever it is, a condition of holiness"), and also Lechler, *apost. u. nachapost. Zeitalt.* p. 49, who nevertheless understands the divine nature of Christ as also included.[1] — ὁρισθέντος] The translation of the Vulgate, *qui praedestinatus est*, based on the too weakly attested reading προορισθέντος (a mistaken gloss), drew forth from old writers (see in Estius) forced explanations, which are now properly forgotten. Ὁρίζειν, however, with the double accusative, means *to designate a person for something, to nominate, to instate* (Acts x. 42 ; comp. Meleager in the *Anthol.* xii. 158, 7: σὲ θεὸν ὥρισε δαίμων), nor is the meaning different here.[2] For although Christ *was* already the Son of God before the creation of the world, and as such was *sent* (viii. 3 ; Gal. iv. 4), nevertheless there was needed a fact, by means of which He should receive, after the humiliation that began with His birth (Phil. ii. 7 f.), *instating* into the rank and dignity of His divine Sonship; whereby also, as its necessary *consequence* with a view to the knowledge and conviction of men, He was legitimately established as the Son. The fact which constituted instatement was the *resurrection*, as the transition to His δόξα ; comp. on Acts xiii. 33 ; and ἐποίησε in Acts ii. 36. Inaccurate, because it confounds that *consequence* with the *thing itself*, is the gloss of Chrysostom: δειχθέντος, ἀποφανθέντος, κριθέντος; and that of Luther: "*shewn.*" Umbreit's rendering is erroneous: "*separated,*" namely from all men. — ἐν

---

[1] A more accurate and precise definition of the idea may be found in Weiss, *bibl. Theol.* p. 313; also Rich. Schmidt, p. 105 f.; Pfleiderer in Hilgenfeld's *Zeitschr.* 1871, p. 169, 503 f.

[2] But not in the sense : *destined to become something*, as Hofmann thinks ; nor generally, in the sense : qui *destinatus* est, but rather : qui *constitutus* est (was *instated*). For otherwise the *aorist* participle would be unsuitable, since it must necessarily indicate an act *following* the γενομένου, etc. ; whereas the divine destination would be *prior* to the birth. Consequently, were that sense intended, it must have been, as in Acts x. 42, ὡρισμένου.

δυνάμει] Not: *through omnipotence* (Umbreit), but: *mightily* (Luther), *forcibly;* for this installation of the Son of God as Son of God was *a work of divine power*, which (see what follows) was accomplished by means of the resurrection from the dead. Thus commanding power, divinely-energetic and effectual, forms the *characteristic quality, in which* the ὁρισμός took place. On ἐν, as paraphrase of the adverb (Col. i. 29; 2 Thess. i. 11), see Bernhardy, p. 209. ἐν δυν. is not, with Melancthon, Schoettgen, Pareus, Sebastian Schmid, and others, including Paulus, Baumgarten-Crusius, Philippi, Mehring, Holsten, Hofmann, and Pfleiderer, to be connected with υἱοῦ Θεοῦ (*as the mightily powerful Son of God*); for it was here of importance to dwell, not on a special *predicate* of the Son of God,[1] but, in contradistinction to the ἐκ σπερμ. Δαυ. κατὰ σάρκα, upon the *divine Sonship in itself;* of which Sonship He was indeed the hereditary possessor, but yet needed, in order to become *instated* in it *with glorious power*, resurrection from the dead. Thus, however, ἐν δυνάμει, even when rightly connected with ὁρισθ., is not, with Chrysostom and Theophylact, to be taken as "per virtutem, i. e. per signa et prodigia" (Calovius, comp. Grotius); nor with Fritzsche: *vi ei datâ;* for Paul himself defines the *how* of the mighty ὁρισμός by: ἐξ ἀναστ. νεκρῶν. This, namely, was the causal fact, *by virtue of which* that ὁρισμός was accomplished; for by the resurrection of Christ, God, who raised Him up (comp. 2 Cor. xiii. 4), accomplished in point of fact His instating declaration: Thou art my Son, this day, etc., Acts xiii. 33. Paul *might* accordingly have written διά, but ἐκ is more expressive of the thought that Christ *in virtue of* the resurrection, etc. On ἐκ, used of causal issuing forth, see Buttmann's *neut. Gr.* p. 281; Ellendt, *Lex.*

---

[1] As if only a change of His *attributes* was concerned, or the transition into the full *reality* of the divine Sonship (Pfleiderer). The question concerned the *installation* of the Son of God as such, as it were His *enthronisation*, which had not taken place previously, but was accomplished by the resurrection with a mighty power. By means of the latter He received—as the Son of God, which from the beginning and even in the days of His flesh He really *was*—a *de facto* instatement, which accomplished itself in a way divinely powerful. What accrued to Him thereby, was not the full *reality* (see viii. 3; Gal. iv. 4), but the full *efficiency* of the Son of God; because He was now exalted above all the limitations of the state of His κένωσις (Phil. ii.; 2 Cor. viii. 9); comp. *e.g.* vi. 9; xi. 33 f., v. 10; 2 Cor. xiii. 4; and numerous other passages. The Son was now the κύριος πάντων, had the name above every name, etc. etc.

Soph. I. p. 550 f. The *temporal* explanation, *since* or *after* (Theodoret, Erasmus, Luther, Toletus, and others, including Reithmayr; comp. Flatt, Umbreit, and Mehring), is to be rejected, because the raising up of Jesus from the dead was itself *the great divine act*, which, completed through the majesty of the Father (vi. 4), powerfully instated the Son in the Son's position and dignities; hence it was also the basis of the apostolic preaching, Acts i. 22, ii. 24 ff., xiii. 30, xvii. 31 f., xxvi. 23; Rom. iv. 24; 1 Cor. xv. 3 ff. We are not to take the *expression* ἐξ ἀναστ. νεκρ., as is often done, for ἐξ ἀναστ. ἐκ νεκρ., the second ἐκ being omitted for the sake of euphony: but it must be viewed *as a general designation of the category* (νεκρῶν, see on Matth. ii. 20): *through resurrection of the dead*, of which category the personal rising of the dead Jesus was the concrete case in point. Comp. xvii. 32. So, also, de Wette, Hofmann; comp. Philippi, who however, following Erasmus and Bengel, introduces also the idea, foreign to this passage, that *our* resurrection is involved in that of Christ. — The following Ἰησοῦ Χριστοῦ is in apposition to τοῦ υἱοῦ αὐτοῦ in v. 3; not necessary in itself, but in keeping with the *fulness* of expression throughout this opening portion of the Epistle, which exhibits a character *of majesty* particularly in vv. 3, 4. — Observe, further, that the exhibition of the holy and exalted nature of Christ in our passage serves to express the high dignity of the apostolic office. Of diversities in faith and doctrine in Rome regarding the person of Christ there is not a trace in the whole Epistle.[1]

Ver. 5. To the general τοῦ Κυρίου ἡμῶν, which designates Christ as *the Lord of Christians in general*, Paul now adds the special relation in which *he himself* stands to this common κύριος. He entertained too lively a consciousness of the bliss and dignity of that relationship, not to set it forth once more (comp. ver. 1) in this overflowing salutation; this time, however, with closer reference to the *readers*, in accordance with his definite character as Apostle of the *Gentiles*. — Vv. 5, 6 are not to be enclosed in a parenthesis; and only a comma should be placed after ver. 6. — δι' οὗ] *through whom*, denotes nothing else than the *medium;* nowhere, not even in Gal. i. 1, the *causa principalis*. The view of the Apostle is, as Origen rightly perceived, that he had

[1] Comp. Gess, *von d. Pers. Chr.* p. 56.

received grace and apostleship through the mediation of Christ, through whom God called him at Damascus. Regarding Gal. i. 1, see on that passage. — ἐλάβομεν] He means *himself* alone, especially since in the address he specifies no joint author of the letter; not however—as Reiche, following Estius and many others, thinks—using the plural *out of modesty* (in the solemnity of an official epistolary greeting ?), but rather (comp. iii. 9) in accordance with the custom, very common among Greek authors, of speaking of themselves in the plural of category (Krüger, § 61, 2 ; Kühner, *ad Xen. Mem.* i. 2, 46). This is, no doubt, to be traced back to the conception "I and my equals;" but this original conception was in course of use entirely lost. The opinion, therefore, that Paul here includes along with himself the other apostles (Bengel, van Hengel) is to be all the more rejected as unsuitable, since the subsequent ἐν πᾶσι τοῖς ἔθνεσιν points to *Paul himself* alone as the *Apostle of the Gentiles*. To understand Paul's *official assistants* as included (Hofmann) is forbidden by the subsequent ἀποστολήν, which does not mean *mission* in general, but, as invariably in the N. T., specially *apostleship*. — χάριν κ. ἀποστολὴν] *grace* (generally) *and* (in particular) *apostleship*. Χάριν is to be understood, not merely of *pardoning* grace (Augustine, Calvin, Calovius, Reiche, Tholuck, Olshausen, and others), or of the extraordinary *apostolic gifts of grace* (Theodoret, Luther, and others, including Flatt and Mehring); for such special references must be demanded by the context; but on the contrary generally of the *entire divine grace*, of which Paul was made partaker through Christ, when he was arrested by Him at Damascus in his career which was hateful to God (Phil. iii. 12; 1 Cor. xv. 10), converted, enlightened (Gal. i. 16), and transferred into the communion of God's beloved ones and saints. The special object (Gal. i. 16) and at the same time the highest evidence of this χάρις which he had received, was his reception of the ἀποστολή,[1] and that for the Gentile world. *Others* find here a ἓν διὰ δυοῖν (Chrysostom, Beza, Piscator, Grotius, Glass, Rich. Simon, Wetstein, Semler, Koppe, Böhme, Fritzsche, Philippi, and others): χάριν ἀποστολῆς. This might certainly be justified

---

[1] Augustine aptly remarks: "Gratiam cum omnibus fidelibus, apostolatum autem non cum omnibus communem habet." Comp. Bengel: "*Gratia* et singularis gratiae mensura *apostolis* obtigit."

in linguistic usage by the explicative καί (Fritzsche, *ad Matth.* p. 856; Nägelsbach, z. *Ilias,* iii. 100); but it arbitrarily converts two elements, which taken separately yield a highly appropriate sense, into one, and fails to recognise—what is involved in the union of the general and the particular—the fulness and force of the discourse moving the grateful heart. This remark applies also against Hofmann, according to whom the Apostle terms one and the same vocation "*a grace and a mission;*" in which view ἀποστ. is erroneously rendered (see above), and in consequence thereof εἰς ὑπακ. π. is then joined merely to χάρ. κ. ἀπ., and not also to ἐλάβ. — εἰς ὑπακ. πίστ.] Object of the ἐλάβ. χάρ. κ. ἀποστ.: *in order that obedience of faith may be produced, i.e. in order that people may subject* themselves to the faith, in order that they *may become believing.* Comp. xvi. 26; Acts vi. 7; 2 Cor. x. 5 f.; 2 Thess. i. 8. To take πίστις for *doctrina fidei* (Beza, Toletus, Estius, Bengel, Heumann, Cramer, Rosenmüller, Flatt, Fritzsche, Tholuck, and others), is altogether contrary to the linguistic usage of the N. T., in which πίστις is always *subjective* faith, although often, as in the present instance, conceived of *objectively,* as a *power.* Comp. xvi. 26; Gal. i. 23. The *activity* of faith *in producing works* (Reithmayr), however, is not contained in the expression. The πίστις is, according to Paul, the conviction and confidence (*assensus* and *fiducia*) regarding Jesus Christ, as the only and perfect Mediator of the divine grace, and of eternal life, through His work of atonement. Faith *alone* (to the exclusion of works) is the causa apprehendens of the salvation promised and obtained through Christ; but, because it transfers us into living and devoted fellowship with Him, altogether of a moral character, it becomes the subjective moral power of the new life regenerated through the power of the Holy Spirit—of the life *in* Christ, which, however, is the necessary consequence, and never the ground of justification. See Luther's Preface. — The *genitive* πίστεως, in accordance with the analogy of the expressions kindred in meaning ὑπακοὴ τοῦ Χριστοῦ in 2 Cor. x. 5, and ὑπακ. τῆς ἀληθείας in 1 Pet. i. 22, necessarily presents itself (comp. Acts vi. 7; Rom. x. 16; 2 Thess. i. 8; also 2 Cor. ix. 13) as denoting that to which the obedience is rendered; not (Grotius, following Beza) the *causa efficiens:* " ut Deo obediatur per fidem," in which explanation, besides, the " Deo " is arbitrarily introduced.[1] Hofmann is also wrong in taking the genitive πίστεως as *epexegetical* (an obedience *consisting in faith*). — ἐν πᾶσι τοῖς ἔθνεσιν] is to be joined with εἰς ὑπακ. πίστεως, *beside which it stands;* the ἔθνη, however, are not all *nations* generally, inclusive of the Jews (so most expositors, including Rückert, Reiche, Köllner, Fritzsche, Baur), but, in accordance with the historical destination of the Apostle (Gal. i. 16; Acts ix. 15, xxvi. 17 f.), and in consequence of the repeated prominence of his calling as *Gentile Apostle* in our letter (ver. 13, xi. 13, xv. 16), all *Gentile* nations, to which also the Romans belonged (Beza, Tholuck, Philippi, de Wette, Baumgarten-Crusius, van Hengel, Ewald, Hofmann and others); and these regarded not from a *geographical* point of view (Mangold, p. 76), but from *a popular* one, as גוים; which precludes us from thinking—not as to a section, but at any rate as to the *mass*, of the Roman congregation—that it was *Jewish*-Christian. This his apostolic calling *for the Gentiles* is meant by Paul in *all* passages where he describes the ἔθνη as the object of his labours (Gal. i. 16, ii. 2, 8, 9; Eph. iii. 1, 8; Col. i. 27; 1 Thess. ii. 16). — ὑπὲρ τοῦ ὀνόμ. αὐτοῦ] belongs, in the most natural connection, not to ἐλάβ..... ἀποστ. (Rückert) or to δι' οὗ .... ἔθνεσιν (de Wette, Mehring, Hofmann), but to εἰς ὑπακοὴν .... ἔθνεσιν; " in order to produce obedience to the faith among all Gentile nations *for the sake of* (for the glorifying of, comp. Acts v. 41; Phil. ii. 13) *His name.*" Acts ix. 15, xv. 26, xxi. 13; 2 Thess. i. 12, serve to illustrate the matter referred to. The idea of wishing to exclude the glorifying of *his own* name (Hofmann) is not for a moment to be imputed to the Apostle. He would have needed a very special motive for doing so.

Ver. 6. Application of the contents of ver. 5 to the relation in which the Apostle stood to his readers, whereby he indicates how he is officially entitled to address them also, teaching, exhorting, and so forth — ἐν οἷς ἐστε καὶ ὑμεῖς κλητοὶ 'I. X.] To be written thus, without a comma after ὑμεῖς, with Heu-

[1] So also van Hengel, on the ground of passages like v. 19; Phil. ii. 12, where however the sense of obedience *to God* results from the *context;* and Ernesti, *Urspr. d. Sünde*, II. p. 281 ff., who urges against our view that it makes ὑπὲρ τοῦ ὀνόμ. αὐτοῦ superfluous. But the glory of Christ is precisely the lofty end of all ὑπακούειν τῇ πίστει. Where it takes place, it is acknowledged that Jesus Christ is Lord, Phil. ii. 11.

mann, Lachmann, Tischendorf, de Wette, Hofmann, and Bisping: *among whom also are ye called (ones) of Jesus Christ.* Among the Gentile nations the Roman Christians were, like other Gentile-Christian churches, called of the Lord; amidst the Gentile world, nationally belonging to it (in opposition to Mangold's mere geographical interpretation), they also shared this high distinction. The reference of the καὶ to *Paul* (Th. Schott), and consequently the interpretation: *as I, so also ye,* is erroneous, because the Apostle has asserted concerning himself something far higher than the mere Christian calling. The common interpretation of κλητοὶ ’I. X. as an *address* (so too Rückert, Fritzsche, Philippi, van Hengel, Mehring) makes the ἐν οἷς ἐστε κ. ὑμ. quite a meaningless assertion; for Bengel's suggestion for meeting the difficulty, that ἐν οἷς has the implied meaning: among which *converted* nations, is purely arbitrary. — Since the *calling* (to the Messianic salvation; see on Gal. i. 6; also 1 Cor. vii. 17) is invariably ascribed by Paul to *God* (viii. 30, ix. 24; 1 Cor. i. 9, vii. 15, 17; 1 Thess. ii. 12; 2 Thess. ii. 14; comp. Usteri, p. 281; Weiss, *bibl. Theol.* § 127; what Schmidt urges in opposition, in Rudelbach's *Zeitschr.* 1849, II. p. 188 ff. is untenable) we must explain it, not as: *called by Christ* (Luther, Rückert, Mehring, Hofmann, and others), but as: *called* (by God) *who belong to Christ* (so Erasmus, Beza, Estius, and most modern commentators, also Winer, p. 183). The genitive is *possessive,* just as in the analogous τοὺς ἐκλεκτοὺς αὐτοῦ in Matth. xxiv. 31. With the substantive nature of κλητός (comp. Buttmann, *neut. Gr.* p. 147) the genitive by no means admits merely the interpretation which points to the *calling subject,* as in 2 Sam. xv 11; 1 Kings i. 41, 49; Zeph. i. 7; but admits of very different references, as *e.g.* in Homer, *Od.* xvii. 386, κλητοί γε βροτῶν are not those called *by* mortals, but those who are called *among* mortals (genitive *totius*).

Ver. 7. Now for the first time, brought by ver. 6 nearer to his readers, Paul passes from the throng of the great intervening thoughts, ver. 2 ff., in which he has given full and conscious expression to the nature and the dignity of his calling, to the formal *address* and to the apostolic *salutation.* — πᾶσι κ.τ.λ.] directs the letter to *all beloved of God who are in Rome,* etc., and therefore to the *collective Roman Christian church,* Phil. i. 1; Eph. i. 1;

Col. i. 1),[1] but not, as Tholuck thinks (comp. Turretin, Wolf, and Böhme), at the same time also to those foreign Christians who were accidentally staying in Rome, for against this view ver. 8, in which ὑπὲρ πάντων ὑμῶν can only refer to the Romans, is decisive. The πᾶσι would be self-obvious and might have been dispensed with, but in this Epistle, just because it is so detailed and is addressed to a great church still far away from the Apostle, πᾶσι carries with it a certain *diplomatic* character. Similarly, though from other grounds, Phil. i. 1. — ἀγαπητ. Θεοῦ, κλητοῖς ἁγίοις] Characteristic special analysis of the idea "*Christians*" in accordance with the high privileges of their Christian condition. For, as reconciled with God through Christ, they are *beloved of God* (v. 5 ff., viii. 39; Col. iii. 12); and, as those who through the divine *calling* to the Messianic salvation have become separated from the κόσμος and *consecrated to God*, because members of the new covenant of grace, they are *called saints*; comp. 1 Cor. i. 2. This *saintship* is produced through the *justification* of the called (viii. 30), and their accompanying subjection to the *influence of the Holy Spirit* (1 Cor. i. 30). De Wette erroneously interprets. "those who are called to be saints." So also Baumgarten-Crusius. The calling always refers to the salvation of the Messiah's kingdom. But that the ἁγιότης is to be understood in that Christian *theocratic* sense after the analogy of the Old Testament קדוש, and not of *individual moral holiness* (Pareus, Toletus, Estius, Grotius, Flatt, Glöckler, de Wette, and others), is plain from the very fact, that *all* Christians *as* Christians are ἅγιοι. — χάρις . . . . εἰρήνη] See Otto, in the *Jahrb. f. d. Theol.* 1867, p. 678 ff. Χάρις is the disposition, the subjective feeling in God and Christ, which the Apostle wishes to be entertained towards and shown to his readers; εἰρήνη is the actual result, which is produced through the manifestation of the χάρις: *grace* and *salvation* (שָׁלוֹם), the latter in every aspect in which it presents itself as the Christian issue of the χάρις. Comp. Melancthon. The

---

[1] With these parallels before us, it is unreasonable to ask why Paul does not designate the readers as a *church*. Bengel and van Hengel are of opinion that no regular congregational bond was as yet in existence. Th. Schott thinks that Paul as yet stood in no relation whatever to the church. The ὄντες ἐν Ῥώμῃ κ.τ.λ. *are* the church, and it is to the *churches* that he has written where he does not write to specified *persons*.

specifically Christian element in this salutation[1] lies in ἀπὸ Θεοῦ πατρὸς .... Χριστοῦ. Comp. 1 Cor. i. 3; 2 Cor. i. 2; Eph. i. 2; Phil. i. 2; 1 Thess. i. 1; 2 Thess. i. 1 f.; 1 Tim. i. 2; 2 Tim. i. 2; Tit. i. 4; Philem. 3. The special rendering of εἰρήνη, *peace*, which, following Chrysostom and Jerome, the majority, including Reiche, Olshausen, Tholuck, Philippi, Umbreit and others retain (the higher peace which is given, not by the world, but by the consciousness of divine grace and love, see especially Umbreit, p. 190 ff.), must be abandoned, because χάρις καὶ εἰρήνη represent the general epistolary χαίρειν (Acts xv. 23; James i. 1), and thus the *generality* of the salutation is expressed in a way characteristically Christian. — πατήρ ἡμῶν means God, in so far as we, as Christians, are His children through the υἱοθεσία (see on Gal. iv. 5; Rom. viii. 15). — καὶ κυρίου] *i.e.* καὶ ἀπὸ κυρίου, not, as Glöckler, following Erasmus, takes it, "and the Father of our Lord Jesus Christ," for against this view stands the decisive fact that God is never called *our and* Christ's Father; see also Tit. i. 4; 2 Tim. i. 2. The formal equalisation of God and Christ cannot be certainly used as a proof (as Philippi and Mehring contend) of the divine nature of Christ—which, however, is otherwise firmly enough maintained by Paul—since the different *predicates* πατρός and κυρίου imply the different conceptions of the causa *principalis* and *medians*. For this purpose different *prepositions* were not required; comp. on Gal. i. 1.

Vv. 8-15. First of all the Apostle now—as under various forms in all his epistles, with the exception of that to the Galatians (also not in 1 Timothy and Titus)—expresses with thanksgiving towards God his pious joy at the faith of his readers; and then assures them of his longing to be with them and to labour among them personally. The thanksgiving is *short*, for it relates to a church not only personally unknown to him, but also far removed from the sphere of labour which he had hitherto occupied; but the *expression* of it is in accordance with the position of the church in the metropolis of the world.

Ver. 8. Πρῶτον μέν] To that, which Paul desires *first of all* to write, there was meant to be subjoined *something further*, possibly by ἔπειτα δέ. But, amidst the ideas that now crowd

---

[1] Regarding Otto's attempted derivation of it from the *Aaronic* benediction, see on 1 Cor. i. 3.

upon him, he abandons this design, and thus the μέν remains
alone. Comp. iii. 2 ; and on Acts i. 1 ; 1 Cor. xi. 18 ; Schaefer,
ad Dem. IV. p. 142 ; Hartung, *Partikell.* II. p. 410. — τῷ Θεῷ μου]
οὗ εἰμί, ᾧ καὶ λατρεύω, Acts xxvii. 23; comp. 1 Cor. i. 4 ; Phil. i. 3,
iv. 19; Philem. 4. — διὰ 'Ιησοῦ Χριστοῦ] These words—to be
connected with εὐχαριστῶ, not with μου, as Koppe and Glöckler
think, against which vii. 25 and Col. iii. 17 are clearly decisive—contain the *mediation, through which* the εὐχαριστῶ takes
place. The Apostle gives thanks not on his own part and independently of Christ, not δι' ἑαυτοῦ, but is conscious of his
thanksgiving *being conveyed through Jesus Christ, as one who is
present to his grateful thoughts;* in so far, namely, as that for
which he thanks God is vividly perceived and felt by him to
have been brought about through Christ. Comp. on Col. iii. 17;
Eph. v. 20. Thus Christ is the mediating *causal agent* of the
thanksgiving. To regard Him as its mediating *presenter* (Origen, Theophylact, Bengel, and others, including Hofmann) cannot be justified from Paul's other writings, nor even by Heb. xiii.
15. Theodore of Mopsuestia well observes : τοῦ Χριστοῦ ταύτης
ἡμῖν τῆς εὐχαριστίας τὴν αἰτίαν παρασχομένου. — ἡ πίστις ὑμῶν]
quite simply : *your faith* (on Christ); the praiseworthy character of
the πίστις is only set forth by the *context* (καταγγέλλ. ἐν ὅλῳ τ. κ.)
afterwards. Everywhere one hears your faith openly spoken of.
Comp. xvi. 19. Observe how this flattering expression of the
Apostle and the *thanksgiving* coupled with it, as also the
στηριχθῆναι κ.τ.λ., in vv. 11, 12, point to the church not as
Jewish-Christian but as *Pauline.* Mangold's reference to Phil.
i. 15-18, in opposition to this inference, leaves out of view the
quite different *personal situation* under which the latter was
written. Comp. on Phil. i. 18, *note.* — ἐν ὅλῳ τ. κόσμῳ] a popular
hyperbole, but how accordant with the position of the church in
that city, towards which the eyes of the whole world were
turned ! Comp. 1 Thess. i. 8. It is, moreover, obvious of itself,
that the subjects of the καταγγέλλειν are the *believers.* As to
the unbelievers, see Acts xxviii. 22.

Ver. 9. Γάρ] The pith of the following *proof of the assurance
conveyed in ver.* 8 lies in ἀδιαλείπτως, not in the desire to come to
Rome, which is not subjoined till ver. 10 (Th. Schott). The interest
felt by the Apostle in the Romans, which was so vivid that he *un-*

ceasingly remembered them, etc., had even now urged him to his εὐχαριστῶ τῷ Θεῷ κ.τ.λ. — μάρτυς .... Θεός] The asseveration in the form of an oath (comp. 2 Cor. i. 23, xi. 31; Phil. i. 8) is intended solemnly to strengthen the impression of what he has to say; viewed with reference to the circumstance which might readily excite surprise, that he, the Apostle of the Gentiles, had never yet laboured in the church—which nevertheless was Pauline—of the capital of the Gentile world. See vv. 10-13. The hypothesis of "*iniquos rumores*," that had reached his ears from Rome (van Hengel), is unnecessary and unsupported by any trace in the letter. — ᾧ λατρεύω κ.τ.λ.] added to strengthen the asseveration with respect to its sacred conscientiousness: *to whom I render holy service in my spirit*, i.e. in my moral self-consciousness, which is the living inner sphere of that service.[1] This ἐν τῷ πν. μου, on which lies the practical stress of the relative clause, excludes indeed all λατρεύειν of a merely external kind, exercising itself in works, or even impure; but is not intended to suggest a definite *contrast* to this, which would here be without due motive. It is rather the involuntary expression of the profoundly vivid *feeling of inward experience.* The Apostle knows and feels that the depths of his innermost life are pervaded by his λατρεύειν. Comp. ᾧ λατρεύω .... ἐν καθαρᾷ συνειδήσει, in 2 Tim. i. 3; also Heb. xii. 28. Τὸ πνεῦμα μου cannot be the Holy Spirit (Theodoret),[2] but Paul bore the *witness* of that Spirit in *his own* spirit (viii. 16; ix. 1.). — ἐν τῷ εὐαγγ. τ. υἱοῦ αὐτοῦ] *in the gospel of His Son*, which I preach, defend, etc. That is the great *sphere to which He is called* in the service of God, in the consciousness of which he is impelled by an inward necessity to devote to his readers that fervent sympathy of which he assures them. Grotius and Reiche think there is an implied contrast to the λατρεία ἐν τῷ νόμῳ, which however is quite foreign to the connection. Can we think of a side-glance at the Jewish style of teaching—when the discourse breathes only love and warmth of affection ? — ὡς ἀδιαλ.] ὡς does not stand for ὅτι (as following the Vulgate, the majority, including Fritzsche, think), but ex-

---

[1] Comp. Ernesti, *Urspr. d. Sünde*, II. p. 89 f.; see also on John iv. 23.

[2] Holsten also (=. *Ev. d. Paul. u. Petr.* p. 386) understands it of the Holy Spirit as *bestowed* on the Apostle (μου). See, against this view, Rich. Schmidt, *Paul. Christol.* p. 33 ff.

presses the *manner* (the degree). God is my witness, *how* unceasingly, etc. Comp. Phil. i. 8; 2 Cor. vii. 15; 1 Thess. ii. 10; Acts x. 28; Calvin; Philippi; van Hengel; see also Ellendt, *Lex. Soph.* II. p. 1000. The idea of modality must be everywhere retained, where ὡς takes the place of ὅτι. See the passages in Heindorf, *ad Plat. Hipp. maj.* p. 281, Jacobs. *ad Ach. Tat.* p. 566. — μν. ὑμ. ποιοῦμ.] *make mention of you,* viz. *in my prayers.* See ver. 10. Comp. Eph. i. 16; Phil. i. 3; 1 Thess. i. 2.

Ver. 10. Πάντοτε . . . δεόμενος] annexes to ὡς ἀδιαλ. the *more precise definition: in that* (so that) *I always* (each time) *in my prayers request.* ἐπί, which is to be referred to the idea of definition of time (Bernhardy p. 246), indicates the form of action which takes place. Comp. 1 Thess. i. 2; Eph. i. 16; Philem. 4; Winer, p. 352 [E.T. 470]. — εἴπως ἤδη ποτέ] *if perhaps at length on some occasion.* For examples of ἤδη, *already* (Baeumlein, *Part.* p. 138 ff.), which, comparing another time with the present, conveys by the reference to something long hoped for but delayed the idea *at length,* see Hartung, *Partikel.* I. p. 238; Klotz, *ad Devar.* p. 607; comp. Phil. iv 10, and the passages in Kypke. Th. Schott incorrectly renders πάντοτε, *under all circumstances,* which it never means, and ἤδη ποτέ as if it were ἤδη νῦν or ἄρτι. The mode of expression by εἴπως implies somewhat of modest fear, arising from the thought of possible hindrances.[1] — εὐοδωθήσομαι] *I shall have the good fortune.* The active εὐοδοῦν is seldom used in its proper signification, *to lead well, expeditum iter praebere,* as in Soph. *O. C.* 1437; Theophr. *de caus. pl.* v. 6, 7; LXX. Gen. xxiv. 27, 48; the passive, however, never means *via recta incedere, expeditum iter habere,* but invariably (even in Prov. xvii. 8) metaphorically: *prospero successu gaudere.* See Herod. vi. 73; 1 Cor. xvi. 2; 3 John 2; LXX. 2 Chron. xiii. 12; Ps. i. 3, and frequently; Ecclus. xi. 16, xli. 1; Tob. iv. 19, v. 16; Test. XII. Patr. p. 684. Therefore the explanation of *a prosperous journey,* which besides amounts only to an accessory modal idea (Beza, Estius, Wolf, and many others following the Vulgate and Oecumenius; including van Hengel and Hofmann), must be rejected, and not combined with ours (Umbreit). — ἐν τῷ θελ. τ. Θεοῦ] *in virtue of the will of God;* on this will the εὐοδωθ. causally depend.

Ver. 11. Ἐπιποθῶ] not *valde* cupio, but denoting the *direction*

---

[1] Comp. xi. 14; and on Phil. iii. 11; 1 Macc. iv. 10.

of the longing. Comp. on 2 Cor. v. 2; Phil. i. 8. — χάρισμα πνευματικόν] Paul calls that, which he intends to communicate to the Romans through his longed-for personal presence among them (ἰδεῖν; comp. Acts xix. 21, xxviii. 20) *a spiritual gift of grace;* because in his apprehension all such instruction, comfort, joy, strengthening, etc., as are produced by means of his labours, are regarded not as procured by his own human individuality, but as a result which the πνεῦμα ἅγιον works by means of him—the gracious working of the Spirit, whose organ he is. While it was highly arbitrary in Toletus, Bengel, Michaelis and others to refer the expression to the *apostolic miraculous gifts*—against which the εὐαγγελίσασθαι in ver. 15 is conclusive—it was a very gratuitous weakening of its force to explain it (as is done by Morus, Rosenmüller, Köllner, Maier, Th. Schott) as a *gift referring to the* (human) *spirit;* "a gift *for the inner life,*" Hofmann. In such an interpretation the specifically *Christian* point of view (1 Cor. xii. 4; comp. εὐλογία πνευματική, Eph. i. 3) is left out of account; besides, πνευματικόν would imply nothing characteristic in that case; for that Paul did not desire to communicate any gifts of another sort, *e.g.* external, would be taken for granted. — The expression τι . . . χάρ. is *modest* (μετριάζοντος, Oecumenius). Note also the arrangement by which the words are made to *stand apart*, and this delicate τι, the substantial χάρισμα, and the qualifying πνευματικόν, are brought into the more special prominence.[1] — εἰς τὸ στηρ. ὑμᾶς] Object of the intended communication of such a gift; *that ye may be established*, namely, in the Christian character and life. See ver. 12; comp. Acts xvi. 5; Rom. xvi. 25; 1 Thess. iii. 2. The στηρίξαι is conceived as being divinely wrought by means of the Spirit, hence the *passive* expression; it was to be accomplished however, as Paul hoped, *through* him as the instrument of the Spirit. Mangold, p. 82, has, without any ground in the text, assumed that this establishment has reference to " their abandoning their Jewish-Christian *scruples regarding the mission to the Gentiles,*" whereas ver. 12 rather testifies to the *Pauline* Christianity of the Romans. This remark applies also against Sabatier, p. 166, who understands " une

---

[1] On μεταδιδόναι τινί τι (instead of τινί τινος), comp. 1 Thess. ii. 8 ; Tob. vii. 9 ; 2 Macc. i. 35. So sometimes, although seldom, in classic authors, Herod. viii. 5, ix. 34 ; Xen. *Anab.* iv. 5, 5 ; Schnef. *Melet.* p. 21 ; Kühner, II. i. p. 295.

conception de l'évangile de Jésus plus large et plus spirituelle."

Ver. 12. Τοῦτο δέ ἐστι] *This, however*, which I have just designated as my longing (namely, ἰδεῖν ὑμᾶς, ἵνα . . . στηριχθ. ὑμᾶς) *means, thereby I intend to say nothing else than*, etc. By this modifying explanation, subjoined with humility, and expressed in a delicate complimentary manner (Erasmus puts the matter too strongly, " pia *vafrities* et sancta *adulatio*"), Paul guards himself, in presence of a church to which he was still a stranger, from the possible appearance of presumption and of forming too low an estimate of the Christian standpoint of his readers.[1]
— συμπαρακληθῆναι] must be understood not, with the Peschito, Vulgate, Valla, Erasmus, Luther, Piscator, de Dieu, and many others, including Koppe and Ewald, in the sense of *comfort* or of *refreshment* (Castalio, Grotius, Cramer, Rosenmüller, Böhme)— which it would be necessary that the context should call for, as in 1 Thess. iii. 2 ; 2 Thess. ii. 17, but which it here forbids by the general ἰδεῖν ὑμᾶς, ἵνα κ.τ.λ.—but in the quite general sense of *Christian encouragement and quickening*. The συμ.—however is not to be explained by ὑμᾶς καὶ ἐμαυτόν; on the contrary, the ἐν ὑμῖν renders it necessary that *Paul alone* should be conceived as the subject of συμπαρακληθῆναι. He desires to be quickened among the Romans (ἐν ὑμῖν) *at the same time with them*, and this by the faith common to both, theirs and his, which should mutually act and react in the way of the Christian sympathy that is based on specific harmony of faith. That the *readers* are not the subject of the συμπαρακλ. (Fritzsche, van Hengel) is certain from ἐν ὑμῖν, which, if it meant *in animis vestris* (van Hengel), would be a perfectly superfluous addition. — The compound συμπαρακλ. occurs only here in the N. T., and is not found in the LXX. or Apocr.; but see Plat. *Rep.* p. 555 A; and Polyb. v. 83, 3. — ἡ ἐν ἀλλήλοις πίστις, more significant of the

[1] The delicate turn which he gives to the matter is this: "*to see you, in order that I*," etc., means nothing more than " *to be quickened along with and among you*," etc. Consequently συμπαρακλ. is parallel to the ἰδεῖν ; for both infinitives must have the same subject. If συμπαρακλ. κ.τ.λ. had been meant to be merely a delicate explanation of στηριχθῆναι ὑμᾶς (the *usual* exposition after Chrysostom), then ἐμέ must necessarily have been added to συμπαρακλ. Grotius aptly says: " συμπαρακλ. regitur ab ἐπιποθῶ." The true interpretation is given also by Bengel and Th. Schott ; comp. Olshausen, Ewald, and Hofmann, who erroneously imputes to me the common view.

hearty character of the faith than ἡ ἀλλήλων πίστις, is the faith of both viewed in its mutual identity, so that the faith which lives in the one lives also in the other. — ὑμῶν τε καὶ ἐμοῦ] placed in this order with delicate tact.

Ver. 13. My longing towards you has *often* awakened in me the *purpose* of coming to you, in order also among you etc. Paul might have placed a καί before προεθ., but was not *obliged* to do so (in opposition to Hofmann's objection); and he has not put it, because he did not *think* of it. The discourse proceeds from the *desire* (ver. 11) to the *purpose*, which is coming nearer to realisation. Hence it is the less necessary to transfer the weight of the thought in ver. 13 to the clause expressive of purpose (Mangold). — οὐ θέλω δὲ ὑμ. ἀγν.] The Apostle lays stress on this communication. Comp. on xi. 25. The δέ is the simple μεταβατικόν. — καὶ ἐκωλ. ἄχρι τοῦ δεῦρο] is a parenthesis separated from the structure of the sentence, so that ἵνα attaches itself to προεθ. ἐλθ. πρ. ὑμ. The καί, however, is not to be taken as adversative, as Köllner still thinks (see, in opposition to this, Fritzsche), but as the simple *and* marking the sequence of thought, which here (comp. John xvii. 10) intervenes *parenthetically*. For the view which makes it still dependent on ὅτι, so that it introduces the second part of what the readers are to know (Hofmann), is precluded by the following clause of purpose, which can only apply to that *resolution* so often formed. — δεῦρο] used only here in the N. T. as a particle *of time*, but more frequently in Plato and later authors; see Wetstein. *That by which* Paul had been hitherto hindered, may be seen in xv. 22; consequently it was neither by the devil (1 Thess. ii. 18) nor by the Holy Spirit (Acts xvi. 6 f.). Grotius aptly observes (comp. xv. 22): "Magis urgebat necessitas locorum, in quibus Christus erat ignotus." — ἵνα τινὰ καρπὸν κ.τ.λ.] is entirely parallel in sense with ἵνα τι μεταδῶ κ.τ.λ. in ver. 11, and it is a gratuitous refining on the figurative καρπόν to find specially indicated here the *conversion of unbelievers beyond the range which the church had hitherto embraced* (Hofmann); comp. also Th. Schott, and even Mangold, who takes the Apostle as announcing his desire *to take in hand the Gentile mission* also among his readers, so that the καρπός would be *Gentiles to be converted*. No; by καρπόν Paul, with a complimentary egotism flattering to the readers, describes that which his personal labours among the Romans would have effected—consequently what had been said without metaphor in ver. 11—according to a current figure (John iv. 36, xv. 16; Phil. i. 22; Col. i. 6), as *harvest-fruit* which he would have *had* among them, and which as the produce of his labour would have been his (ideal) *possession* among them. But in this view the literal sense of ἔχειν (comp. vi. 21 f.) is not even to be altered by taking it as *consequi* (Wolf, Kypke, Koppe, Köllner, Tholuck, and others). To postpone the *having* the fruit, however, till the *last* day (Mehring) is quite alien to the context. — καθὼς καὶ ἐν τοῖς λοιπ. ἔθν.] *as also among the remaining nations, i.e. Gentiles* (see on ver. 5), namely, I have fruit. In the animation and fulness of his thought Paul has inserted twice the καί of comparison, inasmuch as there was present to his mind the twofold conception: (1) "among you also,[1] as among;" and (2) "among you, as also among." So frequently in Greek authors. See Baeumlein, *Partikell.* p. 153; Stallbaum, *ad Plat. Gorg.* p. 457 E; Winer, p. 409 [E. T. 547]. There is therefore no grammatical reason for commencing the new sentence with καθώς (Mehring), nor is it in accordance with the repetition of the ἐν.

Vv. 14, 15. Fuller explanation regarding the previous ἵνα τινὰ καρπ. σχῶ καὶ ἐν ὑμῖν, καθὼς καὶ ἐν τ. λοιπ. ἔθνεσιν. — Respecting βάρβαροι (ὄνομα τὸ οὐχ Ἑλληνικόν, Ammonius), which, according to Greek feeling and usage, denotes generally all *non-Greeks* (Plat. *Polit.* p. 262 D)—all who were strangers to Greek nationality and language—see Dougt. *Anal.* II. p. 100 f.; Hermann, *Staatsalterth.* § 6, 1. How common it was to designate all nations by thus dividing them into Ἑλλ. κ. βάρβ., see in Wetstein and Kypke, with examples from Philo in Loesner, p. 243.

---

[1] That the "you" must mean the Roman *Christians*, and not the still *unconverted* Romans (Th. Schott), is clearly shown by all the passages, from ver. 8 onwards, in which the ὑμεῖς occurs; and especially by the ὑμῖν τοῖς ἐν Ῥώμῃ in ver. 15. As regards their *nationality*, they belong to the category of *Gentiles.* Comp. xi. 13, xvi. 4; Gal. ii. 12, 14; Eph. iii. 1. But if Paul is the *Apostle of the Gentiles*, the Gentiles already converted also belong to his apostolic sphere of labour, as, *e.g.*, the Colossians and Laodiceans, and (vv. 5, 6) the Romans. Schott is compelled to resort to very forced suggestions regarding ἐν ὑμῖν and ὑμῖν, especially here and in ver. 15; as also Mangold, who can only find therein a *geographical* designation (comp. Hofmann: "he addresses them as a *constituent portion of the people of Rome*"). Comp. on ver. 15.

Of course the Hellenes included the Jews also among the βάρβαροι (a view which is attributed even to Philo, but without sufficient ground), while the Jews in their turn applied this designation to the Hellenes. See Grimm on 2 Macc. ii. 21, p. 61. Now it may be asked: *did Paul include the Romans among the "Ελληνες or among the βάρβαροι?* The latter view is maintained by Reiche and Köllner, following older writers; the former is held by Ambrosiaster, Estius, Kypke, and others, and the former alone would be consistent with that delicacy which must be presumed on the Apostle's part, as in fact, since Hellenic culture had become prevalent in Rome, especially since the time of Augustus, the Roman community was regarded from the Roman point of view as separated from the *barbaria*, and only nations like the Germans, Scythians, etc., were reckoned to belong to the latter. Comp. Cicero, *de fin.* ii. 15, "non solum *Graecia* et *Italia*, sed etiam omnis *barbaria*." But the following σοφοῖς τε καὶ ἀνοήτοις, as also the circumstance that the Romans, although they separated themselves from the barbarians (*Greek* authors included them among these, Polyb. v. 104, 1, ix. 37, 5, Krebs and Kypke *in loc.*), are nowhere reckoned among the *Hellenes* or designated as such, make it evident that the above question is to be entirely *excluded* here, and that Paul's object is merely to set forth generally his obligation as Apostle of the Gentiles in its *universality*. This he does in the form of a twofold division, according to *nationality*, and according to *condition of culture*, so that the thought which he would express is: I am in duty bound to *all* Gentiles, *without distinction of their nationality or of their culture;* therefore I am ready, to you also etc. — ὀφειλέτης] Paul regards the divine obligation of office, received through Christ (ver. 5), as the undertaking of a *debt*, which he has to discharge by preaching the Gospel among all Gentile nations. Comp., in reference to this subject, Acts xxvi. 17 f.; Gal. ii. 7; 1 Cor. ix. 16. — οὕτω] *so*, that is, *in accordance with this relation*, by which I am in duty bound to the Ἕλλησι τ. κ. βαρβ., to the σοφ. τ. κ. ἀνοήτ. It does not refer to καθώς, ver. 13, which is dependent on the preceding καὶ ἐν ὑμῖν, but gathers up in itself the import of Ἕλλησι .... εἰμι : *so then, ita, sic igitur.* See Hermann, *ad Luc. de hist. conscr.* p. 161; Buttmann, *neut. Gr.* p. 307. Bengel well says: "est quasi ephiphonema et illatio a toto ad partem insignem." — The οὕτω τὸ κατ' ἐμὲ πρόθυμον (sc. ἐστί) is to be translated: *accordingly, the inclination on my part* [lit. *the on-my-part inclination*] *is*, so that τὸ belongs to πρόθυμον, though the expression τὸ κατ' ἐμὲ πρόθυμον is not substantially different from the simple τὸ πρόθυμον μου, but only more significantly indicative of the idea that Paul *on his part* was willing, etc. Comp. on Eph. i. 15. He says therefore: *in this state of the case the inclination which exists on his side is, to preach to the Romans also*. At the same time κατ' ἐμὲ is purposely chosen out of a feeling of dependence on a higher Will (ver. 10), rather than the simple τὸ πρόθυμον μου, instead of which τὸ ἐμοῦ πρόθυμον would come nearer to the expression by κατ' ἐμέ. On the substantival πρόθυμον, in the sense of προθυμία, comp. 3 Macc. v. 26; Plat. *Leg.* ix. p. 859 B; Eur. *Med.* 178; Thuc. iii. 82, 8; Herodian, viii. 3, 15. The above connection of τὸ .... πρόθυμον is adopted by Seb. Schmid, Kypke, Reiche, Fritzsche, Philippi, van Hengel, Mehring, and others. So also Th. Schott, who however takes οὕτω in a *predicative* sense; as does likewise Hofmann: *Thus the case stands as to the fact and manner of the inclination on my part.* This however is the less appropriate, because ver. 14 contains, not the mode, but the regulative basis of the προθυμία of ver. 15. If τὸ κατ' ἐμέ be taken *by itself*, and not along with πρόθυμον, there would result the meaning: *there is, so far as I am concerned, an inclination;* comp. de Wette. But, however correct in linguistic usage might be τὸ κατ' ἐμέ (see Schaefer, *ad Bos. Ell.* p. 278; Matthiae, p. 734), which would here yield the sense *pro mea virili*, as in Dem. 1210, 20, the πρόθυμον without a verb would stand abruptly and awkwardly, because not the mere copula ἐστί, but ἐστί in the sense of πάρεστι, *adest*, would require to be supplied. Beza, Grotius, Bengel, Tholuck, Rückert, Köllner, Baumgarten-Crusius, take τὸ κατ' ἐμέ as a periphrasis for ἐγώ, so that πρόθυμον must be taken as the predicate (*I on my part am disposed*). Without sanction from the *usus loquendi;* what is cited by Köllner from Vigerus, p. 7 f., and by Tholuck, is of a wholly different kind. The Greek would express this meaning by τὸ γ' ἐμὸν πρόθυμον (Stallbaum, *ad Plat. Rep.* p. 533 A). — καὶ ὑμῖν] as also included in that general obligation of mine; and not: although ye belong to the σοφοί (Bengel, Philippi), which the text does not suggest. But τοῖς ἐν Ῥώμῃ is added with emphasis, since Rome ("caput et theatrum orbis terrarum," Bengel) could least of all be exempted from the task assigned to the Apostle of the Gentiles. Hofmann erroneously holds (comp. Mangold, p. 84) that Paul addresses the readers by ὑμῖν, not in their character as *Christians*, but as *Romans*, and that εὐαγγελίσασθαι means the preaching to those still *unconverted;* comp. Th. Schott, p. 91. No, he addresses the *Christian church in Rome*, to which he has not yet preached, but wishes to preach, the tidings of salvation, which they have up to the present time received from others. As in *every* verse, from the 6th to the 13th, so also here the ὑμεῖς can only be the κλητοὶ Ἰ. Χ., ver. 6 f., in Rome. See besides, against Mangold, Beyschlag in the *Stud. u. Krit.* 1867, p. 642 f.

Vv. 16, 17. Transition to the theme (οὐ γὰρ ἐπαισχ. τ. εὐαγγ.), and the theme itself (δύναμις .... ζήσεται).

Ver. 16. Γάρ] Paul confirms negatively his προθυμία.... εὐαγγελίσασθαι, for which he had previously assigned a positive motive. — οὐ γὰρ ἐπαισχ. τ. εὐαγγ.] Written, no doubt, with a recollection of what he had experienced in other highly civilized cities (Athens, Corinth, Ephesus), as well as, generally, in reference to the contents of the Gospel as a preaching of the *cross* (1 Cor. i. 18).[1] Hence the *negative* form of the expression, as in contrast with the feeling of *shame* which that experience *might* have produced in him, as if the Gospel were something worthless, through which one could gain no honour and could only draw on himself contempt, mockery, etc. Comp. 2 Tim. i. 12. — ἐπαισχύνομαι (Plat. *Soph.* p. 247, D; 2 Tim. i. 8), and αἰσχύνομαι, with accusative of the object; see Kühner, II. i. p. 255 f.; Bernhardy, p. 113.— δύναμις γὰρ Θεοῦ ἐστιν] Ground of the οὐκ ἐπαισχ. τ. εὐαγγ. *Power of God* (genitive of the *subject*) is the Gospel, in so far as God works by means of the message of salvation. By awaking repentance, faith, comfort, love, peace, joy, courage in

---

[1] From his own point of view, viz. that the church in Rome was *Jewish-Christian*, Mangold, p. 98 f., suggests *theocratic* scruples on the part of the readers regarding the *Apostle's universalism*. An idea inconsistent with the notion conveyed by ἐπαισχ., and lacking any other indication whatever in the text; for the subsequent Ἰουδαίῳ τε πρῶτον κ.τ.λ. cannot have been designed cautiously to meet such doubts (see, on the other hand, ii. 9); but only to serve as expression of the *objective* state of the case as regards the historical order of salvation, in accordance with the doctrinal development of *principles* which Paul has in view.

life and death, hope, etc., the Gospel manifests itself as *power*, as a mighty potency, and that *of God*, whose revelation and work the Gospel is (hence τὸ εὐαγγ. τοῦ Θεοῦ, xv. 16; 2 Cor. xi. 7; 1 Thess. ii. 2). Comp. 1 Cor. i. 18, 24. The expression asserts more than that the Gospel is "a powerful means in the hand of God" (Rückert), and is based on the fact that it is the living self-manifestation and effluence of God, as ῥῆμα Θεοῦ (Eph. vi. 17). Paul knew how to honour highly the message of salvation which it was his office to convey, and he was not ashamed of it. Here also, as in vv. 1, 9, τὸ εὐαγγ. is not the *work* or *business* of conveying the message (Th. Schott), but the *message itself*. — εἰς σωτηρίαν] Working of this power of God: *unto salvation*, consequently *with saving power*. And *what* salvation is here meant, was understood by the reader; for σωτηρία and σώζεσθαι are the standing expressions for *the eternal salvation in the Messianic kingdom* (comp. ζήσεται, ver. 17), the opposite of ἀπώλεια (Phil. i. 28; comp. θάνατος, 2 Cor. ii. 16). Comp. generally, James i. 21, τὸν λόγον τὸν δυνάμενον σῶσαι τὰς ψυχὰς ὑμῶν. As to *how* the Gospel works salvation, see ver. 17. — παντὶ τῷ πιστεύοντι] shows *to whom* the Gospel is the power of God unto salvation. *Faith* is the condition on the part of man, without which the Gospel cannot be to him effectually that power; for in the unbeliever the causa apprehendens of its efficacy is wanting. Comp. ver. 17. Melancthon aptly says: "Non enim ita intelligatur haec efficacia, ut si de calefactione loqueremur: ignis est efficax in stramine, etiamsi stramen nihil agit." — παντί gives emphatic prominence to the *universality*, which is subsequently indicated in detail. Comp. iii. 22. — Ἰουδαίῳ τε πρῶτον κ. Ἕλληνι] τε .... καί denotes the equality of what is added. See Hartung, *Partikell.* I. p. 99; Baeumlein, *Part.* p. 225. πρῶτον expresses the *priority;* but not merely in regard to the divinely appointed order of *succession*, in accordance with which the preaching of the Messiah was to begin with the Jews and thence extend to the Gentiles, as Chrysostom, Theodoret, Theophylact, Grotius, and many others, including Olshausen, van Hengel and Th. Schott, have understood it; but in reference to the *first claim* on the Messianic salvation in accordance with the promise, which was in fact the ground of that external order of *succession* in the communication of the Gospel. So Erasmus, Calovius, and others, including Reiche, Tholuck, Rückert, Fritzsche, de Wette, Philippi,

Ewald, Hofmann. That this is the Pauline view of the relation is plain from iii. 1 f.; ix. 1 ff.; xi. 16 ff.; xv. 9; comp. John iv. 22; Matth. xv. 24; Acts xiii. 46. The Jews are the υἱοὶ τῆς βασιλ., Matth. viii. 12. — Ἕλληνι] denotes, in contrast to Ἰουδαίῳ, all *Non-Jews*. Acts xiv. 1; 1 Cor. x. 32 *al*.

Ver. 17 illustrates and gives a reason for the foregoing affirmation: δύναμις Θεοῦ ἐστιν εἰς σωτ. π. τ. πιστ., which could not be the case, unless δικαιοσύνη Θεοῦ κ.τ.λ. — δικαιοσύνη Θεοῦ] That this does not denote, as in iii. 5, an attribute of God,[1] is plain from the passage cited in proof from Hab. ii. 4, where, by necessity of the connection, ὁ δίκαιος must denote the person who is in the state of the δικαιοσύνη Θεοῦ. Comp. iii. 21 ff. It must therefore be *an ethical relation of man* that is meant; and the genitive Θεοῦ must (otherwise in Jas. i. 20)[2] be rendered as the *genitive of emanation from*, consequently: *rightness which proceeds from God, the relation of being right into which man is put by God* (*i.e.* by an act of God declaring him righteous). Comp. Chrysostom, Bengel, and others, including Rückert, Olshausen, Reiche, de Wette, Winer, p. 175 [E. T. 232]; Winzer (*de vocib.* δίκαιος, δικαιοσύνη, *et* δικαιοῦν *in ep. ad Rom.* p. 10); Bisping, van Hengel, Ernesti, *Urspr. d. Sünde*, I. p. 153; Mehring; also Hofmann (comp. his *Schriftbew.* I. p. 627); Holsten, z. *Ev. d. Paul. u. Petr.* p. 408 f.; Weiss, *bibl. Theol.* p. 330 f.; Rich. Schmidt, *Paulin. Christol.* p. 10. This interpretation of the genitive as gen. *originis*, acutely and clearly set forth anew by Pfleiderer (in Hilgenfeld's *Zeitschr.* 1872, p. 168 ff.), is more specially evident from iii. 23, where Paul himself first explains the expression δικαιοσύνη Θεοῦ, and that by δικαιούμενοι δωρεὰν τῇ αὐτοῦ χάριτι, which is turned in ver. 26 to the active form: δικαιοῦντα τὸν ἐκ πίστεως; comp. ver. 30, viii. 33, according to which the genitive appears equivalent to ἐκ Θεοῦ (Phil.

---

[1] It has been understood as the truthfulness of God (Ambrosiaster); as the *justitia Dei essentialis* (Osiander); as the *justitia distributiva* (Origen, and several of the older expositors, comp. Flatt); as the goodness of God (Schoettgen, Semler, Morus, Erchl); as the *justifying righteousness* of God (Märcker). According to Ewald it is the divine righteousness regarded as power and life-blessing, in the goodness of which man may and must fully participate, if he would not feel its sting and its penalty. Comp. Matthias on iii. 21: a righteousness, *such as belongs to God*, consequently, "a righteousness which exists also *inwardly* and is in every respect *perfect*."

[2] Where what is meant is *the rightness required by God*, which man is supposed to realise through exerting himself in works.

iii. 9), in contrast to the ἐμή and ἰδία δικαιοσύνη (Rom. x. 3), and to the δικαιοῦν ἑαυτόν (Luke xii. 15). The passage in 2 Cor. v. 21 is not opposed to this view (as Fritzsche thinks); see *in loc.;* nor are the expressions δικαιοῦσθαι ἐνώπιον Θεοῦ (iii. 20), and παρὰ Θεῷ (Gal. iii. 11), for these represent a special form under which the relation is conceived, expressing more precisely the *judicial* nature of the matter. Hence it is evident that the interpretation adopted by many modern writers (including Köllner, Fritzsche, Philippi, Umbreit), following Luther: "righteousness *before God*," although correct in point of substance, is unsuitable as regards the analysis of the genitive, which they take as genitive of the *object.* This remark applies also against Baur, who (*Paulus*, II. p. 146 ff.) takes the genitive *objectively* as the δικαιοσύνη determined by the idea of God, adequate to that idea; whilst in his *neutest. Theol.* p. 134, he prefers to take the genitive *subjectively:* the righteousness *produced* through God, *i.e.* "the manner in which God places man in the adequate relation to Himself."—The following remarks may serve exegetically to illustrate the *idea* of δικαιοσύνη Θεοῦ, which in the Gospel is revealed from faith:—Since God, as the holy Lawgiver and Judge, has by the law imposed on man the task of keeping it entirely and perfectly (Gal. iii. 10), He can only receive and treat as a δίκαιος (*who is such, as he should be*) —as one normally guiltless and upright, who should be so, therefore, *habitually*—the person who keeps the whole law; or, in other words, only the man who is perfectly obedient to the law can stand to God in the relation of δικαιοσύνη. Such perfection however no man could attain; not merely no Gentile, since in his case the natural moral law was obscured through immorality, and through disobedience to it he had fallen into sin and vice; but also no Jew, for natural desire, excited by the principle of sin in him through the very fact of legal prohibition, hindered in his case the fulfilment of the divine law, and rendered him also, without exception, morally weak, a sinner and object of the divine wrath. If therefore man was to enter into the relation of a righteous person and thereby of a future participator in the Messianic blessedness, it was necessary that this should be done by means of an extraordinary divine arrangement, through which grace and reconciliation should be imparted to the object of wrath, and he should be put forward for the judgment of God as righteous. This arrangement has been effected through the sending of His Son and His being given up to His bloody death as that of a guiltless sacrifice; whereby God's counsel of redemption, formed from eternity, has been accomplished,—objectively for all, subjectively to be appropriated on the part of individuals through faith, which is the ὄργανον ληπτικόν. And, as this plan of salvation is the subject-matter of the *Gospel*, so in this *Gospel* that which previously, though prefigured by the justification of Abraham, was an unrevealed μυστήριον, namely, *righteousness from God*, is revealed (ἀποκαλύπτεται), inasmuch as the Gospel makes known both the accomplished work of redemption itself and the means whereby man appropriates the redemption, namely, *faith in Christ*, which, *imputed* to him as righteousness (iv. 5), causes man to be regarded and treated by God out of grace and δωρεάν (iii. 24) as righteous (δίκαιος), so that he, like one who has perfectly obeyed the law, is certain of the Messianic bliss destined for the δίκαιοι.[1] The so-called obedientia Christi *activa* is not to be included in the *causa meritoria* of the divine justification; but is to be regarded as the

[1] Justification is simply imputative, an actus *forensis*, not *inherent*, and therefore not a *gradual* process, as Romang anew maintains, but produced by the imputation of faith. The new moral life in Christ is the necessary *consequence* (Rom. vi. 8), so that regeneration *comes after* justification—a divine order of salvation inconsistent with all Osiandrian views. See Ritschl, in the *Jahrb. f. Deutsche Theol.* 1857, p. 795 ff., *altkath. Kirche*, p. 76 ff. The regenerate life is neither a *part* (Baumgarten-Crusius) nor the *positive side* (Baur) of justification, the conception of which is not to be referred either to the *consciousness* of liberation from guilt given with conversion (Schleiermacher); or to the unity of forgiveness with the *instilling of love* (Marheineke); or to an *anticipation of the judgment of God* on faith in respect to the divine *life* which develops itself from it as its *fruit* (Rothe, Martensen, Hundeshagen, and others, including Tholuck on v. 9, and Catholics like Döllinger, see on iv. 3)—so that, with regard to its *truth* it would have to be made dependent on *sanctification* (Nitzsch), or the *dying out of sin* (Beck), and so forth,—or to the establishment of the *new sanctified humanity* in the person of Christ (Menken-Hofmann). The *Form. Conc.*, p. 687, rightly warns: "ne ea, quae fidem praecedunt et ea quae eam sequuntur, articulo de justificatione, tanquam ad justificationem pertinentia, admisceantur." Respecting the sensus *forensis* of justification, which is by no means a product of mediæval scholasticism (in opposition to Sabatier, p. 263), comp. Köstlin in the *Jahrb. f. Deutsche Theol.* 1856, p. 89 ff.; and in its purely exegetical aspect, especially Wieseler on Gal. ii. 16, Pfleiderer in Hilgenfeld's *Zeitschr.* 1872, p. 161 ff., and Weiss, *bibl. Theol.* § 112. We may add that with Luther's doctrine of justification Zwingli substantially concurs. See, for defence of the latter (against Stahl), Ritschl, *Rechtfert. u. Versöhnung*, 1870, I. p. 165 ff.

fulfilment of a *preliminary condition* necessary to the death of Jesus, so far as the justification of man was objectively based on the latter; without the complete *active* obedience of Christ (consequently without His sinlessness) His *passive* obedience could not have been that *causa meritoria* (2 Cor. v. 21). — ἀποκαλύπτεται] *is revealed;* for previously, and in the absence of the Gospel, the δικαιοσύνη Θεοῦ was and is something quite hidden in the counsel of God, the knowledge of which is first given *in the Gospel* (comp. xvi. 25; Acts xvii. 30). The prophecies of the Old Testament were only *preparatory* and *promissory* (ver. 2), and therefore were only the *means of introducing* the evangelical revelation itself (xvi. 26). The *present* is used, because the Gospel is conceived of in its continuous proclamation. Comp. the perfect, πεφανέρωται, iii. 21, and on the other hand the historical aorist φανερωθέντος in xvi. 26. Through the ἀποκάλυψις ensues the φανεροῦσθαι, through the *revelation* the *being manifest* as object of knowledge. — ἐκ πίστεως εἰς πίστιν] may not be connected with δικαιοσ. (Luther, Hammond, Bengel, Koppe, Rückert, Reiche, Tholuck, Philippi, Mehring, and others), but rather—as the only arrangement which the position of the words admits without arbitrariness—with ἀποκαλύπτεται. So also van Hengel and Hofmann; comp. Luke ii. 35. The δικαιοσύνη Θεοῦ, namely, is revealed in the Gospel ἐκ πίστεως, *inasmuch as in the Gospel faith on Christ is made known as the subjective cause from which righteousness comes.* Thus the Gospel, as the ῥῆμα τῆς πίστεως (x. 8) and λόγος τῆς καταλλαγῆς (2 Cor. v. 19), makes the divine righteousness become manifest *from faith,* which it in fact preaches as that which becomes imputed; for him who does *not* believe the ἀκοὴ πίστεως (Gal. iii. 2), it leaves this δικαιοσύνη to remain a locked-up *unrevealed* blessing. But it is not merely ἐκ πίστεως, but also εἰς πίστιν; *to faith* (comp. 2 Cor. ii. 16). Inasmuch, namely, as righteousness is revealed in the Gospel *from* faith, faith is *aimed at, i.e.* the revelation spoken of proceeds from faith and is *designed to produce faith.* This sense, equivalent to "*ut fides habeatur,*" and rightly corresponding alike with the simple words and the context, is adopted by Heumann, Fritzsche, Tholuck, Krehl, Nielsen, and van Hengel. It is not "too meaningless" (de Wette), nor "saying pretty nearly nothing" (Philippi); but is on the contrary emphatically appropriate to the purpose of representing faith as the *Fac totum* ("prora et puppis," Bengel, comp. Baur, II. p. 161). See also Hofmann, *Schriftbew.* I. p. 629 f. Comp. vi. 19; 2 Cor. ii. 16. Therefore εἰς πίστιν is not to be taken as *equivalent* to εἰς τὸν πιστεύοντα, *for the believer* (Oecumenius, Seb. Schmid, Morus, Rosenmüller, Rückert, Reiche, de Wette, Olshausen, Reithmayr, Maier, and Philippi), a rendering which should have been precluded by the abstract correlative ἐκ πίστεως. Nor does it mean: *for the furtherance and strengthening of faith* (Clem. Al. *Strom.* v. 1, II. p. 644 Pott., Theophylact, Erasmus, Luther, Melancthon, Beza, Cornelius à Lapide, and others, including Köllner; comp. Baumgarten-Crusius, Klee, and Stengel); for the thought: "from an *ever new*, never tiring, *endlessly progressive* faith" (Ewald; comp. Lipsius, *Rechtfertigungsl.* p. 7, 116, and Umbreit), is here foreign to the connection, which is concerned only with the great fundamental truth in its simplicity; the case is different in 2 Cor. iii. 18. Quite arbitrary, moreover, was the interpretation: "*ex fide legis in fidem evangelii*" (Tertullian; comp. Origen, Chrysostom, Theodoret: δεῖ γὰρ πιστεῦσαι τοῖς προφήταις, καὶ δι' ἐκείνων εἰς τὴν τοῦ εὐαγγελίου πίστιν ποδηγηθῆναι, Zeger, and others). Finally, to take πίστιν as *faithfulness*, and to understand πίστις εἰς πίστιν in the sense of *faith in the faithfulness of God* (Mehring), is to introduce what is neither in the words nor yet suggested by the context. Ewald in his *Jahrb.* IX. p. 87 ff., interprets: *faith in faith*, the reference being to the faith with which man meets the *divine* faith in his power and his good will (?). But the idea of "faith from beneath on the faith from above," as well as the notion generally of God *believing* on men, would be a paradox in the N. T., which no reader could have discovered without more clear and precise indication. After ἐκ πίστ. every one could not but understand εἰς πίστ. also as meaning *human* faith; and indeed everywhere it is man that believes, not *God*. — καθὼς γέγραπται] represents what has just been stated, δικαιοσύνη .... πίστιν, as taking place *in accordance with a declaration of Scripture*, consequently according to the necessity of the divine counsel of salvation. *He who from faith* (on Christ) *is righteous* (transferred into the relation of the δικαιοσύνη Θεοῦ) *shall live* (be partaker of the Messianic eternal life). This, as the Messianic sense intended to be conveyed by the Spirit of God (2 Peter i. 21) in the prophetic words, Hab. ii. 4, "*the righteous shall by his faithfulness*[1] *live*" (attain the theocratic life-blessedness), is recognised by Paul, and expressed substantially in the language of the LXX., rightly omitting the μου, which they inaccurately add to πίστεως. In doing so Paul *might*, in accordance with the Messianic reference of the passage, connect ἐκ πίστεως (בֶּאֱמוּנָתוֹ)—seeing that on this causal definition the *stress* of the expression lies—with ὁ δίκαιος; because, if the *life* of the righteous has πίστις as its cause, his δικαιοσύνη itself can have no other ground or source. That he has *really* so connected the words, as Beza and others rightly perceived (see especially Hölemann, *de justitiae ex fide ambab. in V. T. sedibus*, Lips. 1867), and not, as most earlier expositors have supposed (also de Wette, Tholuck, Delitzsch, on Hab. *l.c.*, Philippi, Baumgarten-Crusius, van Hengel, Ewald, and Hofmann), ἐκ πίστ. ζήσεται, is plain from the connection, according to which it is not the *life* ἐκ πίστ., but *the revelation of righteousness* ἐκ πίστ. that is to be confirmed by the Old Testament. The case is different in Heb. x. 38. See further, generally, on Gal. iii. 11.— The δέ is, without having any bearing on the matter, adopted along with the other words from the LXX. Comp. on Acts ii. 17. A contrast to the unrighteous who shall die (Hofmann) is neither here nor in Hab. ii. 4 implied in the text.

Vv. 18-32. Proof of ver. 17 deduced from experience, and that in the first instance with respect to *Gentile* humanity (the proof in regard to the *Jews* begins at ch. ii.).

Ver. 18. This great fundamental proposition of the Gospel, ver. 17, is proved (γάρ) agreeably to experience, by the fact that, where there is no πίστις, there is also no ἀποκάλυψις of righteousness, but only of the wrath of God. "Horrendum est initium ac fulmen," Melancthon, 1540. — ἀποκαλύπτεται] Emphatically placed, in harmony with the ἀποκαλ. in ver. 17, at the beginning. — ὀργὴ Θεοῦ] The antithesis of δικαιοσ. Θεοῦ, ver. 16. The ὀργή of God is not to be explained with several of the Fathers (in Suicer), Erasmus, and many later authorities, as *poena divina*, which is nothing but a rationalizing interchange of ideas, but rather in the

---

[1] This *faithfulness*, in the prophet's sense, the אֱמוּנָה, and the πίστις in the *Christian* sense, have the same fundamental idea, *trustful self-surrender* to God. Comp. Umbreit, p. 197.

proper literal sense: *wrath*, an affection of the personal God, having a necessary connection with His love. The wrath of God, the reality of which is indisputable as the very presupposition of the work of atonement, is the love of the holy God (who is neither neutral nor one-sided in His affection) for all that is good in its energy as antagonistic to all that is evil.[1] Even Lactantius has aptly remarked, *de ira Dei*, v. 9: "Si Deus non irascitur impiis et injustis, nec pios justosque diligit; in rebus enim diversis aut in utramque partem moveri necesse est, aut in neutram." See on Matth. iii. 7; Eph. ii. 3. — $ἀπ'$ $οὐρανοῦ$] is neither to be connected with $ὀργὴ$ $Θεοῦ$, as Beza, Estius, and many others hold, nor with the bare $Θεοῦ$ (Mehring), but, as the order of the words and the parallel definition $ἐν$ $αὐτῷ$ in ver. 17 require, belongs to $ἀποκαλύπτεται$; so that heaven, the dwelling-place and throne of God (comp. on Matth. vi. 9), is designated as the place from which the $ἀποκάλυψις$ of the $ὀργὴ$ $Θεοῦ$ issues. "*Majestatem* irati Dei significat," Bengel. The revelation of righteousness takes place $ἐν$ $εὐαγγελίῳ$, ver. 17, as something spiritually brought home to the consciousness through the medium of the Gospel; but that of the divine wrath descends *from heaven*, manifested as a divine matter of fact; by which description, however, the *destructive* character of this working of divine power is not expressed (Th. Schott), although it is in fact implied in the entire context. *But what revelation of divine wrath is meant?* Paul himself supplies the information in ver. 24 ff., in which is described what God in His sufficiently well-grounded (vv. 19-23) wrath did ($παρέδωκεν$ $αὐτούς$). God's wrath therefore is revealed from heaven *in this way*, that those who are the objects of it are given up by God to terrible retribution in unchastity and all vice. Against this interpretation (comp. Mehring), which is adopted also by Tholuck, Weber (*vom Zorne Gottes*, p. 89), and Th. Schott, it cannot be objected, with Hofmann, that Paul must have written $ἀπεκαλύφθη$; for he here in fact expresses the *general* proposition of experience, to which the concrete *historical* representation subsequently shall correspond; the divine *axiom* is placed first (*present*), and then the history of it follows (*aorist*). Irrelevant is also the objection of Philippi, that $ἀποκαλύπτειν$ always denotes

---

[1] The idea of the divine $ὀργή$ is diametrically opposed to every conception of sin as a necessity interwoven with human development.

a *supernatural* revelation. For ἀποκαλύπτειν means to *reveal* what was previously unknown, what was veiled from our cognition, *so that it now becomes manifest;* and, in reference to this, it is a matter of indifference whether the revelation takes place in a natural or in a supernatural manner.[1] The *mode* of revealing is not indicated in the word itself, but in the context; and hence according to the connection it is used also, as here, of a revelation *in fact*, by which a state of things previously unknown comes to our knowledge (Matth. x. 26; Luke ii. 35; 2 Thess. ii. 3, 6, 8). Moreover, even according to our interpretation, a *divine* revelation is meant, by which there is certainly brought to light a μυστήριον, namely, the connection of the phenomenon with the divine ὀργή. According to others, Paul means the *inward* revelation of the divine wrath, given by means of *reason and conscience* (Ambrosiaster, Wolf, and others, including Reiche and Glöckler), in support of which view they appeal to ver. 19. But, on the contrary, ἀπ' οὐρανοῦ requires us to understand an ἀποκάλυψις *cognisable by the senses;* and ver. 19 contains not the *mode* of the manifestation of wrath, but its *moving cause* (διότι). Others hold that the ἀποκάλυψις of the divine wrath has come *through the Gospel* ("continens minas," Grotius), and that ἐν αὐτῷ is to be again supplied from ver. 17. So Aquinas, Bellarmine, Corn. à Lapide, Estius, Grotius, Heumann, Semler, Morus, Böhme, Benecke, Maier; comp. Umbreit, who includes also the Old Testament. It is decisive against this view that ἀπ' οὐρανοῦ, just because it is parallel to ἐν αὐτῷ in ver. 17, lays down a mode of manifestation quite different from ἐν αὐτῷ. Had the latter been again in Paul's mind here, he would have repeated it with emphasis, as he has repeated the ἀποκαλύπτεται. Others hold that the manifestation of wrath *at the general judgment* is meant (Chrysostom, Theodoret, Theophylact, Oecumenius, Toletus, Limborch, Koppe, Philippi, Reithmayr, and Ewald). The present, considered in itself, might be chosen in order to express a vivid realisation of the future, or might be accounted for by the ἐν αὐτῷ, which, it is alleged, is to be again mentally supplied (Ewald); but the former explanation is to be rejected on account of the preceding purely present ἀποκαλ. in ver. 17; and against the latter may be

[1] In this case it cannot make any difference whether *God* is or is not the revealing subject, as is most plainly seen from Matth. xvi. 17.

urged the very fact, that ἐν αὐτῷ is not repeated. Had this been the meaning, moreover, the further course of the exposition must have borne reference to the general judgment, which it by no means does; and therefore this interpretation is opposed to the connection, as well as unwarranted by ii. 5 (where the mention of the revelation of judgment belongs to quite a different connection); and not required by the idea of ἀποκαλύπτειν itself, since that idea is adequately met by the divine matter-of-fact revelation of wrath here intended (see above), and besides, the word is repeated intentionally for rhetorical effect. Lastly, while others have contented themselves with leaving the ἀποκάλυψις here *in its entire generality* (Olshausen, Tholuck; comp. Calovius), and thus relieved themselves from giving any explanation of it, the reference to the religion of the O. T. (Bengel and Flatt) seems entirely arbitrary and groundless, and the interpretations which apply it to *evils generally* affecting the world as an expression of the divine wrath (Hofmann), or to the external and internal *distress of the time* (Baumgarten-Crusius), are too general and indefinite, and thereby devoid of any concrete import in keeping with the text. — ἐπὶ πᾶσ. ἀσέβ. κ. ἀδικ. ἀνθρ.] contains the *hostile direction* (comp. Dem. 743, 22) of the ἀποκαλύπτεται .... οὐρανοῦ: *against every ungodliness and immorality of men*, which, etc. Ἀσέβεια and ἀδικία (Plat. *Prot.* p. 323 E; Xen. *Cyr.* viii. 8, 7; Tittmann, *Synon. N. T.* p. 48) are distinguished as *irreligiousness* and *immorality*, so that both describe the *improbitas*, but under different aspects, in reference to the fear of *God* and to the standard of *morals;* hence the former, as involving the idea of impiety, is the stronger expression. Comp. Dem. 548, 11: ἀσέβημα, οὐκ ἀδίκημα μόνον. That the distinction between them is not to be understood, with Köllner, following Theophylact, Grotius, Calovius, Wolf, and many others, *as profanitas in Deum* and *injuria in proximum*, is proved by the following ἐν ἀδικίᾳ κατεχ. — τῶν τ. ἀληθ. ἐν ἀδικ. κατεχ.] *who keep down the truth through immorality*, do not let it develop itself into power and influence on their religious knowledge and their moral condition. The article (*quippe qui*) introduces that *characteristic* of the ἀνθρώπων, not yet more precisely defined, which excites the divine wrath. Rightly in the Vulgate: *corum qui*. See Winer, p. 127 [E. T. 174]. It may be paraphrased: "*of those, I mean, who.*" Comp. Kühner, *ad Xen. Anab.* ii. 7, 13. Bengel, moreover, aptly remarks: " veritas in mente nititur et urget, sed homo eam impedit." This is the peculiar, deeply unfortunate, constant self-contradiction of the heathen character. Comp. Nägelsbach, *Homer. Theol.* I. p. 11 ff. On κατέχειν, *to hinder,* comp. 2 Thess. ii. 6; Luke iv. 42; 1 Macc. vi. 27; Plat. *Phaed.* p. 117 C; Soph. *El.* 754; Pind. *Isthm.* iii. 2, and Dissen *in loc.* Against the interpretation of Michaelis, Koppe and Baur, who take κατέχειν here as meaning *to possess* (1 Cor. vii. 30; 2 Cor. vi. 10), " who possess the truth in unrighteousness, who know what God's will is, and yet sin," ver. 21 is decisive, where the continuous *possession* of the truth is *negatived* by ἐματαιώθησαν .... καρδία; wherefore also it cannot be rendered with Melancthon and van Hengel: who hold the truth *in the bondage of immorality* (vii. 6; Gen. xxxix. 20, xlii. 19). The ἀλήθεια is correctly interpreted in the sense of divine *truth generally;* the *mode of revelation,* in which it is presented to man's knowledge, is furnished by the context, here, by ver. 19 f., as the truth apparent by natural revelation in the works of God; not therefore in the sense of the *doctrine of the Gospel,* which is hindered in its diffusion by Jews and Gentiles (Ammon, comp. Ewald). — ἐν ἀδικίᾳ] *instrumental.* To make it equivalent to ἀδίκως (Reiche, following Theophylact, Beza, Calvin, Piscator, Raphel, and others; comp. ἐν δυνάμει in ver. 4) arbitrarily deprives the representation of an element essential to its fulness and precision, and renders it tame; for it is self-evident that the κατέχειν τ. ἀλ. is unrighteous or sinful, but not so much so that it takes place *through sin.* — Finally, it is to be noted that Paul, in ἀνθρώπ. (correlative of Θεοῦ) τῶν τ. ἀλήθ. ἐν ἀδικ. κατεχ., expresses himself quite *generally,* making apparent by ἀνθρώπ. the *audacity* of this *God-*opposing conduct; but he means the *Gentiles,* as is indicated even by ἐν ἀδικίᾳ (comp. 1 Cor. vi. 1), and as is confirmed beyond doubt by the continuation of the discourse in ver. 19 ff. Koppe supposed that Paul meant the Jews especially, but included also the Gentiles; Benecke, that he speaks of the whole human race in general, which view Mehring specially defends. But the peculiar character of what is contained in vv. 21-32 shows that the Jews are to be entirely excluded from the description which is carried on to the end of the chapter. It is not till ch. ii. 1 that the discourse passes over to them, and makes them suddenly see themselves reflected in the Gentile mirror.

Ver. 19. Διότι] *propterea quod*—only to be separated by a comma from the foregoing—specifies *more precisely* the *causal relation, on account of which* the wrath of God comes upon such men, etc. (ver. 18). They keep down the truth through immorality; if they did so out of ignorance, they would be excusable: but they do not do so out of ignorance, and *therefore* God's wrath is manifested against them. This view of the connection is *suggested* by the literal meaning of διότι itself, and *confirmed* by εἰς τὸ εἶναι αὐτοὺς ἀναπολογ. Comp. Hofmann. So also Fritzsche, who, however, takes διότι as equivalent to γάρ, as does also Philippi,—a use of it that never occurs, not even in Acts xviii. 10. This linguistically erroneous interpretation of διότι condemns also the view of Tholuck, Rückert, de Wette, and Reithmayr, who discover here the *proof, that* the Gentiles *keep down the truth* by immorality; or (so Th. Schott) that Paul rightly describes them as κατέχοντες κ.τ.λ. No; *for the very reason that* they *have* the γνωστὸν τοῦ Θεοῦ, which renders them *inexcusable*, does the wrath of God go forth against the κατέχοντες; ver. 18. — τὸ γνωστὸν τοῦ Θεοῦ] *that which is known concerning God*, not: that which is *knowable* concerning God, a signification which, though adopted by Origen, Theophylact, Oecumenius, Erasmus, Beza, Castalio, Calvin, Piscator, Estius, Grotius, Wolf, Koppe, Rückert, Kollner, Baumgarten-Crusius, Maier, Ewald, Umbreit, Mehring, Hofmann, and others, is never conveyed by γνωστός in the N. T. or in the LXX. and Apocrypha, though it frequently occurs in classic authors (see the passages from Plato quoted by Ast, *Lex.* I. p. 401; Dorvill. *ad Charit.* p. 502; Hermann, *ad Soph. Oed. T.* 361; comp. ἄγνωστος, which in Plato invariably means *unknowable*). In all the places where it occurs in the Scriptures, as also, though less frequently, in the classics (Xen. *Cyr.* vi. 3, 4; Arrian. *Epict.* ii. 20, 4; Aesch. *Choeph.* 702; Beck, *Antiatt.* p. 87, 25), it means *quod notum est* (Vulgate), and is therefore equivalent to γνωτός or γνώριμος, also in Acts iv. 16; Ecclus. xxi. 7. The opposite: ἄγνωστος, Acts xvii. 23. Comp. Luther, 1545: "*das* (nicht: *dass*) man weiss, *das* (nicht: *dass*) Gott sei." That which is *known* of God excludes that which needed a special revelation to make it known, as in particular the contents of the Gospel; the former is derived from the general revelation of nature. If we should take γνωστόν as *knowable*, the assertion of the Apostle would be incorrect without some limiting qualification; for the positively revealed belonged to that which was *knowable*, but not to that which was *known* of God,[1] into which category it was brought only through special revelation, which it would otherwise not have needed. — ἐν αὐτοῖς] *i.e. in their consciousness*, ἐν ταῖς καρδίαις αὐτῶν, ii. 15. Comp. Gal. i. 16. The explanation *inter ipsos*, which Erasmus and Grotius (both referring it arbitrarily to the Gnosis of the *philosophers* among the Gentiles), Köllner and Baumgarten-Crusius give, is to be rejected for this reason, that αὐτοῖς ἐφανέρωσε, compared with νοούμενα καθορᾶται, points to a manifestation of the γνωστόν τοῦ Θεοῦ which is *inward*, although conveyed through the revelation of nature. — ἐφανέρωσε] God—and this subject is again named with emphasis—*has laid it clearly* before them, made it lie openly before their view as an object of knowledge. Comp. on the matter itself Acts xiv. 17, xvii. 26 f.; 1 Cor. i. 21.

Ver. 20 f. Τὰ γὰρ ἀόρατα .... θειότης] Giving a reason for, and explaining, the previous ὁ Θεὸς γὰρ αὐτοῖς ἐφανέρωσε. — τὰ ἀόρατα αὐτοῦ] *His invisible things*, the manifold invisible attributes, that constitute His nature. Paul himself explains it afterwards by ἡ ἀΐδιος αὐτοῦ δύναμις καὶ θειότης; therefore it is not *actiones Dei invisibiles* (Fritzsche; comp. Theodoret). — νοούμενα καθορᾶται] *through the works are seen becoming discerned;* νοούμενα defines the *manner* in which the καθορᾶται takes place, otherwise than through the senses (the νοεῖν, ἀλλ' οὐκ ὄμμασι θεωρεῖν, Plat. *Rep.* p. 529 B), in so far as it is effected by means of *mental discernment*, by the agency of *intelligent perception*. The καθορᾶται forms with ἀόρατα a striking oxymoron, in which the compound selected for that purpose, but not elsewhere occurring in the N. T., heightens still further the idea conveyed by the simple form. Comp. Xen. *Cyr.* iii. 3, 31.: εἰ γὰρ .... ἡμᾶς οἱ πολέμιοι θεάσονται

---

[1] Which, however, is not to be transformed, with Fritzsche, Tholuck, Krehl, and others, into the subjective *scientia Dei*—which has no precedent in usage, is unsuitable to the following φανερόν ἐστι, and is not to be supported even by the LXX. Gen. ii. 9; in which passage, if the text be not corrupted, τὸ ξύλον τοῦ εἰδέναι γνωστόν καλοῦ κ. πονηροῦ must be rendered: the tree by which they were to learn what is known of good and evil, *i.e.* by which they were to become aware of that which they—by the very enjoyment—had known of good and evil.

.... πάλιν καθορῶντες ἡμῶν τὸ πλῆθος. Pind. *Pyth.* ix. 45.: οἶσθα.... εὖ καθορᾷς. On the oxymoron itself, comp. Aristotle, *de mundo*, 6, p. 399, 21. Bekk: ἀθεώρητος ἀπ' αὐτῶν τῶν ἔργων θεωρεῖται (ὁ θεός). — τοῖς ποιήμασι] embraces all that God *as Creator* has produced, but does not at the same time include His governing in the world of history, as Schneckenburger thinks, *Beitr.* p. 102 f.; for מַעֲשֶׂה, with which ποίημα corresponds (LXX. Eccles. iii. 11, vii. 13, *al.*), is the *formal* expression for God's works of creation; as also Paul himself, in Eph. ii. 10, describes the renewing of man as analogous to creation. It is only of the works of creation that the Apostle could assert what he here says, especially as he adds ἀπὸ κτίσεως κόσμου. Since, moreover, τοῖς ποιήμασι, *by means of the works*, contains the *instrumental* definition appended to νοούμενα καθορᾶται,[1] ἀπὸ κτίσ. κόσμου cannot be taken in a causal sense (see Winer, p. 348 [E. T. 463]), as the *medium cognoscendi* (so Luther and many others, including Calovius, Pearson, Homberg, Wolf, Heumann, Morus and Reithmayr), but only in the sense of temporal beginning: *since* the creation of the world they are so perceived. — ἥ τε ἀΐδιος αὐτοῦ δύν. κ. θειότης] A more precise definition of the previous τὰ ἀόρατα αὐτοῦ. Ἀΐδιος, *everlasting*, belongs to both substantives; but καί annexes the general term, the category, of which the δύναμις is a species. See Fritzsche *ad Matth.* p. 786. Its relation to the preceding τέ consists in its completing the climax and cumulation, for which τέ prepares the way. Hartung, *Partikell.* I. p. 98. Hofmann is unsupported by linguistic usage in inferring from the position of τέ, that ἀΐδιος is not meant to apply also to θειότης. It is just that position that makes ἀΐδιος the common property of both members (see especially Hartung, *l.c.* p. 116 f.), so that, in order to analyse the form of the conception, we may again supply ἡ ἀΐδιος αὐτοῦ after καί (Stallbaum, *ad Plat. Crit.* p. 43 B.; Schaefer, *Poet. gnom.* p. 73; Schoemann, *ad Is.* p. 325 f.; also Winer, p. 520 [E. T. 727]). The θειότης is the totality of that which God is as a Being

---

[1] Not merely to νοούμενα (Hofmann), which is closely bound up with καθορᾶται as showing the *manner* of it, so that both *together* are defined instrumentally by τοῖς ποιήμασι. On νοεῖν, as denoting the *intellectual animadvertere* in seeing (Hom. *Il.* λ. 599, in the inverse position: τὸν δὲ ἰδὼν ἐνόησε), comp. Nägelsb. z. *Ilias*, p. 416, ed. 3; Duncan, ed. Rost, p. 787.

possessed of divine attributes, as θεῖον, the collective sum of the divine realities.[1] This comprehensive sense must by no means be limited. The eternal *power*—this aspect of His θειότης which comes into prominence at first and before all others—and the *divinity* of God in its collective aspect, are rationally perceived and discerned by means of His works. Arbitrary is the view of Reiche, who holds that Paul means especially *wisdom and goodness*, which latter Schneckenburger conceives to be intended; and also that of Hofmann (comparing Acts xvii. 29; 2 Pet. i. 4), that the *spiritual nature* of the divine being is denoted. We may add that Rückert holds the strange view, that θειότης, which could not properly be predicated of God, is only used here by Paul for want of another expression. It might be and was necessarily said of God, as being the only adequate comprehensive expression for the conception that was to be denoted thereby. For analogous references to the physico-theological knowledge of God, see Wetstein, and Spiess, *Logos spermaticos*, 1871, p. 212. The suggestion of Philo as the Apostle's source (Schneckenburger) is out of the question. Observe further how completely, in our passage, the *transcendental* relation of God to the world—the negation of all identity of the two—lies at the foundation of the Apostle's view. It does not exclude the *immanence* of God in the world, but it excludes all *pantheism*. See the passages from the O. T. discussed in Umbreit. — εἰς τὸ εἶναι αὐτοὺς ἀναπολ.] has its logically correct reference to the immediately preceding τὰ γὰρ ἀόρατα.... θειότης, and therefore the *parenthesis*, in which Griesbach and others have placed τὰ γὰρ ἀόρ..... θειότης, must be expunged. The εἰς cannot be said of the *result*, as Luther, and many others, including Reiche, Köllner, de Wette, Rückert, Fritzsche, Reithmayr, Philippi, Ewald, following the Vulgate (*ita ut sint inexcusabiles*), have understood it; for the view,

---

[1] On the difference between this word and θεότης (Col. ii. 9), which denotes *Deitas, Godhead*, the *being God*, see Elsner, *Obss.* p. 6, and Fritzsche *in loc.* Van Hengel has erroneously called in question the distinction. In Wisd. xviii. 9, namely, ὁ τῆς θειότητος νόμος is not the law *of the Godhead*, but the law whose nature and character is *divinity*,—of a divine kind; and in Lucian, *de Calumn.* 17, ἡ Ἡφαιστίωνος θειότης is the *divinity* of Hephaestion, his divine *quality*. In Plutarch θειότης very frequently occurs. Appropriately rendered in Vulgate by *divinitas*.

F

which takes it of the *purpose*, is not only required by the prevailing usage of εἰς with the infinitive[1] (see on 2 Cor. viii. 6), but is also more appropriate to the connection, because the καθορᾶται is conceived as a result effected through God's revelation of Himself (ver. 19), and consequently the idea of the divine purpose in εἰς τὸ εἶναι κ.τ.λ. is not to be arbitrarily dismissed. Comp. Erasmus ("ne quid haberent" etc.), Melancthon ("*propter quas causas* Deus" etc.), Beza, Calvin ("*in hoc ut*"), Bengel and others. But Chrysostom, even in his time, expressly opposes this view (comp. also Oecumenius), and at a later period it became a subject of contention between the *Lutherans* and the *Reformed*. See Calovius. The view, which interprets it of the *result*, hesitates to admit the conception of a divine *decree*, under which Paul places the inexcusableness of men; and yet not only *may* this stand to the perception of God from His works which has existed since the beginning in the relation of *result*, but, in accordance with the thoroughly Scriptural idea of destiny (comp. *e.g.* v. 20), it *must* stand to it in the relation of that *decree*. In *this* connection, which inserts the results in the divine *counsel*, the inexcusableness of man appears as *telically given* with the self-manifestation of God. Ver. 21, as in general even ver. 18, contains the perverse conduct of men manifesting itself in the course of human history, *on account of which* God, who foresaw it, has in His natural self-manifestation made their inexcusableness His aim. *Inexcusable* they are intended to be; and that indeed *on account of the fact, that, although they had known God* (namely from that natural revelation), *they have not glorified Him as God.* — διότι] as in ver. 19, only to be separated by a comma from what precedes: inexcusable *on this account, because.* — γνόντες] not: cum agnoscere *potuissent* (Flatt, Nielsen; also as early as Oecumenius); nor yet: although they *knew* God, so that it would be *contemporaneous* with οὐχ .... ἐδόξασαν. So Philippi and van Hengel;

---

[1] Εἰς, with an infinitive having the article, is not used in a single passage, of the Epistle to the Romans in particular, in any other than a *telic* sense. See i. 11, iii. 26, iv. 11, 16, 18, vi. 12, vii. 4, 5, viii. 29, xi. 11, xii. 2, 3, xv. 8, 13, 16. Far too hastily de Wette terms this interpretation in our passage *senseless*, and Baumgarten-Crusius agrees with him. Tholuck calls it grammatical terrorism. Hofmann recognises the telic view as the true one in all cases where εἰς is used with the infinitive.

also Delitzsch, *bibl. Psychol.* p. 346. They had attained the knowledge from the revelation of nature (for to this, according to vv. 19, 20, we must refer it, and not, with Rückert, to the history in Genesis of the original revelation), but only *actu directo*, so far as that same self-manifestation of God had presented itself objectively to their cognition; the *actus reflexus* remained absent (comp. Delitzsch, p. 347), and with them who keep down the truth ἐν ἀδικίᾳ, ver. 18, the issue was not to the praise of God, etc.; so that γνόντες is thus *previous* to the οὐχ .... ἐδόξασαν. Paul sets forth the historical *emergence* of that for which they were inexcusable. They *had* known God, and yet it happened that they did not praise Him, etc. — οὐχ ὡς Θεὸν ἐδόξασαν ἢ ηὐχαρ.] It would have been becoming for them to have rendered to God as such, agreeably to His known nature, praise and thanks; but they did neither the one nor the other. Regarding ὡς in the sense: *according to the measure of His divine quality*, comp. on John i. 14. The *praising* and *thanksgiving* exhaust the notion of the *adoration*, which they should have offered to God. — ἀλλ' ἐματ. ἐν τοῖς διαλ. αὐτῶν] *but they were frustrated in their thoughts* (comp. 1 Cor. iii. 20), so that the conceptions, ideas, and reflections, which they formed for themselves regarding the Deity, were wholly devoid of any intrinsic value corresponding with the truth. Comp. Eph. iv. 17. The ματαιότης is a specific attribute of heathenism. Jer. ii. 5; 2 Kings xvii. 5; Ps. xciv. 11. Comp. also Acts xiv. 15; Judith vi. 4. — καὶ ἐσκοτίσθη κ.τ.λ.] forms a climax to the foregoing. Comp. Eph. iv. 18, i. 18. Their heart that had been rendered by the ἐματαιώθησαν unintelligent, incapable of discerning the true and right, became *dark*, completely deprived of the light of the divine ἀλήθεια that had come to them by the revelation of nature. καρδία, like לֵב, denotes the whole *internal seat of life*, the power which embraces all the activity of reason and will within the personal consciousness. Comp. on Eph. i. 18; Delitzsch, p. 250. To take ἀσύνετος here in a *proleptic* sense (see on Matth. xii. 13) is quite inappropriate, because it destroys the climax. Comp. moreover on ἀσύνετος, Wisd. xi. 15; as also on the entire delineation of Gentile immorality, ver. 20 ff.; Wisd. xiii.–xv. This passage as a whole, and in its details, presents unmistakeable reminiscences of this section of the book of

Wisdom. See Nitzsch in the *Deutsch. Zeitschr.* 1850, p. 387; Bleek in the *Stud. u. Krit.* 1853, p. 340 f. Without reason Tholuck argues against this view.

Vv. 22, 23. In a *false conceit of wisdom* (comp. 1 Cor. i. 17 ff.) this took place (viz. what has just been announced in ἐματαιώθησαν .... καρδία), and what a horrible *actual result* it had! — The construction is independent, no longer hanging on the διότι in ver. 21 (Glöckler, Ewald); the *further* course of the matter is described. *While they said that they were wise* (comp. 1 Cor. iii. 21), *they became foolish.* Comp. Jer. x. 24 f. This becoming foolish must be understood as something *self-incurred*—produced through the conceit of independence—as is required by the description of God's *retribution* on them in ver. 24; therefore the "*dirigente Deo,*" which Grotius understands along with it in accordance with 1 Cor. i. 21, is here foreign to the connection. The explanation of Köllner, Baumgarten-Crusius, and others, including Usteri: "*they have shown themselves as fools,*" is erroneous, because the aorist passive in ver. 21 does not admit of a similar rendering. —For examples of φάσκειν, *dictitare*, in the sense of *unfounded* assertion (Acts xxiv. 9, xxv. 19; Rev. ii. 2), see Raphel, *Xenoph.* and Kypke. Comp. Dem. *Phil.* i. 46, iii. 9; Herodian, iii. 12, 9. Their pretended wisdom was a μάταιος δοξοσοφία, Plat. *Soph.* p. 231 B. We may add that this definition is not aimed at the Gentile *philosophers,* who came much later and in fact did *not* do what is declared in ver. 23 (comp. Calvin), but generally at the *conceit of wisdom* (1 Cor. i. 21), which is necessarily connected with an estrangement from divine truth, and from which therefore idolatry also, with its manifold self-invented shapes, must have proceeded. For heathenism is not the primeval religion, from which man might gradually have risen to the knowledge of the true God, but is, on the contrary, the result of a falling away from the known original revelation of the true God in His works. Instead of the practical recognition and preservation of the truth thus given comes the self-wisdom rendering them foolish, and idolatry in its train. — καὶ ἤλλαξ. κ.τ.λ.] *and they exchanged the majesty of the imperishable God for a likeness of an image of a perishable man,* etc., *i.e.* instead of making, as they ought to have done, the glory of the eternal God manifested to them in the revelation of nature—כְּבוֹד יְהוָה, *i.e.* His glorious perfection (ver. 20)—the object of their adoration, they chose for that purpose *what was shaped like an image of a perishable man*, etc.; comp. Ps. cvi. 20; Jer. ii. 11. The ἐν (comp. Ecclus. vii. 18) is *instrumental*, as is elsewhere the simple dative (Herod. vii. 152; Soph. *Niob.* fr. 400, Dind.): thereby, that they made and adored such an ὁμοίωμα, and on the other hand rejected the gl y of God, which they ought to have worshipped. Comp. LXX. Ps. *l.c.*; ἠλλάξαντο τὴν δόξαν αὐτῶν ἐν ὁμοιώματι μόσχου. On the *genitive* εἰκόνος comp. also 1 Macc. iii. 48; Rev. ix. 7; and on ὁμοίωμα itself in the sense of *likeness*, v. 14, vi. 5, viii. 3; Phil. ii. 7; Ecclus. xxxviii. 28; 2 Kings xvi. 10; Isa. xl. 18; 1 Sam. vi. 5; Plat. *Phaedr.* p. 250 A; *Parm.* p. 132 D. It is not mere *similarity*, but *conformity* with the object of comparison concerned as agreeing therewith in appearance; see also Holsten, *z. Ev. des Paul. u. Petr.* p. 440; Pfleiderer in Hilgenfeld's *Zeitschr.* p. 523 f. — καὶ πετειν. κ. τετραπ. κ. ἑρπ.] No doubt as Paul, in using ἀνθρώπου, thought of the forms of the Hellenic gods, so in πετειν. κ.τ.λ. he had in his mind the Egyptian worship of animals (Ibis, Apis, serpents). Philo, *Leg. ad. Caj.* p. 566, 570. For passages from profane authors respecting the *folly* (at which the φθαρτοῦ here also points) of image-worship, see especially Dougtaeus, *Anal.* 69, p. 102, Grotius and Wetstein. We may add that, like the previous φθαρτοῦ ἀνθρώπου, the genitives πετεινῶν κ.τ.λ. are dependent on εἰκόνος, not on ὁμοιώματι (van Hengel), which is less natural and not required by the singular εἰκόνος, that in fact refers to *each particular instance* in which a man, birds, etc. were copied for purposes of divine adoration by means of statues and other representations.

Ver. 24. *Wherefore* (as a penal retribution for their apostasy) *God also gave them up in the lusts of their hearts to impurity.* καὶ, *also*, indicates the giving up as a thing *corresponding* to the guilt. Comp. on Phil. ii. 9. — ἐν ταῖς ἐπιθ. τ. κ. αὐτ.] contains that, *in which they were involved*, *i.e.* the moral condition in which they were found when they were given up by God to impurity. Comp. ver. 27; Eph. ii. 3; Bernhardy, p. 209. The *instrumental* rendering (Erasmus, Er. Schmid, Glöckler and Krehl) is unnecessary, because the immediate literal sense of ἐν is quite sufficient, and the former is less suitable as to sense, since it conveys something which is obvious of itself. — παρέδωκεν] expresses the *real active giving up* on the part of God. The favourite explanation of it by εἴασε, so often resorted to since Origen and Chrysostom, is nothing but a rationalising gloss at variance with the literal meaning. To the Apostle God is the *living* God, who does not passively *permit* the retributive consequences of fidelity or of apostasy—thus, as it were, letting *them run their course,* as an artificer does with his wheel work—but Himself, everywhere active, pervades and effectively develops the arrangements which He has made. If then God has so arranged that man by apostasy from Him should fall into moral impurity, and that thus sin shall be punished by sin (and this connection of sin with sin is in accordance both with experience and Scripture, Is. vi. 10; Job viii. 4; Ps. lxix. 28, lxxxi. 13; Mark iv. 12), this arrangement can only be carried out in reality through the effective action of its originator; and God Himself must give up the apostates unto impurity, inasmuch as it is by *His* doing that that moral connection is in point of fact accomplished. Comp. Acts vii. 42; Rom. ix. 19; also 2 Thess. ii. 11 f.; and the rabbinical passages quoted by Schoettgen, especially from *Pirke Aboth*, c. 4 : "Festina ad praeceptum leve tanquam ad grave, et fuge transgressionem; praeceptum enim trahit praeceptum, et transgressio transgressionem : quia merces praecepti praeceptum est, et transgressionis transgressio." Consequently, if the understanding of παρέδωκεν in its strictly proper and positive meaning is quite in keeping with the universal agency of God, in His physical and moral government of the world, without, however, making God appear as the author of sin, which, on the contrary, has its root in the ἐπιθυμίαι τ. καρδ., we must reject as insufficient the *privative* interpretation[1] that became current after Augustine and Oecumenius, which Calovius has adopted in part, and Rückert entirely. Comp. Philippi, who thinks of the withdrawal of the Divine Spirit and its results, though in the sense of a positive divine infliction of punish-

---

[1] It is at bottom identical with the *permissive* rendering. Therefore Chrysostom not only explains it by εἴασεν, but illustrates the matter by the instance of a general who *leaves* his soldiers in the battle, and thus deprives them of his aid, and abandons them to the enemy. Theodoret explains it : τῆς οἰκείας προμηθείας ἐγύμνωσε, and employs the comparison of an abandoned vessel. Theophylact illustrates the παρέδωκεν by the example of a physician who gives up a refractory patient (παραδίδωσιν αὐτὸν τῷ ἐπὶ πλέον νοσεῖν).

ment. This withdrawal, through which man is left in the lurch by God, is the immediate negative *precursor* of the παρέδωκεν (Ecclus. iv. 19). Reiche thinks that Paul here avails himself, with more or less consciousness of its being erroneous, of the general view of the Jews regarding the origin of the peculiar wickedness of the Gentiles (Ps. lxxxi. 13; Prov. xxi. 8; Ecclus. iv. 19; Wisd. x. 12, xiii. 1; Acts vii. 42); and that this representation of moral depravity as a divine punishment is to be distinguished from the Christian doctrinal system of the Apostle. But how very inconsistent it is with the character of Paul thus consciously to bring forward what is erroneous, and that too with so solemn a repetition (vv. 26, 28)! And is it not an arrangement accordant with experience, that apostasy from God is punished by an ever deeper fall into immorality? Can this arrangement, made as it is by God "justo judicio" (Calvin), be carried out otherwise than by God? Analogous are even heathen sayings, such as Aesch. *Agam.* 764 ff., and the heathen idea of the θεοβλάβεια; comp. also Ruhnken, *ad Vellej.* ii. 57, 3. But just as man, while his fidelity is rewarded by God through growth in virtue, remains withal free and does not become a virtuous machine; so also he retains his freedom, while God accomplishes the development of His arrangement, in accordance with which sin is born of sin. He *gives himself* up (Eph. iv. 19), while he *is* given up by God to that tragic *nexus* of moral destiny; and he becomes no machine of sin, but possesses at every moment the capacity of μετάνοια, which the very reaction resulting from the feeling of the most terrible misery of sin—punished through sin—is designed to produce. Therefore, on the one hand, man always remains responsible for his deterioration (ver. 32, ii. 6, iii. 5, vii. 14); and, on the other, that punishment of sin, in which the teleological law of the development of evil fulfils itself, includes no contradiction of the holiness of God. For this reason the view of Köllner—that the Apostle's idea is to be separated from its Jewish and temporal form, and that we must assume as the Christian truth in it, that the apostasy of men from God has brought them into deepest misery, as certainly as the latter is self-inflicted—is a superfluous unexegetical evasion, to which Fritzsche also has recourse. — ἀκαθαρσίαν] *spurcitia, impurity,* and that *lustful* (comp. Gal. v. 19; Eph. iv. 19; Col.

iii. 5), as is plain from the following context; not generally: "all action and conduct dishonouring the creaturely glory of man" (Hofmann). The τοῦ ἀτιμάζεσθαι may be taken either as the genitive of the purpose: *that* they might be dishonoured (Rückert, Philippi, van Hengel), or as the genitive of more precise definition depending on ἀκαθαρσ. (impurity of *the becoming dishonoured, i.e.* which *consisted therein;* so Fritzsche, Winer, Tholuck and de Wette). The latter (see Buttmann, *neut. Gr.* p. 230 f.) is the more probable, partly because the ἀτιμάζεσθαι κ.τ.λ. already constitutes the impurity itself, and does not merely attend it as a result; and partly on account of the parallel in ver. 28, where ποιεῖν κ.τ.λ. is likewise *epexegetical*. ἀτιμάζεσθαι is not however the *middle*, whereby the αὐτοπαθές would be expressed, for which there is no empirical usage, but the *passive: that their bodies were dishonoured among themselves*, mutually. This ἐν ἑαυτοῖς refers to the persons (αὐτῶν, not to be written αὑτῶν), not asserting that the ἀτιμάζεσθαι takes place *on themselves*, which is in fact already conveyed by τὰ σώματα αὐτῶν,[1] but rather based on the nature of participation in unchastity, according to which they bring *one on the other reciprocally* the dishonouring of the body. In this personal reciprocity of those who practise unchastity with each other lies the characteristic abominableness of the dishonouring of the body; and this point is designated by ἐν ἑαυτοῖς more expressly, because in contrast to non-participating third persons, than it would have been by ἐν ἀλλήλοις (Kühner, *ad Xen. Mem.* ii. 6, 20).—The *vices of unchastity*, which moreover are still here referred to quite generally (it is otherwise in ver. 26 f.), and not specially as unnatural, according to their disgraceful nature, in whatever forms they may have been practised, are specifically *heathen* (in fact, even partially belonging to the heathen *cultus*), as a consequence of apostasy from the true God (comp. 1 Thess. iv. 5). As they again prevail even among Christians, wherever this apostasy spreads through unbelief, they must verify even in Christendom their *heathen* nature, and, along with the likewise

---

[1] Hofmann refers the reading which he follows, ἐν αὐτοῖς, to the σώματα, but explains this: the body of each person *in himself;* consequently, as if the expression were ἐν ἑαυτοῖς, and that in the sense *in semet ipsis*. With the reading ἐν αὐτοῖς we should rather render it simply: in order that *among them* (*i.e. in their common intercourse*) their bodies should be dishonoured. Such was to be the course of things among them.

essentially heathen πλεονεξία, pre-eminently exclude from the salvation of the Messiah (Eph. v. 5 f.; Col. iii. 5 ; 1 Cor. vi. 9 f.).— With ἀτιμάζ. τ. σώμ. compare the opposite, 1 Thess. iv. 4, where τὸ ἑαυτοῦ σκεῦος must be explained of the body as the vessel of the Ego proper.

Ver. 25. Οἵτινες μετήλλαξαν κ.τ.λ.] *as those who exchanged*, etc. In this description of the character of those who are given up, attached to ver. 24, Paul makes once more apparent the motive which determined God to give them up. The words are a renewed tragic commentary (comp. vv. 22, 23) on the διό, ver. 24. On ὅστις, *quippe qui*, which brings up the class to which one belongs, and thereby includes the specification of the reason, see Hermann, *ad Soph. Oed. R.* 688 ; Matthiae, p. 1073. Hofmann erroneously makes a relative protasis begin with οἵτινες, with which then διὰ τοῦτο κ.τ.λ., ver. 26, would be connected by way of apodosis : *them, who exchanged* etc., God *has therefore* given up. This would not be inconsistent with αὐτούς in ver. 26, which would then be resumptive ; but the very praise of God, in which ver. 25 terminates, and still more the concluding ἀμήν, which can only indicate the end of the sentence (comp. ix. 5, xi. 36 ; Gal. i. 5 ; Eph. iii. 21), ought to have decidedly precluded such a forced intermixture of sentences, which is not to be justified by subtleties.—The compound μετήλλ. (*exchanged*) is more significant than ἤλλαξαν (*changed*) in ver. 23. — τὴν ἀλήθ. τοῦ Θεοῦ] to be taken entirely in harmony with the expression τὴν δόξαν τοῦ Θεοῦ in ver. 23 ; therefore τοῦ Θεοῦ is to be taken as genitive of the *subject*: *the truth of God*, the true divine reality,[1] so as to make it in point of actual meaning, though not in the abstract form of the conception, identical with : "*true God*" (Luther, and most expositors, including Rückert, de Wette, Tholuck, Fritzsche, Philippi, van Hengel). It is differently rendered by Wolf, whom Köllner follows : *the truth revealed* to the Gentiles *by God*. Reiche and Mehring (following Pareus, Camerarius, Estius, Seb. Schmid, and Cramer) take it as *the true knowledge of God*, so that Θεοῦ would be genitive of the *object*. Compare Piscator, Usteri and Glöckler, who understand by it the original consciousness of God. Opposed to these views is the exact parallel in which ver. 25 stands to ver. 23, so that τοῦ Θεοῦ ought not to be taken without necessity

---

[1] Not "the truth, *which God Himself is*" (Hofmann) ; but that, *which God is in true reality*. That is just the adequate substance of His δόξα.

as having a different reference in the two verses. τὴν ἀλήθ. τ. Θεοῦ is explained concretely by τὸν κτίσαντα in the second half of the verse. — ἐν τῷ ψεύδει] *with the lie;* ἐν as in ver. 23. By this Paul means, in contrast to τὴν ἀλήθ. τ. Θεοῦ (but otherwise than in iii. 7), *the false gods,* which are κατ' ἐξοχὴν the ψεῦδος *in concreto,* the negation of the truth of God. Comp. on 1 Cor. viii. 4 f., x. 20. Grotius has aptly said: "pro Deo vero sumserunt imaginarios." Comp. Is. xliv. 20; Jer. iii. 10, xiii. 25, xvi. 19, *al.;* Philo, *vit. Mos.* p. 678 C, p. 679 A. — καὶ ἐσεβάσθησαν .... κτίσαντα] more precise explanation of the first clause of the verse. — ἐσεβ. κ. ἐλάτρ.] The former is *general (coluerunt),* the latter took place through *sacrifices,* and other definite *rites* and *services;* hence Paul designates his own specific service of God in ver. 8 by λατρεύω. σεβάζομαι, in Homer: *to be afraid of* (*Il.* vi. 167, 417), is employed in the later Greek like σέβομαι in the sense *to revere,* Orph. *Arg.* 550, Aq. *Hos.* x. 5. In the N. T. it only occurs here. — τῇ κτίσει] Corresponding with the verb standing next to it, so that the accusative is to be supplied with ἐσεβ. See Matthiae, § 428, 2. — παρὰ τ. κτίσαντα] in the sense of *comparison: prae creatore,* in which case the context alone decides whether the preference of the one before the other is only *relative,* or whether it *excludes* the latter altogether (see on Luke xviii. 14; and van Hengel on our passage). The second case is that which occurs here, in accordance both with the nature of the case, seeing that the Gentiles did not worship the Creator at all, and with the immediate connection (μετήλλαξαν .... ἐν τῷ ψεύδει). The sense therefore substantially amounts to *practerito creatore* (Hilary), or *relicto creatore* (Cyprian), *i.e.* they honoured the creature and *not* the Creator, whom they ought to have honoured. Theophylact says aptly, with reference to the *comparative* παρά: ἐκ τῆς συγκρίσεως τὸ ἔγκλημα ἐπαίρων. So in substance also Beza, Estius, and others, including Reiche, Tholuck, Olshausen, de Wette, Baumgarten-Crusius, Krehl, Reithmayr, Maier, Philippi, van Hengel. The *relative* interpretation: *more than the Creator* (Vulgate, Erasmus, Luther, Castalio, Grotius, Ammon, Rückert, and others), is therefore in point of fact erroneous. The *contra creatorem,* which Hammond, Koppe, Flatt, Fritzsche and Mehring find here, may likewise be traced to the sense of comparison (see Bernhardy, p. 259; Winer, p.

377 [E. T. 504]; and the passages from Plato in Ast. *Lex.* III. p. 28), but has against it the fact, that in the whole context Paul presents the matter in the light of a μετάλλαξις, of an *exchanging* the true for the false, not of *hostility* to the true. From that point of view the Gentiles have worshipped the creature, and not the Creator. Quite parallel is παρ' ἐκεῖνον in Luke, xviii. 14, Lachm. — The doxology: *who is praised*, בָּרוּךְ, not: *celebrandus* (comp. on Eph. i. 3; 2 Cor. xi. 31; Mark xiv. 61), *for ever! Amen,*—is a natural effusion of deeply-moved piety, called forth by the detestable contrast of the Gentile abominations just described, without any further special design (Koppe: " ne ipse in majestatem divinam injurius videri possit;" comp. Tholuck).

Vv. 26, 27. Διὰ τοῦτο] Beginning an independent sentence (against Hofmann, see on ver. 25), refers to the description οἵτινες.... κτίσαντα contained in ver. 25. The giving up is set forth *once more* (comp. ver. 24, διό) as the punishment of apostasy, and now indeed with such increasing force of delineation, that out of the category which is kept quite general in ver. 24 *unnatural sensual abominations* are specially adduced. — εἰς πάθη ἀτιμίας] Genitive of quality. Comp. on πνεῦμα ἁγιωσύνης in ver. 4, and Bornemann, *Schol. in Luc.* p. 21. Parallel to the *passions of a disgraceful character* is εἰς ἀκαθαρσίαν in ver. 24; comp. Col. iii. 5; but the stronger expression here selected prepares the way for the following description of a peculiarly abominable form of vice. Still the *unnatural* element is not implied in πάθη ἀτιμίας itself (Hofmann: they are a dishonouring, not merely of the *body*, but of "*humanity*"), since morally dishonouring passions are the agents, not only in the case of unnatural, but also in that of natural unchastity. — Respecting τὲ γάρ, *namque, for ....indeed* (vii. 7; 2 Cor. x. 8), see Hermann, *ad Soph. Trach.* 1015; Hartung, I. p. 115; Klotz, *ad Devar.* p. 749 ff. — The expressions θήλειαι and ἄρσενες, their *females* and their *males*, not γυναῖκες and ἄνδρες, are chosen *because* the predominant *point of view is simply that of sex;* Reiche thinks: out of contempt, because the words would also be used of beasts; but in fact, such unnatural things are foreign to the very beasts. Besides, the words are used even of the gods (Homer, *Il.* viii. 7, and frequently). — τὴν φυσικὴν χρῆσιν] of *their* sex, not: of the *male*, which is unsuitable to the vice indicated. Regarding χρῆσις in the sense of sexual use, see Wetstein and Kypke, also Coray, *ad Heliodor. Aeg.*, p. 31. — How very prevalent among the Gentiles (it was found also among the Jews, see Schoettgen, *Hor. in loc.*) was the so-called *Lesbian vice*, λεσβιάζειν (Lucian, *D. Mer.* 5. 2), women with women abusing their sex (*tribades*, in Tertullian *frictrices*), see Salmasius, *foen. Trapez.* p. 143 f., 152 f.; and the commentators on Ael. *V. H.* iii. 12. Comp. the ἑταιρίστριαι in Plat. *Symp.* p. 191 E, and the ἀσέλγεια τριβακή in Luc. *Amor.* 28; and see Ruhnken, *ad Tim.* p. 124, and generally Rosenbaum, *Gesch. d. Lustseuche im Alterth.* ed. 2, 1845. — That ὁμοίως δὲ καί after the preceding τέ makes the latter an *anakoluthon*, is commonly assumed, but altogether without foundation, because in τὲ γάρ the τέ does not necessarily require any correlative. See Klotz *l.c.* If it were put correlatively, we should have in ὁμοίως δὲ καί the other corresponding member really present (as is actually the case, *e.g.* in Plat. *Symp.* p. 186 E), which however would in that case inappropriately stand out with *greater emphasis* and *weight* than the former[1] (Stallbaum, *ad Plat. Polit.* p. 270 D, *Rep.* p. 367 C; Dissen, *ad Pind. Ol.* viii. 56; Klausen, *ad Aesch. Choeph.* p. 199). The reading τέ (instead of δέ) in Elz., as well as the entire omission of the particle (C, min., Origen, Jerome), is a too hasty emendation. — ἐξεκαύθησαν] Stronger than the simple form. Comp. Alciphr. iii. 67; ἐξεκαύθην εἰς ἔρωτα. Such a *state* is the πυροῦσθαι in 1 Cor. vii. 9. Moreover, Paul represents here not the heat that *precedes* the act of unchastity, but that which is kindled *in the act itself* (κατεργαζόμενοι .... ἀπολαμβάνοντες). — ἄρσενες ἐν ἄρσεσι] *whilst they, males on males, performed the* (known, from ver. 26) *unseemliness*. On the emphatic juxtaposition of ἄρσ. ἐν ἄρσ. comp. generally Lobeck, *ad Aj.* 522, and in particular Porphyr. *de abstin.* iv. 20; and Wetstein *in loc.* On κατεργαζεσθαι, which is used both of evil (ii. 9, vii. 9, xv. 17 f.) and good (v. 3, xv. 18; Phil. ii. 12), but which, as distinguished from ἐργάζεσθαι, always expresses the

---

[1] Hofmann thinks that with ὁμοίως δὲ καί κ.τ.λ. the argument ascends *to the greater danger for the continuance of the human race*. But that is a purely imported thought. The Apostle's point of view is the *moral* ἀτιμία, which, in the case of female depravity, comes out *most glaringly*. And therefore Paul, in order to cast the most tragic light possible on these conditions, puts the brief delineation of female conduct in the foreground, in order then symmetrically to subjoin, with ὁμοίως δὲ καί, the *male* vice as the second part of the filthy category

bringing to pass, the *accomplishment*, comp. especially ii. 9, and van Hengel thereon; 1 Cor. v. 3; 2 Cor. vii. 10, and the critical remarks thereon. On ἀσχημ. see Gen. xxxiv. 7. — τὴν ἀντιμισθίαν κ.τ.λ.] The *aberration*, which Paul means, see in vv. 21-23, 28; it is the aberration *from God to idols*, not that implied in the *sexual perversion of the divine order* (Hofmann), which perversion, on the contrary, is brought by διό in ver. 24, and by διὰ τοῦτο in ver. 26, under the point of view of penal *retribution* for the πλάνη. By the *recompense* for the πλάνη Paul does not at all mean that the men " *have that done to them by their fellows, which they themselves do to theirs*" (Hofmann), but rather, in harmony with the connection of cause and effect, the abominable *unnatural lusts* just described, to which God has given up the Gentiles, and thereby, in recompensing godlessness through such wicked excesses (ver. 18), revealed His ὀργή. Therefore also ἣν ἔδει is added, namely, in accordance with the necessity of the holy divine order. See vv. 24, 26, 28. On ἀντιμισθία comp. 2 Cor. vi. 13; Clem. Cor. II. 1. It occurs neither in Greek authors, who have the adjective ἀντίμισθος (Aesch. *Suppl.* 273), nor in the LXX. or Apocrypha. — ἐν ἑαυτοῖς] *on themselves mutually* (ἐν ἀλλήλοις), as in ver. 24. It enhances the *sadness* of the description. For a number of passages attesting the prevalence of unchastity between man and man, especially of paederastia among the Gentiles, particularly the Greeks (it was forbidden to the Jews in Lev. xviii. 22), see Becker, *Charikl.* I. p. 346 ff.; Hermann, *Privatalterth.* § 29; Bernhardy, *Griech. Lit.* ed. 2, p. 50 ff. Moreover, Bengel aptly observes regarding the whole of this unreserved exposure of Gentile unchastity : " In peccatis arguendis saepe scapha debet scapha dici. Pudorem praeposterum ii fere postulant, qui pudicitia carent.... Gravitas et ardor stili judicialis proprietate verborum non violat verecundiam." Observe, nevertheless, how the Apostle delineates the *female* dishonour in less concrete traits than the male. He touches the matter in ver. 26 briefly and clearly enough, but with delicate avoidance of detailed description.

Ver. 28. From the previous exclusive description of the sensual vice of the Gentiles, Paul now proceeds to a summary enumeration of yet other vices to which they had been given up by God in punishment of their apostasy. — καθώς] is not causal, but *quemadmodum*. The giving them up was something *corresponding* to their disdainful rejection of the knowledge of God, *proportionate* as punishment. — οὐκ ἐδοκίμασαν] *they deemed God not worth* (1 Thess. ii. 4); οὐ γὰρ ἀγνοίας, ἀλλὰ μελέτης εἶναι φησὶ τὰ τολμήματα, Chrysostom. — ἔχειν ἐν ἐπιγνώσει] Their γνῶναι τὸν Θεόν, derived from the revelation of nature (ver. 21), ought to have been brought by cultivation to an ἐπιγνῶναι, that is, to a penetrating and living knowledge of God (see on Eph. i. 17; 1 Cor. xiii. 12); thus they would have attained to the having God ἐν ἐπιγνώσει; but they would not, and so became τὰ ἔθνη τὰ μὴ εἰδότα τὸν Θεόν, 1 Thess. iv. 5; Gal. iv. 8; Eph. ii. 12; Acts xvii. 30. On ἔχειν ἐν with an abstract noun, which represents the object as appropriated in the action, so that it is *possessed* in the latter (here in ἐπιγνῶναι), comp. Locella, *ad Xen. Eph.* p. 255. Similar is ἐν ὀργῇ ἔχειν, and the like, Krüger on *Thucyd.* ii. 8, 3. — εἰς ἀδόκ. νοῦν] An ingenious paronomasia with οὐκ ἐδοκίμ., to set forth the more prominently the *recompense*, to which the emphatically repeated ὁ Θεός also contributes: as they did not esteem God worthy, etc., God gave them up *to an unworthy*, reprobate νοῦς (the collective power of the mind's action in theoretic and moral cognition[1]). The rendering *judicii expers* (Beza, Glöckler and others) is opposed to the genius of the language, even as Bengel turns it, and Weiss, *bibl. Theol.* p. 280, defines it. The ἀδόκιμον of the νοῦς is its blameworthiness according to an *objective* moral standard, but does not express the mode of thinking which they themselves must condemn *among one another* (Th. Schott; comp. Hofmann), which is neither to be taken by anticipation from ver. 32, nor extracted from μή. — ποιεῖν τὰ μὴ καθήκοντα] *to do what is not becoming*, what is not moral. Comp. 3 Macc. iv. 16. The Stoical distinction between καθῆκον and κατόρθωμα Paul has not thought of (as Vitringa conceives). The infinitive is epexegetical: *so that they do*. The participle with μή indicates *the genus of that which is not seemly* (Baeumlein, *Partik.* p. 296); τὰ οὐ καθήκοντα (comp. Eph. v. 4), would be the *unseemly*. The *negative* expression is correlate to the ἀδόκιμος νοῦς.

---

[1] Comp. on vii. 23, and Kluge in the *Jahrb. f. D. Th.* 1871, p. 329. The νοῦς is ἀδόκιμος when, not receptive for divine truth, it does not determine the ethical conduct in accordance with it.

Vv. 29-31. Πεπληρωμένους πάσῃ ἀδικίᾳ] a more precise definition of ποιεῖν τὰ μὴ καθήκ.: *as those who are full of every unrighteousness* (ver. 18). This is the *general* statement, and all the points subsequently introduced are its several *species*, so that μεστοὺς φθόνου and then ψιθυριστὰς κ.τ.λ. are *appositions* to πεπληρ. π. ἀδικ. Similar catalogues of sins are 2 Cor. xii. 30; Gal. v. 19 ff.; Eph. v. 3 f.; 1 Tim. i. 9 f.; 2 Tim. iii. 2 ff. — πονηρία.... κακίᾳ] *malignity* (malice), comp. Eph. iv. 31; Col. iii. 8; Tit. iii. 3 .... *vileness* (meanness), the latter, in Aristotle and other writers, opposed to ἀρετή, and translated in Cicero, *Tusc.* iv. 15, 34, by *vitiositas*. Comp. 1 Cor. v. 8. — φόνου] Conceived here as the *thought* which has filled the man, the μερμηρίζειν φόνον, Homer, *Od.* xix. 2, comp. Acts ix. 1. On the paronomasia with φθόνου comp. Gal. v. 21. The latter is just the σημεῖον φύσεως παντάπασι πονηρᾶς, Dem. 499, 21. — κακοηθείας] *malicious disposition*, whose peculiarity it is ἐπὶ τὸ χεῖρον ὑπολαμβάνειν τὰ πάντα (Aristotle, *Rhet.* ii. 13). As the context requires a special vice, we may not adopt, with Erasmus, Calvin, and Homberg, the general signification *perversitas, corruptio morum* (Xen. *Cyn.* xiii. 16; Dem. 542, 11; Plat. *Rep.* p. 348 D). See regarding the word generally Homberg, *Parerg.* p. 196; Kypke, II. p. 155 f. — ψιθυρ.] *whisperers, talebearers*, consequently secret slanderers (Dem. 1358, 6); but κατάλαλοι, calumniators, detractors *generally*, not precisely *open ones* (Theophylact, Köllner, de Wette and others). Comp. ψιθυρισμούς τε καὶ καταλαλιάς, Clem. *Cor.* i. 35. The construction of καταλάλους as an adjective with ψιθυρ. (Hofmann), must be rejected, because none of the other elements has an adjectival definition annexed to it, and because καταλάλ. would not add to the notion of ψιθυρ. anything characteristic in the way of more precise definition. ψιθυρ. would be better fitted to form a limiting definition of καταλ. But in 2 Cor. xii. 20 also, both ideas stand independently side by side. — θεοστυγεῖς] *hated by God*, *Deo odibiles* (Vulgate). This *passive* rendering of the word which belongs especially to the tragedians (Pollux, i. 21), so that it is equivalent to Θεῷ ἐχθαιρόμενος (comp. Soph. *Aj.* 458), is clearly attested by the *usus loquendi* as the only correct one. See Eurip. *Troad.* 1213, *Cycl.* 395, 598, Neophr. *ap.* Stob. *serm.* 20, p. 172. Comp. θεοστύγητος in Aesch. *Choeph.* 635, Fritzsche *in loc.*, and Wetstein. Since no passage whatever supports the *active* signification, and since even Suidas and Oecumenius clearly betray that they knew the active meaning adopted by them to be a deviation from the usage of the ancient writers,[1] we must reject, with Koppe, Rückert, Fritzsche, de Wette, Philippi, Baumgarten-Crusius, and Hofmann, the interpretation, *Dei osores*, that has been preferred by the majority since the time of Theodoret.[2] Even the analogous forms that have been appealed to, θεομισής, βροτοστυγής (Aesch. *Choeph.* 51, *Prom.* 799), are to be taken as *passives*, and therefore testify against the active interpretation.[3] Comp. θεοβλαβής, stricken of God, Herod. viii. 137, *al.* In particular, θεομισής is quite the same as θεοστυγής, the opposite of θεοφιλής, beloved of God. (See Plat. *Rep.* p. 612 E, *Euth.* p. 8 A; Dem. 1486, ult.; Arist. *Ran.* 443.) Comp. θεῷ μισητοί, Wisd. xiv. 9; and, as regards the idea, the Homeric ὅς κε θεοῖσιν ἀπέχθηται μακάρεσσιν, *Od.* κ. 74. The accentuation θεόστυγης, approved of even by Grotius and Beza, to distinguish it from the passive θεοστυγής, is nothing but an ancient (Suidas) unsupported fiction. See Buttmann, II. p. 371 Winer, p. 53 [E. T. 61]. *God-hating* is expressed by μισόθεος, Lucian, *Tim.* 35, Aesch. *Ag.* 1090; comp. φιλόθεος, *God-loving*. The adoption, nevertheless, of the active sense was occasioned by the consideration: "ut in passivo positum dicatur, nulla est ratio, quum P. hic homines ex vitiis evidentibus reos faciat," Calvin; but even granting a certain unsuitableness in the pas-

---

[1] Suidas says: Θεοστυγεῖς θεομίσητοι, οἱ ὑπὸ Θεοῦ μισούμενοι καὶ οἱ Θεὸν μισοῦντες· παρὰ δὲ τῷ ἀποστόλῳ θεοστυγεῖς οὐχὶ οἱ ὑπὸ Θεοῦ μισούμενοι, ἀλλ' οἱ μισοῦντες τὸν Θεόν. Oecumenius : Θεοστυγεῖς δὲ οὐ τοὺς ὑπὸ Θεοῦ μισουμένους, οὐ γὰρ αὐτῷ τοῦτο δεῖξαι πρόκειται νῦν, ἀλλὰ τοὺς μισοῦντας Θεόν. These *negative* definitions, which both give, manifestly point to the use of the word in other authors, from which Paul here departs. It is doubtful whether Clement, *Cor.* I. 35, where there is an echo of our passage, had in view the active or the passive sense of θεοστυγεῖς. He uses indeed the evidently active θεοστυγία, but adds at the close of the list of sins : ταῦτα οἱ πράσσοντες στυγητοὶ τῷ Θεῷ ὑπάρχουσιν. Chrysostom does not express his opinion regarding the word.

[2] The *Dei osores* was taken to refer to the heathen vice of wrath against the gods conceived as possessing human passions. See Grotius and Reiche. Others have understood it variously. Tholuck thinks of accusers of providence, *Promethean characters;* Ewald, of *blasphemers of God;* Calvin, of those who have a horror of God *on account of His righteousness*. Thus there is introduced into the general expression what the context gives no hint of. This applies also to Luther's gloss: "the real *Epicureans*, who live as if there were no God."

[3] Even in Clem. *Hom.* i. 12, there is nothing whatever in the connection opposed to the passive rendering of θεοστυγεῖς.

sive sense, still we should not be justified in giving an explanation contrary to the *usus loquendi;* we should be obliged to abide by the view that Paul had mixed up a less suitable term among the others. But this objection is diminished, if we take θεοστ., in accordance with the idea of divine holiness, as a characteristic designation of *infamous evil-doers* in general. So Fritzsche, and also Philippi. Comp. Plat. *Legg.* viii. p. 838 B: θεομισῆ .... καὶ αἰσχρῶν αἴσχιστα. And it vanishes altogether, if, leaving the word in its strict signification, *hated of God,* we recognise in it a *summary judgment of moral indignation respecting all the preceding particulars;* so that, looking back on these, it forms a resting point in the disgraceful catalogue, the continuation of which is then carried on by ὑβριστὰς κ.τ.λ. According to Hofmann, θεοστυγ. is an *adjective* qualifying ὑβριστάς. But we do not see why precisely this single point[1] in the entire catalogue, *insolence* (the notion of which is not to be arbitrarily heightened, so as to make it denote " the *man-despiser who treads upon his fellows*"), among so many particulars, some of them even worse, should be accompanied by an epithet, and one, too, of so extreme severity. — The continuation begins with a threefold description of *self-exaltation,* and that in a descending climax. Regarding the distinction between ὑβρισταί, the *insolent* (qui prae superbia non solum contemnunt alios, sed etiam contumeliose tractant, comp. 1 Tim. i. 13), ὑπερήφανοι, the *proud* (who, proud of real or imaginary advantages, despise others), and ἀλαζόνες (*boasters, swaggerers,* without exactly intending to despise or insult others with their vainglory), see Tittmann, *Synon. N. T.* p. 73 f. Comp. Grotius and Wetstein; on ἀλαζ. especially Ruhnk. *ad Tim.* p. 28, Ast, *ad Theophr. Char.* 23. If ὑπερηφ. be taken as *adjective* with the latter (Hofmann), then the vice, which is invariably and intrinsically immoral,[2] would be limited merely to a particular *mode* of it.—ἐφευρ. κακῶν] *devisers* (Anacr. xli. 3) *of evil things,* quite general; not to be limited to things of

---

[1] For neither καταλάλ. nor ὑπερηφ. are to be taken as adjectives. See on those words. Hofmann seems to have adopted such a view, merely in order to gain analogies in the text for his inappropriate treatment of the objectionable θεοστυγεῖς as an adjective.

[2] See Xen. *Mem.* i. 7, 1 ff., where ἀλαζονεία is the antithesis of ἀρετή. It belongs to the category of the ψεύδεσθαι, Aesch. *adv. Ctesiph.* 99; Plat. *Lys.* p. 218 D. Compare also 2 Tim. iii. 2; Clem. *Cor.* I. 35.

luxury, with Grotius; nor, with Hofmann, to *evils* which they desire to *do to* others. Comp. 2 Macc. vii. 31, and the passages from Philo in Loesner; also Tacit. *Ann.* iv. 11, and Virg. *Aen.* ii. 161. — ἀσυνέτους] *irrational, unreflecting*, who, in what they do and leave undone, are not determined by the σύνεσις, by morally intelligent insight. Luther rightly says: "Mr. Unreason going rashly to work [Hans Unvernunft, mit dem Kopfe hindurch]." So also Ecclus. xv. 7. The rendering *devoid of conscience* (according to Suidas) deviates from the proper signification of the word. — ἀσυνθέτους] makes a paronomasia with the foregoing, and means, not *unsociable* (Castalio, Tittmann, Ewald, comp. Hofmann), for which there is no warrant of usage, but *covenant-breakers* (Jer. iii. 8, 10 f.; Suidas, Hesychius; see also Dem. 383, 6). On ἀστόργ. (without the natural affection of love) and ἀνελεήμ. (unmerciful), see Tittmann, *Synon.* p. 69. — The *succession* of the accumulated particulars is not arranged according to a *systematic* scheme, and the construction of such a scheme leads to arbitrary definition of the import of individual points; but still their distribution is so far in accordance with approximate categories, that there are presented: — 1*st*, The *general* heathen vices, πεπληρωμένους .... κακίᾳ; 2nd, *dispositions inimical* to others, μεστοὺς .... κακοηθείας, and calumniatory *speeches*, ψιθυρ., καταλάλ.; both series concluding with the general θεοστυγεῖς; then, 3*rd*, The *arrogant* character, ὑβριστὰς .... ἀλαζόνας; and finally, 4*th*, A series of negative particulars (all with a privative), but headed by the positive, general ἐφευρ. κακῶν. This negative series portrays the want of dutiful affection in family life (γον. ἀπειθ.), of intelligence (ἀσυνέτ.), fidelity (ἀσυνθ.), and love (ἀστόργ. ἀνελ.), — consequently the want of every principle on which moral action is based.

Ver. 32. Οἵτινες] *quippe qui, of such a character, that they*, cannot be the specification of a reason, as in ver. 25, and cannot consequently be intended to repeat once more the laying of the blame on themselves, since ver. 32 merely continues the description of the wickedness. It rather serves to introduce the *awful completion of this description of vice;* and that in such a way, that the Gentile immorality is brought clearly to light as *an opposition to knowledge and conscience*, and is thereby at the last very evidently shown to be wholly inexcusable (comp. ii. 1). — τὸ δικαίωμα τ. Θεοῦ] *i.e. that which God as Lawgiver and Judge has ordained; what He has determined, and demands, as right.* Comp. Krüger on *Thuc.* i. 41, 1; and see on v. 16. Paul means the natural law of the moral consciousness (ii. 15), which determines: ὅτι οἱ τὰ τοιαῦτα πράσσοντες κ.τ.λ. This ὅτι κ.τ.λ. therefore is not to be treated as a parenthesis. — ἐπιγνόντες] *although they have discerned* (comp. on ver. 28), not merely γνόντες; but so much the greater is the guilt. — θανάτου] What in the view of the heathen was conceived of as *the state of punishment in Hades* (comp. Philippi and Weiss, *bibl. Theol.* p. 277), which was incurred through vice and crime, Paul designates, in accordance with the truth involved in it (comp. Plat. *Rep.* p. 330 D), from *his* standpoint as θάνατος, and by this he means *eternal death* (comp. 2 Thess. i. 8); not *temporal* (Bengel, van Hengel, Mehring); or *execution* (Grotius, Hofmann); also not indefinitely *severe punishments*,[1] *the misery of sin*, and so forth (so even Fritzsche and de Wette). — συνευδοκ. τοῖς πράσσ.] *they are consenting with them that do them* (comp. Luke xi. 48; Acts viii. 1; 1 Cor. vii. 12; 1 Macc. i. 60; 2 Macc. xi. 24). They not only *do* those things, but are also in their moral judgment (so wholly antagonistic to conscience has the latter become in the abandonment unto which God has decreed them, ver. 28) *in agreement* with *others* who so act. Bengel well remarks: " pejus est συνευδοκεῖν; nam qui malum patrat, sua sibi cupiditate abducitur," etc., and how sharply are we otherwise ourselves accustomed to see and judge the mote in the eye of another! (Matth. vii. 3). This climax[2] to the description of immorality, moreover, is neither to be referred with Grotius and Baumgarten-Crusius to the philosophers, who approved of several vices (paederastia, revenge, etc.) or regarded them as *adiaphora;* nor with Heumann and Ewald to the magistrates, who left many crimes unpunished and even furthered them by their own example; but, in harmony with the quite general delineation of Gentile depravity, to be taken as a general feature marking the latter, which is thus laid bare in the deepest

---

[1] Melancthon says well against this view: " P. non loquitur de politica gubernatione, quae tantum externa facta punit : verum de judicio proprio in cujusque conscientia intuente Deum."

[2] The *climax* lies necessarily in ἀλλὰ καὶ (in opposition to Reiche, *Comm. crit.* p. 6).

slough of moral perversity. — The πράσσοντες and πράσσουσι are more *comprehensive* than the simple ποιοῦσιν (do), designating the *pursuit* of these immoralities as the aim of their activity. See on John iii. 20. Comp. Rom. ii. 3, vii. 15, xiii. 4; Dem. *de cor.* 62: τί προσῆκον ἦν ἑλέσθαι πράττειν κ. ποιεῖν.

CHAPTER II.

Ver. 5. After ἀποκαλ. D*** K L ℵ**, min., and several versions and Fathers, including Or., read καί, which is adopted by Mill, Wetst. Matth. and Fritzsche.[1] Against it is the greatly preponderant authority of the uncials, and the suspicion of having been added by way of relief to the accumulation of genitives. — Ver. 8. μέν after ἀπειθ. is wanting in B D* G ℵ*, and is omitted by Lachm. and Tisch. (8), but was easily passed over from inattention as seeming superfluous.—The order ὀργὴ καὶ θυμός (thus also Lachm. and Tisch.) is decisively attested. — Ver. 13. The article before νόμου, which Elz. and Fritzsche read both times, but which Lachm. and Tisch. both times omit, is wanting in A B D E (which however has it in the first case) G ℵ, 31, 46, Damasc.; and betrays itself in the general form of the saying as inserted in order to denote the Mosaic law. — Ver. 14. ποιῇ] Lachm. and Tisch. read ποιῶσιν, following A B ℵ, min., Clem. Or. Damasc. (D* G have ποιοῦσιν). The plural is an amendment suggested by the context. — Ver. 16. Instead of ὅτε Lachm. following A and some Fathers, has ᾗ.; an interpretation; as is also ἐν ᾗ ἡμέρᾳ in B. — Ver. 17. εἰ δέ] The too weakly attested Recepta ἴδε or ἰδέ is either a mere copyist's error, or an alteration to get rid of the supposed anakoluthon. See Reiche, *Comm. crit.*

Ver. 1.—ch. iii. 20. Having shown, ch. i. 18-32, in the case of the *Gentiles*, that they were strangers to the δικαιοσύνη Θεοῦ, Paul now, ch. ii.-iii. 20, exhibits the same fact with reference to the Jews, and thus adduces the second half of the proof as to the *universal* necessity of justification by *faith*. Naturally the Apostle was chiefly concerned with this *second* half of the proof, as the ἀδικία of heathenism was in itself clear; but we see from ch. ii. that the detailed character of that delineation of Gentile wickedness was intended at the same time as a mirror for degenerate Judaism, to repress all Jewish conceit. Comp. Mangold, p. 102.

[1] Defended also by Philippi and Reiche, *Comm. crit.*, who thinks that the καί has been rejected on account of ἀποκαλ. appearing not to receive more precise definition. See on the other hand van Hengel.

Ver. 1. Διό] refers back to the *main tenor of the whole previous exposition* (vv. 18-32), and that indeed in its more special aspect as setting forth the moral condition of heathenism in respect to its *inexcusableness*. This reference is confirmed by the fact, that ἀναπολόγητος εἶ is said with a manifest glancing back to i. 20; it is laid down by Paul as it were as a finger-post for his διό. The reference assumed by Reiche, Fritzsche, Krehl, de Wette, and older writers, to the proposition in ver. 32, that the rightful demand of God adjudges death to the evil-doers; or to the *cognizance* of that verdict, in spite of which the Gentiles were so immoral (Philippi, Baur, Th. Schott, Hofmann, Mangold), has against it the fact that this thought formed only a *subsidiary sentence* in what went before; whereas here a new section begins, at the head of which Paul very naturally has placed a reference, even expressly marked by ἀναπολόγητος, to the entire section ending with ver. 32, over which he now throws once more a retrospective glance. The connection of ideas therefore is: "*wherefore*," *i.e.* on account of that abomination of vice pointed out in vv. 18-32, "*thou art inexcusable*," etc.; "*for*"—to exhibit now more exactly this "*wherefore*"—*wherein thou judgest the other, thou condemnest thyself, because thou doest the same thing.* In other words: before the mirror of this Gentile life of sin all excuse vanishes from thee, O man who judgest, for this mirror reflects thine own conduct, which thou thyself therefore condemnest by thy judgment. A deeply tragic *de te narratur!* into which the proud Jewish consciousness sees itself all of a sudden transferred. A proleptic use of διό (Tholuck) is not to be thought of; not even γάρ is so used in the N. T. (see on John iv. 44), and διό neither in the N. T. nor elsewhere.—ὦ ἄνθρωπε πᾶς ὁ κρίνων] Just as Paul, i. 18, designated the Gentiles by the general term ἀνθρώπων, and only brought forward the special reference to them in the progress of the discourse; so also he now designates the *Jews*, not as yet by name (see this first at ver. 17), but generally by the address ἄνθρωπε, which however already implies a trace of reproach (ix. 20; Luke xii. 14; Plat. *Prot.* p. 330 D, *Gorg.* p. 452 B, and the passages in Wetstein, Ellendt, *Lex. Soph.* I. p. 164), while at the same time he makes it by his πᾶς ὁ κρίνων sufficiently apparent that he is no longer speaking of the class already delineated, but is turning now to the *Jews* contrasted with them; for the self-righteous *judging* respecting the *Gentiles* as rejected of God (Midr. Tillin f. 6, 3; Chetubb. f. 3, 2; and many other passages) was in fact a *characteristic of the Jews*. Hence all the more groundless is the hasty judgment, that this passage has *nothing whatever to do* with the contrast between Jews and Gentiles (Hofmann). Comp. ver. 17 ff. And that it is the *condemning* κρίνειν which is meant, and not the moral capacity of judgment in general (Th. Schott) and its exercise (Hofmann) (comp. on Matth. vii. 9), follows from the subsequent κατακρίνεις more precisely defining its import. Consequently the quite general interpretation (Beza, Calovius, Benecke, Mehring, Luthardt, *vom freien Willen*, p. 416) seems untenable, as well as the reference to the *Gentiles* as the judging subjects (Th. Schott), or to all to whom i. 32 applied (Hofmann), or even specially to Gentile *authorities* (Chrysostom, Theodoret, Theophylact, Oecumenius, Cajetanus, Grotius).—Regarding the *nominative* as further ethical epexegesis of the vocative, see Bernhardy, p. 67, Buttmann, *Neut. Gr.* p. 123. — ἐν ᾧ] either instrumental: *thereby, that*, equivalent to ἐν τούτῳ ὅτι (Hofmann); or, still more closely corresponding to the τὰ γὰρ αὐτὰ πράσσεις: *in which thing*, in which point. Comp. xiv. 22. The temporal rendering: *eodem tempore quo* (Köllner, Reithmayr), arbitrarily obscures the moral identity, which Paul intended to bring out. The κατακρίνεις however is not *facto condemnas* (Estius, van Hengel), but the judgment pronounced upon the other is a *condemnatory judgment* upon thyself, namely, because it applies to thine own conduct. On the contrast between ἕτερον and σεαυτόν comp. ver. 21; 1 Cor. x. 24, 29; Gal. vi. 4; Phil. ii. 4. — τὰ αὐτά] *the same sins and vices*, not indeed according to all their several concrete manifestations, as previously described, but according to their essential moral categories; see vv. 17-24. Comp. on the idea John viii. 7. — ὁ κρίνων] with reproachful emphasis.

Ver. 2. Οἴδαμεν] Paul means to pronounce it as *in his own view and that of his readers an undoubted truth* (comp. iii. 19), that the judicial decision which God will one day pronounce, etc. The δέ carries on the discourse, and the entire sentence forms the *propositio major* to what is now (ver. 3) to be proved, namely, that the person judging (the Jew), who yet makes himself guilty of wickedness similar to the things (τὰ τοιαῦτα) in question, deceives himself if he thinks to escape *the true judgment of God* (ver. 5). Thus τὸ κρῖμα[1] τ. Θεοῦ has the emphasis of contrast with that human judgment so inconsistent with their own conduct. The predicate of being κατὰ ἀλήθειαν ἐπὶ τοὺς κ.τ.λ. belongs not to the latter, but to the *divine* κρῖμα. Th. Schott erroneously emphasises πράσσοντας, dislocating the clear train of thought, as if Paul were treating of the truth that the Gentile's *knowledge* of what was right would not shield him from sin and condemnation. Hofmann also introduces a similar confusion. — κατὰ ἀλήθειαν] contains the *standard*, in accordance with which the judgment of God is pronounced against the τὰ τοιαῦτα πράσσοντες: *in accordance with truth*, so that it is, without error or partiality, entirely adequate to the moral condition of these subjects. Raphel, Köllner, Krehl, Mehring, and Hofmann take it as equivalent to ἀληθῶς, *really* (4 Macc. v. 15; and in Greek writers), so that the meaning would be: it is *in reality* issued over them. But it could not be the object of the Apostle to remind them of the *reality* of the divine judicial sentence, which was under all circumstances undoubted and undisputed, so much as of its *truth*, for the sake of the Jews who fancied that that judgment would condemn the Gentiles, but would spare the descendants of Abraham as such, and on account of their circumcision and other theocratic privileges; by which idea they manifestly denied the ἀλήθεια of the κρῖμα τοῦ Θεοῦ, as if it were an *untrue false* sentence, the contents of which did not correspond to the existing state of the facts.

Ver. 3. Antithesis of ver. 2, "That God judges evildoers according to truth, we know (ver. 2); *but judgest thou* (in the face of that proposition) *that thou shalt . . . . escape?*" This would indeed be at variance with the ἀλήθεια of the judgment. Comp. Matth. iii. 7; and the *passages* from profane writers in Grotius. The *non-interrogative* rendering of vv. 3, 4 (Hofmann) is not called for by the connection with the assertive declaration in ver. 5; it weakens the lively force of the discourse, and utterly fails to suit the ἤ in ver. 4, so prevalent in double questions. — τοῦτο] preparing with emphasis (here: of surprise) for the following ὅτι σὺ

[1] Not κρίμα. With Lachmann it is to be accentuated κρῖμα; see Lobeck, *Paralip.* p. 418. Lipsius is of a different opinion as regards the N. T. (*grammat. Unters.* p 40 f.)

ἐκφ. κ.τ.λ.; Bernhardy, p. 284. — σύ] *Thou* on thy side, as if thou madest an exception; opposed to the Jewish self-conceit (Matth. iii. 7 ff.; Luke iii. 7 f.). The emphasis is not on Θεοῦ (Chrysostom, Theophylact, and others). — ἐκφεύξῃ] not: through *acquittal* (Bengel), comp. Dem. 602, 2, Aristoph. *Vesp.* 157 *al.*, but inasmuch as thou shalt not be subjected to the κρῖμα of God, but shalt on the contrary escape it and be secure afar off from it. Comp. 2 Macc. vi. 26, vii. 35; 1 Thess. v. 3; Heb. ii 3. According to the Jewish illusion only the *Gentiles* were to be judged (Bertholdt, *Christol.* p. 206 ff.), whereas all Israel were to share in the Messianic kingdom as its native children (Matth. viii. 12).

Ver. 4. *Or*—in case thou hast not this illusion—*despisest thou*, etc. The ἤ draws away the attention from the case first put as a question, and proposes another; vi. 3; 1 Cor. ix. 6, and often elsewhere, Baeumlein, *Partikell.* p. 132.—The *despising* the divine goodness is the *contemptuous unconcern as to its holy purpose*, which produces as a natural consequence security in sinning (Ecclus. v. 5 f.). — τοῦ πλούτου τῆς χρηστ.] πλοῦτος, as designation of the "abundantia et magnitudo" (Estius), is a very current expression with the Apostle (ix. 23, xi. 35; Eph. i. 7, ii. 4, 7, iii. 16, Col. i. 27), but is not a Hebraism (Ps. v. 8, lxix. 17 *al.*), being used also by Greek authors; Plat. *Euth.* p. 12 A, and see Loesner, p. 245. — χρηστότητος] is the *goodness* of God, in accordance with which He is inclined to benefit (and not to punish). Comp. Tittmann's *Synon.* p. 195. — ἀνοχή and μακροθ., *patience* and *long-suffering*—the two terms exhausting the one idea—denote the disposition of God, in accordance with which he indulgently tolerates the sins and delays the punishments. See Wetstein, and the passages from the Fathers in Suicer, *Thes.* II. p. 294. Comp. Tittmann, *Synon.* p. 194. — ἀγνοῶν] *inasmuch as it is unknown to thee*, that etc. By this accompanying definition of the καταφρονεῖς the (guilty) *folly* of the despiser is laid bare as its tragic source. Bengel says aptly: "*miratur* Paulus hanc ignorantiam." The literal sense is arbitrarily altered by Pareus, Reiche, de Wette, Maier, and others, who make it denote the not being *willing* to know, which it does *not* denote even in Acts xvii. 23; Rom. x. 3; by Kollner, who, following Grotius, Koppe, and many others, holds it to mean *non considerans*; and also by

Hofmann: "to perceive, as one ought." Comp. 1 Cor. xv. 34. — ἄγει] of *ethical incitement* by influencing the will. Plat. *Rep.* p. 572 D, *al.* See Kypke and Reisig, *ad Soph. O. C.* 253. Comp. viii. 14. But it is not to be taken of the *conatus* (*desires to urge*), but of the standing relation of the goodness of God to the moral condition of man.[1] This relation is an *impelling* to repentance, in which the failure of result on the part of man does not cancel the act of the ἄγει itself. Comp. Wisd. xi. 23; Appian. ii. 63.

— Ver. 5. A vividly introduced contrast to the preceding proposition ὅτι τὸ χρηστὸν .... ἄγει; not a continuation of the question (Lachmann, following Koppe and others; also Baumgarten-Crusius, Ewald), but *affirmative* (by which the discourse becomes far more impressive and striking) as a setting forth of the actual position of things, which is brought about by man through his impenitence, in opposition to the drawing of the divine kindness; for the words can only, in pursuance of the correct *interrogative* rendering of ver. 3, be connected with ver. 4, and not also (as Hofmann holds) with ver. 3. — κατά] *in accordance with*; in a causal sense. Comp. on Phil. iv. 11. On σκληρ. κ. ἀμεταν. καρδ. comp. Acts vii. 31. It is correlative with the previous εἰς μετάνοιαν. — Θησαυρίζεις σεαυτῷ ὀργὴν] Wolf aptly says. "innuitur.... irae divinae judicia paulatim coacervari, ut tandem universa promantur." Comp. Calovius; and see Deut. xxxii. 33-35; Prov. i. 18, ii. 7; Ecclus. iii. 4. For passages of profane writers, where θησαυρός and θησαυρίζειν are used to express the accumulation of evils, punishments, and the like, see Alberti, *Obss.* p. 297; Münthe *in loc.*, from Philo: Loesner, p. 246. The *purposely chosen* word glances back to the previous τοῦ πλούτου κ.τ.λ, and σεαυτῷ, *to thyself*, heightens the *tragic* nature of the foolish conduct that redounds *to one's own destruction*; comp. xiii. 2. — ἐν ἡμέρᾳ ὀργ.] not to be taken with Luther, Beza, Castalio, Piscator, Calvin, Estius, and many others as *in diem irae* (Phil. i. 10; Jude 6; Tob. iv. 9), belongs to ὀργήν: *which breaks out on the day of wrath.* Comp. 1 Thess. iii. 13. Regarding the repetition of ὀργῆς after ὀργήν Bengel correctly remarks: "δεινότης sermonis magna vi." *Whose* wrath, is self-evident, without its being necessary to connect ὀργῆς with Θεοῦ (Hofmann), which

---

[1] Therefore no predestination to damnation can be supposed.

is forbidden by the intervening ἀποκαλ. and by the previous absolutely put ὀργήν. The *article* was not required by ἡμέρᾳ on account of the genitive definitions; 1 Cor. vi. 2; Eph. iv. 30; Phil. i. 6, *al.;* Winer, p. 118 f. [E. T. 155 f.]; Kühner, II. 1, p. 524. —Paul characterises the *day of judgment*, and with what powerful emphasis! by an accumulation of genitives and weighty expressions, with reference to the fate of the *bad* as ἡμέρα ὀργῆς, but with reference to its general destination (afterwards ver. 6 ff. to be further carried out in detail) for *good and bad* as a day ἀποκαλ. δικαιοκρισ. τ. Θεοῦ, *i.e. on which God's righteous judgment* (which until then remains hidden) is *revealed*, publicly exhibited. With the exception of passages of the Fathers, such as Justin, *de resurr.* p. 223, δικαιοκρισία occurs only in an unknown translation of Hos. vi. 5 (where the LXX. read κρίμα) and the the *Test. XII. Patr.* p. 547 and 581.

Ver. 6. Compare Ps. lxii. 13; Prov. xxiv. 12; analogies from Greek writers in Spiess, *Logos spermat.* p. 214. — κατὰ τὰ ἔργα αὐτοῦ] *i.e.* according as shall be commensurate with the moral quality of his actions. On this, and on the following amplification down to ver. 16, it is to be observed :—(1) Paul is undoubtedly speaking of the *judgment of the world*, which God will cause to be held by Christ, ver. 16 ; (2) The *subjects* who are judged are *Jews* and *Gentiles*, ver. 9 ff., consequently *all men*, ver. 16. The distinction, as to whether they are Christians or not, is left out of view in this exposition, as the latter is partly intended to *introduce* the reader to a knowledge of the necessity of justification by faith (down to iii. 20); and it is consequently also left out of view that judgment according to works cannot result in bliss for the unbelievers, because there is wanting to them the very thing whose vital action produces the works in accordance with which the Judge awards bliss, namely, faith and the accompanying regeneration. (3) *The standard of the decision is moral action* and its opposite, vv. 6-10; and this standard is really and in fact the only one, to which at the last judgment all, even the Christians themselves, shall be subjected, and by which their fate for eternity shall be determined, Matth. xvi. 27, xxv. 31 ff.; 2 Cor. v. 10; Gal. vi. 7 ff.; Eph. vi. 8; Col. iii. 24; Rev. ii. 23, xx. 12, xxii. 12. But (4) the relation of moral action in the case of the *Christian* to the *fides salvifica*, as the necessary effect and fruit of which that action must be demanded at the judgment, cannot, for the reason given above under (2), be here introduced into the discussion. (5) On the contrary, *the law* only (in the case of the Jews the Mosaic, in the case of the Gentiles the natural), must be presented as the medium of the decision, ver. 12 ff.; a view which has likewise its full truth (compare what was remarked under (3) above), since the Christian also, because he is to be judged according to his *action*, must be judged *according to law* (compare the doctrine of the *tertius legis usus*), and indeed according to the πλήρωσις τοῦ νόμου introduced by Christ, Matth. v. 17. Comp. xxv. 31 ff.; Rom. xiii. 8-10,—although he becomes partaker of salvation, not through *the merit* of works (a point the further development of which formed no part of the Apostle's general discussion here), but through faith, of which the works are the *practical evidence and measure*.[1] Accordingly the "phrasis legis" (Melancthon) is indeed to be recognised in our passage, but it is to be apprehended in its full truth, which does not stamp as a mere theoretic abstraction (Baur) the contrast, deeply enough experienced by Paul himself, between the righteousness of works and righteousness of faith. It is neither to be looked upon as needing the *corrective* of the Christian plan of salvation; nor as an *inconsistency* (Fritzsche); nor yet in such a light, that the doctrine of justification involves a partial abrogation of the moral order of the world (Reiche), which is, on the contrary, confirmed and established by it, iii. 31. But our passage yields nothing in favour of the possibility, which God may grant to unbelievers, of turning to Christ *after death* (Tholuck), or of becoming partakers of the salvation in Christ in virtue of an exercise of divine power (Th. Schott): and the representation employed for that purpose,— that the life of faith is the *product* of a *previous* life-tendency, and that the ἔργα *perfect* themselves in faith (Luthardt, Tholuck),— is erroneous, because incompatible with the N. T. conception of regeneration as a new creation, as a putting off of the old man, as a having died and risen again, as a being begotten of God through the Spirit, etc. etc. The new life (vi. 4) is the direct

---

[1] It is rightly observed by Calovius: "*secundum opera, i.e.* secundum testimonium operum," is something different from "*propter opera, i.e.* propter meritum operum." Comp. *Apol. Conf. A*, art. 3, and Beza *in loc.*

opposite of the old (vi. 19 ff.). The possibility referred to is to be judged of in connection with the *descensus Christi ad inferos*, but is irrelevant here.

Ver. 7. *To those, who by virtue of perseverance in morally-good work seek to obtain glory and honour and immortality, eternal life* sc. ἀποδώσει. Consequently καθ' ὑπομ. ἔργου ἀγαθ. contains the standard, the regulative principle, by which the seeking after glory, honour, etc. is guided, and ἔργου ἀγαθοῦ,[1] which is not with Beza to be connected with δόξαν, is the genitive of the object to which the ὑπομονή refers (1 Thess. i. 3; Polyb. iv. 51, 1; Theophr. *Char.* 6, 1); while δόξαν κ. τιμὴν κ. ἀφθαρσ. is an exhaustive description of the future salvation according to its *glorious appearing* (2 Cor. iv. 17; Matth. xiii. 43), according to the *honour* united with it (for it is the prize of victory, 1 Cor. ix. 25; Phil. iii. 14; 2 Tim. iv. 8; James i. 12; 1 Pet. v. 4, the joint heirship with Christ, viii. 17, the reigning along with Him, 2 Tim. ii. 12), and according to its *imperishableness* (1 Cor. xv. 52 ff.; Rev. xxi. 4; 1 Pet. i. 4). Paul presents the moral effort under a character thus *specifically Christian*, just because he can attribute it only to *Christian* Jews and Gentiles; and hence he is only able to give his description of this first half of the subjects of future judgment, notwithstanding the generality of his language, in the *Christian* form, in which alone it really takes place. In keeping with this is also the ζωὴν αἰώνιον, *i.e.* eternal life in the kingdom of the Messiah, v. 21, vi. 22 f.; Gal. vi. 8. The above *construction* of the words is already followed by Theophilus, *ad Autol.* i. 20, *ed. Wolf*, and by most expositors, including Tholuck, Rückert, Köllner, de Wette, Olshausen, Philippi, Maier, van Hengel, Umbreit. The objection raised against it by Reiche and Hofmann, that according to the analogy of ver. 6 καθ' ὑπομ. ἔργ. ἀγ. must contain the standard of the ἀποδώσει, and cannot therefore belong to ζητοῦσι, is untenable, because καθ' ὑπομ. ἔργ. ἀγ., though attached to ζητοῦσι, nevertheless does contain (indirectly) the standard of ἀποδώσει; so

---

[1] The singular without the article indicates the thing *in abstracto;* the rule is for every given case: *perseverance in good work.* The idea that the *work of redemption* is referred to (Mehring, in accordance with Phil. i. 6), so that ὑπομ. ἔργ. ἀγ., would be equivalent to ὑπακοὴ πίστεως, ought to have been precluded by the parallel in ver. 10. Comp. ver. 2.

that there remains only an immaterial difference, which however is in fact very consonant to the lively versatility of the Apostle's thought. Still less weight attaches to the objection, that to seek glory and honour is not in itself a praiseworthy thing; for the *moral* tenor of the ζητεῖν δόξαν κ.τ.λ. (comp. Matth. vi. 33; John v. 44) is most definitely assured by καθ' ὑπομ. ἔργ. ἀγ. Utterly unfounded, in fine, is the objection of clumsiness (Hofmann); the symmetrical fulness of vv. 7, 8, has a certain solemnity about it. Reiche and Hofmann, following Oecumenius,[1] Estius, and others, arrange it so that to δόξαν κ. τιμ. κ. ἀφθαρσίαν they supply ἀποδώσει, whilst ζητοῦσι is to be combined with ζωὴν αἰών. and regarded as an apposition or (Hofmann) reason assigned to τοῖς μέν, and καθ' ὑπομ. ἔργ. ἀγ. is the standard of ἀποδώσει. Substantially so also Ewald. No syntactic objection can be urged against this rendering; but how tamely and heavily is the ζητοῦσι ζωὴν αἰών. subjoined! Paul would have written clearly, emphatically, and in harmony with the contrast in ver. 8: τοῖς .... ἀγαθοῦ ζωὴν αἰ. ζητοῦσι δόξαν κ. τιμ. κ. ἀφθ.

Ver. 8. Τοῖς δὲ ἐξ ἐριθείας] sc. οὖσι: paraphrase of the substantive idea, to be explained from the conception of the moral condition as drawing its origin thence (comp. iii. 26; iv. 12, 14; Gal. iii. 10; Phil. i. 17, *al.*). See Bernhardy, p. 288 f. Comp. the use of υἱοί and τέκνα in Eph. ii. 2. We are precluded from taking (with Hofmann) ἐκ in a causal sense (*in consequence of* ἐριθεία), *and as belonging to* ἀπειθ. κ.τ.λ. by the καί, which would here express the idea, unsuitable to the connection: *even* (Baeuml. *Partik.* p. 150, also Xen. *Mem.* i. 3, 1). This καί, the simple *and*, which is not however with Hofmann to be interpreted as if Paul had written μᾶλλον or τοὐναντίον ("*instead of seeking after eternal life, rather*," etc.), clearly shows that τοῖς δὲ ἐξ ἐριθείας is to be taken *by itself*, as it has been correctly explained since the time of the Vulgate and Chrysostom. — ἐριθεία] is not to be derived from ἔρις or ἐρίζω, but from ἔριθος, *a hired*

---

[1] Τὸ ὑπερβατὸν οὕτω τακτέον· τοῖς καθ' ὑπομονὴν ἔργου ἀγαθοῦ ζητοῦσι ζωὴν αἰώνιον, ἀποδώσει δόξαν καὶ .... ἀφθαρσίαν. But there is no ground whatever for the assumption of a hyperbaton, in which Luther also has entangled himself. Very harshly Bengel, Fritzsche, and Krehl separate τοῖς καθ' ὑπομ. ἔργου ἀγ. from what follows, and supply οὖσι; and then take δόξαν .... ζητοῦσι as apposition to τοῖς .... ἔργου, but make ζωὴν αἰ. likewise dependent on ἀποδώσει.

labourer,[1] *a spinner* (Homer, xviii. 550, 560; Hesiod, ἔργ. 600 f.; Dem. 1313, 6; LXX. Is. xxxviii. 12; hence ἐριθεύω, *to work for hire* (Tob. ii. 11), then also: *to act selfishly, to lay plots.* Compare ἐξεριθεύεσθαι, Polyb. x. 25, 9, and ἀνεριθεύτος (*without party intrigues*) in Philo, p. 1001 E. ἐριθεία has therefore, besides the primary sense of *work for hire*, the twofold ethical signification (1) *mercenary greed;* and (2) *desire of intrigue, pursuit of partisan courses;* Arist. *Pol.* v. 2 f. See Fritzsche, *Excursus* on ch. ii.; regarding the composition of the word, see on 2 Cor. xii. 20. The latter signification is to be retained in *all* passages of the N. T. 2 Cor. xii. 20; Gal. v. 20; Phil. i. 16, ii. 3; James iii. 14, 16. — οἱ ἐξ ἐριθείας are therefore the *intriguers, the partisan actors;* whose will and striving are conducive not to the *truth* (for that in fact is a power of an entirely different kind, opposed to their character), but to *immorality;* wherefore there is added, as further characterizing them: καὶ ἀπειθοῦσι. Compare Ignatius, *ad Philad.* 8, where the opposite of ἐριθ. is the χριστομάθεια, *i.e. the discipleship of Christ,* which excludes all selfish partisan effort. *Haughtiness* (as van Hengel explains it), and the *craving for self-assertion* (Mehring and Hofmann) are combined with it, but are not what the word itself signifies. The interpretation formerly usual: *qui sunt ex contentione* (Vulg.), *those fond of strife* (Origen, Chrysostom, Oecumenius, Theophylact, Erasmus, Luther, Beza, Calvin, etc.), which was understood for the most part as *those rebelling against God*, is based partly on the erroneous derivation from ἔρις, partly on the groundless assumption that in the other passages of the N. T. the sense of *quarrelsomeness* is necessary. Since this is not the case, Reiche's conjecture is irrelevant, that the *vulgar usus loquendi* had erroneously derived the word from ἔρις and had *lent* to it the corresponding signification. Köllner explains it rightly as *partisanship,* but gratuitously assumes that this was a special designation for "*godless character*" in general. So in substance also Fritzsche: "*homines nequam.*" The very addition, further describing these men, καὶ ἀπειθοῦσι .... ἀδικίᾳ, quite allows us to suppose that Paul had before his mind the strict and proper meaning of the word *partisanship;* and it is therefore unwarrant-

---

[1] See Valck. *ad Theocr. Adoniaz.* p. 373. Compare συνέριθος frequent in Greek authors.

able to base the common but linguistically erroneous explanation on *the affinity between the notions* of partisanship and of contentiousness (Philippi). The question to be determined is not the category of ideas to which the ἐριθεύειν belongs, but the definite individual idea which it expresses. — ὀργὴ κ. θυμός] sc. ἔσται. In the animation of his description Paul has broken off the construction previously followed. To connect these words with what follows (Mehring) disturbs unnecessarily the important symmetry of the passage. On the distinction between the two words, see Tittmann's *Synon.* p. 131 ff. θυμός : *vehement passion*, in Cic. *Tusc.* iv. 9, 21 rendered *excandescentia*, here, as also in Gal. v. 20, Eph. iv. 31, Col. iii. 8, Rev. xvi. 19, xix. 15, often also in the O. T. and the Apocrypha, made known by its combination with ὀργή, and by its being put last as the more vehement, as the holy divine *wrath.* Compare Isoc. xii. 81 : ὀργῆς κ. θυμοῦ μεστοί. Herodian, viii. 4, 1 : ὀργῇ κ. θυμῷ χρώμενος. Lucian, *de calumn.* 23, *al.*

Vv. 9, 10. Emphatic recapitulation of vv. 7 and 8, inverting the order, and in addition, giving special prominence to the universality of the retribution. The placing the *penal* retribution first gives to this an aspect the more threatening and alarming, especially as the terms expressing it are now *accumulated* in one breath. — θλῖψις κ. στενοχωρία] *Tribulation* and *anguish*, sc. ἔσται. The calamity is thus described as pressing upon them from without (θλῖψις), and as felt inwardly with the sense of its being beyond help (στενοχ.), viii. 35 ; 2 Cor. iv. 7, vi. 12; compare LXX. Is. xxx. 6 ; Deut. xxviii. 53. — ἐπὶ πᾶσαν ψυχὴν ἀνθρ.] denotes not simply "*upon every man*" (so even Philippi), but "*upon every soul which belongs to a man*" who practises evil. The ψυχή is thereby designated as that which is affected by the θλῖψ. κ. στενοχ. (Acts ii. 43 ; Matth. xxvi. 28, *al.*) ; comp. Winer, p. 147 [E. T. 194]. It is the part which *feels* the pain.[1] — πρῶτον] Quite as in i. 16. The Jews, as the people of God, in possession of the revelation with its promises and threatenings, are therefore necessarily also those upon whom the retribution of judgment—not the reward merely, but also the punishment— has to find *in the first instance its execution*. In both aspects they have the *priority* based on their position in the history of

---

[1] See Ernesti, *Urspr. d. Sünde*, II. p. 101 ff.

salvation as the theocratic people, and that as certainly as God is impartial. "Judaei particeps Graecus," Bengel. The Jewish conceit is counteracted in the first clause by Ἰουδαίου τε πρῶτον, in the second by καὶ Ἕλληνι, and counteracted with sternly consistent earnestness. The second πρῶτον precludes our taking the first as *ironical* (Reiche). — εἰρήνη] *welfare*, by which is intended that of the Messiah's kingdom, as in viii. 6. It is not materially different from the ἀφθαρσία and ζωὴ αἰώνιος of ver. 7; the totality of that which had already been described in special aspects by δόξα and τιμή (comp. on ver. 7).—Regarding the distinction between ἐργαζ. and κατεργαζ. (*works* and *brings to pass*) see on i. 27.

Ver. 11. Ground assigned for vv. 9 and 10, so far as concerns the Ἰουδ. π. κ. Ἕλλην. — προσωποληψία] Partial preference from personal considerations. See on Gal. ii. 6. Melancthon: "dare aequalia inequalibus vel inequalia aequalibus." The ground specified is directed against the Jewish theocratic fancy. Comp. Acts x. 34 f.; Ecclus. xxxii. (xxxv.) 15.

Ver. 12. Assigns the ground in point of fact for the proposition contained in ver. 11, in special reference to the future judgment of condemnation.[1] — ἀνόμως] *i.e. without the standard of the law* (without having had it). Comp. 1 Cor. ix. 21; Wisd. xvii. 2. Those whose sins were not transgressions of the Mosaic law (but of the moral law of nature), the sinful Gentiles, shall be transferred into the penal state of eternal death without the standard of the law, without having their condemnation decided in accordance with the requirements of a νόμος to which they are strangers. The ἀπολοῦνται, which is to set in at the final judgment, not through natural necessity (Mangold), is the opposite of the σωτηρία, i. 16, of the ζήσεται, i. 17, of the ζωὴ αἰώνιος, ii. 7, of the δόξα κ.τ.λ., ii. 10; comp. John iii. 15; Rom. xiv. 15; 1 Cor. i. 18. This very ἀπολοῦνται should of itself have precluded commentators from finding in the second ἀνόμως an element of *mitigation* (Chrysostom, Theophylact, Oecumenius), as if it was meant to exclude the *severity* of the law. The

---

[1] Only in reference to the judgment *of condemnation*, because the idea of a Messianic bliss of unbelievers was necessarily foreign to the Apostle; as indeed in vv. 7 and 10 he was under the necessity of describing those to whom Messianic bliss was to be given in recompense, in terms of a *Christian* character.

immoral Gentiles may not hope to remain unpunished on account of their non-possession of the law; punished they shall be independently of the standard of the law. This is the confirmation of the ἀπροσωποληψία of God on the one side, in regard to the *Gentiles*.—The καί before ἀπολ. is the *also* of a corresponding relation, but not between ἀνόμως and ἀνόμως, as if Paul had written καὶ ἀνόμ. ἀπολ., but between ἥμαρτον and ἀπολ.: as they have *sinned* without law, so shall they *also perish* without law. In this way ἀνόμως retains the emphasis of the specific *how*. Compare the following. The *praeterite* ἥμαρτον is spoken from the standpoint of the time of the judgment. — καὶ ὅσοι ἐν νόμῳ κ.τ.λ.] This gives the other aspect of the case, with reference to the *Jews*, who do not escape the judgment (of condemnation) on account of their privilege of possessing the law, but on the contrary are to be judged *by means of the law*, so that sentence shall be passed on them in virtue of *it* (see Deut. xxvii. 26; comp. John v. 45). — ἐν νόμῳ] Not *on the law* (Luther), which would be εἰς νόμον, but the opposite of ἀνόμως: *with the law, i.e.* in possession of the law, which they had as a standard,[1] Winer, p. 361 [E. T. 482]. On νόμος without the article, used of the *Mosaic law*, see Winer, 117 [E. T. 152]. So frequently in the Apocrypha, and of particular laws also in classical writers. To question this use of it in the N. T. (van Hengel, Th. Schott, Hofmann, and others) opens the way for artificial and sometimes intolerable explanations of the several passages. — κριθήσ.] an unsought change of the verb, suggested by διὰ νόμου.

Ver. 13 proves the correctness of the proposition, so much at variance with the fancy of the Jews, ὅσοι ἐν νόμῳ ἥμαρτον, διὰ νόμου κριθήσονται.—The placing of vv. 13-15 *in a parenthesis*, as after Beza's example is done by Grotius, Griesbach, and others, also by Reiche and Winer, is to be rejected, because ver. 13, which cannot be placed in a parenthesis *alone* (as Koppe and Mehring do), is closely joined with what immediately precedes, and it is only in ver. 14 that an intervening thought is introduced by way of illustration. The parenthesis is (with Baumgarten-Crusius) to be limited to vv. 14, 15, as is done also

---

[1] This opposition does not extend beyond the νόμον μὴ ἔχειν and νόμον ἔχειν, ver. 14. Therefore ἐν νόμῳ is not: *within the law* as the divine order of common life (comp. iii. 19) as Hofmann takes it.

by Lachmann. See on ver. 16. — οἱ ἀκροαταί] A reference to the public reading of the Thorah on the Sabbath. Comp. Acts xv. 21; 2 Cor. iii. 14; John xii. 34; Josephus, *Antt.* v. 1, 26, v. 2, 7. The *substantive* brings out more forcibly than the *participial* form of expression would have done the *characteristic* feature: *those, whose business is hearing.* Compare Theile, *ad Jac.* i. 22, p. 76. — παρὰ τῷ Θεῷ] ἐνώπιον αὐτοῦ iii. 20, *according to God's judgment.* 1 Cor. iii. 9; 2 Thess. i. 6; Winer, p. 369 [E. T. 492]. — δικαιωθήσ.] *They shall be declared as righteous, normal.* See on i. 17. This οἱ ποιηταὶ νόμου δικαιωθήσονται is the general fundamental law of God who judges with righteousness (Gal. iii. 12); a fundamental law which required to be urged here in proof of the previous assertion ὅσοι ἐν νόμῳ ἥμαρτον, διὰ ν. κριθήσ. Compare Weiss, *bibl. Theol.* § 87. How in the event of its being impossible for a man to be a true ποιητὴς νόμου (iii. 9 ff.) faith comes in and furnishes a δικαιοσύνη ἐκ πίστεως, and then how man, by means of the καινότης ζωῆς (vi. 4) attained through faith, must and can fulfil (viii. 4) the law completed by Christ (the νόμος τοῦ πνεύματος τῆς ζωῆς, viii. 2), were topics not belonging to the present discussion. Compare on ver. 6. "Haec descriptio est justitia legis, quae nihil impedit alia dicta de justitia fidei," Melancthon.

Vv. 14-16. The οἱ ποιηταὶ νόμου δικαιωθήσονται just asserted did not require proof with regard to the Jews. But, as the regulative principle of the last judgment, it could not but appear to need proof with regard to the *Gentiles*, since that fundamental rule might seem to admit of no application to those who sin ἀνόμως and perish ἀνόμως. Now the *Gentiles*, though beyond the pale of the Mosaic law and not incurring condemnation according to the standard of that law, yet possess in the moral law of nature a certain substitute for the Mosaic law not given to them. It is in virtue of this state of things that they present themselves, not as excepted from the above rule οἱ ποιηταὶ νόμου δικαιωθ., but as subjected to it; namely, in the indirect way that they, although ἄνομοι in the positive sense, have nevertheless in the natural law a substitute for the positive one—which is apparent, as often as Gentiles do by nature that which the positive Mosaic law not given to them enjoins. The connection may therefore be paraphrased somewhat thus: "*With right and reason I say: the doers of the law shall be justified; for as to the case of the*

Gentiles, that ye may not regard them as beyond reach of that rule, it is proved in fact by those instances, in which Gentiles, though not in possession of the law of Moses, do by nature the requirements of this law, that they are the law unto themselves, because, namely, they thereby show that its obligation stands written in their hearts," etc. It is to be observed at the same time that Paul does not wish to prove a justification of the *Gentiles* really *occurring* as a *result* through the fulfilment of their natural law—a misconception against which he has already guarded himself in ver. 12,—but he desires simply to establish the *regulative principle* of justification through the law in the case of the Gentiles. Real actual justification by the law takes place neither among Jews nor Gentiles; because in no case is there a complete fulfilment, either, among the Jews, of the revealed law or, among the Gentiles, of the natural law—which in fact is only a substitute for the former, but at the same time forms the limit beyond which their responsibility and their judgment cannot in principle go, because they have nothing higher (in opposition to Philippi, who refers to the πλήρωμα νόμου, xiii. 10).—The connection of thought between ver. 14 and what precedes it has been very variously apprehended. According to Koppe (compare Calvin, Flatt, and Mehring) vv. 14-16 prove the condemnation of the Gentiles asserted in ver. 12, and ver. 17 ff. that of the Jews; while ver. 13 is a parenthesis. But, seeing that in the whole development of the argument γάρ always refers to what immediately precedes, it is even in itself an arbitrary proceeding to make ὅταν γάρ in ver. 14, without any evident necessity imposed by the course of thought, refer to ver. 12, and to treat ver. 13, although it contains a very appropriate reason assigned for the second part of ver. 12, as a parenthesis to be broken off from connection with what follows; and decisive against this view are the words ἢ καὶ ἀπολογουμένων in ver. 15, which place it beyond doubt that vv. 14-16 were not intended as a proof of the ἀπολοῦνται in ver. 12. Philippi regards ver. 14 as establishing only the first half of ver. 13: "not the hearers of the law are just before God, for even the Gentiles have a law, *i.e.* for even the Gentiles are ἀκροαταὶ τοῦ νόμου." But we have no right to exclude thus from the reference of the γάρ just the very assertion immediately preceding, and to make it refer to a purely negative clause which had merely served to pave the way for this assertion. The reference to the negative half of ver. 13 would only be warranted in accordance with the text, had Paul, as he might have done, inverted the order of the two parts of ver. 13, and so given to the negative clause the second place.[1] And the less *could* a reader see reason to refer the γάρ to this negative clause in the position in which the Apostle has placed it, since ver. 14 speaks of Gentiles who *do* the law, by which the attention was necessarily directed, not to the negative, but to the affirmative, half of ver. 13 (οἱ ποιηταὶ κ.τ.λ.).[2] Such a mode of presenting the connection is even more arbitrary than if we should supply after ver. 13 the thought: " *and therewith also the Gentiles*" (Köllner and others), which however is quite unnecessary. Our view is in substance that given already by Chrysostom (οὐκ ἐκβάλλω τὸν νόμον, φῆσιν, ἀλλὰ καὶ ἐντεῦθεν δικαιῶ τὰ ἔθνη), Erasmus, and others; more recently by Tholuck, Rückert, Reiche, Köllner, Fritzsche, de Wette, Baumgarten-Crusius, Reithmayr, van Hengel, Ewald, Th. Schott, though with very various modifications.

Ver. 14. Ὅταν] *quando*, supposes a case which may take place at any time, and whose frequent occurrence is possible, as "eventus ad experientiam revocatus" (Klotz, *ad Devar*. p. 689): *in the case if, so often as*. — γάρ] introducing the *proof* that the proposition of ver. 13 also holds of the *Gentiles*. See above. — ἔθνη] not to be understood of the *Gentiles collectively*, to which Reiche, de Wette, Köllner, Philippi refer it—for this must have been expressed by the article (against which view neither ix. 30 nor iii. 29, nor 1 Cor. i. 23, is to be adduced), and the putting of the case ὅταν .... ποιῇ with respect to the heathen generally would be in itself untrue—but Paul means rather *Gentiles among whom the supposed case occurs*. — τὰ μὴ νόμον ἔχοντα] *they who have not the law;* a more precise definition bearing on the case, and bringing forward the point on which here the argument turns. See Winer,

---

[1] Only thus—but not as Paul has actually placed it—could the *negative* clause be regarded as the *chief* thought, for which Philippi is obliged to take it, p. 54 f. 3rd ed.

[2] These reasons may also be urged against Hofmann, who, substantially like Philippi, takes vv. 14-16 as a proof, *that in the matter of righteousness before God nothing can depend on whether one belongs to the number of those who hear the law read to them.*

p. 127 [E. T. 174]. Observe the distinction between μὴ νόμον ἔχ. and νόμον μὴ ἔχ. The former negatives—while the contrast of the φύσει floats before the mind—the possession of the *law*, instead of which they have merely a natural analogue of it (compare Stalb. *ad Plat. Crit.* p. 47 D); the latter negatives the *possession* of the law, which *is wanting* to them, whilst the Jews have it. — φύσει τὰ τοῦ νόμου ποιῇ] Most expositors uphold this connection, including Rückert, 2nd ed. On the other hand Bengel and Usteri join φύσει to μὴ νόμ. ἔχοντα, but thus make it superfluous and even unsuitable, and deprive it of all weight in the connection, especially as the word φύσις has here no other sense than *nativa indoles*, *i.e.* the original constitution given with existence, and not moulded by any extraneous training, culture, or other influence beyond the endowments of nature and their natural development (comp. on Eph. ii. 3); φύσει : " *quia* natura eorum ita fert," Stalb. *ad Plat. Phaedr.* p. 249. The *dative* denotes the mediating cause. And that it is the *moral prompting of conscience left to itself*, which Paul means by φύσει *in contrast to the divine leading of the law*, is plain from ver. 15. The φύσει ποιεῖν lies beyond the sphere of positive revelation and its promptings, leadings, etc. It takes place in virtue of an indoles *ingenita*, not *interventu disciplinae divinae formata*, so that the thought of an operation of grace or of the Logos taking place apart from Christ is quite foreign to this passage, and its affirmation is not in harmony with the *truncus et lapis* of the Formula Concordiae. See the later discussions of dogmatic writers as to this point in Luthardt, *v. freien Willen*, p. 366 ff. — τὰ τοῦ νόμου] *what belongs to the law*, i.e. *its constituent elements, its precepts*. Paul does not say simply τὸν νόμον; for he is thinking not of Gentiles who fulfil the law *as a whole*, but of those who *in concrete cases* by their action respond to the *particular portions* of the law *concerned*. Compare Luthardt *l.c.* p. 409. The close relation, in which the ποιεῖν τὰ τοῦ νόμου here stands to ποιηταὶ νόμου in ver. 13, is fatal to the view of Beza, Joh. Cappell., Elsner, Wetstein, Michaelis, Flatt, and Mehring, who explain it as *quae lex facit*, namely, the commanding, convincing, condemning, etc. — ἑαυτοῖς εἰσὶ νόμος] *They are the law unto themselves*, *i.e.* their moral nature, with its voice of conscience commanding and forbidding, supplies to their own Ego the place of the revealed law possessed by the Jews. Thus in that ποιεῖν they serve for themselves as a regulator of the conduct that agrees with the divine law. For parallels (Manil. v. 495, al.: *ipse sibi lex est*, Arist. Nicom. iv. 14: νόμος ὤν ἑαυτῷ al.) see Wetstein; compare also Porph. *ad Marc*. 25, p. 304.—Observe further that here, where the participle stands *without the article*—consequently not οἱ νόμ. μὴ ἔχοντες (as previously τὰ μὴ .... ἔχοντα)—it is to be resolved by *since* they, *because* they; which however does not convey the idea: because they *are conscious* of the absence of the law (as Hofmann objects), but rather: because this want *occurs* in their case. See Buttmann's *neut. Gr.* p. 301. The resolution by *although* (Th. Schott) is opposed to the connection; that by *while* (Hofmann) fails to convey the definite and logical meaning; which is, that Gentiles, in the cases indicated by ὅταν κ.τ.λ. would not be ἑαυτοῖς νόμος, if they had the *positive* law.—The οὗτοι comprehends emphatically the subjects in question· Kühner, II. 1, p. 568; Buttmann *l.c.* p. 262 f.

Ver. 15. Οἵτινες κ.τ.λ.] *quippe qui.* See on i. 25. The οὗτοι of ver. 14 are characterised, and consequently the ἑαυτοῖς εἰσὶ νόμος, just asserted, is confirmed: *being such as show* (practically by their action, ver. 14, make it known) *that the work of the law is written in their hearts, wherewithal their conscience bears joint witness*, etc.—That ἐνδείκνυνται should be understood of the *practical* proof which takes place by the ποιεῖν τὰ τοῦ νόμου (not by the testimony of conscience, Bengel, Tholuck) is required by the συν in συμμαρτυρούσης, which is not a mere strengthening of the simple word (Köllner, Olshausen; comp. Tholuck, following earlier expositors; see, on the other hand, viii. 16, ix. 1), but denotes *the agreement of the internal evidence of conscience with the external proof by fact.*[1] It is impossible to regard the ἐνδείκ-

---

[1] Where συμμαρτυρεῖν appears to be equivalent to μαρτυρ., it is only an *apparent* equivalence; there is always mentally implied an agreement *with the person for whom witness is borne*, as *e.g.* Thuc. viii. 51, 2; Plat. *Hipp. Maj.* p. 282 B: συμμαρτυρῆσαι δέ σοι ἔχω ὅτι ἀληθῆ λέγεις, if what is meant is not a testimony agreeing with *others* (as Xen. *Hist. Gr.* vii. 1, 2, iii. 3, 2), or, as here, one that agrees with a *thing*, a phenomenon, a proof by fact, or the like. Compare Isoc. p. 47 A. In the passage, Plat. *Legg.* iii. p. 680 D, ξυμμαρτυρεῖν is expressly *distinguished* from μαρτυρ.; for, after the τῷ σῷ λόγῳ ἔοικε μαρτυρεῖν preceding, the ναί· ξυμμαρτυρεῖ γάρ must mean: *he is my joint-witness*, whose evidence agrees with what I say. If the reference of συμ. in our passage to the proof by fact be not adopted, then αὐτοῖς would need be supplied; but wherefore should we do so? According to

νυνται as taking place on the day indicated in ver. 16 (Hofmann), since this day can be no other than that of the last judgment. See on ver. 16. — τὸ ἔργον τοῦ νόμου] The *work relating to the law, the conduct corresponding to it, fulfilling it*. The opposite is ἁμαρτήματα νόμου, Wisd. ii. 12. Compare on Gal. ii. 16. The *singular* is *collective* (Gal. vi. 4), as a summing up of the ἔργα τ. νόμου (iii. 20, 28, ix. 32; Gal. ii. 16, iii. 2, 5, 10). Compare τὰ τοῦ νόμου above. This stands written in their hearts as *commanded, as moral obligation*,[1] as ethical law of nature. — γραπτόν] purposely chosen with reference to the *written* law of Moses, although the moral law is ἄγραφος (Plato. *Legg.* p. 481 B, Thuc. ii. 37, 3, and Krüger, *in loc.* p. 200; Xen. *Mem.* iv. 4, 19; Soph. *Ant.* 450; Dem. 317, 23, 639, 22; Dion. Hal. vii. 41). Compare Jer. xxxi. 33; Heb. viii. 10, and the similar designations among the Rabbins in Buxtorf, *Lex Talm.* p. 852, 1349. The supplying of ὄν serves to explain the adjective, which is used instead of the participle to denote what continues and is constant. Compare Bornemann, *ad Xen. Mem.* i. 5, 1; *Symp.* 4, 25. See the truly classic description of this inner law, and that as divine, in Cicero, *de Republ.* iii. 23; of the Greeks, comp. Soph. *O. T.* 838 ff., and Wunder, *in loc.* — συμμαρτυρούσης αὐτῶν συνειδήσεως, καὶ μεταξὺ κ.τ.λ.] While they make known *outwardly by their action* that the ἔργον of the law is written in their hearts, their *inner moral consciousness* accords with it; namely (1), in reference to their own, *personal* relation: *the testimony of their own consciences*; and (2), in regard to their *mutual* relation: the *accusations* or *vindications*[2] that are carried on between Gentiles and Gentiles (μεταξὺ ἀλλήλων) by their thoughts, by their moral judgments. This view of the sense is required by the correlation of the points αὐτῶν and μεταξὺ ἀλλήλων placed with

Tholuck συμ. indicates merely the agreement of the person witnessing with the contents of his testimony. This is never the case, and would virtually deprive the συμ- of all *significance*.

[1] This inward law is not the conscience itself, but the regulative contents of the consciousness of the conscience; consequently, if we conceive the latter, and with justice (in opposition to Rud. Hofmann, *Lehre vom Gewissen*, 1866, p. 54, 58 f.), as presented in the form of a syllogism, it forms the subject of the major premise of this syllogism. Comp. Delitzsch, *bibl. Psychol.* p. 136 f.

[2] The καί added to the ἤ is based on the view taken of the moral state of the Gentiles, that the κατηγορεῖν forms the *rule*. See Baeumlein, *Partik.* p. 126.

emphasis in the foreground (μεταξὺ occurring in Paul's writings only here, and therefore all the more intentionally *chosen* in this case); so that thus both the *personal individual* testimony of conscience (αὐτῶν) and the *mutual* judgment of the thoughts (μεταξὺ ἀλλήλων), are adduced, as accompanying internal acts, in confirmation of the ἐνδείκνυνται. The Gentiles, who do the requirement of the law, practically show thereby that that requirement is inscribed on their hearts; and this is attested at the same time, so far as concerns the *actors themselves*, by their (following) *conscience*, and, so far as concerns their relation *to other Gentiles*, by the *accusations* or the *vindications* which they reciprocally practise in their moral thoughts, the one making reflections of a condemnatory or of a justifying nature on the other.[1] The prominence thus given to αὐτῶν and μεταξὺ ἀλλήλων, and the antithetical correlation of the two points, have been commonly misunderstood (though not by Castalio, Storr, Flatt, Baumgarten-Crusius), and consequently κ. μετ. ἀλλ. τῶν διαλογ. κ.τ.λ. has been taken merely as *an explanatory description of the process of conscience*, in which the thoughts accuse or vindicate one another (i.e. *one thought the other*); so that ἀλλήλων is referred to the *thoughts*, and not, as is nevertheless required by the αὐτῶν standing in contradistinction to it, to the ἔθνη. This view ought even to have been precluded by attending to the fact that, since συμμαρτ..... συνειδήσεως must, in harmony with the context, mean the *approving* conscience, what follows cannot well suit as an exposition, because in it the κατηγορούντων preponderates. Finally, it was an arbitrary expedient, rendering μεταξὺ merely superfluous and confusing, to *separate* it from ἀλλήλ., and to explain the former as meaning *at a future time*, viz. ἐν ἡμέρᾳ κ.τ.λ. (Koppe), or *between, at the same time* (Köllner, Jatho).

Ver. 16 has its connection with what goes before very variously defined. While Ewald goes so far as to join it with ver. 5, and regards everything intervening as a parenthesis, many, and recently most expositors, have connected it with the immediately preceding συμμαρτ..... ἀπολογ.; in which case, however, ἐν ἡμέρᾳ cannot be taken for εἰς ἡμέραν (Calvin), nor the *present* participles in a *future* sense (Fritzsche), since, in accordance with the

---

[1] Compare Weiss, *bibl. Theol.* p. 277 : "It is testified by the conscience, which teaches them to judge the quality of *their own* and *others'* actions."

context, they are *contemporary with* ἐνδείκνυνται. And for that very reason we must reject the view, which has been often assumed, that Paul suddenly transports himself from the present into the time of the judgment, when the exercise of conscience in the Gentiles will be specially active, and that for this reason he at once adds ἐν ἡμέρᾳ κ.τ.λ. directly without inserting a καὶ τοῦτο μάλιστα, or καὶ τοῦτο γενήσεται, or the like (Rückert, Tholuck, de Wette, Reithmayr, Philippi, van Hengel, Umbreit; comp. Estius). The supposition of such an illogical and violent leap of thought in so clear and steady a thinker as Paul is thoroughly arbitrary and wholly without analogy. Moreover, the simple *temporal* self-judgment of the Gentiles fits into the connection so perfectly, that Paul cannot even have conceived of it as an *anticipation* of the last judgment (Mehring). Quite an incorrect thought, repugnant to ver. 12 and to the whole doctrinal system of the Apostle, is obtained by Luthardt (*v. freien Willen*, p. 410 f.), when, very arbitrarily joining it only with ἢ καὶ ἀπολογουμένων, he discovers here the hope " that to such the reconciling grace of Christ shall one day be extended." This is not confirmed by ver. 26. A relative natural morality never in the N. T. supplies the place of faith, which is the absolutely necessary condition of reconciling grace. Compare iii. 9, 22, vii. 14 ff. *al.* Lastly Hofmann, who formerly held a view similar to Luthardt's (see *Schriftbew.* I. p. 669), now connects ἐν ἡμέρᾳ κ.τ.λ. to ἐνδείκνυνται in such a way, that he explains ver. 16 not at all of the final judgment, but, in contrast even to the latter, of *every day on which God causes the Gospel to be proclaimed among the Gentiles; every* such day shall be for all, who hear the message, *a day of inward judgment;* whoever believingly accepts it, and embraces salvation, thereby proves that he himself demands from himself what the revealed law enjoins on those who possess it. This interpretation, which would require us to read with Hofmann κρίνει (the present) instead of κρινεῖ, is as novel as it is erroneous. For the expressions in ver. 16 are so entirely those formally used to denote the *last judgment* (comp. on ἡμέρᾳ 1 Cor. i. 8, v. 5; 2 Cor. i. 14 *al.*; on κρινεῖ, vv. 2, 3, 5, iii. 6 *al.*; on Θεός as the judge, iii. 6, xiv. 10, 12 *al.*; on τὰ κρυπτά, 1 Cor. iv. 5; on διὰ Ἰησοῦ X. 2 Cor. v. 10; Acts xvii. 31), that nothing else could occur to any reader than the conception of that judgment, which moreover has been present to the mind since ver. 2, and from which even κατὰ τὸ εὐαγγ. μου does not draw away the attention. Every element in Hofmann's exposition is subjectively introduced, so that Paul could not have wrapped up the simple thought, which is supposed to be expressed in so precious a manner, in a more strange disguise— a thought, moreover, which is here utterly irrelevant, since Paul has to do simply with the natural law of the Gentiles in its relation to the revealed νόμος of Judaism, and apart as yet from all reference to the occurrence of their conversion; and hence also the comparison with Heb. iv. 12 is here out of place. The proper view of the passage depends on our *treating as a parenthesis*, not (with Winer and others) vv. 13-15, but with Lachmann, vv. 14, 15. This parenthetical insertion is already *indicated* as such by the fact, that the great judicial proposition previously expressed: οἱ ποιηταὶ νόμου δικαιωθήσονται is in vv. 14, 15 proved only with reference to a *part* of mankind, with regard to which it might seem possibly doubtful: it is *required* by the circumstance, that without it ἐν ἡμέρᾳ has no proper logical reference whatever; and lastly, it is *confirmed* by the consideration that, if it is adopted, the whole is wound up not with an illustration having reference to the Gentiles, but—and how emphatically and solemnly!—with the leading thought of the whole discussion.[1] — τὰ κρυπτὰ τῶν ἀνθρ.] *The hidden things of men, i.e.* everything in their inner or outer life which does not come to the knowledge of others at all, or not according to its moral quality. This *special* characteristic of the judgment is given with reference to ver. 13, inasmuch as it is just *such a judging* that is necessary for, and the preliminary to, the realisation of what is affirmed in ver. 13. — κατὰ τὸ εὐαγγέλ. μου] contains, according to the *usual* view, the accordance of the assertion κρινεῖ ὁ Θεός τὰ κρυπτὰ τ. ἀνθρ. διὰ Ἰ. Χρ. with the Apostle's official proclamation of salvation. But *the fact that* God will judge, etc., was so universally known and so entirely undoubted, that the addition in that sense would have been in the highest degree superfluous; and indeed the μου

---

[1] There is therefore the less reason for assuming with Laurent that ver. 16 was a marginal note of the Apostle on ver. 13, which was copied into the text at the wrong place.

in that case would have no significance bearing on the matter, since *no one* proclaiming the Gospel could call in question that truth. We must therefore explain it, with Pareus, Calovius, and many others, including Umbreit and Hofmann, as referring to the *manner of the* κρινεῖ. Paul was so certain of the sole truth of the Gospel committed to him (xvi. 25; Eph. iv. 20 f.) which he had by revelation of God (Gal. i. 11 f.), that he could not but be equally certain that the future *judgment* would not be held otherwise than *according to his Gospel*, whose contents are conceived as the *standard of the sentence*. In that same Gospel he knew it to be divinely determined, to whom the στέφανος τῆς δικαιοσύνης, the eternal life and its δόξα, or on the other hand its opposite, eternal ἀπώλεια, should be awarded by the judge. But he knew at the same time the axiom announced in ver. 13, with which ver. 16 connects itself, to be not at variance therewith (comp. iii. 31); as indeed on the contrary, it is just in the Gospel that perfection in the fulfilment of the law is demanded, and accordingly (see ch. vi. 8, xiii. 8 ff.) the judicial recompense is determined conformably to the conduct, viii. 4; 2 Cor. v. 10; Eph. v. 5; 1 Cor. vi. 9 f.; Gal. v. 19-23. On μου Calvin's note suffices: *suum appellat ratione ministerii*, and that, to distinguish it from the preaching not of other apostles, but of false, and especially of Judaizing teachers. Comp. xvi. 25; 2 Tim. ii. 8. The mistaken view is held by Origen, Jerome and other Fathers (see Fabricius, *Cod. apocr.* p. 371 f.), that Paul meant by *his* Gospel that of *Luke*. — διὰ Ιησοῦ Χρ.] As He is the Mediator of eternal salvation, so also it is He who is commissioned by God to hold the judgment. Comp. Acts xvii. 30, 31; 1 Cor. iv. 5; 2 Cor. v. 10 *al.*; John v. 27; Matth. xxv. 31.

Vv. 17-24. *The logical connection* of this "oratio splendida ac vehemens" (Estius), introduced once more in lively apostrophe,[1] *with what precedes* is to be taken thus: Paul has expressed in vv. 13-16 the rule of judgment, that not the hearers but the *doers* of the law shall in the judgment be justified. He wishes now vividly to bring home the fact, that the conduct of the Jews, with all their conceit as to the possession and knowledge

---

[1] To the *Jews*, not to the *Jewish-Christians*. Respecting the composition and character of the Roman congregation nothing can be inferred from this rhetorical form of expression. Comp. Th. Schott, p. 188 f.

of the law, is in sharp contradiction to that standard of judgment. The δέ and the emphatic σύ are to be explained from the conception of the *contrast*, which the conduct of the Jews showed, to the proposition that only the doers δικαιωθήσονται. As to the *construction* of vv. 17-23, the common assumption of an anakoluthon, by which Paul in ver. 21 abandons the plan of the discourse started with εἰ, and introduces another turn by means of οὖν (see Winer, p. 529 [E. T. 712], Buttmann, p. 331) is quite unnecessary. The discourse, on the contrary, is formed with regular and logically accurate connection as protasis (vv. 17-20) and apodosis, namely thus: *But if thou art called a Jew, and supportest thyself on the law*, etc., down to ver. 20, *dost thou* (interrogative apodosis, vv. 21, 22), *who accordingly* (οὖν, in accordance with what is specified in vv. 17-20) *teachest others, not teach thyself? Stealest thou, who preachest against stealing? Committest thou adultery, who forbiddest adultery? Plunderest thou temples, who abhorrest idols?* These *questions* present the contrast to the contents of the protasis as in the highest degree surprising, as something that one is at a loss how to characterise —and then follows in ver. 23, with trenchant precision, the explanation and decision regarding them in the *categorical* utterance: *Thou, who boastest thyself of the law, dishonourest God by the transgression of the law*, a result which is then in ver. 24 further confirmed by a testimony from the O. T. Ver. 23 also might indeed (as commonly explained) be taken as a *question;* but, when taken as *declaratory*, the discourse presents a form far more finished, weighty and severe. Paul himself, by abandoning the participial expression uniformly employed four times previously, seems to indicate the cessation of the course hitherto pursued. According to this exposition of the connection, in which it must not be overlooked that *the force of the* οὖν *in ver.* 21 *is limited solely to the relation of the* ὁ διδάσκων ἕτερον *and the following participles to what has been said before*,[1] we must reject the view of Benecke, Glöckler, and Hofmann that the apodosis only begins with ver. 23, but in ver. 21 f. there is a

---

[1] This is the well-known *epanaleptic* οὖν, gathering up and resuming what had been said previously. Regarding the frequency of its use also in Greek writers to introduce the apodosis, especially after a *lengthened* protasis, see Hartung, *Partikell.* II. p. 22 f.; Klotz, *ad Devar.* p. 718. Comp. Bengel on ver. 17.

continuation of the hypothetical protasis—an idea which cannot be tolerated, especially at the beginning of the new form of discourse (the antithetical), without repetition of the εἰ. Paul would have written εἰ οὖν ὁ διδάσκων κ.τ.λ. (compare Baeumlein, *Partik.* p. 178). Th. Schott erroneously finds in ἐπαναπαύῃ and καυχᾶσαι the apodosis, which is then explained.

Vv. 17-20 contain the protasis, whose tenor *of censure* (called in question without ground by Th. Schott and Hofmann) reveals itself at first gently, but afterwards, ver. 19 f., with greater force. — Ἰουδαῖος ἐπονομάζῃ] *if thou art named " Jew."* This was the theocratic title of honour opposed to heathenism (יהודה יה, see Philo, *Alleg.* I. p. 55 B, *de plant. Noë*, p. 233 A). Comp. Rev. ii. 9. So much the less therefore is ἐπονομάζ. to be here understood of a *surname* (Bengel). Full effect is given to the compound in classic writers also by the notion of name-giving, *imposing the name*. See Plat. *Crat.* p. 397 E, p. 406 A ; *Phaedr.* p. 238 A *al.;* Xen. *Occ.* 6, 17; Thuc. ii. 29, 3; Polyb. i. 29, 2 ; comp. Gen. iv. 17, 25 f. Van Hengel arbitrarily imports the idea : *pro veteri* nomine (Israelitarum) *novum substituens.* — ἐπαναπαύῃ τῷ νόμῳ] *acquiescis, thou reliest* (Mic. iii. 11 ; 1 Macc. viii. 12; see Wetstein) *on the law*, comp. John v. 45, as if the possession and knowledge of it were to thee the guarantee of salvation. The rest, *of not being obliged first of all to seek* what God's will is (Hofmann), cannot be meant; since such a seeking cannot be separated from the possession of the law, but is on the contrary directed to that very law (see ver. 18). But in the law the Jew saw the *magna charta of his assurance of salvation*. He *relied* upon it. — ἐν Θεῷ] As being the exclusive Father and Protector of the nation. Comp. Gen. xvii. 7; Is. xlv. 25; Jer. xxxi. 33. Observe the climax of the three points in ver. 17. The ἐν with καυχ. (2 Cor. x. 15; Gal. vi. 13), a verb which in Greek authors is joined with ἐπί or εἰς or the accusative, denotes that, *wherein* the καυχ. *rests*, according to the analogy of χαίρειν, τέρπεσθαι ἐν (Bernhardy, p. 211 ; Kühner, II. 1, p. 403). — Ver. 18, τὸ θέλημα] κατ' ἐξοχήν. *Whose* will it was, that was to be obeyed on the part of man, was obvious of itself. Comp. on ὄνομα Acts v. 41. — δοκιμάζεις τὰ διαφέρ.] *Thou approvest the excellent.* Respecting the *lexical* correctness of this rendering comp. on Phil. i. 10. Its correctness *in accordance with the connection* is plain from the climactic relation, in which the two elements of ver. 18 must stand to each other. "Thou knowest the will of God and approvest (theoretically) the excellent"—therewith Paul has conceded to the Jews all possible *theory* of the ethical, *up to the limit of practice*. Others, taking δοκιμάζειν as *to prove*, explain τὰ διαφέροντα as meaning *that which is different;* and this either (comp. Heb. v. 14) of the *distinction between right and wrong* (Theodoret, Theophylact, Estius, Grotius and others, including Reiche, Rückert, Tholuck, Fritzsche, Krehl, Philippi, van Hengel, Th. Schott), or *that which is different from the will of God*, i.e. what is wrong, sinful (Clericus, Glöckler, Mehring, Hofmann; compare Beza). But, after γινώσκεις τὸ θέλημα, how tame and destructive of the climax is either explanation! The Vulgate rightly renders: "probas utiliora." Compare Luther, Erasmus, Castalio, Bengel, Flatt, Ewald. — κατηχούμ. ἐκ τ. νόμου] *Being instructed out of the law* (through the public reading and exposition of it in the synagogues, comp. ἀκροάται, ver. 13), namely as to the will of God, and as to that which is excellent. — Vv. 19, 20 now describe, *with a reference* not to be mistaken (in opposition to Th. Schott and Hofmann) *to the Jewish presumption and disposition to proselytize* (Matth. xxiii. 15), the influence which the Jews, in virtue of their theoretic insight, fancied that they exercised over the *Gentiles*. The accumulated asyndetic designations of the same thing lend lively force to the description. They are not to be regarded with Reiche as reminiscences from the Gospels (Matth. xv. 14; Luke xx. 32, ii. 32); for apart from the fact that at least no canonical Gospel had at that time been written, the figurative expressions themselves which are here used were very current among the Jews and elsewhere. See, *e.g.* Wetstein on Matth. xv. 14. Observe, further, that Paul does not continue here with the conjunctive καί, but with the adjunctive τέ, because what follows contains the conduct determined by and *dependent* on the elements of ver. 18, and not something *independent*. Comp. Ellendt, *Lex. Soph.* II. p. 790. — σεαυτὸν ὁδηγ. κ.τ.λ.] that *thou thyself for thy part*, in virtue of this aptitude received from the law, etc. πέποιθα, accompanied by the accusative with the infinitive, occurs only here in the N. T., and rarely in Greek authors (Aesch. *Sept.* 444). — παιδευτὴν κ.τ.λ.] *trainer of the foolish, teacher of those in nonage.* Comp. Plat. *Pol.* x. p. 598 C: παῖδάς τε καὶ ἄφρονας. — τὴν μόρφωσιν τ. γνώσ. κ. τ. ἀληθ.] *the form of knowledge and of the truth.* In the doctrines and precepts of the law religious knowledge and divine truth, both in the objective sense, attain the conformation and exhibition (Ewald: "embodiment") proper to them, *i.e.* corresponding to their nature (hence τὴν μόρφ.), so that we possess in the law those lineaments which, taken collectively, compose the σχηματισμός (Hesychius) of knowledge and truth and thus bring them to adequate intellectual cognizance. Truth and knowledge have become in the law ἔμμορφος (Plut. *Num.* 8, *Mor.* p. 428 F), or μορφοειδής (Plut. *Mor.* p. 735 A). Paul adds this ἔχοντα τὴν μόρφ. τ. γν. κ. τ. ἀλ. as an illustrative definition (*ut qui habeas*, etc.) to all the points previously adduced; and in doing so he places himself entirely at the Jewish point of view (comp. Wisd. xxiv. 32 ff.), and speaks according to their mode of conception; hence the view which takes μόρφ. here as the mere *appearance* (2 Tim. iii. 5), in contrast to the reality, is quite erroneous (in opposition to τινές in Theophylact, Oecumenius, Pareus, Olshausen). Even Paul himself could not possibly find in the law merely the *appearance* of truth (iii. 21, 31). On μόρφωσις compare Theophrastus, *h. pl.* iii. 7, 4, and διαμόρφωσις in Plut. *Mor.* p. 1023 C.

Vv. 21, 22. Apodosis interrogating with lively indignation. See generally, and respecting οὖν, above on vv. 17-24. The *form* of the questions is expressive of *surprise at the existence* of an incongruity so much at variance with the protases, ver. 17 f.; it must have been in fact *impossible.* So also in 1 Cor. vi. 2.—*Dost thou, who teachest others accordingly, not teach thine own self?* namely, a better way of thinking and living than thou showest by thy conduct. Analogous passages expressing this contrast (comp. LXX. Ps. l. 16 ff.; Ignat. *Eph.* 15) from Greek and Rabbinical authors may be seen in Wetstein.—The following infinitives do not include in themselves the idea of δεῖν or ἐξεῖναι (see Lobeck, *ad Phryn.* p. 753 f.), but find their explanation in the idea of *commanding,* which is implied in the finite verbs; see Kühner, *ad Xen. Mem.* ii. 2, 1, *Anab.* v. 7, 34; Heindorf, *ad Plat. Prot.* p. 346 B; Wunder, *ad Soph. O. C.* 837. — ὁ βδελυσσόμενος τὰ εἴδωλα ἱεροσυλεῖς] *Thou, who abhorrest idols, dost thou plunder temples?* This is necessarily to be understood of the plundering of *idols' temples*, with Chrysostom, Theophylact,[1] Clericus, Wetstein, Koppe, Rosenmüller, Fritzsche, de Wette, Tholuck, Philippi, Mehring (Rückert indecisively); as is required by the antithetic relation in which ἱεροσυλεῖς stands to the βδελυσσόμ. τὰ εἴδωλα. "Thou who holdest all contact with idols as a detestable pollution—dost thou lay plundering hands on their temples?" *Abhorrence of idols* and (not, it might be, temple-destruction, Deut. vii. 25, but greedy) *temple-plundering*[2]—Paul could not have placed at the close of his reproachful questions a contrast between theory and practice more incisively affecting Jewish feeling. That robbery of temples actually occurred among the Jews, may justly be inferred from Acts xix. 37, but especially from Josephus, *Antt.* iv. 8, 10. See also Rabbinical passages in Delitzsch's Hebrew translation, p. 77. It is differently explained by Pelagius, Pareus, Toletus, Grotius, Heumann, Michaelis, Cramer, Reiche, Glöckler, Reithmayr, van Hengel, Ewald, and Hofmann, who understand it of robbing the *Jewish temple* by the embezzlement or curtailment of the temple-moneys and sacrifices (for proofs of this crime, see Josephus, *Antt.* viii. 3, 5 f.), by withholding the temple tribute, and the like. Compare *Test. XII. Patr.* p. 578. Luther, Calvin, Bengel, and others, including Morus, Flatt, Köllner, and Umbreit, interpret it, with still more deviation from the proper sense, as denoting the *"profanatio divinae majestatis"* (Calvin) generally.[3] Compare Luther's gloss, " Thou art a robber of God; for it is God's glory which all who would be holy through works take from Him." Such unjustifiable deviations from the literal sense would not

---

[1] Theophylact (whom Estius follows) very properly refers the ἱεροσυλεῖς to the temples of idols, but limits it to the taking away of the ἀναθήματα. His exposition, moreover, aptly brings out the practical bearing of the point: ἱεροσυλίαν λέγει τὴν ἀφαίρεσιν τῶν ἀνατιθεμένων τοῖς εἰδώλοις. καὶ γὰρ εἰ καὶ ἐβδελύσσοντο τὰ εἴδωλα, ἀλλ᾽ ὅμως τῇ φιλοχρηματίᾳ τυραννούμενοι ἥπτοντο τῶν εἰδωλικῶν ἀναθημάτων δι᾽ αἰσχροκερδίαν.

[2] The objection urged by Reiche and van Hengel, that ἱεροσυλεῖν always refers to temples which the speaker really looks upon as holy places, is irrelevant for this reason, that Paul was obliged to take the word, *which he found existing in the Greek*, in order to indicate temple-robbery, while he has already sufficiently excluded the idea that the temples themselves were sacred in his eyes by τὰ εἴδωλα.

[3] Olshausen thinks that *avarice*, as inward idolatry, is meant.

have been resorted to, if attention had been directed on the one hand to the actual unity of the object in the whole of the antitheses, and on the other to the appropriate climax: *theft, adultery, robbery of idols' temples.*

Ver. 23 gives to the four questions of reproachful astonishment the decisive categorical answer. See above on vv. 17-24. — διὰ τῆς παραβ. τ. νόμου] To this category belonged especially the ἱεροσυλεῖν; for in Deut. vii. 25 f. the *destruction* of heathen statues is enjoined, but the *robbery of their gold and silver* is repudiated. — τὸν θεὸν ἀτιμάζεις] How? is shown in ver. 24. — τὸν θεὸν] who has given the law.

Ver. 24. For confirmation of his τὸν θεὸν ἀτιμάζεις Paul subjoins a *Scripture quotation*, namely Is. lii. 5, in substance after the LXX., not the far more dissimilar passage Ezek. xxxvi. 22 f. (Calvin, Ewald and others), which, according to Hofmann, he is supposed to express according to the Greek translation of Is. *l.c.* "more convenient" for him. But he applies the quotation in such a way that *he makes it his own* by the γάρ not found in the original or the LXX.; only indicating by καθὼς γέγραπται at the close, that he has thus appropriated a *passage of Scripture.* Hence καθὼς γέγ. is placed at *the end*, as is never done in the case of express quotations of Scripture. The historical sense[1] of the passage is not here concerned, since Paul has not quoted it as a fulfilled prophecy, though otherwise with propriety in the sense of iii. 19. — δι᾽ ὑμᾶς] i.e. *on account of your wicked conduct.* — βλασφημεῖται ἐν τοῖς ἔθνεσι] *among the Gentiles*, inasmuch, namely, as these infer from the immoral conduct of the Jews that they have an unholy God and Lawgiver, and are thereby moved to blaspheme His holy name. Comp. Clement, *Cor.* I. 47.

Ver. 25. Having in vv. 17-24 (not merely taken for granted, but) thrown a bright light of illumination on the culpability of the Jews in presence of the law, Paul now briefly and decisively dissipates the fancy of a special *advantage*, of which they were assured through *circumcision*. "*For circumcision indeed*, the advantage of which thou mightest perchance urge against this condemnation, *is useful, if thou doest the law; but if thou art a transgressor of the law, thou hast as circumcised no advantage over the*

---

[1] It refers to God's name being dishonoured through the enslaving of the Jews by their tyrants.

uncircumcised." — γάρ therefore annexes a *corroboration* of the closing result of vv. 23, 24, and does so by excluding every advantage, which the Jew transgressing the law might fancy himself possessed of, as compared with the Gentile, in virtue of circumcision. *Stat sententia!* in spite of thy circumcision! Hofmann is the less justified, however, in taking the μέν *elliptically*, with the suppression of its antithesis (Hartung, *Partikell.* II. p. 414, and generally Baeumlein, *Part.* p. 163), since against its correspondence with the immediately following δέ no well-founded logical objection exists. — περιτομή] *circumcision*, without the article. It is not however, with Köllner and many others, to be taken as a description of *Judaism* generally; but definitely and specially of *circumcision*, to which sacrifice of the body—consecrating men to membership of the people of God (Ewald, *Alterth.* p. 127), and meant to be accompanied by the inner consecration of moral holiness (see on ver. 28)—the theocratic Jewish conceit attributed the absolute value of a service rendering them holy and appropriating the Abrahamic promises. — ὠφελεῖ] seeing that it transfers into the communion of all blessings and promises conferred by God on His covenant people; which blessings and promises, however, are attached to *the observance of His law* as their condition (Gen. xvii. 1 ff.; Lev. xviii. 5; Deut. xxvii. 26; Gal. v. 3), so that circumcision points at the same time to the new covenant, and becomes a sign and seal of the righteousness that is by faith (see on iv. 11). This however the Apostle has *not* yet in view *here.* — ἐὰν νόμ. κ.τ.λ.] Not *on the presupposition* that, but rather, as also the two following ἐάν: *in the case* that, Winer, p. 275 [E. T. 366]. — ἀκροβυστία γέγονεν] Has become עָרְלָה, has lost, for thee, every advantage which it was designed to secure to thee over the uncircumcised, so that thou hast now no advantage over the latter, and art, just as he is, no member of God's people. Paul conceives of the latter as a *holy* people, like the invisible church of God, in which the mortua membra of the people have no part. The same idea is illustrated concretely by R. Berechias in *Schemoth Rabb.* f. 138, 13: "Ne haeretici et apostatae et impii ex Israelitis dicant: Quandoquidem circumcisi sumus, in infernum non descendimus. Quid agit Deus S. B.? Mittit angelum et praeputia eorum attrahit, ita ut ipsi in infernum descendant." See other similar passages in Eisenmenger's *entdeckt. Judenth.* II. p. 339 f. — γέγονεν] Present of the completed action ; vii. 2 ; xiv. 23 ; John xx. 23. It is the emergent *ethical result, which takes place.*

Ver. 26. Interrogative inference of the corresponding inverse relation, drawn from ver. 25.— ἡ ἀκροβυστία αὐτοῦ] referring to the concrete ἀκρόβυστος understood in the previous ἀκροβυστία. See Winer, p. 138 [E. T. 182]. — τὰ δικαιώματα τ. νόμου φυλ.] The same as τὰ τοῦ νόμου ποιεῖν in ver. 14, as also the following τ. νόμον τελοῦσα of ver. 27.[1] A "*perfect, deep inner*" fulfilment of the law (Philippi), is a gratuitous suggestion, since there is no modal definition appended. Paul means *the* observance of the Mosaic legal precepts (respecting δικαιώματα comp. on i. 32 and v. 16), which in point of fact takes place when the Gentile obeys the moral law of nature, ver. 14 f. — εἰς περιτ. λογισθήσεται] *will be reckoned as circumcision* (εἰς in the sense of the result ; see ix. 8 ; Acts xix. 27 ; Is. xl. 17 ; Wisd. ix. 6 ; Theile, *ad Jac.* p. 138). The *future* is not that of the logical certainty (Mehring and older expositors), or of the result (Hofmann), which latter sense would be involved in a form of expression corresponding to the γέγονε ; but the glance of the Apostle extends (see ver. 27) to the *last judgment.* To the uncircumcised person, who observes what the law has ordained, *i.e.* the moral precepts of the law, shall one day be awarded the same salvation that God has destined, subject to the obligation of fulfilment of the law, for those who through circumcision are members of His people. As to the thought comp. Matth. viii. 11, iii. 9 ; 1 Cor. vii. 19 ; Gal. v. 6. The reference to *proselytes of the gate* (Philippi) is not only arbitrary, but also incorrect, because the text has in view the pure contrast between circumcision and uncircumcision, without any hint of an intermediate stage or anything analogous thereto. The proposition is to be retained in its unlimited expression. The mediation,

---

[1] τὸν νόμον τελεῖν means, as in James ii. 8, *to bring the law into execution.* It is only distinguished from φυλάσσειν and τηρεῖν νόμον by its representing the same thing on its *practical* side, so far as the law is *accomplished* by the *action* which the law demands. Comp. Plat. *Legg.* xi. p. 926 A, xii. p. 958 D ; Xen. *Cyr.* viii. 1, 1 ; Soph. *Aj.* 528 ; Lucian. *d. Morte Peregr.* 33. On the whole, -ελεῖν frequently answers to the idea *patrare, facere.* (Ellendt, *Lex. Soph.* II. p. 804.)

however, which has to intervene for the circumcised as well as for the uncircumcised, in order to the procuring of salvation *through faith*, is still left unnoticed here, and is reserved for the subsequent teaching of the Epistle. See especially ch. iv.

Ver. 27 is regarded by most modern expositors, including Rückert, Reiche (undecidedly), Köllner, Fritzsche, Olshausen, Philippi, Lachmann, Ewald and Mehring, as a *continuation of the question*, so that οὐχί is again understood before κρινεῖ. But the sequence of thought is brought out much more forcibly, if we take ver. 27 as *affirmative*, as the reply to the question contained in ver. 26 (as is done by Chrysostom, Erasmus, Luther, Bengel, Wetstein and others; now also by Tholuck, de Wette, van Hengel, Th. Schott, Hofmann). In this case the placing κρινεῖ first conveys a strong emphasis; and καί, as often in classic authors (Thiersch, § 354, 5 b.; Kühner, *ad Xen. Mem.* ii. 10, 2) is the simple *and*, which annexes the answer to the interrogative discourse as if in continuation, and thus assumes its affirmation as self-evident (Ellendt, *Lex. Soph.* I. p. 880). *And the natural uncircumcision, if it fulfils the law, shall judge*, i.e. exhibit in thy full desert of punishment (namely, *comparatione sui*, as Grotius aptly remarks[1]), *thee, who,* etc. Compare, on the idea, Matth. xii. 41; the thought of the *actual direct* judgment on the last day, according to 1 Cor. vi. 2, is alien to the passage, although the *practical indirect* judgment, which is meant, belongs to the future judgment-day. — ἡ ἐκ φύσεως ἀκροβ.] *The uncircumcision by nature, i.e.* the (persons in question) uncircumcised in virtue of their Gentile birth. This ἐκ φύσεως, which is neither, with Koppe and Olshausen, to be connected with τὸν νόμ. τελ., nor, with Mehring, to be taken as equivalent to ἐν σαρκί, is in itself superfluous, but serves to heighten the contrast διὰ γρ. κ. περιτ. The idea, that this ἀκροβυστία is a περιτομή ἐν πνεύματι, must (in opposition to Philippi) have been indicated in the text, and it would have no place in the connection of our passage; see ver. 29, where it first comes in. — τὸν διὰ γράμμ. κ. περιτ.

---

[1] Not so, that God in judging will apply the Gentile obedience of the law as a *standard for estimating* the Jewish transgression of it (Th. Schott), which is gratuitously introduced. The *standard* of judgment remains the law of God (ver. 12 f.); but the *example* of the Gentile, who has fulfilled it, exposes and *practically condemns* the Jew who has transgressed it.

παραβ. νόμου] *who with letter and circumcision art a transgressor of the law.* διά denotes the surrounding circumstances *amidst which, i.e.* here according to the context: *in spite of which* the transgression takes place.¹ Compare iv. 11, xiv. 20; Winer, p. 355 [E. T. 475]. Others take διά as instrumental, and that *either:* διὰ νόμου.... προαχθείς (Oecumenius; comp. Umbreit) or: "*occasione legis*," (Beza, Estius, and others; comp. Benecke), *or:* "who transgressest the law, and art *exhibited* as such by the letter," etc. (Köllner). But the former explanations introduce a foreign idea into the connection; and against Köllner's view it may be urged that his declarative rendering weakens quite unnecessarily the force of the contrast of the two members of the verse. For the most natural and most abrupt contrast to the *uncircumcised* person who keeps the law is he, who *transgresses* the law *notwithstanding letter and circumcision*, and is consequently all the more culpable, because he offends against written divine direction (γραμμ.) and theocratic obligation (περιτ.)

Vv. 28, 29. Proof of ver. 27. *For the true Judaism* (which is not exposed to that κρινεῖ) *resides not in that which is external, but in the hidden world of the internal.* — ὁ ἐν τῷ φανερῷ] i.e. ὅς ἐν τῷ φ. ἐστι (see Bornemann, *Schol. in Luc.* p. 116): *for he is not a Jew, who is so openly*, i.e. not he who shows himself to be an Ἰουδαῖος in external visible exhibition (in profession, circumcision, dress, ceremonial service, and the like) is a genuine, ἀληθινός, Ἰουδαῖος answering to the idea. See Matthiae, p. 1533, Buttmann, *neut. Gr.* p. 335 f. The second half of ver. 28, in which ἐν σαρκί forms an apposition to ἐν τῷ φανερῷ, more precisely defining it, is to be taken as quite parallel. — Ver. 29 is usually rendered: *But he who is a Jew in secret* (scil. *is a true Jew), and circumcision of the heart, in the spirit, not in the letter* (scil. *is true circumcision*). But against this view it may be urged that ὁ ἐν τῷ κρυπτῷ is so completely parallel to the ὁ ἐν τῷ φανερῷ in ver. 28, that a different mode of connection cannot but seem forced. Hence the following construction and exposition result more naturally (comp. Luther, Erasmus, and others; also Fritzsche): *But he is a Jew* (in the true sense) *who*

---

¹ Th. Schott arbitrarily: who with the possession of the law and circumcision *does not cease* to be a transgressor and *to pass for such*.

is so in secret (in the invisible inner life), *and* (instead of now saying, in parallel with ver. 28: ἡ ἐν τῷ κρυπτῷ περιτομή, Paul defines both the ἐν τῷ κρυπτῷ and the true spiritual meaning of περιτομή more precisely, and says) *circumcision of the heart resides* (the ἐστί to be supplied) *in the spirit, not in the letter.*[1] Stripped of figure, περιτομὴ καρδίας is: *the separation of all that is immoral from the inner life;* for circumcision was accounted even from the earliest times as σύμβολον ἡδονῶν ἐκτομῆς (Philo). See Lev. xxvi. 41; Deut. x. 16, xxx. 6; Jer. iv. 14, ix. 26; Ez. xliv. 7; compare Phil. iii. 3; Col. ii. 11; Acts vii. 51; Philo, *de Sacrif.* p. 58: περιτέμνεσθε τὰς σκληροκαρδίας, τόδε ἐστι τὰς περιττὰς φύσεις τοῦ ἡγεμονικοῦ, ἃς αἱ ἄμετροι τῶν παθῶν ἔσπειράν τε καὶ συνηύξησαν ὁρμαὶ καὶ ὁ κακὸς ψυχῆς γεωργὸς ἐφύτευσεν, ἀφροσύνη, μετὰ σπουδῆς ἀποκείρεσθε. See also Schoettgen, *Hor.* p. 815. The uncircumcised heart is ἀμετανόητος, ver. 5. — ἐν πνεύματι] is the power, *in which* the circumcision of the heart finds its *causal ground*, namely, *in the Spirit*, i.e. in the *Holy* Spirit, through whose power it takes place, *not in the letter*, which effects the outward circumcision by its commandment. In true Judaism also the Holy Ghost is the divine active principle (comp. vii. 14). So much the less reason is there for making πνεῦμα in our passage mean the true Jewish *public spirit* proceeding from God (de Wette, comp. Tholuck); or the *spirit of the law*, in contrast to its outward observance (van Hengel, who wrongly urges the absence of the article); or the *new life-principle in man*, wrought in him by the Spirit of God (Rückert, comp. Luther's gloss); on the contrary, the πνεῦμα is to be left as the objective, concrete *divine* πνεῦμα, as the *Holy Spirit* in the definite sense, and as distinguished from the spiritual conditions and tendencies which He *produces*. The correct and clear view is held by Grotius, Fritzsche, and Philippi; compare Hofmann. Others, as Theodore of Mopsuestia, Oecumenius (Chrysostom and Theophylact express themselves very indefinitely), Erasmus, Beza, Toletus, Heumann, Morus, Rosenmüller, Reiche, Mehring, take πνεῦμα as meaning *the spirit of*

---

[1] Ewald, who likewise follows our construction in the first clause of the verse, takes in the second half of it καρδίας as predicate: *and circumcision is that of the heart*. But in that case, since περιτομή *in itself* would be the *true* circumcision, we should expect the article before it.

man. But that the circumcision of the heart takes place in the spirit of man, is self-evident; and the similar contrast between πνεῦμα and γράμμα, vii. 6 and 2 Cor. iii. 6, clearly excludes the reference to the human spirit. — οὗ] *of which*, is *neuter*, and refers to the entire description of the true Jewish nature in ver. 29. The epexegetical relative definition bears to it an *argumentative* relation: *id quod laudem suam habet* etc. οὗ γε would be still more emphatic. To interpret it as *masculine* with reference to Ἰουδαῖος (Augustine, Erasmus, Beza, Bengel, and many others; including Reiche, Rückert, Köllner, de Wette, Olshausen, Tholuck, Fritzsche, Philippi, Ewald, and Hofmann; compare van Hengel), is, especially seeing that Paul has not written ὧν, as in iii. 8 (Schoem. *ad Is.* p. 243), a very unnecessary violence, which Grotius, who is followed by Th. Schott, makes still worse by twisting the construction as if the ἐστίν of ver. 28 stood immediately before οὗ (*it is not the evident Jew*, etc., *whose praise*, etc.). As is often the case in classic authors, the neuter of the relative belongs to the entire sentence; see especially Richter, *de anac. gr. linguae*, § 28; Matthiae, II. p. 987 f. — ὁ ἔπαινος] *i.e. the due praise* (not *recompense*). See on 1 Cor. iv. 5. Compare, on the matter itself, John v. 44, xii. 43. Oecumenius rightly says: τῆς γὰρ κρυπτῆς καὶ ἐν καρδίᾳ περιτομῆς οὐκ ἔσται ἐπαινέτης ἄνθρωπος, ἀλλ' ὁ ἐτάζων καρδίας καὶ νεφροὺς Θεός. Compare the δόξα Θεοῦ iii. 23. This *praise* is the holy *satisfaction* of God [His being *well-pleased*], as He has so often declared it to the righteous in the Scriptures.—Observe how perfectly analogous ver. 28 f. in its tenor of thought is to the idea of *the invisible church*. Compare on ver. 25.

CHAPTER III.

Ver. 2. μὲν γάρ] Lachm. following B D* E G, min. vss., Chrys. Aug. reads μέν. The γάρ was easily lost in consequence of its seeming unnecessary, and of the recollection of i. 8; but is supported by 1 Cor. xi. 18. — Ver. 9. προεχόμεθα] D* G 31, Syr. Erp. Chrys. ms. Theodoret have προκατέχομεν (or κατέχ.) περισσόν, and, with several other authorities, omit οὐ πάντως. This προκατ. περισσ. is an erroneous gloss; and the omission of οὐ πάντως is explained by its being no longer suitable after the adoption of τί οὖν προκατέχομεν περισσόν; see Reiche, *Comm. crit.* — Ver. 11. In important codices the article is wanting before συνίων and ἐκζητῶν. But see LXX. Ps. xiv. 2. — Ver. 22. καὶ ἐπὶ πάντας] is wanting in A B C P ℵ*, Copt. Aeth. Arm. Erp. Clem. Or. Cyr. Aug. Deleted by Lachm. and Tisch. 8. But when we consider that a gloss on εἰς πάντας was quite unnecessary, and on the other hand that καὶ ἐπὶ πάντας was equally unnecessary to complete the sense, we may assume that the twice repeated πάντας may have even at a very early date occasioned the omission of καὶ ἐπὶ πάντας. — Ver. 25. τῆς πίστ.] τῆς is wanting in C* D* F G ℵ, min., and several Fathers (A and Chrys. omit the whole διὰ τ. πίστ.). Suspected by Griesb., and deleted by Lachm. and Tisch. Still the omission of the article might easily occur if the copyist, as was natural, glanced back at διὰ πίστ., ver. 22. — Ver. 26. πρὸς ἔνδειξ.] Following A B C D* P ℵ, min., we should read with Lachm. and Tisch. πρὸς τὴν ἔνδειξ. The article was passed over in accordance with ver. 25. — Ἰησοῦ is wanting in F G 52 It.; and is expanded in other authorities (Χριστοῦ Ἰησοῦ, or τοῦ κυρίου ἡμ. Ἰησοῦ Χριστοῦ). Notwithstanding the preponderating testimony in its favour, it is properly deleted by Fritzsche and Tisch. 7. Supplied from looking back to ver. 22. — Ver. 28. γάρ] Elz. and Tisch. 7. read οὖν, against very preponderating testimony, by which also the arrangement δικ. πίστ. ἄνθρωπον (Elz.: π. δ. ἄ.) is confirmed. Since according to the different modes of apprehending the connection, the emendation might be οὖν as well as γάρ, external attestation only can here be regarded as decisive. — Ver. 29. The reading μόνων (so Tisch. 7. instead of μόνον) is insufficiently attested by B, min. and Fathers; and arose easily out of the context. — οὐχὶ καί] Elz.: οὐχὶ δὲ καί, against decisive testimony. The δέ was easily introduced into the text by the contrast, whether the two questions might be taken separately, or together as one. — ἐπείπερ] A B C D** ℵ, min., Clem. Or. Cyr. Didym. Damasc.: εἴπερ. Recommended by Griesb.; adopted by Lachm. and Tisch. 8. But how easily may the ἐπείπερ, only occurring here in the N. T., and therefore unfamiliar to the copyists, have been exchanged for the familiar εἴπερ!

Vv. 1,[1] 2. As an inference (οὖν) from ii. 28, 29, the objection might now be made from the Jewish standpoint against the Apostle, that he quite does away with the advantage of Judaism and the benefit of circumcision. This objection he therefore raises *in his own person*, in order to remove it himself immediately, ver. 2 ff. — τὸ περισσὸν κ.τ.λ.] the *superiority* (Matth. v. 47, xi. 9; Plat. *Ap. S.* p. 20 C; Lucian. *Prom.* 1; Plut. *Demosth.* 3) of the Jew, *i.e.* what he *has as an advantage* over the Gentile, the Jewish *surplus*. The following ἤ (or, to express it in other words) τίς ἡ ὠφέλ. τ. περιτ. presents substantially the same question in a more specific form. — πολύ] *Much*, namely, is the περισσόν of the Jew or the benefit of circumcision.[2] The neuter comprehends the answer to both; and it must not therefore be said that it applies only to the first question, leaving the second without further notice. It is moreover clear from what precedes and follows, that Paul meant the περισσόν not in a moral, but in a theocratic sense; comp. ix. 4 f. — κατὰ πάντα τρόπον] *in*

---

[1] On chap. iii. see Matthias, *exeget. Abhandlung über vv.* 1-20 (a school-programme), Hanau 1851; and the same author's work: *das dritte Kap. d. Br. an d. Röm*, *ein exeg. Versuch*, Cassel 1857; James Morison, *A critical exposition of the Third Chapter of Paul's Epistle to the Romans*, Lond. 1866.

[2] This answer is *the Apostle's*, not the reply of a *Jew* asserting his περισσόν, whom Paul then interrupts in ver. 4 with μὴ γένοιτο (Baur in the *theol. Jahrb.* 1857, p. 69) —a breaking up of the text into dialogue, which is neither necessary nor in any way indicated, and which is not supported by any analogy of other passages. According to Mehring Paul has written ver. 2, and in fact onward to ver. 8, as the sentiments of a Jew to be summarily dealt with, who in πρῶτον had it in view to enumerate yet further advantages, but whose mouth was closed by ver. 9. The unforced exposition of the successive verses does not permit this view; and ii. 25-29 is not at variance with ver. 2, but, on the contrary, leaves sufficiently open to the Apostle the recognition of Jewish privileges, which he begins to specify; comp. ii. 25 and ix. 4 f.

every way (Xen. *Anab.* vi. 6, 30), in whatever light the matter may be considered. See examples in Wetstein. The opposite: κατ' οὐδένα τρόπον, 2 Macc. xi. 31; Polyb. iv. 84, 8, viii. 27, 2. It is an undue anticipation to take the expression as *hyperbolical* (Reiche), since we do not know how the detailed illustration, which is only begun, would be further pursued. — πρῶτον] *first of all, firstly,* it is a prerogative of the Jew, or advantage of circumcision, that etc. The Apostle consequently begins to illustrate the πολύ according to its individual elements, but, just after mentioning the first point, is led away by a thought connected with it, so that all further enumeration (possibly by εἶτα, Xen. *Mem.* iii. 6, 9) is dropped, and not, as Grotius strangely thinks, postponed to ix. 4. Compare on i. 8; 1 Cor. xi. 18. As the μέν was evidently meant to be followed by a corresponding δέ, it was a mere artificial explaining away of the interruption of the discourse, to render πρῶτον *praecipue* (Beza, Calvin, Toletus, Estius, Calovius, Wolf, Koppe, Glöckler, and others; compare also Hofmann: "before all things"), or to say with Th. Schott, that it indicates the *basis* from which the πολύ *follows*. — ὅτι ἐπιστ. τ. λόγια τ. Θεοῦ] *that they* (the Jews) *were entrusted with the utterances of God,* namely, in the holy Scriptures given to them, devoutly to preserve these λόγια as a Divine treasure, and to maintain them for all ages of God's people as their and their children's (comp. Acts ii. 39) possession. On the Greek form of expression πιστεύομαί τι (1 Cor. ix. 17; Gal. ii. 7), see Winer, p. 244 [E. T. 326]. — τὰ λόγια τ. Θεοῦ] *eloquia Dei.* That by this general expression (χρησμοὺς αὐτοῖς ἄνωθεν κατηνεχθέντας, Chrysostom), which always receives its more precise definition from the context (Acts vii. 38; Heb. v. 12; 1 Pet. iv. 11; compare the passages from the Septuagint in Schleusner, *Thes.* III. p. 464, from Philo in Loesner, p. 248; and see especially Bleek on *Heb.* II. 2, p. 114 f.), Paul means here κατ' ἐξοχὴν the Messianic *prophetic-utterances,* is shown by ver. 3, where the ἀπιστία of the Jews leaves no room for mistake as to the contents of the λόγια. Compare αἱ ἐπαγγελίαι, ix. 4. These λόγια τ. Θεοῦ are contained not *merely* in the prophets proper (Acts iii. 24), but even in the Pentateuch (covenant with Abraham, the promise of Moses); yet the law is *not* meant, nor even *jointly* included (Matthias), against which ver. 3 testifies. Just as little is there meant: *all making known* of God *in the history of salvation*" (Hofmann), which is too general, and is extended by Hofmann even to the *New Testament* revelations. Regarding the *classic* use of λόγια,[1] *prophecies,* see Krüger on Thuc. ii. 8, 2, and generally Locella, *ad Xen. Eph.* p. 152 f.

Ver. 3. Not an objection to the preceding, but *a guarantee of the* ἐπιστεύθ. τὰ λόγια τ. Θεοῦ *just mentioned,* as something that has not been cancelled and revoked through the partial unbelief of the people. "*For how? what is the case?*[2] *If some refused the faith, will their unbelief make void the faithfulness of God?*" will it produce the effect that God shall now regard the promises once committed to the Jews as void, and Himself as no longer bound to His word therein pledged? The ἠπίστησαν and the ἀπιστία are by the context necessarily referred to the λόγια τ. Θεοῦ; the unbelief of a part of the Jews in the promises manifested itself, namely, by their rejecting the Messiah who had appeared according to the promise. So in substance also Matthias, who nevertheless apprehends the notion of ἀπιστ. as *unfaithfulness* towards what was entrusted to them, which the τίνες did not use for the purpose of letting themselves be led thereby to Christ. But ἀπιστεῖν and ἀπιστία (even in 2 Tim. ii. 13) mean specifically throughout the N. T. (see in this Epistle iv. 20, xi. 20, 23; compare Morison, p. 23) *unbelief,* not *unfaithfulness*, although Hofmann also ultimately comes to adopt this notion. This remark also applies against the supposition of Köllner, de Wette, Mehring, and older writers, that Paul meant the *unfaithfulness* (the *disobedience*) of the Jews *in the times before Christ*.[3] Such a view is opposed to the context; and must not the idea, that the earlier breaches of covenant on the part of the Jews

---

[1] The word is not a *diminutive form* (Philippi, who finds in it the usual *brevity* of oracular utterances), but the neuter form of λόγιος. The diminutive conception, *little utterances,* is expressed not by λόγιον, but by λογίδιον, Plat. *Eryx.* p. 401 E. This applies also in opposition to Morison.

[2] τί γάρ; compare Phil. i. 18. Elz., Bengel, and Lachm. place the sign of interrogation after τινές. Van Hengel follows them, also Th. Schott and Hofmann. It is impossible to decide the question. Still, even in classic authors, the τί γάρ; standing alone is frequent, "ubi quis cum alacritate quadam ad novam sententiam transgreditur," Kühner, *ad Xen. Mem.* ii. 6, 2; Jacobs. *ad Del. epigr.* vi. 60; Baeumlein, *Partik.* p. 73 f.

[3] Especially would τινες be quite unsuitable, because it would be absolutely untrue. *All* were disobedient and unfaithful. See ver. 9 ff.

might possibly annul the λόγια, have been wholly strange to Paul and his Jewish readers, since they knew from experience that, even when the Jews had heaped unfaithfulness upon unfaithfulness, God always committed to them anew, through His prophets, the promises of the Messiah ? In the mind of the Apostle the idea of the πάρεσις τῶν προγεγονότων ἁμαρτημάτων was fixed (ver. 25; Acts xvii. 30). Therefore we cannot understand (with Philippi) unbelief in the promises shown in the period *before Christ* to be here referred to. But according to the doctrine of faith in the promised One who had come, as the condition of the Messianic salvation, the doubt might very easily arise: May not the partial *unbelief* of the Jews *since the appearance of Christ*, to whom the λόγια referred, possibly cancel the divine utterances of promise committed to the nation ? Notwithstanding the simple and definite conception of ἀπιστεῖν throughout the N. T., Hofmann here multiplies the ideas embraced so as to include as well disobedience to the law as unbelief towards the Gospel and unbelief towards the prophetic word of promise—a grouping together of very different significations, which is the consequence of the erroneous and far too wide sense assigned to the λόγια τ. Θεοῦ. — τὴν πίστιν τ. Θεοῦ] The genitive is necessarily determined to be the genitive of the subject, partly by ἡ ἀπιστία αὐτῶν, partly by ver. 4, and partly by Θεοῦ δικαιοσ. in ver. 5. Therefore: the *fides Dei* in keeping the λόγια, *keeping His word*, in virtue of which He does not abandon His promises to His people.[1] Compare 2 Tim. ii. 13, and the frequent πιστὸς ὁ Θεός, 1 Cor. i. 9, x. 13; 2 Cor. i. 18 *al.*—Observe further that Paul designates the unbelievers only by τινές, *some*, which is not *contemptuous* or *ironical* (Tholuck, Philippi; compare Bengel), nor intended as a *milder* expression (Grotius), but is rather employed *to place in a stronger light the negation of the effect* under discussion; and, considering the relative import of τινές, it is not at variance with the

---

[1] It is the *fides, qua Deus promissis stat*, not in reality different from the idea of the ἀληθής in ver. 4. The word πίστις, however, is *selected* as the correlative of ἀπιστία. Despite the Jewish ἀπιστία it continues the case, not that God *has been* πιστός (in that, namely, He has spoken among the people, Hofmann thinks), but that He *is* πιστός, in that, namely, He does not allow Himself to be moved by that ἀπιστία τινων to become likewise ἄπιστος, which He would be, if He left His own λόγια committed to the Jews unfulfilled. He will not allow this case of the annulling of His πίστις to occur. Compare 2 Tim. ii. 13.

truth, for although there were *many* (τινές καὶ πολλοί γε, Plat. *Phaed.* p. 58 D), still they were not *all.* Compare xi. 17, and on 1 Cor. x. 7; Krüger, § 51, 16, 14.

Ver. 4. *Let it not be (far be it)! but God is to be truthful, i.e.* His truthfulness is to be the actual result produced (namely, in the carrying out of His Messianic plan of salvation), *and every man a liar.* To this it *shall* come ; the development of the holy divine economy to this final state of the relation between God and men, is what Paul knows and *wishes.* — μὴ γένοιτο] The familiar formula of negation by which the thing asked is repelled with abhorrence, corresponding to the חָלִילָה (Gen. xliv. 17; Josh. xxii. 29; 1 Sam. xx. 2), is used by Paul particularly often in our Epistle, elsewhere in Gal. ii. 17, iii. 21, 1 Cor. vi. 15, always in a dialectic discussion. In the other writings of the N. T. it occurs only at Luke xx. 16, but is current in later Greek authors (Raphel, *Arrian. in loc.;* Sturz, *de dial. Al.* p. 204). — γινέσθω] not equivalent to φανεροῦσθω, ἀποδεικνύσθω (Theophylact), but *the historical result* which shall *come to pass,* the *actual Theodicée* that shall *take place.* This indeed in reality amounts to a φανεροῦσθαι, but it is expressed by γινέσθω, according to its objective reality, which demonstrates itself. In that which God (and man) does, He *becomes actually* what according to His *nature He is.* — πᾶς δὲ ἄνθρ. ψεύστ.] By no means unessential (Rückert), or merely a concomitant circumstance (Th. Schott), is designed, and that all the more forcibly without a preceding μέν, to appropriate the ἀλήθεια *exclusively* to God, in contrast to ἠπίστ. τινες, ver. 3, outbidding this τινές by πᾶς. Every man is a *liar,* if he does not perform the service to which he has become bound, as is brought to light in the case of the τινές by their ἀπιστία, since as members of the people of God they had bound themselves to faith in the divine promises. That Paul had Ps. cxvi. 11 in view (Calvin, Wolf, and many others) is the more doubtful, seeing that he immediately quotes *another* passage. — ὅπως ἂν δικ. κ.τ.λ.] Ps. li. 6 exactly after the LXX. Independently of the more immediate connection and sense of the original text, Paul seizes on *the type* of the relation discussed by him, which is involved in the words of the Psalm, in the form in which they are reproduced by the LXX.[1] and that in the sense:

---

[1] The inaccuracies in the translation of the LXX. must be candidly acknow-

that thou mayest be justified, i.e. acknowledged as faultless and upright, *in thy words, and prevail* (in substance the same as the previous δικαιωθῇς) *when thou disputest*, namely, with men against whom thou defendest and followest out thy right. From this second clause results that πᾶς δὲ ἄνθρ. ψεύστης. The exact appropriateness of this view in the connection is decisive against the explanation commonly adopted formerly after the Vulgate and Luther, and again preferred by Mehring, which takes κρίνεσθαι as *passive* (*when thou art subjected to judgment*). On the use of the *middle*, *to dispute with*, compare LXX. Job ix. 3, xiii. 19, and other passages in Schleusner, *Thes. III.* p. 385 f. *This* use has been properly maintained by Beza, Bengel, and others; also Matthias, Tholuck, Philippi, van Hengel, Ewald, Hofmann, and Morison. Compare 1 Cor. vi. 1; Matth. v. 40. — ἐν τοῖς λόγοις σου] *i.e. in that which thou hast spoken.* And that is the *category* to which *those* λόγια belong, as to which the Apostle has just repelled the idea that God will not keep them on account of the ἀπιστία of the τινές and will thereby prove untrue. The sense " *in sententia ferenda*," when thou passest a sentence (Philippi), cannot be taken out of ἐν τ. λόγ. σου, since God is not represented as *judge*, but as *litigant*, over whom the justifying judicial decision is pronounced. The view of Hofmann is also erroneous: that it denotes the *accusations, which God may bring against men.* For the text represents God indeed as the party gaining the verdict and prevailing, but not as the accuser preferring *charges;* and the λόγοι, in respect of which He is declared justified, point back so directly to the λόγια in ver. 2, that this very correlation has occasioned the selection of the particular passage from Ps. li. — νικᾶν, like *vincere*, used of prevailing in a process; compare Xen. *Mem.* iv. 4, 17; Dem. 1436, 18 *al.* The opposite: ἡττᾶσθαι — On ὅπως (here *in order that in the event of decision*) see Hartung, *Partikell.* II. p. 286, 289; Klotz, *ad Devar.* p. 685.

Vv. 5, 6. In vv. 3 and 4 it was declared that the unbelief of a part of the Jews would not make void the truthfulness of God, but that, on the contrary, the latter should be triumphantly

---

ledged; still they do not yield any essential difference of sense from the idea of the original text. These inaccuracies consist in תִּזְכֶּה (*insons sis*) being rendered in the LXX. by νικήσῃς, and בְשָׁפְטֶךָ (*cum judicas*) being translated ἐν τῷ κρίνεσθαί σε.

justified. But how easily might this be misconstrued by a Jew of the common type as a pretext for his immorality: "the unrighteousness of man in fact brings out more clearly the righteousness of God, and therefore may not be righteously punished by God!" To preclude this misconception and false inference, which so abruptly run counter to his doctrine of universal human guilt, and to leave no pretext remaining (observe beforehand the τί οὖν; προεχόμεθα in ver. 9), Paul, having in view such thoughts of an antagonist, proposes to himself and his readers the question: "*But if our unrighteousness show forth the righteousness of God, what shall we say* (infer)? *Is God then unrighteous, who inflicteth wrath?*" And he disposes of it in the first instance by the categorical answer (ver. 6): *No, otherwise God could not be judge of the world.* The assumption, that this question is *occasioned really and seriously* by what goes before, and called forth from the Apostle himself (Hofmann), is rendered untenable by the very addition κατὰ ἄνθρωπον λέγω. — ἡ ἀδικία ἡμῶν] Quite general: our *unrighteousness*, abnormal moral condition. To this general category belongs also the ἀπιστία, ver. 3. Paul has regarded the possible Jewish misconception, the notion of which occasions his question, as a *general*, but for that reason all the more dangerous inference from vv. 3 and 4, in which the *words* ἀδικία and δικαιοσύνη are suggested by the passage from the Psalms in ver. 4. — ἡμῶν] is said certainly in the character of *the ἀδικοί in general*, and stands in relation to the πᾶς δὲ ἄνθρωπος ψεύστης in ver. 4. But as the whole context is directed against the *Jews*, and the application to *these* is intended in the general expressions, and indeed expressly made in ver. 19, Paul speaks here also in such a way that the *Jewish* consciousness, from which, as himself a Jew, he speaks, lies at the bottom of the *general* form of his representation. — The protasis εἰ .... συνίστησι is a *concessum*, which is in itself correct (ver. 4); but the *inference*, which the Jewish self-justification might draw from it, is rejected with horror. Observe in this protasis the emphatic juxtaposition ἡμῶν Θεοῦ; and in the apodosis the accent which lies on ἄδικος and τὴν ὀργήν. — Θεοῦ δικαιοσ. συνίστησι] *proves God's righteousness* (comp. v. 8; 2 Cor. vi. 4, vii. 11; Gal. ii. 18; Susann. 61; frequently in Polyb Philo, etc.); makes it apparent beyond doubt, that God is without fault, and such as He must be. The contrast to ἡ ἀδικία ἡμῶν requires δικαιοσ. to be taken thus generally, and forbids its being explained of a particular attribute (*truth:* Beza, Piscator, Estius, Koppe, and others; *goodness:* Chrysostom, Theodoret, Grotius, Rosenmuller), as well as its being taken in the sense of i. 17 (van Hengel). — The τί ἐροῦμεν (3 Esr. viii. 82) is used by Paul only in the Epistle to the Romans (iv. 1, vi. 1, vii. 7, viii. 31, ix. 14, 30). Compare, however, generally on such questions arousing interest and enlivening the representation, Blomfield, *Gloss. in Aesch. Pers.* 1013, Dissen, *ad Dem. de cor.* p. 346 f. — μὴ ἄδικος ὁ Θεὸς ὁ ἐπιφ. τ. ὀργήν] This question[1] is so put that (as in ver. 3) a *negative* answer is expected, since Paul has floating before his mind an impious objection conceived of κατὰ ἄνθρωπον. See Hermann, *ad Viger.* p. 789, 810; Hartung, *Partikell.* II. p. 159; Baeumlein, p. 302 f. Hence: *God is not unrighteous then, who dealeth wrath?* This in opposition to Rückert and Philippi, who make the questioner expect an *affirmative* answer, which can never be the case. In those passages in Greek authors, where an affirmative reply notwithstanding follows, it invariably does so *contrary to the expectation* of the questioner; see Kühner, II. 2, p. 1024. ἄδικος, prefixed with emphasis, is, on account of its relation to ὁ ἐπιφ. τ. ὀργήν, to be understood in the strict judicial signification *unrighteous*, which is confirmed by vv. 6 and 7. For examples of ἐπιφέρειν used to express the practical infliction of wrath or punishment see Raphel, *Polyb.;* Kypke, II. p. 160. The *article* with the participle indicates the relation as *well-known;* and τὴν ὀργήν (Sin.* adds αὐτοῦ) denotes the wrath definitely conceived of as *judicial*, inflicted at the judgment. Compare Ritschl, *de ira Dei,* p. 15. — κατὰ ἄνθρωπον λέγω] To preclude his being misunderstood, as if he were asking εἰ δὲ ἡ ἀδικία ἡμῶν.... μὴ ἄδικος κ.τ.λ. from his own enlightened Christian view, Paul remarks parenthetically that he says this *according to a human standard* (Bernhardy, p. 241), after the fashion of ordinary humanity, quite apart from his own higher standpoint of divine enlightenment, to which the idea expressed

---

[1] After μή, ἐροῦμεν is not again to be understood, and then ἄδικος κ.τ.λ. to be taken as a question ensuing *thereon* (Mangold, p. 106). A breaking up of the construction without due ground. Compare, rather, ix. 14, a passage which in form also is perfectly parallel to this one.

in that question would be foreign, and speaking only in accordance with mere human reason. Compare 1 Cor. ix. 8; Gal. iii. 15; Soph. *Aj.* 761: κατ' ἄνθρωπον φρονεῖ. "I say this just as an ordinary man, not under the influence of the divine Spirit, may well say it." Respecting the expression κατὰ ἄνθρ., which is capable according to the context of great variety of meaning, compare Fritzsche *in loc.* It is wrongly inferred from κατὰ ἄνθρ. λέγω that the question μὴ ἄδικος κ.τ.λ. was meant to receive an affirmative answer, because as a negative query it would not be κατὰ ἄνθρ. (see Philippi). But this view overlooks the fact that the whole thought, which is implied in the question calculated though it is for a negative reply,—the thought of the unrighteousness of God in punishing—can in fact only be put into expression κατὰ ἄνθρωπον; in the higher Christian insight a conception so blasphemous and deserving of abhorrence can find neither place nor utterance. The apology however, involved in κατὰ ἄνθρ. λέγω, is applicable only to *what goes before*, not to *what follows*, to which Mehring, Th. Schott and Hofmann refer it. This is the more obvious, since what immediately follows is merely a repudiating μὴ γένοιτο, and the ἐπεί κ.τ.λ., which assigns the ground for this repudiation, is by no means an idea outside the range of revelation, the application of which to a *rational inference*, and one too so plainly right, cannot transfer it to the lower sphere of the κατὰ ἄνθρ. λέγειν.— Ver. 6. ἐπεί] gives the ground of the μὴ γένοιτο; *for* (if the God who inflicts wrath is *unrighteous*) *how will it be possible that He shall judge the world?* The *future* is to be left in its purely *future* sense, since it refers to a future act taking place at any rate, as to which the only difficulty would be to see *how it was to be accomplished*, if, etc. On ἐπεί, *for otherwise*, see Buttmann, *neut. Gr.* p. 308. κρινεῖ has the emphasis.— τὸν κόσμον is to be taken, with most expositors, generally as meaning *all mankind* (compare ver. 19). To be judge of the world and yet, as ἐπιφέρων τ. ὀργ., to be ἄδικος, is a contradiction of terms; the certainty that God is the former would become an impossibility if He were the latter. Compare Gen. xviii. 25. Koppe, Reiche, Schrader, Olshausen, and Jatho, following older authorities, take it only of the *Gentile world* (xi. 12; 1 Cor. vi. 2, xi. 32); "In that case God could not punish even the Gentile world for its idolatry, since it is only in contrast therewith that the true worship of God appears in its full value" (Reiche) But, in this explanation, the very essential idea: "*since* . . . . *appears*" has first of all to be *imported*, an expedient which, in presence of the simplicity and clearness of our view, cannot but seem arbitrary. Even the following proof, ver. 7 f., does not present a reference directly to the judgment of the *Gentiles*. The argument itself rests on the premiss that God can carry out the *judgment* of the world only as One who is *righteous* in His decreeing of wrath. The opposite would be impossible, not only subjectively, in God Himself (Th. Schott), but also objectively, as standing in contradiction to the notion of a world-judgment. See ver. 7 f. This proposition however is so perfectly *certain* to the *consciousness of faith*, out of which Paul asserts it, that there is no ground either for complaining of the *weakness* of the proof (Rückert), or for reading the thoughts that form the proof between the lines (Fritzsche and Mehring, with varying arbitrariness); the more especially as afterwards, in ver. 7, a still further *confirmation* of the ἐπεί . . . . κόσμον follows.

Ver. 7 f. The ἐπεὶ πῶς κρινεῖ ὁ Θεὸς τ. κόσμ. receives its *illustrative confirmation;* for as to the case of God, who would thus be *unrighteous* and nevertheless is to *judge* the world, every ground for judging man as a sinner must be superseded by the circumstance already discussed, viz. that His truth has been *glorified* by man's falsehood (ver. 4 f.); and (ver. 8) as to the case of man himself, there would result the principle directly worthy of condemnation, that he should do evil in order that good might come. Comp. Th. Schott, and in substance also Hofmann and Morison. The argument accordingly rests on the basis, that in the case put (ἐπεί from ver. 6) the relation of God to the judgment of the world would yield two absurd consequences. (See this, as early as Chrysostom.) Another view is that of Calvin, Beza, Grotius, Wolf, and many others, including Rückert, Köllner, Tholuck, Philippi and Umbreit, that the objection of ver. 5 is here amplified. But it is quite as arbitrary and in fact impossible (hence Philippi resorts to the violent expedient of putting in a parenthesis not only κατὰ ἄνθρ. λέγω, but also μὴ γένοιτο . . . . κόσμον), with the reference of γάρ, to overleap entirely ver. 6, as it is strange to make the discourse so completely abrupt and to represent the

Apostle as making no reply at all to the first part of the alleged amplification of the objection (to ver. 7), and as replying to the second part (ver. 8) only by an *anathema sit !* (ὧν τ. κρ. ἔνδ. ἔ.). Against the view of Reiche, who, following Koppe, Rosenmüller, and Flatt, thinks that the *Gentile* is introduced as speaking in ver. 7 (compare Olshausen), we may decisively urge the close connection therewith of ver. 8, *where Paul includes himself also*, but does not "take speech in hand again" (Reiche). See besides on τὸν κόσμον, ver. 6.— ἀλήθεια and ψεύσματι are terms chosen in reference to ver. 4, because the question proposed in ver. 5 was in fact suggested by that verse; but they represent, as ver. 5 proves, the ideas of δικαιοσύνη and ἀδικία; hence: *the moral truth*, *i.e.* the holy righteousness of God (see on John iii. 21; Eph. v. 9; Phil. iv. 8), and *the moral falsehood*, *i.e.* the immorality (Rev. xxii. 15), wickedness of man.[1] — ἐπερίσσευσεν εἰς τ. δόξ. αὐτοῦ] *has abounded richly to His glory*, that is, has shown itself in superabundant measure, which redounds to His glory. The stress of this protasis lies on ἐν τῷ ἐμῷ ψεύσματι. — The *aorist* denotes the result of the having abounded, which subsists at the day of judgment (realised as present by τί . . . . κρίνομαι) as up to that point accomplished fact. — ἔτι] namely, after that assumed result has occurred. — κἀγώ] emphasising the contradictory relation to the contents of the protasis, according to which this ἐγώ seems actually to have *deserved* something of God: *even I* (Baeumlein, *Partik.* p. 150) who have notwithstanding glorified God through my ψεῦσμα. So in substance ("*just I*" according to Hermann, *ad Viger.* p. 837) also Tholuck and Morison; compare Philippi: "*even I still.*" There lies in the expression something of boldness and defiance; but it is not equivalent to καὶ αὐτός, or αὐτός ἐγώ, to the meaning of which Th. Schott and Hofmann ultimately bring it ("*even personally still*"). We may add that this first person, individualising just like the preceding one (ἐν τ. ἐμῷ ψ.), of course represents *the sinner in general* (with an intended application to the *Jews*, see on ver. 5 f) and not *the Apostle himself*, as Schrader and Fritzsche think. Against this latter theory it is decisive that κρίνομαι after ver. 6 must indicate,

---

[1] Those who take ver. 7 f. as spoken in the person of the *Gentile* (see especially Reiche) explain the ἀλήθεια Θεοῦ of the true religion (how entirely opposed to ver. 4 !), ψεύσματι of idolatry, and ἁμαρτωλός as Gentile.

not the judgment of enemies, but necessarily the *divine* act of judging. — ὡς ἁμαρτ.] *as a sinner*, not "*as a Gentile*" (Reiche, Mehring), and others.—Ver. 8. καὶ μή] Before μή we must again supply τί: *and why should we not*, etc. Respecting τί μή, *quidni*, see Hartung, *Partikell.* II. p. 162. Accordingly, as καί continues the question, only a comma is to be placed after κρίνομαι. — As regards the construction, Paul has dropped the plan of the sentence begun with καὶ μή (*and why should we not do evil*, etc.), being led away from it by the inserted remark, and has joined ὅτι ποιήσωμεν *in direct address* (*let us do*) to the λέγειν, so that ὅτι is *recitative*. But on account of this very blending there is no necessity either to make a parenthesis or to supply anything. For similar attractions (compare especially Xen. *Anab.* vi. 4, 18) in which the discourse is interrupted by an intervening clause, and then continued in a regimen dependent on the latter and no longer suitable to the beginning, see Hermann *ad Viger.* p. 745, 894; Bernhardy, p. 464; Dissen, *ad Dem. de cor.* p. 346, 418; Krüger, *gramm. Unters.* p. 457 ff. Many erroneous attempts have been made by commentators (see the various explanations in Morison) to bring out an unbroken construction, as *e.g.* the supplying of ἐροῦμεν or some such word after μή (Erasmus, Calvin, Wolf, Koppe, Benecke, and others, also van Hengel). Even the expedient of Matthias is untenable.[1] The same may be said of that of Hofmann, who supplies an ἐστίν after καὶ μή, and renders: "*Why does it not happen to me according to that, as* (καθώς) *we are slandered*," etc. But if it is quite gratuitous to supply ἐστί, it is still more so to make this ἐστί equivalent to γίνεται μοι. Besides the negation, which, according to our construction,

---

[1] He brings forward the modal definition: ὡς ἁμαρτωλός as the main element; then the modality of the κρίνομαι opposed to this is καὶ μὴ καθὼς βλασφημ. κ.τ.λ.: "Why then am even I still judged like a *sinner*, and not rather according to that, which we are slanderously reported of, and which some affirm that we say: namely, *according to this*, Let us do evil, that *good* may come ?" Instead of saying: καὶ μὴ ὡς ποιήσας τὰ ἀγαθά, Paul, in the indignation of excited feeling, gives to the thought which he had begun the different turn which it presents in the text. With this artificial interpretation, we must remember that Paul would have written καὶ οὐ instead of καὶ μή, since it is an objective relation that is here in question (compare Col. ii. 8 *al.*); that instead of καθώς we should have expected the repetition of the ὡς; and that the notion of κρίνειν, as it prevails in the connection (compare also the following τὸ κρῖμα), does not suit the assumed thought, ὡς ποιήσας τὰ ἀγαθά. Comp. also Morison, p. 79.

harmonises with the deliberative sense, would necessarily be not μή but οὐ, since it would negative the reality of the εἶναι understood (1 Cor. vi. 7; Luke xix. 23, xx. 5 *al.*). The correct view is held also by Winer and Buttmann (p. 235, 211), Philippi and Morison. — καθὼς βλασφημ.] *as we (Christians) are calumniated*, namely, as if we did evil in order that, etc. Then the following καὶ καθώς .... λέγειν contains the accusation, current possibly in Rome also, that the Christians were in the habit of repeating this maxim even as a doctrinal proposition. As to the distinction between φημί (to assert) and λέγω, compare on 1 Cor. x. 15. What may have occasioned such slanders against the Christians? Certainly their non-observance of the Mosaic law, to which they ventured to deem themselves not bound, in order to gain eternal life by the grace of God through faith in the redemptive work of Christ, which was an offence to the Jews. The plural is not to be referred to *Paul alone*, which would be arbitrary on account of the preceding singular; the Christians are conceived as *Pauline* (comp. Acts xxi. 21); and on the part of Jews and Judaizers (τινές, *certain people*, as in 1 Cor. xv. 12) are slanderously and falsely (for see v. 20, vi. 1, 15 ff.) accused of *doing evil that good might come* (might ensue as result). Under this *general category*, namely, the calumniators reduced the bearing of the Christians, so far as the latter, without regulating their conduct by the Mosaic law, were nevertheless assured, and professed, that they should through faith in Christ obtain the divine blessings of salvation. That general accusation was an injurious abstract inference thence deduced. — ὧν] *i.e.* of those, who follow this principle destructive of the whole moral order of God. They form the nearest logical subject. With just indignation the Apostle himself, having a deep sense of morality, makes us feel in conclusion by ὧν τὸ κρῖμα κ.τ.λ. how *deserving of punishment* is the consequence, which, if God be regarded as an unrighteous judge of the world, must ensue for moral conduct from the premiss that God is glorified by the sin of men. The reference of ὧν to the *slanderers* (Theodoret, Grotius, Tholuck, Mehring, Hofmann) is unsuitable, because it separates the weighty closing sentence from the argumentation itself, and makes it merely an accessory thought. — τὸ κρῖμα] The definite judicial sentence, decree of punishment at the last judgment. — ἔνδικον] *accordant with jus-*

tice, rightful. Compare Heb. ii. 2. Frequently used in classic writers.

Ver. 9. When Paul, in vv. 6-8, has defended the righteousness of God as decreeing wrath (ver. 5) in the face of the proposition, correct in itself, that human sin turns out to God's glory, he has thereby also deprived the sinner of all the *defence*, which he might derive from the misapplication of that proposition. This position of the case, as it results from vv. 6-8 (οὖν), he now expresses, and that in the lively form of an interrogation, here accompanied by a certain triumph: *What then? Are we in the position to apply a defence for ourselves?* We cannot therefore with most expositors (including Tholuck, Philippi, Bisping) assume that Paul here reverts to ver. 1.—That the punctuation should not be τί οὖν προεχόμεθα; (as it is given by Oecumenius, 1 Koppe, Th. Schott) is plain from the answer, which is not οὐδὲν πάντως, but οὐ πάντως. And that in adopting the general inclusive form Paul speaks from the standpoint of the *Jewish* consciousness, and not in the person of the *Christians* (Hofmann), is apparent from the context both before (see vv. 3, 5, 7) and after ('Ιουδαίους τε καὶ Ἕλλ., and see ver. 19).— τί οὖν] sc. ἐστί (Acts xxi. 22; 1 Cor. xiv. 15, 26), *what takes place then?* how is then the state of the case? Compare vi. 15, xi. 7; frequent in classical writers; comp. on vv. 3, 5.— προεχόμεθα] *Do we put forward* (anything) *in our defence?* Is it the case with us, that something serves us as a defence, that can secure us against the punitive righteousness of God? προέχειν, which in the active form means *to hold before, to have in advance, to bring forward*, and intransitively *to be prominent*, also *to excel* (see Wetstein, also Reiche, *Comment. crit.* I. p. 24), has in the middle simply the signification *to hold before oneself, to have before oneself*, either in the *proper* sense, *e.g.* of holding forth spears for defence (Hom. *Il.* xvii. 355), or of having oxen in front (*Od.* iii. 8), or of holding in front the ram's head (Herod. ii. 42), etc., or in the *ethical* sense: *to put forward*, πρόσχημα ποιεῖθαι, *to apply something for one's own defence*, as in Soph. *Ant.* 80: σὺ μὲν τάδ᾽ ἂν προὔχοι᾽, Thuc. i. 140, 5 and Krüger *in loc.*, and also Valckenaer, *ad fr. Callim.* p. 227. More frequent in Greek writers is the form προΐσχεσθαι, in this sense, as *e.g.* Thuc. i. 26, 2. Compare also πρόφασιν προΐσχεσθαι, Herod. vi. 117, viii. 3; Herodian, iv. 14, 3; Dem.

in *Schol. Hermog.* p. 106, 16 : προΐσχεσθαι νόμον. This sense of the word is therefore rightly urged by Hemsterhuis, Venema, Koppe, Benecke, Fritzsche ("*utimurne praetextu?*"), Krehl, Ewald, Morison; compare also Th. Schott. This explanation is the only one warranted by linguistic usage,[1] as well as suited to the connection (see above). The most usual rendering (adopted by Tholuck, Köllner, de Wette, Rückert, Baumgarten-Crusius, Philippi, Baur, Umbreit, Jatho, and Mangold) is that of the Peschito and Vulgate (*praecellimus eos?*), and of Theophylact: ἔχομέν τι πλέον .... καὶ εὐδοκιμοῦμεν οἱ Ἰουδαῖοι, ὡς τόν νόμον καὶ τὴν περιτομὴν δεξάμενοι. Compare Theodoret: τί οὖν κατέχομεν περισσόν; Philippi: "Have we any advantage for ourselves?" and now also Hofmann (who held the right view formerly in his *Schriftbew.* I. p. 501): "Do we raise ourselves above those, upon whom God decrees His judgment of wrath?" But the mere *usus loquendi*, affording not a single instance of the *middle* employed with the signification *antecellere, raising oneself above, surpassing*, or the like, decisively condemns this usual explanation in its different modifications.[2] And would not the answer οὐ πάντως, in whatever sense we take it, so long as agreeably to the context we continue to

[1] Also adopted by Valck. *Schol. in Luc.* p. 258. Still he would read προεχώμεθα and take τί οὖν προεχ. together. But the absolute position of προεχ., which has been made an objection to our explanation (Rückert, Tholuck, de Wette, Philippi, Hofmann), does not affect it, since all verbs, if the object be self-evidently implied in the idea itself, may be used so that we can mentally supply a τί (Winer, p. 552 [E. T. 742]). And the *subjunctive*, which van Hengel also regards as necessary with our view, is not required; the indicative makes the question more definite and precise (Winer, p. 267 [E. T. 354]). Ewald likewise reads τί οὖν προεχώμεθα (subjunctive); but expunges γάρ afterwards, and takes οὐ interrogatively, "*What shall we now put forward in defence? did we not already, at the outset, prove altogether that Jews,*" etc. But the omission of γάρ is only supported by D*. Van Hengel despairs of a proper explanation, and regards the text as corrupt.

[2] Reiche (and similarly Olshausen) retains the same exposition in his exegetical Commentary; but takes προεχ. as *passive, are preferred*, referring in support of his view to Plut. *de Stoic. contrad.* 13 (*Mor.* p. 1038 C), where however, in τοῖς ἀγαθοῖς πᾶσι ταῦτα προσήκει κατ' οὐδὲν προεχομένοις ὑπὸ τοῦ Διός, the meaning of this προεχομένοις is *becoming surpassed*. In his *Commentar. crit.* I. p. 26 ff., he has passed over to the linguistically correct rendering *praetexere*, but understands nevertheless the first person of Paul himself, and that in the sense: "*num Judaeis peccandi praetextum porrigo?*" But the middle means invariably to hold something (for protection) before *oneself;* as προφασίζομαι also, by which Hesychius properly explains the word, always refers to the subject, which excuses *itself* by a pretext.

understand as the subject the *Jewish*, not the Christian *we* (as Hofmann takes it), be at variance with the answer πολὺ κατὰ πάντα τρόπον given in ver. 2 ? The shifts of expositors to escape this inconsistency (the usual one being that Paul here means *subjective* advantages in respect of justification, while in ver. 2 he treats of *objective* theocratic advantages) are forced expedients, which, not at all indicated by any clause of more precise definition on the part of Paul himself, only cast suspicion on the explanation. Wetstein, Michaelis, Cramer, Storr, and recently Matthias, take προεχ. as the passive : *are surpassed:* "Stand we (at all) at a disadvantage ? Are we still surpassed by the Gentiles?" Compare Xen. *Anab.* iii. 2, 19 ; Plut. *Mor.* p. 1038 C. But how could this question be logically *inferred* from the foregoing without the addition of other thoughts ? And in what follows it is not the sinful equality of the *Gentiles* with the Jews, but that of the *Jews* with the Gentiles which is made conspicuous. See also ver. 19. Mehring, in thorough opposition to the context, since not a single hint of a transition to the Gentiles is given, makes the question (comp. Oecumenius, 2), and that in the sense "Are we at a disadvantage?" be put into the mouth even of a *Gentile.* — οὐ πάντως] Vulgate: *nequaquam*; Theophylact: οὐδαμῶς. This common rendering (compare the French *point de tout*) is, in accordance with the right explanation of προεχόμεθα, the only proper one. The expression, instead of which certainly πάντως οὐ *might* have been used (1 Cor. xvi. 12), is quite analogous to the οὐ πάνυ, where it means *in no wise*,[1] as in Xen. *Mem.* iii. 1, 11 ; *Anab.* i. 8, 14 ; Herodian, vi. 5, 11 ; Dem. *Ol.* iii. 21 ; Plat. *Lach.* p. 189 C ; Lucian, *Tim.* 24 (see Hartung, *Partikell.* II. p. 87), so that the negative is not transposed, and yet it does not cancel the idea of the adverb, but on the contrary is strengthened by the adverb. By this means the emphatic affirmation, which would have been given by the πάντως alone, is changed into the opposite.[2] Compare Winer, p. 515 f. [E. T. 693]. The comparison with לֹא־כֹל (Buttmann, *neut. Gr.* p. 334) is utterly foreign, since the expression is a pure Greek one. Compare Theognis, 305, Bekker :

---

[1] Those passages where οὐ πάνυ negatives with a certain subtlety or ironical turn (*not quite, not just*), are not cases here in point ; see Schoemann, *ad Is.* p. 276.

[2] Bengel : "Judaeus diceret πάντως, at Paulus *contradicit.*"

οἱ κακοὶ οὐ πάντως (by no means) κακοὶ ἐκ γαστρὸς γεγόνασιν. *Ep. ad Diogn.* 9: οὐ πάντως ἐφηδόμενος (by no means rejoicing) τοῖς ἁμαρτήμασιν ἡμῶν, ἀλλ' ἀνεχόμενος. Perfectly similar is also the Homeric οὐ πάμπαν, *decidedly not;* see Nägelsbach on the *Iliad*, p. 146, ed. 3; Duncan, *Lex. Hom.* ed. Rost, p. 888. Compare οὐδὲν πάντως, Herod. v. 34, 65. The explanation, on which van Hengel also insists: *not altogether,* not in every respect (Grotius, Wetstein, Morus, Flatt, Köllner, Matthias, Umbreit, Mehring and Mangold), as in 1 Cor. v. 10, fails to tally with the true explanation of προεχόμεθα and the unrestricted character of the following proof. — προῃτιασάμεθα] namely, not just from ver. 5 onward (Hofmann), but, in accordance with the following Ἰουδαίους τε κ. Ἕλληνας, in ii. 1 ff. as to the *Jews,* and in i. 18 ff. as to the *Gentiles*.[1] It is therefore as in i. 5 and frequently elsewhere, the plural *of the author,* not: *we Christians* (Hofmann). As to the construction, πάντας may either be joined as an adjective to Ἰουδ. τ. κ. Ἕλλ., or as a substantive to the infinitive, in either case expressing the idea of *all collectively, nemine excepto.* The latter mode of connection is preferable, because it gives a more marked prominence to the idea of totality, which harmonises with the following vv. 10-12. Hence: *we have before brought the charge against Jews and Gentiles, that all,* etc. Comp. Hofmann and Morison. There is elsewhere no instance of the compound προαιτ.; the Greeks use προκατηγορεῖν. — ὑφ' ἁμαρτ. εἶναι] They are—while still unregenerate, a more precise definition that is self-evident—all *under sin,* an expression denoting not merely a state of sin in general, but moral *dependence* on the *power* of sin. Compare vii. 25; Gal. iii. 22. But if this be the case with *Jews* and Gentiles (not merely on the *Gentile* side), then the Jew, after the way of escape indicated in ver. 5 has been cut off by vv. 6-8, has no defence left to him as respects his liability to punishment any more than the Gentile.[2] Accordingly the idea of *liability to punishment* is not yet *expressed* in ὑφ' ἁμαρτ. εἶναι, but is meant only to be *inferred* from it.

[1] Paul however does not say *Gentiles and Jews,* but the converse, because here again, as in previous cases where both are grouped together (in the last instance ii. 9 f.), he has before his mind the divine historical order, which in the very point of sinfulness tells against the Jew the more seriously.

[2] For statements of Greek writers regarding the universality, without any exception, of sin see Spiess, *Logos spermat.* p. 220 f.

Vv. 10-18. Conformity with Scripture of the charge referred to, Ἰουδαίους τε καὶ Ἕλλην. πάντ. ὑφ' ἁμ. εἶναι, so far (ver. 19) as this charge cuts off from the Jews every προέχεσθαι of ver. 9. — The recitative ὅτι introduces citations from Scripture very various in character, which after the national habit (Surenhusius, καταλλ. *thes.* 7) are arranged in immediate succession. They are taken from the LXX., though for the most part with variations, partly due to quotation from memory, and partly intentional, for the purpose of defining the sense more precisely. The arrangement is such that testimony is adduced for—1*st*, the *state* of sin generally (vv. 10-12); 2*nd*, the *practice* of sin in word (vv. 13, 14) and deed (vv. 15-17); and 3*rd*, the sinful *source* of the whole (ver. 18). More artificial schemes of arrangement are not to be sought (as *e.g.* in Hofmann), not even by a play on numbers.[1] — οὐκ ἔστι δίκαιος οὐδὲ εἷς] *There exists not a righteous person* (who is such as he ought to be), *not even one.* Taken from Ps. xiv. 1, where the Sept. has ποιῶν χρηστότητα instead of δίκαιος; Paul has put the latter on purpose at once, in accordance with the aim of his whole argument, prominently to characterise the ὑφ' ἁμαρτ. εἶναι as a want of δικαιοσύνη. Michaelis regards the words as *the Apostle's own*, " under which he comprehends all that follows." So also Eckermann, Koppe, Köllner and Fritzsche. But it is quite at variance with the habit of the Apostle, after using the formula of quotation, to prefix to the words of Scripture a summary of their contents; and this supposition is here the more improbable, seeing that the Apostle continues in ver. 11 in the words of the same Psalm, with the first verse of which our passage substantially agrees. — Regarding οὐδὲ εἷς see on 1 Cor. vi. 5, and Stallbaum, *ad Plat. Symp.* p. 214 D. — Ver. 11 is from Ps. xiv. 2, and so quoted, that the *negative* sense which results indirectly from the text in the Hebrew and LXX. is expressed by Paul directly: *there exists not the understanding one* (the practically wise, *i.e. the pious one*; see Gesenius, *Thes. s. v.* הכם): *there exists not the seeker after God* (whose thoughts and endeavours are directed towards God,

---

[1] According to Hofmann the first and second parts consist each of *seven* propositions. Thus even the conclusion of ver. 12, οὐκ ἔστιν ἕως ἑνός, is to be reckoned as a separate proposition ! How all the parallelism of Hebrew poetry is mutilated by such artifices !

Heb. xi. 6, and see Gesenius, *s. v.* דָּרַשׁ). The article denotes the *genus* as a definite *concrete* representing it. Compare Buttmann's *neut. Gr.* p. 253 f. On the idea, which is also classical, of sin as *folly*, see Nägelsbach, *Hom. Theol.* VI. 2. — The form συνίων (so accentuated by Lachmann; compare Buttmann, I. p. 543), or συνιῶν (though the former is the more probable; compare Winer, p. 77 f. [E. T. 97], also Ellendt, *Lex. Soph.* II. p. 768), is the usual one in the Sept. (instead of συνιείς, Ps. xxxiii. 15). Ps. xli. 1; Jer. xxx. 12; 2 Chron. xxxiv. 12 *et al.* — ἐκζητ.] stronger than the simple form; compare 1 Pet. i. 10; very frequent in the LXX. — Ver. 12. From Ps. xiv. 3 closely after the LXX. ἐξέκλιναν, namely from the right way, denotes the demoralisation (see Gesenius, *s. v.* סוּר), as does also ἠχρειώθησαν, נֶאֱלָחוּ: they have *become useless*, corrupt, good for nothing, ἀχρεῖοι (Matth. xxv. 30); Polyb. i. 14, 6, i. 48, 9. The following ποιῶν χρηστότητα is correlative. This ἅμα (*altogether*) ἠχρειώθ. has still πάντες for its subject. — ἕως ἑνός] The οὐκ ἔστιν holds *as far as to one* (inclusively), so that therefore not one is excepted. Compare Jud. iv. 16. Hebraism, see Ewald, *Lehrb.* § 217, 3. The Latin *ad unum omnes* is similar. — Ver. 13 as far as ἐδολ. is from Ps. v. 10, and thence till αὐτῶν from Ps. cxl. 4, both closely after the LXX.[1] — τάφος ἀνεῳγμ. ὁ λάρ. αὐτ.] Estius: "Sicut sepulcrum patens exhalat tetrum ac pestiferum foetorem, ita ex ore illorum impuri, pestilentes noxiique sermones exeunt." Comp. Pelagius, Bengel, Tholuck, Mehring and Hofmann. But it is more in harmony with the further description, as well as the parallel in Jer. v. 16 (where the quiver of the Chaldeans is compared with an open grave), to find the comparison in the point that, when the godless have opened their throats for lying and corrupting discourse, it is just as if a grave stood opened (observe the *perfect*) to which the corpse ought to be consigned for decay and destruction.[2] So certainly and unavoidably corrupting is their discourse. Moreover λάρυγξ, which is here to be taken in its original sense (as organ of *speech*, not equivalent to φάρυγξ, the

---

[1] The MSS. of the LXX. which read the whole passage vv. 13-18 at Ps. xiv. 3, have been interpolated from our passage in Christian times. See Wolf, *Cur.* on ver. 10.

[2] The metaphorical representation in classical passages, in which, *e.g.*, the Cyclops is termed ζῶν τύμβος (*Anth. Pal.* xiv. 109, 3), or the vultures ἔμψυχοι τάφοι (Gorgias, *ap. Longin.* 3), is not similar.

gullet) is more forcibly graphic than στόμα, representing the speech as passionate *crying*. Compare λαρυγγίζειν, Dem. 323, 1, and λαρυγγισμός, of crying lustily. — ἐδολιοῦσαν] *they were deceiving*. The imperfect denotes what had taken place as continuing up till the present time; and on this form of the third person plural, of very frequent occurrence in the LXX., see Sturz, *Dial. Al.* p. 60; Ahrens, *Dial.* II. p. 304, I. p. 237. — ἰὸς ἀσπίδων] *The poison of asps*, a figure for the insidiously corrupting. See similar passages in Alberti, *Obss.* p. 301. — Ver. 14 is from Ps. x. 7, taken freely from the LXX., who however with their πικρίας deviate from the Hebrew מִרְמוֹת, because they either read it otherwise or translated it erroneously. — πικρία, figurative designation of the *hateful nature*. Comp. Eph. iv. 31; Acts viii. 23; James iii. 14; see Wetstein. — Vv. 15-17 are from Is. lix. 7, 8, quoted freely and with abbreviations from the LXX. — ἐν ταῖς ὁδοῖς αὐτῶν] Where they go, is *desolation* (fragments שׁד) *and misery*, which they produce. — ὁδὸν εἰρ. οὐκ ἔγν.] *i.e. a way on which* one walks *peacefully* (the opposite of the ὁδοί, on which is σύντριμμα κ. ταλαιπ.), *they have not known* (2 Cor. v. 21), it has remained strange to them. — Ver. 18 is from Ps. xxxvi. 1. *The fear of God*, which would have preserved them from such conduct and have led them to an entirely different course, is not before their eyes. "There is objectivity ascribed to a condition which is, psychologically, subjective." Morison.

Ver. 19. The preceding quotations ("in quibus magna est verborum atrocitas," Melancthon) were intended to prove that *Jews* and Gentiles are collectively under the dominion of sin (ver. 9); but how easily might it be imagined on the part of the conceited Jews (see especially Eisenmenger's *entdecktes Judenthum*, I. p. 568 ff.) that the above passages of Scripture (of which those in vv. 10, 11 and 12, taken from Ps. xiv., really refer originally to the Gentiles, to Babylon), however they might affect the *Gentiles*, could have no application to themselves, the *Jews*, who had no need therefore to take them to themselves, as if they also were included in the same condemnation. Such a distinction, however, which could only promote a self-exaltation and self-justification at variance with the divine purpose in those declarations of His word, they were to forego, seeing that everything that the Scripture says has its bearing for the Jews. The Apostle therefore now continues, and that with very emphatic bringing out of the ὅσα in the first half of the verse and of the πᾶν and πᾶς in the second: *we know however* (as in ii. 2) *that whatsoever the law saith, it speaketh to those that are in the law*, consequently that the Jews may not except themselves from the reference of *any* saying in Scripture. — ὅσα] *whatsoever*, therefore also what is expressed in such condemnatory passages as the above, without exception. — ὁ νόμος] in accordance with its reference to vv. 10-18, is necessarily to be taken here as designation of the *O. T. generally* (comp. 1 Cor. xiv. 21; John x. 34, xii. 34, xv. 25; 2 Macc. ii. 18); not, with Hunnius, Calovius, Balduin, and Sebastian Schmid, of *the law in the dogmatic* sense (comp. Matthias); or of the *Mosaic law*, as Ammon and Glöckler, Th. Schott and Hofmann take it, confusing in various ways the connection.[1] So also van Hengel, who quite gratuitously wishes to assume an enthymeme with a minor premiss to be understood (*but the law condemns all those sinners*). The designation of the O. T. by ὁ νόμος, which forms the first, and for Israel most important, portion of it, was here occasioned by τοῖς ἐν τῷ νόμῳ, *i.e.* those who are *in the* law as their *sphere of life.* — λέγει . . . . λαλεῖ] All that the law *says* (materially, or respecting its contents, all λόγοι of the law), it *speaks* (speaks out, of the outward act which makes the λόγοι be heard, makes known through speech) to those who, etc. Comp. on John viii. 43; Mark i. 34; 1 Cor. ix. 8, xii. 3. The dative denotes those to whom the λαλεῖν *applies* (Krüger, § 48,

---

[1] According to Hofmann (compare his *Schriftbeweis*, I. p. 623 f.; so too, in substance, Th. Schott) the train of thought is: after ver. 9 ff. the only further question that could be put is, whether anything is given to Christians that exempts them from the general guilt and punishment. The law possibly? No, "*they know that this law has absolutely* (ὅσα) *no other tenor than that which it presents to those who belong to its domain, for this purpose, that the whole world, in the same extent in which it is under sin, must in its own time* (this idea being conveyed by the aorists φραγῇ and γένηται), *when it comes to stand before God its Judge, be dumb before Him and recognise the justice of His condemning sentence.*" This interpretation, obscuring with a far-fetched ingenuity the plain sense of the words, and wringing out of it a tenor of thought to which it is a stranger, is a further result of Hofmann's having misunderstood the προέχομεθα in ver. 9, and having referred it, as also the subsequent προῃτιασάμεθα, *to the Christians* as subject, an error which necessarily deranged and dislocated for him the entire course of argument in vv. 9-20. At the same time it would not be even *historically true* that the law has absolutely no other tenor, etc.

7, 13). Those who have their state of life within the sphere of the law are to regard *whatsoever the law says* as addressed to *themselves*, whether it was meant primarily for Jews or Gentiles. How this solemnly emphatic *quaecunque heaps* upon the Jews the Divine sentence of "guilty," and cuts off from them every refuge, as if this or that declaration did not apply to or concern them! — ἵνα πᾶν στόμα κ.τ.λ.] *in order that every mouth* (therefore also the *Jew*) *may be stopped* (Heb. xi. 33; Ps. cvii. 42; Job v. 16; and see Wetstein), etc. This, viz. that *no one* shall be able to bring forward anything for his justification, is represented in ἵνα —which is not *ita ut*—as *intended* by the speaking law, *i.e.* by God speaking in the law. Reiche unjustly characterises this thought as *absurd* in every view and from every standpoint; the ἵνα πᾶν κ.τ.λ. does not announce itself as the sole and exclusive end, but on the contrary, without negativing other and higher ends, merely expresses one single and special teleological point, which is however the very point which the connection here required to be cited. The *time* to be mentally supplied for φραγῇ and γένηται is the *future* generally reckoned from the present of λαλεῖ, not that of the *final judgment*, which does not harmonise with the thought in ver. 9 to which the series of Scripture testimonies in vv. 10-18 is appended. — ὑπόδικος] *punishable*, κατάκριτος, ἀπαρρησίαστος, Theophylact; frequently used by classic writers, but elsewhere neither in the N. T. nor in the LXX. or Apocrypha. — τῷ Θεῷ] belongs, not to φραγῇ (Matthias), but, after the manner of the more closely defining parallelism, merely to ὑπόδικ. γένηται: *to God*, as the Being to whom the penalty is to be paid. The opposite is ἀναίτιος ἀθανάτοισιν, Hesiod, ἔργ. 825, and θεοῖς ἀναμπλάκητος, Aesch. *Agam.* 352. Comp. Plat. *Legg.* viii. p. 816 B: ὑπόδικος ἔστω τῷ βλαφθέντι, p. 868 D, 11, p. 932; Dem. 518, 3 *al.* — γένηται] The result which is to manifest itself, as in ver. 4. — πᾶς ὁ κόσμος] quite generally (ver. 9); comp. Eph. ii. 3. And if Paul has described[1]

---

[1] From the poetic tenor of the passage ἵνα πᾶν κ.τ.λ. Ewald conjectures that it reproduces a passage from the O. T. that is now *lost*. But how readily may it be conceived that Paul, who was himself of a deeply poetic nature, should, in the vein of higher feeling into which he had been brought by the accumulated words of psalm and prophecy, spontaneously express himself as he has done! That ὑπόδικος does not again occur in his writings, matters not; ἔνδικος also in ver. 8 is not again used.

this generality (comp. also ver. 23) thus "insigni figura et verborum emphasi" (Melancthon), the result extending to *all humanity* is not contradicted by the virtue of *individuals*, such as the patriarchs; for from the ideal, but at the same time legally true (comp. Gal. iii. 10), standpoint of the Apostle this virtuousness is still no δικαιοσύνη (but only a minor degree of the want of it), and does not therefore form an exception from the category of the ὑπόδικον εἶναι τῷ Θεῷ. See ver. 20. Though different as respects degree, yet *all* are affected and condemned by the declarations quoted; *every one* has a share in this corruption.[1]

— Ver. 20. Διότι] *propterea quod*, i. 19, not *propterea* (Beza, Rosenmüller, Morus, Tholuck), is to be divided from the preceding only by a comma, and supplies the objective reason of that ἵνα κ.τ.λ. of the law: *because the relation of righteousness will accrue to no flesh from works of the law*. For if δικαιοσύνη should come from *works of the law*, the *law* would in fact open up the way of righteousness, and therefore that ἵνα πᾶν κ.τ.λ. would not be correct.[2] As to πᾶσα σάρξ, equivalent to πᾶς ἄνθρωπος, but conveying the idea of moral imperfection and sinfulness in presence of God, see on Acts ii. 17; 1 Cor. i. 20; and compare generally on Gal. ii. 16. That with regard to the *Gentiles* Paul is thinking of the *natural law* (ii. 14) cannot be admitted, seeing that in the whole connection he has to do with the law *of Moses*. But neither may *the* thought be imported into the passage with reference to the Gentiles: "if they should be placed under the law and should have ἔργα νόμου" (Rückert, comp. Philippi and Mehring), since, according to the context, it is only with reference to the *Jews* (ver. 19) that the question is dealt with as to no flesh being righteous—a general relation which, as regards the Gentiles, is perfectly self-evident, seeing that the latter are ἄνομοι, and have no ἔργα νόμου in the proper

---

[1] Compare Ernesti, *Urspr. d. Sünde*, II. p. 152 f.

[2] According to Hofmann, in pursuance of his erroneous interpretation of ver. 19, διότι κ.τ.λ. is meant to contain the specification of the reason "*why the word of the law was published to the Jews for no other object, than that the whole world might be precluded from all objection against the condemning sentence of God.*" Compare also Th. Schott. But Paul has not at all expressed in ver. 19 the thought "*for no other object;*" he must in that case, instead of the simple ἵνα which by no means excludes other objects, have written μόνον ἵνα, or possibly εἰς οὐδὲν εἰ μὴ ἵνα, or in some other way conveyed the non-expressed thought.

sense whatever.—Respecting ἔργα νόμου,[1] *works in harmony with the law* of Moses, the ἔργα being the prominent conception, works which are fulfilments of its precepts, comp. on ii. 15. Moreover that it is not specially the observance of the *ritual* portions of the law (Pelagius, Cornelius à Lapide, Semler, Ammon), but that of the *Mosaic law in general* which is meant, is clear partly from the expression itself, which is put without limitation, partly from the contextual relation of the clause to what goes before, and partly from the following διὰ γὰρ νόμου κ.τ.λ., from which the ethical law is so far from being excluded,[2] that it is on the contrary precisely this aspect of the νόμος which is specially meant.— οὐ δικαιωθήσ.] See on i. 17. The *future* is to be understood either of the moral possibility, or, which is preferable on account of iii. 20, purely in the sense of time, and that of the *future generally*: "In every case in which justification (*i.e.* the being declared righteous by God) shall occur, it will not result from," etc., so that such works should be the *causa meritoria*. The reference to the future judgment (Reiche) is controverted by the fact that throughout the entire connection justification is regarded as a relation arising immediately from faith, and not as something to be decided only at the judgment. See ver. 21 ff. and chap. iv. For this reason there is immediately afterwards introduced as the counterpart of the δικαιοσύνη, which comes directly from faith, the ἐπίγνωσις ἁμαρτίας, which comes directly from the law. It is certain, moreover, that in οὐ δικαιωθ. κ.τ.λ. Paul had Ps. cxliii. 2 in view, but instead of πᾶς ζῶν he put πᾶσα σάρξ as more significant for the matter in hand. — *In what sense* now *shall* no one *from works of the law become righteous before God, i.e.* such that God looks upon him as righteous?[3] *Not* in the sense that perfect compliance with the law would be insuffi-

---

[1] For ἔργων νόμου cannot be taken as *law of works*, as Märcker uniformly wishes. Comp. on ii. 15.

[2] Paul always conceives the law as an undivided whole (comp. Usteri, p. 36), while he yet has in his mind sometimes more the ritual, sometimes more the moral, aspect of this one divine νόμος, according to his object and the connection (Ritschl, *altkathol. K.* p. 73). Comp. on Gal. ii. 16.

[3] In opposition to Hofmann, who in his *Schriftb.* I. p. 612 urges the ἐνώπιον αὐτοῦ against the imputative sense of the passive δικαιοῦσθαι, see Wieseler on Gal. p. 192 f. It is quite equivalent to παρὰ τ. Θεῷ, *judice Deo*, Gal. iii. 11. See generally the thorough defence of the *sensus forensis* of δικαιοῦσθαι in the N. T., also from classic authors and from the O. T. in Morison, p. 163 ff.

cient to secure justification, against which the fundamental law of the judge: οἱ ποιηταὶ νόμου δικαιωθήσονται (ii. 13), would be decisive; *but* in the sense that no man, even with an outwardly faultless observance of the law (comp. on Phil. iii. 6), is in a position to offer to it that full and right obedience, which alone would be the condition of a justification independent of extraneous intervention; in fact, it is only through the law that man comes to a clear perception and consciousness of his moral imperfection by nature (his unrighteousness). See Luther's preface. That this was the Apostle's view, is proved by the reason which follows: διὰ γὰρ νόμου κ.τ.λ. See, besides, especially chs. vii. and viii.; Gal. iii. 10. There is here no mention of the *good works of the regenerate*, which however are only the *fruits* of justification, ch. vi. viii. 2 ff.; Eph. ii. 10 *al.* Comp. Philippi and Morison. — διὰ γὰρ νόμου ἐπίγν. ἁμ.] The law, when it places its demands before man, produces in the latter his first *proper recognition* of his moral incongruity with the will of God. "With these words Paul strikes at the deepest root of the matter," Ewald. Respecting γάρ Calvin's note is sufficient: "a contrario ratiocinatur.... quando ex eadem scatebra non prodeunt vita et mors." The propriety of the argument however rests on the fact that the law does not at the same time supply the strength to conquer sin (viii. 3), but stops short at the point of bringing to cognition the "interiorem immunditiem" which it forbids; "hanc judicat et accusat coram Deo, *non tollit*," Melancthon. It is different in the case of civil laws, which are designed merely to do away with the externa scelera, and to judge the works in and for themselves, xiii. 3 ff.

Vv. 21-30. Paul has hitherto been proving that all men are under sin, and guilty before God. This was the preparatory portion of the detailed illustration of the theme set forth in ch. i. 17; for before anything else there had to be recognised the general necessity of a δικαιοσύνη not founded on *the law*—as indeed such a legal righteousness has shown itself to be impossible. Now however he exhibits this δικαιοσύνη provided from another source—the righteousness of God which comes from *faith* to all without distinction, to believing Jews and Gentiles. Hofmann rejects this division, in consequence of his having erroneously taken προεχόμεθα in ver. 9 as the utterance of the *Christians*.

He thinks that the Apostle only now comes to the conclusion, at which he has been aiming ever since the fifth verse: as to what makes Christians, as distinguished from others, assured of salvation.

Ver. 21.[1] Νυνί is usually interpreted here as a pure *adverb of time* ("nostris temporibus hac in parte felicissimis," Grotius). So also Tholuck, Reiche, Rückert, Olshausen, Baumgarten-Crusius, Winzer, Reithmayr, Philippi, van Hengel, Mehring, Th. Schott, and others. But since what precedes was not given as a delineation of the *past*, there appears here not the contrast between two *periods*, but that between two *relations*, the relation of dependence on the law and the relation of independence on the law (διὰ νόμου.... χωρὶς νόμου). Hence with Beza, Pareus, Piscator, Estius, Koppe, Fritzsche, de Wette, Matthias, and Hofmann, we render: *but in this state of the case*. See regarding this dialectic use of the νῦν Hartung, *Partikell.* II. p. 25; Baeuml. *Part.* p. 95; Ellendt, *Lex. Soph.* II. p. 181. Comp. vii. 17; 1 Cor. v. 11, xii. 18, xiii. 13, *al.*; 4 Macc. vi. 33, xiii. 3. By Greek authors νυνί is not thus used, only νῦν. — χωρὶς νόμου] placed with full emphasis at the beginning as the opposite of διὰ νόμου, belongs to πεφαν. Aptly rendered by Luther: "*without the accessory aid of the law*," *i.e.* so that in this revelation of the righteousness of God the law is left out of account. Reiche (following Augustine, *de grat. Chr.* 1, 8, and *de spir. et. lit.* 9, Wolf, and others) joins it with δικαιοσ.: "the righteousness of God as being imparted to the believer without the law, without the Mosaic law helping him thereto." Compare also Winzer, Klee, Mehring. But apart from the *coactior constructio*, with which Estius already found fault, we may urge against this view the parallel of διὰ νόμου, ver. 20, which words also do not belong to ἐπίγνωσις ἁμαρτ. but to the verb to be supplied. — πεφανέρωται] *is made manifest and lies open to view*, so that it presents itself to the knowledge of every one; the present of the completed action, Heb. ix. 26. The expression itself presupposes the previous κρυπτόν (Col iii. 3 f.; Mark iv. 22), *the having been hidden*, in accordance with which the righteousness of God has not yet been the object of experimental perception. To men it was an *unknown treasure*. The *mode* of the πεφανέρωται however consists in the δικαιοσ. Θεοῦ

---

[1] See Winzer, *Comm. in Rom.* iii. 21-28, *Partic.* I. and II. 1829.

having become *actual,* having passed into historical reality, and having been made apparent, which has been accomplished without mixing up the law as a co-operative factor in the matter. — μαρτυρ. ὑπὸ τ. νόμ. κ. τ. προφ.] An accompanying characteristic definition of δικαιοσύνη Θεοῦ, so far as the latter is made manifest: *being witnessed,* etc. If it is thus the case with regard to it, that in its πεφανέρωται it is attested by the witness of the law and the prophets, then this precludes the misconception that the δικαιοσύνη revealed χωρὶς νόμου is opposed or foreign to the O. T., and consequently an innovation without a background in sacred history. Comp. xvi. 26; John v. 39. "Novum testamentum in vetere latet, vetus in novo patet," Augustine. In this case we are not to think of the *moral requirements* (Th. Schott), but of the *collective Messianic types, promises and prophecies* in the law and the prophets, in which is also necessarily comprised the δικαιοσύνη Θεοῦ as that which is necessary to participation in the Messianic salvation. Comp. i. 2, iii. 2; Acts x. 43, xxviii. 23; Luke xxiv. 27; from the law, the testimony of Abraham, iv. 3 ff. and the testimonies quoted in x. 6 ff. — Observe further that μαρτυρουμ. has the emphasis, in contrast to χωρίς, not ὑπὸ τοῦ νόμου (Bengel, Fritzsche and others). We may add Bengel's apt remark: "Lex *stricte* (namely, in χωρὶς νόμου) et *late* (in ὑπὸ τοῦ νόμου) dicitur."

Ver. 22. *A righteousness of God, however,* (mediated) *through faith in Jesus Christ.* On δέ, with the repetition of the same idea, to be defined now however more precisely, the δικαιοσύνη Θεοῦ (not merely δικαιοσύνη, as Hofmann insists contrary to the words); comp. ix. 30. See on Phil. ii. 8. — The genitive Ἰ. Χ. contains the object of faith[1] in accordance with prevailing usage (Mark xi. 22; Acts iii. 16; Gal. ii. 16, 20, iii. 22; Eph. iii. 12, iv. 13;

[1] This view of the genitive is justly adhered to by most expositors. It is with πίστις as with ἀγάπη, in which the object is likewise expressed as well by the genitive as by εἰς. Nevertheless, Scholten, Rauwenhoff, van Hengel and Berlage (*de formulae Paulinae* πίστις Ἰ. Χριστοῦ *signif.*, Lugd. B. 1856) have recently taken it to mean the "fides, quae *auctore* Jesu Christo *Deo* habetur" (Berlage). Against this view we may decidedly urge the passages where the genitive with πίστις is a thing or an abstract idea (Phil. i. 27; 2 Thess. ii. 13; Acts iii. 16; Col. ii. 12); also the expression πίστις Θεοῦ in Mark xi. 22, where the genitive must necessarily be that of the object. Comp. the classical expressions πίστις θεῶν and the like. See besides Lipsius, *Rechtfertigungsl.* p. 109 f.; Weiss, *bibl. Theol.* p. 335.

Phil. iii. 9; James ii. 1). The article before διὰ πίστ. was not needed for the simple reason that δικαιοσύνη Θεοῦ is without it. Therefore, and because the point at issue here was not the mode of becoming manifest, but the specific characterising of the righteousness itself that had become manifest, neither διὰ πίστ. (Fritzsche, Tholuck) nor the following εἰς πάντας κ.τ.λ. (de Wette, Fritzsche, Tholuck, Winer, Mehring and others) is to be made dependent on πεφανέρωται. — εἰς πάντας κ. ἐπὶ π. τ. πίστ.] scil. οὖσα; see Bornemann, *ad Xen. Symp.* 4, 25. The expression is an earnest and significant bringing into prominence of the universal character of this δικαιοσύνη διὰ πίστ. Ἰ. Χ.: *which is for all, and upon all who believe.* Both prepositions denote the direction of aim, in which the δικαιοσύνη presents itself, though with the special modification that under the εἰς lies the notion of *destination* (not "the immanent influx," Reithmayr), under the ἐπί that of *extending itself* over all. On the peculiar habit, which the Apostle has, of setting forth a relation under several aspects by different prepositional definitions of a single word, see Winer, p. 390 [E. T. 521]; compare generally Kühner, II. 1, p. 475 f. While recent expositors (including Rückert, Reiche, Köllner, de Wette) have often arbitrarily disregarded the distinction in sense between the two prepositions,[1] and have held both merely as a *strengthening* of the idea *all* (" for all, for all without exception," Koppe), the old interpreters, on the other hand, forced upon the εἰς and ἐπί much that has nothing at all in common with the relation of the prepositions; *e.g.* that εἰς π. applies to the *Jews* and ἐπὶ π. to the *Gentiles;* thus Theodoret, Oecumenius, and many others, who have been followed by Bengel, Böhme and Jatho (and conversely by Matthias, who explains ἐκ and εἰς in i. 17 in the same way). — οὐ γάρ ἐστι διαστ.] Ground assigned for the πάντας τ. πιστ. " For there is no distinction made, according to which another

---

[1] For in none of the similar passages are the prepositions synonymous. See iii. 20, xi. 36; Gal. i. 1; Eph. iv. 6; Col. i. 16. See also Matthias and Mehring *in loc.* The latter, following out his connection πεφανέρ., explains: "manifested *to* all *men* and *for* all *believers.*" But it is arbitrary to take τοὺς πιστεύοντας as defining only the second πάντας, as Morus and Flatt (see also Morison, p. 229 ff.) have already done. After the emphatic δικαιοσύνη δὲ Θεοῦ διὰ πίστεως the πιστεύειν is so much the specific and thorough mark of the subjects, that τοὺς πιστεύοντας must define the πάντας in *both* instances.

way to the δικαιοσύνη Θεοῦ would stand open for a portion of men, perchance for the Jews," and that just for the reason that (ver. 23) all have sinned, etc.

Ver. 23. Ἥμαρτον] The sinning of every man is presented as a historical fact of the past, whereby the sinful state is produced. The *perfect* would designate it as a completed subsisting fact. Calvin, moreover, properly remarks that according to Paul there is nulla justitia " nisi perfecta et absoluta," and " si verum esset, nos partim operibus justificari, partim Dei gratia, non valeret hoc Pauli argumentum." Luther aptly observes: " They are altogether sinners, etc., is the main article and the central point of this Epistle and of the whole Scripture." — καὶ ὑστερ.] They *have* sinned, and in consequence of this they *lack*, there is *wanting* to them, etc. This very *present* expression, as well as the *present* participle δικαιούμενοι, ought to have kept Hofmann from understanding πάντες of all *believers;* for in their case that ὑστερεῖσθαι no longer applies (v. 1 f., viii. 1 *al.*), and they are not δικαιούμενοι but δικαιωθέντες; but, as *becoming* believers, they would not yet be πιστεύοντες. — τῆς δόξης τ. Θεοῦ] The genitive with ὑστερεῖσθαι (Diod. Sic. xviii. 71; Joseph. *Antt.* xv. 6, 7) determines for the latter the sense of *destitui*. See Lobeck, *ad Phryn.* p. 237. Comp. on 1 Cor. i. 7. They lack *the honour which God gives*,[1] they are destitute of the being honoured by God, which would be the case, if the ἥμαρτον did not occur; in that case they would possess the good pleasure of God, and this, regarded as *honour*, which they would have to enjoy from God: the δόξα τοῦ Θεοῦ. Comp. ii. 29; John xii. 43, compared with v. 44. Köllner's objection to this view, which first offers itself, of τ. Θεοῦ as the genitive auctoris, which is also held by Piscator, Hammond, Grotius, Fritzsche, Reiche, de Wette, Tholuck, and others, following Chrysostom (comp. Philippi), that it is not the fault of men if they should not have an honour, *which proceeds from God*, is of no weight; since it certainly is the fault of men, if they render it impossible for a holy God to give them the honour which proceeds from Him. Moreover, Köllner's own explanation: honour

---

[1] The genitive τ. Θεοῦ cannot, without arbitrariness, be explained otherwise than was done in the case of δικαιοσύνη τ. Θεοῦ. In consequence of his erroneous exposition of δικαιοσ. τ. Θεοῦ (see on i. 17), Matthias understands here "glory *such as is that of God*," *i.e.* the glory of *personal holiness*.

before God (quite so also Calvin; and comp. Philippi), which is said according to the analogy of human relations, in point of fact quite coincides with the above view, since in fact honour *before* God, or *with* God (Winzer), is nothing else than the honour that accrues to us from God's judgment. Comp. Calvin: " ita nos ab humani theatri plausu ad tribunal coeleste vocat." Accordingly, the genitive is here all the less to be interpreted *coram*, since in no other passage (and especially not in δικαιοσ. Θεοῦ, see on i. 17) is there any necessity for this interpretation. This last consideration may also be urged against the interpretation of others: *gloriatio coram Deo;* " non habent, unde coram Deo gloriantur," Estius. So Erasmus, Luther, Toletus, Wolf, Koppe, Rosenmüller, Reithmayr, and others. It is decisive against this view that in all passages where Paul wished to express *gloriatio*, he knew how to employ the proper word, καύχησις (ver. 27; 2 Cor. vii. 14, viii. 24 *al.*). Others, again, following Oecumenius (Chrysostom and Theophylact express themselves too indefinitely, and Theodoret is altogether silent on the matter), explain the δόξα τ. Θεοῦ to mean the *glory of eternal life*, in so far as God *either* has destined it for man (Glöckler), *or* confers it upon him (Böhme, comp. Morison); *or* in so far as it consists in partaking the glory of God (Beza, comp. Bengel and Baumgarten-Crusius). Mehring allows a choice between the two last definitions of the sense. But the following δικαιούμενοι proves that the δόξα τοῦ Θεοῦ cannot in reality be anything essentially different from the δικαιοσύνη Θεοῦ, and cannot be merely future. Utterly erroneous, finally, is the view of Chemnitz, Flacius, Sebastian Schmid, Calovius,[1] Hasaeus, Alting, Carpzov, Ernesti, recently revived by Rückert, Olshausen, and Mangold, that the δόξα τοῦ Θεοῦ is *the image of God;* " *a godlike* δοξα," as Rückert puts it, and thus gets rid of the objection that δοξα is not synonymous with εἰκών. But how arbitrarily is the relation of the genitive thus defined, altogether without the precedent of a similar usage (2 Cor. xi. 2 is not a case in point)! That the *idea* of the *image* of God is not suggested by anything in the *connection* is self-evident, since, as the subsequent δικαιούμενοι κ.τ.λ. abundantly shows, it is the idea of the want of *righteousness* that is

---

[1] He takes δόξα τοῦ Θεοῦ as " gloria homini a Deo concessa in creatione;" this gloria having been the divine image, which we forfeited after the fall.

under discussion. Hofmann and Ewald have explained it in the same way as Rückert, though they take the genitive more accurately (a δόξα such as God Himself possesses). The latter[1] understands "the glory of God which man indeed has by creation, Ps. viii. 8, but which by sin he may lose for time and eternity, and has now lost." Compare Hofmann: "Whatsoever is of God has a share, after the manner of a creature, in the glory of God. If this therefore be not found in man, the reason is that he has forfeited the relation to God in which he was created." But even apart from the fact that such a participation in the glory of God had been lost already through the fall (v. 12; 1 Cor. xv. 22), and not for the first time through the individual ἥμαρτον here meant, it is decisive against this exposition that the participation in the divine δόξα nowhere appears as an original blessing that has fallen into abeyance, but always as something to be conferred only at the Parousia (v. 2; 1 Thess. ii. 12); as the συνδοξασθῆναι with Christ (viii. 17 f.; Col. iii. 4); as the glorious κληρονομία of God (comp. also 2 Tim. iv. 8; 1 Pet. v. 4); and consequently as the *new* blessing of the *future aἰών* (1 Cor. ii. 9). That is also the proleptic ἐδόξασε in viii. 30, which however would be foreign to the present connection.

Ver. 24. Δικαιούμενοι] does not stand for the finite tense (as even Rückert and Reiche, following Erasmus, Calvin and Melancthon, think); nor is, with Ewald, ver. 23 to be treated as a parenthesis, so that the discourse from the accusative in ver. 22 should now resolve itself more freely into the nominative, which would be unnecessarily harsh. But the participle introduces the *accompanying relation*, which here comes into view with the ὑστεροῦνται τῆς δόξης τ. Θεοῦ, namely, that of the *mode of their δικαίωσις: so that*, in that state of destitution, *they receive justification in the way of gift*. Bengel aptly remarks: "repente sic panditur scena amoenior." The participle is not even to be resolved into καὶ δικαιοῦνται (Peschito, Luther, Fritzsche), but the relation of becoming justified is to be left in the *dependence* on the want of the δόξα Θεοῦ, in which it is conceived

---

[1] Similarly already Melancthon: "gloria Dei, i.e. *luce Dei fulgente in natura incorrupta*, seu *ipso Deo* carent, ostendente se et accendente ardentem dilectionem et alios motus legi congruentes sine ullo peccato." Previously (1540) he had explained: "gloria, quam Deus approbat."

and expressed. Against the Osiandrian misinterpretations in their old and new forms see Melancthon, *Enarr.* on ver. 21; Kahnis, *Dogm.* 1. p. 599 ff.; and also Philippi, *Glaubenslehre*, IV. 2, p. 247 ff. — δωρεάν] *gratuitously* (comp. v. 17, and on the *adverb* in this sense Polyb. xviii. 17, 7; 1 Macc. x. 33; Matth. x. 8; 2 Thess. iii. 8; 2 Cor. xi. 7) they are placed in the relation of righteousness, so that this is not anyhow the result of their own performance; comp. Eph. ii. 8; Tit. iii. 5. — τῇ αὐτοῦ χάρ. διὰ τῆς ἀπολ. τῆς ἐν X. Ἰ.] *in virtue of His grace through the redemption that is in Christ Jesus.* This redemption is that which *forms the medium of* the justification of man taking place gratuitously through the grace of God. By the position of the words τῇ αὐτοῦ χάριτι, the divine grace, is, in harmony with the notion of δωρεάν, emphasised precisely as the *divine*, opposed to all *human* co-operation; comp. Eph. ii. 8. In ἀπολύτρωσις (comp. Plut. *Pomp.* 24, Dem. 159, 15) the special idea of *ransoming* (comp. on Eph. i. 7; 1 Cor. vi. 20; Gal. iii. 13) is not to be changed into the general one of the Messianic *liberation* (viii. 23; Luke xxi. 28; Eph. i. 14, iv. 30; and see Ritschl in the *Jahrb. f. d. Theol.* 1863, p. 512); for the λύτρον or ἀντίλυτρον (Matth. xx. 28; 1 Tim. ii. 6) which Christ rendered, to procure for all believers remission of guilt and the δικαιοσύνη Θεοῦ, was His blood, which was the atoning sacrificial blood, and so as equivalent accomplished *the forgiveness of sins, i.e.* the essence of the ἀπολύτρωσις. See ver. 25; Eph. i. 7; Col. i. 14; Heb. ix. 15; comp. on Matth. xx. 28; 1 Cor. vi. 20; Gal. iii. 13; 2 Cor. v. 21. *Liberation from the sin-principle* (from its dominion) is not the essence of the ἀπολύτρωσις itself (Lipsius, *Rechtfertigungsl.* p. 147 f.), but its *consequence* through the Spirit, if it is appropriated in faith (viii. 2). Every mode of conception, which refers redemption and the forgiveness of sins not to a real atonement through the death of Christ, but subjectively to the dying and reviving with Him guaranteed and produced by that death (Schleiermacher, Nitzsch, Hofmann, and others, with various modifications), is opposed to the N. T.—a mixing up of justification and sanctification. Comp. on ver. 26; also Ernesti, *Ethik d. Ap. P.* p. 27 f. — ἐν X. Ἰησοῦ] *i.e.* contained and resting in Him, in His person that has appeared as the Messiah (hence the Χριστῷ is placed first). To what extent, is shown in ver. 25.

—Observe further that justification, the causa efficiens of which is the divine grace (τῇ αὐτοῦ χάριτι), is here represented as obtained by means of the ἀπολύτρωσις, but in ver. 22 as obtained by means of *faith*, namely, in the one case *objectively* and in the other *subjectively* (comp. ver. 25). But even in ver. 22 the objective element was indicated in πίστ. Ἰησοῦ Χριστοῦ, and in ver. 24 f. *both* elements are more particularly *explained*.

Ver. 25. See on ver. 25 f. Ritschl, in the *Jahrb. f. Deutsche Theol.* 1863, p. 500 ff.; Pfleiderer in Hilgenfeld's *Zeitschr.* 1872, p. 177 ff.; the critical comparison of the various explanations in Morison, p. 268 ff. — ὃν προέθετο κ.τ.λ.] *whom God has openly set forth for Himself.*[1] This signification, familiar from the Greek usage (Herod. iii. 148, vi. 21; Plat. *Phaed.* p. 115 E; Eur. *Alc.* 667; Thuc. ii. 34, 1, 64, 3; Dem. 1071, 1; Herodian, viii. 6, 5; also in the LXX.), is decidedly to be adopted on account of the correlation with εἰς ἔνδειξιν κ.τ.λ. (Vulgate, Pelagius, Luther, Beza, Bengel and others; also Rückert, de Wette, Philippi, Tholuck, Hofmann and Morison); and not the equally classic signification: *to propose to oneself*, adopted by Chrysostom, Oecumenius, Theophylact, Toletus, Pareus, de Dieu, Elsner, Heumann, Böhme, Flatt and Fritzsche (i. 13; Eph. i. 9; 3 Macc. ii. 27): "quem *esse voluit* Deus piaculare sacrificium," Fritzsche.[2] In that case an infinitive must have been required; and it was with the *publicity* of the divine act before the whole world that the Apostle was here concerned, as he has already indicated by πεφανέρωται in ver. 21. Matthias explains it: whom He caused *to be openly made known, to be preached.* But the classical use of προτίθημι, in the active and middle, in the sense of *promulgare* is here foreign, since it refers to the summoning or proclamation of *assemblies* (Soph. *Ant.* 160, and Hermann *in loc.;* Lucian, *Necyom.* 19, and Hemsterhuis *in loc.;* Dion. Hal. vi. 15 *al.;* see

---

[1] Which has been done by the *crucifixion.* Compare the discourse of Jesus where He compares Himself with the serpent of Moses, John iii. Christ has been thus *held up to view* as ἱλαστήριον. In Greek authors the word προτίθεσθαι is specially often used to express the exhibition of dead bodies (Kruger *on Thuc.* ii. 34, 1; Stallbaum, *ad Plat. Phaed.* p. 115 E). We are not to suppose however that *this* usage influenced the Apostle in his choice of the word, since he had Christ before his eyes, not as a dead body, but as shedding His blood and dying.

[2] Ewald has in the translation *predestined*, but in the explanation *exhibited.* Van Hengel declares for the latter.

Schoem. *Comit.* p. 104; Dorvill. *ad Charit.* p. 266 f.) or to the promulgation of *laws*. Besides the ἔνδειξις τῆς δικαιοσύνης of God rests, in fact, not on the *preaching* of the atoner, but on the work of *atonement itself*, which God accomplished by the προέθετο κ.τ.λ. — God's *own participation* therein (for it was *His* ἱλαστήριον, willed and instituted *by Himself*) which is expressed by the *middle*, is placed beyond question by the εἰς ἔνδειξιν κ.τ.λ., and decisively excludes Hofmann's conception of the death of Christ as a *befalling*. Compare on ver. 26. — ἱλαστήριον] is the neuter of the adjective ἱλαστήριος, used as a substantive, and hence means simply *expiatorium* in general, without the word itself conveying the more concrete definition of its sense. The latter is supplied by the *context*. Thus, for example, in the LXX. (in the older profane Greek the word does not occur) the lid of the ark of the covenant, the *Kapporeth*, as the *propitiatorium* operculum, is called τὸ ἱλαστήριον (see below), which designation has become technical, and in Ex. xxv. 17 and xxxvii. 6 receives its more precise definition by the addition of ἐπίθεμα. They also designate the ledge (choir) of the altar for burnt offerings, the עֲזָרָה (Ez. xliii. 15, 17, 20) in the same way, because this place also was, through the blood of reconciliation with which it was sprinkled, and generally as an altar-place, a place of atonement. When they render כַּפְתֹּר in Amos ix. 1 (*knob*) by ἱλαστήριον, it is probable that they *read* כַּפֹּרֶת. See generally Schleusner, *Thes.* III. p. 108 f. The word in the sense of *offerings* of atonement does not occur in the LXX., though it is so used by other writers, so that it may be more specially defined by ἱερόν or θῦμα. Thus in Dio Chrys. *Orat.* xi. 1, p. 355 Reiske: ἱλαστήριον Ἀχαιοὶ τῇ Ἀθηνᾷ τῇ Ἰλιάδι, where a *votive gift* bears this inscription, and is thereby indicated as an offering of atonement, as indeed votive gifts generally fall under the wider idea of offerings (Ewald, *Alterth.* p. 96; Hermann, *gottesd. Alterth.* § 25, 1); again in Nonnus, *Dionys.* xiii. p. 383: ἱλαστήρια (the true reading instead of ἱκαστήρια) Γοργοῦς. 4 Macc. xvii. 22: διὰ τοῦ αἵματος τῶν εὐσεβῶν ἐκείνων καὶ τοῦ ἱλαστηρίου τοῦ[1] θανάτου αὐτῶν. Hesych.: ἱλαστήριον· καθάρσιον. Comp. Schol. Apoll. Rhod. ii. 487, where λωφήϊα ἱερά is ex-

---
[1] The article is, critically, uncertain; but at all events the blood is conceived as atoning *sacrifice*-blood; comp. ver. 19.

plained by ἐξιλαστήρια; also the corresponding expressions for sacrifices, σωτήριον (Xen. *Anab.* iii. 2, 9; v. 1, 1; LXX. Ex. xx. 24); καθάρσιον (Herod. i. 35; Aeschin. p. 4, 10); καθαρτήριον (Poll. i. 32); χαριστήριον (Xen. *Cyr.* iv. 1, 2; Polyb. xxi. 1, 2); εὐχαριστήριον (Polyb. v. 14, 8). Compare also such expressions as ἐπινίκια θύειν; and see generally Schaefer, *ad Bos. Ell.* p. 191 ff. Even in our passage the context makes the notion of an atoning *sacrifice* (comp. Lev. xvii. 11) sufficiently clear by ἐν τ. αὐτοῦ αἵματι; compare Pfleiderer *l.c.* p. 180. The interpretation *expiatory sacrifice* is adopted by Chrysostom (who at least represents the ἱλαστήρ. of Christ as *the antitype of the animal offerings*), Clericus, Bos, Elsner, Kypke, and others, including Koppe, Flatt, Klee, Reiche, de Wette, Köllner, Fritzsche, Tholuck, Messner and Ewald; Weiss (*bibl. Theol.* p. 324) is in doubt between this and the following explanation.[1] Others, as Morus, Rosenmüller, Rückert, Usteri and Glöckler, keep with the Vulgate (*propitiationem*) and Castalio (*placamentum*), to the general rendering: *means of propitiation*. So also Hofmann (comp. *Schriftbew.* II. 1, p. 338 f.), comparing specially 1 John iv. 10, and σωτήριον in Luke ii. 30; and Rich. Schmidt, *Paul. Christol.* p. 84 ff. But this, after the προέθετο which points to a definite public appearance, is an abstract idea inappropriate to it (as "*propiatition*"), especially seeing that ἐν.... αἵματι belongs to προέθετο, and seeing that the view of the death of Jesus as the concrete propitiatory *offering* was deeply impressed on and vividly present to the Christian consciousness (Eph. v. 2; 1 Cor. v. 7; Heb. ix. 14, 28; 1 Pet. i. 19; John i. 29, xvii. 19 *al.*). Origen, Theophylact, Erasmus, Luther, Calvin, Piscator, Pareus, Hammond, Grotius, Calovius, Wolf, Wetstein, and others; also Olshausen, Tholuck (ed. 5), Philippi, Umbreit, Jatho, Ritschl in the *Jahrb. f. Deutsche Theol.* 1863, p. 247, and *altkathol. Kirche*, p.

[1] Estius also explains *victimam* ... *propitiatoriam*, but yet takes ἱλαστ. as *masculine*. It was already taken as *masculine* (propitiator) in the Syriac (compare the reading *propitiatorem* in the Vulgate) by Thomas Aquinas and others; also Erasmus (in his *translation*), Melancthon and Vatablus; more recently also by Vater, Schrader, Reithmayr and van Hengel. But to this it may be objected that there is no example of ἱλαστήριος used with reference to *persons*. This remark also applies against Mehring, who interprets *powerful for atonement*. Kahnis, *Dogm.* I. p. 584, and similarly Mangold, properly retain the rendering: *expiatory offering;* and even Morison recognises the sacrificial conception of the "*propitiatory*," although like Mehring he abides in substance by the idea of the adjective.

85; Weber, *vom Zorne Gottes*, p. 273; Delitzsch *on Heb.* p. 719, and in the illustrations to his *Hebrew translation*, p. 79; Märcker, and others, have rendered ἱλαστήριον in quite a special sense, namely, as referring to the canopy-shaped *cover suspended over the ark of the covenant* (see Ewald, *Alterth.* p. 164 ff.), on which, as the seat of Jehovah's throne, the blood of the sacrifice was sprinkled by the high priest on the great day of atonement (Ex. xxv. 22; Num. vii. 89; Lev. xvi. 13 ff.; Keil, *Arch.* I. § 84, and generally Lund, *Jüd. Heiligth.* ed. Wolf, p. 37 ff.), and which therefore, regarded as the vehicle of the divine grace (see Bähr, *Symbolik*, I. p. 387 ff.; Hengstenberg, *Authent. des Pentateuches*, II. p. 642; Schulz, *alttest. Theol.* I. p. 205), typified Christ as the atoner.[1] That the Kapporeth was termed ἱλαστήριον is not only certain from the LXX.[2] (Ex. xxv. 18, 19, 20, xxxi. 7 *al.*), but also from Heb. ix. 5, and Philo (*vit. Mos.* p. 668, *D* and *E; de profug.* p. 465 A), who expressly represents the covering of the ark as a symbol of the ἵλεω δυνάμεως of God. Compare also Joseph. *Antt.* iii. 6, 5. There is consequently nothing to be urged against this explanation, either as respects the *usus loquendi* or as respects the idea, in accordance with which Christ, the bearer of the divine glory and grace, sprinkled with His own sacrificial blood, would be regarded as the antitype of the Kapporeth. But we may urge against it: (1) that τὸ ἱλαστηρ. does not stand with the article, as in the Sept. and Heb. ix. 5, although Christ was to be designated as the realised idea of the definite and in fact singly existing כפרת (τὸ ἀληθινὸν ἱλαστήριον, Theodoret); (2) that even though the term ἱλαστήριον, as applied to the cover of the ark, was certainly familiar to the readers from its use by the LXX., nevertheless this name, in its application to Christ, would come in here quite *abruptly*, without anything in the context preparing the way for it or leading to it; (3) that προέθετο would in that case be inappropriate, because the ark of the covenant, in the Holy of Holies, was removed from the view of the people;

---

[1] So also Funke, in the *Stud. u. Krit.* 1842, p. 314 f. The old writers, and before them the Fathers, have in some instances very far-fetched points of comparison. Calovius, *e.g.*, specifies five: (1) quoad causam efficientem; (2) quoad materiam (gold and not perishable wood—divine and human nature); (3) quoad numerum (only one); (4) quoad objectum (all); (5) quoad usum et finem.

[2] The LXX. derived the word Kapporeth, in view of the idea which it represented, from כפר, *condonavit*. Comp. also the *Vulgate* ("*expiatorium*").

(4) that, if Christ were really thought of here as כפרת, the following εἰς ἔνδειξιν τῆς δικαιοσύνης αὐτοῦ would be inappropriate, since the כפרת must have appeared rather as the ἔνδειξις of the divine *grace* (comp. Heb. iv. 16); (5) and lastly, that the conception of Christ as the antitype of the cover of the ark is found nowhere else in the whole N. T., although there was frequent opportunity for such expression; and it is therefore to be assumed that it did not belong to the apostolic modes of viewing and describing the atoning work of Christ. Moreover, if it is objected that this interpretation is unsuitable, because Christ, who shed His own blood, could not be the cover of the ark sprinkled with foreign blood, it is on the other hand to be remembered that the Crucified One sprinkled with His own blood might be regarded as the cover of the ark with the same propriety as Christ offering His own blood is regarded in the Epistle to the Hebrews as High Priest. If, on the other side, it is objected to the interpretation *expiatory offering* (see Philippi), that it does not suit προέθετο because Christ offered Himself as a sacrifice to God, but God did not present Him as such to humanity, the objection is untenable, since the idea that *God* has given Christ to death pervades the whole N. T.—not that God has thereby *offered* Christ as a sacrifice, which is nowhere asserted, but that He *has set forth* before the eyes of the universe Him who is surrendered to the world by the very fact of His offering Himself as a sacrifice in obedience to the Father's counsel, as such actually and publicly, namely, on the cross. An exhibition *through preaching* (as Philippi objects) is not to be thought of, but rather the divine *act of redemption* which took place through the sacrificial death on Golgotha. — διὰ τῆς πίστεως] may be connected either with προέθετο (Philippi, following older writers) or with ἱλαστήριον (Rückert, Matthias, Ewald, Hofmann, Morison, and older expositors). The latter is the right construction, since faith, as laying hold of the propitiation, is the very thing by which the ἱλαστήριον set forth becomes *subjectively effective;* but not that whereby the *setting forth itself*, which was an *objective fact* independent of faith, has been accomplished.[1] Hence: *as a sacrifice producing the*

---

[1] Even had no one believed on the Crucified One—a contingency indeed, which in view of the divine πρόγνωσις could not really occur—He would still have

ἱλάσκεσθαι *through faith*. Without faith the ἱλαστήριον would not be actually and in result, what it is in itself; for it does not reconcile the unbeliever. — ἐν τῷ αὐτοῦ αἵματι] belongs to προέθετο κ.τ.λ. God has set forth Christ as an effectual expiatory offering through faith *by means of His blood;* i.e. in that He caused Him to shed His blood, in which lay *objectively* the strength of the atonement.[1] Observe the position of αὐτοῦ. "*quem* proposuit *ipsius* sanguine." Krüger, § 47, 9, 12. Comp. xi. 11; Tit. iii. 5; 1 Thess. ii. 19; Heb. ii. 4 *al*. Comp. ver. 24. Still ἐν τ. αὐτ. αἵμ. is not to be joined with ἱλαστήριον in such a way as to make it the parallel of διὰ τ. πίστ. (Wolf, Schrader, Köllner, Reithmayr, Matthias, Mehring, Hofmann, Mangold, and others); for εἰς ἔνδειξιν κ.τ.λ. requires that ἐν τ. αὐτ. αἵμ. shall be the element defining more closely *the divine act of the* προέθετο κ.τ.λ., by which the divine righteousness is apparent; wherefore also ἐν. τ. αὐτ. αἵμ. is placed immediately before εἰς ἔνδειξιν κ.τ.λ., and not before ἱλαστήριον (against Hofmann's objection). Other writers again erroneously make ἐν . . . . αἵματι dependent on πίστεως (Luther, Calvin, Beza, Seb. Schmid, and others; also Koppe, Klee, Flatt, Olshausen, Tholuck, Winzer, and Morison), joining διὰ τ. πίστ. likewise to ἱλαστήριον: *through faith on His blood.* In that case ἐν would not be equivalent to εἰς, but would indicate the *basis* of faith (see on Gal. iii. 26); nor can the absence of the article after πίστ. be urged against this rendering (see on Gal. *l.c.*): but the ἐν τῷ αὐτ. αἵμ. becomes in this connection much too subordinate a point. Just *by means of the shedding of His blood* was the setting forth of Christ for a propitiatory offering accomplished; in order that through this utmost, highest, and holiest sacrifice offered for the satisfaction of the divine justice—through the blood of Christ —that justice might be brought to light and demonstrated. From *this* connection also we may easily understand why ἐν τῷ αὐτ. αἵμ.,

been set forth as a propitiatory offering, though this offering would not have subjectively benefited any one.

[1] This ἐν τῷ αὐτοῦ αἵματι secures *at all events* to the Apostle's utterance the conception of a *sacrifice* atoning, *i.e.* doing away the guilt, whichever of the existing explanations of the word ἱλαστήριον we may adopt. This also applies against Rich. Schmidt *l.c.*, according to whom (comp. Sabatier, p. 262 f.) the establishment of the ἱλαστήριον consisted in God actually passing sentence on sin itself in the flesh of His Son, and wholly abolishing it as an objective power exercising dominion over humanity—consequently in the destruction of the sin-principle. Regarding viii. 3 see on that passage.

which moreover, following ἱλαστήριον, was a matter of course, is added at all; though in itself unnecessary and self-evident, it is added with all the more weight, and in fact with solemn emphasis. For just in the blood of Christ, which God has not spared, lies the proof of His righteousness, which He has exhibited through the setting forth of Christ as an expiatory sacrifice; that shed blood has at once satisfied His justice, and demonstrated it before the whole world. On the *atoning*, actually *sin-effacing* power of the blood of Christ, according to the fundamental idea of Lev. xvii. 11 (compare Heb. ix. 22), see v. 9; Matth. xxvi. 28; Acts xx. 28; Eph. i. 7; Col. i. 14; Rev. v. 9 *al.*; 2 Cor. v. 14, 21; Gal. iii. 13 *al.* Comp. Kahnis, *Dogm.* I. p. 270 ff., 584 f. Reiche considers that διὰ τῆς πίστ. should be coupled with δικαιούμ., and ὃν .... ἱλαστ. should be a parenthesis, whilst ἐν τ. αὐτ. αἵμ. is to be co-ordinated with the διὰ τ. πίστ. But by this expedient the discourse is only rendered clumsy and overladen. — εἰς ἔνδειξ. τ. δικ. αὐτοῦ] purpose of God in the προέθετο .... αἵματι. The δικαιοσύνη is *righteousness*, as is required by the context (διὰ τ. πάρεσιν .... ἐν τῇ ἀνοχῇ τ. Θεοῦ), not: *truth* (Ambrosiaster, Beza, Turretin, Hammond, Locke, Böhme), or *goodness* (Theodoret, Grotius, Semler, Koppe, Rosenmüller, Morus, Reiche, also Tittmann, *Synon.* p. 185)—significations which the word never bears. It does not even indicate the *holiness* (Fritzsche, Reithmayr, Klaiber, Neander, Gurlitt in the *Stud. u. Krit.* 1840, p. 975· Lipsius, *Rechtfertigungsl.* p. 146 ff.); or the righteousness, *including grace* (Ritschl); or generally the Divine *moral order of justice* (Morison); or the *self-equality of God* in His bearing (Hofmann); but in the strict sense the opposite of ἄδικος in ver. 5, the *judicial* (more precisely, the punitive) *righteousness* (comp. Ernesti, *Urspr. d. Sünde*, I. p. 169 ff.), which had to find its holy satisfaction, but received that satisfaction in the propitiatory offering of Christ, and is thereby practically demonstrated and exhibited. On ἔνδειξις, in the sense of *practical proof*, comp. 2 Cor. viii. 24, and on εἰς Eph. ii. 7: ἵνα ἐνδείξηται. Following ver. 26, Chrysostom and others, including Krehl and Baumgarten-Crusius, take it unsatisfactorily as *justifying* righteousness. Anselm, Luther, Elsner, Wolf, and others, also Usteri, Winzer, van Hengel and Mangold, hold that it is, as in ver. 21, the *righteousness, that God gives*. On the other hand, see the immediately following εἰς.... δίκαιον. — διὰ τὴν πάρεσιν κ.τ.λ.] *on account of the passing by of sins that had previously taken place*, i.e. *because He had allowed the pre-Christian sins to go without punishment*, whereby His righteousness had been lost sight of and obscured,[1] and therefore came to need an ἔνδειξις for men.[2] Thus the atonement accomplished in Christ became "the divine Théodicée for the past history of the world" (Tholuck), and, in view of this ἔνδειξις, that πάρεσις ceases to be an enigma. — πάρεσις, which occurs only here in the N. T. (see however Dionys. Hal. vii. 37; Phalar. *Epist.* 114; Xen. *de praef. eq.* 7, 10; and Fritzsche *in loc.*; Loesner, p. 249); erroneously explained by Chrysostom as equivalent to νέκρωσις, is distinguished from ἄφεσις in so far as the omission of punishment is conceived in πάρεσις as a *letting pass* (ὑπεριδών, Acts xvii. 30; comp. xiv. 16), in ἄφεσις (Eph. i. 7; Col. i. 14) as a *letting free*. Since Paul, according to Acts *l.c.*, regarded the non-punishment of pre-Christian sins as an "overlooking" (comp. Wisd. xi. 23), we must consider the peculiar expression, πάρεσις, here as *purposely chosen*. Comp. παριέναι, Ecclus. xxiii. 2. If he had written ἄφεσις, the idea would be, that God, instead of retaining those sins in their category of guilt (comp. John xx. 23), had *let them free, i.e.* had *forgiven* them.[3] He has not forgiven them, however, but only *let them go unpunished* (comp. 2 Sam. xxiv. 10), *neglexit*. The wrath of God, which nevertheless frequently burst forth (comp. i. 17 ff.) in the ages before Christ over Jews and Gentiles (for Paul, in his perfectly general expressions, has not merely the former in view), was not an adequate recompense counterbalancing the sin, and even increased it (i. 24 ff.); so

---

[1] Compare J. Müller, *v. d. Sünde*, I. p. 352, ed. 5.

[2] The explanation that "διά here indicates that, *whereby* the δικαιοσύνη manifests itself" (Reiche; so also Benecke, Koppe, and older expositors) is incorrect, just because *Paul* in *all* cases (even in viii. 11 and Gal. iv. 13) makes a sharp distinction between διά with the accusative and with the genitive. This interpretation has arisen from the erroneous conception of δικαιοσύνη (as *goodness* or *truth*).

[3] In ἄφεσις the guilt and punishment are *cancelled;* in πάρεσις both are tacitly or expressly left undealt with, but in their case it may be said that "*omittance is not acquittance*." For the idea of *forgiveness* ἄφεσις and ἀφιέναι alone form the standing mode of expression in the N. T. And beyond doubt (in opposition to the view of Luther and others, and recently Mangold) Paul would here have used this form, had he intended to convey that idea. The πάρεσις is intermediate between pardon and punishment. Compare Ritschl in the *Jahrb. f. D. Th.* 1863, p. 501.

I. M

that God's attitude to the sin of the time before Christ, so long as it was not *deleted* either by an adequate punishment, or by atonement, appears *on the whole* as a *letting pass* (comp. Acts xiv. 16) and overlooking. As the correlative of πάρεσις, there is afterwards appropriately named ἀνοχή (comp. ii. 4), not χάρις, for the latter would correspond to ἄφεσις, Eph. i. 7. — The *pre-Christian sins* are not those of individuals prior to their conversion (Mehring and earlier expositors), but the sum of the sins of *the world before Christ*. The ἱλαστήριον of Christ is the epoch and turning-point in the world's history (comp. Acts xvii. 30, xiv. 16. — ἐν τῇ ἀνοχῇ τ. Θεοῦ] *in virtue of the forbearance* (tolerance, comp. ii. 4) *of God*,[1] contains the ground which is the motive of the πάρεσις. It is not to be attached to προγεγ. (Oecumenius, Luther, and many others; also Rückert, Gurlitt, Ewald, van Hengel, Ritschl, and Hofmann), which would yield the sense *with* or "*during* the forbearance of God." Against this view we may urge the very circumstance that the *time* when the sins referred to took place is already specified by προγεγονότων, and expressed in a way simply and fully corresponding with the contrast of the νῦν καιρός that follows, as well as the special pertinent reason, that our mode of connecting ἐν τ. ἀνοχῇ τ. Θ. with διὰ τ. πάρεσιν κ.τ.λ. brings out more palpably the antithetical relation of this πάρεσις to the divine δικαιοσύνη. Moreover, as ἀνοχή is a moral attribute, the *temporal* conception of ἐν is neither indicated nor appropriate. What is indicated and appropriate is simply the use, so common, of ἐν in the sense of the ethical ground. Reiche connects ἐν τῇ ἀνοχῇ τ. Θεοῦ with εἰς ἔνδ. τ. δικ. αὐτ., making it co-ordinate with the διὰ .... ἁμαρτ.: "the δικαιοσύνη showed itself positively in the forgiveness of sins, negatively in the postponement of judgment." Incorrect, on account of the erroneous explanation of διά and δικαιοσ. thus necessitated.—Our whole interpretation of the passage from διὰ τ. πάρεσιν to Θεοῦ is not at variance (as Usteri thinks) with Heb. ix. 15; for, if God has allowed pre-Christian sins to pass, and then has exhibited the

---

[1] Paul writes Θεοῦ, not again αὐτοῦ, because he utters the διὰ τὴν πάρεσιν .... Θεοῦ from *his own* standpoint, so that the subject is presented *objectively*. Comp. Xen. *Anab.* i. 9, 15. But even apart from this the repetition of the noun instead of the pronoun is of very frequent occurrence in all Greek authors, and also in the N. T. (Winer, p. 136 [E. T. 180]).

atoning sacrifice of Christ in proof of His righteousness, the death of Christ must necessarily be the λύτρον for the transgressions committed under the old covenant, but passed over for the time being. But there is nothing in our passage to warrant the reference to the sins of the people of *Israel*, as in Heb. *l.c.* (in opposition to Philippi).

Ver. 26. Πρὸς τὴν ἔνδειξιν] Resumption of the εἰς ἔνδειξιν in ver. 25, and that without the δέ, ver. 22 (comp. on Luke i. 71); while εἰς is exchanged for the equivalent πρός unintentionally, as Paul in ver. 30, and also frequently elsewhere (comp. on Eph. i. 7 and Gal. ii. 16) changes the prepositions.[1] The article, however (see the critical notes), serves to set forth the *definite*, historically *given* ἔνδειξις, which is in accord with the *progress* of the representation; for Paul desires to add now with corresponding emphasis the *historical* element ἐν τῷ νῦν καιρῷ not previously mentioned. The resumption is in itself so obvious, and also in such entire harmony with the emphasis laid upon the ἔνδειξις τῆς δικαιοσύνης αὐτοῦ as the chief point, that for this very reason the interpretation of Rückert and Gurlitt (comp. Beza), which joins πρὸς τὴν ἔνδειξιν κ.τ.λ. with διὰ τ. πάρεσιν.... Θεοῦ, and takes it as the aim of the πάρεσις or the ἀνοχή (Baumgarten-Crusius; comp. Hofmann and Th. Schott), at once falls to the ground. Mehring, rendering πρός *in reference to* or in *view of*, understands the δικαιοσύνη in ver. 26 to mean *imputed* righteousness, and finds the ἔνδειξις of the latter, ver. 26, in the *resurrection* of Jesus; but a decisive objection to his view is that Paul throughout gives no hint whatever that his expressions in ver. 26 are to be taken in any other sense than in ver. 25; and a reference to the resurrection in particular is here quite out of place; the passage goes not beyond the atoning *death* of Christ. — εἰς τὸ εἶναι κ.τ.λ. cannot stand in an epexegetical relation to the previous εἰς ἔνδειξιν κ.τ.λ. because that ἔνδειξις has in fact already been doubly expressed, but now the *further* element καὶ δικαιοῦντα κ.τ.λ. is added, which first brings into full view the teleology of the ἱλαστήριον. εἰς τὸ εἶναι κ.τ.λ. is therefore the definition presenting the final aim of the whole affirmation from ὃν προέθετο to καιρῷ. It is its keystone: *that He may be just and justifying the believers*, which is to be taken as the

[1] Comp. Kühner, II. 1, p. 475 f.

intended *result* (comp. on ver. 4): in order that, through the ἱλαστήριον of Christ, arranged in this way and for this ἔνδειξις, He may manifest Himself as One who is Himself righteous, and who makes the believer righteous (comp. ἱλαστήρ. διὰ τ. πίστεως, ver. 25). He desires to be *both*, the one not without the other. The εἶναι however is the *being* in the *appearance* corresponding to it. The "*estimation* of the *moral public*" (Morison) only ensues as the *consequence* of this. Regarding τὸν ἐκ πίστ. comp. on οἱ ἐξ ἐριθείας, ii. 8. The αὐτόν however has not the force of *ipse* or even *alone* (Luther), seeing it is the subject of the two predications δίκαιον κ. δικαιοῦντα; but it is the simple pronoun of the third person. Were we to render with Matthias and Mehring[1] καὶ δικαιοῦντα: *even when* He justifies, the καί would be very superfluous and weakening; Paul would have said δίκαιον δικαιοῦντα, or would have perhaps expressed himself pointedly by δίκαιον κ. δικαιοῦντα ἀδίκους ἐν πίστεως Ἰ. Observe further that the *justus et justificans*, in which lies the *summum paradoxon evangelicum* as opposed to the O.T. *justus et condemnans* (according to Bengel), finds its solution and its harmony with the O. T. in τὸν ἐκ πίστεως (see chap. iv., i. 17). The Roman Catholic explanation of *inherent* righteousness (see especially Reithmayr) is here the more inept. It is also to be remarked that according to vv. 24-26 *grace* was the *determining ground* in God, that prompted Him to permit the atonement. He purposed thereby indeed the revelation of His *righteousness;* but to the carrying out of that revelation just *thus*, and not otherwise, namely *through the* ἱλαστήριον *of Christ*, He was moved by His own χάρις. Moreover the ἔνδειξις of the divine *righteousness* which took place through the atoning death of Christ necessarily presupposes the *satisfactio vicaria* of the ἱλαστήριον. Hofmann's doctrine of atonement (compensation)[2]

---

[1] They are joined by Ernesti, *Ethik d. Ap. P.* p. 32.

[2] "In consequence of man's having allowed himself to be induced through the working of Satan to sin, which made him the object of divine wrath, the Triune God, in order that He might perfect the relation constituted by the act of creation between Himself and humanity into a complete fellowship of love, has had recourse to the most extreme antithesis of Father and Son, which was possible without self-negation on the part of God, namely, the antithesis of the Father angry at humanity on account of sin, and of the Son belonging in sinlessness to that humanity, but approving Himself under all the consequences of its sin even unto the transgressor's death that befell Him through Satan's agency; so that, after Satan had done on Him the utmost which he was able to do to the sinless One in

does not permit the simple and—on the basis of the O. T. conception of atoning sacrifice—*historically definite* ideas of vv. 25, 26, as well as the unbiassed and clear representation of the ἀπολύτρωσις in ver. 24 (comp. the λύτρον ἀντί, Matth. xx. 28, and ἀντίλυτρον, 1 Tim. ii. 6) to subsist alone with it. On the other hand these ideas and conceptions *given* in and homogeneously pervading the entire N. T., and whose meaning can by no means be evaded, exclude the theory of Hofmann, not merely in form but also in substance, as a deviation evading and explaining away the N. T. type of doctrine, with which the point of view of a "*befalling,*" the category in which Hofmann invariably places the death of Jesus, is especially at variance. And *Faith* in the atoning death has not justification merely "*in its train*" (Hofmann *in loc.*), but justification takes place subjectively *through faith* (vv. 22, 25), and indeed in such a way that the latter is *reckoned* for righteousness, iv. 5, consequently *immediately* (ἐξαίφνης, Chrysostom).

Ver. 27. Paul now infers (οὖν) from vv. 21-26—in lively interchange of question and answer, like a victor who has kept the field—that Jewish boasting (not human boasting generally, Fritzsche, Krehl, Th. Schott) is excluded.[1] The *article* indicates that which is known, and has been before mentioned (ii. 17 ff.),

consequence of sin, without obtaining any other result than His final standing the test, the relation of the Father to the Son was now a relation of God to *the humanity beginning anew in the Son*,—a relation no longer determined by the sin of the race springing from Adam, but by the righteousness of the Son." Hofmann in the *Erl. Zeitschr.* 1856, p. 179 f. Subsequently (see espec. *Schriftb.* II. 1, p. 186 ff.) Hofmann has substantially adhered to his position. See the literature of the entire controversy carried on against him, especially by Philippi, Thomasius, Ebrard, Delitzsch, Schneider, Weber, given by the latter, *vom Zorne Gottes*, p. xliii. ff. ; Weizsäcker in the *Jahrb. f. Deutsche Theol.* 1858, p. 154 ff. It is not to the *ecclesiastical* doctrine, but to Schleiermacher's, and partially also Mencken's subjective representation of it, that Hofmann's theory, although in another form, stands most nearly related. Comp. on ver. 24; and for a more detailed account Ritschl, *Rechtfertigung und Versöhnung*, 1870, I. p. 569 ff., along with his counter-remarks against Hofmann at p. 575 ff. As to keeping the Scriptural notion of imputed righteousness clear of all admixture with the moral change of the justified, see also Köstlin in the *Jahrb. für Deutsche Theol.* 1856, p. 105 ff., 118 ff., Gess, in the same, 1857, p. 679 ff., 1858, p. 713 ff., 1859, p. 467 ff.; compared however with the observations of Philippi in his *Glaubenslehre*, IV. 2, p. 237 ff., 2nd edition.

[1] Hofmann's misconception of ver. 9 still affects him, so as to make him think here of *Christian* καύχησις. Comp., for the right view, especially Chrysostom.

looking back to vv. 9 and 1. — ποῦ] As it were, seeking that which has vanished from the sphere of vision, Luke viii. 25; 1 Cor. i. 20, xv. 55; 1 Pet. iv. 18; 2 Pet. iii. 4; also frequently used thus by classic writers.—The καύχησις is not *the object of boasting* (Reiche), which would be καύχημα, but the *vaunting* itself, which is presented with vivid clearness as that which no longer exists. — ἐξεκλείσθη] οὐκ ἔτι χώραν ἔχει, Theodoret. — διὰ ποίου νόμου;] scil. ἐξεκλείσθη, not δικαιούμεθα, which Mehring, following Michaelis, wholly without logical ground wishes to be supplied. The exclusion, namely, must necessarily have ensued through a *law* no longer allowing the καύχησις; but *through what sort of a law?* of what nature is it? Is it one that demands *works?* No, but a law *of faith.* In these *attributes* lies the ποιότης of the law, which is the subject of inquiry. This cannot have the quality of the Mosaic law, which insists upon *works*, but thereby fosters and promotes the parade of work-righteousness (ii. 17); it must, on the contrary, be a law that requires *faith*, as is done by the Christian plan of salvation, which prescribes the renunciation of all merit through works, and requires us to trust solely in the grace of God in Christ. The Christian plan of salvation *might* be included under the conception of a νόμος, because *the will of God* is given in it by means of the Gospel (comp. 1 John iii. 23), just as in the O. T. revelation by means of the Mosaic law. And the expression was *necessary* in the *connection*, because the question διὰ ποίου νόμου; required both the old and new forms of the religious life to be brought under the one conception of νόμος. Therefore the literal sense of νόμος remains unchanged, and it is neither *doctrine* (Melancthon and many others) nor *religious economy*. Comp. ix. 31.

Ver. 28 gives the ground of the οὐχί κ.τ.λ. — λογιζόμεθα] οὐκ ἐπὶ ἀμφιβολίας λέγεται (Theodore of Mopsuestia): *censemus*, we *deem*, as in ii. 3, viii. 18; 2 Cor. xi. 5. The matter is set down as something that has now been brought between Paul and his readers to a common ultimate judgment, whereby the victorious tone of ver. 27 is not *damped* (as Hofmann objects), but is on the contrary confidently *sealed.* — πίστει] On this, and not on δικαιοῦσθαι (Th. Schott, Hofmann), lies the emphasis in accordance with the entire connection; χωρὶς ἔργ. νόμου is correlative. Paul has conceived λογ. γ. δικ. *together*, and then placed first *the* word which has the *stress;* compare the critical observations. The dative denotes the procuring cause or medium, just like διὰ πίστεως. Bernhardy, p. 101 f. The word "*alone*," added by Luther—formerly an apple of discord between Catholics and Lutherans (see the literature in Wolf)—did not belong to the *translation* as such,[1] but is in *explanation* justified by the context, which in the way of dilemma "cuts off all works utterly" (Luther), and by the connection of the Pauline doctrinal system generally, which excludes also the fides *formata*. See *Form. Conc.* p. 585 f., 691. Comp. on Gal. ii. 16, Osiander in the *Jahrb. f. Deutsche Theol.* 1863, p. 703 f.; Morison *in loc.* All fruit of faith follows justification by faith; and there are no degrees in justification.[2] — χωρὶς ἔργ. νόμου] Without the co-operation therein of works of the law (ver. 20), which, on the contrary, remain apart from all connection with it. Comp. ver. 21. — On the quite general ἄνθρωπον, *a man,* comp. Chrysostom: τῇ οἰκουμένῃ τὰς θύρας ἀνοίξας τῆς σωτηρίας, φησὶν, ἄνθρωπον, τὸ κοινὸν τῆς φύσεως ὄνομα θείς. See afterwards περιτομὴν .... καὶ ἀκροβυστ., ver. 30. Comp. Gal. ii. 16.

Ver. 29. *Or*—in case what has just been asserted in ver. 28 might still be doubted—is it only *Jews* to whom God belongs? and not also *Gentiles?* He must, indeed, have only been a God for the Jews, if He had made justification conditional on works of the law, for in that case it could only be destined for Jews,[3] insomuch as they only are the possessors of the law. Consequently vv. 29, 30 contain a further closing thought, crowning the undoubted accuracy of the confidently expressed λογιζόμεθα κ.τ.λ. in ver. 28. The supplying of a predicative Θεός (Hofmann, Morison, and earlier expositors) is superfluous, since the prevailing usage of εἶναι τίνος is amply sufficient to make it intelligible, and it is quite as clear from the context that the relationship which is meant is that of being God to the persons in question.—How much the ναὶ καὶ ἐθνῶν, said without any limita-

---

[1] Luther has not added it in Gal. ii. 16, where the Nürnberg Bible of 1483 reads "*only* through faith."

[2] Comp. Riggenbach (against Romang) in the *Stud. u. Krit.* 1868, p. 227 ff.

[3] Not for Gentiles also, unless they become proselytes to Judaism, whereby they would cease to be Gentiles.

tion whatever—in their case, as with Ἰουδαίων, God is conceived as protecting them, and guiding to salvation—run counter to the degenerate theocratic exclusiveness; see on Matth. iii. 9, and in Eisenmenger's *entdeckt. Judenth.* I. p. 587 f. But Paul speaks in the certain assurance, which had been already given by the prophetic announcement of Messianic bliss for the Gentiles, but which he himself had received by revelation (Gal. i. 16), and which the Roman church, a Pauline church, itself regarded as beyond doubt.

Ver. 30 is to be divided from the previous one merely by a comma. Regarding ἐπείπερ, *whereas* (in the N. T. only here) introducing something undoubted, see Hermann, *ad Viger.* p. 786; Hartung, *Partikell.* I. p. 342 f.; Baeumlein, p. 204.—The *unity* of God implies that He is God, not merely of the Jews, but also of the Gentiles; for otherwise another special Deity must rule over the Gentiles, which would do away with monotheism. — ὃς δικαιώσει] *who shall* (therefore) *justify.* This exposition contains that which necessarily follows from the unity of God, in so far as it conditions for *both* parties *one* mode of justification (which however must be χωρὶς ἔργων, ver. 28). For Jews as well as for Gentiles He must have destined the way of righteousness *by faith* as the way of salvation. The *future* is neither put for δικαιοῖ (Grotius, and many others), nor to be referred with Beza and Fritzsche to the time of the final judgment, nor to be taken as the future *of inference* (Rückert, Mehring, Hofmann), but is to be understood as in ver. 20 *of every case of justification to be accomplished.* Erasmus rightly says, "Respexit enim ad eos, qui adhuc essent in Judaismo seu paganismo."— The exchange of ἐκ and διὰ is to be viewed as accidental, without real difference, but also without the purpose of avoiding misconception (Mehring). Comp. Gal. ii. 16, iii. 8; Eph. ii. 8. Unsuitable, especially for the important closing thought, is the view of Calvin, followed by Jatho, that there is an irony in the difference: "Si quis vult habere differentiam gentilis a Judaeo, hanc habeat, quod ille *per* fidem, hic vero *ex* fide justitiam consequitur." Theodore of Mopsuestia, Wetstein, Bengel, Hofmann, and others explain it by various other gratuitous suggestions;[1]

---

[1] Bengel: "Judaei pridem in fide fuerant; gentiles fidem ab illis recens nacti erant." Comp. Origen. Similarly Matthias: in the case of the circumcised

van Hengel is doubtful.—The interchange of πίστεως and τῆς πίστ. (*from faith—through the faith*), in which the *qualitative* expression advances to *the concrete with the article*, is also without special design, as similar accidental interchanges often occur in parallel clauses (Winer, p. 110 [E. T. 149]).

Ver. 31—iv. 24. *The harmony of the doctrine of justification by faith with the law, illustrated by what is said in the law regarding the justification of Abraham.* — The new chapter should have begun with ver. 31, since that verse contains the theme of the following discussion. If we should, with Augustine, Beza, Calvin, Melancthon, Bengel, and many others, including Flatt, Tholuck, Köllner, Rückert, Philippi, van Hengel, Umbreit, and Mehring, assume that at iv. 1 there is again introduced something new, so that Paul does not carry further the νόμον ἱστῶμεν, v. 31, but in iv. 1 ff. treats of a new objection that has occurred to him at the moment, we should then have the extraordinary phenomenon of Paul as it were dictatorially dismissing an objection so extremely important and in fact so very naturally suggesting itself, as νόμον οὖν καταργοῦμεν κ.τ.λ., merely by an opposite assertion, and then immediately, like one who has not a clear case, leaping away to something else. The more paradoxical in fact after the foregoing, and especially after the apparently antinomistic concluding idea in ver. 30, the assertion νόμον ἱστῶμεν must have

faith appears as the *ground*, in that of the uncircumcised as the *means* of justification; ἐκ πίστ. signifies: *because* they believe, διά τ. πίστ.: *if* they believe. In the case of the circumcised faith is presupposed as covenant-faithfulness. Comp. also Bisping. According to Hofmann, Paul is supposed to have said in the case of the circumcised *in consequence of faith*, because these wish to become righteous in consequence of legal works; but in the case of the uncircumcised *by means of faith*, because with the latter no other possible way of becoming righteous was conceivable. In the former instance faith is the preceding condition; in the latter the faith existing for the purpose of justification (therefore accompanied by the article) is the means, by which God, who works it, helps to righteousness. This amounts to a subjective invention of subtleties which are equally incapable of proof as of refutation, but which are all the more groundless, seeing that Paul is fond of such interchanges of prepositions in setting forth the same relation (comp. ver. 25 f., and on 2 Cor. iii. 11, and Eph. i. 7). How frequent are similar interchanges also in classic authors! Moreover, in our passage the stress is by no means on the prepositions (Hofmann), but on περιτομήν and ἀκροβυστίαν. And as to the variation of the prepositions, Augustine has properly observed (*de Spir. et lit.* 29) that this interchange serves *non ad aliquam differentiam*, but *ad varietatem locutionis*. Comp. on ἐκ πίστεως δικαιοῦν (here said of *Jews*) also of *Gentiles*, Gal. iii. 8; Rom. ix. 30, and generally i. 17.

sounded, the more difficult becomes the assumption that it is merely an anticipatory declaration abruptly interposed (see especially Philippi, who thinks that it is enlarged on at viii. 1 ff.); and the less can ver. 20, διὰ γ. νόμου ἐπίγνωσις ἁμαρτ. be urged as analogous, since that proposition had really its justification there in what preceded. According to Th. Schott, νόμος is not meant to apply to the Mosaic law at all, but to the fact that, according to ver. 27, *faith* is a νόμος, in accordance with which therefore Paul, when making faith a condition of righteousness, ascribes to himself not abrogation of the law, but rather an establishment of it, setting up merely what God Himself had appointed as the method of salvation. The discourse would thus certainly have a conclusion, but by a jugglery[1] with a word (νόμος) which no reader could, after ver. 28, understand in any other sense than as the Mosaic law. Hofmann explains substantially in the same way as Schott. He thinks that Paul conceives to himself the objection that in the doctrine of faith there might be found a doing away *generally of all law*, and now in opposition thereto declares that that doctrine does not exclude, but includes, the fact that *there is a divine order of human life* (?).

Ver. 31. Οὖν] The Apostle infers for himself from his doctrine of justification ἐκ πίστεως .... χωρὶς ἔργων νόμου—just discussed —a possible objection and reproach: *Do we then make away with the law (render it invalid) through faith?* — νόμον] emphatically put first, and here also to be understood neither of the moral law, nor of every law in general, nor of the entire O. T., but, as is proved by the antithesis between νόμος and πίστις and the reference as bearing on ver. 28, of the *Mosaic law.* Comp. Acts xxi. 28, Gal. iv. 21 f. — διὰ τῆς πίστ.] *i.e. thereby*, that we assert *faith* as the condition of justification. — νόμον ἱστῶμεν] Not: *we let the law stand* (Matthias), but: *we make it stand*, we produce the result *that it*, so far from being ready to fall, in reality *stands upright* (βεβαιοῦμεν, Theodoret) in its authority, force, and obligation. Comp. 1 Macc. xiv. 29, ii. 27; Ecclus. xliv. 20-22. This ἱστάνειν of the law, whereby there is secured to it stability and authority instead of the καταργεῖσθαι, takes place by means of (see ch. iv.) the Pauline doctrine demonstrating and

---

[1] This objection in no way affects the question διὰ ποίου νόμου, ver. 27 (in opposition to Hofmann's objection) where the very ποίου *placed along with it* requires the general notion of νόμου.

making good the fact that, and the mode in which, justification by the grace of God through faith is already taught in the law, so that Paul and his fellow teachers do not come into antagonism with the law, as if they desired to abolish and invalidate it by a new teaching, but, on the contrary, by their agreement with it, and by proving their doctrine from it, secure and confirm it in its position and essential character.[1] — The νόμον ἱστῶμεν, however, is so little at variance with the *abrogation* of the law *as an institute of works obligatory in order to the becoming righteous*, which has taken place through Christianity (x. 4; 2 Cor. iii. 7; Gal. iii. ; Rom. vii. 4; Gal. ii. 19; Col. ii. 14), that, on the contrary, the law *had to fall* in this aspect, in order that, in another aspect, the same law, so far as it teaches *faith* as the condition of the δικαιοσύνη, might be by the gospel imperishably *confirmed* in its authority, and even, according to Matth. v. 17, *fulfilled.* For in respect of this assertion of the value of faith the law and the gospel appear one. — If the νόμον ἱστῶμεν and its relation to the abrogation of the law be defined to mean that "from faith proceeds the *new obedience*, and the *love* develops itself, which is the πλήρωμα νόμου, xiii. 10" (Philippi; comp. Rückert, Krehl, Umbreit, Morison), as Augustine, Melancthon, who nevertheless mixes up with it very various elements, Luther, Calvin, Beza, Vatablus, Calovius, and others assumed (comp. also *Apol. C. A.* p. 83, 223), the further detailed illustration of ch. iv. is quite as much opposed to this view, as it is to *the* interpretations which conceive the law as *pedagogically* leading to Christ (Grotius, Olshausen), or as *fulfilled* in respect of its *object*, which is *justification* by faith (Chrysostom, Oecumenius, Theophylact, and others[2]). In the case of the two latter views, faith appears as something *added to* the law, which is just what Paul *combats* in ch. iv. On the form ἱστῶμεν, from ἱστάω, see Matthiae, p. 482, Winer, p. 75 [E. T. 93]. Still the ἱστάνομεν, recommended by Griesbach and adopted by Lachmann and Tischendorf, has preponderant attestation (so also ℵ*; but ℵ** has ἱστῶμεν), which is here decisive (in opposition to Fritzsche), especially when we take into account the multitude of other forms in MSS. (στάνομεν, ἵσταμεν, συνιστῶμεν, συνιστάνομεν *et al.*).

[1] Comp. Weiss, *Bibl. Theol.* p. 333.
[2] Ὁ γὰρ ἤθελεν ὁ νόμος, τουτέστι τὸ δικαιῶσαι ἄνθρωπον, οὐκ ἴσχυσε δὲ ποιῆσαι, τοῦτο ἡ πίστις τελειοῖ· ὁμοῦ γὰρ τῷ πιστεῦσαι τίνα δικαιοῦται, Theophylact.

CHAPTER IV.

Ver. 1. Ἀβραὰμ .... εὑρηκέναι] Lachm. and Tisch. (8) read εὑρηκ. Ἀβρ. τὸν προπάτορα ἡμῶν, which Griesb. also approved. This *position of the words* has indeed preponderant attestation (A C D E F G ℵ, min., Copt. Arm. Vulg. It. and several Fathers), but may be suspected of being a *transposition* intended to connect κατὰ σάρκα with τὸν πατέρα ἡμ., as in fact this construction was prevalent among the ancients. προπάτορα (Lachm.) though attested by A B C* ℵ, 5, 10, 21, 137, Syr. Copt. Arm. Aeth. and Fathers, appears all the more probably a gloss, since πατέρα here is not used in a spiritual sense as it is afterwards in vv. 11, 12, 17, 18. — Ver. 11. περιτομῆς] Griesb. recommended περιτομήν, which however is only attested by A. C*, min., Syr. utr. Arm. and some Fathers; and on account of the adjoining accusatives very easily slipped in, especially in the position after ἔλαβε. — καὶ αὐτοῖς] καί is wanting in A B ℵ*, min. Ar. pol. Vulg. ms. Orig. in schol. Cyr. Damasc. Condemned by Mill and Griesb., omitted by Lachm. and Tisch. (8). But after the final syllable *NAI* the καί, not indispensable for the sense, was very easily overlooked. On the other hand the ground assumed for its addition, by Reiche, that "the copyists would not have the Jews altogether excluded," cannot be admitted as valid, because in fact the Jews are immediately after, ver. 12, expressly included. — The article before δικαιοσύνην, which Tisch. (8) has omitted, has preponderant attestation. Its omission is connected with the old reading (A) εἰς δικαιοσύνην (comp. ver. 9, v. 3). Ver. 12. τῆς ἐν τῇ ἀκροβ. πίστ.] The reading τῆς πίστ. τῆς ἐν τ. ἀκροβ., recommended by Griesb. and adopted by Scholz, lacks the authority of most and the best uncials, and seems a mechanical alteration after ver. 11. The article τῇ however is, with Tisch. in accordance with decisive testimony, to be deleted, and to be regarded as having been likewise introduced from ver 11 (not as omitted after ver. 10, as Fritzsche thinks). — Ver. 15. οὗ γάρ] A B C ℵ*, min., Copt. Syr. p. (in margin), Theodoret, Theophyl. Ambr. Ruf. read οὗ δέ. Recommended by Griesb. and adopted by Lachm. Fritzsche, Tisch. (8). An alteration, occasioned by the contrast on failing to perceive the appropriateness of meaning in the γάρ. — Ver. 17. ἐπίστευσε] F G and some vss. and Fathers read ἐπίστευσας (so Luther). The κατέναντι οὗ κ.τ.λ. was still regarded as belonging to the passage of Scripture. — Ver. 19. οὐ] Wanting in A B C ℵ, 67**, 93, 137, Syr. Erp. Copt. Chrys. Damasc. Julian. Condemned by Griesb. and deleted by Lachm. and Tisch. (8). But this omission of the οὐ, as well as the very weakly attested ὡς and *licet*, manifestly arose from incorrectly having regard here to Gen. xvii. 17 (as is done even by Buttmann, *ncut. Gr.* p. 305 f. and Hofmann). See the exegetical remarks. — ἤδη] Wanting in B F G 47 *et. al.* and several vss. and Fathers. Bracketed by Lachm. deleted by Fritzsche and Tisch. It is to be regarded as an addition, which suggested itself very easily, whereas there would have been no reason for its omission.

Ver. 1. Οὖν] *Accordingly,* in consequence of the fact that we do not abrogate the law through faith, but on the contrary establish it.[1] This οὖν brings in the *proof* to be adduced from the history of Abraham (" confirmatio ab exemplo," Calvin), for the νόμον ἱστῶμεν just asserted (iii. 31), in the form of an *inference.* For if we should have to say that Abraham our father has attained anything (namely, righteousness) κατὰ σάρκα, that would *presuppose* that the law, which attests Abraham's justification, in nowise receives establishment διὰ τῆς πίστεως (iii. 31). Hence we have not here an objection, but a question proposed in the way of inference by Paul himself, the answer to which is meant to bring to light, by the example of Abraham, the correctness of his νόμον ἱστ. His object is not to let the matter rest with the short and concise dismissal of the question in iii. 31, but to enter into the subject more closely; and this he does now by attaching what he has further to say to the authoritatively asserted, and in his own view established, νόμον ἱστάνομεν in the form of an *inference.* Moreover, the whole is to be taken as *one* question, not to be divided into two by a note of interrogation

---

[1] Observe, in reference to ch. iv. (with iii. 31), of what fundamental and profound importance, and how largely subject to controversy, the relation of Christianity to Judaism was in the Apostolic age, particularly in the case of mixed churches. The minute discussion of this relation, therefore, in a doctrinal Epistle so detailed, cannot warrant the assumption that the church was composed mainly of *Jews,* or at least (Beyschlag) of *proselytes.*

after ἐροῦμεν; in which case there is harshly and arbitrarily supplied to εὑρηκέναι (by Grotius, Hammond, Clericus, Wetstein, and Michaelis) δικαιοσύνην, or at least (van Hengel) the pronoun *it* representing that word, which however ought to have been immediately suggested by the context, as in Phil. iii. 12 (comp. Nägelsbach on *Il.* 1, 76, 302, ed. 3). In the affirmation itself Ἀβρ. is the *subject* (*quid dicemus Abrahamum nactum esse?*). Th. Schott, by an unhappy distortion of the passage, makes him the *object* ("*why should we then say that we have gained Abraham in a fleshly, natural sense for our ancestor?*") This misconception should have been precluded by attending to the simple fact, that in no passage in our Epistle (and in other Epistles the form of expression does not occur) does the τί in τί οὖν ἐροῦμεν mean *why*. Hofmann, who had formerly (*Schriftb.* II. 2, p. 76 ff.) apprehended it in substance much more correctly, now agrees with Schott in so far that he takes τί οὖν ἐροῦμεν as a question by itself, but then explains Ἀβραάμ likewise as the object, so that the question would be, *whether the Christians think that they have found Abraham as their forefather after the flesh?* "The origin of the church of God, to which Christians belong, goes back to Abraham. *In fleshly fashion* he is their ancestor, if the event through which he became such (namely, *the begetting of Isaac*) lie within the sphere of the natural human life; *in spiritual fashion*, on the other hand, if that event belong to the sphere of the history of salvation and its miraculous character, which according to the Scripture (comp. Gal. iv. 23) is the case." This exposition cannot be disputed on linguistic grounds, especially if, with Hofmann, we follow Lachmann's reading. But it is, viewed in reference to the context, erroneous. For the context, as vv. 2, 3 clearly show, treats not of the contrast between the fleshly and the spiritual *fatherhood* of Abraham in the case of Christians, but of the *justification* of the ancestor, as to whether it took place κατὰ σάρκα or by faith. Moreover, if Ἀβρ. was intended to be the object, Paul would have expressed himself as unintelligibly as possible, since in vv. 2, 3 he in the most definite manner represents him as the *subject*, whose action is spoken of. If we take Hofmann's view, in which case we do not at all see why the Apostle should have expressed himself by εὑρηκέναι, he would have written more intelligibly by substituting for this the simple εἶναι, so that

'Αβρ. would have been the subject in the question, as well as in what follows. Finally the proposition that Abraham, as the forefather of *believers as such*, was so *not* κατὰ σάρκα, was so perfectly self-evident, both with reference to the Jewish and the Gentile portion of the Ἰσραὴλ Θεοῦ, that Paul would hardly have subjected it to discussion as the theme of so earnest a question, while yet no reader would have known that in κατὰ σάρκα he was to think of the *miraculous begetting of Isaac*. For even without the latter Abraham would be the προπάτωρ of believers κατὰ πνεῦμα, namely, through his *justification by faith*, ver. 9 ff. — τ. πατέρα ἡμ.] "fundamentum consequentiae ab Abrahamo ad nos," Bengel. Comp. ver. 11 f. ἡμῶν however (comp. James ii. 21) is said from the *Jewish* standpoint, not designating Abraham as the *spiritual* father of the *Christians* (Reiche, Hofmann, Th. Schott), a point that is still for the present (see ver. 11) quite out of view. — κατὰ σάρκα] is, following the Peschito, with most expositors to be necessarily joined to εὕρηκ.; not, with Origen, Ambrosiaster, Chrysostom, Photius, Theophylact, Erasmus, Castalio, Toletus, Calvin, whom Hofmann, Th. Schott, Reithmayr, Volckmar in Hilgenfeld's *Zeitschr.* 1862, p. 221 ff., follow, to τ. πατέρα ἡμ. (not even although Lachmann's reading were the original one); for the former, and not the latter, needed the definition. Abraham has really attained righteousness, only not κατὰ σάρκα, and ἐξ ἔργων in ver. 2 corresponds to the κατὰ σάρκα. Besides with our reading the latter connection is impossible. — The σάρξ on its ethical side[1] is the material-psychic human nature as the life-sphere of moral weakness and of sinful power in man, partly as contrasted with the higher intellectual and moral nature of *the man himself*, which is his πνεῦμα along with the νοῦς (i. 9, vii. 18, 25,

[1] The most recent literature on this subject: Ernesti, *Urspr. d. Sünde*, I. p. 71 ff.; Tholuck in the *Stud. u. Krit.* 1855, 3; Hahn, *Thol. d. N. Test.* I. p. 426 ff.; Delitzsch, *Psychol.* p. 374 ff.; Holsten, *Bedeutung des Wortes σάρξ im N. Test.* 1855, and in *Ev. d. Paul. u. Petr.* p. 365 ff.; Baur in the *Theol. Jahrb.* 1857, p. 96 ff.; and *Neut. Theol.* p. 142 f.; Wieseler *on Gal.* p. 443 ff.; Beck, *Lehrwiss.* § 22; Kling in Herzog's *Encykl.* IV. p. 419 ff.; Hofmann, *Schriftbew.* I. p. 557 ff.; Weber, *vom Zorne Gottes*, p. 80 ff.; also Ritschl, *altkath. Kirche*, p. 66 ff.; Luthardt, *vom freien Willen*, p. 394 ff.; Rich. Schmidt, *Paulin. Christol.* 1870, p. 8 ff.; Weiss, *bibl. Theol.* § 93; Philippi, *Glaubensl.* III. p. 207 ff., and the excursus thereon, p. 231 ff., ed. 2. For the earlier literature see Ernesti, p. 50.

and see on Eph. iv. 23), and partly as opposed to the superhuman *divine* life-sphere and its operation, as here; see the sequel. Hence κατὰ σάρκα is: *conformably to the bodily nature of man in accordance with its natural power*, in contrast to the working of divine grace, by virtue of which the εὑρηκέναι would not be κατὰ σάρκα, but κατὰ πνεῦμα, because taking place through the Spirit of God. Comp. on John iii. 6. Since the ἔργα are products of the human phenomenal nature and conditioned by its ethical determination, not originating from the divine life-element, they belong indeed to the *category* of the κατὰ σάρκα, and ἐξ ἔργων is the correlative of κατὰ σάρκα (wherefore also Paul continues, ver. 2, εἰ γάρ 'Αβρ. ἐξ ἔργων κ.τ.λ.), but they do not exhaust the whole idea of it, as has often been assumed, following Theodoret (κατὰ σάρκα τὴν ἐν ἔργοις, λέγει, ἐπείδηπερ διὰ τοῦ σώματος ἐκπληροῦμεν τὰ ἔργα), and is still assumed by Reiche. Köllner, limiting it by anticipation from ver. 4, holds that it refers to the human mode of *earning wages by labour*. Entirely opposed to the context, and also to the historical reference of ver. 3, is the explanation of *circumcision* (Pelagius, Ambrosiaster, Vatablus, Estius, and others; including Koppe, Flatt, Baur, and Mehring), which Rückert also mixes up, at the same time that he explains it of the ἔργοις. Philippi also refers it to both. — On εὑρηκ., *adeptum esse*, comp. εὑρεῖν κέρδος, Soph. *El.* 1297, ἀρχήν, Dem. 69, 1. The *middle* is still more expressive, and more usual; see Krüger, § 52, 10, 1, Xen. ii. 1, 8, and Kühner *in loc.* The *perfect* infinitive is used, because Abraham *is realised as present;* see ver. 2.

Ver. 2. The question in ver. 1 contained the negative sense, which had therefore necessarily to be limited by κατὰ σάρκα: "We may not assert that Abraham has obtained anything according to the flesh." The reason for this is now assigned (γάρ): "*For, assuming that Abraham has been justified by works*" (as was the Jewish opinion[1]), "*he has cause for boasting,*" namely, that he has attained righteousness through his actions, *but* he has *not* this ground of boasting *with respect to God* (as if

---

[1] In the Talmud it is even inferred from Gen. xxvi. 5 that Abraham kept the whole law of Moses. *Kiddusch* f. 82, 1; *Joma* f. 28, 2; *Beresch. rabba* f. 57, 4. Comp. the passages from Philo quoted by Schneckenburger in the *Stud. u. Krit.* 1833, p. 135.

his justification were the *divine* act), since, namely, in the case supposed it is not *God* to whom he owes the justification, but on the contrary he has *himself* earned it, and God would simply have to acknowledge it as a human self-acquirement. *God* has not, in that supposed case, done anything for him, on account of which he might thus boast *with regard to God* as his justifier; for ἡ τῶν ἀγαθῶν ἔργων πλήρωσις αὐτοὺς στεφανοῖ τοὺς ἐργαζομένους, τὴν δὲ τ. Θεοῦ φιλανθρωπίαν οὐ δείκνυσιν, Theodoret. Comp. also Chrysostom, Oecumenius, and Theophylact. Thus for the proper understanding of this difficult passage (Chrysostom: ἀσαφὲς τὸ εἰρημένον) we must go back to the explanation of the Greek expositors, which is quite faithful both to the words and the context. Comp. on vv. 3, 4. This interpretation, now adopted also by Tholuck (comp. Reithmayr and Th. Schott), has especially *this* advantage, that ἐδικαιώθη is not taken otherwise than in the entire development of the δικαιοσύνη Θεοῦ, not therefore as somewhat *indefinite and general* ("justus apparuit," Grotius), in which case it would remain a question *by whom* Abraham was found righteous (Rückert, Philippi; comp. Beza and others; also Grotius and Koppe, and, with trifling variation, de Wette, likewise Spohn in the *Stud. u. Krit.* 1843, p. 429 ff., Volckmar, and others). That Abraham was justified *with* God was known to no Jew otherwise (comp. Ecclus. xliv. 19 ff.; Manass. 8; Joseph. *Antt.* xi. 5, 7; Eisenmenger, *entdeckt. Judenth.* I. p. 322, 343), and no reader could in accordance with the entire context understand ἐδικαιώθη otherwise, than in this definite sense, consequently in the solemn absolute sense of the Apostle (in opposition to Lipsius, *Rechtfertigungsl.* p. 35). The only question was, *whether* ἐξ ἔργων or ἐκ πίστεως. If we suppose the *former* case, it is indeed for Abraham worthy of all honour, and he may boast of that which he has himself achieved, but with *reference to God*, as if *He* had justified him, he has no ground for boasting.[1] Observe besides, that πρός is used not in the sense of ἐνώπιον, *coram* (Hofmann: *overagainst*), or *apud* (Vulgate), but in accordance

---

[1] Van Hengel places a point after καύχ., and takes ἀλλ' οὐ πρὸς τ. Θεόν as an independent sentence, in which he supplies *secundum literas sacras*, making the sense: "Atqui gloriandi materiam Deum Abrahamo denegare videmus in libris sacris." But that is, in fact, not there. Against my own interpretation in the 1st ed. (making εἰ . . . . ἐδικαιώθη, the *question*, and then ἔχει . . . . Θεόν the *answer* negativing it) see Philippi. The εἰ must be the dialectic *if*.

with the quite common usage of ἔχειν with the object of the thing (to have something to do, to say, to boast, to ask, to censure, etc.), and with specification *of the relation of reference to some one* through πρός τινα. The opposite of ἔχειν καύχημα πρός is ἔχειν μομφὴν πρός, Col. iii. 13. The *special mode* of the reference is invariably furnished by the context, which here, in accordance with the idea of δικαιοσύνη Θεοῦ, suggests the notion that God is the *bestower* of the blessing meant by καύχημα. *To that* the ἔχειν καύχημα of Abraham does *not* refer, if he was justified by *works*. In the latter case he cannot boast of himself: ὁ Θεός με ἐδικαίωσε, Θεοῦ τὸ δῶρον. Reiche and Fritzsche, following Calvin, Calovius, and many others, have discovered here an *incomplete syllogism*, in which ἀλλ' οὐ πρὸς τ. Θεόν is the minor premiss, and the conclusion is wanting, to this effect: "Si suis bene factis Dei favorem nactus est, habet quod apud Deum glorietur . . . . ; sed *non* habet, quod apud Deum glorietur, quum libri s. propter *fidem*, non propter pulchre facta eum Deo probatum esse doceant (ver. 3) . . . . ; non est igitur Abr. ob bene facta Deo probatus," Fritzsche. So in substance also Kraussold in the *Stud. u. Krit.* 1842, p. 783; Baur in the *Theol. Jahrb.* 1857, p. 71; Köstlin in the *Jahrb. f. Deutsche Theol.* 1856, p. 92. Forced, and even contrary to the verbal sense; for through the very *contrast* ἀλλ' οὐ π. τ. Θ. the simple καύχημα is *distinguished* from the καύχημα πρὸς τ. Θεόν, as one that takes place *not* πρὸς τὸν Θεόν. Paul must have written: ἔχει καύχημα πρὸς τὸν Θεόν· ἀλλ' (or ἀλλὰ μὴν) οὐκ ἔχει. Mehring takes ἀλλ' οὐ πρὸς τὸν Θεόν as a *question:* "If Abraham has become righteous by works, he has glory, *but has he it not before God?*" But in what follows it is the very opposite of the affirmation, which this question would imply, that is proved. If the words were interrogative, ἀλλὰ μή must have been used instead of ἀλλ' οὐ (*but yet not before God?*) Hofmann, in consequence of his erroneous exposition of ver. 1, supposes that Paul wishes to explain how he came to propose the question in ver. 1, and to regard an answer to it as necessary. What is here involved, namely, is nothing less than a contradiction between *what Christians say of themselves* (when they deny all possibility of becoming righteous by their own actions), and *what holds good of* "*an Abraham,*" *the father of the people of God.* If the latter has become righteous through his own action, he has glory, and *by this* very *circumstance* his *ancestorship* is distinguished from that of all others. But then the Scripture teaches that what God counted worthy in Abraham was his faith, and it is therefore clear that the glory which he has, if he has become righteous by works, is no glory in presence of God, and consequently *is not fitted to be the basis of his position in sacred history*. This is a chain of ideas imported into the passage; instead of which it was the object of the Apostle himself merely to set forth the simple proposition that Abraham was not justified by works, and not at all to speak of the mode in which the Christian ancestorship of the patriarch came to subsist. — καύχημα (comp. on Phil. i. 26, ii. 16) is throughout the N. T. *materies gloriandi;* as also in the LXX. and Apocrypha; although in classic authors (Pind. *Isthm.* v. 65; Plut. *Ages.* 31) it also occurs as the equivalent of καύχησις, *gloriatio*. In Gal. vi. 4, also, it is joined with ἔχειν.

Ver. 3. I am right in saying: οὐ πρὸς τὸν Θεόν, for Scripture expressly derives the justification of Abraham from his *faith*, not from his *works*, and indeed as something received through *imputation;* so that he consequently possesses, not the previously supposed righteousness of works, but the righteousness of faith as a favour of God, and has ground for boasting of his righteousness *in reference to God*. That righteousness by *works* he would have *earned himself*. Comp. ver. 4. The emphasis lies on ἐπίστευσε and ἐλογίσθη, not on τῷ Θεῷ (Mehring). See ver. 4 f. The passage quoted is Gen. xv. 6, according to the LXX., which renders the active וַיַּחְשְׁבֶהָ by the passive κ. ἐλογίσθη. In the Hebrew what is spoken of is *the* faith which Abraham placed in the divine promise of a numerous posterity, and which God put to his account as righteousness, צְדָקָה, *i.e.* as full compliance with the divine will in act and life; comp. on Gal. iii. 6. *Paul however has not made an unwarrantable use* of the passage for his purpose (Rückert), but has really understood δικαιοσύνη in the dogmatic sense, which he was justified in doing since the imputation of faith as צְדָקָה was essentially the same judicial act which takes place at the justification of Christians. This divine act *began* with Abraham, the father of the faithful, and was not essentially different in the case of later believers. Even in the πιστεύειν τῷ Θεῷ on the part of Abraham Paul has rightly discerned nothing substantially different from the *Christian* πίστις (compare Delitzsch on Gen. *l.c.*), since Abraham's faith had reference to the divine *promise*, and indeed to *the* promise which he, the man trusted by God and enlightened by God, recognised as that which embraced in it the future *Messiah* (John viii. 56). Tholuck, because the promise was a promise of grace, comes merely to the unsatisfactory view of " a *virtual parallel also* with the object of the justifying faith of Christians." Still less (in opposition to Neander and others) can the explanation of the subjective nature of faith in general, without the addition of its specific *object* (Christ), suffice for the conception of Abraham as the father of all believing in *Christ;* since in that case there would only have been present in him a pre-formation of faith as respects its psychological quality generally, and not also in respect of its *subject-matter*, which is nevertheless the specific and distinguishing point in the case of justifying faith. — We may add that our passage, since it expresses not a (mediate) *issuing* of righteousness from faith, but the *imputation* of the latter, serves as a proof of justification being an *actus forensis;* and what the Catholic expositors (including even Reithmayr and Maier) advance to the contrary is a pure subjective addition to the text.[1] It is well said by Erasmus : that is *imputed*, " quod re persolutum non est, sed tamen *ex imputantis benignitate* pro soluto *habetur*." Comp. also Philippi *in loc.*, and Hoelemann, *de justitiae ex fide ambabus in V. T. sedibus*, 1867, p. 8 ff.—Instead of the καί in the LXX., Paul, in order to put the ἐπίστ. with all weight in the foreground, has used δέ, which does not otherwise belong to the connection of our passage. — εἰς δίκ.] Comp. ii. 26. — On the passive ἐλογίσθη see Bernhardy, p. 341 ; Kühner, II. 1, p. 105.

Vv. 4, 5. These verses now supply an illustration of ver. 3 in two *general* contrasted relations, from the application of which— left to the reader—to the case of Abraham the non-co-operation of works (the χωρὶς ἔργων, ver. 6) in the case of the latter's justification could not but be clear. — δέ] is the simple μεταβατικόν. — τῷ ἐργαζομένῳ] *to the worker*, here, as the contrast

---

[1] Not even with the exception of Döllinger (*Christenth. u. K.* p. 188, ed. 2), who says that God accounts the principle of the new free *obedience* (the faith) *as already the whole service to be rendered*, as the *finished* righteousness. Comp. however on i. 17, note.

shows, with the pregnant sense: *to him who is active in works*, of whom the ἔργα are *characteristic*. Luther aptly says: " who deals in works." — ὁ μισθός] *i.e.* the *corresponding* wages (comp. ii. 29), *justa merces*. The opposite: ἡ δίκη, *merita poena;* see Kühner, *ad Xen. Anab.* i. 3, 20. — οὐ λογίζ. κατὰ χάριν, ἀλλὰ κατὰ ὀφείλημα] Comp. Thuc. ii. 40, 4: οὐκ ἐς χάριν ἀλλ' ἐς ὀφείλημα τὴν ἀρετὴν ἀποδώσων. The stress of the contrast lies on κ. χάρ. and κ. ὀφείλ., not in the first part on λογίζεται (Hofmann), which is merely the verb of the Scripture quotation in ver. 3, repeated for the purpose of annexing to it the contrast that serves for its illustration. Not *grace* but *debt* is the regulative standard, according to which his wages are awarded to such an one; the latter are not *merces gratiae*, but merces *debiti*. As in Abraham's case an imputation κατὰ χάριν took place (which Paul assumes as self-evident from ver. 3) he could not be on ἐργαζόμενος; the case of imputation which occurred in relation to him is, on the contrary, to be referred to the opposite category which follows: *but to him that worketh not, but believeth on Him who justifieth the ungodly, his faith is reckoned as righteousness*. Looking to the exact parallel of vv. 4 and 5, the unity of the category of both propositions must be maintained; and ver. 5 is not to be regarded as an application of ver. 4 to the case of Abraham (Reiche), but as likewise a *locus communis*, under which it is left to the reader to classify the case of Abraham in accordance with the above testimony of Scripture. Hence we cannot say with Reiche: " the μὴ ἐργαζόμενος and ἀσεβής is Abraham."[1] On the contrary both are to be kept perfectly general, and ἀσεβής is not even to be weakened as equivalent to ἄδικος, but has been *purposely selected* (comp. v. 6), in order to set forth the saving power of faith[2] by as strong a contrast as possible *to* δικαιοῦντα.

[1] ἀσεβής in his view is an allusion to the earlier idolatry of Abraham, reported by Philo, Josephus, and Maimonides, on the ground of Joshua xxiv. 2. This was also the view of Grotius, Wetstein, Cramer, Michaelis, Rosenmüller, and Koppe; comp. also Döllinger, *Christenth. u. K.* p. 197, ed. 2. The Rabbins have a different tradition, to the effect that Abraham *demolished* the idols of his father Terah, etc.; see Eisenmenger, *entdeckt. Judenth.* I. p. 490 ff., 941.

[2] Consequently *subjective faith* is meant, not its *objective ground*, the righteousness of Christ, *i.e.* according to the *Form. Conc.* p. 884 f., the active and passive obedience of Christ, which is "applied and appropriated" to us through faith. The merit of Christ always remains the causa *meritoria*, to which we are indebted for the imputation of our faith. But the *apprehensio Christi*, which is the essence

— On πιστεύειν ἐπί τινα, expressing faith in *its direction towards some one*, comp. ver. 24; Acts ix. 42, xi. 17; Wisd. xii. 2.

Vv. 6-8. Accordance (καθάπερ) of ver. 5 with an assertion of *David*, that great and revered Messianic authority. That it is only what is said in ver. 5 that is to be vouched by David's testimony, and consequently that the quotation forms only an accessory element in the argument, appears from its being annexed by καθάπερ, from the clear intended relation in which ᾧ ὁ Θεὸς λογ. δικ. appears to λογ. ἡ. πίστ. αὐτ. εἰς δικ. ver. 5, as well as χωρὶς ἔργων to τῷ μὴ ἐργαζ. in the same verse, and from the fact that Paul immediately, in ver. 9, returns to Abraham. Vv. 6-8 cannot therefore be regarded as a second example of justification from the O. T. (Reiche and many others), or even as the starting-point of the reply to the question of ver. 1 (Hofmann). This is forbidden by the proper conception of νόμος in iii. 31, in accordance with which Paul could only employ an example from the *law:* and such an example was that of *Abraham*, Gen. xv., but not that of *David*. — λέγει τ. μακαρ.] *asserts the congratulation;* μακαρισμός does not mean *blessedness*, not even in Gal. iv. 15, see *in loc.* Comp. Plat. *Rep.* p. 591 D; Aristot. *Rhet.* i. 9, 4. — λογίζεται δικαιοσύνην] Here δικαιοσύνη is conceived directly as that, which God reckons to man as his moral status. The expression λογίζεσθαι τινί ἁμαρτίαν is perfectly analogous. In the classics λογίζεσθαι τινί τι is also frequently met with. — χωρὶς ἔργων] belongs to λογίζεται. For, as David represents the λογίζεσθαι δικαιοσύνην as the forgiveness of *sins*, it *must* be conceived by him as ensuing *without any participation* (iii. 21) *of meritorious works.* — μακάριοι κ.τ.λ.] Ps. xxxii. 1, 2 exactly after the LXX. — ἐπεκαλύφθ.] The *amnesty* under the figure of the covering over of sin. Comp. Augustine on Ps. *l.c.*, "Si texit Deus peccata, noluit animadvertere; si noluit animadvertere, noluit punire." Comp. 1 Pet. iv. 8. — οὐ μὴ λογίσηται] *will certainly not impute.* It refers to the future generally, without more precise definition (Hermann, *ad Soph. Oed. C.* 853; Hartung, *Partikel.* II. p. 156 f.), not specially to the *final judgment* (de Wette).

of justifying faith, must not be made equivalent to the *apprehensus Christus* (Calovius; comp. Philippi). The former is the subjective, *which* is imputed; the latter the objective, *on account of which* the imputation by God takes place. The *Formula Concordiae* in this point goes *ultra quod scriptum est*.

Vv. 9, 10. From the connection (καθάπερ, ver. 6) of this Davidic μακαρισμός with what had previously been adduced, vv. 3-5, regarding Abraham, it is now inferred (οὖν) that this declaration of blessedness affects, not the circumcised as such, but *also the uncircumcised;* for Abraham in fact, as an *uncircumcised* person, was included among those pronounced blessed by David. — ἐπὶ τ. περιτ.] The verb obviously to be supplied is most simply conceived as ἐστι (the μακαρισμός *extends to* etc.; comp. ii. 9; Acts iv. 33 *et al.*). Less natural is λέγεται from ver. 6 (Fritzsche); and πίπτει (Theophylact, Bos) is arbitrary, as is also ἦλθεν (Oecumenius), and ἔρχεται (Olshausen). Comp. ver. 13, and see Buttmann, *neut. Gr.* p. 120 f. — ἐπὶ τ. περιτ. κ.τ.λ.] *to the circumcised, or also to the uncircumcised?* The καί shows that the previous ἐπὶ τ. περιτ. is conceived as *exclusive,* consequently without a μόνον. — λέγομεν γάρ κ.τ.λ.] In saying this Paul cannot wish first to explain, quite superfluously, *how he comes to put such questions* (Hofmann), but, as is indicated by λέγομεν, which lays down a proposition as premiss to the argument that follows, he enters on the *proof* (γάρ) from the history of Abraham for the καὶ ἐπὶ τ. ἀκροβ. which is conceived as affirmed. The *present* denotes the assertion pointing back to ver. 3 as continuing: *for our assertion, our proposition is,* etc. The *plural* assumes the assent of the readers. The emphasis however is not on τῷ Ἀβρ. (Fritzsche, de Wette, Baumgarten-Crusius, Maier, Philippi, and others), which Paul would have made apparent by the position of the words ὅτι τῷ Ἀβρ. ἐλογίσθη; nor on ἐλογίσθη, which in that case would necessarily have a pregnant meaning not indicated in the whole connection (as a pure act of grace, independent of external conditions); but on ἡ πίστις εἰς δικαιοσύνην (and thus primarily on πίστις) brought together at the end, by which the import of ver. 3, ἐπίστευσε .... δικαιοσύνην, is recapitulated. — πῶς οὖν ἐλογίσθη] The proposition, *that* to Abraham, etc., is certain; consequently the point at issue is the question *quomodo,* viz. under what *circumstances as to status* (whether in his circumcision, or whilst he was still uncircumcised) that imputation of his faith to him for righteousness took place.[1] Hofmann places

---

[1] Respecting the form of the discourse, Erasmus aptly observes: "Praeter *interrogationis* gratiam multum lucis addit *dilemma,* cujus alteɪ parte

the first mark of interrogation after πῶς οὖν, so that the second question is supposed to begin with ἐλογίσθη. But without sufficient ground, and contrary to the usage elsewhere of the interrogative πῶς by Paul, who has often put τί οὖν thus without a verb, but never πῶς οὖν. We should in such case have to understand ἐλογίσθη; but this word, according to the usual punctuation, is already *present*, and does not therefore *need* to be supplied. — οὐκ ἐν περιτομῇ, ἀλλ' ἐν ἀκροβ.] scil. ὄντι. The imputation in question took place as early as Gen. xv.; circumcision not till Gen. xvii.; the former at least fourteen years earlier.

Ver. 11. An amplification of the οὐκ ἐν περιτ., ἀλλ' ἐν ἀκροβ. viewed as to its historical bearings, showing namely the relation of Abraham's circumcision to his δικαιοσύνη, and therefore only to be separated by a comma from ver. 10. "*And he received a sign of circumcision as seal* (external confirmation, 1 Cor. ix. 2, and see on John iii. 33) *of the righteousness of faith* (obtained through faith, vv. 3, 5), *which he had in uncircumcision.*" That τῆς ἐν τ. ἀκροβ. is not to be connected with δικαιοσ. (Rückert, Reiche) is plain from the following context (πιστευόντων δι' ἀκροβυστίας ver. 11, and τῆς ἐν τῇ ἀκροβ. πίστεως ver. 12). The genitive περιτομῆς is *usually* taken as that of *apposition:* the sign *consisting in circumcision*. But in that case the article could not be omitted before σημεῖον (the absence of it drove van Hengel to the reading περιτομήν, which Hofmann also prefers[1]), since the concrete, historically definite sign would here be meant (compare 2 Cor. v. 5; Eph. ii. 14 *et al.*). It is therefore to be rendered: And *a sign, which took place through circumcision*, a signature which was given to him in the fact that he was circumcised, he received as seal, etc. The *genitive* is thus to be taken simply as *completing* the notion of σημεῖον, *i.e.* as *defining it more precisely* as respects its modal expression. Observe at the same time the dislocation in the order of the words, which brings into emphatic relief the idea of the σημεῖον. According to Gen.

rejecta alteram evincit. Nullum enim argumentandi genus vel apertius vel violentius."

[1] Hofmann explains: and *as a sign* he received circumcision, *as seal* (apposition to σημ.). In that case περιτομήν must have had the *article* (John vii. 22; otherwise in ver. 23). For to take λαμβάνειν περιτομήν as equivalent to περιτέμνεσθαι is forbidden by σημεῖον, with which the περιτομή can be correlative only as a substantive conception.

xi. 17 circumcision was the sign of *the covenant*[1] which God made with Abraham. But with correct dogmatic consistency Paul represents it as the significant mark which had been the seal of the *righteousness by faith*, since in that covenant what God promised was the Messianic κληρονομία (Gen. xv. 5, 18), and Abraham on his part rendered the faith (Gen. xv. 6) which God imputed to him for righteousness. — εἰς τὸ εἶναι αὐτὸν κ.τ.λ.] *in order that he might be*, etc., contains the divinely appointed aim of the σημεῖον ἔλαβε περιτ. κ.τ.λ. This *telic* rendering is grammatically necessary (see on i. 20), as more in keeping with the biblical view (ὁ γὰρ τῶν ὅλων θεὸς προειδὼς ὡς θεὸς, ὡς ἕνα λαὸν ἐξ ἐθνῶν καὶ Ἰουδαίων ἀθροίσει καὶ διὰ πίστεως αὐτοῖς τὴν σωτηρίαν παρέξει, ἐν τῷ πατριάρχῃ Ἀβρ. ἀμφότερα προδιέγραψε, Theodoret), and with the importance of the matter, than the *ecbatic* explanation καὶ οὕτως ἐγένετο πατήρ, which has been justly abandoned of late. — πατέρα πάντων τῶν πιστ. δι' ἀκροβ.] The essence of this spiritual fatherhood is the identity of the relation forming the basis of the sacred-historical connection of all believers with the patriarch without intervention of circumcision—a relation which began with Abraham justified through faith whilst still uncircumcised. Thus the Jewish conception of the national-theocratic childship of Abraham is elevated and enlarged by Paul (comp. Matth. iii. 9; John viii. 37, 39), into the idea of the purely spiritual-theocratic childship, which embraces, not Jews and proselytes as such, but the believers as such—all uncircumcised who believe, and (ver. 12) the believing circumcised. For Abraham's righteousness through faith was attained, when as yet there was no distinction between circumcised and uncircumcised; and to this mode of becoming just before God, independent of external conditions, Christianity by its δικαιοσύνη ἐκ πίστεως leads back again, and continues it. — δι' ἀκροβ.] *with foreskin*, although they are uncircumcised. Comp. on ii. 27, Barnab. *Ep.* 13: τέθεικά σε πατέρα ἐθνῶν τῶν πιστευόντων δι' ἀκροβυστίας τῷ κυρίῳ. — εἰς τὸ λογισθῆναι κ.τ.λ.] is taken by many, including Tholuck and

---

[1] In the Talmud also it is presented as the sign and seal of the *covenant*. See Schoettgen and Wetstein. To the formulary of circumcision belonged the words: "Benedictus sit, qui sanctificat dilectum ab utero, et *signum* (אות) posuit in arue, et filios suos *sigillavit* (חתם) *signo foederis sancti.*" Berachoth f. 13, 1.

Philippi, as a parenthetical illustration of εἰς τὸ εἶναι αὐτὸν πατέρα κ.τ.λ. But as we can attach εἰς τὸ λογισθῆναι κ.τ.λ. without violence or obscurity to πιστευόντων, there is no necessity for the assumption of a parenthesis (which is rejected by Lachmann, Tischendorf, van Hengel, Ewald, Mehring, and Hofmann). Nevertheless εἰς τὸ λογισθ. is not: *who believe on the fact, that* to them also will be imputed (Hofmann), for the object of faith is never expressed by εἰς with a substantival infinitive;[1] but, quite in accordance with the *telic* sense of this form of expression (as in the εἰς τὸ εἶναι previously): who believe (on Christ) *in order that* (according to the divine final purpose ruling therein) *to them also*, etc. — καὶ αὐτοῖς] *to them also*, as to Abraham himself; τὴν δικαιοσύνην expresses the righteousness which is under discussion, that of faith.

Ver. 12. The construction carries onward the foregoing πατέρα πάντων κ.τ.λ.: *and father of circumcision, i.e. father of circumcised persons* (not *of all* circumcised, hence without the article). And in order to express *to what* circumcised persons this spiritual fatherhood of Abraham belongs, Paul adds, by way of more precise definition: *for those* (*dativus commodi*, comp. Rev. xxi. 7; Luke vii. 12) *who are not merely circumcised* (comp. ii. 8), *but also walk in the footsteps*, etc. With this rendering (Chrysostom, Oecumenius, Ambrosiaster, Erasmus, Beza, Calvin, Estius and others; including Ammon, Böhme, Tholuck, Klee, Rückert, Benecke, Reiche, Glöckler, Köllner, de Wette, Philippi, and Winer) it *must* be admitted (against Reiche and Köllner, whose observations do *not* justify the article) that τοῖς is *erroneously* repeated before στοιχοῦσι. Paul *unsuitably* continues with ἀλλὰ καί, just as if he had previously written an οὐ μόνον τοῖς. As any other rendering is wholly inadmissible, and as καὶ τοῖς cannot be an inversion for τοῖς καί (Mehring), we are driven to the assumption of that erroneous insertion of the article, as a negligence of expression. The expression in Phil. i. 29 (in oppo-

---

[1] Not even in ver. 13. And Acts xv. 11, to which Hofmann appeals as an analogous passage, tells directly *against* him, because there the construction of the *infinitive* obtains in the usual way, that *the subject of the governing verb* is understood, as a matter of course, with the infinitive. Comp. Hofmann himself above on ver. 1; Krüger, § 55, 4, 1. Besides the result, according to Hofmann's interpretation, would be an awkward thought, not in keeping with the faith of Abraham.

sition to Fritzsche) would be of the same nature only in the event of Paul having written τοῖς.... οὐ μόνον τοῖς ἐκ περιτομῆς, ἀλλὰ καὶ.... τοῖς στοιχοῦσι κ.τ.λ. Others take τοῖς οὐκ for οὐ τοῖς (as 37, 80, Syr. Arr. Vulg. Slav. and several Fathers read as an emendation), thus making a distinction to be drawn here not between merely circumcised and unbelieving *Jews*, but between *Jews* and *Gentiles* (ἀλλὰ καὶ τοῖς κ.τ.λ.). So Theodoret, Luther, Castalio, Koppe, Storr, Flatt, Schrader (Grotius is doubtful). But such an inversion is as unnatural (comp. ver. 16) as it is unprecedented (it is an error to refer to ii. 27; 1 Thess. i. 8); and how strange it would be, if Paul should have once more brought forward the fatherhood as to the believing Gentiles, but should have left that relating to the Jews altogether without conditioning definition! Hofmann (comp. also his *Schriftbew.* II. 2, p. 82) understands περιτομῆς, after the analogy of ὁ Θεὸς τῆς δόξης κ.τ.λ., as the genitive of *quality* ("a father, *whose fatherhood is to be designated according to circumcisedness;*" as a circumcised person he has begotten Isaac, etc.); then assumes in the case of τοῖς οὐκ ἐκ περιτομῆς μόνον the suppressed antithesis to complete it, ἀλλὰ καὶ ἐκ πίστεως; and finally explains ἀλλὰ καὶ τοῖς στοιχ. as a supplementary addition, while he takes ἀλλὰ καὶ to mean not *but also*, but *also however*. A hopeless misinterpretation! For, as genitive of *quality*, περιτομῆς must have had the article (comp. Acts vii. 2; 2 Cor. i. 3; Eph. i. 17 *al.*), and every reader must have understood περιτομῆς in conformity with πάντων κ.τ.λ., ver. 11, as a specification *whose* father Abraham further is. The reader could all the less mentally supply after τοῖς οὐκ ἐκ περιτ. a *suppressed* contrast, since the *expressed* contrast follows immediately with ἀλλὰ καί; and for *that reason*, again, it could occur to no one to understand this ἀλλὰ καί in any other sense than elsewhere after negations, namely, *but also*, not *also however*. (How inappropriate is Hofmann's citation of Luke xxiv. 22, where no negation at all precedes!) Wieseler's attempt (in Herzog's *Encyklop.* XX. p. 592) is also untenable, since he imports into τοῖς οὐκ ἐκ περιτ. μόνον the sense: "*who do not make circumcision the exclusive condition of salvation*," and likewise renders ἀλλὰ καί *also however;* thus making Paul indicate (1) the Jewish Christians who were not rigid partisans of the law (such as were to be found in Palestine especially), and (2) the Pauline Jewish Christians.

— τοῖς ἴχνεσι κ.τ.λ.] who so walk (see on Gal. v. 25) that they *follow the footsteps* which Abraham has left behind through his faith manifested in his uncircumcised condition, *i.e.* who are believers after the type of the uncircumcised Abraham. The *dative*, commonly taken as *local*, is more correctly, in keeping with the other passages in which Paul uses the dative with στοιχεῖν (Gal. v. 16, 25, vi. 16; Phil. iii. 16), interpreted in the sense of the *norm*.

Ver. 13. Ground assigned for the foregoing, from εἰς τὸ εἶναι αὐτὸν πατέρα onwards. "The father of all believing Gentiles and Jews;" *for it was not the law, but the righteousness of faith, that procured for Abraham or his seed the promise of possessing the world*. Had the law been the agent in procuring that promise, then *the Jews*, as possessors of the law, would be the children of Abraham who should receive what was promised; as it is, however, it must be the *believers*, no matter whether Jews or Gentiles, since not the law has been at work, but on the contrary the *righteousness of faith*. — διὰ νόμου] *through the agency of the law*, is not to be arbitrarily limited (Piscator, Calovius, and others: *per justitiam legis;* Pareus and others: *per opera legis*); for, as the Mosaic law[1] was not yet even in existence, it could *in no way* procure the promise. Hence it is not to be rendered with Grotius: "*sub conditione* observandi legem Mosis," because διὰ δικαιοσ. πίστ. does not admit of a corresponding interpretation. — ἡ ἐπαγγελία] scil. ἐστι. The supplying of this (usually: ἐγένετο) is quite sufficient; comp. on ver. 9. The relation is realised as present. — ἢ τῷ σπέρμ. αὐτοῦ] *neither* to Abraham *nor* to his seed, etc. With ἢ τῷ σπέρμ. αὐτ. Paul takes for granted that the history of the promise in question is known; and *who* are meant by the σπέρμα under the Messianic reference of the promise cannot, according to the context (see especially ver. 11), be doubtful, namely the *believers*, who are the *spiritual* posterity of Abraham (ix. 6 ff.; Gal. iv. 22 ff.); not *Christ* according to Gal. iii. 16 (Estius, Cornelius à Lapide, Olshausen); but also not the *descendants of Abraham proper* (van Hengel). — τὸ κληρ. αὐτ. εἶναι κόσμου] Epexegesis of ἡ ἐπαγγελία. See Kühner, II. 1, p. 518, and *ad Xen. Anab.* ii. 5, 22. The αὐτόν,

---

[1] For to *this* διὰ νόμου must be referred (see ver. 14 ff.) not to *circumcision*, which is brought under the wider conception of the law (Mehring).

referring to Abraham, is so put not because ἡ τ. σπ. αὐτοῦ is only incidentally introduced (Rückert), but because Abraham is regarded as at once the father and representative of his σπέρμα included with him in the promise. — κόσμου] The inheritance of the land of Canaan, which God promised to Abraham for himself and his posterity (Gen. xii. 7, xiii. 14, 15, xv. 18, xvii. 8, xxii. 17; comp. xxvi. 3; Ex. vi. 4), was in the Jewish Christology taken to mean *the universal dominion of the Messianic theocracy*, which was typically pointed at in these passages from Genesis. " Abrahamo patri meo Deus possidendum dedit *coelum et terram*," Tanchuma, p. 165, 1, and see Wetstein. The idea of *Messianic sovereignty over the world*, however, which lies at the bottom of this Jewish particularistic conception, and which the prophets invested with a halo of glory,[1] is in the N. T. not done away, but divested of its Judaistic conception, and raised into a Christological truth, already presented by Christ Himself (comp. Matth. v. 5) though in allegoric form (Matth. xix. 28 ff.; Luke xxii. 30; Matth. xxv. 21). Its necessity lies in the universal dominion to which Christ Himself is exalted (Matth. xxviii. 18; John xvii. 5; Phil. ii. 9 ff.; Eph. iv. 10 *al.*), and in the glorious fellowship of His believers with Him. Now as the idea of this government of the world, which Christ exercises, and in which His believers (the spiritual children of Abraham) are one day to participate, was undeniably also the ideal of Paul (viii. 17; 1 Cor. vi. 2; comp. 2 Tim. ii. 12), it is arbitrary to take κόσμου here otherwise than *generally*, and either to limit it to *the sphere of earth* (Koppe, Köllner, Maier), or to explain it as relating to the dominion of the Jews over the *Gentile world* (van Hengel), or the reception of all peoples into the Messianic kingdom (Beza, Estius and others) or *Messianic bliss* generally (Wetstein, Flatt, comp. Benecke and Glöckler), or the *spiritual* dominion of the world (Baumgarten-Crusius), as even Hengstenberg does: " the world is spiritually conquered by Abraham and his seed" (*Christol.* I. p. 49). The interpretation which takes it to mean the extension of the *spiritual fatherhood over all nations* (Mehring) would only be possible in the absence of ἢ τῷ σπέρματι αὐτοῦ, and would likewise be set aside by the firmly established historical notion of the נחלה. The κληρονόμον

---

[1] Comp. Schultz, *alttest. Theol.* I. p. 225 ff.

εἶναι τοῦ κόσμου of believers is realised in the new glorious world (ἐν τῇ παλιγγενεσίᾳ, Matth. xix. 28, comp. Rom. viii. 18, 2 Pet. iii. 13) after the Parousia; hence the Messianic kingdom itself and all its δόξα, as the completed possession of salvation promised to believers, is designated by the theocratic technical term κληρονομία (see on Gal. iii. 18). — διὰ δικ. πίστ.] Since the νόμος was not the procurer of the promise, but Abraham was righteous through faith (ver. 3), the δικαιοσύνη πίστεως must necessarily have been that which procured the promise (moved God to grant it). See ver. 14. It is true that the promise in question was given to Abraham *prior to* his justification by faith (Gen. xii. 7, xiii. 14 f.); but it was *renewed* to him *subsequently* (xv. 18, xvii. 8); hence we must assume that here Paul had only these latter passages in view.

Vv. 14-17. Proof of the antithesis οὐ διὰ νόμου.... ἀλλα κ.τ.λ. in ver. 13, conducted not historically (as in Gal. iii. 13 ff.), but dogmatically, *a priori*, from the *nature of the law*, from which results the opposite of the latter, the πίστις, as cause of the κληρονομία.

Ver. 14. Here also νόμος is not (as Flatt and others take it) the moral law (to which however the saying may certainly be *applied*), but the *law of Moses*, viewed in *excluding* antithesis to the πίστις. By οἱ ἐκ νόμου, "those of the law" (Luther), are meant those who belong to the law, are *as such* subjected to it; consequently the *Jews* at all events, but just so far as they are *not believers*, not belonging to the Ἰσραὴλ τοῦ Θεοῦ (Gal. vi. 16). The opposite: οἱ ἐκ πίστεως, iii. 26, Gal. iii. 7. That they *wish to attain to the* κληρονομία by the way of the law, is true in itself, but is not expressed in the mere οἱ ἐκ νόμου (in opposition to Hofmann). — κεκένωται ἡ πίστις κ.τ.λ.] *then faith is made void and the promise done away, i.e.* faith is thereby rendered inoperative and the promise of no effect. If it be true that to be subject to the law is the condition of obtaining the possession of the world, nothing further can be said either of a saving power of faith (comp. 1 Cor. i. 17), or of the validity of the promise (comp. iii. 31, Gal. iii. 17). And why not? Because (ver. 15) the law, to which in accordance with that protasis the κληρονομία would be appended, has an operation so entirely opposed to the essence of faith (which trusts in the divine χάρις) and of the promise (which is an emanation from this χάρις), (comp. ver. 16), that it brings about the divine *wrath*, since its result is *transgression*. *On this ground* (διὰ τοῦτο, ver. 16) because the law *worketh wrath*, its relation to the κληρονομία, laid down in ver. 14, cannot exist; but on the contrary the latter must proceed *from faith* that it may be *according to grace*, etc., ver. 16.—The πίστις is the Christian saving faith, of which Abraham's faith was the beginning and type, and the ἐπαγγελία is the Divine promise of the κληρονομία, given to Abraham and his seed, ver. 13.

Ver. 15. On the connection see above. The *assigning of a reason* (γάρ) has reference to the previous κεκένωται ἡ πίστις κ. κατήργ. ἡ. ἐπαγγ., which are closely connected (see ver. 16), and not merely to the κατήργ ἡ ἐπα γγ. (Chrysostom, Fritzsche, Mehring, and others). *The law produces wrath.* It is the *divine* wrath that is meant, not any sort of *human* wrath (against the judgment of God, as Melancthon thought). Unpropitiated, it issues forth on the day of judgment, ii. 5 ff., iii. 5, ix. 22; Eph. ii. 3, v. 6; Col. iii. 6 *al.;* Ritschl, *de ira Dei*, p. 16; Weber, *vom Zorne Gottes*, p. 326 f. — οὗ γὰρ οὐκ ἔστι νόμος κ.τ.λ.] Proof of the proposition that the law worketh wrath: *for where the law is not, there is not even* (οὐδέ) *transgression*, namely, which excites the wrath of God (the Lawgiver). This short, terse and striking *proof*—which is not, any more than the three previous propositions introduced by γάρ, to be reduced to a "*justifying explanation*" (Hofmann), or to be weakened by taking οὐδέ to mean "*just as little*" (Hofmann)—proceeds *a causa ad effectum;* where the *cause* is wanting (namely, παράβασις), there can be no mention of the effect (ὀργή). This *negative* form of the probative proposition includes—in accordance with the doctrine of the Apostle elsewhere regarding the relation of the law to the human ἐπιθυμία (Rom. vii. 7 ff.; 1 Cor. xv. 56; Gal. iii. 19 *al.*), which is kindled on occasion of the law by the power of sin which exists in man—the positive counterpart, that, *where the law is, there is also transgression.* Paul however expresses himself *negatively*, because in his mind the negative thought that the fulfilment of the promise is not dependent on the law still preponderates; and he will not enter into closer analysis of the positive side of it—viz., that faith is the condition—until the sequel, ver. 16 ff. Observe moreover that he has not written οὐδὲ ἁμαρτία, which he could not assert (ver. 13), but οὐδέ παράβασις, as the specific designation of the ἁμαρτία in relation to the *law*, which was the precise point here in question. Comp. ii. 23, 25, 27, v. 14; Gal. ii. 18, iii. 19. Sins *without* positive law (ver. 13) are likewise, and indeed on account of the natural law, ii. 14, objects of the divine wrath (see i. 18 ff.; Eph. ii. 3); but sins *against* a given law are, in virtue of their thereby definite quality of *transgression*, so specifically and specially provocative of wrath in God, that Paul could relatively even deny the imputation of sin when the law was non-existent. See on ver. 13.

Ver. 16 f. Διὰ τοῦτο] Inference from ver. 15, consequently from the wrath-operating nature of the law, on account of which it is so utterly incapable of being the condition of the κληρονομία, that the latter must on the contrary result from the opposite of the law—from faith, etc. Comp. on ver. 14 f. This conclusion is so evident and pertinent that it required only the incomplete, but thus all the more striking expression: "*therefore of faith, in order that according to grace,*" to the end that, etc. — ἐκ πίστεως] scil. οἱ κληρονόμοι εἰσί, according to ver. 14. The supplying, by Fritzsche and others, of ἡ ἐπαγγελία γίνεται or ἐγένετο from ver. 13 is forbidden by the contrast in which ἐκ πίστ. stands to ἐκ νόμου, ver. 14. — ἵνα κατὰ χάριν] The purpose of God in ἐκ πίστεως: "*in order that they might be so by way of grace,*" not by way of merit. Comp. ver. 4 and δωρεάν iii. 24. — εἰς τὸ εἶναι βεβαίαν κ.τ.λ.] contains now in turn the divine purpose,[1] which prevails in the κατὰ χάριν. They shall be heirs *by way of grace;* and *why* by way of grace? *In order that the promise may be sure, i.e.* may subsist in active validity as one to be realised (the opposite of κατήργηται, ver. 14) *for the collective posterity (i.e.* for all believers, see v. 11, 13), *not for those alone, who are such out of the law* (not solely for believers who have become so out of the legal bond of Judaism), *but also for those who are such out of the faith of Abraham,*[2] *i.e.* whose Abrahamic

---

[1] Here also the peculiar deeper scope of the view given is often left unnoticed, and εἰς τὸ εἶναι is taken as *inference:* so that, etc. See on the other hand on i. 20.

[2] ἐν πίστ. Ἀβραάμ goes together (in opposition to Fritzsche, who has conceived the σπέρματι to be supplied as *before* Ἀβρ., and made the genitive Ἀβραάμ dependent on it), since it is not *Jews* and *Christians*, but *Jewish and Gentile believers* who are placed side by side, and in the latter the faith of Abraham (comp. ver. 10) is the characteristic.

kinship is based on Abraham's faith, the uncircumcised believers. Theophylact: παντὶ τῷ σπέρματι, τουτέστι πᾶσι τοῖς πιστεύουσιν· οὐ μόνον τοῖς ἐκ νόμου, τουτέστι τοῖς ἐμπεριτόμοις, ἀλλὰ καὶ τοῖς ἀκροβύστοις, οἵτινες εἰσι σπέρμα Ἀβραὰμ ἐκ πίστεως αὐτῷ γενηθέντες. If anything else than χάρις (such as ὀφείλημα) were the reason determining God to confer the κληρονομία, then both halves of the σπέρμα, in their legal imperfection, would be unsecured with respect to the promise. As it is, however, believing Jews as also believing Gentiles have in the divine χάρις the same guarantee that the κληρονομία shall be imparted to them ἐκ πίστεως. — ὅς ἐστι πατ. πάντ. ἡμῶν] reiterated (comp. vv. 11, 12) solemn setting forth of the fatherhood of Abraham for *all* (πάντων) believers (ἡμῶν), which was indeed the pith and fundamental idea of the entire argument (since ver. 9); there is therefore no new point raised here (Hofmann), but this fatherhood of the patriarch in the history of salvation, already clearly laid down, is summarily expressed afresh, in order (ver. 17), after the insertion of a testimony from Scripture, to present it, by means of κατέναντι οὗ κ.τ.λ., in its holy, divine guarantee and dignity. — ὅτι πατέρα πολλῶν κ.τ.λ.] Gen. xvii. 5, closely after the LXX.; therefore ὅτι, *for*, which in the original text specifies the reason of the name Abraham, is repeated by Paul without any special bearing on his connection, simply as forming part of the words of Scripture. — πατέρα πολλῶν ἐθν.] Aptly explained, in the sense of the Apostle, by Chrysostom and Theophylact: οὐ κατὰ φυσικὴν συγγένειαν, ἀλλὰ κατ' οἰκείωσιν πίστεως. In this spiritual sense—which the passage of Scripture expresses typically—he is constituted by God as father of many nations (in so far, namely, as all believers from among the Jews and all Gentile peoples are to be, in the history of salvation, his spiritual σπέρμα), *i.e. appointed*, and thus *made* so (compare Heb. i. 2; 1 Macc. x. 65, xiv. 34; Hom. *Od.* xv. 253, *Il.* vi. 300; Plat. *Theaet.* p. 169 E; Pind. *Ol.* xiii. 21). Even the original text cannot have meant by גוים merely the twelve tribes of Israel (Hofmann). It means the posterity of Abraham, in so far as Gentile peoples also shall be subjected to it. The Israelite tribes would be עמים. — κατέναντι οὗ ἐπίστ. Θεοῦ] is connected, after the parenthesis (καθὼς .... σε), with ὅς ἐστι πατὴρ πάντ. ἡμῶν. To get rid of the parenthesis by supposing a suppressed *inter-*

vening thought (Philippi), or an *asyndeton*, as if it were καὶ κατέναντι κ.τ.λ. (van Hengel), is a harsh and arbitrary course; while
it is impossible to regard κατέναντι κ.τ.λ. as *explanation* of the
καθὼς γέγραπται (Hofmann), because καθὼς γέγρ. can only be
taken as the quite common (occurring thirteen times in our
Epistle) simple formula for quoting a Scripture proof, and not
as: "*in harmony with* the Scripture passage."— κατέναντι, equivalent to the classical κατεναντίον, means *overagainst* (Mark xi. 2,
xii. 41; Luke xix. 30), *i.e.* here: *in presence of* (κατενώπιον), *coram*,
as after the Heb. frequently in the LXX. and Apocrypha. See
Biel and Schleusner. The *attraction* is to be resolved into:
κατέναντι τοῦ Θεοῦ, κατέναντι οὗ ἐπίστευσε : *coram Deo, coram
quo credidit*.[1] Quite analogous are such passages as Luke i. 4,
περὶ ὧν κατήχηθης λόγων, instead of περὶ τῶν λόγων περὶ ὧν
κατηχ., Matth. vii. 2 *al.* See Bornemann, *Schol. in Luc.* p. 177;
Schmid in the *Tüb. Zeitschr. f. Theol.* 1831, 2, p. 137 ff.; Winer,
p. 155 f. [E. T. 204]; comp. on Acts xxi. 16. So also rightly Philippi
and Hofmann;[2] comp. Märcker. The mode of resolving it adopted
by most commentators (Thomas Aquinas, Castalio, Calvin, Beza,
Er. Schmid, Grotius, Estius, and others; also Tholuck, Rückert,
Reiche, Köllner, Fritzsche, Ewald, van Hengel, Buttmann):
κατέναντι Θεοῦ ᾧ ἐπίστευσε, is at least at variance with the *usual*

---

[1] The *coram, in presence of*, is neither to be explained *ad exemplum* (Chrysostom, Theodoret, Theophylact and others), nor "according to the will" (Reiche,
Krehl and others), nor "according to the judgment" (Rückert, Köllner, Fritzsche,
Maier, Umbreit and others), nor "vi atque potestate divina" (Koppe), nor "before the omniscience of God" (Olshausen), but is to be left without any modifying
explanation. Abraham is *realised as present*, just as he stands πατὴρ πάντων
ἡμῶν *face to face* with the God who had appeared to him, and has become a believer *in conspectu Dei*. This vivid *realisation* of the believing patriarch, as if he
were standing there as father of us all before the face of God, just as formerly in that
sacred moment of history, is a plastic form of presentation which, inaptly condemned by Hofmann, quite accords with the *elevated* and almost poetic *strain* of
the following words. It also fully warrants the coupling of κατέναντι κ.τ.λ. with
ὅς ἐστι πατὴρ πάντων ἡμῶν; it is unnecessary to seek a connection with ὅτι πατέρα
.... τέθεικά σε, either with Bengel, who compares Matth. ix. 6, or with Philippi,
who, thereby getting rid of the parenthesis, inserts after τέθεικά σε the thought:
"and as such he has been appointed."

[2] Who, nevertheless, in consequence of his incorrect view of καθὼς γέγραπται,
professes to illustrate the κατέναντι thus: "*At that time, when he believed, he stood
face to face with God as Him who quickeneth the dead, etc. ; and by the fact, that
God has shown Himself to be just the same as Him before whom he then stood, it
has so come to pass, that he is now before Him the father of us all.*"

mode of attraction, since the attraction of the relative, which, not attracted, would stand in the dative, has no precedent in the N. T., and even in Greek authors very seldom occurs (Kühner, *ad Xen. Mem.* ii. 2, 5, *Gramm.* II. 2, p. 914). Finally, the explanation which takes κατέναντι οὗ as equivalent to κατέναντι τούτου, ὅτι, and the latter as equivalent to ἀνθ' οὗ, *propterea quod*, and in accordance with which Θεοῦ κ.τ.λ. is then taken as *genitive absolute* ("whilst God, who quickeneth the dead, calleth also to that which is not, as though it were present," Mehring), is wrong just because κατέναντι has not the sense supposed. — τοῦ ζωοπ. τ. νεκρούς, καὶ κ.τ.λ.] Distinguishing quality of God as the Almighty, selected with practical reference to the circumstances of Abraham (vv. 18-21): "*Who quickeneth the dead and calleth the non-existent as though it were*," and certainly, therefore, can quicken the decayed powers of procreation, and dispose of generations not yet in existence. A reference to the *offering of Isaac*, whom God could make alive again (Erasmus, Grotius, Baumgarten-Crusius and Mangold), is so foreign to the connection that it would have required definite indication. The ζωοποιεῖν τοὺς νεκρούς is a formal attribute of the almighty God. 1 Sam. ii. 6; Wisd. xvi. 13; Tob. xiii. 2; comp. Deut. xxxii. 9. See also John v. 21; 2 Cor. i. 9; 1 Tim. vi. 13. Origen, Ambrosiaster, Anselm, erroneously hold that the νεκροί are *spiritually* dead, a view which the context must have rendered necessary; comp. Olshausen, who holds that ζωοπ. and καλ. indicate typically the spiritual awakening and the new birth; also Ewald, who will have the application made to the revivifying of the dead Gentiles into true Christians. — καλοῦντος τὰ μὴ ὄντα ὡς ὄντα] *i.e.* "*who utters His disposing decree over that which does not exist, equally as over the existing.*" What a lofty expression of all-commanding power! And how thoroughly in harmony with the then position of Abraham! For as he stood before God and believed (Gen. xv. 6), God had just showed to him the stars of heaven, with the promise οὕτως ἔσται τὸ σπέρμα σου! So that God hereby issued his potent summons (*so shall it be!*) to something that was not (the σπέρμα of Abraham) as though it had been. This explanation (followed also by Rückert and Philippi) is perfectly faithful to the sense of the words, and as much in harmony with the vividly realised situation of

Abraham as it is appropriate to the parallelism; for the latter is *climactic*, leading from the νεκροῖς to the τὰ μὴ ὄντα. καλεῖν, like קרא, does not here mean to *name* (Hofmann, comp. Loesner and Benecke), which would refer to the *name of father* pronounced by God and have in view the divine *knowledge*, but on the contrary, correlative with the mighty ζωοποιεῖν τ. νεκρ. (comp. δυνατός ver. 21), it denotes the call of the Ruler, which He issues to that which is subject to His power. Comp. Ps. l. 1; Is. xl. 26;[1] ὡς is the simple *as* of comparison. Parallels in point are found in Philo, *de Jos.* p. 544 C, where it is said of the force of imagination, that it pictures τὰ μὴ ὄντα ὡς ὄντα; and Artemidor. i. 53, p. 46, ed. Rigalt. where it is said of the painter, that he represents τὰ μὴ ὄντα ὡς ὄντα. Paul could also have, like Clement, *Cor.* II. 1, used τὰ οὐκ ὄντα (the non-existent, Xen. *Mem.* ii. 2, 3), as the contradictory antithesis of τὰ ὄντα (comp. also Plat. *Rep.* p. 476 E); but the negation is conceived subjectively, from the standpoint of the subject who calls: he calls the things, which he knows as non-existent, as if they were. Comp. Xen. *Anab.* iv. 4, 15, and Kühner *in loc.*; Baeumlein, *Partik.* p. 278. Still what Delitzsch, *Psychol.* p. 37 f., deduces from τὰ μὴ ὄντα—that that which enters into historical existence was not previously an absolute nothing, but an object of divine knowledge—is based on the common conception of καλεῖν in the sense of *creative* activity, which is erroneous. No doubt καλεῖν, as is well known, often denotes the *creating* call of God (Isa. xxii. 12, xli. 4, xlviii. 13; 2 Kings viii. 1; Wisd. xi. 25; Philo, *de creat. princ.* p. 728 B, where τὰ μὴ ὄντα ἐκάλεσεν is further defined by εἰς τὸ εἶναι; comp. *de Opif.* p. 13 E). In this case we should have to think by no means of the historical *act of creation out of nothing* (Piscator, Estius and others), but rather, on account of the *present* parti-

---

[1] Quite contrary to the context Erasmus, Ch. Schmid, Koppe and Böhme take καλεῖν in the *dogmatic* sense. And yet even Fritzsche and Mangold have gone over to this explanation: "homines nondum in lucem editos *ad vitam aeternam* invitat." Van Hengel takes καλεῖν as *arcessere*, and τὰ μὴ ὄντα *that which is of no account* (see on 1 Cor. i. 28), so that the sense would be: "quaecunque nullius numeri sunt arcessivit (to the childship of Abraham), quasi sint in pretio." But this peculiar interpretation of μὴ ὄντα and ὄντα must have been specifically suggested by the context, especially as it strips off the whole poetical beauty of the expression.

ciple, either of the *continuous* creative activity (Köllner), or (better still on account of the parallel of ζωοπ.) of an *abiding characteristic* of God generally, from which no time is excluded. But this whole interpretation of καλεῖν is set aside here by ὡς ὄντα. For ὡς cannot be taken for εἰς (Luther, Wolf, and others), because an use so utterly isolated in the N. T. is in itself very improbable, and because, where ὡς stands in classic authors in the sense of εἰς, it is only so used in reference to *persons* (Hermann, *ad Viger.* p. 853; Poppo, *ad Thuc.* III. 1, p. 318 ff.), or, at the most, where what is personal is represented by neuter objects; see Döderlein, *philolog. Beitr.* p. 303 ff. Some desire ὡς ὄντα to be taken for ὡς ἐσόμενα (de Wette), or as a summary expression for εἰς τὸ εἶναι ὡς ὄντα (Reiche, Köllner, Tholuck, de Wette, Bisping), but these expedients are arbitrary in themselves, and, in the case of the latter especially—seeing that ὄντα would have to be taken in the sense of the result, as only adjectives are elsewhere used (see on Matth. xii. 43, and Breitenbach, *ad Xen. Oec.* 4, 7)—ὡς would only be superfluous and confusing.

Vv. 18–21. More particular setting forth of this faith of Abraham, according to its lofty power and strength. Εἶδες πῶς τίθησι καὶ τὰ κωλύματα καὶ τὴν ὑψηλὴν τοῦ δικαίου γνώμην πάντα ὑπερβαίνουσαν, Chrysostom.

Ver. 18. "Ὅς] Parallel to the ὅς ἐστι κ.τ.λ. ver. 16; therefore only a comma or a colon need be put after ὡς ὄντα. — ἐπ' ἐλπίδι] *on hope*, is the basis of the ἐπίστ. Comp. 1 Cor. ix. 10; frequent in Greek authors. See also Tit. i. 2. Abraham's faith was *opposed to hope* (παρ' ἐλπίδα, frequent in classical writers) in its *objective* reference, and yet not ἀνέλπιστος, but rather *based on hope* in its *subjective* reference,—a significant oxymoron. — εἰς τὸ γενέσθαι κ.τ.λ.] Rightly Luther: *in order that he might be.* Comp. Rückert, Tholuck, Philippi. It contains the *end*, ordained by God, of the ἐπίστ., thus exhibiting Abraham's faith in its teleological connection with the divine decree, and that in reference to the word of God, ver. 17; hence, it is less in harmony with the context to take εἰς τὸ γενέσθαι κ.τ.λ. as the purpose of *Abraham*. Ver. 11, εἰς τὸ εἶναι αὐτὸν κ.τ.λ. is quite analogous. Following Beza, many writers (including even Reiche, Köllner, Baumgarten-Crusius, Krehl, Mehring, Hofmann) take εἰς τὸ γεν. as the object of ἐπίστ.; quite contrary to the usage of the N. T.; see on ver. 11. Here, as in every case previously, the object of faith (the divine promise) is quite self-evident. The view which explains it of the *consequence* (Böhme, Flatt, Fritzsche, following older writers) for καὶ οὕτως ἐγένετο, is linguistically erroneous (see on i. 20), and quite at variance with the tenor of the discourse; for in vv. 19-21 *the delineation of the faith itself* is still continued, so that at this stage the *result* (it is introduced in ver. 22) would be quite out of place. — κατὰ τὸ εἰρημ.] belonging to γενέσθαι κ.τ.λ., not to ἐπίστευσε (Hofmann, in accordance with his incorrect view of εἰς τὸ κ.τ.λ.). — οὕτως] What is *meant* by this, Paul assumes to be familiar to his readers; and therefore the corresponding part is by no means wanting. F G and several Fathers (also Vulg. ms.) have after σου the addition: ὡς οἱ ἀστέρες τοῦ οὐρανοῦ καὶ ἡ ἄμμος τῆς θαλάσσης. The first half only is a *proper* gloss; the καὶ ἡ ἄμ. τ. θαλ. does not lie in the οὕτως, Gen. xv. 5, but is imported from Gen. xii. 16.

Vv. 19-21 are still dependent on ὅς, completing the description of the believing Abraham: *and* (who), *because he was not weak in faith, regarded not his own dead body.*[1] Theophylact has properly expressed the *meiosis* in μὴ ἀσθ.: μὴ ἀσθενήσας τῇ πίστει, ἀλλ' ἰσχυρὰν αὐτὴν ἔχων. By μή the ἀσθεν. is negatived from the point of view of the subject. Comp. on ver. 17. — οὐ κατενόησε] *he did not fix his attention thereon.* Comp. Heb. iii. 1, x. 24; Luke xii. 24; Judith x. 14. This remark is no historical blunder inconsistent with Gen. xvii. 17 (de Wette; comp. Rückert), but is quite in harmony with the account given in Gen. xv. 5, 6, where, immediately after the divine promise οὕτως ἔσται τὸ σπέρμα σου, it is said: καὶ ἐπίστευσεν Ἀβρ. τῷ Θεῷ. *This* (and not what is related in Gen. xvii. 17) is the fact which Paul here exhibits in greater detail, inasmuch as he depicts the καὶ ἐπίστευσε of Gen. *l.c.*, in its strength at first negatively (in the non-consideration of bodily obstacles) and then positively. The *immediately decided* faith of Abraham in Gen. xv., to which Paul here refers, is not inconsistent with the subsequent hesitation, Gen. xvii. (the account of which, moreover,

---

[1] *i.e.* his own body: *which was one already dead.* Therefore νενεκρ. without the article. Comp. Kühner, *ad Xen. Anab.* iv. 6, 1; Stallbaum, *ad Plat. Rep.* p. 573 A.

belongs to another author); the latter is a **wavering** which may easily be understood from a psychological point of view. Comp. the doubt of the Baptist as to the Messiahship of Jesus, Matth. xi. 2 ff. — νενεκρωμένον and νέκρωσις conveying the idea of decrepitude with reference to the powers of procreation and of conception respectively. Comp. Heb. xi. 12; Kypke, II. p. 164. — ἑκατονταέτης κ.τ.λ.] *although* so advanced in years that he might naturally have regarded etc., yet he did not do so. The που is the *circiter* in *approximate statements of number;* Herod. i. 119; vii. 5; Diog. L. viii. 86. Comp. Xen. *Oec.* 17, 3. Not used by Paul elsewhere. Abraham was then ninety-nine years old. See Gen. xvii. 1, 17, xxi. 5. "Post Semum nemo centum annorum generasse Gen. xi. legitur," Bengel.[1] — Observe, as to καὶ τ. νέκ., that the negation οὐ κατενόησε extends to both the objects of the sentence. Hofmann's objection to our reading,[2] and his declaration that instead of καί we should expect οὐδέ, are erroneous; see Winer, p. 460 [E. T. 610]; Buttmann, *neut. Gr.* p. 315.[3] The νέκρωσις is the *deadness* of the womb attested as having already set in at Gen. xviii. 11. Was Sarah still to become a mother ἐκ πολιᾶς γαστρός (Pind. *Pyth.* iv. 98)! — εἰς δὲ τὴν ἐπαγγελίαν κ.τ.λ.] The negative proposition in ver. 19 is, in the first place, still more specially *elucidated*, likewise negatively, by εἰς . . . . ἀπιστία (δέ, the epexegetical *autem*), and then the *positive opposite* relation is subjoined to it by ἀλλ' ἐνεδυν. κ.τ.λ. In the former negative illustrative clause the chief element giving *the information* is εἰς τ. ἐπαγγ. τ. Θεοῦ, which is therefore placed first with great emphasis: "*but with regard to the promise of God he wavered not incredulously, but waxed strong in faith,*" etc.

[1] With regard to the children subsequently begotten with Keturah, Gen. xxv. 1 ff., the traditional explanation, already lying at the foundation of Augustine, *de Civ. D.* xvi. 28, is sufficient, viz. that the power of begetting, received from God, continued after the death of Sarah. — On ἑκατονταέτης comp. Pind. *Pyth.* iv. 503. According to the uncertain canon of the old grammarians (see Lobeck, *ad Phryn.* p. 406 f.) it ought to have been written here as an oxytone (so Lachmann) because it is the predicate of a person. Comp. Kuhner, I. p. 420.

[2] With the reading *without* οὐ (see the crit. remarks) the thought conveyed is: *and without having been weak in faith he regarded*, etc., *but did not become doubtful in respect to the promise of God*, etc. Comp. Hofmann. But μὴ ἀσθ. τ. πιστ. would thus be superfluous, and even logically unsuitable in relation to ver. 20. Simply and clearly Paul would only have written: καὶ κατενόησε μὲν τὸ ἑαυτοῖ σῶμα κ.τ.λ. εἰς δὲ τὴν ἐπαγγ. κ.τ.λ.

[3] Comp. also Jacobs, *ad Del. epigr.* vi. 10, *not. crit.*

Since in this way the discourse runs on very simply and suitably to the sense, it is unnecessary to resort to the more awkward suggestion, that Paul already begins the antithetic statement with δέ (*however*, see Hartung, *Partikell.* I. p. 171), to which nevertheless he has again given the emphasis of contrast through the negative and positive forms (Philippi, who, however, admits our view also; comp. Tholuck and others). In no case, however, can it be said, with Rückert, that Paul wished to write εἰς δὲ τ. ἐπαγγ. τ. Θεοῦ ἐπίστ. μηδὲν διακρινόμενος, but that his love for antitheses induced him to divide the idea of ἐπίστ. into its negative and positive elements, and that therefore εἰς should be referred to the ἐπίστ. at first thought of. De Wette (comp. Krehl) conjectures that, according to the analogy of πιστεύειν εἰς, εἰς is the object of διεκρ. It is the quite usual *in regard to, as respects;* see Winer, p. 371 [E. T. 496]. — διακρίνεσθαι] *To waver*, the idea being that of a mental struggle into which one enters, xiv. 23; Matth. xxi. 21; Acts x. 20; see Huther on James i. 6. This usage is so certain in the N. T., that there is no need to translate, with van Hengel: *non contradixit*, referring to Gen. xvii. 17 ff., in which case τῇ ἀπιστίᾳ is supposed to mean : "quanquam in animo volvebat, quae diffidentiam inspirarent." Such a thought is foreign to the connection, in which everything gives prominence to *faith* only, and not to a mere resignation. — τῇ ἀπιστίᾳ is *instrumental*, in the sense of the producing cause, but τῇ πίστει, on account of the correlation with ἀσθεν. τῇ πίστει in ver. 19, is to be taken as the dative of *more precise definition*, consequently : he wavered not *by means of the unbelief* (which in such a case he would have had), but became strong *as respects the faith* (which he had). Hofmann's explanation is erroneous, because not in keeping with the ἀσθεν. τ. πίστ. above He takes τῇ πίστει as causal : *by faith* Abraham was strengthened " *to an action in harmony with the promise and requisite for its realisation.*" This addition, which can hardly fail to convey a very indelicate idea, is a purely gratuitous importation. — ἐνεδυναμώθη] *became strong*, heroic in faith ; passive. Comp. Aq. *Gen.* vii. 20: ἐνεδυναμώθη τό ὕδωρ. Heb. xi. 34 ; Acts ix. 32 ; Eph. vi. 10 ; LXX. Ps. lii. 7 : ἐνεδυναμώθη ἐπὶ τῇ ματαιότητι αὐτοῦ. In Greek authors the word does not occur. —

δοὺς δόξαν τῷ Θεῷ] *while he gave God glory, and*[1] *was fully persuaded* (xiv. 5; Col. iv. 12) *that*, etc. The *aorist* participles put the διδόναι δόξαν κ.τ.λ. not as *preceding* the ἐνεδυναμώθη, or as *presupposed* in it, but as *completed simultaneously with it.* (comp. on Eph. i. 5). — διδόναι δόξαν (נָתַן כָּבוֹד) τῷ Θεῷ denotes generally every act (thinking, speaking or doing) that tends to the glory of God (Josh. vii. 19; Jer. xiii. 16; Esr. x. 11; Luke xvii. 18; John ix. 24; Acts xii. 23); and the context supplies the special reference of its meaning. Here: by recognition of the divine *omnipotence* (not *circumcisione subeunda*, as van Hengel thinks), as is shown by what follows, which is added epexegetically. "Insigne praeconium fidei est, gloriam Deo tribuere," Melancthon. The opposite: 1 John v. 10. — ἐπήγγελται] in a middle sense. Winer, p. 246 [E. T. 328].

Ver. 22. Result of the whole disquisition, emphatically pointing back to ver. 3 (ἐλογίσθη αὐτῷ εἰς δικαιοσύνην). — διὸ καί] *on which account also* (i. 24), namely because Abraham believed so strongly as is described in vv. 18-21. — The *subject* of ἐλογίσθη (*it* was reckoned) is self-evident, viz. the *believing*. Comp. Nägelsbach, *zur Ilias*, p. 60, ed. 3.

Vv. 23-25. Relation of the Scripture testimony as to Abraham's justification to the justification of Christians by faith; with which the proof for the νόμον ἱστῶμεν διὰ τῆς πίστεως (iii. 31) is completed. — δι' αὐτόν] *on his account*, in order to set forth the mode of *his* justification. Then, corresponding thereto: δι' ἡμᾶς. Comp. Beresch R. 40, 8: "Quicquid scriptum est de Abrahamo, scriptum est de filiis ejus." On the idea generally comp. xiv. 4; 1 Cor. ix. 10, x. 6, 11; Gal. iii. 8. — μέλλει λογίζεσθαι] namely the πιστεύειν, which, in accordance with the divine ordination, is to be reckoned to us Christians (μέλλει),—*to us, as those who believe on Him that raised up Jesus.* μέλλει (comp. on viii. 13) is therefore not to be taken for ἔμελλε (Böhme, comp. Olshausen), but contains what God has willed, which shall accomplish itself *continuously* as to *each* concrete case (not for the first time at the judgment, as Fritzsche thinks) where Christ

---

[1] The evidence against καί is too weak. Without it πληροφ. would be *subordinated* to the δοὺς δόξ. τ. Θ. Oecumenius has aptly remarked on πληροφ.: οὐκ εἶπε πιστεύσας, ἀλλ' ἐμφατικώτερον. It corresponds with the *full victory* of the trial of the patriarch's faith at the *close* of its delineation.

is believed on. The ἡμεῖς, *i.e.* the community of believers (not however conceived as *becoming* such, as Hofmann supposes), are the constant recipients of the fulfilment of that which was once written not merely for Abraham's sake but also for theirs. — τοῖς πιστεύουσιν] not: who from time to time *become believing* (Hofmann), which is not consistent with ἡμᾶς, but: quippe *qui credunt*. The ἐπὶ τὸν ἐγείραντα κ.τ.λ. that is added then points out the *specific contents*, which is implied in the μέλλει λογίζεσθαι, for the πιστεύειν that has not yet been more precisely defined. In and with this faith we have constantly the blessing of the λογίζεσθαι divinely annexed to it. Comp. viii. 1. And the ἐπὶ τὸν ἐγείραντα κ.τ.λ. (comp. x. 9) is *purposely chosen* to express the character of the faith, partly on account of the necessary analogy with ver. 17,[1] and partly because the divine omnipotence, which raised up Jesus, was at the same time the strongest proof of divine grace (ver. 25). Regarding ἐπί, comp. on ver. 5 — παρεδόθη] standing designation for the divine surrender of Christ, surrender *unto death* (viii. 32), perhaps after Is. liii. 12. It is at the same time *self-surrender* (Gal. ii. 20; Eph. v. 2), since Christ was obedient to his Father. — διὰ τὰ παραπτ. ἡμῶν] *on account of our sins*, namely, that they might be atoned for by the ἱλαστήριον of Jesus, iii. 24 f., v. 8 f. — διὰ τὴν δικαίωσιν ἡμῶν] *on account of our justification*, in order to accomplish on us the judicial act of transference into the relation of δικαιοσύνη. Comp. v. 18. For this object God raised Jesus from the dead;[2] for the resurrection of the sacrificed One was required to produce in men *the faith*, through which alone the objective fact of the atoning offering of Jesus could have the

---

[1] But in point of fact to "believe on *Christ*" and to "believe on *God* who raised Christ," are identical, because in both cases Christ is the *specific object*.

[2] Compare Weiss, *bibl. Theol.* p. 329. For the view which the older Reformed theologians (comp. also Gerhard in Calovius) took of the state of the case as an *acquittal from our sins*, which was accorded to Christ and to us with Him through His resurrection, see Ritschl, *Rechtfertigung und Versöhnung*, I. p. 283 f. According to Beza, Christ could not have furnished the atonement of our sins, if He had not, as the risen victor, vanquished death. But the case is rather conceived as the converse: Christ could not have risen, if His death had not expiated our sins. In this way Christ has not merely died ὑπὲρ ἡμῶν, but has also been raised again (2 Cor. v. 15); without His saving power, however, having been in itself conditioned only by the resurrection (to which, in the main, the views of Öttinger and Menken ultimately come).

effect of δικαίωσις *subjectively*, because Christ is the ἱλαστήριον διὰ τῆς πίστεως, iii. 25. *Without* His resurrection therefore the atoning work of His death would have remained without subjective appropriation; His surrender διὰ τὰ παραπτ. ἡμῶν would not have attained its end, our justification. Comp. especially 1 Cor. xv. 17; 2 Cor. v. 20 f., xv.; 1 Pet. i. 21. Moreover the two definitions by διά are not two *different* things, but only the two aspects of *the same* exhibition of grace, the negative and the positive; of which, however, the former by means of the parallelism, in which both are put in juxtaposition, is aptly attributed to the death as the *objective* ἱλαστήριον, and the latter to the resurrection, as the divine act that is the means of its *appropriation*.[1] Melancthon has well said: "Quanquam enim *praecessit* meritum, tamen ita ordinatum fuit ab initio, ut tunc singulis *applicaretur*, cum fide acciperent." The latter was to be effected by the *resurrection* of Jesus; the *meritum* lay in His *death*, but the *raising Him up* took place for the δικαίωσις, in which His *meritum* was to be *realised* in the faithful. Comp. viii. 34. Against the Catholic theologians, who referred δικ. to *sanctification* (as Maier, Bisping, Döllinger and Reithmayr still do), see Calovius. Nor is *intercession* even (viii. 34) to be introduced into διὰ τὴν δικαίωσιν ἡμῶν (Calvin and others; also Tholuck and Philippi), since that does not take place to produce the δικαιοσύνη, but has reference to those who are already justified, with a view to *preserve* them in the state of salvation; consequently the δικαίωσις of the subjects concerned *precedes* it.

[1] The reference to the fellowship with the death of Christ, whereby believers have died to their former life, and with His resurrection as an entrance into a new state of life no longer conditioned by the flesh (see Rich. Schmidt, *Paulin. Christol.* p. 74), is inadmissible; because it does not correspond to the prototype of Abraham, which determines the entire representation of justification in this chapter.

CHAPTER V.

Ver. 1. ἔχομεν] Lachm. (in the margin), Scholz, Fritzsche, and Tisch. (8) read ἔχωμεν, following A B* C D K L ℵ*, min., several vss. (including Syr. Vulg. It.) and Fathers. But this reading, though very strongly attested, yields a sense (*let us maintain peace* with God) that is here utterly unsuitable; because the writer now enters on a new and important *doctrinal topic*, and an exhortation at the very outset, especially regarding a subject not yet expressly spoken of, would at this stage be *out of place*.[1] Hence the ἔχομεν, sufficiently attested by B** ℵ** F G, most min., Syr. p. and some Fathers, is to be retained; and the subjunctive must be regarded as having arisen from misunderstanding, or from the hortatory *use* of the passage. — Ver. 2. τῇ πίστει] wanting in B D E F G, Aeth. It.; omitted by Lachm. and Tisch. (7), as also by Ewald. Following ver. 1, it is altogether superfluous; but this very reason accounts for its omission, which secured the direct reference of εἰς τ. χάρ. ταύτ. to προσαγ. The genuineness of τῇ πίστει is also attested by the reading ἐν τῇ πίστει (so Fritzsche) in A ℵ** 93, and several Fathers, which points to a repetition of the final letters of ἐσχήκαμEN. — Ver. 6. After ἀσθενῶν preponderating witnesses have ἔτι, which Griesb. Lachm. and Tisch. (8) have adopted. A misplacement of the ἔτι before γάρ, because it was construed with ἀσθενῶν, along with which it came to be written. Thus ἔτι came in twice, and the first was either mechanically allowed to remain (A C D* ℵ), or there was substituted for it εἴγε (B), or εἰς τί (F G), or εἰ γάρ. The misplacement of the ἔτι came to predominate, because a Church-lesson began with Χριστός. — Ver. 8. ὁ Θεός, which a considerable number of witnesses have before εἰς ἡμᾶς (so Tisch. 7), is wanting in B. But as the love of *Christ*, not that of God, appeared from ver. 7 to be the subject of the discourse, ὁ Θεός was omitted. — Ver. 11. καυχώμενοι] F G read καυχῶμεν; L, min., and several Fathers καυχώμεθα. Also Vulg. It. Arm. Slav. ex-

---

[1] This even, in opposition to the opinion of Tisch. (8), that on account of the weighty testimony in its favour ἔχωμεν cannot be rejected, "*nisi prorsus ineptum sit; ineptum vero non videtur.*" Hofmann also has not been able suitably to explain the ἔχωμεν which he defends. See the exegetical remarks.

press *gloriamur*. An erroneous interpretation. See the exegetical remarks. — Ver. 12. The second ὁ θάνατος is wanting in D E F G 62, It. Syr. p. Aeth. and most Fathers, also Aug. In Syr. with an asterisk; Arm. Chrys. Theodoret place it after διῆλθεν. Tisch. (7) had omitted it. But as the word has preponderant testimony in its favour, and as in order to the definiteness of the otherwise very definitely expressed sentence it cannot be dispensed with, if in both halves of ver. 12 the relation of *sin* and *death* is, as is manifestly the design, to be expressly put forward, ὁ θάνατος omitted by Tisch., must be defended. Its omission may have arisen from its apparent superfluousness, or from the similarity between the final syllables of ἀνθρώΠΟΥΣ and θάνα-ΤΟΣ. — Ver. 14. μή] is wanting in 62, 63, 67**, Or. and others, codd. in Ruf. and Aug., and is declared by Ambrosiaster to be an interpolation. But it is certified partly by decisive testimony in its favour; partly by the undoubted genuineness of the καί; and partly because the μή apparently contradicts the erroneously understood ἐφ' ᾧ (*in quo*) πάντες ἥμαρτον in ver. 12. See Reiche, *Commentar. crit.* I. p. 39 ff. — Ver. 16. ἁμαρτήσαντος] D E F G, 26, 80, and several vss. and Fathers read ἁμαρτήματος, which Griesb. recommended. A gloss occasioned by the antithesis ἐκ πολλ. παραπτωμάτων. — Ver. 17. τῷ τοῦ ἑνὸς παραπτώματι] So also Lachm. and Tisch. (8) following B C K L P ℵ, vss., and Fathers. But A F G read ἐν ἑνὶ παραπτ., D E ἐν τῷ ἑνὶ παραπτ. 47, Or. ἐν ἑνὸς παραπτ. The original reading was most probably the simplest, ἐν ἑνὶ παραπτ., which, though not most strongly, is nevertheless sufficiently attested (also recommended by Griesb. and adopted by Tisch. (7), because from it the rise of the other variations can be very naturally explained. By way of more specific indication in some cases, the article was added (D E), in others ἑνί was changed into ἑνός (47, Or.). But, seeing that in any case the sense was quite the same as in the τῷ τοῦ ἑνὸς παραπτ. read in ver. 15, this was at first written alongside as a parallel, and then taken into the text.

CONTENTS. — Paul has hitherto described the δικαιοσύνη ἐκ πίστεως in respect of its necessity (i. 18–iii. 21); of its nature (iii. 21-30); and of its relation to the law (iii. 31–iv. 25). *He now discusses the blessed assurance of salvation secured for the present and the future* to the δικαιωθέντες ἐκ πίστεως (ver. 1-11); and then —in order clearly to exhibit the greatness and certainty of salvation in Christ, more especially in its *divine world-wide* significance as the blissful epoch-forming counterpart of the *Adamite* ruin—he presents us with a detailed *parallel between this salvation and the misery which once came through Adam* (vv. 12-19), *and was necessarily augmented through the law* (vv. 20, 21).

Ver. 1.[1] Οὖν draws an inference from the whole of the preceding section, iii. 21–iv. 25, and develops the argument in such a form that δικαιωθέντες, following at once on διὰ τὴν δικαίωσιν ἡμ., heads the sentence with triumphant emphasis. What a *blessed assurance of salvation* is enjoyed by believers in virtue of their justification which has taken place through faith, is now to be more particularly set forth; not however in the form of an *exhortation* (Hofmann, in accordance with the reading ἔχωμεν) "to let our relation to God be one of peace" (through a *life* of faith), in which case the emphasis, that obviously rests in the first instance on δικαιωθ. and then on εἰρήνην, is taken to lie on διὰ τοῦ κυρίου ἡμ. Ἰ. Χ.— εἰρήνην ἔχ. π. τ. Θεόν] He who is justified is no longer in the position of one to whom God must be and is hostile (ἐχθρὸς Θεοῦ, ver. 9 f.), but on the contrary he has *peace* (not in a general sense *contentment*, satisfaction, as Th. Schott thinks) in his relation to God. This is *the* peace which consists in the known objective state of reconciliation, the opposite of the state in which one is subject to the divine *wrath* and the *sensus irae*. With justification this peace ensues as its immediate and abiding result.[2] Hence δικαιωθέντες .... ἔχομεν (comp. Acts ix. 31; John xvi. 33). And *through Christ* (διὰ τοῦ κυρίου κ.τ.λ.) as the εἰρηνοποιός is this *pacem obtinere* (Bremi, *ad Isocr. Archid.* p. 111) procured; a truth obvious indeed in itself, but which, in consonance with the strength and fulness of the Apostle's own believing experience, is very naturally again brought into special prominence here, in order to connect, as it were, triumphantly with this objective cause of the state of peace what we owe to it respecting the point in question, ver. 2. There is thus the less necessity for joining διὰ τοῦ κυρίου κ.τ.λ. with εἰρήνην (Stölting); it belongs, like πρὸς τ. Θεόν, in accordance with the position of ἔχομεν, to the *latter* word.— πρός (of the ethical relation, Bernhardy, p. 265), as in Acts ii. 47, xxiv. 16. Comp. Herodian, viii. 7, 8: ἀντὶ πολέμου μὲν εἰρήνην ἔχοντες πρὸς θεούς. Plat. *Pol.* v. p. 465 B: εἰρήνην πρὸς ἀλλήλους

---

[1] On vv. 1-8 see Winzer, *Commentat.* Lips. 1832. On the entire chapter Stölting, *Beiträge z. Exegese d. Paul. Briefe*, Göttingen, 1869, p. 3 ff.

[2] Comp. Dorner, *die Rechtfert. durch den Glauben*, p. 12 f.

οἱ ἄνδρες ἄξουσιν; *Legg.* xii. p. 955 B; *Alc. I.* p. 107 D; Xenoph. and others. It is not to be confounded with the divinely wrought inward state of *mental* peace, which is denoted by εἰρήνη τοῦ Θεοῦ in Phil. iv. 7; comp. Col. iii. 15. The latter is the subjective correlate of the objective relation of the εἰρήνη, which we have πρὸς τὸν Θεόν, although inseparably combined with the latter.

Ver. 2. Δι' οὗ καὶ κ.τ.λ.] Confirmation and more precise definition of the preceding διὰ.... Ἰησοῦ Χ. The καί does not merely append (Stölting), but is rather the "*also*" of *corresponding relation*, giving prominence precisely to what had here an important practical bearing *i.e.* as proving the previous διὰ κυρίου κ.τ.λ. Comp. ix. 24; 1 Cor. iv. 5; Phil. iv. 10. The *climactic* interpretation here (Köllner: "a heightened form of stating the merit of Christ;" comp. Rückert) is open to the objection that the προσαγωγὴ εἰς τ. χάρ. is not something added to or higher than the εἰρήνη, but, on the contrary, the *foundation* of it. If we were to take καὶ.... καί in the sense "*as well .... as*" (Th. Schott, Hofmann), the two sentences, which are not to be placed in special relation to iii. 23, would be made co-ordinate, although the second is the *consequence* of that which is affirmed in the first. — τὴν προσαγωγὴν] *the introduction*,[1] Xen. *Cyrop.* vii. 5, 45; Thuc. i. 82, 2; Plut. *Mor.* p. 1097 E, Lucian, *Zeux.* 6; and see also on Eph. ii. 18. *Through Christ* we have had our introduction to the grace, etc., inasmuch as He Himself (comp. 1 Pet. iii. 18) in virtue of His atoning sacrifice which removes the wrath of God, has become our προσαγωγεύς, or, as Chrysostom aptly expresses it, μακρὰν ὄντας προσήγαγε. In this case the preposition διά, which corresponds with the διά in ver. 1, is fully warranted, because Christ has brought us to

---

[1] Προσαγωγή ought not to be explained as *access* (Vulg. *accessum*, and so most interpreters), but as *leading towards*, the meaning which the word *always* has (even in Eph. ii. 18, iii. 12). See Xen. *l.c.*: τοὺς ἐμοὺς φίλους δεομένους προσαγωγῆς. Polybius uses it to express the bringing up of engines against a besieged town, ix. 41, 1, xiv. 10, 9; comp. i. 48, 2; the bringing up of ships to the shore, x. i. 6; the bringing of cattle into the stall, xii. 4, 10. In Herod. ii. 58 also the literal meaning is: a *leading up, carrying up* in solemn procession. Tholuck and van Hengel have rightly adopted the active meaning in this verse (comp. Weber, *vom Zorne Gottes*, p. 316); whilst Philippi, Umbreit, Ewald, Hofmann (comp. Mehring) abide by the rendering "*access.*" Chrysostom aptly observes on Eph. ii. 18: οὐ γὰρ ἀφ' ἑαυτῶν προσήλθομεν, ἀλλ' ὑπ' αὐτοῦ προσήχθημεν.

grace in His capacity as the divinely appointed and divinely given *Mediator*. Comp. Winer, p. 354 f. [E. T. 473]. — To τ. προσαγ. ἐσχήκ. belongs εἰς τ. χάριν ταύτην; and τῇ πίστει, *by means of faith*, denotes the subjective medium of τ. προσαγ. ἐσχήκαμεν. On the other hand, Oecumenius, Bos, Wetstein, Michaelis, Reiche, Baumgarten-Crusius take τ. προσαγωγ. absolutely, in the sense of *access to God* (according to Reiche as a figurative mode of expressing the *beginning* of grace), and εἰς τὴν χάρ. ταύτ. as belonging to τῇ πίστει. In that case we *must* supply after προσαγ. the words πρὸς τ. Θεόν from ver. 1 (Eph. ii. 18, iii. 12); and we *may* with Bos and Michaelis explain προσαγωγή by the usage of courts, in accordance with which access to the king was obtained through a προσαγωγεύς, *sequester* (Lamprid. in *Alex. Sev.* 4). But the whole of this reading is liable to the objection that πίστις εἰς τὴν χάριν would be an expression without analogy in the N. T. — ἐσχήκαμεν] Not: *habemus* (Luther and many others), nor *nacti sumus et habemus* (most modern interpreters, including Tholuck, Rückert, Winzer, Ewald), but *habuimus*, namely, *when we became Christians*. So also de Wette, Philippi, Maier, van Hengel, Hofmann. Comp. 2 Cor. i. 9, ii. 13, vii. 5. The perfect *realises as present* the possession formerly obtained, as in Plat. *Apol.* p. 20 D, and see Bernhardy, p. 379. — εἰς τὴν χάρ. ταύτ.] The divine grace of which the justified are partakers[1] is conceived as a *field of space*, into which they *have had* (ἐσχήκαμεν) introduction through Christ by means of faith, and in which they now *have* (ἔχομεν) peace with God. — ἐν ᾗ ἑστήκαμεν] does not refer to τῇ πίστει (Grotius), but to the nearest antecedent, τὴν χάριν, which is also accompanied by the demonstrative: *in which we stand*. The joyful consciousness of the present, that the possession of grace once entered upon is *permanent*, suggested the word to the Apostle. Comp. 1 Cor. xv. 1; 1 Pet. v. 12. — καὶ καυχώμεθα] may be regarded as a

[1] For to nothing else than the grace experienced in *justification* can εἰς τ. χάρ. τ. be referred in accordance with the context (δικαιωθέντες)—not to the *blessings of Christianity generally* (Chrysostom and others, including Flatt and Winzer; comp. Rückert and Köllner); not to the *Gospel* (Fritzsche); and not to the εἰρήνη (Mehring, Stölting), which would yield a tame tautology.—The demonstrative ταύτην implies something of triumph. Compare Photius. The joyful consciousness of the Apostle is still full of the high blessing of grace, which he has just expressed in the terms δικαίωσις and δικαιωθέντες.

continuation either of the last relative sentence (ἐν ᾗ ἑστήκ., so van Hengel, Ewald, Mehring, Stölting), or of the previous one (δι' οὗ καὶ κ.τ.λ.), or of the principal sentence (εἰρήν. ἔχομεν). The *last* alone is suggested by the context, because, as ver. 3 shows, a new and independent element in the description of the blessed condition is introduced with καὶ καυχώμεθα. — καυχᾶσθαι expresses not merely the idea of *rejoicing*, not merely "the inward elevating *consciousness*, to which outward expression is not forbidden" (Reiche), but rather the actual *glorying*, by which we praise ourselves as privileged ("what the heart is full of, the mouth will utter"). Such is its meaning in all cases. — On ἐπί, *on the ground* of, *i.e. over*, joined with καυχ. comp. Ps. xlviii. 6; Prov. xxv. 14; Wisd. xvii. 7; Ecclus. xxx. 2. No further example of this use is found in the N. T.; but see Lycurgus in Beck. *Anecd.* 275, 4; Diod. S. xvi. 70; and Kühner, II. 1, p. 436. It is therefore unnecessary to isolate καυχώμεθα, so as to make ἐπ' ἐλπίδι independent of it (iv. 18; so van Hengel). Comp. on the contrary, the σεμνύνεσθαι ἐπί τινι frequent in Greek authors. The variation of the prepositions, ἐπί and in ver. 3 ἐν, is not to be imputed to any set purpose; comp. on iii. 20; iii. 25 f. *al.* — The δόξα τ. Θεοῦ is the glory of God, in which the members of the Messiah's kingdom shall hereafter participate. Comp. 1 Thess. ii. 12; John xvii. 22, also viii. 17; Rev. xxi. 11; 1 John iii. 2; and see Weiss, *bibl. Theol.* p. 376. The reading of the Vulg.: *gloriae filiorum Dei*, is a gloss that hits the right sense. Reiche and Maier, following Luther and Grotius, take the genitive as a *genit. auctoris.* But that God is the giver of the δόξα, is self-evident and does not *distinctively characterize* it. Rückert urges here also his exposition of iii. 23; comp. Ewald. But see on that passage. Flatt takes it as the *approval of God* (iii. 23), but the ἐλπίδι, pointing solely to the glorious future, is decisive against this view. It is aptly explained by Melancthon: "quod Deus sit nos gloria sua aeterna ornaturus, i. e. vita aeterna et communicatione sui ipsius."

Vv. 3, 4.[1] Οὐ μόνον δέ] scil. καυχώμεθα ἐπ' ἐλπίδι τῆς δόξης

---

[1] See a climax of description, similar in point of form in the Tractat. מוטה 9, 15 (see Surenh. III. 309): "Providentia parit alacritatem, alacritas innocentiam, innocentia puritatem, puritas abstinentiam, abstinentia sanctitatem, sanctitas modestiam, modestia timorem, timor sceleris pietatem, pietas spiritum sanctum,

τ. Θεοῦ. Examples of the usage (ver. 11, viii. 23, ix. 10; 2 Cor. viii. 19) may be seen in Kypke, II. p. 165; Vigerus, ed. *Herm.* p. 543; Heind. and Stallb. *ad Phaed.* p. 107 B. Comp. *Legg.* vi. p. 752 A; *Mcn.* p. 71 B. — ἐν ταῖς θλίψ.] *of the tribulations* (affecting us), as commonly in the N. T. ἐν is connected with καυχᾶσθαι (ver. 11; 2 Cor. x. 15; Gal. vi. 13). Comp. Senec. *de prov.* iv. 4: "gaudent magni viri rebus adversis non aliter quam fortes milites bellis triumphant." As to the ground of this *Christian* καύχησις, see the sequel. On the *thing* itself, in which the believer's victory over the world makes itself apparent (viii. 35 ff.), comp. 2 Cor. xi. 30, xii. 9; Matth. v. 10, 12; Acts v. 41; 1 Pet. iv. 12 f. Observe further, how with the joyful assurance of ample experience the triumphant discourse proceeds from the ἐλπὶς τῆς δόξης, as subject-matter of the καυχᾶσθαι, to the direct *opposite* (ἐν ταῖς θλίψεσιν), which may be likewise matter of glorying. Others (Glöckler, Baumgarten-Crusius, Stölting) erroneously render ἐν as *in*, which the contrast, requiring the *object*, does not permit, since ἐν τ. θλ. is not opposed to the ἐν ᾗ in ver. 2. — ὑπομονήν] *endurance* ("in ratione bene considerata stabilis et perpetua permansio," Cic. *de inv.* ii. 54), namely, in the Christian faith and life. Comp. ii. 7; Matth. x. 22, xxiv. 13. Paul lays down the ἡ θλίψις ὑπομ. κατεργάζ. *unconditionally*, because he is speaking of those who have been justified ἐκ πίστεως, in whose case the reverse cannot take place without sacrifice of their faith. — δοκιμήν] *triedness*, 2 Cor. ii. 9, viii. 2, ix. 13; Phil. ii. 22, "quae ostendit fidem non esse simulatam, sed veram, vivam et ardentem," Melancthon. Triedness is *produced* through endurance (not *made known*, as Reiche thinks); for whosoever does not endure thereby becomes ἀδόκιμος. There is here no inconsistency with James i. 3. See Huther. — ἐλπίδα] namely, τῆς δόξης τ. Θεοῦ, as is self-evident after ver. 2. The hope, it is true, already exists before the δοκιμή; nevertheless, the more the Christian has become *tried*, the *more* also will hope (which the ἀδόκιμος loses) consciously possess him. Comp. James i. 12. Hope is therefore present, and yet withal is *produced* by the emergence of the δοκιμή, just as faith may be

et spiritus sanctus resurrectionem mortuorum." In contrast with this, how fervent, succinct, and full of life is the climax in our passage! For other chains of climactic succession, see viii. 29 ff., x. 14 ff.; 2 Pet. i. 5 ff.

present, and yet be still further produced through something emerging (John ii. 11). Comp. Lipsius, *Rechtfertigungsl.* p. 207 f. — Observe further, how widely removed from all fanatical pride in suffering is the reason assigned with conscious clearness for the Christian καυχᾶσθαι ἐν ταῖς θλίψεσι in our passage. In it the ἐλπίς is uniformly meant and designated as the highest subjective *blessing* of the justified person, who is assured of the glorious consummation (not in ver. 3 f. as *conduct* and only in ver. 2 as *blessing*, as Hofmann thinks). Comp. the ἡδεῖα ἐλπίς, which ἀεὶ πάρεστι, in contrast to the ζῆν μετὰ κακῆς ἐλπίδος in Plato, *Rep.* p. 331 A.

Ver. 5. Ἡ δὲ ἐλπίς] not, "*the hope thus established*" (Oecumenius, Olshausen, Stölting), but, in accordance with the analogy of the preceding elements, and without any excluding limitation, *the hope* (of glory), as such, consequently the *Christian* hope. This deceives no one who has it. It is self-evident, and the proof that follows gives information as to the fact, that this is uttered in the consciousness and out of the inward assurance of real living justification by faith.[1] — οὐ καταισχύνει] *maketh not ashamed, i.e.* "habet certissimum salutis (of the thing hoped for) exitum," Calvin, as will be shown at the judgment. "*Spes* erit *res*," Bengel. Comp. ix. 33; Ecclus. ii. 10; Bar. vi. 39; Ps. xxii. 6. Comp. also Plat. *Conv.* p. 183 E, λόγους καὶ ὑποσχέσεις καταισχύνας. *Polit.* p. 268 D; Dem. 314, 9. The expression of triumphant certainty in the *present* is not to be removed by changing it into the *future* (Hofmann, who would read καταισχυνεῖ). — ὅτι ἡ ἀγάπη τ. Θεοῦ κ.τ.λ.] Ground of ἡ δὲ ἐλπίς οὐ καταισχ. The divine love,[2] effectually present in the heart through the Holy Spirit, is to the Christian consciousness of faith the sure pledge that we do not hope in vain and so as to be put to shame at last, but that God will on the contrary fulfil our hope. Θεοῦ is the genitive of the subject; *the love of God to us* (so most expositors following Origen, Chrysostom and Luther), not of the object: *love to God* (Theodoret, Augustine, Anselm and others; including Klee, Glöckler, Umbreit, Hofmann, Stölting),

---

[1] Comp. Düsterdieck in the *Jahrb. f. D. Th.* 1870, p. 668 ff.

[2] As is well said by Calovius: "quae charitas effusa in nobis non qua *inhaesionem subjectivam*, sed qua *manifestationem* et qua *effectum* vel *sensum* ejusdem in cordibus nostris effusum." Comp. Melancthon (against Osiander).

which appears from ver. 8 as incorrect.[1] Comp. viii. 39; 2 Cor. xiii. 13. As respects the justified, the wrath of God has given place to His *love*, which has its presence in them through the Spirit, its dwelling and sphere of action in believing hearts; and thus it is to them, like the Spirit Himself, $ἀρραβων$ of the hoped-for $δόξα$, 2 Cor. i. 22, v. 5.— $ἐκκέχυται$] Figure for abundant, living effective communication (Acts ii. 17, x. 45). The idea of *abundance* is already implied in the sensuous image of outpouring, but may also, as in Tit. iii. 6, be specially expressed. Comp. generally Suicer, *Thes.* I. p. 1075. — $ἐν ταῖς καρδίαις$] denotes, in accordance with the expression of the completed fact, the being spread abroad *in the heart* (motus *in loco*). Comp. LXX. Ps. xlv. 2.— $διὰ πνεύματος κ.τ.λ.$] Through the agency of the Spirit bestowed on us, who is the principle of the real self-communication of God, the divine love is also poured out in our hearts; see viii. 15, 16; Gal. iv. 6.

Ver. 6. Objective actual proof of this $ἀγάπη τ. Θεοῦ$, which through the Spirit fills our heart. Comp. as to the argument viii. 39. "*For Christ, when we were yet weak, at the right time died for the ungodly.*"— $ἔτι$] can in no case belong to $ἀπέθανε$ (Stölting), but neither does it give occasion for any conjecture (Fritzsche: $ἢ τί$). Paul should perhaps have written: $ἔτι γὰρ ὄντων ἡμ. ἀσθενῶν Χριστός κ.τ.λ.$, or: $Χριστὸς γὰρ ὄντων ἡμῶν ἀσθενῶν ἔτι κ.τ.λ.$ (hence the second $ἔτι$ in Lachmann); but amidst the collision of emphasis between $ἔτι$ and the subject both present to his mind, he has expressed himself inexactly, so that now $ἔτι$ *seems* to belong to $Χριστός$, and yet in sense necessarily *belongs*, as in ver. 8, to $ὄντων κ.τ.λ.$[2] Comp. Plat. *Rep.* p.

---

[1] Among Catholics this explanation of *active* love was favoured by the doctrine of the *justitia infusa*.

[2] Van Hengel decides in favour of the reading with the double $ἔτι$ (Griesbach, Lachmann, see the critical remarks); he thinks that Paul had merely wished to say: $ἔτι γὰρ Χ. κατὰ καιρ. ὑπ. ἀσεβ. ἀπέθ.$, but had in dictation for the sake of clearness inserted after $Χριστός$ the words $ὄντων ἡμῶν ἀσθ. ἔτι$. Mehring also follows Lachmann's reading. He thinks that Paul intended to write, with emphatic repetition of the $ἔτι$: $ἔτι γὰρ Χριστὸς, ἔτι ὑπὲρ ἀσεβῶν ἀπέθανε$, but interrupted the sentence by the insertion of $ὄντων ἡμ. ἀσθ.$ Ewald, holding $εἰ γάρ$ or $εἴγε$ to be the original (see critical remarks), and then reading $ἔτι$ after $ἀσθενῶν$, finds in ver. 9 the apodosis of ver. 6, and takes vv. 7, 8 as a parenthesis. Comp. also Usteri, *Lehrbegr.* p. 119. Th. Schott also follows the reading $εἰ γάρ$ (and after $ἀσθ.: ἔτι$), but finds the apodosis so early as ver. 6, by supplying after $ἀσθ. ἔτι$: $ἀπέθανε$; whereas Hofmann (in his *Schriftbew.* II. p. 347), following the same

503 E: ἔτι δὴ ὃ τότε παρεῖμεν νῦν λέγομεν; p. 363 D: οἱ δ' ἔτι τούτων μακροτέρους ἀποτείνουσι μισθούς (where ἔτι ought to stand before μακρ.). Achill. Tat. v. 18: ἐγὼ δὲ ἔτι σοὶ ταῦτα γράφω παρθένος, and see Winer, p. 515 [E. T. 692]. Buttmann, *neut. Gr.* p. 333 f.; and Fritzsche *in loc.* To get rid of this irregularity, Seb. Schmid, Oeder, Koppe, and Flatt have taken ἔτι as *insuper*, and that either in the sense of *adeo* (Koppe, also Schrader), which however it never means, not even in Luke xiv. 26; or so that a "*for further, for moreover*" (see Baeumlein, *Partik.* p. 119) introduces a *second* argument for ἡ δὲ ἐλπὶς οὐ καταισχ. (Flatt, also Baumgarten-Crusius). Against this latter construction ver. 8 is decisive, from which it is clear that vv. 6-8 are meant to be nothing else than the proof of the ἀγάπη τ. Θεοῦ. On ἔτι itself, with the imperfect participle in the sense of *tunc adhuc*, comp. Ellendt, *Lex. Soph.* I. p. 693. It indicates the continued existence, which the earlier condition still had; Baeumlein, p. 118; Schneider, *ad Plat. Rep.* p. 449 C. — ὄντων ἡμ. ἀσθενῶν] *when we were still (ἔτι) without strength*, still had not the forces of the true spiritual life, which we could only receive through the Holy Ghost. The sinfulness is purposely described as *weakness* (need of help), in order to characterise it as the motive for the *love of God* interfering to save. The idea of *disease* (Theodoret: τῆς ἀσεβείας περικειμένων τὴν νόσον; comp. Theophylact, Umbreit and others), or that of *minority* (van Hengel), is not suggested by anything in the context. — κατὰ καιρόν] may either (1) be rendered *according to the time*, according to the nature of the time, so that with Erasmus, Luther, Flacius, Castalio, Pareus, Seb. Schmid, also Schrader and Th. Schott, it would

reading, like Ewald, made ver. 9 fill the place of the apodosis, but now prefers to read ἔτι at the beginning as well as also after ἀσθενῶν, and to punctuate thus: ἔτι γ. Χριστὸς ὄντων ἡμῶν ἀσθενῶν, ἔτι κατὰ καιρὸν ὑπ. ἀσεβ. ἀπέθ. With this reading Hofmann thinks that the second ἔτι begins the sentence anew, so that with Χριστὸς ἀπέθανεν an ἔτι stands twice, the first referring to ὄντων ἡμῶν ἀσθενῶν, and the second to ὑπὲρ ἀσεβῶν. But it is self-evident that thus the difficulty is only *doubled*, because ἔτι would *both times* be erroneously placed, which would yield, especially in the case of the second ἔτι, a strange and in fact intolerable confusion, since there would stand just beside it a *definition of time* (κατὰ καιρόν), to which nevertheless the word elsewhere, so frequently used with definitions of time, is *not* intended to apply—a fact which is not to be disguised by subtleties. Märcker also would read ἔτι twice, but render the first ἔτι "*moreover*," which, however, would be without reference in the text.

have to be connected with ἀσθ.;[1] or (2) it may belong to ὑπὲρ ἀσεβ. ἀπέθανε, and mean, in accordance with the context, either *at the appointed time* (Gal. iv. 4), as it is here taken usually, also by de Wette, Tholuck, Philippi, Maier, Baumgarten-Crusius; or (3) *at the proper time* (see Kypke; comp. Pind. *Isthm.* ii. 32; Herod. i. 30; Lucian, *Philops.* 21; LXX. Is. lx. 22; Job v. 16; xxxix. 18; Jer. v. 24), the same as ἐν καιρῷ, ἐς καιρόν, ἐπὶ καιροῦ; Phavorinus: κατὰ τὸν εὔκαιρον κ. προσήκοντα καιρόν; and so the bare καιρόν (Bernhardy, p. 117), equivalent to καιρίως, the opposite of ἀπὸ καιροῦ and παρὰ καιρόν. In the *first* case, however, κ. κ. would either assign to the ἀσθ. an inappropriate excuse, which would not even be true, since the ἀσθένεια has always obtained since the fall (ver. 13); or, if it was meant directly to disparage the *pre-christian age* (Flacius, "ante omnem nostram pietatem," comp. Stölting and Hofmann), it would characterise it much too weakly. In the *second* case an element not directly occasioned by the connection (proof of God's *love*) would present itself. Therefore the *third* interpretation alone: *at the right time* (so Ewald and van Hengel) is to be retained. The death of Jesus for the ungodly took place *at the proper season*, because, had it not taken place then, they would, instead of the divine grace, have experienced the final righteous outbreak of divine *wrath*, seeing that the time of the πάρεσις, iii. 25, and of the ἀνοχή of God had come to an end. Comp. the idea of the πλήρωμα τῶν καιρῶν, Eph. i. 10; Gal. iv. 4. Now or never was the time for saving the ἀσεβεῖς; now or never was the καιρὸς δεκτός, 2 Cor. vi. 2; and God's love did not suffer the right time for their salvation to elapse, but sent Christ to die for them the sacrificial death of atonement.[2] — ὑπέρ] *for, for the benefit of.*

[1] Comp. Stölting: "*conformably to the time*," *i.e.* as it was *suitable* for the time, namely, the time of ungodliness. Similarly Hofmann, "*in consideration of the time*," which was a time of godlessness, "without the fear of God on the part of individuals making any change thereon."

[2] According to my former explanation of the passage the meaning would be, that, if Christ had appeared and died *later*, they would have perished unredeemed in their ἀσθένεια, and would have had no share in the act of atonement. But this view is untenable; because Paul cannot have looked on the divine proof of love, given in the redeeming death of Christ, otherwise than in a quite general light, *i.e.* as given to all mankind, as it appears everywhere in the N. T. since John iii. 16. Comp. Philippi, with whose view I now in substance concur, although in κατὰ καιρόν, by explaining it as "seasonably," I find more directly an element of the *love*, which the context proposes to exhibit.

Comp. Eur. *Alc.* 701: μὴ θνῆσκ' ὑπὲρ τοῦδ' ἀνδρὸς οὐδ' ἐγὼ πρὸ σοῦ, *Iph. A.* 1389; Soph. *Trach.* 705; *Aj.* 1290; Plat. *Conv.* p. 179 B: ἐθελήσασα μόνη ὑπὲρ τοῦ αὐτῆς ἀνδρὸς ἀποθανεῖν; Dem. 690, 18; Xen. *Cyr.* vii. 4, 9 f.; Isocr. iv. 77; Dio. Cass lxiv. 13; Ecclus. xxix. 15: ἔδωκε γὰρ τὴν ψυχὴν αὐτοῦ ὑπὲρ σοῦ; 2 Macc. vi. 28, vii. 9, viii. 21; comp. also Ignatius, *ad Rom.* 4: ὑπὲρ Θεοῦ ἀποθνήσκω.[1] So in all passages where there is mention of the object of Christ's death. Luke xxii. 19, 20; Rom. viii. 32, xiv. 15; 1 Cor. i. 13; 2 Cor. v. 14; Gal. iii. 13; Eph. v. 1; 1 Thess. v. 9, 10; 1 Tim. ii. 6; Tit. ii. 14. See also Ritschl in the *Jahrb. für Deutsche Theol.* 1863, p. 242. That Paul did not intend by ὑπέρ to convey the meaning *instead of*, is shown partly by the fact, that while he indeed sometimes exchanges it for the synonymous (Bremi, *ad Dem. Ol.* iii. 5, p. 188, Goth.) περί (Gal. i. 4, like Matth. xxvi. 20; Mark xiv. 25), he does not once use instead of it the unambiguous ἀντί (Matth. xx. 28), which must nevertheless have suggested itself to him most naturally; and partly by the fact, that with ὑπέρ as well as with περί he puts not invariably the genitive of the person, but sometimes that of the *thing* (ἁμαρτιῶν), in which case it would be impossible to explain the preposition by *instead of* (viii. 3; 1 Cor. xv. 3). It is true that he has certainly regarded the death of Jesus as an act furnishing the satisfactio vicaria, as is clear from the fact that this bloody death was accounted by him as an expiatory sacrifice (iii. 25; Eph. v. 2; Steiger on 1 Pet. p. 342 f.), comp. αντίλυτρον in 1 Tim. ii. 6; but *in no passage* has he expressed the substitutionary relation *through the preposition*. On the contrary his constant conception is this: the sacrificial death of Jesus, taking the place of the punishment of men, and satisfying divine justice, took place as such *in commodum* (ὑπέρ, περί) *of men*, or —which is the same thing—*on account of their sins* (*in gratiam*), in order to expiate them (περί or ὑπὲρ ἁμαρτιῶν). This we hold against Flatt, Olshausen, Winzer, Reithmayr, Bisping, who take ὑπέρ as *loco*. That ὑπέρ must at least be understood as *loco* in Gal. iii. 13; 2 Cor. v. 14 (notwithstanding ver. 15); 1 Pet. iii. 18 (Rückert, Fritzsche, Philippi), is not correct. See on Gal. *l.c.* and 2 Cor. *l.c.*; Philem. 13 is not *here* a case in point. — ἀσεβῶν]

---

[1] Comp. the compound ὑπερθνήσκειν with genit., so frequent especially in Euripides.

Paul did not write ἡμῶν, in order that after the need of help (ἀσθενῶν) the *unworthiness* might also be made apparent; ἀσεβῶν is the *category*, to which the ἡμεῖς have belonged, and the *strong* expression (comp. iv. 5) is *selected*, in order now, through the contrast, to set forth the more prominently the divine love in its very *strength*.

Vv. 7, 8. Illustrative description (γάρ) of this dying ὑπὲρ ἀσεβῶν as the practical demonstration of the divine love (ver. 8). Observe the syllogistic relation of ver. 8 to ver. 7; which is apparent through the emphatic ἑαυτοῦ.—*Scarce, namely, for a righteous man* (not to mention for ἀσεβεῖς) *will any one die.* This very contrast to the ἀσεβεῖς completely shuts out the *neuter* interpretation of δικαίου (" pro re justa," Melancthon, comp. Olshausen, Jerome, Erasmus, *Annot.* Luther). On account of the same contrast, consequently because of the parallel between ὑπὲρ τοῦ ἀγαθοῦ and ὑπὲρ δικαίου, and because the context generally has to do only with the dying for *persons*, τοῦ ἀγαθοῦ also is to be taken not as neuter,[1] but as masculine; and the article denotes *the definite* ἀγαθός *who is in question* in the case concerned. Since, moreover, an essential distinction between δίκαιος and ἀγαθός (comp. on the contrary Matth. v. 45; further, ἀνὴρ ἀγαθὸς κ. δίκαιος in Luke xxiii. 50; ἡ ἐντολὴ ἁγία κ. δικαία κ. ἀγαθή in Rom. vii. 12; ὁ δίκαιος ἡμῖν ἀναπέφανται ὤν ἀγαθός τε καὶ σοφός, Aesch. *Sept.* 576; Eur. *Hipp.* 427; *Thes.* fr. viii. 2) is neither implied in the context, where on the contrary the contrast to both is ἀσεβῶν and ἁμαρτωλῶν, nor is in the least hinted at by Paul, no explanation is admissible that is based on an essential difference of idea in the two words; such as that τοῦ ἀγαθοῦ should be held to express something *different from* or *higher* than δικαίου. Therefore the following is the only explanation that presents itself as conformable to the words and context: After Paul has said that one will hardly die for a righteous man, he wishes to add, by way of confirmation (γάρ), *that cases of the undertaking such a death might possibly occur*, and expresses this in the form: *for perhaps for the good man one even takes it upon him to die.* Thus the previously asserted ὑπὲρ δικαίου τις ἀποθα-

---

[1] Köster also in the *Stud. u. Krit.* 1854, p. 312, has taken both words as neuter: "hardly does one die for others *for the sake of their* (mere) *right;* sooner at all events *for the sake of the manifestly good*, which they have."

νεῖται, although one assents to it *vix et aegre*, is yet said *with reason,—it may perhaps occur*. Paul has not however written τοῦ δικαίου in the second clause of the verse, as he might have done, but introduces τοῦ ἀγαθοῦ, and prefixes it, in order now to make still more apparent, in the interest of the contrast, the category of the *quality* of the person for whom one may perhaps venture this self-sacrifice. This is substantially the view arrived at by Chrysostom, Theodoret, Theophylact, Erasmus, in the *Paraphr.*, Beza, Calvin (" rarissimum sane inter homines exemplum exstat, ut pro justo mori quis sustineat, *quamquam illud nonnunquam accidere possit*"), Castalio, Calovius, and others; recently again by Fritzsche (also Oltramare and Reithmayr); formerly also by Hofmann (in his *Schriftbew.* II. 1, p. 348). It has been wrongly alleged that it makes the second half of the verse superfluous (de Wette) and weakening (Köllner and Rückert); on the contrary, in granting what may certainly now and again occur, it the more emphatically paves the way for the contrast which is to follow, that God has caused Christ to die for quite other persons than the δικαίους and ἀγαθούς—for us *sinners*. Groundless also is the objection (of van Hengel), that in Paul's writings the repeated τίς always denotes *different* subjects; the indefinite τίς, *one, any one*, may indeed even here represent in the concrete application *different* subjects or the *same*. Comp. 2 Cor. xi. 20. And, even if δικαίου and τοῦ ἀγαθοῦ be regarded as two distinct conceptions, may not the second τίς be *the same* with the first? But the perfect accordance with the words and context, which is only found in the exposition offered, shuts out every other. Among the explanations thus excluded are: (1) Those which take τοῦ ἀγαθοῦ as *neuter*, like the rendering of Jerome, Erasmus, *Annot.* (" bonitatem"), Luther, Melancthon (" pro bona et suavi re, i. e. incitati cupiditate aut opinione magnae utilitatis"), and more recently Rückert (" for the good, *i.e. for what he calls his highest good*"), Mehring ("*for for his own advantage some one perhaps risks even life*"); now also Hofmann (" what is *in itself* and *really* good .... *a moral value*, for which, when it is endangered, one sacrifices life, in order not to let it perish"). — (2) Those explanations which indeed take τοῦ ἀγαθοῦ properly as *masculine*, but yet give self-invented *distinctions of idea* in reference to δικαίου; namely (*a*), the exposition, that ὁ ἀγαθός means *the benefactor: hardly does any one die for a righteous man* (who stands in no closer relation to him); *for for his benefactor one dares perchance* (out of gratitude) *to die.* So Flacius,[1] Knatchbull, Estius, Hammond, Clericus, Heumann, Wolf, and others; including Koppe, Tholuck, Winer, Benecke, Reiche, Glöckler, Krehl, Maier, Umbreit, Bisping, Lechler and Jatho. They take the article with ἀγαθοῦ as: the benefactor *whom he has,* against which nothing can be objected (Bernhardy, p. 315). But we may object that we cannot at all see why Paul should not have expressed *benefactor* by the very current and definite term εὐεργέτης; and that ἀγαθός must have obtained the specific sense of *beneficence* (as in Matth. xx. 15; Xen. *Cyr.* iii. 3, 4, *al. ap.* Dorvill. *ad Charit.* p. 722; and Tholuck *in loc.*) from the *context*—a want, which the mere article cannot supply (in opposition to Reiche). Hence, in order to gain for ἀγαθός the sense *beneficent* in keeping with the context, δίκαιος would have to be taken in the narrower sense as *just* (with Wetstein and Olshausen), so as to yield a climax from the *just* man to the *benevolent* (who renders more than the mere obligation of right binds him to do). An apt illustration of this would be Cicero, *de off.* iii. 15: "Si vir bonus is est, qui prodest quibus potest, nocet nemini, recte *justum* virum, *bonum* non facile reperiemus." But in ver. 8 there is no reference to ἀγαθός in the sense assumed; and the *narrower* sense of δίκαιος is at variance with the contrasting ἁμαρτωλῶν in ver. 8, which demands for δίκ. precisely the *wider* meaning (righteous). Besides the prominence which Paul intends to give to the love of God, which caused Christ to die for *sinners,* while a man hardly dies for a δίκαιος, is weakened just in proportion as the sense of δίκαιος is narrowed. The whole interpretation is a forced one, inconsistent with the undefined τοῦ ἀγαθοῦ itself as well as with the entire context. — (*b*) No better are the explanations which find in τοῦ ἀγαθοῦ *a greater degree of morality* than in δικαίου, consequently a man more worthy of having life sacrificed for him. So, but with what varied distinctions! especially Ambrosiaster (the δίκαιος is such *exercitio,* the ἀγαθός *natura*), Bengel (δίκ. homo *innoxius,* ὁ ἀγαθός, *omnibus pietatis numeris absolutus*

---

[1] *Clav.* I. p. 693. "Vix accidit, ut quis suam vitam profundat pro justissimis; pro eo tamen, *qui alicui valde est utilis,* forsitan mori non recuset."

... v. g. pater patriae), Michaelis, Olshausen, Köllner (δίκ.: legally just, ἀγαθ.: perfectly good and upright), de Wette (δίκ.: *irreproachable*, ἀγαθ.: the *noble*), Philippi and Th. Schott (both substantially agreeing with de Wette), also van Hengel (δίκ.: probus *coram Dco*, i. e. venerabilis, ἀγαθ.: bonus *in hominum oculis*, i. e. amabilis), and Ewald, according to whom δίκ. is *he* "who, in a definite case accused unto death, is nevertheless innocent in that particular case," while the ἀγαθός is " he, who not only in one such individual suit, but predominantly in his whole life, is purely useful to others and guiltless in himself;"[1] comp. Stöltiug, who finds in δίκ. the honest upright man, and in ἀγαθός him whom we *personally esteem and love*. But all these distinctions of idea are artificially created and brought in without any hint from the context.[2] — On τάχα, *fortasse, perhaps indeed*, expressing possibility not without doubt, comp. Xen. *Anab.* v. 2, 17; Philem. 15; Wisd. xiii. 6, xiv. 19. In classic authors most frequently τάχ' ἄν. — καὶ τολμᾷ] *etiam sustinet, he has even the courage*,[3] can prevail upon himself, *audet*. The καί is the *also* of the corresponding relation. In presence of the good man, *he ventures also* to die for him. — We may add, that the words from ὑπὲρ γὰρ τοῦ ἀγαθοῦ down to ἀποθανεῖν are not to be put (with Lachmann) in a *parenthesis*, since, though they form only a subordinate confirmatory clause, they cause no interruption in the construction. — Ver. 8. δέ] Not antithetical (" such are *men*, but such is *God*," Mehring), as if the sentence began with ὁ δὲ Θεός, but rather *carrying* it *onward*, namely, to the middle term of the syllogism (the minor proposition), from which then the conclusion, ver. 9, is designed to result. — συνίστησι] *proves*, as in iii. 5. The accomplished fact of the atoning death is

---

[1] Ewald supposes an allusion to cases like these in 1 Sam. xiv. 45, xx. 17; but that it is also possible, that Paul might have in view Gentile examples that were known to himself and the readers.

[2] Kunze, in the *Stud u. Krit.* 1850, p. 407 ff., also rightly recognises this; but explains the second half, contrary to the words, as if the proposition were expressed conditionally (εἰ καί), "*for if even some one* lightly *ventures* to die for the good man, still however God proves his love," etc. Comp. Erasm. *Paraphr.* — Märcker explains it in the sense of *one friend dying for another;* and suggests that Paul was thinking of the example of Damon and Pythias.

[3] Respecting τολμᾶν see Wetstein, who properly defines it: "quidpiam grave in animum inducere et sibi imperare." Comp. Stallbaum, *ad Plat. Rep.* p. 360 B; Monk, *ad Eur. Alc.* 284; Jacobs in *Addit. ad Athen.* p. 309 f.

conceived according to its *abiding* effect of setting forth clearly the divine love; hence the *present*. The *emphasis* indeed lies in the first instance on συνίστησι (for from this proof as such a further inference is then to be drawn), but passes on strengthened to τὴν ἑαυτοῦ, because it must be God's *own* love, authenticating itself in the death of *Christ*, that gives us the assurance to be expressed in ver. 9. *God Himself*, out of His love for men, has given Christ to a death of atonement; iii. 24, viii. 32; Eph. ii. 4; 2 Thess. ii. 16; John iii. 16; 1 John iv. 10 *et al.* To find in τ. ἑαυτοῦ ἀγαπ. the contrast to *our* love towards *God* (Hofmann; comp. on ver. 5) is quite opposed to the context, which exhibits the *divine* demonstration of love in *Christ's* deed of love. That is the clear relation of ver. 8 to ver. 6 f., from which then the blessed inference is drawn in ver. 9. Hence we are not to begin a *new* connection with συνίστησι δέ κ.τ.λ. (Hofmann, "God lets us know, and gives us to experience that He loves us; and this He does, *because* Christ, etc."). The ὅτι cannot be the *motive* of God for His συνίστησι κ.τ.λ., since He has already *given* Christ *out of* love; it is meant on the contrary to specify the *actual ground of the knowledge* of the divine proof of love (= εἰς ἐκεῖνο, ὅτι, comp. on 2 Cor. i. 18; John ii. 18). — εἰς ἡμᾶς] belongs to συνίστ. — ἔτι ἁμαρτ. ὄντ. ἡμ.] For only through the atoning death of Christ have we become δικαιωθέντες. See ver. 9.

Ver. 9. To prove that hope maketh not ashamed (ver. 5), Paul had laid stress on the possession of the divine love in the heart (ver. 5); then he had proved and characterised this divine love itself from the death of Christ (vv. 6-8); and he now again *infers*, from this divine display of love, from the death of Christ, that the hoped-for eternal salvation is all the more assured to us. — πολλῷ οὖν μᾶλλον] The conclusion does not proceed *a minori ad majus* (Estius and many, including Mehring), but, since the point now turns on the carrying out of the divine act of atonement, *a majori* (vv. 6-8) *ad minus* (ver. 9). — πολλῷ μᾶλλον] expresses the enhancement of certainty, as in vv. 15-17: *much less therefore can it be doubted that*, etc.; νῦν stands in reference to ἔτι ἁμαρτωλῶν ὄντων ἡμῶν in ver. 8. — σωθησόμεθα ἀπὸ τ. ὀργῆς] *we shall be rescued from the divine wrath* (1 Thess. i. 10; comp. Matth. iii. 7), so that the latter, which issues forth at the last judgment (ii. 5, iii. 5), does not affect us. Comp. Winer,

p. 577 [E. T. 743]; Acts ii. 40. This *negative* expression for the attainment of the hoped-for δόξα renders the inference more obvious and convincing. For the positive expression see 2 Tim. iv. 18. — δι' αὐτοῦ] *i.e.* through the operation of the *exalted* Christ, ἐν τῇ ζωῇ αὐτοῦ, ver. 10. — Faith, as the ληπτικόν of justification, is understood as a matter of course (ver. 1), but is not mentioned here, because only what has been accomplished by *God* through *Christ* is taken into consideration. If faith were in the judgment of God the anticipation of moral perfection (but see note on i. 17), least of all could it have been left unmentioned. Observe also how Paul has justification in view as a *unity*, without different degrees or stages.

Ver. 10. More special development (γάρ, *namely*) of ver. 9. — ἐχθροί] namely, *of God*, as is clear from κατηλλ. τῷ Θεῷ. But it is not to be taken in an *active* sense (hostile to God, as by Rückert, Baur, Reithmayr, van Hengel, Mehring, Ritschl in the *Jahrb. f. Deutsche Theol.* 1863, p. 515 f.; Weber, *vom Zorne Gottes*, p. 293, and others); for Christ's death did not remove the enmity of men against God, but, as that which procured their pardon on the part of God, it did away with the *enmity of God against men*, and thereupon the cessation of the enmity of men towards God ensued as the moral consequence brought about by faith. And, with that active conception, how could Paul properly have inferred his πολλῷ μᾶλλον κ.τ.λ., since in point of fact the certainty of the σωθησόμεθα is based on our standing in friendship (grace) with God, and not on our being friendly towards God? Hence the *passive* explanation alone is correct (Calvin and others, including Reiche, Fritzsche, Tholuck, Krehl, Baumgarten-Crusius, de Wette, Philippi, Hofmann): *enemies of God*, *i.e.* those against whom the holy θεοσεχθρία, the ὀργή of God on account of sin, is directed; θεοστυγεῖς, i. 30; τέκνα ὀργῆς, Eph. ii. 3. Comp. xi. 28; and see on Col. i. 21; comp. Pfleiderer in Hilgenfeld's *Zeitschr.* 1872, p. 182. This does not contradict the ἀγάπη Θεοῦ praised in ver. 8 (as Rückert objects), since the very arrangement, which God made by the death of Jesus for abandoning His enmity against sinful men without detriment to His holiness, was the highest proof of His *love* for us (not for our sins).—Consequently κατηλλάγημεν and καταλλαγέντες must also be taken not actively, but *passively*: *reconciled with God*, so that He is no longer hostile towards us, but has on the contrary, on account of the death of His (beloved) Son, abandoned His wrath against us, and we, on the other hand, have become partakers in His grace and favour; for the positive assertion (comp. ver. 1 f.), which is applicable to all believing individuals (ver. 8), must not be weakened into the negative and general conception "that *Christians have not God against them*" (Hofmann). See on Col. i. 21 and on 2 Cor. v. 18. Tittmann's distinction between διαλλάττειν and καταλλάττειν (see on Matth. v. 24) is as arbitrary as that of Mehring, who makes the former denote the *outward* and the latter the *inward* reconciliation. Against this view, comp. also Philippi's *Glaubenslehre*, II. 2, p. 270 ff. — ἐν τῇ ζωῇ αὐτοῦ] *by His life;* more precise specification of the import of δι' αὐτοῦ in ver. 9; therefore not " cum vitae ejus simus participes" (van Hengel, comp. Ewald). The *death* of Jesus effected our reconciliation; all the less can His exalted *life* leave our deliverance unfinished. The *living* Christ cannot leave what His *death* effected without final success. This however is accomplished not merely through His *intercession*, viii. 34 (Fritzsche, Baumgarten-Crusius), but also through His whole working in His kingly office for His believers up to the completion of His work and kingdom, 1 Cor. xv. 22 ff.

Ver. 11. Οὐ μόνον δέ] Since καυχώμενοι cannot stand for the finite tense (as, following Luther, Beza and others, Tholuck and Philippi still would have it) οὐ μόνον δέ cannot be supplemented by σωθησόμεθα (Fritzsche, Krehl, Reithmayr, Winer, p. 329, 543 [E. T. 441, 729], following Chrysostom), so as to make Paul say: we shall be not only *saved* (actually in itself), but also *saved in such a way* that we glory, etc. Moreover, the present καυχᾶσθαι could not supply any modal definition at all of the future σωθησόμεθα. No, the participle καυχώμ. compels us to conceive as supplied to the elliptical οὐ μόνον δέ (comp. on ver. 3) the previous participle καταλλαγέντες (Köllner, Baumgarten-Crusius, Hofmann; formerly also Fritzsche); every other expedient is arbitrary.[1] This supplement however, according to which the two

---

[1] Most arbitrary of all is the view of Mehring, that οὐ μόνον δέ refers back to ἐν τῇ ζωῇ αὐτοῦ; and that Paul would say: not merely on the *life* of Christ do we place our hope, but also on the fact that we now glory in our *unity* with God (?). Th. Schott refers it to σωθησόμεθα, but seeks to make καυχώμενοι suitable

participles answer to each other, is confirmed by the concluding refrain: δι' οὗ νῦν τ. καταλλ. ἐλάβ., which is an echo of the καταλλαγέντες understood with οὐ μόνον δέ.' Accordingly we must render: *not merely however as reconciled, but also as those who glory*, etc. Thus the meaning is brought out, that the certainty of the σωθήσεσθαι ἐν τ. ζωῇ αὐτοῦ (ver. 10) is not only based on the objective ground of the accomplished reconciliation, but has also subjectively its corresponding vital expression in the καυχᾶσθαι ἐν τῷ Θεῷ κ.τ.λ., in which the lofty feeling of the Christian's salvation reveals itself. — ἐν τῷ Θεῷ] Luther's gloss is apt: "that God is ours, and we are His, and that we have in all confidence all blessings in common from Him and with Him." That is the bold and joyful *triumph* of those sure of salvation. — διὰ τ. κυρίου κ.τ.λ.] This glorying *is brought about through Christ*, because He is the author of our new relation to God; hence: δι' οὗ νῦν τ. καταλλ. ἐλάβ. The latter is that κατηλλάγημεν of ver. 10 in its subjective reception which has taken place by faith. — νῦν is to be taken here (differently from ver. 9) in contrast, not to pre-Christian times (Stölting), but to the future glory, in reference to which the reconciliation received in the present time (continuing from the conversion of the subjects of it to Christ) is conceived as its actual ground of certainty.

Vv. 12-19. *Parallel drawn between the salvation in Christ and the ruin that has come through Adam.* — Εἰπὼν, ὅτι ἐδικαίωσεν ἡμᾶς ὁ Χριστός, ἀνατρέχει ἐπὶ τὴν ῥίζαν τοῦ κακοῦ, τὴν ἁμαρτίαν καὶ τὸν θάνατον, καὶ δείκνυσιν ὅτι ταῦτα τὰ δύο δι' ἑνὸς ἀνθρώπου, τοῦ Ἀδάμ, εἰσῆλθεν εἰς τὸν κόσμον..... καὶ αὖ δι' ἑνὸς ἀνῃρέθησαν ἀνθρώπου, τοῦ Χριστοῦ, Theophylact; comp. Chrysostom, who compares the Apostle here with the *physician* who penetrates to the *source* of the evil. Thus the perfect objectivity of the salvation, which man has simply to receive, but in no way to earn, and of which the Apostle has been treating since chap. i. 17, is, by way of a grand conclusion for the section, set forth afresh in fullest light, and represented in its deepest and most comprehensive connection with the history of the world. The whole μυστήριον of the divine plan of salvation and its history is still to be unfolded before the eyes of the reader by referring it to the entire time, in which the salvation is still future, as if therefore Paul had written: οὐ μόνον δὲ σωθησόμεθα, ἀλλὰ καὶ νῦν, or ἐν τῷ νῦν καιρῷ καυχώμεθα.

ere the moral results that are associated with it are developed in chap. vi.

Ver. 12.[1] Διὰ τοῦτο] *Therefore*, because, namely, we have received through Christ the καταλλαγή and the assurance of eternal salvation, ver. 11. The assumption that it refers back to the whole discussion from chap. i. 17 (held by many, including Tholuck, Rückert, Reiche, Köllner, Holsten, Picard) is the more unnecessary, the more naturally the idea of the καταλλαγή itself, just treated of, served to suggest the parallel between Adam and Christ, and the δι' οὗ τὴν καταλλαγὴν ἐλάβομεν in point of fact contains the summary of the whole doctrine of righteousness and salvation from i. 17 onward; consequently there is no ground whatever for departing, as to διὰ τοῦτο, from the connection with what immediately precedes.[2] This remark also applies in opposition to Hofmann (comp. Stölting and Dietzsch), who refers it back to the entire train of ideas embraced in vv. 2-11. A recapitulation of this is indeed given in the grand concluding thought of ver. 11, that it is Christ to whom we owe the reconciliation. But Hofmann quite arbitrarily supposes Paul in διὰ τοῦτο to have had in view an *exhortation* to think of Christ conformably to the comparison with Adam, but to have got no further than this *comparison*. — ὥσπερ] There is here an ἀνανταπόδοτον as in Matth. xxv. 14; and 1 Tim. i. 3. The comparison alone is expressed, but not the thing compared, which was to

---

[1] See Schott (on vv. 12-14) in his *Opusc.* I. p. 313 ff.; Borg, *Diss.* 1839; Finkh in the *Tüb. Zeitschr.* 1830, 1, p. 126 ff.; Schmid in the same, 4, p. 161 ff.; Rothe, *neuer Versuch e. Auslegung d. paul. Stelle Rom.* v. 12-21, Wittemb. 1836; J. Müller, *v. d. Sünde*, II. p. 481, ed. 5; Aberle in the *theol. Quartalschr.* 1854, p. 455 ff.; Ewald, *Adam u. Christus Rom.* v. 12-21, in the *Jahrb. f. bibl. Wissensch.* II. p. 166 ff.; Picard, *Essai exégét. sur Rom.* v. 12 ff. Strassb. 1861; Hofmann, *Schriftbew.* I. p. 526 ff.; Ernesti, *Urspr. d. Sünde*, II. p. 184 ff.; Holsten, z. *Ev. d. Paul. u. Petr.* p. 412 ff.; Stölting, *l.c.* p. 19 ff.; Klöpper in the *Stud. u. Krit.* 1869, p. 496 ff.; Dietzsch, *Adam u. Christus Rom.* v. 12 ff., Bonn 1871. Compare also Lechler's *apost. Zeit.* p. 102 ff.

[2] The close junction with ver. 11 is maintained also by Klöpper, who unsuitably however defines the aim of the section, vv. 12-21, to be, to guard the readers against a timid littleness of faith, as though, notwithstanding justification, they were still with reference to the future of judgment not sure and certain of escaping the divine wrath; a timid mind might see in the tribulations anticipations of that wrath, etc. But how far does the entire confession of vv. 1-11 stand elevated above all such littleness of faith! In the whole connection this finds no place whatever, and receives therefore in vv. 12-21 not the slightest mention or reference.

have followed in an apodosis corresponding to the ὥσπερ. The illustration, namely, introduced in vv. 13, 14 of the ἐφ' ᾧ πάντες ἥμαρτον now rendered it impossible to add the second half of the comparison *syntactically* belonging to the ὥσπερ, and therefore the Apostle, driven on by the rushing flow of ideas to this point, from which he can no longer revert to the construction with which he started, has no hesitation in dropping the latter (comp. generally Buttmann's *neut. Gr.* p. 331; Kühner, II. 2, p. 1097), and in subsequently bringing in *merely* the main tenor of what is wanting by the relative clause attached to Ἀδάμ: ὅς ἐστι τύπος τοῦ μέλλοντος in ver. 14. This ὅς.... μέλλ. is consequently the *substitute* for the omitted apodosis, which, had it not been supplanted by vv. 13, 14, would have run somewhat thus: *so also through one man has come righteousness, and through righteousness life, and so life has come to all.* Calvin, Flacius, Tholuck, Köllner, Baur, Philippi, Stölting, Mangold, Rothe (who however without due ground regards the breaking off as intended from the outset, in order to avoid sanctioning the Apokatastasis) find in ὅς ἐστι τύπ. τ. μέλλ., in v. 14, the resumption and closing of the comparison,[1] not of course in form, but in substance; compare also Melancthon. According to Rückert, Fritzsche (in his commentary), and de Wette, Paul has come, after vv. 13, 14, to reflect that the comparison begun involved not merely *agreement* but also *discrepancy*, and has accordingly turned aside from the apodosis, which must necessarily have expressed the equivalence, and inserted instead of it the opposition in ver. 15. This view is at variance with the entire character of the section, which indeed bears quite especially the stamp of most careful and acute premeditation, but shows no signs of Paul's having been led in the progress of his thought to the opposite of what he had started with. According to Mehring, ver. 15, following vv. 13, 14 (which he parenthesises) is meant to complete the comparison introduced in ver. 12, ver. 15 being thus taken interrogatively. Against this view, even apart from the inappropriateness of taking it as a question, the ἀλλ' in ver. 15 is decisive.

---

[1] The objection of Dietzsch, p. 43, that τύπος asserts nothing real regarding the second member of the comparison, is unsatisfactory, since Paul is just intending to bring forward a very definite special statement regarding the typical relation which he now merely expresses in general terms.

Winer, p. 503 [E. T. 712] (comp. Fritzsche's *Conject.* p. 49) finds the epanorthosis in πολλῷ μᾶλλον, ver. 15, which is inadmissible, because with ἀλλ' οὐχ in ver. 15 there is introduced the *antithetical* element, consequently something *else* than the *affirmative* parallel begun in ver. 12. Others have thought that vv. 13-17 form a parenthesis, so that in ver. 18 the first half of the comparison is resumed, and the second now at length added (Cajetanus, Erasmus Schmid, Grotius, Bengel, Wetstein, Heumann, Ch. Schmid, Flatt, and Reiche). Against this view may be urged not only the unprecedented length, but still more the contents of the supposed parenthesis, which in fact already comprehends in itself the parallel under every aspect. In ver. 18 f. we have *recapitulation*, but not *resumption*. This much applies also against Olshausen and Ewald. Others again have held that ver. 12 contains the protasis and the apodosis completely, taking the latter to begin *either* with καὶ οὕτως (Clericus, Wolf, Glöckler), or even with καὶ διά (Erasmus, Beza, Benecke), both of which views however are at variance with the parallel between Adam and Christ which rules the whole of what follows, and are thus in the light of the connection erroneous, although the former by no means required a trajection (καὶ οὕτως for οὕτω καί). While all the expositors hitherto quoted have taken ὥσπερ as the beginning of the first member of the parallel, others again have thought that it *introduces the second half of the comparison.* So, following Elsner and others, Koppe, who after διὰ τοῦτο conceives ἐλάβομεν καταλλαγὴν δι' αὐτοῦ supplied from ver. 11; so also Umbreit and Th. Schott (for this reason, because we σωθησόμεθα ἐν τῇ ζωῇ αὐτοῦ, Christ comes by way of contrast to stand just as did Adam). Similarly Märcker, who attaches διὰ τοῦτο to ver. 11. These expositions are incorrect, because the *universality* of the Adamite ruin, brought out by ὥσπερ κ.τ.λ., has no point of comparison in the supplied protasis (the explanation is *illogical*); in Gal. iii. 6 the case is different. Notwithstanding van Hengel (comp. Jatho) thinks that he removes all difficulty by supplying ἐστί after διὰ τοῦτο; while Dietzsch, anticipating what follows, suggests the supplying after διὰ τοῦτο: *through one man life has come into the world.* — δι' ἑνὸς ἀνθρώπου] *through one man*, that is, δι' ἑνὸς ἁμαρτήσαντος, ver. 16. *A single* man brought upon all sin and death; *a single* man also righteousness and life. The *causal* relation is based on the fact that sin, which previously had no existence whatever in the world, only began to exist in the world (on earth) by means of the first fall.[1] *Eve*, so far as the matter itself is concerned (Ecclus. xxv. 14; 2 Cor. xi. 3; 1 Tim. ii. 14; Barnab. *Ep.* 12), might as well as *Adam* be regarded as the εἷς ἄνθρ.; the latter, because he sinned as the first man, the former, of whom Pelagius explained it, because she committed the first transgression. Here however, because Paul's object is to compare the One man, who as the bringer of salvation has become the *beginner of the new* humanity, with the One man who as *beginner of the old humanity* became so destructive, in which *collective* reference (comp. Hofmann's *Schriftbew.* I. p. 474) the woman *recedes into the background*, he has to derive the entrance of sin into the world from *Adam*, whom he has in view in δι' ἑνὸς ἀνθρώπου. Comp. 1 Cor. xv. 21 f., 45 f. This is also the common form of Rabbinical teaching. See Eisenmenger's *entdeckt. Judenth.* II. p. 81 f. — ἡ ἁμαρτία] not: *sinfulness, habitus peccandi* (Koppe, Schott, Flatt, Usteri, Olshausen), which the word never means; not *original sin* (Calvin, Flacius, and others following Augustine); but also not merely *actual sin in abstracto* (Fritzsche: "nam ante primum facinus patratum nullum erat facinus"), but rather what sin is according to its idea and essence (comp. Hofmann and Stölting), consequently *the determination of the conduct in antagonism to God*, conceived however as a *force*, as a real power working and manifesting itself—exercising its dominion—in all cases of concrete sin (comp. ver. 21, vi. 12, 14, vii. 8, 9, 17 *al.*). This moral mode of being in antagonism to God became existent in the human world through the fall of Adam, produced death, and spread death over all. Thus our verse itself describes the ἁμαρτία as a real objective *power*, and in so doing admits only of *this* explanation. Compare the not substantially different explanation of Philippi, according to which the actual sin of the world is meant as having come into the world *potentialiter* through Adam; also Rothe, who conceives it to refer to sin as a *principle*, but as active; and Dietzsch. — On εἰς τ. κόσμον, which applies to the *earth* as the dwelling-place *of mankind* (for *in the universe gene-*

---

[1] Not merely *came to light* as *known* sin (Schleiermacher, Usteri). See Lechler, p. 104.

rally sin, the *devil*, was already in existence), comp. Wisd. ii. 24, xiv. 14; 2 John 7; Clem. *Cor.* I. 3; Heb. x. 5. Undoubtedly sin by its entrance into the world came into human *nature* (Rothe), but this is not *asserted* here, however decisively our passage stands opposed to the error of Flacius, that man is in any way as respects his essential nature ἁμαρτία.[1] — The *mode* in which the fall took place (through the *devil*, John viii. 44; 2 Cor. xi. 3) did not here concern the Apostle, who has only to do with the mischievous *effect* of it, namely, that it brought ἁμαρτία into the world, etc. — καὶ διὰ τ. ἁμαρτ. ὁ θάνατος] scil. εἰς τ. κόσμον εἰσῆλθε. The θάνατος is *physical death* (Chrysostom, Theodoret, Augustine, Calovius, Reiche, Fritzsche, Maier, van Hengel, Klöpper, Weiss, and many others), viewed as the separation of the soul from the body and its transference to Hades (not as "citation before God's judgment," Mehring), with which however the conception of the φθορά and ματαιότης of the κτίσις in ch. viii., very different from the θάνατος of men, must not be mixed up (as by Dietzsch), which would involve a blending of dissimilar ideas. The interpretation of bodily death is rendered certain by ver. 14 as well as by the considerations, that the text gives no hint of departure from the primary sense of the word; that the reference to Gen. ii. 17, iii. 19 could not be mistaken by any reader; and that on the basis of Genesis it was a universal and undoubted assumption both in the Jewish and Christian consciousness, that mortality was caused by Adam's sin. See Wisd. ii. 24; John viii. 44; 1 Cor. xv. 21; Wetstein and Schoettgen, *in loc.*; and Eisenmenger's *entdeckt. Judenthum*, II. p. 81 f. Compare, respecting Eve, Ecclus. xxv. 24. Had Paul taken θάνατος in *another* sense therefore, he must of necessity have definitely indicated it, in order to be understood.[2] This is decisive not only against the Pelagian interpretation of *spiritual*

---

[1] Compare Holsten, *zum Ev. d. Paul. u. Petr.* p. 418: who thinks that the unholiness *lying dormant in human nature* first entered *actually* into the visible world as a *reality* in the transgression of Adam; also Baur, *neut. Theol.* p. 191, according to whom the principle of sin, that from the beginning had been *immanent* in man, only came forth *actually* in the παράβασις of the first parent. In this way sin would not have *come into the world*, but must *have been in the world* already before the fall, only not having yet attained to objective manifestation.

[2] This remark holds also against Mau in Pelt's *theol. Mitarb.* 1838, 2, who understands the form of life *after* the dissolution of the earthly life.

death, which Picard has repeated, but also against every combination whatever—whether complete (see especially Philippi and Stölting), or partial—of *bodily, moral* (comp. νεκρός, Matth. viii. 22), and *eternal* death (Schmid, Tholuck, Köllner, Baumgarten-Crusius, de Wette, Olshausen, Reithmayr; Rückert undecidedly); or the *whole collective evil,* which is the consequence of sin, as Umbreit and Ewald explain it; compare Hofmann: "all *that runs counter to the life that proceeds from God,* whether as an *occurrence,* which puts an end to the life wrought by God, or as a *mode of existence* setting in with such occurrence." As regards especially the inclusion of the idea of *moral* death (the opposite of the spiritual ζωή), the words θάνατος and ἀποθνήσκειν are never used by Paul in *this* sense; not even in vii. 10 (see *in loc.*), or in 2 Cor. ii. 16, vii. 10, where he is speaking of *eternal* death.[1] The reference to spiritual death is by no means rendered necessary by the contrast of δικαιοσ. ζωῆς in ver. 18, comp. ver. 21; since in fact the death brought into the world by Adam, although physical, might be contrasted not merely in a Rabbinical fashion, but also generally in itself, with the ζωή that has come through Christ; for to this ζωή belongs also the life of the glorified *body,* and it is a life *not again subject to death.* — καὶ οὕτως] *and in such manner, i.e.* in symmetrical correspondence with this connection between the sin that entered by one man and the death occasioned by it. Fuller explanation is then given, by the ἐφ' ᾧ πάντες ἥμαρτον, respecting the emphatically prefixed εἰς πάντας, to whom death, as the effect of that first sin of the One, had penetrated. Since οὕτως sums up the state of the case previously expressed (comp. *e.g.* 1 Cor. xiv. 25; 1 Thess. iv. 17) any further generalization of its reference can only be arbitrary (Stölting: "through *sin*"). Even the explanation: "in virtue of the causal connection between sin and death" (Philippi and many others) is too general. The οὕτως, in fact, recapitulates the *historical* state of the case just presented, so far as it specifies the *mode in which* death has come to *all,* namely, in *this* way, that *the One* sinned and thereby brought into the world *the death,* which conse-

---

[1] In 2 Tim. i. 10 θάνατος is used in the sense of *eternal* death, which Christ (by His work of atonement) has done away; the opposite of it is ζωή καὶ ἀφθαρσία, which He has brought to light by His gospel. Not less is Eph. ii. 1 to be explained as meaning *eternal* death.

quently became the lot *of all*. — διῆλθεν] *came throughout* (Luke v. 15). This is the progress of the εἰς τὸν κόσμον εἰσῆλθε in its extension to all individuals, εἰς πάντας ἀνθρώπ., which in contrast to the δι' ἑνὸς ἀνθρ. is put forward with emphasis as the main element of the further description, wherein moreover διῆλθεν, correlative to the εἰσῆλθε, has likewise emphasis. On διέρχεσθαι εἰς τινα comp. Plut. *Alcib.* 2. Compare also ἐπί τινα in Ez. v. 17 and Ps. lxxxvii. 17. More frequent in classic authors with the simple accusative, as in Luke xix. 1. — ἐφ' ᾧ πάντες ἥμαρτον][1] *on the ground of the fact that*, i.e. *because, all sinned*, namely (and for this the momentary sense of the aorist is appropriate[2]) when through the One sin entered into the world. Because, when *Adam* sinned, *all* men sinned in and with him, the representative of entire humanity (not: "*exemplo* Adami," Pelagius; comp. Erasmus, *Paraphr.*), death, which came into the world through the sin that had come into it, has been extended to *all* in virtue of this causal connection between the sin that had come into existence through Adam and death. *All* became mortal through Adam's fall, because this having sinned on the part of Adam was a having sinned on the part *of all*; consequently τῷ τοῦ ἑνὸς παραπτώματι οἱ πολλοὶ ἀπέθανον, ver. 15. Thus it is certainly on the ground of Adam that all die (ἐν τῷ Ἀδὰμ πάντες ἀποθνήσκουσιν, 1 Cor. xv. 22), because, namely, when Adam sinned, all sinned, all as ἁμαρτωλοὶ κατεστάθησαν (ver. 19), and consequently the death that came in through his sin can spare none. But it is in a linguistic point of view erroneous, according to the traditional Catholic interpretation after the example of Origen, the Vulgate, and Augustine (Estius, Cornelius

---

[1] The most complete critical comparison of the various expositions of these words may be seen in Dietzsch, p. 50 ff.

[2] Hofmann erroneously holds (*Schriftbew. l.c.*) that the *imperfect* must have been used. What is meant is in fact the *same* act, which in Adam's sin is done by all, not *another contemporaneous* act. Comp. 2 Cor. v. 15. It is mere empty arbitrariness in Thomasius *l.c.* p. 316, to say that our explanation is *grammatically* unjustifiable. Why so? Stölting (comp. Dietzsch) objects to it that then ὁ θάνατος διῆλθεν must also be taken in the momentary sense. But this by no means follows, since ἐφ' ᾧ πάντ. ἥμ. is a special relative clause. Nevertheless even that ὁ θάναρ. διῆλθ. is not something gradually developing itself, but a thing done in and with the sin of the One man. *This One* has sinned and has become liable to death, and thereby *all* have become mortal, because Adam's sin was the sin *of all*.

à Lapide, Klee; not Stengel, Reithmayr, Bisping, and Maier; but revived by Aberle), to take ἐφ' ᾧ as equivalent to ἐν ᾧ, *in quo* scil. *Adamo*, as also Beza, Erasmus Schmid, and others do; compare Irenaeus, *Haer.* v. 16, 3. The *thought* which this exposition yields ("omnes ille unus homo fuerunt," Augustine) is essentially correct, but it was an error to derive it from ἐφ' ᾧ, since it is rather to be derived from πάντες ἥμαρτον, and hence also it is but arbitrarily explained by the sensuous notion of all men having been *in the loins* (Heb. vii. 9, 10) of Adam (Origen, Ambrosiaster, Augustine). Chrysostom gives in general the proper sense, though without definitely indicating how he took the ἐφ' ᾧ: "τί δέ ἐστιν ἐφ' ᾧ πάντες ἥμαρτον; ἐκείνου πεσόντος καὶ οἱ μὴ φαγόντες ἀπὸ τοῦ ξύλου γεγόνασιν ἐξ ἐκείνου πάντες θνητοί." So also substantially Theophylact, though explaining, with Photius, ἐφ' ᾧ as equivalent to ἐπὶ τῷ Ἀδάμ. The right view is taken by Bengel ("quia omnes peccarunt.... *Adamo peccante*"); Koppe ("ipso actu, quo peccavit Adamus"), Olshausen, Philippi, Delitzsch, *Psychol.* p. 126, 369, and Kahnis, *Dogm.* I. p. 590, III. p. 308 f.; comp. also Klöpper.[1] The objection that in this way the essential definition is arbitrarily supplied (Tholuck, Hofmann, Stölting, Dietzsch, and others) is incorrect; for what is maintained is simply that more precise definition of ἥμαρτον, for which the immediate connection has necessarily prepared the way, and therefore no person, from an unprejudiced point of view, can speak of "an abortive product of perplexity impelling to arbitrariness" (Hofmann). Nor is our view at variance with the meaning of οὕτως (as Ernesti objects), since from the point of view of death having been occasioned by Adam's sin (οὕτως) the *universality* of death finds its explanation *in the very fact*, that *Adam's* sin was the sin *of all*. Aptly (as against Dietzsch) Bengel compares 2 Cor. v. 14: εἰ εἷς ὑπὲρ πάντων ἀπέθανε, ἄρα οἱ πάντες ἀπέθανον (namely, *Christo moriente*); see on that passage. Others, and indeed most modern expositors (including Reiche, Rückert, Tholuck, Fritzsche,

---

[1] Who, although avoiding the direct expression of our interpretation, nevertheless in substance arrives at the same meaning, p. 505: "All however sinned, because Adam's sin penetrated to them, inasmuch as God punished the fault of Adam so thoroughly that his sin became shared by all his descendants." For Klöpper properly explains the ἐφ' ᾧ, defining the relation as *imputation* of Adam's sin to all.

de Wette, Maier, Baur, Ewald, Umbreit, van Hengel, Mehring, Hofmann, Stölting, Thomasius, Mangold, and others,) have interpreted ἥμαρτον of *individual* sins, following Theodoret: οὐ γὰρ διὰ τὴν τοῦ προπάτορος ἁμαρτίαν, ἀλλὰ διὰ τὴν οἰκείαν ἕκαστος δέχεται τοῦ θανάτου τὸν ὅρον. Compare Weiss, *bibl. Theol.* p. 263 ; Märcker *l.c.* p. 19. But the taking the words thus of the universal having actually sinned as cause of the universal death (see other variations further on) must be rejected for the simple reason, that the proposition would not even be true ;[1] and because the view, that the death of individuals is the consequence of their own actual sins, would be inappropriate to the entire parallel between Adam and Christ, nay even contradictory to it. For as *the sin of Adam* brought *death* to all (consequently not their own self-committed sin), so did the *obedience of Christ* (not their own virtue) bring *life* to all. Comp. 1 Cor. xv. 22. This objective relation corresponding to the comparison remains undisturbed in the case of our exposition alone, inasmuch as ἐφ' ᾧ πάντ. ἥμαρτ. shows *how* the sin of *Adam* necessarily brought death to *all*. To explain ἥμαρτον again, as is done by many, and still by Picard and Aberle: *they were sinful*, by which is meant *original sin* (Calvin, Flacius, Melancthon in the *Enarr.:* "omnes habent peccatum, scilicet pravitatem propagatam et reatum"), or to import even the idea *poenam luere* (Grotius), is to disregard linguistic usage ; for ἥμαρτον means *they have*

[1] Namely, in respect to the many millions of children who have not yet sinned. The reply made to this, that Paul has had in view only *those capable of sin* (Castalio, Wetstein, Fritzsche and others) is least of all applicable in the very case of this Apostle and of the present acutely and thoroughly considered disquisition, and just as little is an appeal to the *disposition* to sin (Tholuck) which children have (Paul says plainly ἥμαρτον). This way out of the difficulty issues in an exegetical self-deception.—He who seeks to get rid of the question regarding children must declare that it is not here raised, since the passage treats of the human race *as a whole* (comp. Ewald, *Jahrb.* VI. p. 132, also Mangold, p. 118 f.). This would suffice, were the question merely of universal *sinfulness;* for in such a case Paul could just as properly have said πάντες ἥμαρτον here, with self-evident reference to all capable of sin, as in iii. 23. But the question here is the connection between the *sin* of all and the *dying* of all, in which case there emerges *no* self-evident limitation, because *all*, even those still incapable of peccatum actuale, must die. Thus the question as to children still remains, and is only disposed of by *not* taking ἥμαρτον in the sense of having individually sinned ; comp. Dietzsch, p. 57 f. This also applies against Stölting, according to whom Paul wishes to show that sin works death *in the case of all sinners* without exception.

sinned, and nothing more. This is acknowledged by Julius Müller (*v. d. Sünde*, II. p. 416 ff. ed. 5), who however professes to find in ἐφ' ᾧ π. ἥμ. only an *accessory reason* for the preceding, and that in the sense: "*as then*" *all would besides have well deserved this severe fate for themselves by their actual sins.* Incorrectly, because ἐφ ᾧ does not mean "*as then*" or "*as then also*" (*i.e.* ὡς καί); because the statement of the reason is by no means made apparent as in any way merely *secondary* and *subjective*, as Neander and Messner have rationalised it, but on the contrary is set down as the single, complete and objective ground; because its alleged purport would exercise an alien and disturbing effect on the whole development of doctrine in the passage; and because the sense assigned to the simple ἥμαρτον (*this severe fate they would have all moreover well merited*) is purely fanciful. Ernesti takes ἐφ' ᾧ not of the objective ground, but as specifying the *ground of thinking so*, *i.e.* the subjective ground of *cognition*: "*about which there can be no doubt, in so far as* all have in point of fact sinned;" this he holds to be the logical ground for the οὕτως κ.τ.λ. But, as there is no precedent of usage for this interpretation of ἐφ' ᾧ (Phil. iii. 12 is unjustifiably adduced), Ernesti is compelled to unite with ἐφ' ᾧ vv. 13 and 14 in an untenable way. See on ver. 13 f., remark 1, and Philippi, *Glaubensl.* III. p. 222 ff. ed. 2. — Respecting ἐφ' ᾧ, which is quite identical with ἐφ' οἷς, we have next to observe as follows: It is equivalent to ἐπὶ τούτῳ ὅτι, and means *on the ground of the fact that*, consequently in real sense *propterea quod*,[1] *because* (*dieweil*, Luther), of the causa *antegressa* (not *finalis*), as also Thomas Magister and Favorinus have explained it as equivalent to διότι. So in the N. T. at 2 Cor. v. 4 and Phil. iii. 12. Comp. Theophilus, *ad Autol.* ii. 40, ed. Wolf: ἐφ' ᾧ οὐκ ἴσχυσε θανατῶσαι αὐτούς (*because* he was unable to put them to death), Diod. Sic. xix. 98: ἐφ ᾧ .... τὸ μὲν μεῖζον καλοῦσι ταῦρον, τὸ δὲ ἔλασσον μόσχον (*because* they call the greater a bull, etc.); just so ἐφ' οἷς, Plut. *de Pyth. orac.* 29. Favorinus quotes the examples: ἐφ' ᾧ τὴν κλοπὴν

---

[1] Baur also, II. p. 202 (comp. his *neutest. Theol.* p. 138), approves the rendering *because*, but foists on this *because* the sense: "*which has as its presupposition.*" Thus it should be understood, he thinks, also in 2 Cor. v. 4 and Phil. iii. 12; and thus Paul proves from the universality of death the universality of sin. See, in opposition to this logical inversion, Ernesti, p. 212 ff.

εἰργάσω, and ἐφ' οἷς τὸν νόμον οὐ τηρεῖς, κολασθήσῃ. Thomas Magister cites the example from Synesius *ep.* 73 : ἐφ' ᾧ Γεννάδιον ἔγραψεν (*propterea quod* Gennadium accusasset, comp. Herm. *ad Viger.* p. 710). Another example from Synesius (in Devarius, ed. Klotz, p. 88) is : ἐφ' οἷς γὰρ Σεκοῦνδον εὖ ἐποίησας (*on the ground of this, that,* i.e. *because* thou hast done well to Secundus) ἡμᾶς ἐτίμησας, καὶ ἐφ' οἷς οὕτω γράφων τιμᾷς, ἐξηρτήσω σαυτοῦ κ. ἐποίησας εἶναι σούς. See further Josephus, *Antt.* i. 1, 4 : ὁ ὄφις συνδιαιτώμενος τῷ τε Ἀδάμῳ καὶ τῇ γυναικὶ φθονερῶς εἶχεν, ἐφ' οἷς (*propterea quod*) αὐτοὺς εὐδαιμονήσειν ᾤετω πεπεισμένους τοῖς τοῦ Θεοῦ παραγγέλμασι. *Antt.* xvi. 8, 2 : καὶ τὸ δικαίως αὐτοὶ παθεῖν, ἐφ' οἷς ἀλλήλους ἠδίκησαν, προλαμβάνοντες μόνον. Rothe (followed by Schmid, *bibl. Thol.* p. 260) has taken it as : "*under the more definite condition, that*" (ἐπὶ τούτῳ ὥστε), so that individual sins are the consequence of the diffusion of death through Adam's sin over mankind. But this view is wholly without precedent in the usus loquendi, for the very frequent use of ἐφ' ᾧ, *under the condition, that* (usually with the infinitive or future indicative), is both in idea and in practice something quite different; see Kühner, II. 2, p. 1006. Of a similar nature are rather such passages as Dem. 518, 26 : ἐν γὰρ μηδέν ἐστιν, ἐφ' ᾧ τῶν πεπραγμένων οὐ δίκαιος ὢν ἀπολωλέναι φανήσεται (*upon the ground of which* he will not seem worthy, etc.); *de cor.* 114 (twice); as well as the very current use of ἐπὶ τούτῳ, *propterea* (Xen. *Mem.* i. 2, 61), of ἐπ' αὐτῷ τούτῳ, *for this very reason* (Dem. 578, 26 ; Xen. *Cyr.* ii. 3, 10), etc.; and further, such expressions as ἐπὶ μιᾷ δὴ ποτε δίκῃ πληγὰς ἔλαβον (Xen. *Cyr.* i. 3, 16), where ἐπί with the dative specifies the *ground* (Kühner, II. 1, p. 436). Ewald formerly (*Jahrb.* II. p. 171), rejecting the second ὁ θάνατος, explained: " and thus there penetrated to all men *that, whereunto all sinned,*" namely death, which, according to Gen. ii. 17, was imposed as punishment on sin, so that whosoever sinned, sinned so that he had to die, a fate which he might know beforehand. In this way the ἐφ' ᾧ would (with Schmid and Glöckler, also Umbreit) be taken of the *causa finalis* (Xen. *Cyr.* viii. 8, 24 : οὐδέ γε δρεπανηφόροις ἔτι χρῶνται, ἐφ' ᾧ Κῦρος αὐτὰ ἐποιήσατο, iii. 3, 36, ὑπομιμνήσκειν, ἐφ' οἷς τε ἐτρεφόμεθα, Thuc. i. 134, 1, *al.*; and see especially Wisd. ii. 23), and the subject of διῆλθεν (τοῦτο) would be implied in it. But, apart from the genuineness of ὁ θάνατος, which must be defended, there still remains, even with the explanation of ἐφ' ᾧ as final, so long as ἥμαρτον is explained of individual actual sins, the question behind as to the *truth* of the proposition, since not *all*, who die, have actually sinned; and indeed the view of the death of all having been caused by the actual sins of all is incompatible with what follows.[1] See also Ernesti, p. 192 ff.; comp. his *Ethik. d. Ap. P.* p. 16 f. Moreover the *telic* form of expression itself would have to be taken only in an improper sense, instead of that of the necessary, but on the part of the subjects not intended, *result*, somewhat after the idea of fate, as in Herod. i. 68 : ἐπὶ κακῷ ἀνθρώπου σίδηρος ἀνεύρηται. Subsequently (in his *Sendschr. d. Ap. P.*) Ewald, retaining the second ὁ θάνατος, has assumed for ἐφ' ᾧ the signification, *so far as* (so also Tholuck and van Hengel); holding that by the limiting phrase "*so far as they all sinned*," death is thus set forth the more definitely as the result of sin, so that ἐφ' ᾧ corresponds to the previous οὕτως. But even granting the not proved limiting signification of ἐφ' ᾧ (which ἐφ' ὅσον elsewhere has, xi. 13), there still remain with this interpretation also the insurmountable difficulties as to the sense, which present themselves against the reference of ἥμαρτον to the individual sins. Hofmann (comp. also his *Schriftbew.* I. p. 529 f.) refers ἐφ' ᾧ to ὁ θάνατος, so that it is equivalent to οὗ παρόντος : *amidst the presence* of death; making the emphasis to lie on the preposition, and the sense to be : "*death was present at the sinning of all those to whom it has penetrated; and it has not been invariably brought about and introduced only through their sinning, nor always only for each individual who sinned.*" Thus ἐπί might be justified, not indeed in a temporal sense (which it has among poets and later prose writers only in proper statements of time, as in Homer, *Il.* viii. 529, ἐπὶ νυκτί), but perhaps in the sense of *the prevailing circumstance*, like the German "*bei*" [with, amidst] [2]

[1] Along with which it may be observed that there is the less warrant for mentally supplying, in the contrasted propositions on the side of salvation, a condition corresponding to the ἐφ' ᾧ π. ἥμαρτ. (Mangold; ἐὰν πάντες πιστεύσωσιν, which is implicitly involved in λαμβάνοντες, ver. 17), the *more essential* this antitypical element would be.

[2] So also Dietzsch has taken it, in substantial harmony with Hofmann, less artificially, but not more tenably : *amidst the presence of death*. He thinks that

(see Kühner, II. 1, p. 434). But apart from the special tenor of the thought, which we are expected to extract from the bare ἐφ' ᾧ, and which Paul might so easily have conveyed more precisely (possibly by ἐφ' ᾧ ἤδη παρόντι, or οὗ ἤδη παρόντος), this artificial exposition has decidedly against it the fact that the words ἐφ' ᾧ πάντες ἥμαρτον must necessarily contain the argumentative *modal information* concerning the preceding proposition κ. οὕτως εἰς πάντας ἀνθρώπους ὁ θάν. διῆλθεν, which they in fact contain only when our view is taken.[1] They must solve the enigma which is involved in the momentous οὕτως of that clause; and this enigma is solved only by the statement of the reason: *because all sinned*, so that the θανάσιμος ἁμαρτία of Adam was the sin *of all*. Against Hofmann, compare Philippi's *Glaubensl.* III. p. 221 f. ed. 2.

REMARK 1. The Rabbinical writers also derived universal mortality from the fall of Adam, who represented the entire race in such a way that, when Adam sinned, all sinned. See the passages in Ammon, *Opusc. nov.* p. 72 ff. Even perfectly righteous persons are " comprehensi sub poena mortis" (R. Bechai in *Cad hackemach* f. 5, 4). It may reasonably be assumed therefore that the doctrine of the Apostle had, in the first instance, its historical roots in his Jewish (comp. Ecclus. xxv. 23 ; Wisd. ii. 23 f.; xiv. 14) and especially his Rabbinical training, and was held by him even prior to his conversion; and that in his Christian enlightenment he saw no reason for abandoning the proposition, which on the contrary he adopted into the system of his Chris-

the Apostle desires to emphasise the view that death, originating from the One, is and prevails in the world, *quite apart from the sinning of individuals;* that independently of this, and *prior* to it, the universal dominion of death springing from Adam is already in existence. But with what strange obscurity would Paul in that case have expressed this simple and clear idea! How unwarranted it is to attach to his positive expression the negative signification (*apart from, independently of*)! With just as little warrant we should have to attach to the πάντες, since in no case could it include the children who have not yet sinned, a limitation of meaning, which yet it is utterly incapable of bearing after the εἰς πάντας ἀνθρώπους just said. The exposition of Dietzsch, no less than that of Hofmann, is a laboriously far-fetched and mistaken evasion of the proposition clearly laid down by Paul : " *because they all sinned*," namely, when through one man sin came into the world and death through sin.

[1] This applies equally against the similar exposition of Thomasius (*Chr. Pers. u. Werk.* I. p. 316 f.), *amidst the presence of which relation* (ᾧ as neuter). As if previously a "*relation*" had been expressed, and not a *concrete historical fact!* Weisse took ἐφ' ᾧ even as *although*,—a linguistic impossibility, which Finckh also presents.

tian views, and justified by continuing to assert for it in the development of the divine plan of redemption the place which is here assigned to it, as even Christ Himself traces death back to the fall (John viii. 44). Comp. 1 Cor. xv. 22: ἐν τῷ Ἀδὰμ πάντες ἀποθνήσκουσιν, on which our passage affords the authentic commentary. We may add that, when Maimonides is combating (*More Nevoch.* iii. 24) the illusion that God arbitrarily decrees punishments, there has been wrongly found in the dogmatic proposition adduced by him, "*non est mors sine peccato,* neque castigatio sine iniquitate," the *reverse* of the above doctrine (see especially Fritzsche, p. 294). The latter is on the contrary *presupposed* by it.

REMARK 2. That Adam was *created* immortal, our passage does not affirm, and 1 Cor. xv. 47 contains the opposite. But not as if Paul had conceived the first man as *by his nature* sinful, and had represented to himself sin as a *necessary natural quality of the σάρξ* (so anew Hausrath, *neut. Zeitgesch.* II. p. 470), but thus: if Adam had not sinned in consequence of his self-determination of antagonism to God, he would have *become* immortal through eating of the tree of life in Paradise (Gen. iii. 22). As he has sinned, however, the consequence thereof necessarily was *death,* not only for himself, seeing that he had to leave Paradise, but for all his posterity likewise.[1] From this consequence, which the sin of Adam had for *all,* it results, in virtue of the necessary causal connection primevally ordained by God between sin and death, by reasoning back *ab effectu ad causam,* that the fall of Adam was the collective fall of the entire race, in so far as in fact all forfeited Paradise and therewith incurred death. — If ἐφ' ᾧ πάντες ἥμαρτον be explained in the sense of *individual actual sins,* and at the same time the untenableness of the explanation of Hofmann and Dietzsch be recognised, it becomes impossible by any expedients, such as that of Rothe, I. p. 314, ed. Schenkel, to harmonize the view in our passage with that expressed in 1 Cor. xv. 47; but, if it be referred to the *fall of Adam,* every semblance of contradiction vanishes.

Ver. 13 f. *Demonstration,* that the death of all has its ground in the sin of *Adam* and the causal connection of that sin with death. This argument, conducted with great conciseness, *sets out* from the undoubted historical certainty (it is already sufficiently attested in Gen. iv.-vi.) that during the entire period

---

[1] Comp. Jul. Müller, *dogmat. Abhandl.* 1870, p. 89 f. Schultz, *alttest. Theol.* I. p. 394.

prior to the law (ἄχρι νόμου = ἀπὸ Ἀδὰμ μέχρι Μωϋσέως, ver. 14) there was sin in humanity; *then further argues* that the death of individuals, which yet has affected those also who have not like Adam sinned against a positive command, cannot be derived from that sin prior to the law, because in the non-existence of law there is no imputation; *and allows it to be thence inferred* that consequently the death of all has been caused (ἐφ' ᾧ πάντες ἥμαρτον) by the sin of Adam (not by their individual sins). Paul however leaves this *inference* to the reader himself; he does not expressly declare it, but instead of doing so he says, returning to the comparison begun in ver. 12: ὅς ἐστι τύπος τοῦ μέλλοντος, for in that death-working operation of Adam's sin for all lay, in fact, the very ground of the typical relation to Christ. Chrysostom aptly says: εἰ γὰρ ἐξ ἁμαρτίας ὁ θάνατος τὴν ῥίζαν ἔσχε, νόμου δὲ οὐκ ὄντος ἡ ἁμαρτία οὐκ ἐλλογεῖται, πῶς ὁ θάνατος ἐκράτει; ὅθεν δῆλον ὅτι οὐκ αὐτὴ ἡ ἁμαρτία ἡ τῆς τοῦ νόμου παραβάσεως, ἀλλ' ἐκείνη τῆς τοῦ Ἀδὰμ παρακοῆς, αὕτη ἦν ἡ πάντα λυμαινομένη. Καὶ τίς ἡ τούτου ἀπόδειξις; τὸ καὶ πρὸ τοῦ νόμου πάντας ἀποθνήσκειν· ἐβασίλευσε γὰρ κ.τ.λ. Compare Oecumenius. — ἄχρι νόμου] *i.e.* in the period previous to the giving of the law, comp. ver. 14; consequently not during the period of the law, ἕως ὁ νόμος ἐκράτει,[1] Theodoret; comp. Origen, Chrysostom, and Theodore of Mopsuestia. — ἐλλογεῖται] preserved nowhere else except in Boeckh, *Inscript.* I. p. 850 A, 35, and Philem. 18 (text rec.), but undoubtedly meaning: *is put to account* (consequently equivalent to λογίζεται, iv. 4), namely, here, according to the context, *for punishment*, and that *on the part of God;* for in the whole connection the subject spoken of is the divine dealings in consequence of the fall. Hence we are neither to understand *ab judice* (Fritzsche), nor: *by the person sinning;* so Augustine, Ambrosiaster, Luther ("then one does not regard the sin") Melancthon ("non accusatur in nobis ipsis") Calvin, Beza and others, including Usteri, Rückert, J. Müller, Lipsius, Mangold, and Stölting ("there the sinner recognises not his sin as guilt"), whereby a thought quite irrevelant to the argument is introduced. — μὴ ὄντος νόμου] *without the*

---

[1] As is well known, Peyrerius (*Praeadamitae s. exercitat. exeg. in Rom.* v. 12-14, Amst. 1655) referred the νόμου here to the law given to Adam in Paradise; and found thus a proof for his *Preadamites.*

existence of the law; νόμος, as previously ἄχρι νόμου, meaning the *Mosaic* law, and not *any* law generally (Theodore of Mopsuestia, and many others, including Hofmann), as ἁμαρτία already points to the *divine* law. Comp. iv. 15. The proposition itself: "*Sin is not imputed, if the law is absent,*" is set down as something universally *conceded*, as an *axiom;* therefore with repetition of the subject (in opposition to Hofmann, who on account of this repetition separates ἁμαρτία δέ κ.τ.λ. from the first half of the verse and attaches it to what follows), and with the verb in the *present.* The proposition itself, inserted as an intervening link in the argument with the metabatic δέ, without requiring a preceding μέν, which Hofmann is wrong in missing (see Dietzsch and Kühner, II. 2, p. 814), has its truth as well as its more precise application in the fact, that in the absence of law the action, which in and by itself is unlawful, is no *transgression* of the *law* (iv. 15), and cannot therefore be brought into account *as such.* That Paul regarded the matter in this light, and had not, as Hofmann thinks, sinning generally, "as it was one and the same thing in the case of all," in view apart from the sins of individuals, is plain also from καὶ ἐπὶ τοὺς μὴ ἁμαρτ. ἐπὶ τῷ ὁμοιώματι τῆς παραβάσ. Ἀδάμ, in ver. 14. His thought is: If the death of men after Adam had been caused by their own sin, then in the case of all those, who have died during the period from Adam till the law, the sin which they have committed must have been already reckoned to them as transgression of the law, just as Adam's sin was the transgression of the positive divine command, and as such brought upon him death; but this is inconceivable, because the law was not in existence. In this Paul leaves out of consideration the Noachian commands (Gen. ix.), as well as other declarations of God as to His will given before the law, and likewise individual punitive judgments, such as in the case of Sodom, just because he has only the strict idea of real and formal legislation before his mind, and this suggests to him simply the great epochs of the Paradisaic and Sinaitic legislations. A view, which does not subvert the truth of his demonstration, because mankind in general were without law from Adam until Moses, the natural law, because not given positively, remaining out of the account; it makes the act at variance with it appear as sin (ἁμαρτία), but not as παράβασις νόμου, which as such ἐλλογεῖται. — Ver. 14. ἀλλ'] *at, yet,* although sin is not put to account in the absence of the law. It introduces an apparently contradictory phenomenon, confronting the ἁμαρτία οὐκ ἐλλογεῖται κ.τ.λ.; one, however, which just proves that men have died, not through their own special sin, but through the sin of Adam, which was put to their account. ἐβασίλευσεν] prefixed with emphasis: death has not perchance been powerless, no, it has *reigned, i.e.* has exercised its power which deprives of life (comp. vv. 17-21). Hofmann (comp. also Holsten, Aberle, and Dietzsch) finds in the emphatic ἐβασ. the *absolute* and *abiding* dominion, which death has exercised independently of the imputation of sins (ἀλλά being taken as the simple *but*), "just as a king, one by virtue of his *personal* position *once and for all* entitled to do so, exercises dominion over those who, in virtue of their belonging to his domain, are *from the outset subject* to him." But no reader could educe this qualitative definite sense of the βασιλεύειν, with the highly essential characteristic elements ascribed to it, from the mere verb itself; nor could it be gathered from the position of the word at the head of the sentence; on the contrary, it must unquestionably have been *expressed* (by ἐτυράννευσεν possibly, or τυραννικῶς ἐβασίλευσεν) seeing that the subsequent καί (*even* over those, etc.) does not indicate a *mode* of the power of the (personified) death, but only appends the fact of its dominion being without exception. — μέχρι Μωϋσ.] equivalent to ἄχρι νόμου in ver. 13. A distinction of sense between μέχρι and ἄχρι is (contrary to the opinion of Tittmann, *Synon.* p. 33 f.) purely fanciful. See Fritzsche, p. 308 ff. and van Hengel *in loc.* — καὶ ἐπὶ τοὺς μὴ ἁμαρτήσαντας κ.τ.λ.] even over those[1] who have not sinned like Adam, that is, have not like him transgressed a positive divine command. Even these it did not spare. It is erroneous with Chrysostom (but not Theodoret and Theophylact) to connect ἐπὶ τῷ ὁμοιώματι κ.τ.λ. with ἐβασίλ. So Finckh again does, following Castalio and Bengel: "quia illorum eadem atque Adami transgredientis ratio fuit.... i.e. *propter reatum ab Adamo contractum.*" Erroneous for this reason, that Paul, apart from the little children or those other-

[1] βασιλεύειν with ἐπί is a Hebraism (על). Compare Luke i. 33, xix. 14; 1 Sam. viii. 9, 11; 1 Macc. i. 16.

wise incapable of having sin imputed, whom however he must have indicated more precisely, could not conceive at all (iii. 23) of persons who had not sinned (μὴ ἁμαρτήσαντες without any modal addition more precisely defining it), and a limitation *mentally supplied* (*sine lege* peccarunt, Bengel) is purely fanciful. The καί, *even*, refers to the fact that in the period extending from Adam till Moses, excluding the latter, positively given divine commands were certainly transgressed by individuals to whom they were given, but it was not *these merely* who died (as must have been the case, had death been brought on by their own particular sins); it was *also those*,[1] who etc. *Their* sin was not ἐπὶ τῷ ὁμοιώμ. τῆς παραβ. Ἀδάμ (ἐπί used of the *form*, in which anything occurs, see Bernhardy, p. 250); they did not sin in such a way, *that their action was of like shape with the transgression of Adam*, "quia non habebant ut ille *revelatam certo oraculo* Dei voluntatem," Calvin. For other definitions of the sense see Fritzsche, p. 316, and Reiche, *Commentar. crit.* I. p. 45 ff. Reiche himself explains it of those who have transgressed no command *expressly threatening death*. So also Tholuck. But this peculiar limitation is not suggested by the context, in which, on the contrary, it is merely the previous μὴ ὄντος νόμου which supplies a standard for determining the sense of the similarity. According to Hofmann καὶ ἐπὶ τοὺς down to Ἀδάμ is meant to be one and the same with the previous ἀπὸ Ἀδὰμ μέχρι Μωϋσέως, inasmuch as a transgression similar to that of Adam could only then have occurred, "*when God placed a people in the same position in which Adam found himself, when he received a divine command on the observance or transgression of which his life or death depended.*" This misconception, springing from the erroneous interpretation of ἐφ' ᾧ πάντες ἥμαρτον, is already excluded by καί,[2] as well as, pursuant to the tenor of thought, by the fact that in the *pre-legal* period in question all those, who transgressed a command divinely given

---

[1] Consequently the two classes, formed by Paul, are not to be so distinguished that the one shall embrace men before Noah, and the other the Noachian race (van Hengel). *Both* classes are included in the *whole* period from Adam till Moses.

[2] Which necessarily assumes a class of sinners in the pre-legal period, whose sin was homogeneous with that of Adam. This also, in opposition to Mangold, p. 121, and Dietzsch, p. 98; according to whose and Hofmann's definition of the sense, Paul ought either to have omitted the καί altogether, or to have inserted it before ἀπὸ Ἀδάμ.

to them by way of revelation, sinned like Adam. Their sin had thereby the same moral form as the act of Adam; but not only had *they* to die, but also (καί) those who had *not* been in *that* condition of sinning. Death reigned over the latter also.—The *genitive* with ὁμοιώμ. is not that of the *subject* (Hofmann), but of the *object*, as in i. 23, vi. 5, viii. 3; the sins meant are not so conceived of, that the παράβασις of Adam *is* homogeneously *repeated* in them, but so that they are, as to their specific nature, of *similar fashion with it*, and consequently belong to *the same ethical category*. They have morally just the same character. As to ὁμοίωμα see on i. 23. — ὅς ἐστι τύπος τοῦ μέλλοντος] *who*— to educe now from vv. 13, 14 the result introduced in ver. 12, and so to return to the comparison there begun—*is type of the future* (Adam). Theophylact correctly paraphrases: ὡς γὰρ ὁ παλαιὸς Ἀδὰμ πάντας ὑποδίκους ἐποίησε τῷ οἰκείῳ πταίσματι (by bringing upon them death), καίτοι μὴ πταίσαντας, οὕτως ὁ Χριστὸς ἐδικαίωσε πάντας, καίτοι μὴ δικαιώσεως ἄξια ποιήσαντας. Compare 1 Cor. xv. 45. Koppe, following Bengel, takes μέλλ. as *neuter* (*of that, which should one day take place*), and ὅς for ὅ. This agreement of the relative with the following substantive would perhaps be grammatically tenable (Hermann, *ad Viger.* p. 708; Heind. *ad Phaedr.* p. 279), but seeing that Ἀδάμ immediately precedes it, and that the idea of Christ being ὁ ἔσχατος Ἀδάμ is a Pauline idea (1 Cor. *l.c.*), it is quite unjustifiable to depart from the reference of the ὅς to Adam; and equally so to deny to the μέλλων its supplement from the immediately preceding Ἀδάμ, and to take it as "*the man of the future*" (Hofmann), which would nevertheless yield in substance the same meaning.—τύπος] *type*, so that the μέλλων is the *anti*-type (1 Pet. iii. 21). The type is always something historical (a person, thing, saying), which is destined, in accordance with the divine plan, to prefigure something corresponding to it in the future,—in the connected scheme of sacred historical teleology, which is to be discerned from the standpoint of the antitype. Typical historical parallels between Adam and the Messiah (so that the latter is even expressly termed the last Adam) are found also in Rabbinical authors (e.g. *Neve Schalom* f. 160, 2: "Quemadmodum homo primus fuit primus in peccato, sic Messias erit ultimus ad auferendum peccatum penitus;" *Neve Schalom* 9, 9:

Adamus postremus est Messias"), and are based in them on the doctrine of the ἀποκατάστασις πάντων. Compare the passages in Eisenmenger, *entdeckt. Judenth.* II. p. 819, 823 ff. Paul based this typology of his on the *atoning work of Christ* and its results, as the whole discussion shows; hence in his present view Christ as the μέλλων Ἀδάμ is not *still* to come, but is already historical. Comp. Chrysostom; also Theodore of Mopsuestia: ὥσπερ δι' ἐκείνου (Adam) τῶν χειρόνων ἡ πάροδος ἐγένετο, οὕτω διὰ τούτου τῆς τῶν κρειττόνων ἀπολαύσεως τὴν ἀφορμὴν ἐδεξάμεθα. For this reason however ὁ μέλλων may not, with Fritzsche and de Wette, be referred to the last coming of Christ; but must be dated from the time of Adam, in so far, namely, as in looking back to the historical appearance of Adam, Christ, as its antitype, *is* the *future* Adam (comp. ὁ ἐρχόμενος).

REMARK 1. Those who refer ἐφ' ᾧ πάντες ἥμαρτον to the proper sins of individuals, or even to the *principle* of the ἁμαρτία dwelling in them, ought not to find, as Baumgarten-Crusius, Umbreit, and Baur still do, the proof for the πάντες ἥμαρτον in ver. 13 f.; for how in the connection of the passage could any proof for the universality of sin be still required? Certainly just as little as in particular *for the fact*, that, *with death already existing in the world* (Dietzsch), all individuals have *sinned*. Consistently with that reference of the ἐφ' ᾧ π. ἥμαρτον there must rather have been read from ver. 13 f. the proof *for this*, that the death of all results from the proper sins of all. But how variously has this demonstration been evolved! Either: *although sin has not until Moses been imputable according to positive law, yet each one has brought death upon himself by his sin* (ver. 14), *which proves the relative imputation thereof.* So de Wette. Or: *although sin, which even from Adam till Moses was not lacking, be not imputed by a human judge in the absence of positive law, yet the reign of death* (ver. 14) *shows that God has imputed the pre-Mosaic sins.* So Fritzsche. Or: in order to show "*in Adamo causam quaerendam esse, cur hominum peccata mors secuta sit*," Paul declares that death has reigned over all from Adam till Moses, whether they sinned like Adam or differently. So van Hengel; comp. also Weiss, *bibl. Theol.* p. 264. Or: *not even in the period from Adam till Moses was sin absent; but the clear proof to the contrary is the dominion of death in this period.* So Baur, and with a substantially similar view of the mode of inference *ab effectu ad causam*,[1] Rothe also. But however it may

---

[1] According to the correlation of the ideas *sin* and *death*, comp. Baur, *neut. Theol.* p. 138.

be turned, the probative element has first of all to be read into the passage; and even then the alleged proof (ver. 14) would only be a reasoning backwards from the historical *phenomenon* in ver. 14 to the *cause asserted* by ἐφ' ᾧ π. ἥμαρτ., and consequently a mere clumsy argument in a circle, which again *assumes* the assertion to be proved—id quod erat demonstrandum—in the phenomenon brought forward in ver. 14; and moreover utterly breaks down through the proposition that sin is not imputed in the absence of law. Ewald, in his former view (*Jahrb.* II.) rightly deduces from ver. 14: *consequently it only appears the more certain, that death propagated itself to them only by means of Adam's,*" but attributes to this inference, consistently with his view of ἐφ' ᾧ π. ἥμ., the sense: " *that they all sinned unto death just in the same way as, and because, Adam had sinned unto it.*" In his later view (*Sendschr. d. Ap. P.*) he supposes that in connection with ἐφ' ᾧ πάντες ἥμαρτον the possible *doubt* may have arisen, *whether it was so certain that death had come upon those oldest men from Adam till Moses in consequence of their sins?* which doubt Paul properly answers in ver. 13 f., thereby all the more corroborating the truth. But the emergence of a doubt is indicated by nothing in the text; and that doubt indeed would have been dissipated by the very fact that those men were *dead*, which does not prove however that they died *on account of their sins*. Thus also the matter would amount to a reasoning in a circle. According to Tholuck the argument is: *that death has passed upon all through the disposition to death (?) introduced in Adam, and not through their own sins, is plain from the fact, that pre-Mosaic sin, though not positively threatened with death, as in the case of Adam and in the law, was nevertheless placed under its dominion.*" Only thus, he holds, is the logical relation between the clauses apparent. In general this is right; but by this very circumstance Tholuck just attests the correctness of *our* explanation of ἥμαρτον, namely, that it is *not* meant of individual sin. The caution which he inserts against this inference, namely, that Paul regards the actual sins "only as the relatively free manifestations of the hereditary sinful substance," is of no avail, seeing that they remain always acts of individual freedom, even though the latter be only relative, while the argument in our passage is such that the individual's own sins, as cause of death, are *excluded*. Ernesti joins ἁμαρτία δὲ κ.τ.λ. with ἐφ' ᾧ κ.τ.λ.: "since indeed all have sinned, but sin is not placed to account," etc. The ἄχρι .... κόσμῳ, standing in the way, he encloses in a parenthesis. But why this parenthesis? The πάντες ἥμαρτον, in the sense of iii. 23, needed no proof; and it could not occur to any one to date sin only from the epoch of the law. The ἄχρι .... κόσμῳ acquires its pertinent significance when, as an essential element in the syllogistic deduction, it is closely united with the axiom ἁμαρτία δὲ οὐκ ἐλλογ. κ.τ.λ. attached to it, and is not set aside in a parenthesis as if it might equally well have been omitted. According to Holsten the argument turns on the fact that *objective* sin entered the world through Adam, and death along with it; thus death has passed upon *all* because *all* were sinners (in the *objective* sense)—a diffusion by means of one over the whole, which is illustrated by the thought that, while sin was in the world until the law, this sin could not, in the absence of law, be imputed as *subjective* guilt; but death became ruler, in accordance with the objective divine law of the universe, with a tyrannical power not conditioned by the subjects of its rule, even over those who were indeed (*objectively*) sinners, but not (*subjectively*) transgressors like Adam. Holsten has certainly in this way avoided the error of making universal death conditioned by the subjective sin of the individuals; but he has done so by means of a distinction between objective and subjective sins, which is so far from being suggested by the text, that it was just through Adam that the *subjective* sin, joined with the *consciousness of guilt*, entered the world, and therefore the divine action, in decreeing death upon sin, could not be conceived as indifferent to the subjectivity. Hofmann—who sees in ἄχρι .... κόσμῳ a [very unnecessary] ground assigned for the ἐφ' ᾧ π. ἥμαρτον, upon which there follows in ἁμαρτία δὲ κ.τ.λ. a declaration regarding death in the pre-legal period, according to which this could not have been caused by the sinning of that period, seeing that on the contrary the latter took place when death was already present—confuses the entire exposition of the passage, and by his artificial rendering of ἐφ' ᾧ πάντες ἥμαρτον makes the understanding of it *impossible*. In general the entire history of the interpretation of our passage shows that when once the old ecclesiastical explanation of ἐφ' ᾧ (this however taken as *propterea quod*) πάντες ἥμαρτον is regarded as the *Charybdis* to be shunned at all hazards, the falling into the *Scylla* becomes unavoidable. Even Klöpper, in attributing to πάντες ἥμαρτον the underlying thought that Adam's sin penetrated to all, and Dietzsch, by his simplifying and modification of Hofmann's exposition, have not escaped this danger.

REMARK 2. Since Paul shows from the absence of *imputation* (ἐλλογεῖται) in the absence of law, that the death of men after Adam cannot have been occasioned by their own individual sins, but only by Adam's, in which all were partakers in virtue of their connection with him as their progenitor, he must have conceived that Adam's sin brought death not merely to himself but also at the same time to all *by way of imputation;* and therefore the *imputatio peccati Adamitici* in reference to the *death*, to which all are subjected, certainly results from our passage as a Pauline doctrine. But as to *original sin* (not however as to its condemnableness in itself), the testimony of our passage is only indirect, in so far, namely, as the ἐφ' ᾧ πάντες ἥμαρτον, according to its proper explanation and confirmation in ver. 13 f., necessarily presupposes in respect to Adam's posterity the habitual want of justitia originalis and the possession of concupiscence.

REMARK 3. The view of Julius Müller as to an original estate and original fall of man in an extra-temporal sphere (comp. the monstrous opinion of Benecke, p. 109 ff., and in the *Stud. u. Krit.* 1832, p. 616 ff.) cannot be reconciled with our passage and its reference to Gen. iii.[1] See Ernesti, p. 247 ff., and among dogmatic theologians, especially Philippi, III. p. 92 ff.; and (against Schelling and Steffens) Martensen, § 93, p. 202 ff. ed. 2.

Ver. 15. *But not as is the trespass, so also is the gift of grace.* Although Adam and Christ as the heads of the old and new humanity are typical parallels, how *different* nevertheless are the two *facts*, by which the former and the latter stand to one another in the relation of type and antitype (on the one side the παράπτωμα, on the other the χάρισμα)—different, namely (εἰ γὰρ κ.τ.λ.), by the opposite *effects*[2] issuing from those two facts, on which that typical character is based. The question is not as to the different *measure* of efficacious power, for this extends alike in both cases from *one* to *all;* but as to the different specific *kind* of effect; there death, here the rich grace of God —the latter the more undoubted and certain (πολλῷ μᾶλλον), as coming after that deadly effect, which the παράπτωμα had. "*For if* (εἰ purely hypothetical) *through the trespass of one the many died, much more has the grace of God and the gift by grace of the one man Jesus Christ become abundant to the many.*" On τὸ παράπτωμα comp. Wisd. x. 1. The contrast is τὸ χάρισμα, *the work of grace, i.e.* the atoning and justifying act of the divine grace in Christ,[3] comp. ver. 17 ff. — οἱ πολλοί] *the many,*

[1] Nor with the N. T. generally, which teaches an extra-temporal mode of existence *only in the case of Christ.* The extra-temporal condition and fall supposed by Müller are not only *outside* of Scripture, but *at variance with* it.

[2] This contrast forbids the taking ἀλλ' οὐκ . . . . χάρισμα *interrogatively* (Mehring and earlier expositors), and so getting rid of the negation.

[3] The unhappy and happy *consequences* respectively of the παράπτωμα and the χάρισμα are not included in these conceptions themselves (in opposition to

namely, according to ver. 12 (comp. ver. 18), the collective posterity of Adam. It is *in substance* certainly identical with πάντες, to which Mehring reverts; but the *contrast to the* εἷς becomes more palpable and stronger by the designation of the collective mass as οἱ πολλοί. Grotius erroneously says: "*fere omnes*, excepto *Enocho*," which is against vv. 12, 18. Such a unique, miraculous exception is not taken into consideration at all in this mode of looking at humanity as such on a great scale. Erroneous also is the view of Dietzsch, following Beck, that οἱ πολλοί and then τοὺς πολλούς divide mankind into *two classes*, of which the one continues in Adamite corruption (?) while the other is in Christ raised above sin and death. This theory breaks down even on the historical aorist ἀπέθανον and its, according to ver. 12, necessary reference to the *physical* death which was given with *Adam's* death-bringing fall for *all*, so that they *collectively* (including also the subsequent believers) became liable to death through this παράπτωμα. See on ver. 12. It is moreover clear from our passage that for the explanation of the death of men Paul did not regard their *individual* sin as the *causa efficiens*, or even as merely *medians;* and it is a meaning gratuitously introduced, when it is explained: "the many *sinned* and found death, *like* the one Adam," (Ewald, *Jahrb.* II., van Hengel and others). — πολλῷ μᾶλλον] as in ver. 9, of the *logical plus, i.e.* of the degree of the evidence as enhanced through the contents of the protasis, *multo potius*. "If Adam's fall has had so bad an universal consequence, much less can it be doubted that," etc. For God far rather allows His goodness to prevail than His severity; this is the presupposition on which the conclusion rests. Chrysostom has correctly interpreted π. μᾶλλ. in the logical sense (πολλῷ γὰρ τοῦτο εὐλογώτερον), as does also Theodoret, and recently Fritzsche, Philippi, Tholuck (who however takes in the *quantitative* plus as well), van Hengel, Mangold, and Klöpper. The *quantitative* view (Theophylact: οὐ τοσοῦτον μόνον, φησὶν, ὠφέλησεν ὁ

Dietzsch). Nor is παράπτωμα to be so distinguished from παράβασις, that the former *connotes* the unhappy *consequences* (Grotius, Dietzsch). On the contrary, the expressions are popular synonyms, only according to different *figures*, like *fall* (not *falling away*) and *trespass*. Comp. on παράπτ. Ez. xiv. 13, xv. 8, xviii. 24, 26, iii. 20; Rom. iv. 25, xi. 11; 2 Cor. v. 19; Gal. vi. 1; Eph. ii. 1 *et al.*

Χριστὸς, ὅσον ἔβλαψεν ὁ 'Αδάμ; also Erasmus, Calvin, Beza, Calovius and others; and in modern times Rückert, Reiche, Köllner, Rothe, Nielsen, Baumgarten-Crusius, Maier, Hofmann, and Dietzsch) is opposed to the analogy of vv. 17, 18; and has also against it the consideration, that the measure *of punishment* of the παράπτωμα (viz. the *death of all*) was already quantitatively the greatest possible, was absolute, and therefore the measure of the *grace*, while just as absolute (εἰς τοὺς πολλούς), is not greater still than that measure of punishment, but only stands out against the dark background of the latter all the more *evidently* in its rich fulness.[1] — ἡ χάρις τ. Θεοῦ κ. ἡ δωρεά] the former, *the grace of God*, richly turned towards the many, is the principle of the latter (ἡ δωρεά = τό χάρισμα in ver. 15, the gift of justification). The δωρεά is to be understood κατ' ἐξοχήν, without supplying τοῦ Θεοῦ; but the discourse keeps apart with solemn emphasis what is cause and what is effect. — ἐν χάριτι .... Χριστοῦ is not with many expositors (including Rothe, Tholuck, Baumgarten-Crusius, Philippi, Mehring, Hofmann, and Dietzsch) to be joined with ἡ δωρεά (the gift, which is procured through the grace of Christ), but with Fritzsche, Rückert, Ewald, van Hengel, and others, to be connected with ἐπερίσσευσε (*has become abundant through the grace of Christ*)—a construction which is decisively supported, not indeed by the absence of the article, since ἡ δωρεά ἐν χάριτι might be conjoined so as to form one idea, but by *the* reason, that only with this connection the τῷ .... παραπτώματι in the protasis has its necessary, strictly correspondent, correlative in the apodosis. The divine grace and the gift have abounded to the many *through the grace of Christ*, just

[1] The way would have been logically prepared for the *quantitative* plus by the hypothetical protasis only in the event of that which was predicated being in the two clauses *of a similar* (not opposite) *kind;* in the event therefore of its having been possible to affirm a salutariness of the παράπτωμα in the protasis. Comp. xi. 12; 2 Cor. iii. 9, 11; Heb. ix. 13 f., xii. 9, 25. The main objection which Dietzsch (following Rothe) raises against the interpretation of the *logical* plus, *on the ground* that we have here two *historical realities* before us, is by no means tenable. For even in the case of two facts which have taken place, the one may be corroborated and inferred from the other, namely, *as respects its certainty and necessity*. If the *one* has taken place, *it is by so much the more evident* that the *other* also has taken place. The historical reality of the one leaves all the less room for doubt as to that of the other. The second does not in this case require to be something still *future*, especially if it be an occurrence, which does not fall within the range of *sensuous* perception.

as the many died *through the fall of Adam.* The χάρις Ἰησοῦ Χριστοῦ is—as the genitive-relation naturally suggests of itself, and as is rendered obviously certain by the analogy of ἡ χάρις τ. Θεοῦ—*the grace of Jesus Christ,* in virtue of which He found Himself moved to accomplish the ἱλαστήριον, in accordance with the Father's decree, and thereby to procure for men the *divine* grace and the δωρεά. It is not therefore the favour *in which Christ stood with God* (Luther, 1545); nor the grace *of God* received *in the fellowship of Christ* (van Hengel); nor is it the steadily continued, earthly and heavenly, redeeming *efficacy of Christ's grace* (Rothe, Dietzsch). Comp. Acts xv. 11, 2 Cor. viii. 9; Gal. i. 6; Tit. iii. 6; 2 Cor. xii. 8, xiii. 13. The designation of Christ : τοῦ ἑνὸς ἀνθρώπου Ἰ. Χ., is occasioned by the contrast with the one man Adam. Comp. 1 Cor. xv. 21; 1 Tim. ii. 5. To describe the divine glory of this One man (Col. i. 19) did not fall within the Apostle's present purpose; but it was known to the reader, and is presupposed in His χάρις (John i. 64). — τῇ τοῦ] "articuli nervosissimi," Bengel. — εἰς τοὺς πολλούς] belongs to ἐπερίσσ. The πολλοί are likewise here, just as previously, *all mankind* (comp. πάντας ἀνθρώπους, ver. 18). To this multitude has the grace of God, etc., *been plentifully imparted* (εἰς τ. π. ἐπερίσσευσε, comp. 2 Cor. i. 5), namely, from the *objective* point of view, in so far as Christ's act of redemption has acquired for all the divine grace and gift, although the subjective reception of it is conditioned by faith. See on ver. 18. The expression ἐπερίσσευσε (he does not say merely ἐγένετο, or some such word) is the echo of his own blessed experience.

Ver. 16. Continuation of the difference between the gift of grace and the consequence of the fall, and that with reference to the *causal origination* on either side in a *numerical* aspect.[1] — *And not as through one, who has sinned, so is the gift,* i.e. it is not so in its case—the state of the case there is the very reverse—as if it were occasioned δι᾽ ἑνὸς ἁμαρτήσ. (like death

[1] Dietzsch takes it differently, finding the progress of the argument in this, that at the end *a state of life adequate to the divine law* may be established. This view however rests on an erroneous exposition of δικαίωμα (see below), and generally on an erroneous mixing up of sanctification with justification—an intermingling to be avoided throughout the entire train of thought in our passage; comp. Pfleiderer in Hilgenfeld's *Zeitschr.* 1872, p. 167.

through Adam). The δι' ἑνὸς ἁμαρτήσ. indicates the unity of the person and of the accomplished sinful act; comp. Stölting. Beyond the simple ἐστί after δώρημα nothing is to be supplied (so also Mangold), because the words without supplement are quite in accordance with the Greek use of ὡς (Bernhardy, p. 352, Stallbaum, *ad Plat. Sympos.* p. 179 E), and yield an appropriate sense, whereas none of the supplements that have been attempted are suggested by the context. It has been proposed, *e.g.* after ἁμαρτ. to supply θάνατος εἰςῆλθεν (Grotius, Estius, Koppe), or τὸ κρῖμα or κατάκριμα (Bengel, Klee, Reiche, Köllner; or after ὡς: τό (Beza), which is indeed impossible, but is nevertheless resorted to even by de Wette: "and not like *that which originated through one* that sinned, so is the gift," and Tholuck: " the gift has a different character from *that which has come through the one man sinning.*" Comp. Philippi, who like Rückert and Dietzsch supplies merely ἐγένετο after ἁμαρτ. (and then after δωρ.: ἐστί),—which however still yields no complete sentence, since the ἐγένετο is without a subject. The correct view in substance is taken by Rothe, Ewald, and van Hengel; while Fritzsche still calls in the aid of a supplement after ἁμαρτ. (τὸ παράπτωμα ἐγένετο); and Hofmann even wishes mentally to supply to καὶ . . . . δώρημα from what precedes, to which it is attached, εἰς τοὺς πολλοὺς ἐπερίσσευσεν as predicate;[1] whereas Mehring puts his rendering, which erroneously *makes it a question* (comp. on ver. 15), in this form: "*And ought not the gift* to be, *as it* was through *one* that *sinned?*" — τὸ μὲν γὰρ κρῖμα κ.τ.λ.] sc. ἐστί; explanation of the point of difference previously specified: *For the judicial sentence redounds from a single one to a sentence of condemnation, but the gift of grace from many trespasses to a sentence of justification.* — τὸ κρῖμα] quite general: *the sentence which God pronounces as judge;* comp. 1 Cor. vi. 7. For *the kind of sentence,* which this shall prove to be in the concrete result, is indicated only by the following εἰς κατάκριμα. The explanation which refers it to the *divine*

---

[1] It would run thus: "*The gift has not so accrued abundantly to the many and passed over to them, as was the case when such a bestowal ensued through one that sinned.*" This supplement is already guarded against by the fact that κ. οὐχ down to δώρημα is the obvious parallel of οὐχ ὡς τ. παραπτ. down to χάρισμα, and hence, like the latter, may not be supplemented further than by ἐστί. Any other course is arbitrary and artificial.

announcement contained in Gen. ii. 17 (Fritzsche, Dietzsch) is erroneous, because the latter is a threat, and not a κρῖμα; and because the act of Adam must have already preceded the κρῖμα. Others understand by it the *sentence of punishment* pronounced against *Adam*, which has become a sentence of punishment (sentence of death) against his *posterity* (κατάκριμα) (Reiche, Rückert, Nielsen, Baumgarten-Crusius, Krehl, de Wette, Maier, Hofmann); but wrongly, because they thus neglect the pointed interchange of κρῖμα and κατάκριμα, and in εἰς κατάκριμα place the stress on the condemned subject, which however is not even mentioned. Linguistically erroneous is the view of Beza, Calixtus, Wolf, and others, that τ. κρῖμα is the *guilt*. Nor does it mean the *state of being finally adjudged* (Stölting). Philippi, Tholuck, Ewald, and van Hengel hold the right view; while Rothe, with unnecessary refining and gratuitous importation, takes τὸ μέν and τὸ δέ by themselves as subject, κρῖμα and χάρισμα as predicates ("the one effect is a righteous judgment.... the other on the contrary a gift"). Dietzsch still more breaks up the sentence, making κρῖμα and χάρισμα *appositions*, the former to τὸ μέν, and the latter to τὸ δέ. — ἐξ ἑνός] has, like ἐκ πολλῶν παραπτ. afterwards, the chief emphasis; ἑνός is masculine on account of the previous δι' ἑνὸς ἁμαρτήσ., not neuter (παραπτώματος), as Rothe, Mehring, Dietzsch, Stölting and others think. This masculine however does not necessitate our taking πολλῶν also as *masculine* (Hofmann), which would in itself be allowable (comp. on 2 Cor. i. 11), but is here opposed by the consideration that Paul would have expressed the *personal* contrast to ἐξ ἑνός more symmetrically and thoughtfully by the bare ἐκ πολλῶν. The Vulgate gives the right sense: "*ex multis delictis.*" — ἐξ] points to the motive cause, producing the event from itself: *forth from one;* see Kühner, II. 1, p. 399. Just in the same way the second ἐκ. — εἰς κατάκριμα] sc. ἐστί, as in the first half of the verse,[1] "ut una cum praesentibus praeterita tamquam eadem in tabella reprae-

---

[1] In consequence of the way in which Hofmann has supplemented the first half of the verse, we should now take, in the one instance, ἐξ ἑνὸς εἰς κατάκριμα εἰς τοὺς πολλοὺς ἐπερίσσευσεν as predicate to τὸ κρῖμα; and in the other instance, ἐκ πολλῶν παραπτωμάτων εἰς δικαίωμα εἰς τοὺς πολλοὺς ἐπερίσσευσεν as predicate to τὸ χάρισμα,—notwithstanding that in both cases a definition with εἰς is already given by Paul himself. How enigmatically and misleadingly he would have written!

sentet," van Hengel. *One* was the cause (moving the divine righteousness) that the judgment of God presents itself in the result as a punitive judgment (namely, that on account of the sin of one all should die, ver. 12); *many* sins, on the other hand, were the cause (moving the divine compassion) that the gift of grace results *in concreto* as a judgment of justification. In the one case an *unity*, in the other a *multiplicity*, was the occasioning cause. In the second clause also, following the analogy of κρῖμα in the first, τὸ χάρισμα is conceived of generally and abstractly; the χάρισμα redounds in the concrete case εἰς δικαίωμα, when God, namely, forgives the many sins and declares their subjects as righteous. δικαίωμα, which is not, with Dietzsch, to be understood in the sense of *the right framing of life* through sanctification of the Spirit—a view contrary to linguistic usage and the context—is here also (comp. i. 32, ii. 26, viii. 4; Luke i. 6; Heb. ix. 1, 10; Rev. xv. 4; frequently in LXX. and Apocr., see Schleusner, *Thes.* II. p. 167 f.), according to its literal signification, in itself nothing else than *judicial determination, judicial sentence;* but it is to be taken here in the Pauline sense of the divine δικαιοῦν, hence: the *sentence defining righteousness*, the ordinance of God in which He completes the δικαίωσις as *actus judicialis*, the opposite of κατάκριμα. *Condition* of righteousness (Luther and others), "*the actual status of being righteous*" (Hofmann), would be represented by δικαιοσύνη; *satisfaction of justice*, compensation of justice (Rothe, Mehring following Calovius, and Wolf), in accordance with which idea it may even designate *punishment* in classical usage (Plat. *Legg.* ix. p. 864 E), it *might* mean (Aristot. *Eth. Nic.* v. 7, 17: ἐπανόρθωμα τοῦ ἀδικήματος), but never does so in Biblical usage, to which this special definition of the sense is foreign. Paul could convey the sense *declaration as righteous, verdict of justification*, the more appropriately by δικαίωμα, since in Bar. ii. 17 the word is also substantially thus used (δώσουσι δόξαν κ. δικαίωμα τῷ κυρίῳ, in Hades they shall not praise God and *declare Him righteous*). Compare also 2 Sam. xix. 28; Jer. xi. 20; Prov. viii. 20; Rev. xv. 4, and xix. 8.[1] The right view is taken by Fritzsche, Baumgarten-

---

[1] Where τὰ δικαιώματα τῶν ἁγίων are the divine verdicts of justification, which the saints have received. The pure byssus is their symbol. Compare Ewald, *Joh. Schr. in loc.* p. 330. Düsterdieck understands it otherwise (righteous acts).

Crusius, Krehl, Philippi, Tholuck, Ewald, van Hengel, Holsten, Klöpper, and Pfleiderer; Rückert (also Maier) abides by *means of justification*, following merely the form of the word without empirical proof, while de Wette is undecided, and Stölting, without precedent from linguistic usage (comp. above Luther.and Hofmann), understands the *state* of justification into which the *state of grace* (the χάρισμα) has passed. These two conceptions however exclude any idea of succession, and are concurrent.— The addition ζωῆς in D. Vulg. is a correct gloss; comp. ver. 18.

Ver. 17. The τὸ δὲ χάρισμα ἐκ πολλ. παραπτ. εἰς δικαίωμα, just asserted in contrast to the κατάκριμα proceeding from One, has now the seal of *confirmation* (γάρ) impressed on it through the triumphant certainty of the *reign of life*, which must belong to the recipients of the δικαίωμα in the approaching completion of the kingdom through the One Jesus Christ all *the more undoubtedly*, since the παράπτωμα of the One Adam brought death to reign. The effect of the second One (the Adam μέλλων) in the direction of salvation cannot in fact remain behind the effect which proceeded from the first One in the direction of destruction. On this rests the *evidence* of the blissful assurance, which with πολλῷ μᾶλλον stands forth as it were from the gloom of the death previously described (comp. vv. 15, 9). The view that ver. 17 adduces the *proof* of the first half of ver. 16 being *really proved* by its second half (Hofmann), is to be rejected for this very reason, that the demonstration in ver. 16 is so full and clear in itself, especially after ver. 15, that there is no longer any necessity for receiving *proof of its probative power*, and no reader could expect this. It is quite arbitrary in Rothe, especially looking to the regular continuation by γάρ, to take ver. 16 as a parenthesis, and to attach ver. 17 to ver. 15. For other views of the connection see Dietzsch, who, in accordance with his own unsuitable rendering of δικαίωμα, finds here the inner righteous condition of life verified by the final reign of life as its outward manifestation. — διὰ τοῦ ἑνός] *through the medium of the One*, is added, although ἐν ἑνὶ παραπτώματι had been already said (see the critical remarks), in order to prepare the way with due emphasis for the διὰ τοῦ ἑνὸς Ἰησοῦ Χριστοῦ of the apodosis. Comp. on 2 Cor. xii. 7. — πολλῷ μᾶλλον] Here also, as in ver. 15, the *logical plus*, the far greater *certainty* and *evidence*. — οἱ λαμβάνοντες] not those who believingly *accept* (Bengel, Rothe, van Hengel, and others), but simply the *recipients*. The present participle denotes the presence of the time of grace introduced by Christ, which stands in the middle between the former reign of death and the reign of life in the blissful future and determines the subjects of the latter; comp. ver. 11. — τὴν περισσείαν] the *abundant fulness* (comp. ii. 4) of grace, referring to ἐπερίσσευσε in ver. 15. — τῆς χάρ. κ. τ. δωρεᾶς] distinguished, as in ver. 15. But the emphasis of the description, climactic in the enthusiasm of victory, lies in the first instance on χάριτος, and then, as it advances, on δικαιοσύνης, in contrast to the former tragic παράπτωμα. — τῆς δικαιοσ.] is that, in which the δωρεά consists. The whole characteristic description of the subjects by οἱ .... λαμβάνοντες already implies the certainty with which one may reckon in the case of those, who are honoured to receive such abundance, on the final βασιλεύειν ἐν ζωῇ through Christ. — ἐν ζωῇ βασιλεύσουσι] The word βασιλ. itself, and more especially the *future*, renders it certain that the *future* Messianic ζωή is here meant; in which, as the opposite of the θάνατος, the pardoned and justified shall have the joint-dominion of the new world (viii. 21), the κληρονομία and its δόξα (viii. 17), under Christ the Head (1 Cor. iv. 8, vi. 2; 2 Tim. ii. 12), in whose final manifestation their life shall be gloriously manifested (Col. iii. 3 f.). Observe, further, that in the apodosis Paul does not say ἡ ζωή βασιλεύσει ἐπὶ τοὺς .... λαμβάνοντας in accordance with the protasis, but appropriately, and in harmony with the active nature of the relation, *i.e.* of the future glorious liberty of the children of God, places the subjects actively in the foreground, and affirms of *them* the reigning *in* life.—The Ἰησοῦ Χριστοῦ is added *as if in triumph*, in contradistinction to the unnamed but well-known εἷς, who occasioned the dominion of death. Finally, we should not fail to notice how in this passage the glance proceeds from the status *gratiae* (λαμβάνοντες) backward to the status *irae* (ἐβασίλευσε), and forward to the status *gloriae* (βασιλεύσουσι).

Ver. 18 f. Summary recapitulation of the whole parallel treated of from ver. 12 onwards, so that the elements of likeness and unlikeness contained in it are now comprehended in one utterance. Συλλογίζεται ἐνταῦθα τὸ πᾶν, Theodore of Mopsuestia.

The emergence of the ἄρα οὖν now ushering in the conclusion, as well as the corresponding relation of the contents of ver. 18 f. to the indication given by ὅς ἐστι τύπος τοῦ μέλλοντος in ver. 14, carries us back to ver. 12; not merely to ver. 16 f. (de Wette, Fritzsche); or merely to vv. 15-17 (Hofmann, Dietzsch). The right view is taken by Philippi, Ewald, Holsten. — ἄρα οὖν] conclusive: *accordingly then*,[1] in very frequent use by the Apostle (vii. 3, 25, viii. 12, ix. 16, 18, xiv. 12, 19; Gal. vi. 10; Eph. ii. 19 *et al.*), and that, contrary to the classical usage (Herm. *ad Antig.* 628, *ad Viger.* p. 823), at the beginning of the sentence. For the *necessary* (contrary to Mehring's view) *completion* of the two sentences, which are in the sharpest and briefest manner compressed as it were into a mere exclamation (Ewald), it is sufficient simply to supply: *res cessit, it has come*, ἀπεβή (Winer, p. 546 [E. T. 734]), or ἐγένετο (Grotius). See Buttmann's *neut. Gr.* p. 338. *As it therefore has come to a sentence of condemnation for all men through One trespass, so also it has come to justification of life* (which has for its consequence the possession of the future Messianic life, comp. ver. 21; John v. 28, 29) *for all men through One justifying judgment*. The supplying of τὸ κρῖμα ἐγένετο to the first, and τὸ χάρισμα ἐγένετο to the second half (so Fritzsche and Rückert), considering the opposite sense of the two subjects, renders the very compressed discourse somewhat singular. — δι' ἑνὸς δικ.] *through one judicial verdict* (see on vv. 16, 19), namely, that which was pronounced by God on account of the obedience of Christ rendered through His death. In strict logic indeed the δικαίωμα, which is properly the antithesis of κατάκριμα (as in ver. 16), should not be opposed to παράπτωμα; but this incongruity of a lively interchange of conceptions is not un-Pauline (comp. ver. 15). And it is thoroughly unwarranted to assign to δικαίωμα here also, as in ver. 16, significations which it has not; such as *actual status of being righteous* (Hofmann, Stölting), *fulfilment of right* (Philippi, Mangold), *making amends* (Rothe), *righteous deed* (Holsten), *righteous life-condition of Christ* (Dietzsch), with which a new humanity begins, *act of justification* (Tholuck), *virtuousness* (Baumgarten-Crusius), *obedience* (de

---

[1] Ἄρα, "ad internam potius causam spectat," οὖν, "magis ad externam," Klotz, *ad Devar.* p. 717. Comp. p. 173 The ἄρα serves specifically for *dialectic* accuracy; Baeumlein, p. 35; comp. Kühner, II. p. 857.

Wette), and the like—definitions, in which for the most part regard is had to the act of the death of Jesus partly with and partly without the addition of the *obedientia activa* (comp. also Klöpper), while Fritzsche explains it of the incarnation and humiliation of Christ (Phil. ii. 5, 8) as His *recte factum*. Ewald interprets rightly: " through One righteous sentence;" so also van Hengel and Umbreit. This alone is permitted by ver. 16. It is the One declaration of what is now of right, that is, the judicial verdict of the being reconciled, which took place on the part of God on the ground of Christ's sacrificial death—*the consequence therefore, of* His ὑπακοή rendered in death—and which so far may appear as the antithesis to the fall of Adam with the same right as in ver. 15 the grace and gift were adduced as the contrast to that fall. To take the ἑνός as *masculine* (Vulgate, Theodoret, Theophylact, Erasmus, Luther, Calvin, and many others, including Tholuck, Fritzsche, Nielsen, Picard, Klöpper, Philippi, and Hofmann), is, seeing that no article is annexed, unwarranted according to the analogy of the immediate context, vv 17, 19; or Paul would have only expressed himself in a way liable to be misunderstood (how differently in ver 16!). Equally unwarranted is it to conceive the verb to be supplied in the apodosis as *in the future* (Philippi, Dietzsch). The judicial verdict *is given* and *has redounded* once and for ever to justification of eternal life for all; that is the great historical fact of salvation, which Paul has in view and sets forth as a concrete event (not under the point of view of a timeless abstraction, as Rothe thought) without considering how far it is now or in the future appropriated through faith by the subjects.—In both halves of the verse πάντες ἄνθρωποι is simply *all men*, as in ver. 12. At the same time it must be noted that in the second half the relation is conceived in its *objectivity*. On the part of God it has come to justification for *all*; thus the case stands *objectively*; the *subjective attainment* of this universal justification, the realisation of it for the *individuals*, depends upon whether the latter believingly apprehend the δικαίωμα for their own subjective δικαίωσις, or unbelievingly reject it. This dependence on a subjective condition, however, did not belong to the scope of our passage, in which the only object was to set forth the all-embracing blessed objective consequence of the ἓν δικαίωμα, in contrast to the all-destructive objective consequence of the ἕν παράπτωμα. Hence just as little can anything be deduced from our passage as from xi. 32 in favour of a final ἀποκατάστασις. The distinction imported by Hofmann and Lechler: that πάντες ἄνθρωποι means all *without distinction*, and πάντες οἱ ἄνθρωποι, on the other hand, all *without exception*, the *sum total* of mankind, is purely fanciful; πάντες means *omnes, nemine excepto*, alike whether the substantive belonging to it, in accordance with the connection, has or has not the article ("articulus, cum sensus fert additus vel omissus, discrimen sententiae non facit," Ellendt, *Lex. Soph.* II. p. 519). Only when the article stands *before* πάντες (consequently οἱ πάντες ἄνθ.) does *the* distinction emerge, that we have to think of "*cunctos* sive *universos*, i. e. singulos *in unum corpus colligatos*" (Ellendt, p. 521); comp. Krüger, § 50, 11, 12.; Kühner, II. 1, p. 545.

Ver. 19. This final sentence, assigning a reason, now formally by the recurrence of the ὥσπερ points back to ver. 12, with which the whole chain of discourse that here runs to an end had begun. But *that which* is to be established by γάρ is not the *how* of the parallel comparison, which is set forth repeatedly with clearness (in opposition to Rothe), but the blissful conclusion of that comparison in ver. 18: εἰς δικαίωσιν ζωῆς, upon which what is now expressed in ver. 19 impresses *the seal of certainty*. Dietzsch thinks that the purport, which is kept general, of ver. 18 is now to be established from the *personal life*. But the right interpretation of δικαίωμα and of δίκαιοι κατασταθήσονται is opposed to this view. — ἁμαρτωλοὶ κατεστάθ. οἱ πολλοί] *The many were set down as sinners;* for according to ver. 12 ff. they were indeed, through the disobedience of Adam, put actually *into the category of sinners*, because, namely, they sinned in and with the fall of Adam. Thus *through the disobedience of the one man*, because all had part in it, *has the position of all become that of sinners*. The *consequence* of this, that they were subjected to *punishment* (Chrysostom, Oecumenius, Theophylact and others), were *treated* as sinners (Grotius, Flatt, Böhme, Krehl and others), and the like, is *not* here *expressly included*, but after the foregoing is obvious of itself. Fritzsche (comp. Koppe and Reiche) has: through their death they *appeared as sinners*.[1] On the one hand this gratuitously imports

[1] So also Julius Müller, *v. d. Sünde*, II. p. 485, ed. 5, evading the literal sense: "the many have become *declared* (as it were before the divine judgment-seat) as

I.   S

something (through their death), and on the other it does violence to the expression κατεστάθ., which denotes the real putting into the position of sinners, whereby they *de facto* came to stand as sinners,[1] *peccatores constituti sunt* (James iv. 4; 2 Pet. i. 8; Heb. v. 1, viii. 3; 2 Macc. xv. 2; 3 Macc. i. 7; Plat. *Rep.* p. 564 A; *Conv.* p. 222 B; examples from Xenophon in Sturz, II. p. 610), as is required by the ruling normal clause ἐφ᾽ ᾧ πάντες ἥμαρτον in ver. 12. The Apostle might have written ἐγενήθησαν (as Dietzsch explains the κατεστ.), but he has already in view the antithesis δίκαιοι καταστ., and expresses himself in conformity to it: hence also he does not put πάντες (which might have stood in the first clause), but οἱ πολλοί. — διὰ ὑπακοῆς] *through obedience.* The death of Jesus was κατ᾽ ἐξοχήν His *obedience* to the will of the Father, Phil. ii. 8; Heb. v. 8. But this designation is *selected* as the antithesis to the παρακοή of Adam, and all the more certainly therefore it does not here mean "the collective life-obedience" (Lechler, comp. Hofmann, Dietzsch and others), but must be understood as the deed of atonement willed by God (ver. 8 ff.), to which we owe justification, and the *ethical premiss* of which on Christ's side is righteousness of life, although Hofmann improperly rejects this view as a *groundless fancy.* — δίκαιοι κατασταθήσονται] *shall be placed in the category of righteous.* The *future* refers[2] to the future revelation of glory after the resurrection (Reiche, Fritzsche, Klöpper); not to the fact that the multitude of believers is conceived of as not yet completed, and consequently the justifying of them is chiefly regarded as a succession of cases *to come* (comp. iii. 20, 30). The *how* of the δίκαιοι κατασταθ. cannot be found in an *actual becoming righteous*, as result of the divine work of grace, at the

---

sinners through the disobedience of the one man (as the determining initial point of sinful development), by the fact, that they have been subjected to death." See on the other hand Hofmann, who properly urges that they did not become sinners only along with their dying, but immediately through Adam's disobedience. But the *how* of their doing so is in fact just the ἐφ᾽ ᾧ πάντες ἥμαρτον, according to *our* conception of these words.

[1] Dietzsch should not have raised the objection that it ought to have been εἰς ἁμαρτωλούς, or ἐν ἁμαρτωλοῖς. See generally Kühner, II. 1, p. 274.

[2] Corresponding to the βασιλεύσουσι in ver. 17, and hence not to be explained in a mere general way of the certain expectation or conviction (Mehring), as Hofmann also takes it in the sense of μέλλει λογίζεσθαι, iv. 24. Comp. on the other hand ii. 13, 16; and see on Gal. v. 5.

close of the saving process (Dietzsch), which would offend against the whole context since ver. 12, and anticipate the contents of ch. vi. In truth the mode which Paul had in view is beyond doubt, after the development of the doctrine of justification in chs. iii. iv. God has forgiven believers on account of the death of Christ, and counted their faith as righteousness. Thus the obedience of the One has caused that at the judgment the πολλοί shall by God's sentence enter into the category of the righteous,[1] as the disobedience of the One had caused the πολλοί to enter the opposite. In both cases the *causa meritoria* is the objective act of the two heads of the race (the sin of Adam—the death of Christ), to whom belong the πολλοί on both sides; while the *subjective mediating* cause is the individual relation to those acts (communion in Adam's fall—faith). It is a mistake therefore to quote this passage against the Protestant doctrine of justification (Reithmayr and Bisping), as if the making righteous were designated as sanctification. But we are not entitled to carry the comparison between Adam and Christ further than Paul himself has done.

Vv. 20, 21. The comparison between Adam and Christ is closed. But in the middle between the two stood the *law!* How therefore could Paul leave unnoticed *the relation of the law to both*, the relation of this essential intervening element in the divine plan of salvation, the continuity of which was not to be hindered by the law, but, on the contrary, advanced to its blissful goal? The mention of it presented itself necessarily to him, especially after the utterance already contained in ver. 13, even without our thinking of an opponent's objection,[2] or, at least, of persons who fancied that they must themselves furnish something in order to secure for themselves eternal life (Hofmann); but it cannot be regarded as the proper *goal* of the entire discussion (Th. Schott), which would not at all correspond to so succinct an indication. — παρεισῆλθεν] *there came in alongside*

[1] Consequently not through any internal communication or infusion of the moral quality of righteousness; comp. Döllinger, *Christenthum u. K.* p. 200 f. 190, ed. 2. See on the other hand Köstlin in the *Jahrb. f. D. Theol.* 1856, p. 95. Döllinger erroneously explains καταστᾰθῆσ.: "*established in righteousness.*"

[2] So even Cyril and Grotius; compare Mangold. The latter finds here a proof of the preponderantly *Jewish-Christian* character of the readers. But with as little right as it might be found in Gal. iii.

(of the ἁμαρτία, which had already come in, ver. 12) into the world. See Vigerus, ed. Herm. p. 651; and van Hengel *in loc.* Comp. Philo in Loesner, p. 252, especially *de temul.* p. 263 C, where παρεισελθεῖν ἐῶσα means *juxta se intrare sinens.* On the idea comp. Gal. iii. 19. The notion of *secrecy* (Vulgate: *subintravit,* comp. Erasmus, *Annot.*, Send.) is not implied in παρά *in itself,* but would require to be suggested by the *context,* as in Gal. ii. 4; Pol. i. 7, 3; i. 8, 4; ii. 55, 3 (where λάθρᾳ stands along with it); comp. παρεισάγω, παρεισδύω, παρεισφέρω κ.τ.λ., which likewise receive the idea of secrecy only from the context. But this is *not* at all the case here, because this idea would be at variance with the solemn giving of the law (Gal. iii. 19; Acts vii. 33), and the reverence of the Apostle for it (Rom. vii. 12 ff.) Reiche, Rothe, Tholuck, Rückert, and Philippi import the idea that the law is designated as an *accessory* institution, or its coming in as of *subordinate* importance in comparison with that of sin (Hofmann), as an element *not making an epoch* (Weiss, Dietzsch). It *was* not such, Gal. iv. 24, nor is this sense implied in the word itself. Linguistically incorrect (for παρεισέρχ. does not mean coming in *between,* but coming in *alongside*) is the view of others: that it came in the *middle* between Adam (according to Theodoret and Reithmayr, Abraham) and Christ (Calvin, Grotius, Estius, Baumgarten-Crusius, Usteri, Ewald, Bisping and others). Nor does παρεισῆλθεν mean: it came in *in opposition thereto, i.e.* in opposition to *sin* (Mehring). Such a reference must necessarily have been implied, as in Gal. ii. 4, in the context, but would be out of place here on account of the following ἵνα κ.τ.λ., which Mehring inappropriately takes as painful *irony.* Finally that παρά means *obiter, ad tempus* (Chrysostom, Theophylact, Cornelius à Lapide) is a pure fancy. — ἵνα πλεονάσῃ τὸ παράπτ.] *in order that the transgression might be increased.* The παράπτωμα can only be intended in *the* sense in which the reader must have understood it in virtue of the preceding text, ver. 15 ff., therefore of the *Adamite* transgression. This was the concrete destructive evil, which existed in the world as the beginning of sin and the cause of universal death. By the law, however, it was not to be abolished or annulled, but on the contrary (observe the prefixing of πλεονάσῃ) it was to be *increased, i.e.* to obtain accession in more and more παραπτώμασι. If therefore τὸ παράπτωμα is not to be taken collectively (Fritzsche, de Wette, van Hengel and others) just as little is ἵνα πλεονάσῃ to be rationalised so that it may be interpreted *logice*, of greater *acknowledgment* of sin (Grotius, Wolf, Nielsen, Baur), or of the *consciousness of sin* (J. Müller), since the corresponding ὑπερεπερίσσ. cannot be so taken; nor so, that ἵνα is to be explained as ecbatic (Chrysostom, and several Fathers quoted by Suicer, *Thes.* I. p. 1454, Koppe, Reiche), which is *never* correct, and is not justified by the groundless fear of a blasphemous and un-Pauline idea (Reiche). Comp. Gal. iii. 19; 1 Cor. xv. 56; and generally on i. 24. Augustine (in Ps. cii. c. 15) rightly says by way of describing the *intervening* aim referred to: " non crudeliter hoc fecit Deus, sed consilio medicinae;.... augetur morbus, crescit malitia, quaeritur medicus et totum sanatur." — παράπτωμα and ἁμαρτία are not certainly distinguished as Tittmann, *Synon.* p. 47, defines; nor yet, as Reiche thinks, simply thus, that both words indicate the same idea only under different figures (this would be true of παράπτωμα and ἁμαρτήμα); but in this way, that τὸ παράπτωμα invariably indicates only the concrete sin, the sinful deed; while ἡ ἁμαρτία may have as well the concrete (as always when it stands in the plural, comp. on Eph. ii. 1) as the abstract sense. It has the latter sense in our passage, and it appears *purposely chosen*. For if the Adamite transgression, which was present in the world of men as a fact and with its baneful effect, received accession through the law, so that this evil actually existing in humanity since the fall increased, the sum total of sin *in abstracto*, which was among men, was thereby enlarged; the *dominion* of sin became greater, both extensively and intensively (comp. Lipsius, *Rechtfertigungsl.* p. 73). Therefore the discourse *progresses* thus: οὗ δὲ ἐπλεόνασεν ἡ ἁμαρτία, and then ἐβασίλ. ἡ ἁμαρτία. — οὗ] *where*, local, of the *domain, where* etc. This *field* is generally *the world of men*, in which, however, the increase in sin here meant came from the people of the law, from Israel; but without the sphere of the οὗ being limited to the latter, since immediately, in ver. 21, he brings forward the *universal* point of view as it prevails throughout the section (in opposition to Hofmann). The *temporal* rendering: *when* (Grotius, de Wette, Fritzsche, Stölting) is likewise linguistically correct (time being represented *under the aspect of space*, comp. ἀφ' οὗ and the like), but less in harmony with the analogous passages, iv. 15; 2 Cor. iii. 17 (οὗ.... ἐκεῖ). — ὑπερεπερίσσ.] *it became over-great*, supra modum redundavit. The ἐπλεόνασεν had to be *surpassed*. Comp. 2 Cor. vii. 4; 1 Tim. i. 14; Mark vii. 37; 2 Thess. i. 3. But that it had surpassed *itself* (Hofmann), is a definite reference gratuitously introduced. The two correlative verbs are related simply as *comparative* and *superlative*. — ἵνα ὥσπερ κ.τ.λ.] *in order that, just as* (formerly) *sin reigned in virtue of death, so also* (divine) *grace should reign by means of righteousness unto eternal life through Jesus Christ our Lord*. This is the whole blessed aim of the ὑπερεπερίσσ. ἡ χάρις. Rothe incorrectly desires to treat οὗ δὲ ....χάρις as a parenthesis. This proposition is in fact so essential, that it is the necessary premiss for the opening up of that most blessed prospect. See moreover Dietzsch. — ἐν τῷ θανάτῳ] not *unto death* (Luther, Beza, Calvin, and many others), nor yet *in death* as the *sphere* of its rule (Tholuck, Philippi), but *instrumentally*, corresponding to the antithesis διὰ δικαιοσύνης εἰς ζωὴν αἰώνιον (which belong together). Sin has brought death into the world with it, and subjected all to death (ver. 12), ἐφ' ᾧ πάντες ἥμαρτον; thus sin exercised its dominion *in virtue of death*. This dominion however has given way to the dominion of grace, whose rule does not indeed abolish death, which having once entered into the world with sin has become the common lot of all, in itself, but accomplishes its object all the more blissfully, in that it confers a *righteousness redounding to everlasting life*.[1] And grace exercises this bliss-bringing rule *through the merit of its personal Mediator* (πρόξενος, Chrysostom) *Christ*, who has earned it for men through His expiatory death. The *full triumphant conclusion*, διὰ Ἰησοῦ Χριστοῦ τοῦ κυρίου ἡμῶν (comp. vii. 25; 1 Cor. xv. 57 *al.*) belongs to the entire thought ἡ χάρις βασιλεύσῃ.... ζ. αἰώνιον, upon which it impresses the *seal*. Here, also, the δικαιοσύνη is the righteousness of *faith* (not of life).

---

[1] The pregnant sense, which Hofmann, on ver. 14, attributes to the βασιλεύειν, and seeks to apply analogically here also (comp. Dietzsch), is here least of all appropriate.

CHAPTER VI.

Ver. 1. ἐπιμένωμεν] approved by Mill, Griesb. and others; adopted by Lachm. Tisch. and Fritzsche. The *Recepta* is ἐπιμενοῦμεν, contrary to decisive evidence (A B D E F G, min.); also contrary to K P ℵ, min., which have ἐπιμένομεν. Brought into conformity with ἐροῦμεν. — Ver. 11. After μέν Elz. has εἶναι against preponderating evidence. Supplementary addition, which is also variously placed. Notwithstanding Tisch. (8) has adopted it, but before νεκρούς, following B C ℵ*. — τῷ κυρίῳ ἡμῶν also, which Elz. has after Ἰησοῦ, is, according to decisive testimony, not genuine (an ascetic addition). — Ver. 12. ὑπακ. ταῖς ἐπιθ. αὐτοῦ] so also Lachm. and Tisch. following A B C* ℵ, min., and most vss. and Fathers. D E F G Clar. Boern. Iren. Tert. Vict. tunun., have ὑπακούειν αὐτῇ. Preferred by Rinck, and adopted by Scholz and Fritzsche. The reading of Elz.: ὑπακ. αὐτῇ ἐν ταῖς ἐπιθ. αὐτοῦ has least evidence. The most strongly attested ὑπακ. ταῖς ἐπιθ. αὐτοῦ appears to have been the original. From it the ὑπακ. αὐτῇ arose through αὐτῇ being marginally annexed to ταῖς ἐπιθ. αὐτ. as a gloss, to render it apparent, that in the case of the lusts of the body the ἁμαρτία (*original sin*) was to be understood. This gloss was adopted partly *instead of* τ. ἐπιθ. αὐτοῦ (so ὑπακ. αὐτῇ arose); and partly *along with* τ. ἐπιθ. αὐτοῦ, which latter course occasioned a connecting ἐν, and gave rise to the Recepta. — Ver. 15. ἁμαρτήσομεν] A B C D E K L P ℵ, min. and Clem. have ἁμαρτήσωμεν. Recommended by Griesb., adopted by Lachm. Tisch. and Fritzsche, and rightly on account of the decisive evidence in its favour. — Ver. 21. τὸ γὰρ τέλος] Lachm. reads τὸ μὲν γὰρ τέλος in agreement with B D* E F G ℵ* § 73, Syr. p. Theodoret. Rightly: how easily might the μέν *solitarium* be lost under the hands of unskilled copyists! Comp. Buttmann, *neut. Gr.* p. 313.

Chs. vi.-viii. *Moral results from the* δικαιοσύνη Θεοῦ.[1] Chapter

[1] Thus Paul certainly passes over from the field of the *gaining salvation* to that of its moral *preservation;* but not, as Th. Schott thinks, with a view to show the *non-necessity of the law* for the latter and so to *justify his acting as Apostle to the Gentiles*. In ch. vi. the law in fact is mentioned not as unnecessary,

vi. shows how it, so far from furthering immorality, on the contrary excludes the latter from the Christian state, and for the first time rightly establishes, promotes, and quickens true morality. Chap. vii. shows the same in relation to the law; and ch. viii. sets forth the blessed condition of those who as justified are morally free.

Ch. vi. 1-14. *Continuance in sin in order that grace may abound —that is a thing utterly opposed to the fellowship with Christ, into which we are brought by baptism ; for we are thereby rendered dead unto sin, and translated into a new moral life. Correspond therefore* (vv. 12-14) *to this new relation* (your ideal, ver. 14) *by your conduct.*

Ver. 1. Οὖν] In consequence of what is contained in v. 20, 21. — With ἐπιμένωμεν κ.τ.λ. Paul proposes to himself, as a possible inference from what he had just said " de pleonasmo gratiae" (Bengel), the problem, whose solution in the negative was now to be his further theme—a theme in itself of so decisive an importance, that it does not require the assumption of a *Jewish-Christian* church (Mangold) to make it intelligible. On the introduction in *interrogative* form by τί οὖν ἐροῦμεν, comp. Dissen, *ad Dem. de cor.* p. 346 (τί οὖν φημὶ δεῖν;). As however the "*what shall we say then ?*" inquires after a *maxim* in some sort of way to be inferred, the deliberative "*shall we continue, etc. ?*" could at once follow directly, without any need for supplying before it a repeated ἐροῦμεν, or μὴ ἐροῦμεν ὅτι, and for taking ἐπιμένωμεν in a *hortatory* sense (van Hengel, Hofmann). — ἐπιμένειν τῇ ἁμαρτ., *to continue in sin,* not to cease from it. Comp. xi. 22 f.; Col. i. 23; 1 Tim. iv. 16; Acts xiii. 43; Xen. *Hell.* iii. 4, 6 ; *Oec.* 14, 7 : ἐπιμένειν τῷ μὴ ἀδικεῖν.

Ver. 2. Μὴ γένοιτο] *Let it not be* (see on iii. 4), namely, that we continue in sin. — οἵτινες] *as those who,* contains the reason (of the πῶς ἔτι κ.τ.λ.). See on i. 25. The relative clause is put first with rhetorical emphasis, in order at once to make the *absurdity* of the maxim plainly apparent. Comp. Kühner, II. 2, p. 1104; Bernhardy, p. 299. — ἀπεθάν. τ. ἁμαρτ.] *The dying to sin,* which took place by baptism (see ver. 3), is *the abandonment of all life-communion with it experienced in himself* by the

but as the contrast to the state of grace (ver. 14 f.) ; and ch. vii. is occupied with something far loftier than its non-necessity. Of the justification of his apostolic working among the Gentiles, and of its bearing on the law, the Apostle says nothing.

convert (Col. ii. 20; Gal. ii. 19, vi. 14; 1 Pet. ii. 24). Comp. Theodoret: ἠρνήθης, φησὶ, τὴν ἁμαρτίαν καὶ νεκρὸς αὐτῇ γέγονας. This moral change, which has taken place in him, has put an end to the determining influence of sin over him; in relation to it *he has ceased to be still in life.* Similar is the Platonic conception in Macrob. *Somn. Scip.* i. 13: "mori etiam dicitur, cum anima adhuc in corpore constituta corporeas illecebras philosophia docente contemnit et cupiditatum dulces insidias reliquasque omnes exuit passiones." Michaelis, Cramer, Storr, Flatt, Nitzsch (*de discr. revelat.* etc. II. p. 233) take the sense to be: we who *on account of sin* have died (with Christ), *i.e.* who have to regard ourselves as if, on account of sin (or Nitzsch: "ad eripiendam peccati vim mortiferam"), we had ourselves endured what Christ suffered. But in this view the main point "*with Christ*" is arbitrarily imported; and see ver. 11. — πῶς] denotes the *possibility* which is negatived by the question. The *having died to sin*, and the *living* in it (as the life-element, comp. Gal. ii. 20), are mutually exclusive. — ζήσομεν] purely future. How is it possible that we *shall be living* in it (in its fellowship) still (ἔτι), namely, at any future time whatever after the occurrence of that ἀπεθάνομεν? The very weakly attested reading preferred by Hofmann, ζήσωμεν, is only a case of mechanical conformity with ἐπιμένωμεν in ver. 1.

Ver. 3. *Ἤ] or*, if this (ver. 2) should still appear doubtful. See Hartung, *Partikell.* II. p. 61; Baeumlein, *Partik.* p. 132. Comp. vii. 1. — ἀγνοεῖτε] presupposes an *acquaintance* with the moral nature of baptism; it must in fact have been an *experimental* acquaintance. With this *knowledge*, how *absurd* would be that ζήσομεν ἐν αὐτῇ! Comp. 1 Cor. vi. 2. — ὅσοι] *all we who*, not *stronger* than οἵτινες, but put *differently*; not characterising, but designating the *whole collectively*. — ἐβαπτίσθημεν εἰς Χ. Ἰ. εἰς τὸν θάν. κ.τ.λ.] *we, who were baptized in reference to Christ Jesus*[1] (we who through baptism became those specifically

[1] Βαπτίζειν εἰς never means anything else than *to baptize in reference to, in respect to;* and the more special definitions of its import are furnished simply by the context. Comp. on Matth. xxviii. 19; 1 Cor. x. 2; Gal. iii. 27. — On εἰς Χ. Ἰησοῦν comp. Acts ii. 38, viii. 16, xix. 5. Undoubtedly the name "*Jesus*" was named in baptizing. But the conception of *becoming immersed into Christ* (in Rückert and others, and again in Weiss, *bibl. Theol.* p. 343) is to be set aside, and is not to be supported by the figurative expression in Gal. iii. 27. The mystic character of our passage is not produced by so vague a sensuous conception,

belonging to Him), *were baptized in reference to His death* ; *i.e.* we were brought through our baptism into the fellowship of His death; so that we have a real share ethically in His death, through the cessation of all our life for sin. Theodore of Mopsuestia : τὸ βάπτισμα κοινωνοὺς ποιεῖ τοῦ θανάτου τοῦ Χριστοῦ. Ambrosiaster: "cum baptizamur, *commorimur Christo ;*" Bengel : " perinde est, ac si eo momento Christus pro tali homine, et talis homo pro Christo pateretur, moreretur, sepeliretur." This interpretation, namely of the spiritual *fellowship* produced through baptism (prepared for by the repentance and πίστις that preceded baptism, accomplished by the baptism itself, Gal. iii. 27; Col. ii. 11 f.; Tit. iii. 5), is required by the context in ver. 2 (ἀπεθάνομεν), ver. 4 (συνετάφημεν), and ver. 5 f. It is therefore not the idea of *imitation* (Reiche, Köllner, following Grotius and others), but that of the *dying along with* (συσταυροῦσθαι, ver. 6 ; Gal. ii. 20 ; comp. 2 Cor. v. 14) unto which, *i.e.* in order to the accomplishment of which in us, we were baptized. The *efficient cause* of this fellowship of death is the divine grace, which forgives sin and grants the Holy Spirit to him who becomes baptized ; the *means of this grace* is baptism itself; the *appropriating cause* is faith, and the *causa meritoria* the death of Christ.[1] Observe here also, however, that the spheres of justification and sanctification are not intermixed. The justified person becomes sanctified, not the converse. In baptism man receives forgiveness of sins through faith (comp. Acts ii. 38 ; xxii. 16) ; justified by which he also becomes partaker of the virtue of the Holy Spirit in the sacrament unto new life (Tit. iii. 5). " Liberationem a *reatu* peccati vel justificationem consequitur liberatio a *dominio* peccati, ut justificati non vivant peccato, sed peccato mortui

—which moreover has all the passages against it in which βαπτίζειν is coupled with ὄνομα (Matth. xxviii. 19 ; Acts ii. 38, x. 48, xix. 5 ; 1 Cor. i. 13)—but is based simply on the ethical consciousness of that intimate appertaining to Christ, into which baptism translates its recipients.

[1] Namely as the *atoning death* (v. 6, 10, 21), the appropriation of which shall be attended with the saving effect of a new life belonging to Him, 2 Cor. v. 14, 15. If this death thus becomes "*the end, once for all existent, of the relation of the world to God as determined by sin*" (Hofmann), that is the divinely willed *ethical result*, which faith obtains from the ἱλαστήριον, inasmuch as the believer realises his being dead to the power of sin with Christ, who in His expiatory death underwent the killing power of sin and therewith died to that power (vv. 9, 10). Comp. ver. 10 f.

Domino," Calovius. Compare ἀπελούσασθε, ἡγιάσθητε 1 Cor. vi. 11, and the remarks thereon. The *latter* is the fellowship in dying and living with Christ, which is accomplished in baptism by the operation of the Spirit; see on Gal. iii. 27; 1 Cor. xii. 13; Acts xix. 2 f.; Weiss, *bibl. Theol.* p. 345 f. But it is of course obvious that the idea of the baptism of children was wholly foreign to this view of the Apostle based on experience.

Ver. 4. An inference from ver. 3, by which the impossibility indicated in ver. 2 is now made completely evident.—*Buried with Him therefore* (not merely *dead* with Him, but, as the dead Christ was *buried* in order to rise again, *buried with* Him also) *were we, in that we were baptized into His death*. The recipient of baptism, who by his baptism enters into the fellowship of *death* with Christ, is necessarily also in the act of baptism ethically *buried* with Him (1 Cor. xv. 4), because *after* baptism he is spiritually *risen* with Him. In *reality* this burial with Him is not a moral fact *distinct* from the having died with Him, as actual burial is distinct from actual dying; but it sets forth the fulness and completeness of the relation, of which the recipient, in accordance with the *form* of baptism, so far as the latter takes place through κατάδυσις and ἀνάδυσις (see Suicer, *Thes.*), becomes conscious *successively*. The recipient—thus has Paul figuratively represented the process—is conscious, (*a*) in the baptism *generally*: now am I entering into fellowship with the *death* of Christ, εἰς τὸν θάνατον αὐτοῦ βαπτίζομαι; (*b*) in *the immersion in particular*: now am I becoming *buried* with Christ; (*c*) and then, in the emergence: now I *rise* to the new life with Christ. Comp. on Col. ii. 12. — εἰς τὸν θάνατον] is necessarily, after ver. 3, to be joined with διὰ τοῦ βαπτίσμ., in which case, since one can say βαπτίζεσθαι εἴς τι, the connecting article was not required (comp. on Gal. iii. 26; Eph. iii. 13); consequently: *through baptism unto death*. It is not however specially the death of *Christ* that is again meant, as if αὐτοῦ were again annexed; but the description is *generalised*, agreeably to the context, in a way that could not be misunderstood. Whosoever, namely, as Paul has just set forth in ver. 3, has been baptized unto the death of *Christ*, has in fact thereby received baptism *unto death;* *i.e.* such a baptism that, taken away by it from his previous vital activity, he has become one belonging to death, one who has fallen under its sway. This however is just that relation of moral death, which, in the concrete, is the fellowship of the death of *Christ*. The connection with συνετάφ., in which εἰς τ. θάνατον is sometimes referred to the death of *Christ* (Grotius, Baumgarten-Crusius), and sometimes to the death of *sin* (Calovius, Wolf, Winzer, *Progr.* 1831), is erroneous, for this reason, that whosoever is buried does not *come* into death, but *is* in it already; and hence "the becoming buried into death" would yield quite an *incongruous* conception. This also applies against the expedient tried by Hofmann of making θάνατος here the *death-state* of Christ, unto which we were given up. Even in this view that incongruity continues:[1] but after ver. 3 θάνατος can only be again *death* simply, not *state of death* (as if Paul could not have conveyed that sense by εἰς τὸ μνημεῖον, or εἰς τοὺς νεκρούς, or in some other suitable way). Observe, moreover, how Paul here also, since he has the *bodily* resurrection of Christ in view,[2] mentions specially the correlative of the *burial* that preceded it. Comp. on 1 Cor. xv. 4. — ἵνα] *purpose* of the συνετάφημεν.... θάνατον, and this statement of purpose has the chief importance, corresponding to the πῶς ἔτι ζήσομεν ἐν αὐτῇ in ver. 2. — διὰ τῆς δόξ. τ. πατρός] *through the majesty of the Father* was the resurrection of Christ brought about. The δόξα, כָּבוֹד, the glorious collective perfection of God, certainly effected the raising of Jesus chiefly as *omnipotence* (1 Cor. vi. 14; 2 Cor. xiii. 4; Eph. i. 19 f.); but the comprehensive significance of the word— selected with conscious solemnity, and in highest accordance with the glorious victory of the Son—is not to be curtailed on

---

[1] This cannot be got rid of by any artificial turns (like that of Hofmann: "His burial removed Him from the sphere of sin expiated through His death.... whereby His existence in the world of sin *came to a complete close*"). Certainly the θάνατος of the Lord, even regarded as a state, occurred at that great moment when He cries His τετέλεσται and departs; and in nowise has He been *translated* into the θάνατος through His *burial*.

[2] *i.e.* His resurrection *as respects the buried body;* so that the latter no longer remained in the grave, but came forth thence living and immortal. That the body of Christ "*vanished*" and "*made room*" for a new pneumatic body (Holsten, *z. Ev. d. Paul u. Petr.* p. 133), is an unsuitable conception, seeing that the pneumatic body must necessarily have been assumed even in death, and independently of the burial of the old body. Thus the resurrection of Jesus would be nothing else than the change of body that took place in death.

that account (in opposition to Koppe, Baumgarten-Crusius, and earlier expositors). According to the invariable representation of the N. T. *God* is the raiser of Jesus (iv. 24, viii. 11; Acts ii. 24, 31 ff. *et al.;* see on John i. 19); but yet the δόξα of God does not in this case any more than elsewhere in the N. T. denote *God Himself* (Langer, *Judenth. in Paläst.* p. 210 ff.). Erroneously however Theodoret, Theophylact, and several Fathers explain: διὰ τ. δόξ. τ. πατρ., τουτέστι διὰ τῆς οἰκείας θεότητος. Linguistic usage admits as in itself allowable the view of Castalio and Carpzov: "*in paterna gloria* resurrexit," so that διά would be used of the state; to which also van Hengel inclines. But, had Paul desired to express a relation corresponding to the ἐν καιν. ζ. in the apodosis, he must have inserted ἐν also; since the conception of the raising of Jesus *through* the Father was one of so solemn importance, and all the more appropriate here, since believers also owe their moral resurrection-life to the Father of Christ (Eph. ii. 10 *al.*); it is in fact the life of regeneration. Besides, the paterna gloria was attained by Christ only through His *ascension*. See on Luke xxiv. 26. — ἐν καινότητι ζωῆς] *in a new* (moral) *constitution of life;*[1] a stronger way of bringing out the idea of καινότης, than ἐν ζωῇ καινῇ would be, for which it does not stand (in opposition to Grotius, Koppe, Reiche, and others). See Winer, p. 221 [E. T. 309]. Comp. vii. 6. According to van Hengel ζωῆς is the genitive of *apposition:* "in novo rerum statu, *qui vita est.*" But this *qui vita est* is self-evident; and therefore the emphasis must remain upon καινότητι. This newness is the ethical analogue of the new estate in which Christ was alive from the dead, conceived in contrast to the παλαιότης which prevailed prior to baptism. Comp. ver. 8.

Ver. 5. Confirmatory elucidation (γάρ) of the previous ἵνα ὥσπερ κ.τ.λ.—σύμφυτος, which in classic authors usually means *innate, naturally belonging to* (see the passages from Plato in Ast, *Lex.* III. p. 313, Eur. *Andr.* 955; comp. 2 Macc. iii. 22), is here *grown together* (Theophr, *de caus. plant.* v. 5, 2; LXX. Zech. xi. 2; Amos ix. 14). This figurative expression represents the most intimate union of being, like our *coalescent* with anything (qui or quod *coaluit* cum aliqua re). Plat. *Phaedr.* p. 246 A; Aesch.

---

[1] τὴν καινὴν πολιτείαν τὴν κατὰ τὸν παρόντα βίον, ἐκ τῆς τῶν τρόπων γινομένην. Ὅπου γὰρ ὁ πόρνος γένηται σώφρων καὶ ὁ πλεονέκτης ἐλεήμων καὶ ὁ τραχὺς ἥμερος, καὶ ἐνταῦθα ἀνάστασις γέγονεν, Chrysostom.

Ag. and Klausen *in loc.* p. 111. In the classics συμφυής is the more usual form for this idea, especially with γίνεσθαι (Plato, *Soph.* p. 247 D, *Tim.* p. 45 D, p. 88 A; Plut. *Lycurg.* 25). Hence: *For, if we have become* (through baptism, vv. 3, 4) *such as are grown together with that which is the likeness of His death*, (comp. on i. 23), *i.e.* persons, to whose nature it inseparably belongs to present in themselves that which resembles His death, *so also shall we be grown together with the likeness of His resurrection*. On ὁμοίωμα comp. i. 23, v. 14, viii. 3. The rendering of σύμφυτοι by *complantati* (Vulgate, Luther), in connection with which Chrysostom, Origen, Theodore of Mopsuestia, Theodoret, Theophylact, Beza, and others explain the figure of the plant by the *fruits* of the ethical burial, is linguistically incorrect, as if the word came not from συμφύω, but from συμφυτεύω (comp. φυτευτός, l'lat. *Rep.* p. 510 A, ἀφύτευτος, Xen. *Oec.* 20, 22). The interpretation *engrafted* (Erasmus, Calvin, Estius, Cornelius à Lapide, Klee) is likewise without linguistic evidence, and does not suit the abstract τῷ ὁμοιώματι. — τῷ ὁμοιώμ. τοῦ θανάτου αὐτοῦ] *i.e.* the condition corresponding in similarity of form to His death, which has specifically and indissolubly become ours. This *ethical conformity with His death*, however, the growing together with which took place through our baptism, is just that moral death to sin, vv. 3, 4, in which the spiritual communion in death with Christ consists. τ. ὁμ. τ. θ. α. is to be joined with σύμφυτοι (Vulgate, Chrysostom, Beza, Calvin, Estius, Koppe, Tholuck, Rückert, Reiche. Olshausen, de Wette, Philippi, and others; now including Hofmann). Others however take it as the dative of the *instrument*, and supply τῷ Χριστῷ to σύμφυτοι: "*for, if we have entered into close union with Christ through the* ὁμοίωμα *of His death*," etc. So Erasmus, Beza, Grotius, Flatt, Fritzsche, Krehl, Baumgarten-Crusius, Maier, Baur, van Hengel, and Reithmayr; also Weiss, *bibl. Theol.* p. 344. Nevertheless it is arbitrary to *separate* τω ὁμ. from σύμφ. γεγ., seeing that it *stands* beside it and in a structural respect *presents* itself most naturally with it, and also as belonging to it yields a very *appropriate sense*; and on the other hand to attach to σύμφ. a word which Paul *has* not put in, and which he *must have* put in, if he would not lead his readers astray. Still more mistaken is the view of Bisping, that σύμφ. belongs to τοῦ θανάτ. αὐτοῦ, and that τῷ ὁμοιώμ. comes in between them instrumentally. Hofmann has rightly abandoned this tortuous interpretation, which he formerly followed. Comp. on the right connection Cyril, *Catech.* iii. 12; and even *Martyr. Ignat.* 5 : ἐμαυτὸν.... σύμφυτον θέσθαι τῷ τοῦ θανάτου αὐτοῦ ὁμοιώματι. — ἀλλὰ καί] *but also.* ἀλλά, for the speedy and more emphatic introduction of the contrasted element, as frequently also in the classics, at the head of the apodosis; see on 1 Cor. iv. 15; Col. ii. 5. — τῆς ἀναστάσεως] cannot, in keeping with the protasis, depend directly upon the σύμφυτοι to be again understood (Erasmus, Calvin and others; including Rückert, Olshausen, de Wette and Krehl), but only upon the τῷ ὁμοιώματι to be supplied (Beza, Grotius, Estius, and many others; including Winzer, Fritzsche, Baumgarten-Crusius, Maier, Philippi, Tholuck, Ewald, van Hengel, and Hofmann), so that when completed it would run : ἀλλὰ καὶ τῷ ὁμοιώματι τῆς ἀναστάσεως αὐτοῦ σύμφυτοι ἐσόμεθα. The former view is indeed likewise unobjectionable grammatically, for σύμφυτοι may also stand with the genitive (Plat. *Phil.* p. 51 D, *Def.* p. 413 C, Bernhardy, p. 171); but the latter is suggested by the context, and presents itself easily enough and without harshness. Further, it is self-evident, after ver. 4, that in τ. ἀναστ. we are not to think of the resurrection of our *body* (Tertullian, Chrysostom, Ambrosiaster, Oecumenius, Cornelius à Lapide, and others; comp. also Ewald), or of this as *included* (Koppe and Klee). — ἐσόμεθα] receives its only correct interpretation from its relation to, and bearing on, the clause expressive of the purpose, ἵνα.... ἐν καιν. ζ. περιπ. in ver. 4, according to which it must express the *necessarily certain.* Matthiae, p. 1122; Kühner, II. 1, p. 148, ed. 2. Compare πῶς ἔτι ζήσομεν ver. 2. The sense of *willing* ("ut reviviscamus curabimus," Fritzsche) is not suggested by the connection; nor is that of a *summons* (Olshausen, Rückert, and older expositors); but it is rather the expression of what shall certainly be the case, as the consequence of the σύμφυτοι γεγόν. τῷ ὁμοιώμ. τοῦ θανάτου αὐτοῦ assumed as real in the protasis; *it cannot be otherwise ;* with the having become σύμφυτοι this ἐσέσθαι is *given ;* with that fact having begun and taken place is posited this further development, which necessarily attaches itself thereto.

Ver. 6. Τοῦτο γινώσκοντες] Definition to τῆς ἀναστάσ. ἐσόμεθα, which *objective* relation is confirmed by the corresponding experimental *conscious knowledge* (comp. εἰδότες in ver. 9): *since we know this;* not a mere continuation of the construction instead of κ. τοῦτο γινώσκομεν (Philippi), as the participle is never so used, not even in ch. ii. 4; nor yet to be conceived as *in the train* of the ἐσόμεθα (Hofmann), as if Paul had expressed himself by some such word as ὥστε, or with the telic infinitive (γνῶναι). Respecting τοῦτο see on ch. ii. 3. — ὁ παλ. ἡμ. ἄνθρ.] *i.e. our old ego*—our personality in its entire sinful condition before regeneration (John iii. 3; Tit. iii. 5). Comp. Eph. iv. 22; Col. iii. 9. From the standpoint of the καινότης πνεύματος, constituting the Christian self-consciousness, the Christian sees his pre-Christian ethical personality as his *old* self no longer to be found in life, as the person which he had formerly *been* Comp. on 2 Cor. v. 17; Eph. ii. 10. — συνεσταυρώθη] namely, when we were baptized and thereby transplanted into the fellowship of death. See on vv. 3, 4. This special expression of the being killed with Him is selected simply because Christ was slain on the *cross;* not as Grotius and others, including Olshausen, hold: " quia sicut per crucem *non sine gravi dolore* ad exitum pervenitur, ita illa natura (the old man) sine dolore non extinguitur." Compare Umbreit. The simple ἵνα καταργ. is not at all in keeping with this far-fetched reference, which is not supported by Gal. ii. 19 f.; but just as little with the reference to the *disgrace* of crucifixion (Hofmann). — ἵνα καταργ.] Design of the ὁ παλ. ἡμ. ἄνθρ. συνεστ.: *in order that the body of sin might be destroyed,* i.e. *the body belonging to the power of sin,* ruled by sin.[1] Comp. vii. 24. The old man had *such* a body; and *this* σῶμα was to be destroyed, put out of existence by the crucifixion with Christ; consequently not the body *in itself,* but *in so far* as it is the sin-body, becoming determined by sin in its expressions of life to sinful πράξεσι (viii. 13). The propriety of this interpretation appears from vv. 7, 12, 13, 23. Comp. on Col. ii. 11. If we explain it merely of " *the body as seat or organ of sin,*" the idea would not in itself be un-Pauline, as Reiche thinks; for the σῶμα would in fact appear not as the soliciting

---

[1] It is self-evident that Paul might have said also τὸ σῶμα τῆς σαρκός, as in Col. ii. 11. But his whole theme (ver. 1) suggested his saying τῆς ἁμαρτίας. He might even have written merely ἡ σάρξ, but τὸ σῶμα was given in the immediate context (συνεσταυρ.).

agent of sin (not as the σάρξ), but as its vehicle, in itself morally indifferent, but serving sin as the organic instrument of its vital activity (see Stirm in the *Tübing. Zeitschr. f. Theol.* 1834, 3, p. 10 ff.); but καταργηθῇ is decisive against this view. For this could neither mean *destroyed, annihilated*, because in fact even the body of the regenerate is a σῶμα τ. ἁμαρτίας in the sense assumed (ver. 12); nor even *evacuaretur* (Tertullian, Augustine), *rendered inactive, inoperative,* partly because *then* the idea of σάρξ would be assigned to σῶμα, and partly because it is only the conception of the *destruction* of the body which corresponds to the conception of crucifixion. Others take the corpus peccati *figuratively;* either so, that *sin* is conceived *under the figure of a body* with significant reference to its being crucified (so Fathers in Suicer, *Thes.* II. p. 1215, Piscator, Pareus, Castalio, Hammond, Homberg, Calovius, Koppe, Flatt, and Olshausen; also Reiche, conceiving sin as a monster); or, similarly to this mode of apprehending it, in such a way as to find the sense: "*the mass of sin,*" τὴν ἀπὸ τῶν διαφορῶν μερῶν πονηρίας συγκειμένην .... κακίαν, Chrysostom. So Ambrosiaster, Pseudo-Hieronymus, Theophylact, Erasmus, Cornelius à Lapide, Grotius, Estius, Reithmayr and others; so also Calvin, who however takes the corpus peccati as a designation of the natural man itself, which is a *massa, ex peccato conflata.* Philippi also ultimately comes to the *massa peccati*, which is conceived as an organism having members, as σῶμα; so likewise Jatho and Julius Müller, *v. d. Sünde,* I. p. 460, ed. 5; also Baur (" as it were *the substance of sin*"). But all these interpretations are at variance partly with the Pauline *usus loquendi* in general, and partly with ver. 12 in particular, where ἐν τῷ θνητῷ ὑμ. σώματι by its reference to our passage confirms our view of the σῶμα. The right view is held substantially by Theodoret, Theophylact 2, Bengel and others, including Tholuck, Köllner, de Wette, Rückert, Fritzsche, Maier, Nielsen, Hofmann and Weiss; whereas Baumgarten-Crusius, and also Ernesti, *Urspr. d. Sünde,* I. p. 113, convert σῶμα into the idea of *state of life.* — τοῦ μηκέτι δουλ. κ.τ.λ.] " finem abolitionis notat," Calvin. The sin, which is committed, is conceived as a ruler to whom *service* is rendered. See John viii. 34.

Ver. 7. Establishment of the τοῦ μηκέτι δουλ. ἡμ. τῇ. ἁμ. by the general proposition: *whosoever is dead, is acquitted from sin.*

— ὁ ἀποθαν.] is explained by many of *ethical* death. So Erasmus, Calovius, Homberg, Bengel and others, including Koppe, Flatt, Glöckler, Olshausen, Tholuck (who regards sin as *creditor*), de Wette ("whosoever has died to sin, he—alone—is acquitted from sin"), Rothe, Krehl, Philippi (whosoever is ethically dead, over him has sin lost its right to impeach and to control, just as Bengel explains it), also van Hengel, Jatho, and Märcker. But neither the nature of the *general proposition*, which forms in fact the major premiss in the argument, and of which only the *application* is to be made (in the minor proposition) to ethical dying; nor the *tautological* relation, which would result between subject and predicate, can permit this explanation. The conception of *ethical* dying recurs only in *the sequel*, and hence σὺν Χριστῷ is added to ἀπεθάνομεν in ver. 8, so that Paul in this development of his views draws a sharp distinction between the being dead in the spiritual (vv. 6, 8) and in the ordinary sense. We must therefore explain ver. 7 as a general proposition regarding death in the ordinary sense, and consequently regarding *physical* death (so rightly Hofmann), but not specially of the death by *execution*, through which sin is expiated (Alethaeus, Wolf and others; with this view they compare δεδικ., the juristic expression: *he is justified;* see Michaelis' note); for *any such* peculiar reference of the still wholly unrestricted ἀποθανών is forbidden by the very generality of the proposition, although for δεδικαίωται passages might be cited like Plat. *Legg.* II. p. 934 B; Aristot. *Eth.* v. 9. — δεδικ. ἀπὸ τ. ἁμ.] "*The dead person is made just from sin,*" *i.e.* he is in point of fact justified and acquitted from sin, he is placed by death in the position of a δίκαιος, who is such thenceforth; not as if he were now absolved from and rid of the guilt of his sins committed in life, but *in so far as the dead person sins no more*, no longer δουλεύει τῇ ἁμαρτίᾳ, from whose power, as from a legal claim urged against him during his life in the body, he has been actually released by death as through a decree of acquittal. Comp. Köstlin in the *Jahrb. f. Deutsche Theol.* 1856, p. 98 f.; Th. Schott, p. 260, and Hofmann; also Baur, *neut. Theol.* p. 161 f.; Delitzsch, Illustrations to his Hebrew version, p. 84. Just for this reason has Paul added ἀπὸ τῆς ἁμαρτίας (comp. Acts xiii. 38; Ecclus. xxvi. 29; *Test. XII. patr.* p. 541), which would have been quite superfluous, had he taken δεδικαίωται, *justus constitutus est,* in the dogmatic sense of his doctrine of justification. The proposition itself, moreover, *is an axiom of the popular traditional mode of view,* which Paul uses for his purpose as *admitted.* This axiom has also its relative truth, and that partly in so far as the dead person has put off the σῶμα τῆς σαρκός with which he committed his sins (Col. ii. 11), partly in so far as with death the dominion of law over the man ceases (vii. 1), and partly in so far as in death all the relations are dissolved which supplied in life the objects of sinning.[1] For the discussion of the question as to the absolute truth of the proposition, in its connection with Biblical anthropology and eschatology, there was no occasion at all here,[2] where it is only used as an auxiliary clause, and ex concesso. Comp. 1 Pet. iv. 1. Usteri mistakenly explains it: by death man has suffered the *punishment,* and thus *expiated* his guilt. For that Paul does not here express the Jewish dogma: "death as the punishment for sin *expiates* the guilt of sin" (see Eisenmenger, *entdeckt. Judenth.* II. p. 283 f.) is proved partly by the irrelevancy of such a sense to the context (γάρ); and partly by its inconsistency with the doctrines of the Apostle as to justification by faith and as to the judgment, according to which death cannot set free from the guilt-obligation of sin. Ewald makes a *new* idea be brought in at ver. 7: "Even in common life, in the case of one who is dead, the sins of his previous life cannot be further prosecuted and punished, he passes for justified and acquitted of sin ....; if in addition sin as a power has been broken by Christ (ver. 9 f.), then we may assuredly believe," etc., ver. 8. But γάρ in ver. 7 indicates its connection with *what goes before,* so that it is only *with the* δέ in ver. 8 that a new thought is introduced. Besides, we should expect, in the case of the assumed course of thought, an οὖν instead of the δέ in ver. 8. Finally, it is not clear how that rule of common law was to serve as a joint ground for the faith of becoming alive with Christ.

[1] The Greek expositors—who already give substantially our explanation—have confined themselves to this point. Chrysostom: ἀπήλλακται τὸ λοιπὸν τοῦ ἁμαρτάνειν νεκρὸς κείμενος. Theodoret: τίς γὰρ ἐθεάσατο πώποτε νεκρὸν ἢ γάμον ἀλλότριον διορύττοντα, ἢ μιαιφονίᾳ τὰς χεῖρας φοινίττοντα κ.τ.λ. Melancthon compares the proverb: νεκρὸς οὐ δάκνει, Beza the saying of Anacreon: ὁ νεκρὸς οὐκ ἐπιθυμεῖ, Grotius that of Aeschylus: οὐδὲν ἄλγος ἅπτεται νεκρῶν. Comp. Soph. *O. C.* 955.

[2] Compare Melancthon: "Ceterum hoc sciamus, diabolos et omnes damnatos in omni aeternitate horribilia peccata facere, quia sine fine irascuntur Deo," etc.

Ver. 8 f. *Carrying onward* the discussion by the metabatic δέ· and thereby passing from the *negative* side of the having died with Christ as proved in personal consciousness (τοῦτο γινώσκοντες, ver. 6) in. vv. 6, 7, to its *positive* side, which is likewise exhibited as based on the consciousness of faith (πιστεύομεν). " But if we have *died* (according to vv. 6, 7) with Christ, we believe that we shall also *live* with Him, since we know," etc. etc. — πιστεύ-ομεν] expresses, not confidence in the divine aid (Fritzsche), or in the divine promise (Baumgarten-Crusius), or in God not leaving His work of grace in us unfinished (Philippi); but simply the *being convinced of our* συζήσομεν αὐτῷ ; in so far, namely, as the having died with Christ is, seeing that He has risen and dieth no more, in the consciousness of faith the necessary premiss, and thus the ground for belief as to our becoming alive with Him. If the former, the ἀπεθάνομεν σὺν Χριστῷ, be true, we cannot doubt the latter. — συζήσομεν αὐτῷ] must necessarily be understood, in accordance with the preceding and following context (ver. 11), of the *ethical* participation in the new ever-lasting life of Christ. Whosoever has died with Christ is now also of the belief that his life, *i.e.* the positive active side of his moral being and nature, shall be a fellowship of life with the exalted Christ; that is, shall be able to be nothing else than this. This communion of life is the ἐν Χριστῷ and Χριστὸν ἐν ἡμῖν εἶναι. In the full consciousness of it Paul says : ζῶ δὲ οὐκέτι ἐγώ, ζῇ δὲ ἐν ἐμοὶ Χριστός (Gal. ii. 20). At the same time it is not to be explained as if an ἀεί or the like stood beside συζήσομεν (without falling away), as is done by Tholuck; compare Theophylact. Others, in opposition to the context, hold that what is meant is the future participation of Christians in the bliss of the glorified Saviour (Flatt, Reiche, Maier, following Origen, Chrysostom, Theodoret, Grotius, and Heumann); and others still, at variance alike with the definiteness and unity of the sense, interpret it of the earthly moral and the eternal blessed life *together* (Sebastian Schmid, Böhme, Rosenmuller; and not rejected by de Wette). The reference or joint-reference to the future glory is not required either by the *future*, which, on the contrary, demands the same rendering exactly as ἐσόμεθα in ver. 5, nor by πιστεύομεν (see above). — εἰδότες, ὅτι κ.τ.λ.] *Since we know, that*, etc. Were we, namely, obliged to fear that Christ is still subject to the power of death,[1] that his life is not a perfected life, in that case we should lack the adequate secure *ground of faith* for that πιστεύομεν κ.τ.λ. The being assured that Christ liveth eternally and dieth no more (Acts xiii. 34), lends to our faith in our own moral communion of life with Him its basis and firm footing; without that knowledge this faith would be wanting in that which gives it legitimacy and guarantee. For who can cherish the conviction that he stands in that holy communion of resurrection-life with Christ, if he should be compelled to doubt whether his Lord, though indeed risen, might not again fall a victim to death ? This thought would only keep us aloof from that faith and make it a moral impossibility for us since it would set before us the prospect of a similar perishing of the new life which we had gained. Hofmann, who makes a new sentence begin with εἰδότες, which is to continue till ver. 11, might have been warned against doing so by the absence of a particle (οὖν); and should have been decisively precluded from it by the tortuous way in which, if ver. 10 is set aside in a parenthesis, it is necessary to obtain a forced regimen for the passage. — θάνατος αὐτοῦ οὐκέτι κυρ.] no longer dependent on ὅτι, but an independent and therefore all the more emphatic repetition of the important thought: *death is no longer Lord over Him*, has no more power over Him, such as it once had at the crucifixion. Comp. 1 Cor. xv. 25.

Ver. 10. Proof of the θάνατος αὐτοῦ οὐκέτι κυριεύει.[2] — ὃ γὰρ ἀπέθανε] ὃ is in any case the accusative of the object. But whether Paul conceived it as: *for as to what concerns His death* (see Vigerus, ed. Herm. p. 34; Frotscher and Breitenbach, *ad Xen. Hier.* 6, 12; Matthiae, p. 1063), or *what*, i.e. *the death which He died* (so Rückert, Fritzsche, de Wette, Philippi; see Bernhardy, p. 106 f.; comp. on Gal. ii. 20) cannot be determined, since both renderings suit the correct interpretation of what

---

[1] Death *had become* lord over Him, because in obedience to God (Phil. ii. 6 ff.) Christ had subjected Himself to its power, so that He ἐσταυρώθη ἐξ ἀσθενείας (2 Cor. xiii. 4). The κυριεύειν of death over Him was therefore a thing willed by God (v. 8-10), and realised through the voluntary obedience of Jesus. See John x. 18; Matth. xx. 28.

[2] Not a parenthetical *intervening clause* (Hofmann), which is appropriate neither to the essential *importance* of the sentence in the train of thought, nor to the *application* which it receives in ver. 11.

follows. Yet the latter, analogous to the expression θάνατον θανεῖν, is to be preferred as the more simple, and as uniform with Gal. ii. 20. — τῇ ἁμαρτίᾳ ἀπέθ.] the relation of the dative is to be determined from νεκροὺς τῇ ἁμ. in ver. 11; therefore it can be nothing else than what is contained in ἀπεθάν. τῇ ἁμ. in ver. 2 (comp. Hofmann), namely: *he is dead to sin* (dative of reference), *i.e.* His dying *concerned* sin; and indeed so that the latter (namely the sin of the world, conceived as power) has now, after He has suffered death on account of it, become without influence upon Him and has no more power over Him; He submitted Himself to its power in His death, but through that death *He has died to its power*.[1] So also have we (ver. 11) to esteem ourselves as dead to sin (νεκροὺς τῇ ἁμ.), as rescued from its grasp through our ethical death with Christ, in such measure that we are released from and rid of the influence of this power antagonistic to God. The close accordance of this view of τῇ ἁμ. ἀπέθ. with the context (according to vv. 11 and 2) is decisive against the explanations of the dative deviating from it, such as: *ad expianda peccata* (Pareus, Piscator, Grotius, Michaelis, and others including Olshausen); or: *ad expianda tollendaque peccata* (Koppe, Flatt, Reiche, Fritzsche, Philippi); or: *in order to destroy the power of sin* (Chrysostom, Beza, Calvin, Bengel, and others, including Ewald and Umbreit). Rückert, Köllner, and de Wette wish to abide by an *indefinite* reference of the death of Jesus to sin as the remote object; but this simply explains nothing, and leaves only a *formal* parallelism remaining.—ἐφάπαξ] *for once*, with emphasis, excluding repetition, *once for all.* Comp. Heb. vii. 27, ix. 12, x. 10; Lucian, *Dem. euc.* 21. — ζῇ τ. Θεῷ] *vivit Deo*, namely so, that now in His estate of exaltation, after He has through His death died to the power of sin, His life *belongs to God, i.e.* stands to God *in the relation of being dependent on, and of being determined by, Him.* The contrast to the preceding yields the *excluding* sense. Christ's earthly life, namely, was also a ζῆν τῷ Θεῷ, but was at the same time exposed to the death-power of

---

[1] Rich. Schmidt, *Paul. Christol.* p. 55, justly insists that Christ for His own person died to sin, but further on (p. 59), ends in finding an *ideal*, not a real relation. But He died *really* to sin, inasmuch as He took upon Himself, in the death of the cross, the curse of the law; after which human sin had now no longer any power over Him. Compare on ver. 3.

human sin, which is now no longer the case, inasmuch as His life rescued from death is wholly determined by the fellowship with God. This latter portion of the verse belongs also to the proof of ver. 9, since it is in fact just the (exclusive) belonging to God of Christ's life, that makes it certain that death reigns no longer over Him; ὡς ζῶν τῷ Θεῷ he can no longer be παθητός (Acts xxvi. 23), which He previously was, until in obedience to God ἐξ ἀσθενείας He was crucified (2 Cor. xiii. 4).

Ver. 11. Application of ver. 10 to the readers.—Although in ver. 10 there was no mention of a λογίζεσθαι on the part of Christ, we are not, with Griesbach and Koppe, to break up the discourse by the punctuation: οὕτω καὶ ὑμεῖς λογίζεσθε κ.τ.λ. (comp. on the contrary Luke xvii. 10).—*Accordingly reckon ye yourselves also* (like Christ) *as dead*, etc. λογίζεσθε, namely, containing the standard by which they are to apprehend their moral life-position in its reality, is not, with Bengel and Hofmann, to be taken as *indicative*, but rather, seeing that *here* the discourse *passes over* to the second person and *proceeds* in exhortation in ver. 12 ff., with the Vulgate, Chrysostom and Luther, as *imperative*. — ἐν Χρ. Ἰ.] These words, which Rückert, Köllner, de Wette, and others quite arbitrarily join merely with ζῶντας δὲ τ. Θεῷ, belong to both portions of the summons; and do not mean *per Christum* (Grotius and others, including Fritzsche), but denote rather the specific *element, in which* the being dead and living take place, namely, in the ethical bond of fellowship, which is just the εἶναι ἐν Χριστῷ.

Ver. 12 f. Οὖν] in consequence of this λογίζεσθε, for the proof of it in the practice of life. For this *practice* the λογίζεσθαι κ.τ.λ. is meant to be the regulative *theory*. The negative portion of the following exhortation corresponds to the νεκροὺς μὲν τῇ ἁμαρτίᾳ in ver. 11; and the positive contrast ἀλλὰ κ.τ.λ. to the ζῶντας δὲ τῷ Θεῷ. — μὴ βασιλ.] With this *nothing sinful* is admitted (comp. Chrysostom); but on the contrary the influence of the (personified) sin, conquering the moral ego, is *entirely forbidden*,[1] as the whole connection teaches. — ἐν τῷ θνητῷ ὑμ. σώμ.] ἐν simply indicates the seat and sphere, in which the for-

---

[1] But Luther's gloss is good: "Mark, the saints have still evil lusts in the flesh, which they do not follow." Comp. the carrying out of the idea in Melancthon.

bidden dominion would take place (not *by means of*, as Th. Schott thinks). As to θνητῷ, every explanation is to be avoided which takes the word in any other sense than the ordinary one of *mortal* (comp. viii. 11), because it has no other signification (see all the examples in Wetstein), and because the context contains nothing at all in favour of giving any other turn to the notion of the word. We must reject therefore the opinion that it is equivalent to νεκρῷ, as taken in the ethical sense: dead *for sin* (Turretin, Ch. Schmidt, Ernesti, Schleusner, Schrader, and Stengel). Directly affirmed of the body, the mortality could not but be understood by every reader quite definitely as the *physical*. The *purpose* of the epithet however must manifestly result from the relation *of motive*, in which the mortality of the body stands to the prohibition of the reign of sin in the body. And the more precise definition of this motive is to be derived from the previous νεκροὺς μὲν τῇ ἁμαρτιᾷ, ζῶντας δὲ τῷ Θεῷ. If we are convinced, namely, that we are dead for sin and alive for God; if we account ourselves as those who have put off the ethical mortality (ὡς ἐκ νεκρῶν ζῶντας, ver. 13), then it is *an absurdity* to allow sin to reign in the body, which in fact is *mortal*. This quality stands in a relation of *contradiction* to our *immortal* life entered upon in the fellowship of Christ, and thus the dominion, for which we should deliver over our body to sin, would prove that we were not that for which, nevertheless, in genuine moral self-judgment, we have to take ourselves; since in fact the mortal life of the body, if we yield it to the government of sin, excludes the immortal Christian life described in ver. 11. Hofmann imports more into the passage than its connection with ver. 11 suggests; namely the double folly, that such an one should not use the *power*, which the life of Christ gives him over the mortal body and therewith over sin; and that he should permit himself *to be entangled in the death* to which his body falls a victim, while he possesses a life of which also his body would become joint-participant. This is a fine-spun *application* of the true interpretation. Different is the view of Köllner (comp. Calvin: "per *contemtum* vocat mortale"), that it is here hinted how *disgraceful* it is to make the *spirit* subordinate to sin, *which only dwells in the perishable body;* and of Grotius: " de vita altera cogitandum, nec formidandos *labores haud sane diuturnos*" (comp. Chrysostom and Theodoret; so also on the whole Reiche). But the context contains neither a contrast between body and spirit, nor between this and the other life. Flatt thinks that Paul wished to remind his readers of the *brevity of sensual pleasure;* comp. Theophylact. But how little would this be in keeping with the high standpoint of the moral sternness of the Apostle ! According to others, Paul desired to remind them warningly of the *destructiveness* of sin, which had brought death on the body (de Wette, Krehl, Nielsen, Philippi, also Maier). But this point of view as to destructiveness is remote from the connection, in which the pervading theme is rather the *unsuitableness* of the dominion of sin to the communion of death and life with Christ. Others still explain it variously.[1] — σώματι] *body*, as in ver. 6; not a symbolic expression for the entire ego (Reiche, following Ambrosiaster and various early expositors); nor yet body *and soul*, so far as it is not yet the recipient of the Spirit of God (Philippi); for even in all such passages as viii. 10, 13, 23; xii. 1 σῶμα retains purely its signification *body*. But sin reigns in *the body* (comp. on ver. 6), so far as its material substratum is the σάρξ (Col. ii. 11), which, with its life-principle the ψυχή, is the seat and agent of sin (vii. 18 ff. *al*.). Hence the sinful desires are *its* desires (αὐτοῦ), because, excited by the power of sin in the flesh, they are at work in the body and its members (vii. 5, 23; Col. iii. 5). Sin aims at securing obedience to these desires through its dominion in man. Consequently εἰς τὸ ὑπακ. τ. ἐπιθ. αὐτ. implies the—according to ver. 11 absurd—*tendency* of the allowing sin to reign in the mortal body, which the Apostle forbids. — μηδέ] *also especially not* (as *e.g.* 1 Cor. v. 8). — παριστάνετε] *present*, i.e. *place at the disposal, at the service*. Matth. xxvi. 53; Acts xxiii. 24; 2 Tim. ii. 15; Athen. iv. p. 148 B; Lucian, *d. Mar.* 6, 2; Diod. Sic. xvi. 79; Dem. 597 pen. — τὰ μέλη ὑμῶν] *your members*, which sin desires to use as executive organs, tongue, hand, foot, eye, etc. The *mental*

---

[1] Olshausen connects thus: "let not the sin manifesting itself in your mortal body reign in you." In that case Paul must have repeated the article after ἁμ. According to Baur there lies in θνητῷ the idea: "whose mortality can only remind you of that, which it even now is as νεκρὸν τῇ ἁμαρτίᾳ." But, had Paul desired to set forth the moral death through the adjective by way of motive, he must then have written, after ver 11, ἐν τῷ νεκρῷ ὑμῶν σώματι, which after what goes before would not have been liable to any misconception.

powers and activities, feeling, will, understanding, are not included (in opposition to Erasmus, Reiche, Philippi and others); but Paul speaks concretely and graphically of the *members*, in reference to which the mental activities in question are necessarily presupposed. Comp. Col. iii. 5.— ὅπλα ἀδικίας] as *weapons of immorality*, with which the establishment of immorality is achieved. The ἁμαρτία is conceived as a *ruler* employing the members of man as *weapons of warfare*, wherewith to contend against the government of God and to establish ἀδικία (opposite of the subsequent δικαιοσύνης). It injures the figure, to which ver. 23 glances back, to explain ὅπλα (comp. כְּלִי) *instruments*, as is done by many (including Rückert, Köllner, Baumgarten-Crusius, Krehl, Fritzsche, de Wette, and Ewald), a meaning which it indeed frequently bears in classic Greek since Homer (see Duncan, *Lex.* ed. Rost, p. 844), but never in the N. T. Comp. especially 2 Cor. vi. 7, x. 4. — παραστήσατε] the aorist here following the present (comp. Bernhardy, p. 393), marking the immediateness and rapidity of the opposite action which has to set in. It stands to παριστάνετε in a *climactic* relation. See Winer, p. 294 [E. T. 394], Kühner, II. 1, p. 158. — ἑαυτούς] *yourselves, your own persons*, and specially also your members, etc. — ὡς ἐκ νεκρ. ζῶντας] *as those that are alive from the dead* (risen), *i.e.* those who have experienced in themselves the ethical process of having died and attained to the resurrection-life with Christ. Only thus, in the sense of the moral renovation discussed in vv. 2-11—not in the sense of Eph. ii. 1 (Philippi and older expositors)—can it be explained agreeably to the context, especially as ὡς corresponds to the λογίζεσθε κ.τ.λ. in ver. 11. This ὡς, *quippe*, with the participle (as in xv. 15, and very frequently), expresses, namely, the relation of the case, in which what is demanded is to appear to the readers as corresponding to their Christian state, which is described as life from the dead.[1] — τῷ Θεῷ] *belonging to God*, as in vv. 10, 11.

[1] The ὡς is not the "*like*" of comparison (Hofmann, who, following Lachmann, prefers with A B C ℵ the ὡσεί, which does not elsewhere occur in the writings of Paul), but the "*as*" of the *quality*, in which the subjects have to conceive themselves. Comp. Wunder, *ad Soph. Trach.* 394, p. 94 ; Kühner, II. 2, p. 649. According to Hofmann the comparative ὡσεί is only to extend to ἐκ νεκρῶν (and ζῶντας to be predicative): *as living persons like as from the dead*. But such a mere *comparison* would be foreign to the whole context, according to which

Ver. 14. Not the *ground and warrant for* the exhortation (Hofmann), in which case the thought is introduced, that obedience is *dependent on the readers;* but an *encouragement* to do what is demanded in vv. 12, 13, through the *assurance* that therein sin shall not become lord over them, since they are not in fact under the law, but under grace. Comp. the similar encouragement in Phil. ii. 13. In this assurance lies a "dulcissima consolatio," Melancthon, comp. Calvin. They have not to dread the danger of failure. Understood as an expression of *good confidence,* that they would not allow sin to become lord over them (Fritzsche), the sentence would lack an element assigning an *objective* reason, to which nevertheless the second half points. Heumann, Koppe, Rosenmüller, Flatt, and Umbreit take the future *imperatively,* which is erroneous for the simple reason that it is not in the *second* person (Bernhardy, p. 378). — οὐ γάρ ἐστε ὑπὸ νόμον (Gal. iv. 21), ἀλλ' ὑπὸ χάριν: *For not the law, but* divine *grace* (revealed in Christ) *is the power under which you are placed.* This *contrast,* according to which the norm-giving position of the law is *excluded* from the Christian state (it is not merely the *superfluousness* of the law that is announced, as Th. Schott thinks), is the justification of the encouraging assurance previously given. Had they been *under the law,* Paul would not have been able to give it, because the merely commanding law is the δύναμις τῆς ἁμαρτίας (1 Cor. xv. 56), and accumulates sins (v. 20), in which reference he intends to discuss the matter still further in ch. vii. But they stand under a quite different power, *under grace;* and *this* relation of dependence is quite calculated to bring to the justified that consecration of moral strength, which they require against sin and for the divine life (v. 21; vi. 1 ff.). "Gratia non solum peccata diluit, sed ut non peccemus facit," Augustine.

Vv. 15-23. *This* οὐκ εἶναι ὑπὸ νόμον, ἀλλ' ὑπὸ χάριν *does not therefore give us freedom to sin.* From the οὐ γάρ .... χάριν, Christians are *really* alive (with Christ) from the dead, and paralysing the pith of the view, which does not lie in a *quasi,* but in a *tanquam.* The Vulgate renders correctly: "*tanquam ex mortuis viventes.*" He who participates ethically in the resurrection-life of the Lord is *alive from death,* but not alive *as if from death ;* just as little is he *as if alive* from death. Theodore of Mopsuestia rendered the ὡσεί, which he read, in the latter sense; referring it to ἐκ νεκρ. ζῶντας together, and explaining the meaning to be that, previous to the *actual* resurrection, only ἡ κατὰ τὸ δυνατὸν μίμησις is required.

namely, the inference of freedom to sin might very easily be drawn by immoral Christians (comp. ver. 1), which would be exactly the reverse of what the Apostle wished to establish by that proposition (ἁμ. ὑμ. οὐ κυρ. ver. 14). Paul therefore proposes to himself this possible inference and negatives it (ver. 15), and then gives in ver. 16 ff. its refutation. Accordingly vv. 15-23 form only an ethico-polemical preliminary to the positive illustration of the proposition, "ye are not under the law, but under grace," which begins in ch. vii.

Ver. 15. Τί οὖν] sc. ἐστι; *what is then the state of the case?* Comp. iii. 9. Shall this Christian position of ours be misused for sinning?—With the reading ἁμαρτήσομεν the sense would be purely *future: shall we sin?* will this case occur with us? But with the proper reading ἁμαρτήσωμεν Paul asks: *Are we to sin? deliberative* subjunctive as in ver. 1. To the ἐπιμένωμ. τ. ἁμαρτ. in ver. 1 our ἁμαρτήσωμεν stands related *as a climax;* not merely the state of perseverance in sin, but every sinful action is to be abhorred; the former from the pre-Christian time, the latter in the Christian state of grace. — ὅτι οὐκ ἐσμὲν ὑπὸ νόμον κ.τ.λ.] emphatic repetition. Bornemann, *ad Xen. Mem.* iv. 3, 17, *Schol. in Luc.* p. xxxix.

Ver. 16. Paul begins the detailed illustration of the μὴ γένοιτο with an appeal to the consciousness of his readers, the tenor of which corresponds to the saying of Christ: "No man can serve two masters." This appeal forms the *propositio major;* the *minor* then follows in ver. 17 f., after which the *conclusion* is obvious of itself.—" *Know ye not, that, to whom ye yield yourselves as slaves for obedience, ye are slaves of him whom ye obey?*" Here the emphasis is not on ἐστε (slaves *ye are in reality,* as de Wette and others think), or even on the relative clause ᾧ ὑπακούετε (Hofmann), but, as is required by the order of the words, and the correlation with παριστ. ἑαυτούς, on δοῦλοι. Whosoever places *himself* at the disposal of another for obedience as a slave, is no longer free and independent, but is just the *slave* of him whom he obeys. — παριστάνετε] The *present,* as expressing the general proposition which continues to hold good. See Kühner, II. 1, p. 115. — ᾧ ὑπακούετε] *whom ye obey* (erroneously rendered by Reiche and Baumgarten-Crusius: *have to obey*). By this, instead of the simple αὐτοῦ or τούτου, the relation of *subjection*, which was already expressed in the protasis, is once more vividly brought into view: that ye are *slaves* of him, *whom ye*, in consequence of that παριστάνειν ἑαυτοὺς δούλους to him, *obey*. The circumstantiality has a certain earnestness and solemnity. If ye yield yourselves as slaves for obedience, then ye are nothing else than *slaves* in the service *of him* whom ye *obey*. The less reason is there for attaching εἰς ὑπακ. to the apodosis (Th. Schott, Hofmann). — ἤτοι ἁμαρτίας] sc. δοῦλοι.[1] Respecting the disjunctive ἤτοι, *aut sane*, found nowhere else in N. T., see especially Klotz, *ad Devar.* p. 609, Baeumlein, *Partik.* p. 244. It lays strong emphasis on the first alternative. Very frequently thus used in Greek authors. Comp. Wisd. xi. 18. — εἰς θάνατον] result, to which this relation of slavery leads. The θάνατος cannot be *physical* death (Reiche, Fritzsche, van Hengel), since that is not the consequence of individual[2] sin (see on v. 12), and is not averted from the δοῦλος ὑπακοῆς ; nor is it, either generally, the *misery of sin* (de Wette), or specially *spiritual* death, alienation from the true ζωή, an idea which Paul never conveys by θάνατος; but rather, seeing that θάνατος, as is more precisely indicated in ver. 21, and is placed beyond doubt by the contrast of ζωὴ αἰώνιος, must be conceived as the τέλος of the bondage of sin; *eternal* death (Chrysostom, Theophylact, and others, including Rückert, Reithmayr, and Tholuck). Comp. i. 32. This is not at variance with the antithesis εἰς δικαιοσύνην, which is not to be taken (as in ver. 13) in the sense of *moral righteousness* (Philippi and others); for this is not the *result*, but is itself the *essence* of the δοῦλον εἶναι ὑπακοῆς (comp. v. 19), since ὑπακοή, in contradistinction to the ἁμαρτία, is obedience to

[1] Consequently *servants of sin*, who are serviceable to that which is sin ; and then : *servants of obedience*, who are in the service of the opposite of ἁμαρτία, in the service of divine obedience. Hofmann erroneously takes the genitives as genitives of *quality* (servants *who sin* and *who obey*); see Winer, p. 222 [E. T. 297]. What reader could, after δοῦλοι (comp. John viii. 34), have stumbled on this singular relation of quality ; the assumption of which ought to have been precluded by vv. 17, 20. Comp. 2 Pet. ii. 19.

[2] Philippi here observes, with the view of *including* bodily death also in the idea, that it "is personally appropriated and merited by the individual through his own act." This is not Pauline, and is at variance with the true interpretation of the ἐφ᾽ ᾧ πάντες ἥμαρτον in v. 12. It is not with death as it is with the atonement, which is objectively there for all, but must be *appropriated* by something subjective. Comp. 1 Cor. xv. 22. Moreover, such personal appropriation would be inconceivable in the case of all children dying without actual sin.

the divine will. On the contrary δικαιοσύνη, antithetically correlative with the θάνατος, must be conceived as the *final result* of that δοῦλον εἶναι ὑπακοῆς, and apply to the time of final perfection in the αἰὼν μέλλων, when the faithful, who have not relapsed into the service of sin, but in their faith have been servants of obedience, on account of the death of Christ δίκαιοι κατασταθήσονται, ver. 19. It is therefore *the* righteousness which is awarded to them in the *judgment*.[1] If it were the *righteousness of faith* even now attained (Th. Schott), ὑπακοῆς would need to be taken, with Schott, of *becoming a believer* (i. 5), which is contextually inadmissible, since what is spoken of is the state of grace already *existing* (ver. 15), in which service is rendered to the obedience of God only, and not to sin. In accordance with the misconceptions of Hofmann, already noticed in detail (see above), there results as his sense of the whole: "*To whom ye place yourselves as servants at his disposal, ye are servants for the purpose of obedience; ye are so to him whom ye obey, servants either—for there is no third alternative—who act contrary to their master's will and thereby merit death, or such as live in obedience and are therefore righteous in the presence of their master.*" What kind of a θάνατος, and in what sense δικαιοσύνη is meant, is supposed accordingly to be self-evident. And by the following thanksgiving, ver. 17, the Apostle is alleged "*as it were half to take back*" his question, Whether they do not know etc., so that the medium of transition to ver. 17 is "*why yet still the question?*" A series of gratuitously imported fancies.

Ver. 17. *Propositio minor.* — χάρις δὲ τῷ Θεῷ, ὅτι] animated expression of piety; "ardor pectoris apostolici," Bengel. Comp. vii. 25. — ὅτι ἦτε δοῦλοι τ. ἁμ., ὑπηκ. κ.τ.λ.] ἦτε has emphasis: *that ye were slaves of sin* (that this condition of bondage is *past*) etc. Comp. Eph. v. 8. The prefixing of ἦτε, and the non-insertion of a μέν, clearly prove that this is the true interpretation, and not that, by which the main idea is discovered in the *second* half: "non Deo gratias agit, quod servierint peccato, sed quod, qui servierint peccato, postea obedierunt evangelio," Grotius. In that case μέν at least would be indispensable in the first clause. The mode of expression is *purposely chosen*, in order

---

[1] Köstlin has also justly directed attention in the *Jahrb. f. deutsche Theol.* 1856, p. 127, to the *sensus forensis* of δικαιοσύνη in our passage.

to render more forcibly apparent their earlier dangerous condition (whose further delineation in ver. 19, moreover, points to the former *heathenism* of the readers). — ἐκ καρδίας] οὐδὲ γὰρ ἠναγκάσθητε, οὐδὲ ἐβιάσθητε, ἀλλ' ἑκόντες μετὰ προθυμίας ἀπέστητε, Chrysostom. Comp. Job viii. 10; Mark xii. 30; Wisd. viii. 21 *al.*; Theocr. xxix. 4; also ἐκ θυμοῦ, ἐξ εὐμενῶν στέρνων, and similar phrases in Greek writers. The opposite: ἐκ βίας. — εἰς ὃν παρεδ. τύπ. διδ.] may either be resolved: τῷ τύπῳ τῆς διδ., εἰς ὃν παρεδ., with Chrysostom and others, including Rückert, Reiche, Köllner, Tholuck, de Wette, Fritzsche, Winer, and Philippi (see Fritzsche, *Diss.* II. p. 133, *Conject.* p. 34; Bornemann, *Schol. in Luc.* p. 177); or: εἰς τ. τύπ. τῆς διδ., εἰς ὃν παρεδ. (as in iv. 17); or: εἰς τ. τύπ. τῆς διδ., ὃν παρεδ. *i. e.* ὃς παρεδ. ὑμῖν (see Castalio and Grotius on the passage, Kypke, II. p. 167, Ewald and Hofmann). It is decisive in favour of the first mode of resolution that ὑπακούειν εἰς τι is never equivalent to ὑπακούειν τινί;[1] while to take ὑπηκούσατε *absolutely* either in the sense of the obedience *of faith*, i. 5 (Ewald), or in that of *absolute obedience* ("as obedient servants in contrast to sinful ones," Hofmann), is inadmissible, because ὑπηκούσατε in its antithetical correlation with δοῦλοι τῆς ἁμαρτίας needs a more precise definition. And this it has precisely in εἰς ὃν παρεδόθ. κ.τ.λ., which cannot therefore indicate *whereunto* (Ewald and Hofmann) the ὑπακούειν has taken place,—an artificial farfetched expedient, which is wrung from them, in order to get instead of obedience towards the doctrine obedience as *effect of* the doctrine (comp. Matth. xii. 41, where however μετενόησαν stands by its side, which is in fact of itself a complete conception). The τύπος διδαχῆς, εἰς ὃν παρεδ. is usually (and still by Hofmann) understood of *Christian* doctrine generally, so far as it is a definite, express form of teaching. But since the singular expression τύπος does not thus appear accounted for, and since the Roman church was undoubtedly planted through the preaching of *Pauline* Christianity, which is certainly a particular *type*, different from Judaistic forms of Christian teaching and in various points even contrasting with these, it is preferable to understand by it the *distinct expression* which the Gospel

---

[1] In the passages quoted by Kypke from Greek authors ὑπακούειν εἰς τι means to obey *in reference to something*, to be obedient *in a matter*. Reiche's judgment of these passages is erroneous. See on 2 Cor. ii. ~

had received *through Paul,* consequently the doctrinal form *of his* Gospel (ii. 16, xvi. 25), in opposition to anti-Paulinism (Rückert, ed. 1, de Wette, comp. Philippi). This εἰς ὃν παρεδ. is decisive *in favour of* the interpretation "form of doctrine" in an *objective* sense, and against the *subjective* explanation: image of the doctrine, which is impressed *on the heart* (Kypke). Following Theodore of Mopsuestia, Oecumenius, Calvin, Grotius, Calovius, and many others, Reiche (as also Olshausen, Reithmayr and Krehl) take τύπος in the sense of *exemplar, ideal which the doctrine holds up,* consequently in that of the ethical rule, which as model of life is contained in the Gospel (διδαχ.).[1] This is in harmony neither with the ὑπακούειν nor with the εἰς ὃν παρεδ. Unsuitable to the former is also the interpretation of Beza and others, to which Tholuck inclines, that the evangelical doctrine is "quasi instar typi cujusdam, *cui veluti immittamur,* ut ejus figurae conformemur." Van Hengel understands ὑπηκούσατε in the sense of obedience *toward God,* and εἰς as *quod attinet at;* Paul in his view says: "obedivistis Deo ad sequendam quam profiteri edocti estis doctrinae formam." This form of doctrine, to which the Romans were directed at the founding of their church, had been, he conceives, probably more Judaistic than purely Pauline. But against the absolute interpretation of ὑπηκούσ. see above; while the assumption of a τύπος διδαχῆς not truly Pauline is irreconcilable with the expression of thanksgiving, and is not supported by Phil. i. 15, a passage which is to be explained from the peculiar situation of the Apostle. We may add that Paul aptly specialises the ὑπακοή—which was set forth in the major, in ver. 16, quite generally (as obedience to God in general) —*at the subsumption* in the minor, ver. 17, as obedience to *his Gospel.*— παρεδόθ.] τὴν τοῦ Θεοῦ βοήθειαν αἰνίττεται, Chrysostom. The reference to *God,* which is also to be observed for the passives in ver. 18, is plain from χάρις τῷ Θεῷ. That it is not to be taken as *middle (to yield themselves,* so Fritzsche) is shown by the same passives in ver. 18. Παραδίδωμι either with the dative or *with* εἰς, in the sense of delivering over *to the disposal and power of another,* is very current everywhere in Greek literature (Judith x. 15; Rom. i. 26; Xen. *Hell.* 1, 7, 3; Dem.

---

[1] So probably Chrysostom took it, who explains ὁ τύπος τ. διδαχῆς by ὀρθῶς ζῆν καὶ μετὰ πολιτείας ἀρίστης. So also Theophylact.

515, 6, 1187, 5); but whether in a hostile sense or not, is conveyed not by the expression itself, but simply by the context. To the expression itself the abolition of one's own self-determination is essential. So also here. The Christian has at his conversion ceased to be *sui juris*, and has *been given over to the morally regulative power of the Gospel*. On τύπος διδαχῆς comp. Jamblichus, *de Pythag. vit.* 16 : τῆς παιδεύσεως ὁ τύπος, Plat. *Rep.* p. 412 B: οἱ τύποι τῆς παιδείας, p. 397 C : τύπῳ τῆς λέξεως, Jamblichus *l.c.* 23 : τὸν τύπον τῆς διδασκαλίας, Isoc. *Antid.* 186 : ὁ τύπος τῆς φιλοσοφίας.

Ver. 18. "But, freed from sin, ye have become servants of righteousness." This is not to be regarded as the *conclusion* from the two premisses, vv. 16, 17 (Rückert, Reiche), because οὖν is not used, and because substantially the same thought was already contained in ver. 17. Paul rather expresses once more the happy change in his readers just described ; and does so in a thoughtfully chosen antithetical form, no longer however dependent on ὅτι, but independent and thus more emphatic (hence a colon is, with Lachmann, to be inserted before ἐλευθ.). But he leaves the reader to draw for himself the *conclusion*, namely : this μὴ γένοιτο is therefore fully justified. — The δέ is the *autem* of continuation ; the transition, however, is not from activity (ὑπηκούσατε) to passiveness (Hofmann, comp. Th. Schott), for the latter is already given in παρεδόθητε, but from the state of the case expressed in ver. 17 to a striking *specification, in a more precise form*, of the revolution in the relation of service, which was accomplished in them. — ἀπὸ τ. ἁμαρτ.] that is, from the relation of slavery to it. — ἐδουλ. τῇ δικαιοσ.] *ye have been placed in the slave-relation to righteousness ;* a representation of the complete dependence on the moral necessity of being righteous, implied in conversion. On the dative comp. 1 Cor. ix. 19 ; Tit. ii. 3 ; 2 Pet. ii. 19. *This* slavery, where the δικαιοσύνη is the mistress, is consequently the true moral freedom (ἐλευθεροπρεπὲς δὲ ἡ ἀρετή, Plat. *Alc. I.* p. 135 C.). Comp. the similar paradox in 1 Cor. vii. 22.

Ver. 19. Paul had, in vv. 16-18, represented the idea of the highest moral freedom—in a form corresponding indeed with its nature as a moral necessity ("Deo servire vera libertas est," Augustine), but still borrowed from human relations—as δουλεία. He now therefore, not to justify himself, but to induce his

I.   U readers to separate the idea from the form, announces *the fact that*, and the *reason why*, he thus expresses himself regarding the loftiest moral idea in this concrete fashion, derived from an ordinary human relation. *I speak* (in here making mention of *slavery*, vv. 16-18) *what is human* (belonging to the relations of the natural human life) *on account of the* (intellectual) *weakness of your flesh, i.e.* in order thereby to come to the help of this your weakness. For the setting forth of the idea in some such sensuous form is the appropriate means of stimulating and procuring its apprehension in the case of one, whose knowledge has not yet been elevated by divine enlightenment to a higher platform of strength and clearness released from such human forms. Respecting ἀνθρώπινον see the examples in Wetstein. It is the antithesis of θεῖον, Plat. *Rep.* p. 497 C. The expression κατὰ ἄνθρωπον λέγω in ch. iii. 5 is in substance equivalent, since ἀνθρώπινον also necessarily indicates the *form and dress* employed for the idea, for whose representation the Apostle has uttered *what is human*. The σάρξ, however, *i.e.* the material human nature in its psychical determination, as contrasted with the divine pneumatic influence (comp. on iv. 1), is *weak* for religious and moral *discernment*, as well as for good (Matth. xxvi. 41); hence the σοφία σαρκική (2 Cor. i. 12) is foolishness with God (1 Cor. iii. 19). Others, taking it not of intellectual weakness, but of *moral* weakness, refer it to what *follows* (Origen, Chrysostom, Theophylact, Erasmus, Calvin, Estius, Hammond, Wetstein, and others, including Klee, Reithmayr, and Bisping), in the sense: "I do not demand what is too hard (ἀνθρώπ., comp. 1 Cor. x. 13); for although I might require a far higher degree of the new obedience, yet I require only the same as ye have formerly rendered to sin."[1] But the following ὥσπερ .... οὕτω introduces not the equality of the *degree*, but, as is plain from ver. 20, only the comparison in general between the former and the present state. Besides, the demand itself, which by this interpretation would only concern a lower stage of Christian life, would be inappropriate to the morally ideal character of the whole hortatory discourse, which is not injured by the concrete figurative form. This remark also applies to the dismembering explanation

---

[1] So also probably Theodoret: τῇ φύσει μετρῶ τὴν παραίνεσιν· οἶδα γὰρ τὰ ἐν τῷ θνητῷ σώματι κινούμενα πάθη.

of Hofmann (comp. Th. Schott), who makes ἀνθρώπινον λέγω form a parenthesis, and then connects διὰ τὴν ἀσθένειαν τ. σαρκὸς ὑμῶν with ἐδουλώθητε τῇ δικαιοσύνῃ, so that the thought would be: the weakness of our inborn nature gives occasion that our translation into the life of righteousness is dealt with as an *enslavement* thereto, while otherwise it would be simply restoration to the freedom of doing our own will; according to this weakness what is right is not done freely of itself, but in the shape of a *service.* But how could Paul have so *degraded* the moral *loftiness* of the position of the δουλωθέντες τῇ δικαιοσύνῃ! To him they were indeed the δουλωθέντες τῷ Θεῷ (ver. 22), and in his estimation there was nothing morally more exalted than to be δοῦλος Θεοῦ, as Christ Himself was. The Christian has put on Christ in this respect also (Gal. iii. 27), and lives in the spirit of the holiest freedom (2 Cor. iii. 17 f.); his subjection to the service of δικαιοσύνη has not taken place on account of his inborn nature incapacitating him for moral freedom (as though it were a measure of compulsion); but on the contrary he has put off the morally weak old man, and so he lives as a new creature—by means of the newness of the spirit, and in virtue of his communion in the resurrection-life of Christ—in the condition of righteousness, which Paul has here under the designation of *bondage,* accommodating himself by the ordinary human expression to the natural weakness of the understanding, brought into contrast with the having been freed from sin. — ὥσπερ γάρ κ.τ.λ.] *Practical assigning of a reason* for the proposition just affirmed ἀνθρωπίνως in ver. 18, in the form of a *concrete demand.* In opposition to Hofmann, who (at variance with his own interpretation of xiii. 6!) declares it impossible to clothe the assigning of a reason in the dress of an exhortation, see Baeumlein, *Partik.* p. 86. Heb. xii. 3 (see Delitzsch) is to be taken in the same way; comp. James i. 7; and see on 1 Cor. i. 26. Hence: *for, as ye have placed your members at the disposal,* etc., *so now place,* etc. Since the discourse proceeds indeed in the same figurative manner, but yet so that it now assumes the *hortatory* form, ἀνθρώπινον .... σαρκὸς ὑμῶν is not to be put in a parenthesis, but with Fritzsche, Lachmann, and Tischendorf, to be separated from ὥσπερ by a period. — τῇ ἀκαθαρσίᾳ κ. τῇ ἀνομίᾳ] The two exhaust the notion of ἁμαρτία (ver. 13), so that ἀκαθ. characterises sin as morally defiling *the man* (see on i. 24), and ἀνομ. (1 John iii. 4) as a violation of *the divine law* (see Tittmann, *Synon.* p. 48). — εἰς τὴν ἀνομ.] *on behalf of* antagonism to law, *in order that it may be established* (*in facto*). The interpretation εἰς τὸ ἐπιπλέον ἀνομεῖν, Theophylact (so also Oecumenius, Erasmus, Luther, Grotius, Köllner, Ewald, and others), is, in its practical bearing, erroneous, since it is only the yielding of the members to the *principle* of ἀνομία that actually brings the latter *into a concrete reality*. — εἰς ἁγιασμόν] *in order to attain holiness* (1 Cor. i. 30; 1 Thess. iv. 3 f. 7; 2 Thess. ii. 13), moral purity and consecration to God. To be an ἅγιος in mind and walk—that goal of Christian development—is the aim of the man, who places his members at the disposal of δικαιοσύνη as ruler over him. The word ἁγιασμός is found only in the LXX., Apocr. and in the N. T. (in the latter it is always *holiness*, not *sanctification*,[1] even in 1 Tim. ii. 15; Heb. xii. 14; 1 Pet. i. 2), but not Greek writers. In Dion. Hal. i. 21, it is a false reading, as also in Diod. iv. 39. Ἁγιασμόν stands *without the article*, because this highest moral goal is conceived of *qualitatively*.

Vv. 20-22. With γάρ Paul does not introduce an illustration to ver. 19 (Fritzsche), but rather—seeing that ver. 20 through οὖν in ver. 21, as well as through the correlative antithesis in ver. 22, must necessarily form a connected whole in thought with what follows till the end of ver. 22—the *motive* for complying with what is enjoined in ver. 19; and that in such a way, that he first of all *prepares the way* for it by ver. 20, and then in ver. 21 f., leading on by οὖν, *actually expresses* it, equally impressively and touchingly, as respects its deterrent (ver. 21) and inviting (ver. 22) aspects. The fact that he first sets down ver. 20 *for itself*, makes the recollection which he thus calls up more forcible, *more tragic*. Observe also the emphasis and the symmetrical separation of the several words in ver. 20. — ἐλεύθ. ἦτε τῇ δικαιοσ.] *Ye were free in relation to righteousness*, in point of fact independent of its demands, since ye were serving the opposite ruler (the ἁμαρτία). Οὐδὲ γὰρ διενέμετε τῆς δουλείας τὸν τρόπον τῇ δικαιοσύνῃ καὶ τῇ ἁμαρτίᾳ, ἀλλ' ὅλως ἑαυτοὺς ἐξε-

---

[1] In opposition to Hofmann, on ver. 22. But to the Christian consciousness it is self-evident that *holiness* can only be attained under the influence of the Holy Spirit. Comp. Ritschl, *altkath. K.* p. 82.

CHAP. VI. 20-22. 309

διότε τῇ πονηρίᾳ, Chrysostom. A sad truth based on experience! not a flight of irony (Koppe, Reiche, Philippi, and others), but full of deep moral pain. — Ver. 21. οὖν] in consequence of this freedom. — τίνα .... ἐπαισχύνεσθε is with Chrysostom, Oecumenius, Castalio, Beza, Calvin, Grotius, Estius, Wetstein, Bengel, and others, including Winer, Reiche (but see below), Fritzsche, Jatho, and Hofmann (but see below)—in harmony with the punctuation of the *text. rec.*—to be regarded as one connected question, so that the reason to be given for replying in the negative sense to this question is then contained in τὸ γὰρ τέλος ἐκείνων θάνατος; namely, thus: *what fruit, now, had ye then* (when ye were still in the service of sin, etc., ver. 20) *of things, on account of which ye are now ashamed?* i.e. ye had then *no* fruit, *no* moral gain, etc., and the proof thereof is: *for the final result of them* (those things) *is death.* What leads at last to death, could bring you no moral gain. For the grammatical explanation ἐκείνων is to be supplied before ἐφ' οἷς (which in fact is perfectly regular, Winer, p. 149 [E. T. 203]), and to this the ἐκείνων in the probative clause refers. Regarding ἐπαισχ. ἐπί τινι, to be ashamed *over anything* (not merely of the being put to shame *by the fact* of something *not proving to be what* we thought it, as Th. Schott weakens the sense) comp. Xen. *Hell.* v. 4, 33: ἐπὶ τῇ ἡμετέρᾳ φιλίᾳ αἰσχυνθῇς, Plat. *Rep.* p. 396 C: οὐκ αἰσχυνεῖσθαι ἐπὶ τῇ τοιαύτῃ μιμήσει, LXX., Is. xx. 5, i. 29; 1 Macc. iv. 31; also Dem. 426, 10. Reiche makes the double mistake of very arbitrarily referring ἐφ' οἷς to καρπόν, which is to be taken collectively; and of explaining καρπὸν ἔχειν as meaning *to bring forth fruit* (which would be κ. ποιεῖν, φέρειν), so that the sense would be: "what deeds, on account of which ye are now ashamed, proceeded from your service of sin?" Hofmann, resolving the expression into ἐπὶ τούτοις ἃ νῦν ἐπαισχύνεσθε, wishes to take ἐπί in the well-known sense of *addition to,* so that Paul asks: "what fruit had ye then *over and above* those things of which ye are now ashamed?" those things being the former disgraceful *enjoyments,* with which they now desired to have nothing further to do. But how could the reader think of such *enjoyments* without any hint being given by the text? And how arbitrary in this particular place is that interpretation of ἐπί, especially when the verb itself is compounded with ἐπί, and that in the sense: to be ashamed *thereupon*, and accordingly indicates how ἐφ' οἷς is to be resolved and properly understood! See generally on ἐπί with the dative, as specifying the ground with verbs of emotion, Kühner, II. 1, p. 436, and with αἰσχύν. II. 2, p. 381, rem. 6. Many others (Syriac, Theodore of Mopsuestia, Theodoret, Theophylact, Erasmus, Luther, Melancthon, Erasmus Schmid, Heumann, Carpzov, Koppe, Tholuck undecidedly, Rückert, Köllner, de Wette, Olshausen, Baumgarten-Crusius, Lachmann, Tischendorf, Philippi, Reithmayr, Ewald, van Hengel, and Th. Schott) end the question with τότε, so that ἐφ' οἷς νῦν ἐπαισχ. becomes the answer, of which again τὸ γὰρ τέλ. ἐκ θάν. is the proof: "*what sort of fruit had ye then? Things* (ye had as fruit) *of which ye are now ashamed; for the end of them is death.*" Καρπόν is likewise regarded as a figurative description either of *gain* or *reward* ("ignoble and pernicious joys and pleasures," Ewald), or of *actions*, which are the penal consequence of reprobate sentiments. But fatal to all this explanation, which breaks up the passage, is the antithesis in ver. 22, where the *having of fruit*, not its *quality*, is opposed to the preceding; if Paul had inquired in ver. 21 regarding the *quality* of the fruit, he must have used in ver. 22 some such expression as νυνὶ δὲ.... τὸν ἁγιασμὸν ἔχετε τὸν καρπὸν ὑμῶν. Besides, we cannot well see why he should not have written either τίνας καρπούς or ἐφ' ᾧ and ἐκείνου; he would by annexing the *plurals*, though these were in themselves admissible on account of the collective nature of καρπός, have only expressed himself in a fashion obscure and misleading. Finally, it is to be observed that he never attributes καρπόν or καρπούς to immorality; he attributes to it ἔργα (Gal. v. 19), but uses καρπός only of the good; he speaks of the καρπὸς τοῦ πνεύματος, Gal. v. 22; of the καρπὸς τοῦ φωτός, Eph. v. 9; of the καρπὸς δικαιοσύνης, Phil. i. 11; of the καρπ. ἔργου, Phil. i. 22; comp. Rom. i. 13; in fact he *negatives* the idea of καρπός in reference to evil, when he describes the ἔργα τοῦ σκότους as ἄκαρπα, Eph. v. 11; comp. Tit. iii. 14. With this type of conception our interpretation alone accords, by which in the question τίνα καρπὸν κ.τ.λ. (comp. 1 Cor. ix. 18) there is contained the *negation* of καρπός in the service of sin, the ἄκαρπον εἶναι. The most plausible objection to our explanation is this, that in accordance with it ἐφ' οἷς νῦν ἐπαισχ. becomes merely an incidental observation. But an incidental observation may be of great weight in its bearing on the matter in hand. It is so here, where it contains a trenchant argumentative point in favour of replying in a negative sense to the question. Calvin aptly says: "non poterat gravius exprimere quod volebat, quam appellando eorum conscientiam et quasi in eorum persona pudorem confitendo." Compare also Chrysostom. — ἐκείνων] *neuter:* those things, on account of which ye are now ashamed, the *pre-Christian sins and vices.* Bengel well remarks: "remote spectat praeterita." — θάνατος] *death,* i.e. *the eternal* death, whose antithesis is the ζωὴ αἰώνιος, ver. 23 ; not the *physical* (Fritzsche), comp. on ver. 16. — The μέν before γάρ (see the crit. remarks) does not correspond to the following δέ ; on the contrary, we must translate: *for the end indeed* (which however excludes every fruit) is death. See Hartung, *Partikell.* II. p. 414, Winer, p. 534 f. [E. T. 719 f.]. — Ver. 22. νυνὶ δέ κ.τ.λ.] *But now* (ye are no longer without fruit, as formerly; no, now) *ye possess your fruit unto holiness,* so that its possession has as its consequence holiness for you (εἰς consecutive). The ἁγιασμός is consequently not *the fruit* (the moral gain) *itself,* which they already *have* (that would also be at variance with οὕτω νῦν παραστ.....εἰς ἁγιασμόν in ver. 19), but the *state, which the* ἔχειν *of their fruit shall in future bring about.* The *fruit itself*—and καρπός is to be taken, quite as in ver. 21, as ethical product—is consequently the *new, Christian morality* (comp. the καινότης ζωῆς in ver. 4), the Christian virtuous nature which belongs to them (ὑμῶν), and the possession of which leads by the way of progressive development *to holiness.* — τὸ δὲ τέλος ζωὴν αἰών.] *as the final result however* (of this your fruit) *eternal life* in the kingdom of Messiah. *This* possession is now as yet an ideal one (viii. 24). Hofmann erroneously takes τὸ δὲ τέλος *adverbially* (1 Pet. iii. 8 ; comp. on 1 Cor. xv. 24), which is impossible after ver. 21, in accordance with which the word must here also be the emphatic *substantive,* the *finale* of the καρπός; hence also ζωὴν αἰώνιον is dependent not on εἰς (Hofmann), but on ἔχετε. — The circumstance, moreover, that Paul in ver. 22 says δουλωθ. τῷ Θεῷ, while in ver. 18 he has said ἐδουλ. τῇ δικαιοσύνῃ, is rightly illustrated by Grotius: "qui bonitati rebusque honestis servit, et Deo servit, quia Deus hoc semper amavit et in evangelio apertissime praecepit." Comp. xii. 2. And precisely therein lies the true freedom, 1 Pet. ii. 16; John viii. 36.

Ver. 23. Τὰ ὀψώνια] *the wages.* Comp. 1 Cor. ix. 7; Luke iii. 14. Ὀψώνιον κυρίως λέγεται τὸ τοῖς στρατιώταις παρὰ τοῦ βασιλέως δεδομένον σιτηρέσιον, Theophylact. Comp. Photius, 367. See Lobeck, *ad Phryn.* p. 420. The *plural,* more usual than the singular, is explained by the various elements that constituted the original natural payments, and by the coins used in the later money wages. — *The wages which sin gives* stands in reference to ver. 13, where the ἁμαρτία is presented as a ruler, to whom the subjects tender their members as weapons, for which they receive their *allowance!* — θάνατος] as in ver. 22. — τὸ δὲ χάρισμα τ. Θεοῦ] Paul does not say τὰ ὀψώνια here also (" *vile verbum,*" Erasmus), but characterizes what God gives for wages as what it *is* in its specific nature—a *gift of grace,* which is no ἀντιταλαντεύεσθαι (Theodoret). To the Apostle, in the connection of his system of faith and doctrine, this was very natural, even without the supposition of any special design (in order—it has been suggested—to afford no encouragement to pride of virtue or to confiding in one's own merit). — ἐν Χριστῷ κ.τ.λ.] In Christ is the *causal basis,* that the χάρισμα τ. Θεοῦ is eternal life; a triumphant conclusion as in v. 21; comp. viii. 39.

CHAPTER VII.

Ver. 6. ἀποθανόντες] Elz. reads ἀποθανόντος, which was introduced as a conjecture by Beza, without critical evidence, solely on account of some misunderstood words of Chrysostom (see Mill, Bengel, *Appar.*, and especially Reiche, *Comment. crit.* I. p. 50 ff.). The ἀποθανόντες, adopted by Griesb. Matth. Lachm. Scholz, and Tisch., following Erasmus and Mill, is the reading in A B C K L P ℵ, min., and most vss. and Fathers. D E F G Vulg. It. codd. in Ruf. and Latin Fathers read τοῦ θανάτου. Preferred by Reiche. But especially when we consider its merely one-sided attestation (the Oriental witnesses are wanting), it seems to be a gloss having a practical bearing (see ver. 5) on τοῦ νόμου, which has dispossessed the participle regarded as disturbing the construction. — Ver. 13. γέγονε] Lachm. and Tisch. (8), following A B C D E P ℵ, 47, 73, 80, Method. Damasc. read ἐγένετο. Some Latin codd. have *est*. F G have no verb at all. With the preponderance, thus all the more decisive, of the witnesses which favour ἐγένετο, it is to be preferred. — Ver. 14. σαρκικός] The σάρκινος adopted by Griesb. Lachm. Scholz, and Tisch. is attested by A B C D E F G ℵ*, min., and several Fathers. For this reason, and because the ending κός was easily suggested by the preceding πνευματικός, as in general σαρκικός was more familiar to the copyists (xv. 27; 1 Cor. ix. 11; 2 Cor. x. 4; 1 Pet. ii. 11) than σάρκινος (2 Cor. iii. 3), the latter is to be assumed as the original reading. — Ver. 17. οἰκοῦσα] Tisch. (8) reads ἐνοικοῦσα, which would have to be received, if it were attested in more quarters than by B ℵ. — Ver. 18. οὐχ εὑρίσκω] A B C ℵ, 47, 67**, 80, Copt. Arm. Procl. in Epiph. Method. Cyr. codd. Gr. *ap.* Aug. have merely οὔ. Approved by Griesb.; adopted by Lachm. and Tisch. But if there had been a gloss, the supplement would have been παράκειται. The omission on the other hand is explained by the copyist's hurrying on from OYX to the OY at the beginning of ver. 19. — Ver. 20. θέλω ἐγώ] Since ἐγώ is wanting in B C D E F G, min., Arm. Vulg. It. and several Fathers, but is found in 219, Clem. after τοῦτο, in Chrys. before οὐ; and since it is, according to the sense and the analogy of vv. 15, 19, inappropriate, it has rightly been deleted by Lachm. and Fritzsche, and is to be regarded as a mechanical addition from what immediately follows. If ἐγώ were original (and had been omitted in accordance with vv. 15, 19), it must have had the emphasis of the contrast, which however it has not. — Ver. 25. εὐχαριστῶ] Lachm. and Tisch. read χάρις, which Griesb. also approved of, following B and several min., vss. and Fathers. Fritzsche reads χάρις δέ in accordance with C**, ℵ **, min., Copt. Arm. and Fathers. Both are taken from the near, and, in the connection of ideas, analogous vi. 17 (not εὐχαρ. from i. 8). The reading ἡ χάρις τ. Θεοῦ (D E and some Fathers), or ἡ χ. τ. κυρίου (F G), is manifestly an alteration, in order to make the *answer* follow the preceding question.

Vv. 1-6. *The Christian is not under the Mosaic law; but through his fellowship in the death of Christ he has died to the law, in order to belong to the Risen One and in this new union to lead a life consecrated to God.*

Ver. 1.[1] *Ἢ ἀγνοεῖτε*] Paul certainly begins now the detailed illustration, still left over, of οὐ γάρ ἐστε, vi. 14; but he connects his *transition* to it with what immediately precedes, as is clear from the nature of ἤ (comp. vi. 3). Nevertheless the logical reference of ἤ ἀγνοεῖτε is not to be sought possibly in the previous τῷ κυρίῳ ἡμῶν, with which the following κυριεύει is here correlative (Reiche), since that κυρίῳ has in fact no essential importance at all and is for the progress of the thought immaterial; but rather in the leading idea last expressed (ver. 22), and established (ver. 23), *namely, that the Christian, freed from the service of sin and become the servant of God, has his fruit to holiness, and, as the final result, eternal life.* This proposition could not be *truth*, if the Christian were not free *from the law* and did not belong to the Risen Christ instead, etc., vv. 1-6. — ἀδελφοί] address to the *readers collectively* (comp. i. 13), not merely to the *Jewish Christians* (Toletus, Grotius, Estius, Ch. Schmidt, and others, including Tholuck and Philippi), because in that case an addition must have been made excluding Gentile Christians, which however is so far from being contained in γινώσκουσι, especially when it is without the article, that in the case of *Christians generally* the knowledge of the O. T. was of necessity to be presupposed; see below. This applies also against Hofmann's view, that Paul, although avoiding a specific express designation, has in view *that* portion of his readers, which had

---
[1] On the entire chapter, see Achelis in the *Stud. u. Krit.* 1863, p. 670 ff.

not been capable of the misconception indicated in ver. 15. This limitation also—and how easily could the adroit author of the Epistle have indicated it in a delicate way !—cannot be deduced either from ἀδελφοί or from γινώσκουσι κ.τ.λ. — γινώσκ. γὰρ νόμ. λ.] justifies the appeal to the readers' own insight: *for I speak to such as know the law.* We may not infer from these parenthetical words, or from vv. 4-6, that the majority of the Roman congregation was composed of *Jewish-Christians*;[1] for, looking to the close connection subsisting between the Jewish and Gentile-Christian portions of the Church, to the custom borrowed from the synagogue of reading from the Old Testament in public, and to the necessary and essential relations which evangelical instruction and preaching sustained to the Old Testament so that the latter was the basis from which they started, the Apostle might designate his *readers generally* as γινώσκοντες τὸν νόμον, and predicate of them an acquaintance with the law. Comp. on Gal. iv. 21. The less need is there for the assumption of a previous proselytism (de Wette, Beyschlag, and many others), with which moreover the ἀδελφός addressing the readers *in common* is at variance; comp. i. 13, viii. 12, x. 1, xi. 23, xii. 1, xv. 14, 30, xvi. 17.— ὁ νόμος] not *every law* (Koppe, van Hengel); nor the *moral law* (Glöckler); but the *Mosaic*, and that in the usual sense comprehending the whole; not merely of the law of marriage (Beza, Toletus, Bengel, Carpzov, Chr. Schmidt; comp. Olshausen). This is required by the theme of the discussion generally, and by the foregoing γινώσκ. γ. νόμ. λαλῶ in particular.— τοῦ ἀνθρώπου] is not to be connected with ὁ νόμος (Hammond, Clericus, Elsner, and Mosheim), but belongs, as the order of the words demands, to κυριεύει. — ἐφ' ὅσον χρ. ζῇ] *For so long time as he liveth* (ἐπί as in Gal. iv. 1 in the sense of stretching over a period of time, see Bernhardy, p. 252; comp. Nägelsbach, z. *Ilias*, ii. 299, ed. 3, Ast. *Lex. Plat.* I. p. 768), the (personified) law is lord over the man who is subjected to it (τοῦ ἀνθρ.). That ὁ ἄνθρωπος is the subject to ζῇ, is decided by vv. 2, 3, 4. By the assumption of ὁ νόμος as subject

[1] On the contrary, the inference would be : If the Church had been a *Jewish-Christian* one, the γινώσκειν νόμον would in its case have been so entirely *self-evident*, that we should not be able at all to see why Paul should have specially noticed it. But as *converted Gentiles* the readers had become acquainted with the law. This also applies against Holtzmann, *Judenth. u. Christenth*, p. 783.

(Origen, Ambrosiaster, Erasmus, Vatablus, Grotius, Estius, Bengel, Koppe, and Flatt), in which case ζῇ is supposed to signify *viget* or *valet* (in spite of vv. 2, 3), the discourse is quite disarranged; for Paul is not discussing the abrogation of the law, but the fact that the Christian as such is no longer under it. Nor do vv. 2, 3 require ὁ νόμος as subject, because the point there illustrated is, that the death of *the man* (not of the law) dissolves the binding power of the law over him. Comp. Schabb. f. 151, 2: "postquam mortuus est homo, liber est a praeceptis;" Targ. Ps. lxxxviii. 6 in Wetstein on ver. 3. The proposition in vi. 7 is similar, and presupposes this thought. To take ζῇν as equivalent to ζῇν ἐν σαρκί ("so long as the man *continues to lead his old natural life*, he is a servant of the law," Philippi, also Umbreit), is quite opposed to the context: see ζῶντι and ζῶντος in vv. 2, 3, with their antitheses. The *emphasis*, moreover, is not on ζῇ (Hofmann), but, as is shown by the very expression ὅσον, ou ἐφ' ὅσον χρόνον, *for the entire time*, that he lives; it does *not* lose its power over him *sooner* than when he dies; *so long* as he is in life, he remains subject to it. If this is attended to and there is not introduced a wholly irrelevant "*only* so long as he liveth," the thought appears neither trivial nor disproportionate to the appeal to the legal knowledge of his readers. For there is a *peculiarity* of the νόμος in the fact, that it cannot have, like human laws, merely temporary force, that it cannot be altered or suspended, nor can one for a time be exempted from its control, etc. No, *so long* as man's life endures, the dominion of the νόμος over him continues.[1] Nor is the proposition incorrect (because that dominion ceases in the case of the believer, Philipppi); for it simply contains a *general rule of law*, which, it is self-evident, refers to the ἄνθρωπος ἔννομος *as such*. If the Jew becomes a Christian, he *dies* as a Jew (ver. 4), and the rule in question is not invalidated.

Ver. 2. Concrete illustration of the proposition in ver. 1, derived from the relation of the law to *marriage* and its dissolution, which in the woman's case can only take place through the *death* of the husband, so that it is only after that death has occurred that she may marry another. This example, as the tenor

[1] Comp. Th Schott, p. 267; Hofmann formerly held the right view (*Schriftbew.* II. 1, p. 352).

of the following text shows (in opposition to Hofmann), is selected, not because the legal ordinance in question was in its nature the only one that Paul could have employed, but *because* he has it in view to bring forward the union with Christ, which takes place after the release from the law, as analogous to *a new marriage*, and does so in ver. 4. The illustration is only apparently (not really; Usteri, Rückert, and even Umbreit in the *Stud. u. Krit.* 1851, p. 643) *awkward*, in so far namely as the deceased and the person released from the law through the event of death are represented in it as *different*. This appearance drove Chrysostom and his followers to adopt the hypothesis of an inversion of the comparison; thus holding that the *law* is properly the deceased party, but that Paul expressed himself as he has done out of consideration for the Jews (comp. Calvin and others), whereas Tholuck contents himself with the assumption of a (strange) *pregnancy* of expression which would include in the one side the other also; and Umbreit regards "the irregularity in the change of person" as *unavoidable*. But the semblance of inappropriateness vanishes on considering καὶ ὑμεῖς in ver. 4 (see on that passage), from which it is plain that Paul in his illustration, ver. 2 f., follows the view, that the death of the husband implies (in a metaphorical sense by virtue of the union of the two spouses in one person, Eph. v. 28 ff.) *the death of the woman also* as respected her married relation, and consequently her release from the law, so far as it had bound her as a ὕπανδρος γυνή to her husband, so that she may now marry another, which previously she could not do, because the law does *not* cease to be lord over the man *before he is dead*. So in substance also Achelis *l.c.* Consequently ver. 2 f. is not to be taken *allegorically*, but properly and concretely; and it is only in ver. 4 that the allegorical *application* occurs. It has been allegorically explained, either so, that the wife signifies the soul and the husband the sin that has died with Christ (Augustine, comp. Olshausen); *or*, that the wife represents humanity (or the church) and the husband the law, to which the former had been spiritually married (Origen, Chrysostom, Calvin, and others, including Klee, Reiche, and Philippi). But the former is utterly foreign to the theme of the text; and the latter would anticipate the application in ver. 4. — ὕπανδρος] *viro subjecta*, married; also current in later

Greek authors, as in Polyb. x. 26, 3, Athen. ix. p. 388 C; in the N. T. only here. See Wetstein and Jacobs, *ad Ael. N. A.* iii. 42. — τῷ ζῶντι ἀνδρί] *to her* (τῷ) *living husband.* ζῶντι has the emphasis, correlative to the ἐφ᾽ ὅσον χρόνον ζῇ in ver. 1. On δέδεται comp. 1 Cor. vii. 27. — νόμῳ] *by the law.* For by the law of Moses the right of dismissing the husband was not given to the wife (Michaelis, *Mos. R.* § 120 ; Saalschütz, p. 806 f.). Paul however leaves unnoticed *the* case of the woman through *divorce* ceasing to be bound to her husband (Deut. xxiv. 2 ; Kiddusch. f. 2, 1 : " Mulier possidet se ipsam *per libellum repudii* et per mortem mariti"), regarding the matter, in accordance with his scope, only in such a way as not merely seemed to be the rule in the majority of cases, but also harmonized with the original ordinance of the Creator (Matth. xix. 8). — κατήργηται ἀπὸ τ. νόμου τ. ἀνδρ.] that is, *with respect to her hitherto subsisting subordination under the law binding her to her husband she is absolved, free and rid of it.* See on Gal. v. 4. The Apostle thus gives expression to the thought lying at the basis of his argument, that with the decease of the husband the wife also has ceased to exist as respects her legal connection with him; in this legal relation, from which she is fully released, she is no longer existent. Comp. on ἀπό 2 Cor. xi. 3. She is still there, but no longer as bound to that law, to which she died with the death of her husband; comp. ver. 6. The joining of ὁ νόμος with the genitive of the subject concerned (frequent in the LXX.) is very common also in classic authors. Th. Schott, following Bengel, erroneously takes τ. ἀνδρ. as genitive of *apposition;* the law being for the wife *embodied* in the husband. The law that *determines the relation of the wife to the husband* is what is intended, like ὁ νόμος ὁ περὶ τοῦ ἀνδρός; see Kühner, II. 1, p. 287.

Ver. 3. Ἄρα οὖν] See on v. 18. — χρηματίσει] she shall (formally) *bear the name.* See Acts xi. 26; Plut. *Mor.* 148 D; Polyb. v. 27, 2, 5, xxx. 2, 4. The *future* corresponds to the following: ἐὰν γένηται ἀνδρὶ ἑτέρῳ] *if she shall have become joined to another husband* (as wife). Comp. Deut. xxiv. 2 ; Ruth i. 12 ; Judg. xiv. 20 ; Ez. xvi. 8, xxiii. 4. It is not a Hebraism ; see Kypke, II. p. 170 ; Kühner, II. 1, p. 384. — ἀπὸ τοῦ νόμου] *from the law,* so far, that is, as it binds the wife to the husband. From that bond she is now released, ver. 2. — τοῦ μὴ εἶναι κ.τ.λ.] Not a more precise definition (Th. Schott); nor yet a consequence (as *usually* rendered), which is never correct, not even in Acts vii. 19 (see Fritzsche, *ad Matth.* p. 845 ff.); but rather: *in order that she be not an adulteress.* That is the *purpose*, involved in the divine legal ordinance, of her freedom from the law.

Ver. 4. "Ὥστε] does not express the "*agreement*" or the "*harmony*" with which what follows connects itself with the preceding (Hofmann), as if Paul had written οὕτως or ὁμοίως. It is rather the common *itaque* (Vulgate), *accordingly, therefore, consequently*, which, heading an independent sentence, draws an inference from the preceding, and introduces the actual relation which results from vv. 1-3 with respect to Christians, who through the death of Christ are in a position corresponding with that of the wife. This *inference* lays down that legal marriage relation as *type.* — καὶ ὑμεῖς] *ye also*, like the wife in that illustration quoted in vv. 2, 3, who through the death of her husband is dead to the dominion of the law. In this, in the first instance (for the main stress falls on εἰς τὸ γενέσθαι κ.τ.λ.), lies the point of the inference; analogously with the case of that wife Christians also are dead to the law through the death of Christ, because, in their spiritual union with Him, they have suffered death along with Him. Van Hengel takes καὶ ὑμεῖς in the sense : ye also, *like other Christians*, which, however, since ver. 4 begins the application of what had previously been said of the *woman*, is neither in harmony with the text nor rendered necessary by the first person καρποφορ. — ἐθανατ. τῷ νόμῳ] *ye were rendered dead to the law*,[1] so that over you as dead persons it rules no longer (ver. 1). The dative as in vi. 2, 10. The *passive* (not ye *died*) is *selected*, because this (ethical) death of Christians is fellowship with the death of Christ, which was a *violent* one. Therefore: διὰ τοῦ σώμ. τ. X.] *by the fact, that the body of Christ was put to death.* The conception of the participation of believers (as respects their

[1] This is expressed from the *Jewish-Christian* consciousness, nevertheless it includes indirectly the *Gentile-Christians* also ; for without perfect obedience to the law *no man* could have attained to salvation, wherefore also obedience to the law was expected on the part of Judaists from the converted Gentiles (Acts xv.). As the argument advances, the language of the Apostle becomes *communicative*, so that he includes himself with his readers, among whom he makes no distinction. Compare viii. 15 ; Gal. iii. 14, iv. 6. By our passage therefore the readers are not indicated as having been, as respects the majority, Jews or at least proselytes.

inner life and its moral self-consciousness) in the death of their Lord, *according to which the putting to death of their Master included their own putting to death*, is justly assumed by Paul, after ch. vi., as something present to the consciousness of his readers, and therefore views deviating from this (*e. g.* that διὰ τ. σώμ. τ. X. applies to the atoning sacrificial death, which did away the dominion of the law) are to be rejected as here irrelevant, and not in keeping with the proper sense of ἐθανατ. For that ἐθανατ. τ. νόμῳ is meant to be a mild expression for ὁ νόμος ἐθανατώθη, ἀπέθανεν ὑμῖν (Koppe and Klee, following Calvin, Grotius, and others, also several Fathers; comp. on ver. 2), is an assumption as gratuitous, as is a "contraction of the thought and expression," which Philippi finds, when he *at the same time* introduces the conception of the putting to death *of the law* through the body of Christ, which is here alien. — εἰς τὸ γενέσθαι ὑμᾶς ἑτέρῳ] *in order to become joined to another* (than the law)—this is the *object* which the ἐθανατ. τ. νόμῳ κ.τ.λ. had, and thereby the *main point* in the declaration introduced by ὥστε, parallel to the τοῦ μὴ εἶναι κ.τ.λ. in ver. 3. Paul apprehends the relation of fellowship and dependence of the Christian's life to Christ—as he had prepared the way for doing so in vv. 2, 3, and as was in keeping with his mode of view elsewhere (2 Cor. xi. 2; Eph. v. 25 ff.)—under the image of a *marriage connection*, in which the exalted Christ is the husband of His Church that has become independent of the law by dying with Him. — τῷ ἐκ νεκρ. ἐγερθ.] apposition to ἑτέρῳ, in significant historical reference to διὰ τ. σώμ. τ. X. For if Christ became *through His bodily death* our deliverer from the law, we cannot now belong to Him otherwise than as the *Risen One* for a new and indissoluble union. The importance of this addition in its bearing on the matter in hand lies in the καινότης ζωῆς (vi. 3, 11, 13, 22) which, on the very ground of the ethical communion with the Risen One, issues from the new relation. Certainly the death of Christ appears here "as the end of a sin-conditioned state of the humanity to be united in Him" (Hofmann, *Schriftbew.* II. 1, p. 354); but this great moral epoch has as its necessary presupposition just the vicarious atoning power of the ἱλαστήριον which was rendered in the death of Jesus; it could not take place without this and without the faith appropriating it, iii. 21 ff.; v. 1 ff. — ἵνα καρποφ. τ. Θεῷ]

The *aim* not of ἐκ νεκρῶν ἐγερθέντι (Koppe, Th. Schott, Hofmann), but rather—because the *belonging to* is that which conditions the fruit-bearing—of the γενέσθαι ὑμᾶς ἑτέρῳ, τῷ ἐκ νεκρ. ἐγ., consequently the final *aim* of the ἐθανατ. τῷ νόμῳ. There is here (though van Hengel and others call it in question, contrary to the clear connection) a continuation of the figure of marriage with respect to its *fruitfulness* (Luke i. 42; Ps. cxxvii. 3, Symm. and Theod. Ps. xci. 15). The morally holy walk, namely, in its consecration to God is, as it were, the fruit which issues from our fellowship of life with Christ risen from the dead as from a new marriage-union, and which *belongs in property* to God as the lord-paramount of that union (the supreme ruler of the Messianic theocracy); the bringing forth of fruit takes place *for God*. The opinion of Reiche and Fritzsche that καρποφ. taken in the sense of the *fruit of marriage* yields an *undignified* allegory (the figure therefore is to be taken as borrowed from a field or a tree, which Philippi, Tholuck, and Reithmayr also prefer) is untenable, seeing that the union with Christ, if regarded as a *marriage* at all, must also necessarily, in accordance with its moral design, be conceived of as a *fruitful marriage*.[1]

Ver. 5. Confirmation of the ἵνα καρποφ. τ. Θεῷ. That we should bring forth fruit to *God*, I say with justice; for formerly under the law we bore fruit to *death*, but now (ver. 6) our position is quite different from what it was before. — ὅτε ἦμεν ἐν τῇ σαρκί] This is the positive and characteristic expression for the negative: when we were not yet made dead to the law. Then the σάρξ—the materially human element in us, in its psychically determined antagonism to the Divine Spirit and will—was the life-element in which we moved. Comp. viii. 8 f.; 2 Cor. x. 3. We are ἐν τ. σώματι, 1 Cor. v. 3 (2 Cor. xii. 2), even after we have died with Christ, because that is an *ethical* death; but for that very reason we are now, according to the holy self-consciousness of the new life of communion with the Risen One, no longer ἐν τ. σαρκί; and our body, although we still as respects its material

---

[1] This view is the one perfectly consistent with the context, and should not be superseded by the prudery of modern canons of taste (Fritzsche terms it *jejunam et obscoenam*). Theodoret already has the right view : καὶ ἐπειδὴ συνάφειαν κ. γάμον τὴν εἰς τὸν κύριον προσηγόρευσε πίστιν, εἰκότως δείκνυσι καὶ τὸν τοῦ γάμου καρπόν. Comp. Theophylact.

substance live in the flesh (Gal. ii. 20), is ethically not a σῶμα τῆς σαρκός any more, Col. ii. 11. The interpretation of Theodoret: τῇ κατὰ νόμον πολιτείᾳ (so also Oecumenius), though hitting the approximate meaning of the matter, has its inaccurate arbitrariness exposed by the reason assigned for it: σάρκα γὰρ τὰς τῇ σαρκὶ δεδομένας νομοθεσίας ὠνόμασε, τὰς περὶ βρώσεως κ. πόσεως. The description ἐν τῇ σαρκί must supply the ethical conception which corresponds with the contents of the apodosis. Therefore we may not render with Theodore of Mopsuestia: *when we were mortal* (the believer being no longer reckoned as mortal); but the *moral* reference of the expression requires at least a more precise definition of the contents than that the existence of the Christian had ceased to be *an existence locked up in his inborn nature* (Hofmann). — τὰ παθ. τῶν ἁμαρτ.] *the passions through which sins are brought about*, of which the sins are the actual *consequence*. On παθήματα compare Gal. v. 24, and παθή, i. 26. They are the passive excitations (often used by Plato in contrast to ποιήματα), which one experiences (πάσχει). Comp. esp. Plat. *Phil.* p. 47 C. — τὰ διὰ τ. νόμου] sc. ὄντα, *which are occasioned by the law;* How? see vv. 7, 8. It is erroneous in Chrysostom and Grotius to supply φαινόμενα. Comp. rather 1 Cor. xv. 56. — ἐνηργεῖτο] *were active*, middle, not passive (Estius, Glöckler) which would be contrary to Pauline usage. See 2 Cor. i. 6, iv. 12; Eph. iii. 20; Gal. v. 6; Col. i. 29; 1 Thess. ii. 13; 2 Thess. ii. 7. The Greeks have not this use of the middle. — ἐν τ. μέλ. ἡμ.] *in our members* (as in ver. 23 and vi. 13) they were the active agent. — εἰς τὸ καρποφ. τ. θανάτῳ] This is the *tendency* (the parallel ἵνα καρποφ. τ. Θεῷ in ver. 4 is decisive here against the interpretation, everywhere erroneous, of the *consequence*) which the passions of sin, in their operation in our members, had with us · *that we should bring forth fruit unto death*, that is, divested of figure: *that we should lead a life falling under the power of death*. The subject ἡμᾶς is supplied, as often along with the infinitive (comp. Kühner, ad *Xen. Mem.* iii. 6, 10; *Anab.* ii. 1, 12), naturally and easily from the immediately preceding ἡμῶν (comp. 1 Cor. viii. 10; 2 Thess. iii. 9; Heb. ix. 14). There is therefore the less reason to depart from the mode of conception prevailing in ver. 4, and to understand the παθήματα as the fruit-bearing subjects (Hofmann; comp. Vulgate, Luther, Calvin, and others), in which case there is imported the conception that the occurrence is something *foreign to the man himself* (Hofmann). The θάνατος, personified as the lord-paramount opposed to τῷ Θεῷ in ver. 4, is not *physical* (Fritzsche) but *eternal* death, vi. 21, 23, which is incurred through sinful life. The καρποφ. however retains here the figure of the *fruit of marriage*, namely, according to the context, of the marriage with the law (ver. 4), which is now dissolved since we have died with Christ. Comp. Erasmus, *Paraph.*: "ex infelici matrimonio infelices foetus sustulimus, quicquid nasceretur morti exitioque gignentes." In Matth. xii. 39 the conception is different. But comp. James i. 15.

Ver. 6. κατηργ.] See on ver. 2. — ἀποθανόντες ἐν ᾧ κατειχ.] *dead* (see ver. 4) *to that* (neuter) *wherein we were held fast.* So also Fritzsche and Reiche in his *Comm. crit.* The construction is consistent and regular, so that τούτῳ is to be understood before ἐν ᾧ (Winer, p. 149 f. [E. T. 203 f.]). That wherein we were held fast (as in a prison), is self-evident according to the text; not as the *government of sin* (van Hengel, Th. Schott), or as the σάρξ (Hofmann), but as the *law* in whose grasp we were. Comp. Gal. iii. 28. Were we with the majority (including Rückert, de Wette, Köllner, Krehl, Philippi, Maier, Winer, Ewald, Bisping, and Reithmayr) to take ἐν ᾧ as *masculine* (and how unnecessarily!), the ἀποθανόντες as modal definition of κατηργ. would have an isolated and forlorn position; we should have expected it behind νυνὶ δέ. — ὥστε δουλεύειν κ.τ.λ.] actual result, which has occurred through our emancipation from the law: *so that we* (as Christians) *are serviceable in newness of spirit, and not in oldness of letter;* that is, so that our relation of service is in a new definite character regulated by spirit, and not in the old constitution which was regulated by literal form. That the δουλεύειν in καινότης πνεύμ. was a service of *God*, was just as obvious of itself to the consciousness of the readers, as that in παλαιότης γράμμ. it had been a service *of sin* (vi. 20). On account of this self-evident *diversity* of reference no definition at all is added. On the οὐ in the contrast (not μή) see Buttmann, *neut. Gr.* p. 300. — ἐν indicates the sphere of activity of the δουλεύειν, and is to be understood again along with παλ.; comp. ii. 29. The qualitatively expressed πνεύματος, meaning in concrete application the *Holy* Spirit as the efficient principle of the Christian life, and the qualitative γράμματος, characterising the law according to its nature and character as non-living and drawn up in letters, are the specifically heterogeneous factors on which the two contrasted states are dependent. The παλαιότης —in accordance with the nature of the relation in which the law, presenting its demands in the letter but not inwardly operative, stands to the principle of sin in man—was *necessarily* sinful (not merely in actual abnormality, as Rothe thinks; see ver. 7 ff., and comp. on vi. 14); just as on the other hand the καινότης, on account of the vitally active πνεῦμα, must also necessarily be moral. Where this is contradicted by experience and the behaviour of the Christian is immoral, there the πνεῦμα has ceased to operate, and a καινότης πνεύματος is in fact not present at all. Paul however, disregarding such abnormal phenomena, contemplates the Christian life as it is constituted in accordance with its new, holy, and lofty nature. If it is otherwise, it has fallen away from its specific nature and is a *Christian* life no longer.

END OF VOLUME FIRST.

NEW SERIES

OF THE

FOREIGN THEOLOGICAL LIBRARY.

The Issue for 1882 *comprises—*
DORNER'S SYSTEM OF CHRISTIAN DOCTRINE. Vols. III. and IV. (completion).
WEISS'S BIBLICAL THEOLOGY OF THE NEW TESTAMENT. Vol. I.
MARTENSEN'S CHRISTIAN ETHICS. (Social Ethics.)

1880.—GODET'S COMMENTARY ON THE EPISTLE OF ST. PAUL TO THE ROMANS. Vol. I.
HAGENBACH'S HISTORY OF DOCTRINES. Vols. I. and II.
DORNER'S SYSTEM OF CHRISTIAN DOCTRINE. Vol. I.

1881.—GODET'S COMMENTARY ON THE EPISTLE OF ST. PAUL TO THE ROMANS. Vol. II.
DORNER'S SYSTEM OF CHRISTIAN DOCTRINE. Vol. II.
MARTENSEN'S CHRISTIAN ETHICS. (Individual Ethics.)
HAGENBACH'S HISTORY OF DOCTRINES. Vol. III. (completion).

The FOREIGN THEOLOGICAL LIBRARY was commenced in 1846, and from that time to this Four Volumes yearly (or 148 in all) have appeared with the utmost regularity.

The Publishers decided to begin a NEW SERIES with 1880, and so give an opportunity to many to subscribe who are possibly deterred by the extent of the former Series.

With this view, Messrs. CLARK beg to announce as in preparation
DR. KEIL'S HANDBOOK OF BIBLICAL ARCHÆOLOGY.
GOEBEL'S PARABLES OF JESUS.
REUSCH'S BIBLE AND NATURE.
WEISS'S LIFE OF CHRIST.

From time to time other works will be added to this list; but the Publishers are sanguine enough to believe that a Series containing the works of writers so eminent, upon the most important subjects, cannot fail to secure support.

The Binding of the Series is modernized, so as to distinguish it from the former Series.

The Subscription Price will remain as formerly, 21s. annually for Four Volumes, payable in advance.

A SELECTION OF TWENTY VOLUMES
FOR FIVE GUINEAS

May be had from the Volumes issued previously to New Series, viz.:—
Works mentioned on pages 2, 3, 4.

[See pages 2, 3, 4.

T. and T. Clark's Publications.

MESSRS. CLARK allow a SELECTION of TWENTY VOLUMES (*or more at the same ratio*) from the Volumes issued previously to New Series (*see below*),

At the Subscription Price of Five Guineas.

NON-SUBSCRIPTION PRICES WITHIN BRACKETS.

Dr. Hengstenberg.—**Commentary on the Psalms.** By E. W. HENGSTENBERG, D.D., Professor of Theology in Berlin. In Three Vols. 8vo. (33s.)

Dr. Gieseler.—**Compendium of Ecclesiastical History.** By J. C. L. GIESELER, D.D., Professor of Theology in Göttingen. Five Vols. 8vo. (£2, 12s. 6d.)

Dr. Olshausen.—**Biblical Commentary on the Gospels and Acts.** Adapted especially for Preachers and Students. By HERMANN OLSHAUSEN, D.D., Professor of Theology in the University of Erlangen. In Four Vols. 8vo. (£2, 2s.)—**Commentary on the Romans.** In One Vol. 8vo. (10s. 6d.)—**Commentary on St. Paul's First and Second Epistles to the Corinthians.** In One Vol. 8vo. (9s.)—**Commentary on St. Paul's Epistles to the Philippians, to Titus, and the First to Timothy.** In continuation of the Work of Olshausen. By LIC. AUGUST WIESINGER. In One Vol. 8vo. (10s. 6d.)

Dr. Neander.—**General History of the Christian Religion and Church.** By AUGUSTUS NEANDER, D.D. Nine Vols. 8vo. (£3, 7s. 6d.)

Prof. H. A. Ch. Hävernick.—**General Introduction to the Old Testament.** By Professor HÄVERNICK. One Vol. 8vo. (10s. 6d.)

Dr. Müller.—**The Christian Doctrine of Sin.** By Dr. JULIUS MÜLLER. Two Vols. 8vo. (21s.) New Edition.

Dr. Hengstenberg.—**Christology of the Old Testament, and a Commentary on the Messianic Predictions.** By E. W. HENGSTENBERG, D.D. Four Vols. (£2, 2s.)

Dr. M. Baumgarten.—**The Acts of the Apostles; or, The History of the Church in the Apostolic Age.** By M. BAUMGARTEN, Ph.D. Three Vols. (£1, 7s.)

Dr. Stier.—**The Words of the Lord Jesus.** By RUDOLPH STIER, D.D., Chief Pastor and Superintendent of Schkeuditz. In Eight Vols. 8vo. (£4, 4s.)

Dr. Carl Ullmann.—**Reformers before the Reformation, principally in Germany and the Netherlands.** Two Vols. 8vo. (£1, 1s.)

Professor Kurtz.—**History of the Old Covenant; or, Old Testament Dispensation.** By Professor KURTZ of Dorpat. In Three Vols. (£1, 11s. 6d.)

Dr. Stier.—**The Words of the Risen Saviour, and Commentary on the Epistle of St. James.** By RUDOLPH STIER, D.D. One Vol. (10s. 6d.)

Professor Tholuck.—**Commentary on the Gospel of St. John.** One Vol. (9s.)

Professor Tholuck.—**Commentary on the Sermon on the Mount.** One Vol. (10s. 6d.)

Dr. Hengstenberg.—**On the Book of Ecclesiastes.** To which are appended: Treatises on the Song of Solomon; the Book of Job; the Prophet Isaiah; the Sacrifices of Holy Scripture; and on the Jews and the Christian Church. In One Vol. 8vo. (9s.)

Dr. Ebrard.—**Commentary on the Epistles of St. John.** By Dr. JOHN H. A. EBRARD, Professor of Theology. In One Vol. (10s. 6d.)

Dr. Lange.—**Theological and Homiletical Commentary on the Gospels of St. Matthew and Mark.** By J. P. LANGE, D.D. Three Vols. (10s. 6d. each.)

Dr. Dorner.—**History of the Development of the Doctrine of the Person of Christ.** By Dr. I. A. DORNER, Professor of Theology in the University of Berlin. Five Vols. (£2, 12s. 6d.)

Lange and Dr. J. J. Van Oosterzee.—**Theological and Homiletical Commentary on the Gospel of St. Luke.** Two Vols. (18s.)

Dr. Ebrard.—**The Gospel History: A Compendium of Critical Investigations in support of the Historical Character of the Four Gospels.** One Vol. (10s. 6d.)

Lange, Lechler, and Gerok.—**Theological and Homiletical Commentary on the Acts of the Apostles.** Edited by Dr. LANGE. Two Vols. (21s.)

Dr. Hengstenberg.—**Commentary on the Gospel of St. John.** Two Vols. (21s.)

Professor Keil.—**Biblical Commentary on the Pentateuch.** Three Vols. (31s. 6d.)

T. and T. Clark's Publications. 3

CLARK'S FOREIGN THEOLOGICAL LIBRARY—Continued.

Professor Keil.—Commentary on Joshua, Judges, and Ruth. One Vol. (10s. 6d.)
Professor Delitzsch.—A System of Biblical Psychology. One Vol. (12s.)
Dr. C. A. Auberlen.—The Divine Revelation. 8vo. (10s. 6d.)
Professor Delitzsch.—Commentary on the Prophecies of Isaiah. Two Vols. (21s.)
Professor Keil.—Commentary on the Books of Samuel. One Vol. (10s. 6d.)
Professor Delitzsch.—Commentary on the Book of Job. Two Vols. (21s.)
Bishop Martensen.—Christian Dogmatics. A Compendium of the Doctrines of Christianity. One Vol. (10s. 6d.)
Dr. J. P. Lange.—Commentary on the Gospel of St. John. Two Vols. (21s.)
Professor Keil.—Commentary on the Minor Prophets. Two Vols. (21s.)
Professor Delitzsch.—Commentary on Epistle to the Hebrews. Two Vols. (21s.)
Dr. Harless.—A System of Christian Ethics. One Vol. (10s. 6d.)
Dr. Hengstenberg.—Commentary on Ezekiel. One Vol. (10s. 6d.)
Dr. Stier.—The Words of the Apostles Expounded. One Vol. (10s. 6d.)
Professor Keil.—Introduction to the Old Testament. Two Vols. (21s.)
Professor Bleek.—Introduction to the New Testament. Two Vols. (21s.)
Professor Schmid.—New Testament Theology. One Vol. (10s. 6d.)
Professor Delitzsch.—Commentary on the Psalms. Three Vols. (31s. 6d.)
Dr. Hengstenberg.—The Kingdom of God under the Old Covenant. Two Vols. (21s.)
Professor Keil.—Commentary on the Books of Kings. One Volume. (10s. 6d.)
Professor Keil.—Commentary on the Book of Daniel. One Volume. (10s. 6d.)
Professor Keil.—Commentary on the Books of Chronicles. One Volume. (10s. 6d.)
Professor Keil.—Commentary on Ezra, Nehemiah, and Esther. One Vol. (10s. 6d.)
Professor Keil.—Commentary on Jeremiah. Two Vols. (21s.)
Winer (Dr. G. B.)—Collection of the Confessions of Christendom. One Vol. (10s. 6d.)
Bishop Martensen.—Christian Ethics. One Volume. (10s. 6d.)
Professor Delitzsch.—Commentary on the Proverbs of Solomon. Two Vols. (21s.)
Professor Oehler.—Biblical Theology of the Old Testament. Two Vols. (21s.)
Professor Christlieb.—Modern Doubt and Christian Belief. One Vol. (10s. 6d.)
Professor Godet.—Commentary on St. Luke's Gospel. Two Vols. (21s.)
Professor Luthardt.—Commentary on St. John's Gospel. Three Vols. (31s. 6d.)
Professor Godet.—Commentary on St. John's Gospel. Three Vols. (31s. 6d.)
Professor Keil.—Commentary on Ezekiel. Two Vols. (21s.)
Professor Delitzsch.—Commentary on Song of Solomon and Ecclesiastes. One Vol. (10s. 6d.)
Gebhardt (H.)—Doctrine of the Apocalypse. One Vol. (10s. 6d.)
Steinmeyer (Dr. F. L.)—History of the Passion and Resurrection of our Lord. One Vol. (10s. 6d.)
Haupt (E.)—Commentary on the First Epistle of St. John. One Vol. (10s. 6d.)
Hagenbach (Dr. K. R.)—History of the Reformation. Two Vols. (21s.)
Philippi (Dr. F. A.)—Commentary on Romans. Two Vols. (21s.)

And, in connection with the Series—

Murphy's Commentary on the Book of Psalms. *To count as Two Volumes.* (12s.)
Alexander's Commentary on Isaiah. Two Volumes. (17s.)
Ritter's (Carl) Comparative Geography of Palestine. Four Volumes. (32s.)
Shedd's History of Christian Doctrine. Two Volumes. (21s.)
Macdonald's Introduction to the Pentateuch. Two Volumes. (21s.)
Gerlach's Commentary on the Pentateuch. 8vo. (10s. 6d.)
Dr. Hengstenberg.—Dissertations on the Genuineness of Daniel, etc. One Vol.

The series, in 155 Volumes (including 1882), price £40, 13s. 9d., forms an *Apparatus* without which it may be truly said *no Theological Library can be complete;* and the Publishers take the liberty of suggesting that no more appropriate gift could be presented to a Clergyman than the Series, in whole or in part.

*** No DUPLICATES *can be included in the Selection of Twenty Volumes; and it will save trouble and correspondence if it be distinctly understood that* NO LESS *number than Twenty can be supplied, unless at non-subscription price.*

Subscribers' Names received by all Retail Booksellers.

LONDON: (*For Works at Non-subscription price only*) HAMILTON, ADAMS, & CO.

FOREIGN THEOLOGICAL LIBRARY.

ANNUAL SUBSCRIPTION: One Guinea for Four Volumes, Demy 8vo.

N.B.—Any *two* Years in this Series can be had at Subscription Price. *A single Year's Books* (except in the case of the current Year) *cannot be supplied separately.* Non-subscribers, price 10s. 6d. each volume, with exceptions marked.

1 8 6 4— Lange on the Acts of the Apostles. Two Volumes.
Keil and Delitzsch on the Pentateuch. Vols. I. and II.

1 8 6 5— Keil and Delitzsch on the Pentateuch. Vol. III.
Hengstenberg on the Gospel of John. Two Volumes.
Keil and Delitzsch on Joshua, Judges, and Ruth. One Volume.

1 8 6 6— Keil and Delitzsch on Samuel. One Volume.
Keil and Delitzsch on Job. Two Volumes.
Martensen's System of Christian Doctrine. One Volume.

1 8 6 7— Delitzsch on Isaiah. Two Volumes.
Delitzsch on Biblical Psychology. (12s.) One Volume.
Auberlen on Divine Revelation. One Volume.

1 8 6 8— Keil's Commentary on the Minor Prophets. Two Volumes.
Delitzsch's Commentary on Epistle to the Hebrews. Vol. I.
Harless' System of Christian Ethics. One Volume.

1 8 6 9— Hengstenberg on Ezekiel. One Volume.
Stier on the Words of the Apostles. One Volume.
Keil's Introduction to the Old Testament. Vol. I.
Bleek's Introduction to the New Testament. Vol. I.

1 8 7 0— Keil's Introduction to the Old Testament. Vol. II.
Bleek's Introduction to the New Testament. Vol. II.
Schmid's New Testament Theology. One Volume.
Delitzsch's Commentary on Epistle to the Hebrews. Vol. II.

1 8 7 1— Delitzsch's Commentary on the Psalms. Three Volumes.
Hengstenberg's Kingdom of God under the Old Testament. Vol. I.

1 8 7 2— Keil's Commentary on the Books of Kings. One Volume.
Keil's Commentary on the Book of Daniel. One Volume.
Keil's Commentary on the Books of Chronicles. One Volume.
Hengstenberg's History of the Kingdom of God. Vol. II.

1 8 7 3— Keil's Commentary on Ezra, Nehemiah, and Esther. One Volume.
Winer's Collection of the Confessions of Christendom. One Volume.
Keil's Commentary on Jeremiah. Vol. I.
Martensen on Christian Ethics.

1 8 7 4— Christlieb's Modern Doubt and Christian Belief. One Vol.
Keil's Commentary on Jeremiah. Vol. II.
Delitzsch's Commentary on Proverbs. Vol. I.
Oehler's Biblical Theology of the Old Testament. Vol. I.

1 8 7 5— Godet's Commentary on St. Luke's Gospel. Two Volumes.
Oehler's Biblical Theology of the Old Testament. Vol. II.
Delitzsch's Commentary on Proverbs. Vol. II.

1 8 7 6— Keil's Commentary on Ezekiel. Two Volumes.
Luthardt's Commentary on St. John's Gospel. Vol. I.
Godet's Commentary on St. John's Gospel. Vol. I.

1 8 7 7— Delitzsch's Commentary on Song of Solomon and Ecclesiastes.
Godet's Commentary on St. John's Gospel. Vols. II. and III.
Luthardt's Commentary on St. John's Gospel. Vol. II.

1 8 7 8— Gebhardt's Doctrine of the Apocalypse.
Luthardt's Commentary on St. John's Gospel. Vol. III.
Philippi's Commentary on the Romans. Vol. I.
Hagenbach's History of the Reformation. Vol. I.

1 8 7 9— Philippi's Commentary on the Romans. Vol. II.
Hagenbach's History of the Reformation. Vol. II.
Steinmeyer's History of the Passion and Resurrection of our Lord.
Haupt's Commentary on the First Epistle of St. John. One Volume.

_{*} *For New Series commencing with* 1880, *see page* 1.

T. and T. Clark's Publications.

In Twenty Handsome 8vo Volumes, SUBSCRIPTION PRICE £5, 5s.,

MEYER'S
Commentary on the New Testament.

'Meyer has been long and well known to scholars as one of the very ablest of the German expositors of the New Testament. We are not sure whether we ought not to say that he is unrivalled as an interpreter of the grammatical and historical meaning of the sacred writers. The Publishers have now rendered another seasonable and important service to English students in producing this translation.'—*Guardian.*

(Yearly Issue of Four Volumes, 21s.)
Each Volume will be sold separately at (on an average) 10s. 6d. *to Non-Subscribers.*

CRITICAL AND EXEGETICAL
COMMENTARY ON THE NEW TESTAMENT.
By Dr. H. A. W. MEYER,
OBERCONSISTORIALRATH, HANNOVER.

The portion contributed by Dr. MEYER has been placed under the editorial care of Rev. Dr. DICKSON, Professor of Divinity in the University of Glasgow; Rev. Dr. CROMBIE, Professor of Biblical Criticism, St. Mary's College, St. Andrews; and Rev. Dr. STEWART, Professor of Biblical Criticism, University of Glasgow.

1st Year—Romans, Two Volumes.
Galatians, One Volume.
St. John's Gospel, Vol. I.

2d Year—St. John's Gospel, Vol. II.
Philippians and Colossians, One Volume.
Acts of the Apostles, Vol. I.
Corinthians, Vol. I.

3d Year—Acts of the Apostles, Vol. II.
St. Matthew's Gospel, Two Volumes.
Corinthians, Vol. II.

4th Year—Mark and Luke, Two Volumes.
Ephesians and Philemon, One Volume.
Thessalonians. (*Dr. Lünemann.*)

5th Year—Timothy and Titus. (*Dr. Huther.*)
Peter and Jude. (*Dr. Huther.*)
Hebrews. (*Dr. Lünemann.*)
James and John. (*Dr. Huther.*)

The series, as written by Meyer himself, is completed by the publication of Ephesians with Philemon in one volume. But to this the Publishers have thought it right to add Thessalonians and Hebrews, by Dr. Lünemann, and the Pastoral and Catholic Epistles, by Dr. Huther. So few, however, of the Subscribers have expressed a desire to have Dr. Düsterdieck's Commentary on Revelation included, that it has been resolved in the meantime not to undertake it.

'I need hardly add that the last edition of the accurate, perspicuous, and learned commentary of Dr. Meyer has been most carefully consulted throughout; and I must again, as in the preface to the Galatians, avow my great obligations to the acumen and scholarship of the learned editor.'—BISHOP ELLICOTT *in Preface to his* '*Commentary on Ephesians.*'
'The ablest grammatical exegete of the age.'—PHILIP SCHAFF, D.D.
'In accuracy of scholarship and freedom from prejudice, he is equalled by few.'—*Literary Churchman.*
'We have only to repeat that it remains, of its own kind, the very best Commentary of the New Testament which we possess.'—*Church Bells.*
'No exegetical work is on the whole more valuable, or stands in higher public esteem. As a critic he is candid and cautious; exact to minuteness in philology; a master of the grammatical and historical method of interpretation.'—*Princeton Review.*

In Twenty-four Handsome 8vo Volumes, Subscription Price £6, 6s. 0d.,

Ante=Nicene Christian Library.

A COLLECTION OF ALL THE WORKS OF THE FATHERS OF THE CHRISTIAN CHURCH PRIOR TO THE COUNCIL OF NICÆA.

EDITED BY THE

REV. ALEXANDER ROBERTS, D.D., AND JAMES DONALDSON, LL.D.

MESSRS. CLARK are now happy to announce the completion of this Series. It has been received with marked approval by all sections of the Christian Church in this country and in the United States, as supplying what has long been felt to be a want, and also on account of the impartiality, learning, and care with which Editors and Translators have executed a very difficult task.

The Publishers do not bind themselves to *continue* to supply the Series at the Subscription price.

The Works are arranged as follow:—

FIRST YEAR.

APOSTOLIC FATHERS, comprising Clement's Epistles to the Corinthians; Polycarp to the Ephesians; Martyrdom of Polycarp; Epistle of Barnabas; Epistles of Ignatius (longer and shorter, and also the Syriac version); Martyrdom of Ignatius; Epistle to Diognetus; Pastor of Hermas; Papias; Spurious Epistles of Ignatius. In One Volume.
JUSTIN MARTYR; ATHENAGORAS. In One Volume.
TATIAN; THEOPHILUS; THE CLEmentine Recognitions. In One Volume.
CLEMENT OF ALEXANDRIA, Volume First, comprising Exhortation to Heathen; The Instructor; and a portion of the Miscellanies.

SECOND YEAR.

HIPPOLYTUS, Volume First; Refutation of all Heresies, and Fragments from his Commentaries.
IRENÆUS, Volume First.
TERTULLIAN AGAINST MARCION.
CYPRIAN, Volume First; the Epistles, and some of the Treatises.

THIRD YEAR.

IRENÆUS (completion); HIPPOLYTUS (completion); Fragments of Third Century. In One Volume.
ORIGEN: De Principiis; Letters; and portion of Treatise against Celsus.

CLEMENT OF ALEXANDRIA, Volume Second; Completion of Miscellanies.
TERTULLIAN, Volume First; To the Martyrs; Apology; To the Nations, etc.

FOURTH YEAR.

CYPRIAN, Volume Second (completion); Novatian; Minucius Felix; Fragments.
METHODIUS; ALEXANDER OF LYcopolis; Peter of Alexandria; Anatolius; Clement on Virginity; and Fragments.
TERTULLIAN, Volume Second.
APOCRYPHAL GOSPELS, ACTS, AND Revelations; comprising all the very curious Apocryphal Writings of the first three Centuries.

FIFTH YEAR.

TERTULLIAN, Volume Third (completion).
CLEMENTINE HOMILIES; APOSTOlical Constitutions. In One Volume.
ARNOBIUS.
DIONYSIUS; GREGORY THAUMAturgus; Syrian Fragments. In One Volume.

SIXTH YEAR.

LACTANTIUS; Two Volumes.
ORIGEN, Volume Second (completion). 12s. to Non-Subscribers.
EARLY LITURGIES AND REMAINing Fragments. 9s. to Non-Subscribers.

Single Years cannot be had separately, unless to complete sets; but any Volume may be had separately, price 10s. 6d.,—with the exception of ORIGEN, Vol. II., 12s., and the EARLY LITURGIES, 9s.

T. and T. Clark's Publications. 7

In Fifteen Volumes, demy 8vo, Subscription Price £3, 19s.
(*Yearly issues of Four Volumes,* 21s.)

The Works of St. Augustine.

EDITED BY MARCUS DODS, D.D.

SUBSCRIPTION:
Four Volumes for a Guinea, *payable in advance* (24s. when not paid in advance).

FIRST YEAR.

THE 'CITY OF GOD.' Two Volumes.
WRITINGS IN CONNECTION WITH the Donatist Controversy. In One Volume.
THE ANTI-PELAGIAN WORKS OF St. Augustine. Vol. I.

SECOND YEAR.

'LETTERS.' Vol. I.
TREATISES AGAINST FAUSTUS the Manichæan. One Volume.
THE HARMONY OF THE EVANgelists, and the Sermon on the Mount. One Volume.
ON THE TRINITY. One Volume.

THIRD YEAR.

COMMENTARY ON JOHN. Two Volumes.
ON CHRISTIAN DOCTRINE, ENCHIRIDION, ON CATECHIZING, and ON FAITH AND THE CREED. One Volume.
THE ANTI-PELAGIAN WORKS OF St. Augustine. Vol. II.

FOURTH YEAR.

'LETTERS.' Vol. II.
'CONFESSIONS.' With Copious Notes by Rev. J. G. PILKINGTON.
ANTI-PELAGIAN WRITINGS. Vol. III.

Messrs. CLARK believe this will prove not the least valuable of their various Series. Every care has been taken to secure not only accuracy, but elegance.
It is understood that Subscribers are bound to take at least the issues for two years. Each volume is sold separately at 10s. 6d.

'For the reproduction of the "City of God" in an admirable English garb we are greatly indebted to the well-directed enterprise and energy of Messrs. Clark, and to the accuracy and scholarship of those who have undertaken the laborious task of translation.' —*Christian Observer.*
'The present translation reads smoothly and pleasantly, and we have every reason to be satisfied both with the erudition and the fair and sound judgment displayed by the translators and the editor.'—*John Bull.*

SELECTION FROM
ANTE-NICENE LIBRARY
AND
ST. AUGUSTINE'S WORKS.

THE Ante-Nicene Library being now completed in 24 volumes, and the St. Augustine Series being also complete (*with the exception of the* 'LIFE') in 15 volumes, Messrs. CLARK will, as in the case of the Foreign Theological Library, give a Selection of 20 Volumes from both of those series at the *Subscription Price* of FIVE GUINEAS (or a larger number at same proportion).

LANGE'S COMMENTARIES.

(*Subscription price, nett*), 15s. each.

THEOLOGICAL AND HOMILETICAL COMMENTARY ON THE OLD AND NEW TESTAMENTS. Specially designed and adapted for the use of Ministers and Students. By Prof. JOHN PETER LANGE, D.D., in connection with a number of eminent European Divines. Translated, enlarged, and revised under the general editorship of Rev. Dr. PHILIP SCHAFF, assisted by leading Divines of the various Evangelical Denominations.

OLD TESTAMENT—14 VOLUMES.

I. **GENESIS.** With a General Introduction to the Old Testament. By Prof. J. P. LANGE, D.D. Translated from the German, with Additions, by Prof. TAYLER LEWIS, LL.D., and A. GOSMAN, D.D.

II. **EXODUS.** By J. P. LANGE, D.D. LEVITICUS. By J. P. LANGE, D.D. With GENERAL INTRODUCTION by Rev. Dr. OSGOOD.

III. **NUMBERS AND DEUTERONOMY.** NUMBERS. By Prof. J. P. LANGE, D.D. DEUTERONOMY. By W. J. SCHROEDER.

IV. **JOSHUA.** By Rev. F. R. FAY. **JUDGES** and **RUTH.** By Prof. PAULUS CASSELL, D.D.

V. **SAMUEL,** I. and II. By Professor ERDMANN, D.D.

VI. **KINGS.** By KARL CHR. W. F. BAHR, D.D.

VII. **CHRONICLES,** I. and II. By OTTO ZÖCKLER. **EZRA.** By FR. W. SCHULTZ. **NEHEMIAH.** By Rev. HOWARD CROSBY, D.D., LL.D. **ESTHER.** By FR. W. SCHULTZ.

VIII. **JOB.** With an Introduction and Annotations by Prof. TAYLER LEWIS, LL.D. A Commentary by Dr. OTTO ZÖCKLER, together with an Introductory Essay on Hebrew Poetry by Prof. PHILIP SCHAFF, D.D.

IX. **THE PSALMS.** By CARL BERNHARDT MOLL, D.D. With a new Metrical Version of the Psalms, and Philological Notes, by T. J. CONANT, D.D.

X. **PROVERBS.** By Prof. OTTO ZÖCKLER, D.D. **ECCLESIASTES.** By Prof. O. ZÖCKLER, D.D. With Additions, and a new Metrical Version, by Prof. TAYLER LEWIS, D.D. **THE SONG OF SOLOMON.** By Prof. O. ZÖCKLER, D.D.

XI. **ISAIAH.** By C. W. E. NAEGELSBACH.

XII. **JEREMIAH.** By C. W. E. NAEGELSBACH, D.D. **LAMENTATIONS.** By C. W. E. NAEGELSBACH, D.D.

XIII. **EZEKIEL.** By F. W. SCHRÖDER, D.D. **DANIEL.** By Professor ZÖCKLER, D.D.

XIV. **THE MINOR PROPHETS. HOSEA, JOEL,** and **AMOS.** By OTTO SCHMOLLER, Ph.D. **OBADIAH** and **MICAH.** By Rev. PAUL KLEINERT. **JONAH, NAHUM, HABAKKUK,** and **ZEPHANIAH.** By Rev. PAUL KLEINERT. **HAGGAI.** By Rev. JAMES E. M'CURDY. **ZECHARIAH.** By T. W. CHAMBERS, D.D. **MALACHI.** By JOSEPH PACKARD, D.D.

THE APOCRYPHA. (*Just published.*) By E. C. BISSELL, D.D. One Volume.

NEW TESTAMENT—10 VOLUMES.

I. **MATTHEW.** With a General Introduction to the New Testament. By J. P. LANGE, D.D. Translated, with Additions, by PHILIP SCHAFF, D.D.

II. **MARK.** By J. P. LANGE, D.D. **LUKE.** By J. J. VAN OOSTERZEE.

III. **JOHN.** By J. P. LANGE, D.D.

IV. **ACTS.** By G. V. LECHLER, D.D., and Rev. CHARLES GEROK.

V. **ROMANS.** By J. P. LANGE, D.D., and Rev. F. R. FAY.

VI. **CORINTHIANS.** By CHRISTIAN F. KLING.

VII. **GALATIANS.** By OTTO SCHMOLLER, Ph.D. **EPHESIANS** and **COLOSSIANS.** By KARL BRAUNE, D.D. **PHILIPPIANS.** By KARL BRAUNE, D.D.

VIII. **THESSALONIANS.** By Drs. AUBERLIN and RIGGENBACH. **TIMOTHY.** By J. J. VAN OOSTERZEE, D.D. **TITUS.** By J. VAN OOSTERZEE, D.D. **PHILEMON.** By J. VAN OOSTERZEE, D.D. **HEBREWS.** By KARL B. MOLL, D.D.

IX. **JAMES.** By J. P. LANGE, D.D., and J. J. VAN OOSTERZEE, D.D. **PETER** and **JUDE.** By G. F. C. FRONMÜLLER, Ph.D. **JOHN.** By KARL BRAUNE, D.D.

X. **THE REVELATION OF JOHN.** By Dr. J. P. LANGE. Together with double Alphabetical Index to all the Ten Volumes on the New Testament, by JOHN H. WOODS.

CHEAP RE-ISSUE OF
STIER'S WORDS OF THE LORD JESUS.

To meet a very general desire that this now well-known Work should be brought more within the reach of all classes, both Clergy and Laity, Messrs. CLARK are now issuing, for a limited period, the *Eight* Volumes, handsomely bound in *Four*, at the *Subscription Price* of

TWO GUINEAS

As the allowance to the Trade must necessarily be small, orders sent either direct or through Booksellers must *in every case* be accompanied with a Post Office Order for the above amount.

'The whole work is a treasury of thoughtful exposition. Its measure of practical and spiritual application, with exegetical criticism, commends it to the use of those whose duty it is to preach as well as to understand the Gospel of Christ.'—*Guardian.*

New and Cheap Edition, in Four Vols., demy 8vo, *Subscription Price* 28s.,

THE LIFE OF THE LORD JESUS CHRIST:

A Complete Critical Examination of the Origin, Contents, and Connection of the Gospels. Translated from the German of J. P. LANGE, D.D., Professor of Divinity in the University of Bonn. Edited, with additional Notes, by MARCUS DODS, D.D.

'We have arrived at a most favourable conclusion regarding the importance and ability of this work—the former depending upon the present condition of theological criticism, the latter on the wide range of the work itself; the singularly dispassionate judgment of the Author, as well as his pious, reverential, and erudite treatment of a subject inexpressibly holy. . . . We have great pleasure in recommending this work to our readers. We are convinced of its value and enormous range.'—*Irish Ecclesiastical Gazette.*

BENGEL'S GNOMON—CHEAP EDITION.
GNOMON OF THE NEW TESTAMENT.

By JOHN ALBERT BENGEL. Now first translated into English. With Original Notes, Explanatory and Illustrative. Edited by the Rev. ANDREW R. FAUSSET, M.A. The Original Translation was in Five Large Volumes, demy 8vo, averaging more than 550 pages each, and the very great demand for this Edition has induced the Publishers to issue the *Five* Volumes bound in *Three*, at the *Subscription Price* of

TWENTY-FOUR SHILLINGS.

They trust by this still further to increase its usefulness.

'It is a work which manifests the most intimate and profound knowledge of Scripture, and which, if we examine it with care, will often be found to condense more matter into a line than can be extracted from many pages of other writers.'—*Archdeacon* HARE.

'In respect both of its contents and its tone, Bengel's Gnomon stands alone. Even among laymen there has arisen a healthy and vigorous desire for scriptural knowledge, and Bengel has done more than any other man to aid such inquirers. There is perhaps no book every word of which has been so well weighed, or in which a single technical term contains so often far-reaching and suggestive views. . . . The theoretical and practical are as intimately connected as light and heat in the sun's ray.'—*Life of Perthes.*

Just published, in demy 4to, Third Edition, price 25s.,

BIBLICO-THEOLOGICAL LEXICON OF NEW TESTAMENT GREEK.

By HERMANN CREMER, D.D.,
PROFESSOR OF THEOLOGY IN THE UNIVERSITY OF GREIFSWALD.

TRANSLATED FROM THE GERMAN OF THE SECOND EDITION

(WITH ADDITIONAL MATTER AND CORRECTIONS BY THE AUTHOR)

By WILLIAM URWICK, M.A.

'Dr. Cremer's work is highly and deservedly esteemed in Germany. It gives with care and thoroughness a complete history, as far as it goes, of each word and phrase that it deals with. . . . Dr. Cremer's explanations are most lucidly set out.'—*Guardian.*

'It is hardly possible to exaggerate the value of this work to the student of the Greek Testament. . . . The translation is accurate and idiomatic, and the additions to the later edition are considerable and important.'—*Church Bells.*

'A valuable addition to the stores of any theological library. . . . It is what it claims to be, a Lexicon, both biblical and theological, and treats not only of words, but of the doctrines inculcated by those words.'—*John Bull.*

'We very heartily commend this goodly volume to students of biblical literature.'—*Evangelical Magazine.*

'We cannot find an important word in our Greek New Testament which is not discussed with a fulness and discrimination which leaves nothing to be desired.'—*Nonconformist.*

'Cremer's Lexicon is, and is long likely to be, indispensable to students whether of theology or of the Bible, and must always bear witness to his scholarship, erudition, and diligence.'—*Expositor.*

'A work of immense erudition.'—*Freeman.*

'This noble edition in quarto of Cremer's Biblico-Theological Lexicon quite supersedes the translation of the first edition of the work. Many of the most important articles have been re-written and re-arranged. . . . We heartily congratulate Mr. Urwick on the admirable manner in which he has executed his task, revealing on his part adequate scholarship, thorough sympathy, and a fine choice of English equivalents and definitions.'—*British Quarterly Review.*

'As an aid in our search, we warmly commend the honest and laborious New Testament Lexicon of Dr. Cremer.'—*London Quarterly Review.*

'The judiciousness and importance of Dr. Cremer's design must be obvious to all students of the New Testament; and the execution of that design, in our judgment, fully establishes and justifies the translator's encomiums.'—*Watchman.*

'A majestic volume, admirably printed and faultlessly edited, and will win gratitude as well as renown for its learned and Christian Author, and prove a precious boon to students and preachers who covet exact and exhaustive acquaintance with the literal and theological teaching of the New Testament.'—*Dickinson's Theological Quarterly.*

Second Edition in preparation,

FINAL CAUSES.

By PAUL JANET, Member of the Institute, Paris.

Translated from the French by William Affleck, B.D.

CONTENTS.—PRELIMINARY CHAPTER—The Problem. BOOK I.—The Law of Finality. BOOK II.—The First Cause of Finality. APPENDIX.

'This very learned, accurate, and, within its prescribed limits, exhaustive work. . . . The book as a whole abounds in matter of the highest interest, and is a model of learning and judicious treatment.'—*Guardian.*

'Illustrated and defended with an ability and learning which must command the reader's admiration.'—*Dublin Review.*

'A great contribution to the literature of this subject. M. Janet has mastered the conditions of the problem, is at home in the literature of science and philosophy, and has that faculty of felicitous expression which makes French books of the highest class such delightful reading; . . . in clearness, vigour, and depth it has been seldom equalled, and more seldom excelled, in philosophical literature.'—*Spectator.*

'A wealth of scientific knowledge and a logical acumen which will win the admiration of every reader.'—*Church Quarterly Review.*

Just published, in demy 8vo, price 10s. 6d.,

THE BIBLE DOCTRINE OF MAN.

(Seventh Series of Cunningham Lectures.)

By JOHN LAIDLAW, D.D.,

Professor of Systematic Theology, New College, Edinburgh.

'An important and valuable contribution to the discussion of the anthropology of the sacred writings, perhaps the most considerable that has appeared in our own language.'
—*Literary Churchman.*

'The work is a thoughtful contribution to a subject which must always have deep interest for the devout student of the Bible.'—*British Quarterly Review.*

'Dr. Laidlaw's work is scholarly, lucid, able, interesting, and valuable. . . . Thoughtful and devout minds will find much to stimulate, and not a little to assist, their meditations in this learned and, let us add, charmingly printed volume.'—*Record.*

'On the whole, we take this to be the most sensible and reasonable statement of the Biblical psychology of man we have met.'—*Expositor.*

'The book will give ample material for thought to the reflective reader; and it holds a position, as far as we know, which is unique.'—*Church Bells.*

'The Notes to the Lectures, which occupy not less than 130 pages, are exceedingly valuable. The style of the lecturer is clear and animated; the critical and analytical judgment predominates.'—*English Independent.*

Just published, Second Edition, demy 8vo, 10s. 6d.,

THE HUMILIATION OF CHRIST,

IN ITS PHYSICAL, ETHICAL, AND OFFICIAL ASPECTS.

By A. B. BRUCE, D.D.,

PROFESSOR OF DIVINITY, FREE CHURCH COLLEGE, GLASGOW.

'Dr. Bruce's style is uniformly clear and vigorous, and this book of his, as a whole, has the rare advantage of being at once stimulating and satisfying to the mind in a high degree.'—*British and Foreign Evangelical Review.*

'This work stands forth at once as an original, thoughtful, thorough piece of work in the branch of scientific theology, such as we do not often meet in our language. . . . It is really a work of exceptional value; and no one can read it without perceptible gain in theological knowledge.'—*English Churchman.*

'We have not for a long time met with a work so fresh and suggestive as this of Professor Bruce. . . . We do not know where to look at our English Universities for a treatise so calm, logical, and scholarly.'—*English Independent.*

By the same Author.

Just published, Second Edition, demy 8vo, 10s. 6d.,

THE TRAINING OF THE TWELVE;

OR,

Exposition of Passages in the Gospels exhibiting the Twelve Disciples of Jesus under Discipline for the Apostleship.

'Here we have a really great book on an important, large, and attractive subject—a book full of loving, wholesome, profound thoughts about the fundamentals of Christian faith and practice.'—*British and Foreign Evangelical Review.*

'It is some five or six years since this work first made its appearance, and now that a second edition has been called for, the Author has taken the opportunity to make some alterations which are likely to render it still more acceptable. Substantially, however, the book remains the same, and the hearty commendation with which we noted its first issue applies to it at least as much now.'—*Rock.*

'The value, the beauty of this volume is that it is a unique contribution to, because a loving and cultured study of, the life of Christ, in the relation of the Master of the Twelve.'—*Edinburgh Daily Review.*

T. and T. Clark's Publications.

WORKS BY THE LATE
PATRICK FAIRBAIRN, D.D.,
PRINCIPAL AND PROFESSOR OF THEOLOGY IN THE FREE CHURCH COLLEGE, GLASGOW.

In crown 8vo, price 6s.,

PASTORAL THEOLOGY: A Treatise on the Office and Duties of the Christian Pastor. With a Biographical Sketch of the Author.

'This treatise on the office and duties of a Christian pastor, by the late Professor Fairbairn, is well deserving thoughtful perusal. Throughout the volume, however, there is a tone of earnest piety and practical good sense, which finds expression in many profitable counsels, embodying the result of large experience and shrewd observation. . . . Much of the volume is devoted to the theory and practice of preaching, and this part we can most heartily commend; it is replete with valuable suggestions, which even those who have had some experience in the ministry will find calculated to make them more attractive and efficient preachers.'—*Christian Observer.*

In crown 8vo, price 7s. 6d.,

THE PASTORAL EPISTLES. The Greek Text and Translation. With Introduction, Expository Notes, and Dissertations.

'We cordially recommend this work to ministers and theological students.'—*Methodist Magazine.*
'We have read no book of his with a keener appreciation and enjoyment than that just published on the Pastoral Epistles.'—*Nonconformist.*

In Two Volumes, demy 8vo, price 21s., Sixth Edition,

THE TYPOLOGY OF SCRIPTURE, viewed in connection with the whole Series of the Divine Dispensations.

In demy 8vo, price 10s. 6d., Fourth Edition,

EZEKIEL, AND THE BOOK OF HIS PROPHECY: An Exposition. With a new Translation.

In demy 8vo, price 10s. 6d., Second Edition,

PROPHECY, viewed in its Distinctive Nature, its Special Functions, and Proper Interpretation.

In demy 8vo, price 10s. 6d.,

HERMENEUTICAL MANUAL; or, Introduction to the Exegetical Study of the Scriptures of the New Testament.

In demy 8vo, price 10s. 6d.,

THE REVELATION OF LAW IN SCRIPTURE, considered with respect both to its own Nature and to its Relative Place in Successive Dispensations. (The Third Series of the 'Cunningham Lectures.')

PROFESSOR GODET'S WORKS.

In Three Volumes, 8vo, price 31s. 6d.,
A COMMENTARY ON
THE GOSPEL OF ST. JOHN.
By F. GODET, D.D.,
PROFESSOR OF THEOLOGY, NEUCHATEL.

'This work forms one of the battle-fields of modern inquiry, and is itself so rich in spiritual truth that it is impossible to examine it too closely; and we welcome this treatise from the pen of Dr. Godet. We have no more competent exegete, and this new volume shows all the learning and vivacity for which the Author is distinguished.'—*Freeman.*

In Two Volumes, 8vo, price 21s.,
THE GOSPEL OF ST. LUKE.
Translated from the Second French Edition.

'Marked by clearness and good sense, it will be found to possess value and interest as one of the most recent and copious works specially designed to illustrate this Gospel.'—*Guardian.*

In Two Volumes, 8vo, price 21s.,
ST. PAUL'S EPISTLE TO THE ROMANS.

'We have looked through it with great care, and have been charmed not less by the clearness and fervour of its evangelical principles than by the carefulness of its exegesis, its fine touches of spiritual intuition, and its appositeness of historical illustration.'—*Baptist Magazine.*

Just published, in crown 8vo, price 6s.,
DEFENCE OF THE CHRISTIAN FAITH.
TRANSLATED BY THE
Hon. and Rev. Canon LYTTELTON, M.A.,
RECTOR OF HAGLEY.

'This volume is not unworthy of the great reputation which Professor Godet enjoys. It shows the same breadth of reading and extent of learning as his previous works, and the same power of eloquent utterance.'—*Church Bells.*

'Professor Godet is at once so devoutly evangelical in his spirit and so profoundly intelligent in his apprehension of truth, that we shall all welcome these contributions to the study of much debated subjects with the utmost satisfaction.'—*Christian World.*

Just published, in demy 8vo, Fourth Edition, price 10s. 6d.,
MODERN DOUBT AND CHRISTIAN BELIEF.
A Series of Apologetic Lectures addressed to Earnest Seekers after Truth.
By THEODORE CHRISTLIEB, D.D.,
UNIVERSITY PREACHER AND PROFESSOR OF THEOLOGY AT BONN.

Translated, with the Author's sanction, chiefly by the Rev. H. U. WEITBRECHT, Ph.D., and Edited by the Rev. T. L. KINGSBURY, M.A.

'We recommend the volume as one of the most valuable and important among recent contributions to our apologetic literature. . . . We are heartily thankful both to the learned Author and to his translators.'—*Guardian.*

'We express our unfeigned admiration of the ability displayed in this work, and of the spirit of deep piety which pervades it; and whilst we commend it to the careful perusal of our readers, we heartily rejoice that in those days of reproach and blasphemy so able a champion has come forward to contend earnestly for the faith which was once delivered to the saints.'—*Christian Observer.*

DR. LUTHARDT'S WORKS.

In Three handsome crown 8vo Volumes, price 6s. each.

'We do not know any volumes so suitable in these times for young men entering on life, or, let us say, even for the library of a pastor called to deal with such, than the three volumes of this series. We commend the whole of them with the utmost cordial satisfaction. They are altogether quite a specialty in our literature.'—*Weekly Review.*

APOLOGETIC LECTURES
ON THE
FUNDAMENTAL TRUTHS OF CHRISTIANITY.
Fifth Edition.

By C. E. LUTHARDT, D.D., Leipzig.

'From Dr. Luthardt's exposition even the most learned theologians may derive invaluable criticism, and the most acute disputants supply themselves with more trenchant and polished weapons than they have as yet been possessed of.'—*Bell's Weekly Messenger.*

APOLOGETIC LECTURES
ON THE
SAVING TRUTHS OF CHRISTIANITY.
Fourth Edition.

'Dr. Luthardt is a profound scholar, but a very simple teacher, and expresses himself on the gravest matters with the utmost simplicity, clearness, and force.'—*Literary World.*

APOLOGETIC LECTURES
ON THE
MORAL TRUTHS OF CHRISTIANITY.
Third Edition.

'The ground covered by this work is, of course, of considerable extent, and there is scarcely any topic of specifically moral interest now under debate in which the reader will not find some suggestive saying. The volume contains, like its predecessors, a truly wealthy apparatus of notes and illustrations.'—*English Churchman.*

In Three Volumes, 8vo, price 31s. 6d.,

ST. JOHN'S GOSPEL DESCRIBED AND EXPLAINED ACCORDING TO ITS PECULIAR CHARACTER.

'Full to overflowing with a ripe theology and a critical science worthy of their great theme.'—*Irish Ecclesiastical Gazette.*

Just published, in demy 8vo, price 9s.,

ST. JOHN THE AUTHOR OF THE FOURTH GOSPEL.
By Professor C. E. LUTHARDT,
Author of 'Fundamental Truths of Christianity,' etc.

Translated and the Literature enlarged by C. R. Gregory, Leipzig.

'A work of thoroughness and value. The translator has added a lengthy Appendix, containing a very complete account of the literature bearing on the controversy respecting this Gospel. The indices which close the volume are well ordered, and add greatly to its value.'—*Guardian.*

'There are few works in the later theological literature which contain such a wealth of sober theological knowledge and such an invulnerable phalanx of objective apologetical criticism.'—*Professor Guericke.*

Crown 8vo, 5s.,

LUTHARDT, KAHNIS, AND BRÜCKNER.
The Church: Its Origin, its History, and its Present Position.

'A comprehensive review of this sort, done by able hands, is both instructive and suggestive.'—*Record.*

HANDBOOKS FOR BIBLE CLASSES.

'These volumes are models of the *multum in parvo* style. We have long desired to meet with a Series of this kind—Little Books on Great Subjects.'—*Literary World*.

THE EPISTLE OF ST. PAUL TO THE GALATIANS.
With Introduction and Notes [*Price* 1s. 6d.
By THE REV. PROFESSOR JAMES MACGREGOR, D.D.

THE POST-EXILIAN PROPHETS— HAGGAI, ZECHARIAH, MALACHI.
With Introduction and Notes [*Price* 2s.
By MARCUS DODS, D.D.
'Thoughtful, suggestive, and finely analytical.'—*Evangelical Magazine*.

THE LIFE OF CHRIST.
By REV. JAMES STALKER, M.A. [*Price* 1s. 6d.
'As a succinct, suggestive, beautifully written exhibition of the life of our Lord, we are acquainted with nothing that can compare with it.'—*Christian World*.

THE CHRISTIAN SACRAMENTS.
By PROFESSOR JAMES S. CANDLISH, D.D. [*Price* 1s. 6d.
'An admirable manual; sound, clear, suggestive, and interesting.'—*Free Church Record*.

THE BOOKS OF CHRONICLES.
By REV. PROFESSOR MURPHY, BELFAST. [*Price* 1s. 6d.
'We know no Commentary on the Chronicles to compare with this, considering the small size and cost.'—*Wesleyan Methodist Magazine*.

THE WESTMINSTER CONFESSION OF FAITH.
With Introduction and Notes [*Price* 2s.
By REV. JOHN MACPHERSON, M.A.
'This volume is executed with learning, discrimination, and ability.'—*British Messenger*.

THE BOOK OF JUDGES.
By REV. PRINCIPAL DOUGLAS. [*Price* 1s. 3d.
'This volume is as near perfection as we can hope to find such a work.'—*Church Bells*.

THE BOOK OF JOSHUA.
By REV. PRINCIPAL DOUGLAS. [*Price* 1s. 6d.

THE EPISTLE TO THE HEBREWS.
By REV. PROFESSOR A. B. DAVIDSON. [*Price* 2s. 6d.

SCOTTISH CHURCH HISTORY.
By REV. NORMAN L. WALKER, M.A. [*Price* 1s. 6d.

THE CHURCH.
By REV. PROFESSOR WM. BINNIE, D.D., [*Price* 1s. 6d.

www.ingramcontent.com/pod-product-compliance
Lightning Source LLC
Chambersburg PA
CBHW030344230426
43664CB00007BB/526